Windows XP Cookbook™

Other Microsoft Windows resources from O'Reilly

Related titles
Windows XP Hacks
Windows XP in a Nutshell

Windows XP Annoyances for Geeks
Windows XP Pocket Reference

Windows Books Resource Center
windows.oreilly.com is a complete catalog of O'Reilly's Windows and Office books, including sample chapters and code examples.

O'REILLY NETWORK
oreillynet.com is the essential portal for developers interested in open and emerging technologies, including new platforms, programming languages, and operating systems.

Conferences
O'Reilly brings diverse innovators together to nurture the ideas that spark revolutionary industries. We specialize in documenting the latest tools and systems, translating the innovator's knowledge into useful skills for those in the trenches. Visit *conferences.oreilly.com* for our upcoming events.

O'REILLY NETWORK Safari Bookshelf
Safari Bookshelf (*safari.oreilly.com*) is the premier online reference library for programmers and IT professionals. Conduct searches across more than 1,000 books. Subscribers can zero in on answers to time-critical questions in a matter of seconds. Read the books on your Bookshelf from cover to cover or simply flip to the page you need. Try it today with a free trial.

Windows XP Cookbook™

Robbie Allen and Preston Gralla

O'REILLY®

Beijing · Cambridge · Farnham · Köln · Paris · Sebastopol · Taipei · Tokyo

Windows XP Cookbook™
by Robbie Allen and Preston Gralla

Published by O'Reilly Media, Inc., 1005 Gravenstein Highway North, Sebastopol, CA 95472.

O'Reilly books may be purchased for educational, business, or sales promotional use. Online editions are also available for most titles (*safari.oreilly.com*). For more information, contact our corporate/institutional sales department: (800) 998-9938 or *corporate@oreilly.com*.

Editor:	Simon St.Laurent
Production Editor:	Adam Witwer
Production Services:	Argosy Publishing
Cover Designer:	Ellie Volckhausen
Interior Designer:	David Futato

Printing History:

August 2005:	First Edition.

 This book uses RepKover™, a durable and flexible lay-flat binding.

ISBN: 0-596-00725-6
[M]

Table of Contents

Preface . . . . **xvii**

1. Introduction **1**

    Approach to the Book   2

    At Least Three Ways to Do It   2

    Where to Find the Tools   3

    Running Tools with Alternate Credentials   3

    A Brief Word on Windows Scripting   4

    Where to Find More Information   5

2. Operating System Installation and Maintenance **8**

    2.0 Introduction   8

    2.1 Preparing to Install Windows XP   8

    2.2 Installing from a CD or DVD   11

    2.3 Installing from a Network Share   14

    2.4 Installing from an Unattended Installation   15

    2.5 Cloning Windows XP Installations   20

    2.6 Installing from Remote Installation Services (RIS)   21

    2.7 Troubleshooting Installation Problems   25

    2.8 Upgrading to Windows XP   28

    2.9 Creating a Multiboot Installation   30

    2.10 Troubleshooting Multiboot Problems   31

    2.11 Activating Windows XP   32

    2.12 Viewing the Installed Service Pack and Hotfixes   34

    2.13 Installing a Hotfix   36

    2.14 Installing a Service Pack   37

    2.15 Slipstreaming a Service Pack or Hotfix into a Build   39

2.16 Configuring Automatic Updates   40

2.17 Disabling the Windows Firewall After Installation   43

2.18 Keeping an Installation Process Worm- and Virus-Free   44

3. Managing Hardware and Devices **46**

3.0 Introduction   46

3.1 Adding Hardware   47

3.2 Resolving Unknown Devices   49

3.3 Repairing a Missing Modem   50

3.4 Recovering from a Bad Device Driver Update   51

3.5 Using the Last Known Good Configuration
to Resolve Hardware Problems   52

3.6 Running Windows in Safe Mode   53

3.7 Using System Restore to Recover from a Hardware-Induced Problem   55

3.8 Resolving Device Conflicts   56

3.9 Resolving USB Bandwidth Problems   58

3.10 Resolving Hung USB Devices   59

3.11 Keeping USB Devices from Disappearing   61

3.12 Curing Stubborn USB Devices   62

3.13 Revealing Hidden Devices   64

3.14 Checking Drivers with the Driver Verifier Tool   65

3.15 Resolving Printer Timed-Out and Not Ready Problems   66

3.16 Troubleshooting Local Printing Problems   66

3.17 Printing to a USB Printer from DOS   68

3.18 Resolving Failed Network Printing with Internet Connection Sharing   69

3.19 Interpreting Device Manager Error Codes   70

3.20 Troubleshooting Sound Problems   71

3.21 Troubleshooting Video Problems   73

3.22 Troubleshooting Video Monitor Problems   74

3.23 Stopping LCD Monitor Resolution Messages   75

3.24 Interpreting Windows INF Files   76

3.25 Figuring out AUTORUN.INF Files   79

3.26 Correcting Parameters in BIOS   81

3.27 Troubleshooting CD Autorun Software Installation Problems   83

3.28 Troubleshooting CD-ROM and DVD-ROM Reading Problems   84

3.29 Resolving DVD Reading and DVD Movie Problems   86

3.30 Restoring Access to CD-ROMs   87

4. Installing, Uninstalling, and Working with Applications **88**

    4.0 Introduction 88

    4.1 Uninstalling "Unremovable" Components 88

    4.2 Removing Unruly Applications 91

    4.3 Removing Stubborn Uninstall Entries
from Already Uninstalled Programs 93

    4.4 Changing the Default Location for Installing Applications 94

    4.5 Launching Applications with Keyboard Shortcuts 95

    4.6 Customizing the Way Applications Open
Using Switches and Parameters 97

    4.7 Running Older Applications 100

    4.8 Using the Application Compatibility Toolkit
to Solve Compatibility Problems 102

    4.9 Troubleshooting Application Compatibility 105

    4.10 Running DOS Programs in Their Own Optimized Environments 106

    4.11 Forcing Older Programs to Use Windows XP Common Controls 107

    4.12 Using Keyboard Application Shortcuts 109

    4.13 Moving a New Microsoft Application
to Another Windows XP System 111

    4.14 Remotely Installing a Microsoft Application Using Group Policy 113

    4.15 Remotely Redeploying a Microsoft Application Using Group Policy 115

    4.16 Remotely Uninstalling a Microsoft Application Using Group Policy 116

5. Customizing the Interface **118**

    5.0 Introduction 118

    5.1 Getting Rid of Undeletable Desktop Icons 120

    5.2 Changing "Unchangeable" Desktop Icons and System Objects 124

    5.3 Showing Your XP Version on Your Desktop 126

    5.4 Turning Off Balloon Tips 127

    5.5 Cleaning Your Desktop Automatically 128

    5.6 Adding an Address Bar to the Taskbar 129

    5.7 Adding a Shortcut to a Disk, Folder,
or Internet Address to the Taskbar 130

    5.8 Hiding Specific Icons in the Notification Area 130

    5.9 Hiding All Icons in the Notification Area 132

    5.10 Controlling the Start Menu's Frequently Used Programs List 133

    5.11 Customizing the Start Menu's Pinned Programs List 136

    5.12 Displaying Control Panel Applets in a Cascading Menu 137

    5.13 Hiding and Recategorizing Control Panel Applets 138

5.14 Customizing Right-Click Menu Choices in Windows Explorer 142

5.15 Changing the Resolution of Thumbnails in Windows Explorer 147

5.16 Improving Laptop and LCD Resolution with ClearType 149

5.17 Converting to the Classic Windows Interface 150

5.18 Using TweakUI 153

5.19 Using Group Policy Editor to Alter the Interface 153

5.20 Saving Your Desktop Settings 156

5.21 Fixing the Start Shortcut Menu 157

5.22 Troubleshooting My Recent Documents 158

6. System Properties, Startup, and Shutdown **160**

6.0 Introduction 160

6.1 Automatically Setting the Time on a Domain-Connected PC 160

6.2 Automatically Setting the Time on a PC Not Connected to a Domain 162

6.3 Changing the System Name 165

6.4 Create a Multiboot Menu 167

6.5 Using Virtual PC to Run Multiple Operating Systems Simultaneously 172

6.6 Performing a Clean Boot 174

6.7 Shutting Down Unnecessary Programs
and Services that Run on Startup 175

6.8 Speeding Up Shutdown Time 181

6.9 Changing Your Boot Screen 182

6.10 Personalizing Your PC's Sounds 183

6.11 Creating Power Schemes 185

6.12 Extending Battery Life on a Laptop 187

6.13 Changing the Location of Your Startup Folders 189

6.14 Disabling Error Reporting 190

6.15 Creating Environment Variables 193

6.16 Creating a Reboot or Shutdown Shortcut 196

6.17 Scheduling a Reboot 196

6.18 Speeding Up System Startup 197

7. Disks, Drives, and Volumes **200**

7.0 Introduction 200

7.1 Viewing the Disk, Drive, and Volume Layout 202

7.2 Converting a Basic Disk to Dynamic 204

7.3 Enabling Disk Performance Statistics 205

7.4 Formatting a Volume 206

7.5   Setting the Drive Letter of a Volume   207

7.6   Setting the Label of a Volume   208

7.7   Cleaning Up a Volume   209

7.8   Defragmenting a Volume   211

7.9   Compressing a Volume   213

7.10   Checking a Volume for Errors   215

7.11   Making a Disk or Volume Read-Only   216

7.12   Mapping a Network Drive   218

7.13   Creating a Virtual Drive to Another Drive or Folder   220

7.14   Finding Large Files and Folders on a Volume   221

7.15   Enabling Disk Quotas   224

7.16   Limiting a User to a Specified Disk Quota   226

7.17   Viewing Disk Quota Usage   228

8. Files, Folders, and Shares **230**

8.0   Introduction   230

8.1   Creating and Deleting a File   232

8.2   Creating and Deleting a Folder   233

8.3   Undeleting a File   235

8.4   Securely Deleting a File   235

8.5   Viewing the Properties of a File or Folder   237

8.6   Creating a Shortcut   239

8.7   Creating a Link or Junction Point   242

8.8   Creating a Program Alias   244

8.9   Searching for Files or Folders   245

8.10   Copying, Moving, or Renaming a File or Folder   246

8.11   Comparing Files or Folders   248

8.12   Hiding a File or Folder   249

8.13   Making a File or Folder Read-Only   251

8.14   Compressing a File or Folder   252

8.15   Encrypting a File or Folder   255

8.16   Replacing a File That Is in Use   256

8.17   Taking Ownership of a File or Folder   258

8.18   Finding Out Who Opened or Modified a File Last   259

8.19   Finding Open Files   261

8.20   Finding the Process That Has a File Open   262

8.21   Viewing File Activity   263

8.22   Performing an Action on Several Files at Once   264

8.23   Creating and Deleting Shares   266

8.24	Viewing Shares	267
8.25	Restricting Access to a Share	269
8.26	Enabling Web Sharing	270
8.27	Publishing a Share in Active Directory	271

9. The Registry **273**

9.0	Introduction	273
9.1	Creating and Deleting a Key	275
9.2	Setting a Value	277
9.3	Setting Keys or Values Using Group Policy	280
9.4	Exporting Registry Files	281
9.5	Importing Registry Files	282
9.6	Searching the Registry	283
9.7	Comparing the Registry	284
9.8	Restricting Access to the Registry	285
9.9	Backing Up and Restoring the Registry	287
9.10	Creating a Registry Link	289
9.11	Monitoring Registry Activity	290
9.12	Viewing Processes That Have a Registry Key Open	292

10. Processes, Tasks, and Services **294**

10.0	Introduction	294
10.1	Viewing the Running Processes	295
10.2	Viewing the Properties of a Process	297
10.3	Viewing the Resources a Process Is Using	298
10.4	Suspending a Process	302
10.5	Killing a Process	303
10.6	Running a Task with Alternate Credentials	304
10.7	Running a Task on a Remote System	306
10.8	Running a Task Automatically via the Registry	308
10.9	Running a Task Automatically via Login Scripts	310
10.10	Running a Task via Group Policy	312
10.11	Viewing All Automatic Tasks	314
10.12	Scheduling a Task	314
10.13	Viewing Scheduled Tasks	317
10.14	Deleting a Scheduled Task	318
10.15	Troubleshooting Scheduled Tasks	320
10.16	Starting and Stopping a Service	321
10.17	Running Any Program or Script as a Service	322

10.18 Setting the Startup Type of a Service 325
10.19 Setting the Account and Password of a Service 327
10.20 Performing an Action Automatically When a Service Fails 329
10.21 Viewing the Antecedent and Dependent Services for a Service 330
10.22 Viewing the Service Load Order 333
10.23 Viewing the Startup History of a Service 335
10.24 Granting Permissions to Manage One or More Services 336

11. Digital Media **339**
11.0 Introduction 339
11.1 Ripping Digital Music 339
11.2 Creating a Playlist 343
11.3 Burning a CD 344
11.4 Troubleshooting CD Burning 346
11.5 Playing Internet Radio Stations 350
11.6 Protecting Your Privacy in Windows Media Player 351
11.7 Searching Through Digital Media Collections Using Metadata 354
11.8 Capturing Video to Your PC 356
11.9 Making Your Own DVDs 360
11.10 Converting Images Easily Between Graphics Formats 362
11.11 Processing Images for Email and the Web 364

12. Network Configuration **367**
12.0 Introduction 367
12.1 Viewing the Network Configuration 368
12.2 Disabling a Connection 371
12.3 Configuring an IP Address 373
12.4 Renewing or Releasing a DHCP IP Address 375
12.5 Configuring DNS Settings 377
12.6 Registering DNS Records or Flushing the DN Cache 380
12.7 Finding a Computer's Active Directory Site 381
12.8 Managing Routes 383
12.9 Viewing the Open Ports and Connections 385
12.10 Troubleshooting Network Connectivity Problems 387
12.11 Configuring TCP/IP Filtering 388
12.12 Measuring Link Speed and Latency Between Two Hosts 391
12.13 Installing the IPv6 Stack 392

13. The Internet **394**

   13.0 Introduction   394

   13.1 Using a HOSTS File to Speed Up Web Access   395

   13.2 Troubleshooting DNS Problems   396

   13.3 Installing Internet Information Services (IIS)   399

   13.4 Using the IIS MMC Snap-in to Manage Your Internet Servers   401

   13.5 Setting Up and Configuring a Telnet Server   403

   13.6 Use the Telnet Administrator to Manage a Telnet Server   405

   13.7 Customizing Internet Explorer's Logo and Titlebar   406

   13.8 Blocking Pop Ups   409

   13.9 Protecting Your Privacy by Handling Cookies Properly   412

   13.10 Protecting Yourself Against Spyware   416

   13.11 Customizing Internet Explorer Security Settings   419

   13.12 Allowing Programs to Bypass the Windows Firewall   422

   13.13 Tracking Firewall Activity with a Windows Firewall Log   426

   13.14 Protecting Yourself with the ZoneAlarm Firewall   428

   13.15 Surfing the Web Anonymously   431

   13.16 Finding and Reading RSS Feeds   432

14. Wireless Networking **434**

   14.0 Introduction   434

   14.1 Installing a Wireless Adapter   434

   14.2 Installing a Wireless Router   438

   14.3 Connecting to Your Wireless Network   440

   14.4 Troubleshooting WiFi Network Connections   442

   14.5 Speeding Up a WiFi Network   445

   14.6 Keeping Your WiFi Network Secure   447

   14.7 Setting Up WiFi Encryption   450

   14.8 Mixing 802.11b and 802.11g Devices   455

   14.9 Setting Up an Ad Hoc Wireless Network   456

   14.10 Connecting to a Hotspot   458

   14.11 Sending Email from a Hotspot   460

   14.12 Stopping Hotspot "Stuttering"   463

   14.13 Protecting Yourself at Hotspots   464

15. User, Group, and Computer Accounts **467**

   15.0 Introduction   467

   15.1 Creating a User Account   469

   15.2 Unlocking a User   471

15.3 Troubleshooting Account Lockout Problems 473

15.4 Viewing and Modifying the Account Lockout and Password Policies 474

15.5 Enabling and Disabling a User Account 478

15.6 Setting a User's Password 480

15.7 Setting a Domain User's Account Options 483

15.8 Setting a Domain User's Profile Attributes 485

15.9 Finding a Domain User's Last Logon Time 487

15.10 Creating a Group Account 488

15.11 Viewing the Members of a Group 491

15.12 Viewing a User's Group Membership 493

15.13 Adding and Removing Members of a Group 495

15.14 Creating a Computer Account 497

15.15 Joining a Computer to a Domain 499

15.16 Renaming a Computer 501

15.17 Resetting a Computer Account 504

16. Event Logs and Log Files **507**

16.0 Introduction 507

16.1 Creating an Event 509

16.2 Viewing Events 510

16.3 Creating a New Event Log 512

16.4 Viewing the Size of an Event Log 514

16.5 Setting the Maximum Size of an Event Log 515

16.6 Setting the Event Log Retention Policy 516

16.7 Clearing the Events in an Event Log 518

16.8 Restricting Access to an Event Log 519

16.9 Searching an Event Log 520

16.10 Searching the Event Logs on Multiple Systems 522

16.11 Archiving an Event Log 524

16.12 Finding More Information about an Event 525

16.13 Triggering an Action When an Event Occurs 526

16.14 Troubleshooting a Corrupt Event Log 528

16.15 Enabling Boot Logging 529

16.16 Enabling User Environment Logging 530

16.17 Enabling NetLogon Logging 531

16.18 Enabling Windows Installer Logging 532

16.19 Enabling Windows Time Service Logging 534

16.20 Enabling Outlook Logging 535

16.21 Troubleshooting Application Failures with the Dr. Watson Logs 536

17. Security and Auditing **538**

   17.0 Introduction   538

   17.1 Analyzing Your Security Configuration   540

   17.2 Enabling Auditing   542

   17.3 Renaming the Administrator and Guest Accounts   544

   17.4 Disabling or Removing Unused Accounts, Services, and Software   547

   17.5 Enabling Screen Saver Locking   547

   17.6 Disabling Storage of the LM Password Hash   550

   17.7 Requiring Strong Passwords   550

   17.8 Getting Notified of New Security Vulnerabilities   552

18. Performance Tuning **553**

   18.0 Introduction   553

   18.1 Speeding Up System Performance with the Task Manager   553

   18.2 Tracking System Performance with the Performance Console   558

   18.3 Using Memory More Efficiently   563

   18.4 Balancing System Performance and Visual Effects   567

   18.5 Optimizing Page File Size   568

   18.6 Cleaning Up Your Hard Disk   570

   18.7 Converting Your Hard Disk to NTFS   573

   18.8 Disabling Startup Services and Programs   575

   18.9 Removing Unnecessary Items from the Notification Area   579

   18.10 Improving Startup Performance   580

19. Backup and Recovery **581**

   19.0 Introduction   581

   19.1 Performing a Backup   581

   19.2 Restoring from Backup   586

   19.3 Using Automated System Recovery   587

   19.4 Creating an ASR Disk "After the Fact"   588

   19.5 Using System Restore to Revive a Broken Machine   589

   19.6 Disabling System Restore Remotely   592

   19.7 Retrieving a Shadow Copy of a Corrupted or Deleted File   593

   19.8 Using XCOPY for Interim Backups   595

   19.9 Using the Recovery Console During Boot Failures   596

   19.10 Creating a Password Reset Disk   598

   19.11 Recovering and Decrypting an Encrypted File or Folder   599

   19.12 Backing up and Restoring Activation Data   601

   19.13 Auditing Backup and Restore Actions   602

   19.14 Caring for Backup Media   602

20. Crashes and Errors **605**

    20.0 Introduction   605

    20.1 Using Safe Mode   605

    20.2 Using Last Known Good Configuration   606

    20.3 Using Boot Log to Trace Problems   607

    20.4 Using VGA Mode to Solve Video Problems   608

    20.5 Using Recovery Console   609

    20.6 Repairing AUTOEXEC.NT or CONFIG.NT Errors   610

    20.7 Fixing Cryptographic Services Error   611

    20.8 Fixing NTOSKRNL Errors   612

    20.9 Fixing a HAL Error   613

    20.10 Fixing Corrupted or Missing \WINDOWS\SYSTEM32\CONFIG Errors   614

    20.11 Fixing NTLDR or NTDETECT Not Found Errors   615

    20.12 Configuring Error Reporting   616

    20.13 Troubleshooting Blue Screen Error Messages   617

    20.14 Setting Up and Using Dr. Watson to Troubleshoot Errors   619

Appendix: Summary of Windows XP Versions and Service Packs **623**

Index **631**

Preface

There are literally thousands of programs, tools, commands, screens, scripts, buttons, tabs, applets, menus, and settings contained within Windows XP. And it has only been in the last couple of years that Microsoft's documentation has actually been more of a help than a hindrance. But it still isn't enough. What Windows XP users and administrators really need is a quick and easy way to find what they need to get done what they need to. There are plenty of books that will go into all sorts of detail about the theory behind a particular technology or application, but what if you don't need that? What if you know the theory but just can't remember the exact command-line or graphical sequence to customize the interface or check on the running processes? There are very few books that cut through the fluff and provide you the essentials for getting the job done. This book is intended to do just that.

Based on our own experience, hours of research, and years of hanging out on newsgroups and mailing lists, we've compiled over 300 recipes that should answer many of the "How do I..." questions one could pose about Windows XP.

Who Should Read This Book

Windows XP Cookbook will be useful to anyone that has to use, deploy, administer, or automate Windows XP. But this isn't a typical end user book; we cover the spectrum of topics involved with running Windows XP in both small and large environments. As a result, IT professionals and system administrators will get the most out of the book and find it a great day-to-day reference. Also, power users will find *Windows XP Cookbook* a great source for information on tweaking XP and getting the most out of their systems.

If you like the format of this book but crave more recipes on Active Directory or Windows Server 2003, take a look at *Active Directory Cookbook* and *Windows Server Cookbook,* also from O'Reilly.

What's in This Book

This book consists of 20 chapters. Here is a brief overview of each chapter:

- , *Introduction*, sets the stage by covering our approach to the book, where you can find the tools used in the book, and where to find additional information outside of the book.

- Chapter 2, *Operating System Installation and Maintenance*, covers tasks related to installing and upgrading Windows XP, installing hotfixes and service packs, and performing initial system configuration.

- Chapter 3, *Managing Hardware and Devices*, covers adding and managing hardware, troubleshooting hardware-related problems, resolving device conflicts, and dealing with USB devices and printers.

- Chapter 4, *Installing, Uninstalling, and Working with Applications*, covers remotely installing, uninstalling, and redeploying applications using Group Policy, dealing with installation and uninstallation problems, changing the default location for installing applications, customizing application launches, and resolving compatibility problems between applications and XP.

- Chapter 5, *Customizing the Interface*, covers customizing the desktop, controlling and customizing the Start menu, and customizing the Control Panel and Windows Explorer.

- Chapter 6, *System Properties, Startup, and Shutdown*, covers creating a multiboot menu, running multiple operating systems in addition to XP, performing a clean boot, halting services that run at startup, changing your boot screen, speeding up startup and shutdown times, disabling error reporting, and customizing reboots.

- Chapter 7, *Disks, Drives, and Volumes*, covers disk quotas, converting between disk types, creating drives, mapping drives, and managing volumes.

- Chapter 8, *Files, Folders, and Shares*, covers file and folder manipulation, creating shortcuts and links, modifying file properties, and managing share points.

- Chapter 9, *The Registry*, covers basic Registry administration. It includes recipes on how to create and delete Registry keys and values, exporting and importing Registry files, restricting access to the Registry, and monitoring Registry activity.

- Chapter 10, *Processes, Tasks, and Services*, covers both basic and advanced process and task management including how to create, suspend, and kill processes, and schedule tasks. Additionally, starting and stopping services, running scripts as services, searching for services, and viewing various service properties is covered.

- Chapter 11, *Digital Media*, covers ripping and burning digital music, using Windows Media Player, playing Internet radio stations, using media metadata, converting images between graphics formats, capturing video, and making DVDs.

- Chapter 12, *Network Configuration*, covers tasks related to configuring network adapters, viewing network configuration, viewing network traffic, and installing IPv6 support.

- Chapter 13, *The Internet*, covers speeding up web access, troubleshooting DNS problems and Internet connections, working with Internet Information Services (IIS) and Telnet servers, customizing Internet Explorer, blocking pop ups, handling cookies, protecting yourself against spyware, and using firewalls.

- Chapter 14, *Wireless Networking*, covers working with XP's wireless client, installing a wireless router, wireless security, troubleshooting wireless networking, and using hotspots.

- Chapter 15, *User, Group, and Computer Accounts*, covers how to create and administer local and domain user, group, and computer accounts.

- Chapter 16, *Event Logs and Log Files*, covers how to create and view events, create and manage event logs, search event logs, and enable various system logging.

- Chapter 17, *Security and Auditing*, covers several tasks related to securing Windows XP, including auditing, screen saver locking, enabling strong passwords, and disabling unused accounts.

- Chapter 18, *Performance Tuning*, covers tracking and speeding up system performance, using RAM more effectively, optimizing pagefile size, cleaning your hard disk, and converting a hard disk to NTFS.

- Chapter 19, *Backup and Recovery*, covers making backups, restoring from backups, using Automated System Recovery, using System Restore, retrieving a shadow copy, using XCOPY, using the Recovery Console, creating a password reset disk, and backing up, auditing backup and restore, caring for backup media, and restoring activation data.

- Chapter 20, *Crashes and Errors*, covers using Safe Mode and the Last Known Good Configuration, using a boot log to trace problems, using the Recovery Console, repairing Autoexec.nt or Config.nt errors, fixing a wide variety of XP errors, configuring error reporting, and using Dr. Watson to troubleshoot errors.

The Appendix provides an overview of the major Windows XP versions including service packs 1 and 2.

This book covers hundreds of tasks you'll need to do at one point or another with Windows XP. If you feel something important has been left out that should be included, let us know. We'll work to get it into a future edition. For contact information, see the "We'd Like Your Feedback!" section later in the preface.

Using Code Examples

This book is here to help you get your job done. In general, you may use the code in this book in your programs and documentation. You do not need to contact us for permission unless you're reproducing a significant portion of the code. For example, writing a program that uses several chunks of code from this book does not require permission. Selling or distributing a CD-ROM of examples from O'Reilly books *does* require permission. Answering a question by citing this book and quoting example code does not require permission. Incorporating a significant amount of example code from this book into your product's documentation *does* require permission.

We appreciate, but do not require, attribution. An attribution usually includes the title, author, publisher, and ISBN. For example: "*Windows XP Cookbook,* by Robbie Allen and Preston Gralla. Copyright 2005 O'Reilly Media, Inc., 0-596-00725-6."

If you feel that your use of code examples falls outside fair use or the permission given here, feel free to contact us at *permissions@oreilly.com*.

Safari® Enabled

 When you see a Safari® Enabled icon on the cover of your favorite technology book, it means the book is available online through the O'Reilly Network Safari Bookshelf.

Safari offers a solution that's better than e-books. It's a virtual library that lets you easily search thousands of top technology books, cut and paste code samples, download chapters, and find quick answers when you need the most accurate, current information. Try it for free at *http://safari.oreilly.com*.

Conventions in This Book

The following typographical conventions are used in this book:

Constant width
> Indicates command-line elements, computer output, code examples, and registry keys.

Constant width italic
> Indicates placeholders (for which you substitute an actual name) in examples and in Registry keys.

Constant width bold
> Indicates user input.

Italic
> Introduces new terms and URLs, commands, file extensions, filenames, directory or folder names, and UNC pathnames.

Indicates a tip, suggestion, or general note. For example, we'll tell you if you need to use a particular version or if an operation requires certain privileges.

 Indicates a warning or caution. For example, we'll tell you if Active Directory does not behave as you'd expect or if a particular operation has a negative impact on performance.

We'd Like Your Feedback!

The information in this book has been tested and verified to the best of our ability, but mistakes and oversights do occur. Please let us know about errors you may find, as well as your suggestions for future editions, by writing to:

O'Reilly Media, Inc.
1005 Gravenstein Highway North
Sebastopol, CA 95472
800-998-9938 (in the U.S. or Canada)
707-829-0515 (international or local)
707-829-0104 (fax)

You also can send us messages using email. To be put on our mailing list or to request a catalog, send email to:

info@oreilly.com

To ask technical questions or comment on the book, send email to:

bookquestions@oreilly.com

For corrections and amplifications to this book, check out O'Reilly Media's online catalog at:

http://www.oreilly.com/catalog/windowsxpckbk/

Acknowledgments

Thanks to O'Reilly for signing this book and sticking with it through the delays. We'd also like to thank our editor Simon St.Laurent for being patient with us and providing words of encouragement throughout the process.

Jim Aspinwall, author of several books including *PC Hacks* (O'Reilly), wrote Chapters 3 and 20 and The Appendix. Jonathan Hassell, author of *Learning Windows Server 2003* (O'Reilly) among others, wrote Chapters 2 and 19. We appreciate their help without which the book might have never been completed. We would also like to thank Wei-Meng Lee for his initial contribution to Chapter 19.

Jim and Jonathan also served as technical reviewers along with Eric Cloninger, all of whom caught numerous oversights and mistakes which made the book much better as a result. We'd like especially to highlight Eric's thoughtful and thorough feedback.

Preston thanks, as always, his wife Lydia, and children Gabe and Mia.

Robbie would like to thank his lovely wife, Janet, for her support and friendship.

CHAPTER 1

Introduction

The Windows operating system (OS) has come a long way in the last 10 years. In the early days of Windows NT, system crashes were common annoyances that users and administrators had to learn to deal with. There were few tools to manage the OS, and the ones that were available, mainly of the graphical variety, were limited in functionality and didn't scale well. Also at that time, Microsoft was not yet serious about providing intuitive scripting interfaces or mechanisms to deploy configuration changes, which would allow administrators to automate repetitive tasks. The result was that administrators were forced to do a lot with little.

The tides changed dramatically with the release of Windows 2000, which turned out to be much more scalable and manageable. Microsoft began to improve in the management areas it had previously lacked by adding more tools and introducing several new scripting interfaces that were robust and easy to use.

But in many ways, Windows 2000 felt like a first version release of a major piece of software, which it was. Windows 2000 did a lot of things right, but there were still major gaps in terms of usability and features. Windows XP, Microsoft's latest client OS, is a much more mature platform. It isn't as big of an upgrade as Windows NT to Windows 2000, but Microsoft smoothed out a lot of the rough edges that were present in Windows 2000.

You can't get all of this capability wrapped up into a single OS without some trade-offs. To be able to take full advantage of Windows XP, you have to know lots of gory technical details. You have to know how to navigate through the hundreds of dialogs and menus. You have to know which command-line utilities are available to accomplish various tasks, where to find them, and which options you should use for each utility. You have to know what scripting interfaces are available to automate tasks so you can keep your support costs low. We take it for granted, but that is a lot for any one person to know. We've been doing Windows system administration for nine years and we still have a difficult time recalling the correct tool or command or scripting interface for certain tasks.

And that is the purpose of this book: to be a comprehensive reference so we don't have to waste time (and brain cells) trying to remember that WMI doesn't have any scripting interfaces for creating or modifying pagefiles; or how to use Group Policy to run a task on a group of workstations; or how to find all of the files that are currently open on a system. This book covers installation, configuration, and maintenance duties for Windows XP, but it also covers a great deal more.

Approach to the Book

If you are familiar with the O'Reilly cookbook format that you can find in other popular books such as *Active Directory Cookbook*, *Perl Cookbook*, or *Windows Server Cookbook*, then the layout of this book will not be new to you. It is composed of 20 chapters, each containing 10 to 30 recipes that describe how to perform a particular task. Within each recipe are four sections: *Problem*, *Solution*, *Discussion*, and *See Also*. The Problem section briefly describes the task the recipe addresses and when you might need to use it. The Solution section contains step-by-step instructions on how to accomplish the task. Depending on the task, there could be several sets of solutions covered. The Discussion section goes into detail about the solution(s). The See Also section contains references to additional sources of information that can be useful if you still need more information after reading the discussion. The See Also section may reference other recipes, Microsoft Knowledge Base (MS KB) (*http://support.microsoft.com/*) articles or documentation from the Microsoft Developers Network (MSDN) (*http://msdn.microsoft.com*).

At Least Three Ways to Do It

People like to work in different ways. Some prefer graphical user interfaces (GUI) while others like command-line interfaces (CLI). And experienced system administrators like to automate tasks using scripts. Since people prefer different methods, and no one method is necessarily better than another, we decided to write solutions to recipes using as many of each as is available. That means instead of just a single solution per recipe, we include several using GUI, CLI, and scripting examples. That said, some recipes cannot be accomplished with one of the three methods or it may be very difficult to do with a particular method. In that case, we cover only the applicable methods.

In the GUI and CLI solutions, we use standard tools that are either provided with the operating system or available for download from Microsoft's web site. But because there is a lot of good freeware and shareware out there, we also include a section on applicable tools you can download that can help you accomplish the task.

We took a similar approach with the scripting solutions. While one of the authors prefers Perl, we focus on VBScript due to its widespread use among Windows administrators. It is also the most straightforward from a coding perspective when using Windows Management Instrumentation (WMI) and Windows Script Host (WSH). For those familiar with other languages such as Visual Basic, Perl, and JScript, it is very easy to convert code from VBScript. For those of you who wish that all of the solutions were written with Perl instead of VBScript, you are in luck. On the book web site we've posted companion Perl scripts for each VBScript example. Go to *http://www.rallenhome.com/books/* to download the code.

Where to Find the Tools

For the GUI and CLI solutions to mean much to you, you need access to the tools that are used in the examples. For this reason, in the majority of cases and unless otherwise noted, we used only tools that are part of the default operating system or available in the Resource Kit or Support Tools.

The Windows Server 2003 and Windows 2000 Resource Kit tools can be installed on Windows XP and provide numerous utilities that aid administrators in their daily tasks. More information on the Resource Kit can be found at the following web site: *http://www.microsoft.com/windows/reskits/*. Some of the Resource Kit tools are free; for others you must buy the Resource Kit.

Windows Support Tools also includes many "must have" tools for people who work with Windows XP. The installation MSI for the Windows Support Tools can be found on an XP CD in the *\support\tools* directory.

Running Tools with Alternate Credentials

A best practice for managing Windows XP systems is to create separate administrator accounts and grant them elevated privileges, instead of letting administrators use their normal user account that they use to access network resources. This is beneficial because an administrator who wants to use elevated privileges has to log on explicitly through an admin account instead of having privileges all the time, which could lead to accidental changes. With the separate account method, the administrator would need alternate credentials to use tools to administer systems unless he or she logged on (locally or with Terminal Services) to the target machine using admin credentials.

There are several ways to specify alternate credentials when running tools. Many GUI and CLI tools have a user and password authentication option. If the tool you want to use does not have that option you can use the *runas.exe* command instead. The following command runs the *enumprop.exe* command under the credentials of the administrator account in the *rallencorp.com* domain:

```
> runas /user:administrator@rallencorp.com /netonly "enumprop LDAP://dc1/
dc=rallencorp,dc=com"
```

Sometimes it is convenient to create an MMC console that runs under administrator privileges. In this case, simply use *mmc.exe* as the command to run from *runas*:

```
> runas /user:administrator@rallencorp.com /netonly "mmc.exe"
```

This will create an empty MMC console from which you can add consoles for any snap-in that has been installed on the local computer. This is beneficial because all of the consoles that you add will be run under that administrative account. If you don't want to type that command over and over, simply create a shortcut on your desktop and put the command as the target path. By doing this you eliminate one of the common complaints about using alternate credentials, that is, it makes the job more tedious.

 The /netonly option is necessary if the user you are authenticating with does not have local logon rights on the computer from which you are running the command, or if you want to authenticate with an account from a non-trusted domain.

There is another option for running MMC snap-ins or any GUI program with alternate credentials. Click on the Start menu and browse to the tool you want to open, hold down the Shift key, and then right click on the tool. If you select Run As, you will be prompted to enter alternate credentials with which to run the tool.

A Brief Word on Windows Scripting

Much has been said over the years about how unfriendly the Windows OS is to experienced power users and system administrators who want to automate tasks with scripts. We're pleased to say that Microsoft has made some great strides in this area over the last four or five years so that now there are very few tasks that you cannot automate with a script.

Microsoft has developed three primary scripting interfaces over the years: WSH, WMI, and ADSI. Note that we said that these are interfaces, not languages. In generic terms, a scripting interface is just a framework for how a script calls functions or methods to perform tasks. WSH is the scripting engine that acts as the interpreter for the scripting languages that are native to Windows (i.e., VBScript and Jscript). It has an interface for doing basic scripting such as printing out to a console or displaying a dialog box, processing command-line arguments, and other basic system administration tasks such as reading and writing files and manipulating the Registry. WMI is the high octane system management interface. With it you can query and often configure many of the components within Windows. WMI is to computers what ADSI is to Active Directory. ADSI is the primary scripting interface for querying and manipulating objects in Active Directory. You can also use it to manage local users and groups on a computer as well as the IIS Metabase.

Where to Find More Information

While it is our hope that this book provides you with enough information to perform the majority of Windows system administration tasks you are likely to do, it is not realistic to think every possible task can be covered. In fact, there are easily another five or six chapters we could have included in this book, but due to space and time considerations it was not possible for this edition. There is a wealth of additional resources and information you can find on the Internet or in a bookstore. In this section we cover some of the ones we use most frequently.

Help and Support Center

Windows XP comes with a new feature called the Help and Support Center, which is available directly off the Start menu. It is a great resource of information and it serves as the central location to obtain help information about the operating system, applications, and installed utilities.

Command-Line Tools

If you have any questions about the complete syntax or usage of a command-line tool we use in the book, you should first take a look at the help information available with the tool. The vast majority of CLI tools provide syntax information by simply passing /? as a parameter. For example:

```
> netsh /?
```

Microsoft Knowledge Base (MS KB)

The Microsoft Help and Support web site is a great source of information and is home to the Microsoft Knowledge Base (MS KB) articles. Throughout the book we include references to pertinent MS KB articles where you can find more information on a topic. You can find the complete text for a KB article by searching on the KB number at the following web site: *http://support.microsoft.com/default.aspx*. You can also append the KB article number to the end of this URL to go directly to the article: *http://support.microsoft.com/?kbid=*.

Microsoft Developers Network (MSDN)

MSDN contains a ton of information on Windows XP and programmatic interfaces such as WMI. Throughout the book we'll sometimes reference MSDN pages in recipes where applicable. Unfortunately, there is no easy way to reference the exact page we're referring to unless we provided the URL or navigation to the page, which would more than likely change by the time this book is printed. Instead, we provide the name of the title of the page, which you can use to search on via the following site: *http://msdn.microsoft.com/library/*.

Web Sites

These web sites are great starting points for information that helps you perform the tasks covered in this book:

Microsoft Windows XP Home Pages – http://www.microsoft.com/windowsxp/
> This site is the starting point for Windows XP information provided by Microsoft. It contains links to whitepapers, case studies, and tools.

Microsoft Webcasts – http://support.microsoft.com/default.aspx?scid=fh;EN-US;pwebcst
> Webcasts are on-demand audio/video technical presentations that cover a wide range of Microsoft products. There are numerous webcasts related to Windows XP technologies that cover such topics as installing service packs, configuring home networking, and troubleshooting startup and shutdown problems.

Google – http://www.google.com/
> Google should be one of your primary starting points for locating information. Google is often quicker and easier to use to search the Microsoft web sites (e.g., MSDN) than the search engines provided on those sites.

MyITForum – http://www.myitforum.com
> The MyITForum site has very active online forums for various Microsoft technologies. It also has a large repository of scripts.

LabMice – http://www.labmice.net/
> The LabMice web site contains a large collection of links to information on Windows XP including MS KB articles, whitepapers, and other useful web sites.

Robbie Allen's Home Page – http://www.rallenhome.com/
> One of the author's personal web sites, which has information about the books he's written and links to download the code contained in each (including this book).

Microsoft Technet Script Center – http://www.microsoft.com/technet/community/scriptcenter/default.mspx
> This site contains a large collection of WSH, WMI, and ADSI scripts.

Newsgroups

Many of the Windows XP related Microsoft newsgroups are very active and have one or more of Microsoft's Most Valuable Professionals (MVPs) actively responding to questions. If you have a question and can't find an answer, try posting to the pertinent newsgroup.

These are general-purpose Windows XP newsgroups:

- microsoft.public.windowsxp.general
- comp.windows.misc

Here are some of the newsgroups that cover a specific Windows XP technology:

- microsoft.public.windowsxp.configuration_manage
- microsoft.public.windowsxp.customize
- microsoft.public.windowsxp.help_and_support
- microsoft.public.windowsxp.security_admin
- microsoft.public.windowsxp.setup_deployment

These are the scripting-related newsgroups:

- microsoft.public.windowsxp.wmi
- microsoft.public.scripting.vbscript
- microsoft.public.scripting.wsh
- microsoft.public.adsi.general
- microsoft.public.active.directory.interfaces

If you have a question about a particular topic, a good starting point is to search the newsgroups using Google Groups (*http://groups.google.com/*). Just like Google's web search engine, Google's group search engine is an invaluable resource.

Magazines

A good way to stay current with the latest industry trends and system administration techniques is by reading magazines. Here are a few good ones you should consider subscribing to:

Windows IT Pro Magazine – http://www.windowsitpro.com/
This is a general-purpose monthly magazine for system administrators who support Microsoft products. The articles contributed by industry experts are informative and provide unique insight into common issues system administrators face.

Windows Scripting Solutions – http://www.winnetmag.com/WindowsScripting/
This is a useful monthly newsletter that covers all aspects of scripting in the Windows environment. You'll see a little bit of everything in this newsletter.

Security Administrator – http://www.winnetmag.com/WindowsSecurityIndex.cfm
Security is an important part of any system administrator's job these days. With this news letter you'll be able to stay abreast of the latest Windows security issues.

Operating System Installation and Maintenance

2.0 Introduction

Windows installations have matured over the years and have become the gold standard for user-friendly setup procedures across all different platforms. Most users will encounter the installation process only once—when they first purchase Windows XP—and those who buy computers with Windows XP pre-installed are subjected to even less of the installation procedure. Thus, the majority of advice in this book will be about using and administering Windows XP after it is installed.

However, there are always some things to remember when preparing for a Windows XP deployment, creating customized installations of multiple operating systems, and keeping those deployments up to date, and that is the focus of this chapter. You'll find recipes that include very generic solutions, as sometimes there is only one way to do it, but you'll also find other recipes including both GUI and command line methods, and some recipes on updating Windows XP that include Group Policy methods.

2.1 Preparing to Install Windows XP

Problem

You want to get ready to install Windows XP on your machine.

Solution

You'll need the following items handy to complete the installation:

- The XP professional installation CD, if you're using this type of medium for the installation
- The product key for your version, which can be found on the back of the CD jewel case for retail versions. For network installations and other volume

editions, you'll need to check with the person in your organization that is in charge of licensing.

- Details about your Internet or network connection, such as whether you are assigned an IP address or obtain one automatically from your provider via DHCP, usernames and passwords, and miscellaneous server addresses. You can probably find all of this information in a welcome letter or packet you received from your Internet service provider when you signed up.

- The name of your computer, and the name of the workgroup or domain to which it belongs. For machines that will join a domain, you'll need an account on the domain and the password associated with that account. For workgroup installations, all you need is the name of the workgroup.

If you have a machine currently running another version of Windows, and you wish to upgrade to Windows XP, run the Windows XP Upgrade Advisor, which you can download from the Microsoft web site at *http://www.microsoft.com/windowsxp/pro/ upgrading/advisor.mspx*. The Upgrade Advisor examines your system's hardware and software and lets you know whether Windows XP will run on the system. It will also ping Microsoft's web site and let you know of any updates you can download that will further prepare your system for the upgrade, and even install those updates for you if you'd like.

> The code that makes the Windows XP Upgrade Advisor work is taken directly from the Windows XP installation code, so while you are running the tool, you may see messages that imply you're installing the OS. You can safely ignore that insinuation.

Finally, perform a bit of house cleaning on your system to make sure everything is in as tip-top a shape as possible. Try the following steps:

1. Go to Control Panel and Add/Remove Programs, and remove anything you haven't used in the last six months. These programs take up hard disk space, litter the Registry with entries, and generally make upgrading more complex. Before you uninstall, however, make sure you have the original installation disks for the software so you can re-install if needed.

2. Go to your computer manufacturer's web site and check to see whether you have the latest BIOS version. Most modern manufacturers post updated BIOS revisions every six to twelve months, and it's best to have this piece of hardware as updated as possible before you upgrade, as the installation process uses the BIOS extensively.

3. Get rid of the temporary files that are probably littering your computer. Look in directories such as *C:\Temp*, *C:\Windows\Temp*, or *C:\WINNT\Temp*. Also, delete any temporary Internet files from Internet Explorer by opening IE and going to Tools and Options. On the General tab, under Temporary Internet Files, click the Delete button. Also, empty your Recycle Bin as well.

4. Uninstall your antivirus software. Chances are that there is an updated version available specifically for Windows XP that you can install after Setup is finished, and in the interim, antivirus software can have nasty interactions with XP's installation method.

5. Of course, defragmenting your hard drive is a great anti-problem strategy.

Discussion

One of the early decisions you'll need to make when installing Windows XP on a system you already own is whether to perform a clean installation of the OS or to upgrade your existing version of Windows to Windows XP. There are a couple of schools of thought on the matter.

Advocates of clean installations subscribe to the theory of Windows rot: that is, the performance and age of a Windows installation are inversely proportional. As Windows installations get older, a lot of trash and detritus builds up in key areas of the OS, including temporary folders, the Registry, startup groups, Internet Explorer's add-on manager, and so on. Couple that with the high likelihood that your system is infested with spyware, old cookies, and adware, and many administrators and computer experts believe that anytime you want to change your installed operating system, you should completely format your hard drive and install cleanly. Of course, the downside of this method is that you need to reinstall all of your regularly used applications, restore your data from a backup, and reconfigure your desktop settings, wallpaper, favorites, fonts, and other preferred customizations.

On the other hand, upgrade installations have become increasingly refined, accurate, and problem-free in recent years. Windows XP's installation program is hard to kill, and if it encounters a problem upon upgrade, it can usually work around it. By performing an upgrade, you maintain your current settings, there's no need for a lengthy data restoration process, and you don't need to reinstall all of your applications. The flip side, however, is that all of the junk and unwanted software travels with you on the journey between operating systems, and over time that can cause real performance and stability problems.

The debate can rage on and on, but the real decision maker for you should be the amount of time and effort you're willing to invest in the move to Windows XP. If your primary aim is a clean system and you have an entire weekend and perhaps longer to see the process through to completion, then go with the clean install. If you need to get Windows XP running in an afternoon, then use the upgrade installation.

See Also

Recipe 2.8 for more on upgrading to Windows XP, the PC Pitstop XP Readiness Test site at *http://www.pcpitstop.com/xpready/xptests.asp*, WSC's "Upgrading to Windows XP" site at *http://aumha.org/win5/a/xpupgrad.htm*, and Microsoft's "Get Ready to Set Up Windows XP Professional" page at *http://www.microsoft.com/windowsxp/ using/setup/getstarted/intro.mspx*

2.2 Installing from a CD or DVD

Problem

You have a CD or DVD of Windows XP, and you want to perform a clean installation of Windows XP on your computer using it.

Solution

It's a fairly effortless procedure to install Windows XP onto systems.

1. Turn the system power on and insert the Windows XP CD into the drive. If you receive a prompt to select from what location to boot, choose the option to boot off the CD. The system will boot a minimal, text-only version of Windows XP into main memory and begin the initial installation procedure.

2. Select the Clean Install option.

3. Read the terms of the license agreement. If you accept (which, of course, you have to do in order to continue installation), hit F8 to continue.

4. Partition your disk, as described in the Discussion section. Figure 2-1 shows the disk partitioning screen.

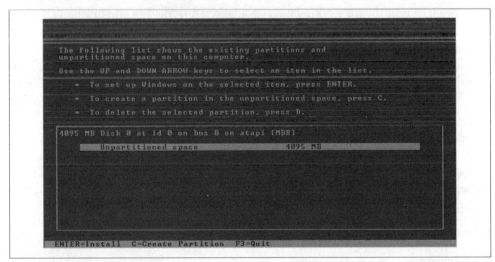

Figure 2-1. The disk partitioning screen

5. Select the file system with which you want the partition formatted and press Enter to start the format. The remainder of this book will assume your Windows XP installation resides on a partition formatted with the NTFS file system.

This process can take up to one hour to complete, depending on the size and speed of your drive. If your hard drive is new or you have already formatted it, you can choose the Quick Format option for near-immediate results.

6. Enter the location where you want the actual Windows XP system files. We recommend accepting the default location, *%systemroot%\windows*.

7. Wait for the file copy to finish. If you are downloading the files via a modem, this can take up to five minutes. Once the copy is complete, the system will reboot, and the next portion of the installation will commence in graphical mode.

8. Choose the regional settings for this computer. You can change the language, locale, and keyboard settings depending on your geographical location. Click Next.

9. Enter your name and organization, and then click Next.

10. Choose the unique name of this computer using alphanumeric characters. The name can be up to 15 characters long and should not contain spaces. Click Next.

11. Generate and enter a password for the administrator account. Be sure to remember this information. If you write it down, store the paper in a secure location, as this password allows for full control of your system.

12. Adjust the time zone and machine time and date on the next screen. Click Next.

13. The network components of Windows XP are installed next. This step includes the following processes:

    a. Detecting the network adapter or adapters installed in the machine. This is usually automatic, as Windows XP knows of a lot of network cards and can install drivers without the need for your input.

    b. Confirming the selection of network protocols. On modern networks, you will typically want the Client for Microsoft Networks, File and Print Sharing for Microsoft Networks, and the TCP/IP protocol. The "typical settings," as shown in Figure 2-2, will install these automatically.

    c. Creating or joining an existing workgroup or domain. If you'd like to join a domain, you'll need a domain username and password. For workgroups, just the name will suffice.

14. Finally, files are copied and settings are finalized. This step can take an additional 20 minutes.

Your installation will be complete once the system restarts.

Discussion

The installation process is trivial for the vast majority of users. Here are some things to expect and note during the process:

There are some options when it comes to slicing and dicing the disk space on a machine that will run Windows XP. You can, of course, create a new partition on

---

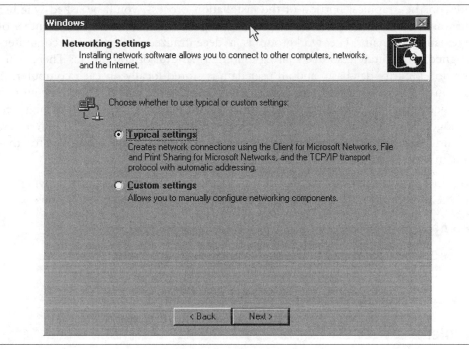

Figure 2-2. The networking options selection screen

either a nonpartitioned portion of a disk or by deleting an existing partition to make room for a new one. You can also install Windows XP to an existing disk partition if there's enough free disk space.

How much disk space? A general guide is that the partition that Windows XP will reside on ought to be at least 1.5 GB in size, and preferably more. It's also recommended by most computer experts that you keep the system files separate from your individual data files—at the very least, keep your personal data on a separate partition, and even better, on a separate disk. Having separate partitions ensures the security of the your personal files if the operating system ever becomes corrupted, whereas having separate disks affords that security as well as increased I/O performance because of less disk seeking.

Along with partitioning comes the choice of file systems. Windows XP supports two: NTFS and FAT32. NTFS is the file system native to Windows NT-based operating systems, and it supports the full range of built-in security features, automatic file compression, and file encryption. FAT32, while a venerable standard that has a place in systems where legacy compatibility is crucial, does not offer the security features of NTFS and therefore should be a last resort. However, you can convert an existing FAT32 system to NTFS at a later time; reversion to a FAT system from NTFS is not possible with Windows XP's built-in disk management tool suite.

Later, in the graphical portion of the installation process, you'll be asked whether you want to create or join an existing workgroup or make this machine a member of an existing domain. The workgroup is a decentralized collection of computers designed to facilitate resource sharing among a handful of computers. There is no common security database, and all user data is stored locally on each computer. A domain is a group of network resources as designed by the network administrator so that their security databases may be centralized and shared. Domains allow for a central logon and easier management of its member clients and servers. To join a new machine to a domain, that domain must already exist and the controller for that domain must be available to the new machine.

One final tip: to speed up the installation process, you might consider copying the entire CD to your local hard drive, thus removing the need for a slow CD drive.

See Also

Recipe 2.9 for creating multiboot installations

2.3   Installing from a Network Share

Problem

You want to install Windows XP from a file share located on your network.

Solution

Without a lot of work, you can only do this from a machine running an existing copy of Windows XP. This of course means that you'll have to perform either an upgrade to your current operating system or a multiboot installation, in which a clean copy of XP is installed alongside your current operating system.

To run XP's installation program from a network share:

1. Boot your existing version of Windows on your target machine.
2. Browse to the network location where the Windows XP distribution files are located.
3. Run *WINNT32.EXE*.

The Setup program will run and create a local copy of the Windows XP distribution files that are located on the file share. Once the copy process is complete, Windows will prompt you to reboot. After the restart, you can now follow the instructions, beginning with step 8, which can be found in Recipe 2.2.

Discussion

Installing XP from a network share isn't a very efficient way to distribute XP to multiple machines unless you have only a handful of systems on your network. The most

---

common reason to install the operating system this way is to share out one CD or DVD drive across the network and not shuffle CDs around to multiple machines. However, for any more than five computers, we recommend finding an alternate method of installation, particularly using the client deployment features of Windows Server 2003.

See Also

Recipe 2.6 for installing from Remote Installation Services

2.4   Installing from an Unattended Installation

Problem

You want to use a script file to have a completely "hands-free" installation of Windows XP, particularly for use on multiple computers.

Solution

Using a graphical user interface

Use Setup Manager to generate an unattended setup file based on your responses to different prompts.

1. On the Windows XP distribution CD, navigate through the *Support\Tools* folder hierarchy.
2. Double-click the *deploy.cab* file.
3. Select all files inside the new folder, and select Copy to Folder from the Edit menu.
4. Copy the files to a directory on your hard disk. You may need to create this directory using the Make New Folder button.
5. Inside the new folder, launch Setup Manager by double-clicking on *setupmgr.exe*.

Once Setup Manager has started, you'll be prompted either to create a new answer file or to edit an existing one. Choose to create a new one, and click Next. Now, you're presented with several options, depending on the particular application for which your new answer file will be used. You can create a basic unattended setup answer file, one that can automate the mini-Setup program inside an installation that has been run through the SYSPREP utility (more on this later), or a file that will control installations started with RIS, or Remote Installation Services. Both of these are covered later in this chapter. For now, select to create a normal, basic unattended setup answer file, and click Next.

The next screen prompts you to choose the operating system for which you're creating an unattended install—you can create files for all editions of Windows XP and all editions of Windows Server 2003 except Datacenter, too, so the Setup Manager utility is more useful than it might otherwise appear. Choose to install Windows XP and click Next. At this point, you can now choose what level of "hands-off" you wish to achieve: a completely hands-on installation with customized defaults read from the answer file, a fully hands-off installation that is started from the command line and not finished until Windows XP is completely installed, and most options in between. Choose Fully Automated to get the full breadth of options that Setup Manager can manage, and click Next.

Here, Setup Manager offers to assist you in creating a distribution share on your network, a file share that contains an entire copy of the Windows distribution files for the purposes of kicking off network-based automated installation sequences. For our purposes, click on "No, this answer file will be used to install from a CD," since we just need to create an answer file, not generate an infrastructure for more complex rollouts. Click Next, accept the End-User License Agreement, and click Next once more. You have completed the wizard portion of the Setup Manager process, and the screen shown in Figure 2-3 is shown.

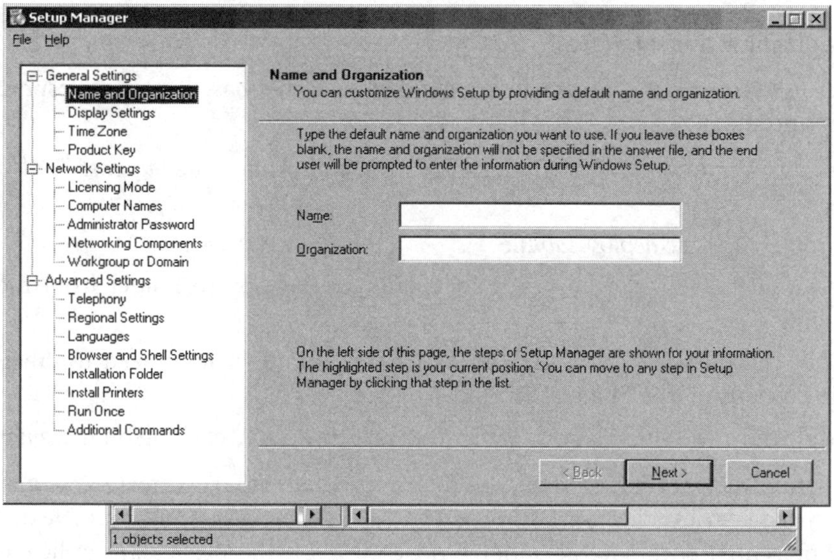

Figure 2-3. Setup Manager's detailed configuration screen

The remaining portion of Setup Manager involves customizing the many details of a Windows XP installation.

1. The first section, General Settings, allows you to enter your name and organization, and display settings like color depth and resolution, your time zone, and your Windows product key. Enter the appropriate values and click Next in each section.

2. The Computer Names screen appears. You have some options as far as assigning names to newly deployed computers: you can type in the names directly into Setup Manager, import names from a text file, or tell Setup to automatically generate them based on the values entered for the name and organization earlier in the process. Click Next to proceed.

3. Now, you need to generate an administrator password. Since you've chosen the fully automated type of answer file, the option for the user to provide a password is not available. Instead, you enter one yourself. Click Next to move on.

4. You're prompted on the next screen to select the appropriate networking components for these systems. The typical settings use DHCP to get an IP address and installs file sharing capabilities. You can also select a static IP address. Click Next once you've configured the relevant options.

5. On the Workgroup or Domain page, choose whether to be a part of a workgroup or join an existing security domain. Also specify the names of either the workgroup or the domain to join. Click Next.

6. You're now in the Advanced Settings portion of Setup Manager, and the first screen is very, very useful: it allows you to determine exactly what parts of Windows are installed on a machine. Now you can get rid of Games or not install IIS on all of your machines by default, a useful feature of the Windows installation program that Microsoft inexplicably removed first in Windows 2000 Professional and then in all later versions. Select the appropriate Windows components to include or not install, and click Next.

7. The Telephony Settings page appears. Enter your area code and outside dialing preferences, and then to proceed, click Next.

8. On the next page, adjust any regional settings, like keyboard, currency, time zone, and the like. Click Next, and again, specify your region-specific language settings. Click Next when you are finished.

9. The Browser and Shell Settings page appears. Using this feature, you can customize Internet Explorer's home page, security, and personalization settings, so that these are automatically set up during installation. Click Next once you've configured these options appropriately.

10. Specify the name of the folder where the Windows system files should reside. This is also known as the SYSTEMROOT for other purposes, like in the context of the Recovery Console. Click Next to continue.

11. The Install Printers screen appears. Here, you can specify the names of network printers that will be automatically configured and already available to the new installation. You can specify any number of network printers. This is a big win for all network administrators. Click Next once you've entered your list of printers.

12. The Run Once page allows you to specify commands and programs that will run after the first boot of the newly installed operating system—that is, just after it's finished. This is useful if you have batch files to run only once after a machine is installed. These settings are stored in the Windows Registry. Click Next.

13. The Additional Commands screen appears. These commands are executed at the end of Setup, but before the first restart. This feature is great if you're interested in installing the Recovery Console automatically after an installation is completed. To continue, click Next.

14. Finally, you'll be prompted to select a location for the answer file. Select one, click OK, and you have successfully created your answer file.

 Before using your unattended installation script, you'll need to rename it from *UNATTEND.TXT* to *WINNT.SIF*. Refraining from doing so will result in a nonfunctional script.

You can see a sample SIF file, generated by Setup Manager, in the Discussion section of this recipe.

Using a command-line interface

To begin an unattended setup using a script, you first need to call *WINNT32.EXE* from the command line using the following, assuming your script is in *C:\Deploy*:

```
> Winnt32 /unattend:c:\deploy\winnt.sif
```

Another method is a bit less keyboard interactive but requires more manual labor: if you use the distribution CD-ROM to install Windows XP and you boot directly from it, Setup will look for a file on a floppy in the A drive named *WINNT.SIF*. If it finds one, Setup will read the instructions from it; if it doesn't, then Setup will continue along a normal, user-interactive process.

Discussion

Perhaps the simplest method of automating Windows XP deployment is to use unattended setup answer files. These files use a syntax not unlike that found in Windows 3.1's old INI files, providing answers for questions like computer name, your CD key, your name, where you live, and the like.

Here is a sample unattended setup file (known as an SIF file):

```
[data]
floppyless = "1"
msdosinitiated = "1"
OriSrc = "\\%SERVERNAME%\RemInst\%INSTALLPATH%\%MACHINETYPE%"
OriTyp = "4"
LocalSourceOnCD = 1
DisableAdminAccountOnDomainJoin = 1
```

```
[SetupData]
OsLoadOptions = "/noguiboot /fastdetect"
SetupSourceDevice = "\Device\LanmanRedirector\%SERVERNAME%\RemInst\%INSTALLPATH%"

[Unattended]
OemPreinstall = yes
OemPnpDriversPath = \Drivers\Nic
DriverSigningPolicy = Ignore
FileSystem = LeaveAlone
ExtendOEMPartition = 0
TargetPath = \WINDOWS
OemSkipEula = yes
InstallFilesPath = "\\%SERVERNAME%\RemInst\%INSTALLPATH%\%MACHINETYPE%"
LegacyNIC = 1

[UserData]
FullName = "%USERFIRSTNAME% %USERLASTNAME%"
OrgName = "%ORGNAME%"
ComputerName = %MACHINENAME%
ProductID = "ABCDE-12345-FGHIK-67890-LMNOP"

[GuiUnattended]
OemSkipWelcome = 1
OemSkipRegional = 1
TimeZone = %TIMEZONE%
AdminPassword = "*"

[Display]
BitsPerPel = 24
XResolution = 1024
YResolution = 768
VRefresh = 60

[Networking]

[NetServices]
MS_Server=params.MS_PSched

[Identification]
JoinDomain = %MACHINEDOMAIN%
DoOldStyleDomainJoin = Yes

[RemoteInstall]
Repartition = Yes
UseWholeDisk = Yes

[OSChooser]
Description ="Windows XP with Service Pack 2"
Help ="Automatically installs Microsoft Windows XP Professional without prompting the
user for input."
LaunchFile = "%INSTALLPATH%\%MACHINETYPE%\templates\startrom.com"
ImageType =Flat
Version="5.1 (0)"
```

See Also

Recipe 2.5 for cloning Windows XP installations, Recipe 2.6 for installing from Remote Installation Services, Recipe 2.17 for slipstreaming a service pack or hotfix into a build, and MS KB 155197, "Unattended Setup Parameters" for information on each setting in the SIF file

2.5   Cloning Windows XP Installations

Problem

You have one machine that you'd like to clone onto multiple machines.

Solution

Use SYSPREP to accomplish this. First, configure and arrange the initial machine as you like it, using the local administrator account. Then:

1. Create a new local administrator. See Chapter 15 for instructions on creating local users.
2. Log out of the local administrator account and log in to the new account you created.
3. Navigate to the System applet inside Control Panel. Under the Advanced tab, click the User Profiles button.
4. Select the one called Administrator that has the local machine's name in it, and click Copy To.
5. Click Change in the Permitted to Use section.
6. Select Everyone in the list. This gives permission for anybody logged into the computer to use the contents of the profile. Click OK.
7. Click OK to get out of the Copy To dialog box.
8. Finally, copy the contents of the *Documents and Settings\Administrator* folder to *Documents and Settings\Default Users*. Ensure that you are displaying hidden files and folders so that you copy all configuration files.
9. Now, run SYSPREP with the following command:

   ```
   > sysprep –reseal –quiet –mini –pnp
   ```

SYSPREP will strip the SIDs off the system, scrub any personal identifying information from the image, and then shut down the machine. From that point, use a drive copying utility to move the images to multiple machines.

Once the copy is complete, reboot the computer without the floppy and proceed through mini-Setup again, so that all personal information can be restored and new SIDs can be generated. Do this on the cloned computers and the original "prototype" computer.

Discussion

Products like Symantec Ghost are often the quickest way to lay down an image of a drive onto multiple systems at once. The downside is that by taking what amounts to a photograph of a machine, any security identifiers (SIDs) that are stored on the machine are replicated in that image to other machines. The result would be multiple machines with identical SIDs, which can cause a lot of problems on your network.

Ghost and DriveImage have SID generators built in, but Microsoft doesn't support that. The company wants you to use SYSPREP instead, which scrubs SIDs from an image in a supported fashion so that you can clone a machine easily.

SYSPREP works with other operating systems besides Windows XP; however, SYSPREP will not image a domain controller, a certificate server, or a member of a cluster.

See Also

Recipe 2.4 for installing from an unattended installation, and "Customizing SYSPREP Installations" (*http://www.microsoft.com/resources/documentation/Windows/XP/all/reskit/en-us/Default.asp?url=/resources/documentation/windows/xp/all/reskit/en-us/prbc_cai_oziz.asp*)

2.6   Installing from Remote Installation Services (RIS)

Problem

You want to use a menu-based system to deploy Windows XP on systems without similar hardware (in other words, machines unsuitable for cloning).

Solution

You can use a feature of Windows 2000 Server and Windows Server 2003, called Remote Installation Services (RIS), to deploy Windows images onto systems with varied hardware bases. Here's how.

RIS depends on the ability to network-boot your client computers and transfer the image to them. The process to do so depends somewhat on the client computer: some corporate-targeted PCs have options in the machine's BIOS to boot from the network, usually found in the area that determines the boot order of the storage devices. Other computers offer an option directly during the POST process to press F12 or some similar key to perform a network service boot (the Compaq Armada E550 I'm using to write this now uses the latter method, whereas the Dell Precision Workstation that is my main desktop computer uses F10).

However, some older computers—and yes, some newer computers as well—don't have the option to boot to the network in their BIOS or during POST. In this case, you'll need to use the RIS remote boot disk, mentioned earlier in this chapter as the saving grace for some machines. The Windows Server 2003 RIS disk supports 32 network adapters, all of which are PCI cards. If your Ethernet card is on that list, then RIS will work even if the machine doesn't directly support PXE, the Preboot eXecution Environment. To generate the network boot disk, navigate to the *\RemoteInstall\ Admin\i386* directory on your RIS server machine, and double-click on *RBFG.EXE*. It will prompt you to insert a disk which it will then format and reconstruct as the RIS remote boot disk.

On to actually performing the deployment: insert the boot floppy or select the option to boot from the network, which applies in your case. If you use the boot floppy, you will see a screen similar to the following:

```
Microsoft Windows Remote Installation Boot Floppy
Copyright 2001 Lanworks Technologies Co., a subsidiary of 3Com Corporation
All rights reserved.
3Com 3C90XB / 3C90XC Etherlink PCI
Node: 00115A5E3E12
DHCP....
TFTP..........
Press F12 for network service boot
```

During that process, no matter which method you use to activate the network boot, the computer contacts a DHCP server and requests an address. That address is sent in a packet, containing a pointer to a server that has files needed to continue to RIS boot process. These files are transferred using the TFTP protocol, a cousin of the commonly found FTP protocol. Once the boot files are transferred, the program prompts you to confirm that you want to boot from the network. Press F12 to confirm this, and the blue-screened, text-based Client Installation Wizard will appear. Then, follow these steps:

The first screen prompts you to enter your username, password, and account domain membership information. Do so, and then press Enter.

You'll now be asked whether you want to do an automatic or custom setup or if you'd like to restart a previous failed setup attempt. Automatic setups generate the computer name from a combination of your username and the computer's MAC address and set up an unattended installation with all the defaults. They can also retrieve existing data from Active Directory with regard to computer name and identification if you're redeploying a machine already in the directory. Custom setups allow you to define a specific computer name for each RIS installation whether or not the machine is already in the directory. Restarting a failed setup attempt is as functional as it is obvious.

When using the Custom Setup option, you will be expected to know the location in Active Directory that the computer account should be located. If you do not specify a location, the default [domainname.com]/Computers, the computer's organizational unit, will be the home of the newly deployed machine.

Then, confirm your selections, and press Enter. The installation will begin.

Discussion

If you're thinking of using RIS on your network, here are some things to keep in mind.

- All client machines must support the PXE boot feature somehow. This is the stickler here. PXE, or Pre-boot eXecution Environment, allows a computer's BIOS to hand off boot control to the Ethernet card installed on the computer. The Ethernet card searches for an authorized DHCP server, applies the address assigned by that server, and then launches a TFTP transfer client that downloads the necessary files to boot into the Client Installation Wizard—the first step of a RIS installation. If your network card doesn't support PXE booting, then you can't get on the network and therefore can't take advantage of RIS. However, if you're the owner of one of around 20 specific models of network cards, you are in luck: Microsoft provides a network boot disk with takes care of the PXE logic for the network card, enabling you to use RIS on a machine that would otherwise not qualify. There have been many promises on the part of Microsoft to expand this boot disk's coverage of network cards—claims of such modifications date back before the release of Windows 2000—but as of yet, there have been no additions.

- Laptops MUST be able to boot off the network. The aforementioned boot floppy works with only two PC Card-based Ethernet adapters and those are fairly old. So laptops that aren't the most recent will likely still need to be deployed manually, or at least without RIS. However, notebook manufacturers have begun to include built-in Ethernet connections using the miniPCI standard, and these are commonly PXE compliant. If it's time to reevaluate your baseline corporate laptop configuration, you would do well to ensure that your laptops are PXE compliant.

- RIS imaging, using either a scripted install or a flat image installation, can only handle the C drive. If you have a computer with multiple physical disks, RIS will only transfer an image *of* a C drive *to* a C drive, and nothing else. RIS will only build images of C drives, and it will only service C drives on the client side. This works similarly for partitions, although you should be careful about partitioning since RIS tends to reformat the entire hard disk, which will blow away your existing partitions as well. Either pay careful attention when performing RIS deployments to computers with many partitions, or use another scheme to organize your computers.

- You must have a separate partition or physical disk on the server to use for the RIS subsystem. RIS cannot cope with having Windows system files on the same volume where flat images and other images are located. This is mainly because of interactions between critical copies of active Windows system files and the Single Instance Storage Groveler service, or SIS, which allows one copy of one file to be placed on a disk, and links to be placed in all other locations on the disk where a copy of that file resided. It's like mail aliasing, in that small links to one copy of one file save space that would otherwise be wasted with multiple copies of the same file. Enterprises with eight different Server 2003 images available to RIS obviously have eight copies of many files. SIS reduces the disk space usage eight-fold.

Software requirements are a little less stringent than the hardware RIS needs. You must have a DHCP server on your network, and you must be conducting RIS deployments in an Active Directory-based domain. RIS cannot handle static IPs, mainly because the PXE protocol has no such provision for them. RIS also uses DHCP as a mechanism to control the entry of unauthorized RIS servers to your network: before a RIS server can be used for deployments, it must be authorized within the Active Directory.

See Also

Chapter 2, *Learning Windows Server 2003* (O'Reilly), MS KB 304314, "How to Deploy Windows XP Images from Windows 2000 RIS Servers," and MS KB 891275, "How to Set Up, Configure, and Use Remote Installation Services in Windows 2000"

2.7 Troubleshooting Installation Problems

Problem

You're having problems with Windows XP's installation process and want to know where to look for trouble.

Solution

Here are some common problems and suggested workarounds:

Disk space errors
If you're getting messages like "Not enough disk space for installation," then perhaps it's time to look at your partitioning scheme and create another partition from any existing free space on the hard disk. If you don't have any free space left, you'll almost positively have to delete files on the original partition to

make space for the installation. However, if you have a larger drive available, you can clone your smaller drive to the larger one and remove this limitation.

Windows simply won't boot

Make sure that all the installed hardware is detected, and make sure that all of the hardware in your system is listed on the Hardware Compatibility List, which can be found from the Microsoft web site at *http://www.microsoft.com/windows/reskits/webresources*.

STOP messages

Check the Microsoft Knowledge Base at *http://support.microsoft.com* by entering the code for the STOP error that's displayed on the blue error screen. Chances are, there are good workarounds for the error you're seeing listed there. STOP messages are usually caused by either unstable hardware or incorrect driver installations, so again, double-check to make sure your hardware is on the HCL.

Setup fails during text mode

Try to remove legacy boot devices, like old CD-ROM drives or floppy drives, on modern systems because these settings cannot be reliably detected and accounted for by the Setup program. Also, make sure that the Plug and Play operating system option is disabled in the BIOS.

Setup fails during GUI mode

The easiest fix is to simply restart; Setup will figure out where it stopped responding and continue its operations from there. Problems usually creep up at the beginning of GUI mode setup because of the device detection phase. If Setup is freezing midway through the process, it could be because of a failure on the part of the Optional Component Manager (OCM or OC Manager), which handles the installation of external components that have their own setup routines. Finally, if Setup is failing toward the end of the process, it's probably an error with the computer configuration phase, where registration of object linking and embedding (OLE) control dynamic-link libraries (DLLs) is occurring.

Disk I/O and file copy errors

It's possible that your hard disk is defective, or at least that it contains defective sectors. You also might need to replace RAM. Of course, the obvious problem might be defective media, too.

The Discussion section lists more advanced troubleshooting techniques.

Discussion

While the vast majority of the time Windows XP will install without a hitch, there are some issues (a piece of malfunctioning hardware, a power failure during installation, or a faulty download of a dynamic update) that can cause the installation process to fail. Luckily, there are ways to recover from a bugged-out installation.

Starting over

Sometimes it can be easier to cut your losses and start an installation over from the beginning, particularly if an error early in the process is preventing you from proceeding. The installation process changes three things on your drive, all of which need to be reversed to restart the installation (unless, of course, you want to format the hard drive and therefore aren't concerned with data loss):

- Setup also constructs the *win_nt.~bt* directory to store boot files, which instruct your computer to boot into Setup's "post-first" phases (that is, all phases after the initial reboot). This should be removed.

- Setup modifies your *boot.ini* file with a line something like this:

    ```
    Multi(0)disk(0)rdisk(0)partition(2)\$win_nt$.~bt="Microsoft Windows XP
    Professional Setup"
    ```

    This line needs to be removed as well.

- Setup creates the *win_nt.~ls* directory and copies all files to the system in this directory in order to have data to work with if it cannot access the setup CD. This should also be removed, if it exists. (Some installation scenarios don't require its creation.)

At this point, no traces of the previous setup attempt remain on the machine, and you are free to start the installation process over.

The recovery console

For more serious problems with installation, or if you have a once-functional installation that seems to have failed, Microsoft has provided a tool that might let you make changes to rescue that system from the jaws of certain death. Around since Windows 2000, the Recovery Console is a text-based operating system extension that allows you direct access to the disk on which Windows XP is installed and similar access to key configuration files and data. It also provides a convenient way around DOS's inability to read NTFS-formatted drives, which is an issue any administrator with troubleshooting experience has come up against.

To use the Recovery Console, you must first set it up. If you are using a working Windows XP system, it's prudent to go ahead and set the console up; that way, if it fails, using the console is as simple a procedure as selecting it from the startup menu at first boot. To do so, simply run `winnt32 /cmdcons` from within Windows. Setup will copy files and modify your boot configuration file to list the console within its options. Now you're prepared for disaster, should it ever strike. It's a good idea to make a habit of installing the console when you first install Windows XP: it's not a difficult process and it can be automated using the `/firstboot` option in a pre-install script, which we'll cover later in this chapter.

There are reports that the winnt32 /cmdcons command does not appear to work if you have updated to Service Pack 2 via Windows Update. You may receive a message stating "Setup cannot continue because the version of Windows on your computer is newer than the version on the CD." To work around this, create a slipstreamed setup CD, as shown in Recipe 2.15.

If, on the other hand, you're working on the failed system, you can still set up the console; you'll just have to delve into Windows Setup in order to do so. Boot off the Windows XP CD-ROM or DVD, select the option to repair an existing installation, choose to do so using the Recovery Console, and Windows will copy the files and make the boot modifications for you and launch the console.

Once the console has launched, it's a two-step process to the command line:

1. Select the installation to repair.
2. Enter the administrator credentials for that installation.

Windows will approve your password and then dump you at a DOS-like prompt. You can move around the file system with the common DOS commands, like CD, DEL, FORMAT, and the like, but there are also several special commands detailed in Table 2-1 that control special functions peculiar to the console.

Table 2-1. Selected commands for the Recovery Console

Command name	Function
DISABLE	Prevents a service, named in the argument syntax of this command, from starting up upon a normal boot.
DISKPART	Executes a disk partitioning utility much like that used in the initial text-based phase of Setup.
ENABLE	Explicitly instructs a service named in the argument syntax of this command to start upon a normal boot.
FIXBOOT	Like the old fdisk /mbr command from DOS days, this will restore boot sector information and make the drive contained in the argument syntax the default drive for booting.
FIXMBR	This command is like FIXBOOT, but it will only touch the master boot record of the drive; it won't alter default boot drives or create BOOT.INI files.
HELP	Lists all commands available in the Recovery Console.
LISTSVC	For use with the DISABLE and ENABLE commands, this lists all available services that can be started and stopped.
LOGON	Logs you out of an existing console and lets you select another installation on which to perform recovery functions.
SYSTEMROOT	Goes to the default Windows directory without grappling with unwieldy "CD" (change directory) commands.

The Recovery Console makes it easy to correct simple errors that used to require reinstallation. It's a good idea, held over from Windows 2000, but yet still unknown to many.

See Also

Recipe 2.10 for troubleshooting multiboot problems, and MS KB 243996, "How to Enable Verbose Logging in Windows 2000 GUI-Mode Setup"

2.8   Upgrading to Windows XP

Problem

You want to install your copy of Windows XP over your existing operating system, thereby preserving your current applications, settings, and data.

Solution

Insert your Windows XP CD into the drive, and allow the automatic menu to appear. Click on the Install Windows XP option, and wait for Setup to launch.

One of the first things you will see upon the upgrade process beginning is a prompt, asking whether you want to connect to the Web to update the install routine. This is known as the Dynamic Update process, and updates to the Setup program itself are downloaded to make sure it's completely up to date before the OS upgrade commences.

A few steps later, the Setup program will generate a report from the Upgrade Advisor. You were introduced to this program in Recipe 2.1. If you haven't yet run the tool, leave the default and let Setup identify possible problems it thinks will crop up, including both hardware and software compatibility issues.

Then, simply follow the procedure in Recipe 2.2, beginning with step 8 after your first reboot.

Discussion

Upgrading to Windows XP is uneventful. You might think this section is ridiculously short, but in reality, Microsoft has done such a good job addressing upgrade scenarios that they really are simple, almost akin to applying a service pack. (After all, it's not a big confidence booster in a core operating system when upgrades completely fail.)

The only key to an even smoother installation is to ensure that your existing Windows operating system is configured exactly as you want it, and that all third-party software installed on the system, be it application software or drivers, is compatible with Windows XP. It can be a nasty surprise to launch the newly upgraded system and see a blue screen before ever logging on.

A note for older hardware owners: even if the compatibility test gives a green light, upgrading Windows 95 and Windows ME systems with older hardware specifically not detected or known to XP can be very traumatic. Relying on the compatibility checker is not the best method. Emphasis must be placed on checking at a minimum each and every hardware vendor for Windows 2000 or Windows XP drivers and doing BIOS updates if available.

But other than that, for the vast majority of users, upgrades to XP are mind-numbingly easy.

Editions

If you purchased the lower-cost Upgrade edition of Windows XP, you'll find it works best when you run the Setup program over your existing operating system. However, contrary to popular belief, you *are* allowed to use the upgrade media to perform a clean install on a system. You will be prompted to insert media from previous versions of Windows to justify your upgrade. The valid versions include:

- Windows NT Workstation, Versions 3.51 and 4.0
- Windows 2000 Professional
- Windows 95
- Windows 98 (original and second editions)
- Windows Millennium Edition

See Also

The Windows Support Center's "Upgrading to Windows XP" site at *http://aumha.org/win5/a/xpupgrad.htm*

2.9 Creating a Multiboot Installation

Problem

You want to install Windows XP, but you also want to keep your current installation of Windows intact.

Solution

You can install more than one OS on your machine. When you first turn on the computer, or every time you restart, you can then select which operating system you want to use. This is called "multibooting."

To multiboot Windows XP with Windows 95, 98, ME, or MS-DOS:

1. Make sure your hard disk is formatted with either FAT or FAT32.

2. Install the operating systems that will co-boot with Windows XP, in the following order as applicable: MS-DOS, Windows 95 or 98, Windows ME. Follow the normal installation procedure for the operating system.

3. Install Windows XP, selecting a different volume for the XP installation when you are prompted to select the target disk for installation.

To multiboot Windows NT 4.0 with Windows XP:

1. Make sure your hard disk is formatted with FAT, FAT32, or NTFS.

2. Install Windows NT 4.0, using the normal installation procedure for the operating system.

3. Upgrade the NT installation to at least Service Pack 5, in order to install the support for the latest NTFS version used in Windows XP.

4. Install Windows XP, selecting a different volume for the XP installation when you are prompted to select the target disk for installation.

Finally, once your installations are completed, to specify the default operating system that your computer will boot with, do the following from within Windows XP:

1. Go to Start, and open the Control Panel.

2. Double-click System, and then on the Advanced tab, under Startup and Recovery, click the Settings button.

3. Under System Startup, select the operating system you'd like to boot with by default, and then click OK.

Discussion

Be sure to perform complete backups of your system before you create a multiboot installation. While the multiboot installation itself is relatively safe, there is a chance you won't be able to get back to your existing operating system if you do it.

Also, keep the following in mind:

- You can't use both Windows 95 and 98 on the same computer.

- In order to obtain support for Microsoft, each copy of a Windows OS must be installed at least on separate volumes, if not on separate disks. You can make a multibooting scenario work when you install two or more copies of Windows on the same disk volume, but the company won't support it if you have problem. The only exception to this is if you are installing multiple copies of Windows XP only.

- You can't install Windows XP on compressed drives that were compressed using tools or programs other than the Windows-integrated NTFS compression utility.

- Use a different computer name for each operating system on the same computer that is joined to a Windows domain. For workgroups, this is not required.
- If you want to install an application for each OS to use, you must perform the installation on each OS. The applications cannot share installation data from the other operating systems on your hard drives.

See Also

Recipe 2.10 for troubleshooting multiboot problems, and MS KB 306559, "How to Create a Multiple-Boot System in Windows XP"

2.10   Troubleshooting Multiboot Problems

Problem

You are having problems with more than one operating system installed on your computer, and you need to know where to start looking to fix it.

Solution

If you receive the following error:

```
Windows XP could not start because the following files were missing or corrupted:
WINDOWS\SYSTEM32\CONFIG\SYSTEM NTLDR MISSING
You can try to repair this file by starting the Windows Setup program from original
floppies or boot from CD-ROM.
Select 'r' at first screen to repair
```

this probably happened because you installed Windows NT after Windows XP, or because you reinstalled Windows NT. The easiest fix is to start the Recovery Console, as described in Recipe 2.7, and at the prompt, type fixboot.

If your dual-boot with Windows NT isn't working, check out the following suggestions:

- Make sure your hard drive is formatted with FAT16 or NTFS, not FAT32.
- Upgrade your NT installation, if you can access it, to at least Service Pack 5 and preferably Service Pack 6a.

If you get the following message in one of your installations:

```
iexplore caused an Invalid Page Fault in module kernel32.dll
```

then you need to reinstall each of your operating systems on a separate partition, if not a separate hard drive altogether. This is a confirmed error in the interactions between multiple operating systems on the same disk. Multiple installations of Windows XP, however, do not see this error.

If you don't see a boot menu when starting your computer, you probably installed another operating system after Windows XP. Reinstall Windows XP to correct the error. Windows XP must always be the last OS installed.

If you can't get both Windows 95 and Windows 98 installations working, quit trying. These operating systems are so closely related that they use the same boot file, so using both operating systems on the same computer isn't possible.

Discussion

If you don't have the Recovery Console installed, and you need to replace the boot files as described in the Solution section, then boot with another operating system and copy *NTLDR* and *NTDETECT.COM* from the *I386* folder of the Windows XP distribution CD to the root of your first hard drive. If you're using MS-DOS to perform this copy and restore, then you'll probably need to change the attributes on the files using the following DOS commands:

```
> attrib ntdetect.com -r -s -h
> attrib ntldr -r -s -h
```

See Also

Recipe 2.7 for troubleshooting installation problems, and MS KB 315233, "Windows XP Does Not Start on a Computer that is Configured for Dual Booting"

2.11   Activating Windows XP

Problem

You need to activate Windows XP.

Solution

Using a graphical user interface

To activate over the Internet:

1. Open the Start menu.
2. Navigate through All Programs → Accessories → System Tools.
3. Click on Activate Windows.
4. Click the first Yes option to activate Windows over the Internet and then click Next.
5. Select whether to register at the same time. While activation doesn't require any personal information from you, registration does. We'll assume you select No. Click Next.
6. The wizard will pause for a few seconds, and return a success message.

To activate over the telephone:

1. Open the Start menu.
2. Navigate through All Programs → Accessories → System Tools.

3. Click on Activate Windows.

4. Click the second Yes option to activate Windows over the telephone.

Using a command-line interface

Open a command prompt, switch to the *C:\WINDOWS\SYSTEM32\OOBE* directory, and enter msoobe /a. Then follow step 4 in either section above, depending on your preferred method of activation. (You can't script the activation process, but you can script launching the activation wizard.)

Discussion

Activation is new to Windows XP and the latest versions of Microsoft Office and is Microsoft's way of enforcing their single-use licenses for these products. Previously, nothing more than dire warnings and license agreement acknowledgments prevented users from installing a single, purchased copy of Windows on more than one computer. The company decided that this abuse was too rampant to ignore and thus built product activation technology into Windows XP.

Product activation is actually fairly simple: within the first 30 days of installing XP, you must instruct the computer to contact Microsoft either over the Internet or by using a modem and give Microsoft's activation system information about the hardware on which XP is currently installed. Your computer then receives a release code, which officially activates the system and allows you to continue running XP without further interruption. However, upon each boot, Windows checks to make sure the hardware on which it is installed is the same and that the release code it received from the activation process is till applicable. If not, then Windows functionality is greatly restricted until you contact Microsoft to obtain a new release code.

To derive the hardware information that your system sends to Microsoft for activation, Windows looks at the following devices and generates a number based on the first device of each type it finds:

- Display adapter
- SCSI adapter
- IDE adapter, which generally identifies the motherboard
- Network card and its corresponding MAC address
- A range of RAM amount—usually identified as 64–128 MB, 128–256 MB, 256–512 MB, and so on
- Processor type and serial number, if available
- Hard drive device and volume serial number (VSN)
- CD-ROM / CD-RW / DVD-ROM

This number is then recorded on your hard drive. Each time Windows boots, it checks to make sure the hardware that derived the number is the same. If not, the activation sequence is retriggered.

See Also

Microsoft's activation web site: *http://www.microsoft.com/piracy/activation.mspx*, and "How activation works with volume licenses" at *http://www.microsoft.com/piracy/activation_volumefaq.mspx*

2.12 Viewing the Installed Service Pack and Hotfixes

Problem

You need to determine the installed service pack and any installed patches and fixes on a given machine.

Solution

Using a graphical user interface

To determine the current level of service pack, right-click on My Computer and select Properties. On the General tab, you'll see the current service pack.

To determine any hotfixes that are installed, go to Control Panel and double-click on Add/Remove Programs. Click the Change/Remove Programs button in the left pane, and make sure the Show Programs checkbox is ticked at the top of the window. You'll see the hotfixes listed—they are under Windows XP-Software Updates.

Using a command-line interface

To determine the current level of service pack, run winver from the command line. A box will pop up showing the current service pack level at the end of the version string.

To determine the installed hotfixes, run systeminfo from the command line, and look under the Hotfixes section. A sample report looks like the following:

```
Host Name:                JONLAPTOP
OS Name:                  Microsoft Windows XP Professional
OS Version:               5.1.2600 Service Pack 2 Build 2600
OS Manufacturer:          Microsoft Corporation
OS Configuration:         Standalone Workstation
OS Build Type:            Uniprocessor Free
Registered Owner:         Jonathan Hassell
Registered Organization:  Jonathan Hassell Omnimedia
Product ID:               55274-770-4137265-22643
Original Install Date:    12/28/2004, 8:52:38 PM
System Up Time:           1 Days, 17 Hours, 14 Minutes, 17 Seconds
System Manufacturer:      Dell Computer Corporation
System Model:             Latitude D600
```

```
System type:                  X86-based PC
Processor(s):                 1 Processor(s) Installed.
                              [01]: x86 Family 6 Model 9 Stepping 5
GenuineIntel ~597 Mhz
BIOS Version:                 DELL   - 27d40907
Windows Directory:            C:\WINDOWS
System Directory:             C:\WINDOWS\system32
Boot Device:                  \Device\HarddiskVolume2
System Locale:                en-us;English (United States)
Input Locale:                 en-us;English (United States)
Time Zone:                    (GMT-05:00) Eastern Time (US & Canada)
Total Physical Memory:        511 MB
Available Physical Memory:    80 MB
Virtual Memory: Max Size:     2,048 MB
Virtual Memory: Available:    2,002 MB
Virtual Memory: In Use:       46 MB
Page File Location(s):        C:\pagefile.sys
Domain:                       WORKGROUP
Logon Server:                 \\JONLAPTOP
Hotfix(s):                    16 Hotfix(s) Installed.
                              [01]: File 1
                              [02]: File 1
                              [03]: File 1
                              [04]: File 1
                              [05]: File 1
                              [06]: File 1
                              [07]: File 1
                              [08]: Q147222
                              [09]: S867460 - Update
                              [10]: KB834707 - Update
                              [11]: KB873339 - Update
                              [12]: KB885835 - Update
                              [13]: KB885836 - Update
                              [14]: KB886185 - Update
                              [15]: KB887797 - Update
                              [16]: KB890175 - Update
NetWork Card(s):              2 NIC(s) Installed.
                              [01]: Intel(R) PRO/Wireless LAN 2100 3A Mini PCI Adapter
                                    Connection Name: Wireless Network Connection
                              [02]: Broadcom 570x Gigabit Integrated Controller
                                    Connection Name: Local Area Connection
                                    DHCP Enabled:    Yes
                                    DHCP Server:     192.168.0.1
                                    IP address(es)
                                    [01]: 192.168.0.102
```

Discussion

You can run the systeminfo tool remotely. To obtain the report on another computer, run systeminfo /s system and replace "system" with the name of the remote computer. You will of course need valid logon credentials for the remote system.

See Also

Microsoft's "Take Command-Line Control of WMI," at *http://www.microsoft.com/technet/prodtechnol/windows2000serv/maintain/featusability/wmic.mspx*, Recipe 2.13 for installing a hotfix, and Recipe 2.15 for installing a service pack

2.13   Installing a Hotfix

Problem

You need to install a hotfix to update your Windows XP installation.

Solution

Using a graphical user interface

The easiest way to get and install hotfixes is through Windows Update. Open Internet Explorer, and browse to *http://www.windowsupdate.com*. Choose the Express Install option on the page that comes up (you may need to wait a few seconds as the dynamic parts of the page initialize), and then select the updates you'd like. Click Install, confirm your selections, and click Install Now. You'll receive a dialog box informing you of how the patching is doing, and you may be prompted to restart when the patch has been successfully applied.

If you have a standalone copy of a patch, there are a couple of ways to open it. From a GUI:

1. Double-click on the hotfix to execute it.
2. Select whether to backup files or not, and then click Next.
3. Click Next to install the hotfix.

Depending on the type and depth of the patch, you may be required to restart your computer for the hotfix to take effect.

Using a command-line interface

If you have a standalone copy of a patch, the way to open it from the command line is simply to type the name of the patch and press Enter. Command-line patch execution is useful for scripting, so if you have an emergency patch to deploy to several computers at once, you can put the patch command in a login script and so the patch will deploy the next time a user logs on.

Discussion

In early 2004, Microsoft standardized the names for hotfixes. A typical hotfix name is in the format *Q987654_wxp_sp3_x86_en.exe*, where:

- *987654* is the knowledge base article that describes the problem
- *wxp* is the operating system for which the fix is applicable
- *sp3* is the next service pack version of which the fix will be a part
- *x86* is the processor type for the fix
- *en* is the language of the fix

See Also

Recipe 2.16 for configuring Automatic Updates

2.14   Installing a Service Pack

Problem

You need to install a service pack for Windows XP.

Solution

Using a graphical user interface

Download the service pack file to a known location, and then navigate to that place on your file system. Double-click the file, select whether to make backups of critical system files before the service pack is installed, and then click Next. The service pack will be applied.

This process can take anywhere from 5 to 20 minutes. You'll be required to restart your machine.

You can also obtain service packs from Windows Update now. See Recipe 2.13 for instructions on how to get hotfixes and other updates from *http://windowsupdate.com*.

Using Group Policy

You can use the IntelliMirror software distribution functionality of Group Policy to deploy service packs to Windows XP machines that are members of domains. You will need to install the Administrative Tools pack from the Windows Server 2003 CD on your XP workstation.

1. Expand the service pack into a folder on a file server, and share this folder.
2. In the Active Directory Users and Computers console, right-click the organizational unit (OU) where you want to create the Group Policy, and then click Properties.
3. Make a new Group Policy object (GPO) and edit it.

4. Select Computer Configuration → Software Settings → Software Installation and make a new package.

5. Browse to the *update.msi* file in your shared distribution folder that you created in step 1. Make sure you browse to the network location for the file, and not through a local path.

The next time Group Policy is refreshed on your client machines, the service pack will be deployed.

Using a command-line interface

Enter the name of the service pack downloadable file on the command line, and press Enter.

Discussion

If you are using the command line and do not want the service pack installation prompts to appear on your screen, add the /q switch to the command.

Turning on Automatic Updates should also install service packs for you, if you don't want to do it yourself. For more information on this, see Recipe 2.16.

See Also

"Deploying Windows XP Service Pack 2 in Enterprise Environments," at *http://www.microsoft.com/technet/prodtechnol/winxppro/deploy/sp2entdp.mspx*

For advice on any problems that might result from installing Service Pack 2, check out the following article: *http://www.windowsdevcenter.com/pub/a/windows/2004/09/28/sp2_woes.html*.

2.15 Slipstreaming a Service Pack or Hotfix into a Build

Problem

You want the latest service pack files to be included in the distribution media or location from which you deploy Windows XP to clients.

Solution

To slipstream a service pack into a build, follow these steps.

1. Create a directory called *c:\winsp*, and copy the downloaded service pack file there. I'll assume the service pack file is named *ws2k3sp3.exe*.

2. Extract the service pack to that directory by executing the following command from the command line or from Start → Run: ws2k3sp3.exe -x.

---

3. Now, update the files from the regular Windows distribution CD with the new service pack files by executing the following command from the command line or from Start → Run: D:\wins2k3sp3\i386\UPDATE\UPDATE.EXE -S:C:\windist.

The files are updated and the process is complete. Slipstreaming is an easy way to make sure new systems are updated before they're ever put into production.

To apply hotfixes to an installation while it's in progress, you must use an unattended installation and call the *cmdlines.txt* file. The following steps are necessary:

1. Create a distribution folder.

2. Create the answer file *unattend.txt* by using the Setup Manager tool. *unattend.txt* will contain any computer-specific information needed by the commands in the *cmdlines.txt* file.

3. Create the *cmdlines.txt* file by using the Setup Manager tool. *cmdlines.txt* is a file that contains the commands that would run during the GUI installation. These commands can be hotfix installation commands as well.

4. Add the *I386* folder from the Windows installation CD-ROM to the distribution folder.

5. Add the *unattend.txt* and *cmdlines.txt* files to the \I386\OEM subfolder.

6. Add hotfix executable files to the \I386\OEM subfolder. (Hotfix files are named six-digit-number.exe, where the six digit number is the number assigned to the hotfix.) Hotfix files can be downloaded from Microsoft's web site.

7. Add lines to the *cmdlines.txt* file, which is a file that must be available if a Windows automated installation requires the running of different code (for example, installation of applications or addition of hotfixes) after the operating system is installed. Thus, to install the hotfix *Q123456.exe*, you use this line in the [Commands] section of the *cmdlines.txt* file:

        "Q123456 /q"

Discussion

Since deployment and initial installation is now so convenient, you will likely find yourself longing for a streamlined post-setup process. One of the most common tasks that must be performed before you can hand off a computer to an employee is installing the latest service pack. This is especially important in light of the latest wave of worm attacks: newly installed machines can be infected with these worms before you even have a chance to install patches!

All hope is not lost, however. Using a special command line function of the service pack executable, you can instruct any Microsoft NT operating system-based service pack to replace old files in a central distribution share with updated ones. This process, known as slipstreaming, works very well with RIS images, because you already have the requisite distribution share. Let's walk through the process. You'll need the network/administrative (in other words, the full) version of the service pack for your respective platform.

To have RIS installations apply hotfixes, you must do the following:

- Ensure that patches reside on an accessible network share.
- Configure RIS to install the appropriate service pack.
- Add script lines to the [GuiRunOnce] section of the unattended installation file, as shown in Recipe 2.4.

See Also

Recipe 2.4 for installing from an unattended installation, and Recipe 2.6 for installing from Remote Installation Services

2.16   Configuring Automatic Updates

Problem

You want to configure your Windows XP computers to automatically download updates from Windows Update without administrator or user intervention.

Solution

Using a graphical user interface

From the Start menu, right-click on My Computer and select Properties. On the Automatic Updates tab, you can select how the updating should work. You can select to download recommended updates for the system automatically and install them at the specified time, to only download updates and then prompt you for installation, to only notify you of the availability of updates and leave it to you to download and apply them, or to turn off Automatic Updates entirely.

Using Group Policy

These Group Policy settings for configuring Automatic Updates can be found under Computer Configuration → Windows Settings.

Configure Automatic Updates
  This option specifies whether this computer will receive security updates and critical bug fixes. The first option has the currently logged on user notified before downloading updates, and notified again before installing the downloaded updates. The second option has updates automatically downloaded, but not installed until a logged on user acknowledges their presence and authorizes the installation. The third option has updates automatically downloaded and installed on a schedule that you can set in the appropriate boxes on the sheet. If

you configure clients to download and install updates, it only schedules them to download at the time you specify. The updates don't actually get installed until the next day at the time when the workstation normally checks for new patches.

Reschedule Automatic Updates scheduled installations

This option specifies the amount of time to wait after booting before continuing with a scheduled installation that was missed previously. If the status is set to Enabled, a missed scheduled installation will occur the specified number of minutes after the computer is next started. If the status is set to Disabled or Not Configured, a missed scheduled installation will simply roll over to the next scheduled installation.

No auto-restart for scheduled Automatic Updates installations

This option designates whether a client computer should automatically reboot when an update that is just installed requires a system restart. If the status is set to Enabled, Automatic Updates will not restart a computer automatically during a scheduled installation if a user is logged in to the computer, instead notifying the user to restart the computer to complete the installation. If the status is set to Disabled or Not Configured, Automatic Updates will notify the user that the computer will automatically restart in five minutes to complete the installation.

Using the Registry

The following Registry changes can be made to configure Automatic Updates.

To enable or disable Automatic Updates

Create the value NoAutoUpdate in the HKEY_LOCAL_MACHINE\SOFTWARE\Policies\Microsoft\Windows\WindowsUpdate\AU key. The value is a DWORD with possible values 0 (enabled) or 1 (disabled).

To configure the update download and notification behavior

Create the value AUOptions in the HKEY_LOCAL_MACHINE\SOFTWARE\Policies\Microsoft\Windows\WindowsUpdate\AU key. The value is a DWORD that includes integers 2 (notify of download and notify before installation), 3 (automatically download but notify before installation), and 4 (automatically download and schedule the installation).

To schedule an automated installation

Create the values ScheduledInstallDay and ScheduledInstallTime in the HKEY_LOCAL_MACHINE\SOFTWARE\Policies\Microsoft\Windows\WindowsUpdate\AU key. The value for each is a DWORD. For ScheduledInstallDay, the range is from 0 to 7, with 0 indicating every day and 1 through 7 indicating the days of the week, Sunday through Saturday, respectively. For ScheduledInstallTime, the range is from 0 to 23, signifying the hour of the day in military time.

To specify how long to wait before completing a missed installation

Create the value `RescheduleWaitTime` in the `HKEY_LOCAL_MACHINE\SOFTWARE\`
`Policies\Microsoft\Windows\WindowsUpdate\AU` key. The value is a DWORD that
ranges from 1 to 60, measured in minutes.

To specify whether to restart a scheduled installation with a currently logged in non-administrative user

Create the `NoAutoRebootWithLoggedOnUsers` value in the `HKEY_LOCAL_MACHINE\`
`SOFTWARE\Policies\Microsoft\Windows\WindowsUpdate\AU` key. The value is a
DWORD that can be zero, which indicates that a reboot will indeed take place,
or one, which indicates the reboot will be postponed while a user is logged on.

Use the following .REG file to automate Registry changes. Below is a sample file that
you can modify according to the settings mentioned previously:

```
Windows Registry Editor Version 5.00

[HKEY_LOCAL_MACHINE\SOFTWARE\Policies\Microsoft\Windows\WindowsUpdate]
"WUServer"="http://YOUR-SUS-SERVER"
"WUStatusServer"="http://YOUR-SUS-SERVER"

[HKEY_LOCAL_MACHINE\SOFTWARE\Policies\Microsoft\Windows\WindowsUpdate\AU]
"RescheduleWaitTime"=dword:00000003
"NoAutoRebootWithLoggedOnUsers"=dword:00000000
"NoAutoUpdate"=dword:00000000
"AUOptions"=dword:00000004
"ScheduledInstallDay"=dword:00000000
"ScheduledInstallTime"=dword:00000006
"UseWUServer"=dword:00000001
```

Discussion

The Group Policy and Registry settings also work if you have a Software Update Services server running on your network.

See Also

MS KB 294871, "Description of the Automatic Updates feature in Windows," and
MS KB 328010, "How to configure automatic updates by using Group Policy or Registry settings."

2.17 Disabling the Windows Firewall After Installation

Problem

You want the Windows Firewall in Windows XP Service Pack 2 or higher to automatically be disabled when a machine first boots after installation, for compatibility reasons with existing software you have deployed.

Solution

In Windows XP Service Pack 2, the Windows Firewall is automatically enabled at all times, including when the machine boots immediately after installation is completed. You can disable this by doing the following:

Using a graphical user interface

Unfortunately, you can't disable the firewall automatically after booting through the GUI. However, it's a painless procedure to quickly disable it after installation:

1. Open the Control Panel.
2. Double-click on the Windows Firewall icon.
3. On the General tab, click the Off radio button.
4. Click OK.

The firewall is now disabled.

Using Group Policy

If your machines are participating in a domain environment and you have access to Group Policy settings for the domain, you can disable the firewall through that method. If you use Group Policy, the settings will automatically be applied as soon as the machine boots the first time. The correct Group Policy object is Computer Configuration/Administrative Templates/Network/Network Connections/Windows Firewall/Domain Profile/Windows Firewall. Disable the setting "protect all network connections."

Using a command-line interface

The netsh utility can turn the firewall on and off, depending on the current firewall profile. To disable the firewall on a machine in a domain environment, use the following command:

```
> netsh firewall set opmode mode=DISABLE profile=DOMAIN
```

Or, if you are using a standalone machine, the following command will disable the firewall:

```
> netsh firewall set opmode mode=DISABLE profile=STANDARD
```

If you use unattended setup files, you can add the following lines to the appropriate SIF file to create a new firewall profile which has the firewall itself turned off:

```
[WindowsFirewall]
Profiles = WindowsFirewall.TurnOffFirewall

[WindowsFirewall.TurnOffFirewall]
Mode = 0
```

Discussion

For machines running a version of Windows XP earlier than Service Pack 2, you cannot turn the Internet Connection Firewall (ICF) off within unattended setup files. You'll need to disable the ICF however you wish once the machine has booted after installation.

2.18   Keeping an Installation Process Worm- and Virus-Free

Problem

In this day and age of worms that proliferate in minutes, you want to keep machines you're installing free of worms and viruses during the actual setup process itself.

Solution

Here are some tips on avoiding a pre-installation worm infestation:

Perform your installation behind a firewall.   Even if you purchase a cheap home/ small office-style firewall and router device, that should help deflect the fiercest of worms from your vulnerable machines.

Disconnect the computer from the network and join a domain after install.   If you aren't making use of RIS and have regular CD media, consider simply removing the network cable from the computer during the installation. There's really no effective difference in joining a domain during the installation or joining it after you've had a chance to boot the system and install protective software.

Use a private RIS server placed behind your firewall.   If you have a spare license of Windows 2000 Server or Windows Server 2003, you can install a RIS machine behind a firewall but disconnected from the Internet, and you can commence network installations on that private network, safely guarded from the perils of the open Internet connection.

Use a CD with a slipstreamed service pack.   If you must install with an active network connection, at least use the most updated copy of the installation materials you can. This will at a minimum prevent historic worms from infecting during installation, but it's a less desirable choice because new threats may exist that can penetrate the machine during the setup process.

Use a separate VLAN on your network to quarantine machines being installed.   If you have rather sophisticated switches and network management gear, you can filter traffic to and from a certain VLAN and effect a poor man's quarantine, so if you set up machines within that VLAN, you've added another layer of protection. Of course, you'll want to install antispyware and virus protection as soon as possible.

Discussion

If at all possible, the best solution is to use a firewall, however inexpensive, for installations where a network connection is required. Of course, you can absolutely protect against Internet-borne viruses by installing Windows XP with no connection to the network.

See Also

Recipe 2.15 for slipstreaming a service pack into new installation media

CHAPTER 3
Managing Hardware and Devices

3.0   Introduction

Hardware provides a foundation for software—BIOS, operating systems, and applications programs—to do its work. Earlier PC operating systems—CP/M, DOS, and Windows 1.x–3.x—interacted with but rarely intervened between software and hardware. Programs could reach out and touch discrete CPU, memory, disk drive, and COM-port bits at will. Ever since OS/2 and Windows NT, through Windows 95, 98, Me, 2000, and XP, operating systems have become significantly more involved in both isolating hardware from applications—to provide for better security, reduce device conflicts—and embracing hardware to create a richer user experience.

The first 20 years of PC hardware saw constant contention over architecture limitations, connections, I/O port standards, and driver conflicts that led to many errors, lockups, and nonfunctional systems. In recent years PC hardware has evolved away from pushy and proprietary hardware implementations to better standards supporting more cooperation and interoperability with fewer conflicts, not to mention universal technologies that also work in and with Apple and Unix products. There are still many exclusive PC-only products in use by many users, but eventually we will have only hardware based on ubiquitous standards that make products more economical and interchangeable with other systems.

Legacy devices had obscure and often complex configuration requirements. Today's Plug and Play products let you seamlessly move from a PC to a Mac as often as you like without the base computers and operating systems freaking out. Also, while it may now be unusual to find a modem that uses an old serial COM port, or a printer that uses the old parallel LPT-port, an add-in card that uses an 8-bit ISA-slot, or software that comes on 5.25" diskettes, they still exist and are supported by most PCs and their operating systems alongside newer technologies.

Plug and Play is Microsoft and the PC industry's first effort at trying to eliminate the technical barriers of switches, jumpers, and obscure configuration details that befuddle users and technicians, and keep consumers from tackling the marvels of PCs. It is supposed to provide for the automatic detection and nonconflicting configuration of hundreds of types of hardware devices, from keyboards to network cards, FLASH memory chips, and digital cameras. These are excellent benefits, but they only succeed when all the devices and the system BIOS work properly together.

Plug and Play support began as early as Windows 95 Supplemental Release 1, and it has improved with each subsequent version of Windows. Plug and Play itself has not changed substantially, but has definitely benefited over time from more cooperation among hardware vendors and driver software programmers. While much progress has been made in bringing along Plug and Play with PCI, USB, IEEE-1394/ FireWire™, AGP, PCI-X, ATA, and S-ATA, they all have new and different configuration and operational issues when we get to current hardware and Windows XP. Windows XP itself does not have a lot to do with Plug and Play except to listen to what the BIOS tells Windows about the system and attached devices, but Windows can vividly reveal the symptoms associated with poor Plug and Play performance and general hardware misbehavior that you need to know about and be able to resolve.

PC administrators constantly add, troubleshoot, upgrade, and reconfigure hardware, from system boards to myriad USB devices, and have to deal with system BIOS updates, changing BIOS and I/O device parameters, and digging in to Windows' Device Manager. In this chapter you will explore and learn about many different aspects of hardware and drivers related to Windows XP, what you need to know about devices and configuring them, as well as interactions among other devices and software.

3.1   Adding Hardware

Problem

You want to manually add a new hardware component because Windows did not recognize it, or Windows found your new hardware but previously installed hardware disappeared.

Solution

Using the BIOS

1. Press the appropriate key(s) to access the built-in BIOS setup program. Typically, pressing the DEL or F2 key will access setup, although some systems use F1, F10, Ctrl+Alt+S, or ESC.

2. Locate the selection for Reset NVRAM, Reset ESCD, or Reset Plug and Play.

3. Select Yes or Reset.

4. Save the settings and restart your PC.

Using a graphical user interface

1. Right-click My Computer.
2. Select Properties.
3. Select the Hardware tab.
4. Click the Device Manager button.
5. Right-click the computer icon at the top of the list.
6. Select Scan for hardware changes.
7. If the Device Manager finds new devices it will automatically locate and install drivers or prompt you for the location of suitable driver files. Device Manager may also find devices that conflict with others and display the yellow exclamation point icon alerting you to problems that need further investigation, covered in Recipes 3.2 and 3.7.

Using a command-line interface

1. Download DEVCON from *http://support.microsoft.com/default.aspx?scid=kb;EN-US;Q311272*, then uncompress and save the files to a known location on your hard drive—*C:\DEVCON* seems like a friendly location.
2. Go to Start, select Run, then type in CMD and click OK.
3. In the command prompt window navigate to the folder DEVCON is stored in—*C:\DEVCON\i386* for most of us.
4. Type in the following command to force Windows to re-evaluate the system for new devices:

    > devcon rescan

5. Type in the following command to all of the devices Windows knows about:

    > devcon findall *

6. Scroll through the command-prompt window to see whether your devices have been discovered.

Discussion

Occasionally, a slow or conflicted Plug and Play device may not be immediately or automatically recognized or reconfigured by the BIOS upon booting, or by Windows' hardware detection. Detection failure could be caused by a Plug and Play device not responding to new discovery by the BIOS, or by one of the devices being unable to use an alternative available interface. Also, Windows may not be able to address a new device because it is busy with other tasks and misses the new device notification from the Hardware Abstraction Layer. Resetting Plug and Play enumeration in the BIOS or telling Windows' Device Manager to "look again" using Device Manager's scan process or DEVCON to tell Windows to re-eunumerate devices should fix this problem.

See Also

Microsoft's web sites provide considerable information toward getting Plug and Play and Windows to cooperate. Check out the details at *www.microsoft.com/resources/ documentation/Windows/XP/all/reskit/en-us/prdh_dmt_pjoy.asp* and *www.microsoft. com/windowsxp/using/setup/learnmore/devicemgr.mspx*.

3.2   Resolving Unknown Devices

Problem

You want to install new hardware but the Add New Hardware wizard fails to recognize the connection of a new device or fails to find an appropriate driver.

Solution

Using a graphical user interface

1. Disconnect the device from the PC to prevent recurring detection.
2. Uninstall the device driver:
    a. Right-click My Computer, select Properties.
    b. Select the Hardware tab then click Device Manager.
    c. Double-click Other Devices to expand, right-click the unknown device listed, and select Uninstall.
    d. Confirm the removal of the device, and then click OK to close the dialogs.
3. Install the proper device driver:
    a. Place the CD-ROM for the device in your CD or DVD drive.
    b. Run the setup program for the device software from the CD-ROM and follow the instructions, which usually include being prompted to reconnect the device and letting the Add New Hardware wizard find and associate the appropriate driver. (If you've lost the CD-ROM for your device, it's time for a visit to the hardware manufacturer's web site to download a current driver, install or unzip the files, and browse to the location of the files so Windows can install them.)

Discussion

Because many device manufacturers don't register their devices and drivers with Microsoft, Windows XP does not always have a reference point to find appropriate drivers. This symptom is frequently experienced when connecting a new USB device before installing the device driver for the device. Plug and Play may extract and present the proper make and model information from the attached device, but without a known driver, Windows banishes it as an "unknown device." Installing the device driver after the fact will not fix the problem because the device is already committed to the unknown category, so the "unknown device" must first be removed, and then you must install the proper driver before reconnecting the device. Unknown devices may be the modern-day "DLL hell" of Windows past.

See Also

Microsoft is quite familiar with the "unknown device" conundrum and offers several suggestions at MS KB 314464, "How to troubleshoot unknown devices that are listed in Device Manager in Windows XP," MS KB 161220, "Removing Unknown Device in Device Manager Hangs Computer," and MS KB 187723, "Plug and Play Printer Is Detected as an Unknown Device."

3.3   Repairing a Missing Modem

Problem

Your modem does not work under Windows XP after upgrading the OS.

Solution

Using a graphical user interface

1. Uninstall the device driver, if present.
   a. Right-click My Computer, and select Properties.
   b. Select the Hardware tab, then click Device Manager.
   c. Double-click on Modems to expand the listing, right-click the modem listed, and select Uninstall.

      - or -

      Double-click Other Devices to expand, right-click PCI Simple Communication Controller, and select Uninstall.
   d. Confirm the removal of the device, then click OK to close the dialogs.
2. Install generic modem driver:
   a. Right-click My Computer, and select Properties.
   b. Select the Hardware tab, then click Device Manager.
   c. Double-click on Modems to expand the listing, right-click the modem listed, and select Uninstall.

      - or -

      Double-click Other Devices to expand, right-click PCI Simple Communication Controller, and select Uninstall.
   d. Confirm the removal of the device, then click OK to close the dialogs.

Rockwell/Conextant modem chips found in many popular modems—included with off-the-shelf PCs in particular, but also older pre-Windows XP modems—may not be supported in XP without new drivers. The best thing to do is to obtain generic Rockwell modem drivers for the HSF (Soft 56k PCI) and HCF (USB) models of modem chips from the Conexant web site at *http://www.conexant.com/customer/md_driverdownload.jsp*, or visit the web site of your modem's manufacturer for XP drivers, then follow step 1 above to remove the wrong driver before installing new drivers.

Discussion

This problem usually occurs when Windows 95, 98, or ME is upgraded to Windows XP, if the old modem is based on the Rockwell or other chipset and the proper drivers are not included in Windows XP. A generic modem type or updated generic driver will provide basic support for the modem. Upgrading to more up-to-date drivers suitable for Windows 2000 or XP will get you up and running.

See Also

A few independent web sites offer a wealth of information about the Rockwell modem chipset commands and drivers for myriad modems using the chip. Looking up *www.modemhelp.net/r/rockwell.shtml* and *members.shaw.ca/reboot/*, or *www.modemsite.com/56k/rockhcf.asp*, will put you deep in the middle of modem nirvana to get these devices up and running.

3.4 Recovering from a Bad Device Driver Update

Problem

A recently updated device driver fails.

Solution

1. Log on with an account that has administrator rights.
2. Click Start, right-click My Computer, and select Properties.
3. Select the Hardware tab, then click Device Manager.
4. In the device list, double-click the device branch for the type of device you need to roll back (e.g., Network adapters).
5. Right-click the specific device, then click Properties.
6. Select the Driver tab, then click Roll Back Driver.
7. Click Yes when you receive the following message:

    ```
    Are you sure you would like to roll back to the previous driver?
    ```

8. The previous device driver is restored. Click Close.

9. Quit Device Manager, then click OK and restart Windows.

Discussion

Windows XP is smart enough to remember driver changes and provides an automatic way to roll back to the previously installed driver. Rolling back to a previous driver can save you a great deal of time and frustration, if you are aware of the specific change you made to your hardware. If the device driver update you did fails completely, preventing you from using the system, then you may have to perform this step in Safe Mode or use Recipe 3.5 to get the system back to a previous state. Windows System Restore is an alternative solution that will roll back more than just your hardware configuration, since it rolls back all software and Registry changes as well.

See Also

Driver rollback is a feature unique to Windows XP and will likely be in future versions of Windows. Microsoft is generous about its coverage of this feature in several knowledge base articles, including those found at *http://www.microsoft.com/windowsxp/pro/using/itpro/hardware/driverrollback.asp*, MS KB 83922, "A device does not work after you try to update the driver by using Windows Update"; *http://www.microsoft.com/windowsxp/compatibility*, *http://www.microsoft.com/windowsxp/using/helpandsupport/learnmore/russel_02october14.mspx*, and *http://www.microsoft.com/windowsxp/using/setup/expert/mcfedries_03may12.mspx*.

3.5   Using the Last Known Good Configuration to Resolve Hardware Problems

Problem

A device you recently installed, or that has failed, can force Windows into the boot menu or prevent Windows from booting up.

Solution

1. During Windows startup press the F8 key to access the Start menu.

2. Using the cursor keys, select Last Known Good Configuration.

3. Press the Enter key to restart.

Discussion

Windows saves Registry data about the last time the system started and ran properly, which is known as the Last Known Good Configuration. When you make this selection from the Start menu, Windows replaces settings known to work from a prior complete startup into the Registry and restarts using them. Using this method has one small flaw in that an automatically configured Windows installation with the SYSPREP utility and then setup scripts may use generic drivers and settings, setting the system to use new drivers at next restart and leaving the system with a prior good configuration to go back to. SYSPREP is a Microsoft tool that removes all traces of prior users, custom settings, mapped drives, network connections, PC hostname—everything that reveals how a system administrator or another user has configured the system. SYSPREP allows administrators to configure new PCs and then give their users a fresh, clean XP experience the first time they boot up, without someone else's clutter in the way.

Since you may not be able to restart and access Window's System Restore feature, the Last Known Good Configuration feature is a subset of a full System Restore Point, which will roll back all Windows changes since a given time. This feature reverts your system to working hardware configurations without affecting software or system configuration changes. If using the Last Known Good Configuration option does not work, you need to boot to Safe Mode to run System Restore, or finally, sadly, reinstall Windows, and provide known good drivers.

See Also

Snippets of details about the Last Known Good Configuration can be found throughout the Web. Most compelling are tips to disable the feature should you find yourself stuck and not wanting to use the last boot configuration. Check out *http://www. compphix.com/somefactaboutlastknowngoodconfig.html*, *http://www.windowsitpro.com/ Article/ArticleID/14852/14852.html*, and *http://www.winguides.com/registry/display. php/851/.*

3.6   Running Windows in Safe Mode

Problem

You cannot start Windows normally. Windows hangs when the GUI should be presented, or after the GUI starts but devices do not function properly.

Solution

Using a command-line interface

1. Restart your computer, and then press F8 during the initial startup to start your computer in Safe Mode.
2. Windows will begin to boot, but much more slowly than normally. It carefully picks and chooses default drivers and avoids loading noncritical services and resident applications.

3. Log on using an account with administrator rights.

4. Click OK when Windows presents its very obvious "running in Safe Mode" dialog.

5. You are left with Windows displayed in 640×480×16-color resolution and an annoying "Safe Mode" background. At this point Windows is pretty much powerless, though sometimes simply booting into Safe Mode and restarting can be enough to clear Windows' mind and let it start normally.

6. If Windows cannot restart normally after a pass through Safe Mode, repeat from step 1, but stay in Safe Mode without restarting and follow the next step.

7. Use Device Manager to disable or remove recently installed, conflicting, or suspect devices to get Windows back to a bootable state. Restart the system to learn whether you've found and removed the troublesome device.

Discussion

Safe Mode lets you "get under the hood" of Windows without the clutter of excess services, drivers, and resident programs, including some viruses and spyware. It gives you raw, brute force control over troublesome configuration items stemming from recently installed or corrupt hardware or software. In Safe Mode you have full access to everything Device Manager knows about the system hardware so you can remove devices, update or roll back device drivers, and even reset the configuration data of legacy devices to match their true hardware settings. You also have access to the Registry Editor and services console to remove or disable troublesome services and programs.

Safe Mode does not allow you to use Add/Remove Programs because the Windows installer service is not running and some uninstall processes simply will not run in Safe Mode.

By coincidence, just running in Safe Mode can allow Windows' Device Manager to reset device configurations without troublesome drivers in the way, allowing Windows to restart normally without your having to touch a thing. With all these subtle yet powerful benefits Safe Mode can be your best friend in times of Windows' seemingly unreasonable confusion about what and how it should run.

3.7 Using System Restore to Recover from a Hardware-Induced Problem

Problem

You cannot start Windows normally or even in Safe Mode.

Solution

Using a graphical user interface

1. Log on to Windows using an account with administrator rights.
2. Navigate Start → All Programs → Accessories → System Tools, and then click System Restore.
3. On the Welcome to System Restore page, click Restore My Computer to an Earlier Time, then click Next.
4. On the Select a Restore Point Page, click the most recent or a specific checkpoint in the On This List, click a Restore Point list, then click Next.
5. Click OK to accept the changes listed.
6. Click Next on the Confirm Restore Point Selection page.
7. After the system restarts, log on using an account with administrator rights.
8. Click OK to acknowledge the System Restore Restoration Complete page.

Using a command-line interface

1. Restart your computer, and then press F8 during the initial startup to start your computer in Safe Mode with a command prompt.
2. Log on using an account with administrator rights.
3. Enter the following command at the command prompt:

   > `%systemroot%\system32\restore\rstrui.exe`

4. Press the Enter key and follow the instructions to restore your computer to a previous state.

Discussion

The Windows System Restore feature saves entire System and User Registry databases on a daily basis (if configured to do so), when new devices are installed, or on demand. These saved databases can be recalled as necessary or desired to return your entire system to a previously known state. Because System Restore takes your entire system back to a prior time and state, all devices and applications changed since a prior restore may not function correctly after restoration, so you should use it with caution. If you know you've only made one or a few configuration changes, then the Last Known Good Configuration is a less aggressive means to go back to a working condition than going back in time. Safe Mode is a better option if you are able to isolate a single change in the system and undo it or remove a device or driver that caused a problem.

See Also

Microsoft's FAQs about System Restore at *http://www.microsoft.com/technet/ prodtechnol/winxppro/plan/faqsrwxp.mspx* is one of many references about this feature. Configuring System Restore is covered at *http://msdn.microsoft.com/library/en-us/sr/sr/ configuring_system_restore.asp*. General instructions for the use of System Restore may be found at *http://www.kellys-korner-xp.com/xp_restore.htm*.

3.8   Resolving Device Conflicts

Problem

A device stops functioning after a new device is connected, or a newly connected device fails to function.

Solution

Using Device Manager

1. To determine which devices have conflicts, click Start then right-click My Computer and select Properties.

2. Select the Hardware tab, then click Device Manager.

3. Review the list of device types for any expanded entries, and specifically individual devices marked with an exclamation point surrounded by a yellow dot. This indicates either a nonfunctioning device or a device with resources in conflict with another device.

4. Double-click the device with the yellow exclamation point to access its properties.

5. Select the Resources tab and note the entries under Resource Settings and the Conflicting Device List for details on the specific nature of the conflict. Most likely you will find a conflict between two COM ports, two LPT ports, or with a sound, video, or network card conflicting with another such device.

6. You have the ability to change resource assignments for some devices if the Settings Based On, Use Automatic Settings, and Change Settings controls are not grayed out. There is an important distinction here—you cannot change the resources a devices uses from within Windows. Doing so would violate Plug and Play and the Hardware Abstraction Layer rules. Here you can only tell Windows what the resources for the device are or will be once you reconfigure the device outside of Windows, and most likely by changing settings on the hardware itself with the system powered off and the device removed. Instead of making changes here and now, note which devices conflict, then reconfigure or remove the conflicting device and let Plug and Play determine the new configuration.

Using BIOS settings

1. Restart your PC and press the appropriate key(s) to access the built-in BIOS setup program. Typically, pressing the DEL or F2 key will access setup, though some systems use F1, F10, Ctrl+Alt+S, or ESC.

2. Within the BIOS setup program, locate the menu selection and entries for configuration of peripheral or I/O devices. This varies from PC to PC, make and model to make and model—consult the documentation for your PC.

3. There are several possible items to check, reconfigure, or reset—the address and IRQ settings for COM and LPT ports, built-in/internal sound cards, and MIDI ports, assign or unassign IRQ for video, USB, or other devices that may present such options. Refer to Table 3-1 below for typical resource assignments for common I/O devices.

4. After determining and setting a new configuration or AUTO mode, save your settings, exit setup, and restart your PC. The Plug and Play BIOS will detect the changes and refresh Windows' Device Manager accordingly.

Using hardware configurations

1. Remove the conflicting hardware device.

2. Consult the documentation for the device for options to reconfigure I/O addresses and IRQ assignments, then reconfigure the device for proper resource settings, referring to Table 3-1 below as appropriate.

3. Replace the device in your PC.

4. Restart your PC, and let Plug and Play detect the changes and update Windows.

Table 3-1. Common legacy I/O device resource settings

Device	I/O address	Interrupt / IRQ
COM1	3F8-3FFh	4
COM2	2F8-2FFh	3
COM3	3E8-3EFh	4
COM4	2E8-2EFh	3
LPT1	378-37Fh	7
LPT2	278-27Fh	5
Sound	220-2FFh	5, 10, 11
IDE Interface 1	1F0-1F7h	14
IDE Interface 2	170-177h	15

Discussion

In these days of Plug and Play devices it is rare, but not impossible, to have a resource conflict between two devices. Most conflicts are the result of installing an older-style modem or COM-port expansion card, an old SCSI card, or a sound card with improper settings. Even among Plug and Play devices, not all of them play well with others, and some simply will not respect the presence and configuration of devices already in the system. If two Plug and Play devices cannot resolve their conflicts by forcing a reset of NVRAM or Plug and Play settings through the BIOS, you may have to remove one of them and replace it with another make or model of device that behaves properly.

See Also

For a very complete and detailed discussion of legacy/non-Plug and Play hardware configurations, and how Plug and Play really works, obtain a copy of *IRQ, DMA & I/O* by Jim Aspinwall, and refer to the Plug and Play specification at *http://www. microsoft.com/whdc/system/pnppwr/pnp/default.mspx*.

3.9 Resolving USB Bandwidth Problems

Problem

You receive an error message: USB Controller Bandwidth Exceeded.

Solution

1. Stop your audio or video device.
2. Disconnect all other devices from the USB port you are using for your audio or video streaming device, or reconnect only the audio or the video device to another port or hub on another port.
3. Restart your audio or video device.
4. Do not connect new devices to the same port or hub as the streaming device.

Discussion

USB host ports are limited to a total maximum bandwidth—high-speed USB 1.1 devices are capable of moving data at a maximum rate of 12MBps, while low-speed hosts provide 1.5MBps data rates. USB 2.0 devices can theoretically move data at 480 MBps. When a streaming device begins to stream, it reserves bandwidth on the port the device is connected to, limiting the remaining bandwidth available for other devices. A new device may demand additional bandwidth that the port cannot provide. By using a separate USB host port for streaming devices and another host port for additional devices, you can avoid the bandwidth limitations. Note that USB hubs do not constitute host ports but are merely expansions of a main USB host. Bandwidth reservation and limiting bandwidth available to other devices is considered "by design" according to USB specifications and does not indicate a problem with your hardware.

See Also

The true Univeral Serial Bus (USB) specification and FAQs about USB are available at *http://www.usb.org*. You will find additional information at *http://www.intel.com/technology/usb/* and *http://computer.howstuffworks.com/usb.htm*.

3.10   Resolving Hung USB Devices

Problem

You are having problems with a USB device—one or more devices stop functioning or the system hangs when another device is connected.

Solution

Ensure the device driver is installed first

A majority of USB problems occur from connecting the device before Windows knows what the device is, so it cannot find or install the proper device driver. This results in the device being classified as an "unknown device" to Device Manager and it will stay there forever until corrected. To clear an unknown device:

1. Disconnect the USB device.
2. Click Start, then right-click My Computer and select Properties.
3. Select the Hardware tab, then click Device Manager.
4. Review the device list to find Unknown Device.
5. Right-click Unknown Device, and select Uninstall and follow the prompts to remove the device. Close the Device Manager and My Computer Properties dialogs.
6. Install the device drivers for your USB product, then follow the instructions to know when it is OK to connect the device.
7. Connect the device only when prompted.

Ensure adequate power to device

A single USB device may draw a maximum of 500 mA or 2.5 watts from any single USB hub connection. Some hubs cannot provide enough power for one or more devices that draw maximum power. Try disconnecting all other USB devices, then connect only the problematic device to see whether it functions properly. If it does, you will need to use a separately powered hub for one or more devices to ensure there is enough power for all of them.

Reset hardware

Shut down your PC. Disconnect the power from all devices. Restart your PC and boot fully into Windows. Reconnect the power to your devices to allow Plug and Play settings to refresh.

Use the root hub

To avoid data signal and cabling problems, if the device is plugged into a secondary hub, disconnect it from the secondary hub and reconnect it to the root hub (direct USB port) on your PC. If the device is already connected to the root hub (main system), try connecting it to a USB hub to improve power and signal conditioning.

Change cables

Not all cables are created equal or are of high-enough quality to pass data signals properly for high-speed USB 1.1 or higher-speed USB 2.0 devices. Try a shorter cable or a cable from a different manufacturer.

Configure the USB root hub to use an IRQ

1. Click Start, then right-click My Computer and select Properties.
2. Select the Hardware tab, then click Device Manager.
3. Under Universal Serial Bus Controllers, locate the Standard OpenHCD USB Host Controller entries.
4. Right-click each of the Standard OpenHCD USB Host Controller items, and select Properties, then the Resources tab.
5. In the Resource type column under Resource Settings, make sure there is an IRQ assignment listed. If no IRQ assignment is shown, you need to go into BIOS setup to configure the USB controller hardware to use an IRQ.
6. Restart your PC and access the BIOS setup program.
7. Find the parameters for assigning an IRQ to the USB interface and set it to Yes or Enable.
8. Restart your PC and recheck the USB devices for proper functionality.

Update your PC's BIOS firmware

It is not unusual to learn that the BIOS that runs your PC's system board has a few kinks and flaws. Plug and Play features existed long before USB devices were invented, so the implementation of Plug and Play in your BIOS may not be up to the task of properly handling USB. Check your PC maker's web site for BIOS revisions for your system board, and download and install the latest version.

Discussion

USB technology is perhaps the most practical method for connecting peripherals ever conceived for a computer system. The number of devices that use USB has grown tremendously since its initial implementation—almost anything you want to connect to a PC is available in USB versions and many items are only available in USB. USB, however, is not foolproof—BIOS, USB chipsets, adequate power supply, proper cabling, and well-designed software device drivers must all work together to provide that true Plug and Play experience for everything from PDAs to video cameras and MP3 players. USB devices themselves do not often fail, so it is important to verify all of the elements that allow USB to work. The examples above are very common and reliable methods to ensure your USB devices works with your computer.

See Also

Comprehensive information about how USB works with Windows XP may be found at *http://www.microsoft.com/whdc/system/bus/USB/default.mspx*. A general overview of USB features and functions may be found at *http://www.microsoft.com/windowsxp/using/networking/learnmore/jones_02august05.mspx*.

3.11 Keeping USB Devices from Disappearing

Problem

Every so often, a USB device fails to be recognized and usable even though it has been connected for as long as the PC has been running.

Solution

Using the USB cable

1. Unplug the USB device and wait for Windows to signal the disconnect, or for 30 to 60 seconds to be sure Windows knows the device is gone.
2. Reconnect the USB device and wait for Windows to recognize it again.

Using a graphical user interface

1. Click Start, then right-click My Computer and select Properties.
2. Select the Hardware tab, then click Device Manager.
3. Locate and expand the device type of interest—Network adapters, or other.
4. Locate the device of interest, right-click on it, then select Properties.
5. If the device properties dialog includes a power management tab, click on it.

6. Uncheck the box next to Allow the Computer to Turn Off This Device to Save Power.

7. Click OK, then close Device Manager.

Discussion

Windows power management will turn off devices when the system goes into standby and may also do so when a screen saver kicks in. Some USB devices do not reset and come back to life after being told to power off and then come back on later, but they do OK if completely disconnected and reconnected. Changing the power management characteristics for a device can keep it from losing power and getting confused. This symptom can also affect built-in and PCI network adapters that support and comply with power management.

See Also

Power management is a significant topic of discussion among PC and peripheral design engineers at both the hardware and software/driver levels. Microsoft and Intel are the best sources for information on how chipsets and Windows support power management. For details, visit the following web pages: *http://www.microsoft.com/whdc/archive/winpowmgmt.mspx*, *http://www.microsoft.com/whdc/system/pnppwr/powermgmt/devicepm.mspx*, *http://www.microsoft.com/whdc/resources/respec/specs/pmref/default.mspx*, *http://www.microsoft.com/resources/documentation/Windows/XP/all/reskit/en-us/prdh_dmt_xapo.asp*, and *http://www.intel.com/intelpress/samples/ppm_chapter.pdf*.

3.12 Curing Stubborn USB Devices

Problem

Your new USB device is discovered and becomes an "Unknown Device" or fails to work even if listed properly in Device Manager.

Solution

Try using hardware alternatives:

- Connect USB 1.1 devices to USB 1.1 ports or hubs.
- Connect USB 2.0 devices to USB 2.0 ports or hubs.
- Connect the USB device to a root hub.
- Connect the USB device to a powered hub.
- Install a USB add-in PCI card to avoid motherboard and BIOS problems.

Discussion

If a new USB device is detected by Windows XP and the Found New Hardware Wizard appears, you at least know your system has some USB functionality. You need to resolve hardware issues with signal quality and compatibility—proper timing and getting a clean signal between a USB device and host are critical. However, you do not have any control over the USB host device, how it handles signals, or how the BIOS or native device drivers handle the host components.

You can, however control the connection points to a certain extent, by choosing which port you connect the device to on your PC. Most USB 1.1 devices will work when connected to USB 2.0 ports and hubs, which should down-shift to USB 1.1 specifications, but you may find that using a USB 1.1 port or hub is required. As well, most USB 2.0 devices will work when connected to USB 1.1 ports and hubs, but the performance will drop to USB 1.1 specifications, so you'll want to use a USB 2.0 port or hub.

Devices that get their power from the USB connection must be provided the right voltage and adequate current capacity to function. While all USB ports provide power, not all of them provide enough power for all of the devices you want to use. Plain USB hubs get their power from the host port. This arrangement may not provide adequate power, so opting for powered hubs is a good choice. Fortunately, USB is quite expandable by adding or daisy-chaining hubs, and if each hub provides power, every device should get what it needs. If you have two or more devices that require a lot of power, such as web cameras, separate their connections to different hubs to avoid overloading a single powered hub. Without detailed testing in somewhat of a "lab environment" it is not easy to tell if a port or hub is really delivering the power it says it will, so it can be easier to simply change brands or models of hubs until you get adequate power.

Laptops and system boards with built-in USB hosts are subject to the whims of BIOS and device drivers. Using a PC card or PCI-based USB host adapter and appropriate driver can separate native hardware problems and give XP something you both can work with.

See Also

The best guides to troubelshooting USB problems under Windows XP may be found in MS KB 310575, "General USB troubleshooting in Windows XP," and on Microsoft's web site at *www.microsoft.com/resources/documentation/Windows/XP/all/reskit/en-us/Default.asp?url=/resources/documentation/Windows/XP/all/reskit/en-us/prdh_dmt_nrtj.asp*

3.13   Revealing Hidden Devices

Problem

You want to find a hidden device that you've never heard of but that a program says you have installed.

Solution

Using a graphical user interface

1. Click Start, then right-click My Computer and select Properties.
2. Select the Hardware tab, then click Device Manager.
3. Select View, then select Show Hidden Devices from the menu.
4. Note the appearance of dozens of new items appearing under Network adapters, system devices, and a new non-Plug and Play drivers device grouping.

Discussion

For security and management reasons, Windows XP separates software from your PC's hardware through a part of the operating system called the Hardware Abstraction Layer, or HAL. Unlike the old days of DOS where software had direct, uncoordinated, and often catastrophic access directly to hardware devices, the HAL is like a huge secure device driver overseeing all things hardware connected to the operating system, requiring that programs send data to and get data from hardware through it. This provides security benefits to data and stability to the operating system, and helps negotiate or avoid software and device conflicts. If a piece of software needs to work with a piece of hardware, it must do so with a device driver, which accesses the hardware through the HAL.

Many programs can attach themselves to your system as if they were a piece of hardware, by using device drivers so they can control specific features of real hardware devices or the data passing to and from them. Examples are video card acceleration and tweaking utilities, data transfer accelerators, virus protection, and desktop firewalls for networking.

Just like normal device drivers, the device drivers associated with applications can be removed by right-clicking them and selecting Uninstall, but you have to be able to see them first, so we use this recipe to make them visible.

See Also

Tidbits of information about hidden devices and safely removing them can be found at *www.tech-recipes.com/windows_installation_tips504.html*, *http://www.techzonez.com/forums/showthread.php?t=13418*, and in *Windows XP Hacks*, published by O'Reilly.

Some relevant information from *Windows XP Hacks* can be found at *www.oreilly.com/catalog/winxphks2/chapter/hack116.pdf*.

3.14   Checking Drivers with the Driver Verifier Tool

Problem

You need to determine which drivers are loaded and the characteristics about them.

Solution

Using a graphical user interface

1. Click Start, then select Run.
2. Type in verifier and click OK.
3. In the Driver Verifier Manager dialog, with the Create standard settings radio button selected under Select a Task, click Next.
4. To see the analysis of all drivers on your system, select the Automatically Select All Drivers Installed on This Computer radio button, and click Finish.
5. Your choices will be stored and you will receive a pop-up indicating that you must reboot for the changes to take effect. Click OK, then reboot at your convenience.
6. After rebooting your PC, rerun Verifier to see the analysis of all running drivers and the state they are in. Driver Verifier will, per Microsoft, tell you a variety of things as described in the Discussion section.

Discussion

Windows' device driver verification tool will trace the loading and activity of any device driver you choose. This tool is intended for developers and low-level system engineers, but it can tell you which drivers are or have been loaded during Windows operation and help you debug them in case you experience system or device crashes.

See Also

Details on the parameters, use, and results of the Driver Verifier Manager can be found in MS KB 244617, "How to Use Driver Verifier to Troubleshoot Windows Drivers."

3.15 Resolving Printer Timed-Out and Not Ready Problems

Problem

You experience no printing, or slow or failed/timed-out printing symptoms from DOS programs under Windows XP. Printer output is garbled or incomplete.

Solution

Using a graphical user interface

1. Click Start, then select Printers and Faxes.
2. Right-click the icon for your printer, then select Properties.
3. Select the Ports tab.
4. If your printer is connected to your PC through an LPT port, highlight the port and click the Configure Port... button. You cannot change the configuration of USB or network ports.
5. In the Configure LPT Port dialog you will see a default Transmission Retry with a value of 90 seconds. Change this value to 15, then click OK.

Discussion

Because Windows isn't really intended to support DOS and DOS hardware devices, the print spooler and HAL drivers may send data prematurely to the printer driver or wait too long to send data to an LPT-port-connected printer from a DOS program, and then time out before the printer acknowledges it is ready to or has accepted data. Setting a shorter timeout period for the LPT port time out forces the print spooler driver to send data sooner and get the printer to start producing the desired output.

See Also

Broader coverage of DOS and Windows printing problems can be found at *http://www.superflow.com/support/support-dynosoft-prntprobs.htm*.

3.16 Troubleshooting Local Printing Problems

Problem

You cannot print to a local printer.

Solution

1. Test the parallel port driver and the hardware. If the printer is connected to an LPT (parallel) port, see whether you can print from a command prompt.

   If the printer is not a PostScript printer, type **dir > lpt1** at a command prompt and press Enter. You may have to do this more than once to fill the print buffer on some printers.

   Page-oriented printers (for example, laser printers) generally do not start to print until a form-feed PCL command is sent or until more information than just a page is present in the buffer.

   Running the dir > lpt1 command from the C:\Windows directory will fill the page buffer.

2. If you can successfully print from a command prompt (step 1 above), the parallel port driver and the hardware are working correctly. This eliminates the Graphics Device Interface (GDI) and the driver as possible causes. If the output is printed to the printer from the dir command, the print driver or printer configuration is probably the source of the problem.

3. Check the documentation for your printer to determine if it requires a plain LPT port, and EPP, or an ECP parallel port configuration. This configuration must be set in the system BIOS to match the printer. Windows will detect this configuration change and install the appropriate driver for the port.

4. See whether the printer cable meets the IEEE 1284 specification. If the cable does meet the specification, the cable itself is marked accordingly.

5. Make sure that no devices other than the printer are connected to the port and that no scanners, switch boxes, and so on are between the computer and the printer.

Discussion

Local printer ports can be a bit tricky if they are not configured properly or use the wrong cable to connect them to the PC. There are four hardware configurations possible in the system BIOS for most the LPT/parallel ports—Normal or Output Only, Bi-Directional, Enhanced Parallel Port (EPP), and Enhanced Capability Port (ECP). Normal or Output Only is typical for most older dot-matrix and laser printers that do not communicate ink or toner status back to the PC. ECP mode is typical for later model laser and ink-jet printers that tell the PC about toner or ink status levels. If you have the correct printer driver installed, printing problems can be resolved easily with the proper port setting and cable.

See Also

Excellent references to resolving printing problems can be found at *http://www. computerhope.com/issues/ch000248.htm* and *http://h10025.www1.hp.com/ewfrf/wc/ genericDocument?lc=en&cc=ca&docname=bpy20814*

3.17   Printing to a USB Printer from DOS

Problem

You need to print from DOS or command-line programs but have a USB printer.

Solution

Using a graphical user interface

1. Click Start, then select Printers and Faxes.
2. Right-click the icon for your printer, then select Sharing.
3. Select the Share This Printer radio button, then type in a name for the shared printer.
4. Click OK to close the dialog, saving the results.
5. Once the printer is shared it can be mapped to an LPT port assignment that DOS understands by following the next steps for using a command-line interface to complete this recipe.

Using a command-line interface

Use the following command:

```
> net use lpt1: \\localhost\<printername> /persistent:yes
```

where *<printername>* is the name you gave the printer share in step 3 above. Then run the following command:

```
> dir > lpt1:
```

This will print out a list of your current directory. When you need to print from a DOS program, make sure the program is set to use LPT1 so the printed output will go through the LPT1 port assignment to the newly shared USB printer.

Discussion

DOS is not aware of and does not support USB devices. To print from a DOS program using a USB printer you have to fool XP into thinking it's sharing a local printer and capture all print data sent to that local printer as if it had an LPT-attached device. The NET USE solution is a simple, eloquent workaround to bridge old technology to new.

See Also

HP has lots of information available at *h20000.www2.hp.com/bizsupport/TechSupport/Document.jsp?objectID=bpl11166*.

3.18 Resolving Failed Network Printing with Internet Connection Sharing

Problem

You cannot print to a networked printer after setting up Internet Connection Sharing.

Solution

Using the printer's setup features

1. Access the configuration menu for your networked printer or network printer adapter.

2. Change the network address of the printer to a value within the same 192.168.0.x TCP/IP subnet that Internet Connection Sharing uses. Valid addresses are 192.168.0.1 through 192.168.0.254, although your PCs are probably using the first few addresses, so setting the address to 192.168.0.10 should work.

3. Go to the Start menu, or through the Control Panel, and select Printers and Faxes.

4. Remove the networked printer, then select Add a Printer and reinstall the printer using its new IP address (step 2) for the TCP/IP port, or rerun the printer's installation software and configure it with the new address.

5. Repeat steps 3 and 4 on every PC that uses the networked printer so all of them can communicate with it on the proper subnet.

6. Send a test page from each PC to the network printer to be sure things are properly set up.

Discussion

Internet Connection Sharing uses the 192.168.0.x TCP/IP subnet for all computers that use this feature to communicate between networked/LAN-based computers to the Internet connection on the PC that is sharing the connection. If your LAN uses a different TCP/IP subnet, and your other PCs and printer may be able to communicate with each other, but they will no longer be able to communicate with the PC that has ICS installed and running. The necessary correction is to configure all PCs and networked devices to use the ICS-compatible network addresses.

This situation applies if you are using a printer that has a TCP/IP connection, or a network printer adapter, and your workstations print directly to its IP address. This does not apply if you share a printer from another computer or on a server.

See Also

Generic networked printer troubleshooting is covered at *www.microsoft.com/ hardware/broadbandnetworking/10_ts_printeronecomputer.mspx*, while print server related troubleshooting is well-covered at *http://www.windowsdevcenter.com/pub/a/ windows/2004/09/28/printer_problems.html*.

3.19 Interpreting Device Manager Error Codes

Problem

One or more hardware devices are not functioning and you find error codes in the Properties for the device in Device Manager.

Solution

Using a graphical user interface

1. Click Start, then right-click My Computer, and select Properties.
2. Select the Hardware tab, then click Device Manager.
3. Locate and expand the device type of interest—Network adapters, or other.
4. Locate the device of interest, right-click it, and select Properties.
5. Under Device Status you will see either "The device is working properly" or error codes related to the type of failure, which may be interpreted and acted upon from the details provided at *http://support.microsoft.com/default. aspx?scid=kb;en-us;310123*.
6. Translating the error codes into corrective steps typically reveals the need to replace or update the device driver, reinitializing Plug and Play as detailed in Recipe 3.1, or powering off both the PC and the device and restarting them to clear a hardware malfunction.
7. After taking the appropriate corrective step indicated by Microsoft's error code translations, follow steps 1 through 5 above to verify that the driver is working properly.

Discussion

We wish Microsoft and most PC experts who do know what these error codes mean would put them into plain English, but cryptic numeric error codes seem to be the norm. Errors such as those listed above are not uncommon, and neither are their causes, or the solutions. Most such errors are the result of changes in the system, or the occasional outright failure of a system component or peripheral. If the suggested fixes are ineffective it is time to consider replacing the afflicted component.

See Also

The Windows XP Resource Kit online documentation provides a wealth of information about Device Manager and device troubleshooting at *http://www.microsoft. com/resources/documentation/Windows/XP/all/reskit/en-us/Default.asp?url=/resources/ documentation/Windows/XP/all/reskit/en-us/prjk_dec_lgsc.asp*.

3.20   Troubleshooting Sound Problems

Problems

You suffer from one of the following problems:

- You do not hear sound from your computer's speakers or headphones.
- A sound is played, but then stops suddenly or the sound skips or misses in some areas.
- The sound is distorted or scratchy.
- The computer stops responding (hangs) when a sound is played or the computer restarts when a sound is played.
- You receive an error message when you try to play sound. For example, you may receive any one of the following error messages:

  ```
  MIDI output error detected.

  No wave device that can play files in the current format is installed.

  The CD Audio device is in use by another application.

  WAV sound playback error detected.

  Your audio hardware cannot play files like the current file.
  ```

Solution

1. First, verify connections and settings:
   a. Be sure you have made the proper connections between your PC or sound card. It is very easy to confuse the icons for line, speaker, and auxillary input/output jacks.
   b. Be sure you have the proper power to your amplified speakers.
   c. Double-click the Volume Control (speaker) icon in the Tool TrayCheck to access the complete set of playback controls, then verify that none of the controls for Master Volume, WAV, or other sound sources are set to mute.

2. Next, check sound files and disks for corruption:

    a. Try other sound files. The one you selected may be corrupt.

    b. Check your disk drive for errors using CHKDSK.

    c. If the sound stops coincident with mouse movement, network activity, or other events on your system, check the sound card for conflicts in Device Manager and resolve the conflicts by resetting Plug and Play in BIOS or reconfiguring the sound card address, IRQ, and DMA settings to nonconflicting values.

3. Next, verify the proper input and output connections suitable for the sound source and speaker type:

    a. If the source of the sound is an external device such as an MP3 or CD player, make sure it is connected to the line input connection for your sound card.

    b. Check the documentation for your speakers to determine if they should be connected to the speaker or line out connectors on your sound card, and reconnect accordingly.

4. Next, verify the configuration of the sound card relative to other hardware:

    a. Open Device Manager to look for indications of a conflict—perhaps a newly installed sound card assumed the resources of another device, or another new device assumed the resources of the sound device. Resolve the conflict by resetting Plug and Play in BIOS, or reconfiguring the sound card or other device.

    b. It is possible the device driver for your sound card or another device is causing an error that Windows cannot recover from forcing it to restart. Uninstall then upgrade the device driver for your sound card or other new device.

5. Lastly, ensure your sound card supports and that you have the proper drivers installed for the type of file you are trying to open:

    a. Your sound device may not support MIDI files. Check the documentation for your sound device.

    b. Most sound cards support MIDI as well as WAV and other file types, but the driver that translates MIDI files to play them may not be installed or may be corrupt. Uninstall then reinstall or upgrade the drivers for your sound device.

Discussion

Playing sounds can be a more complex task than displaying high-resolution graphics. Windows must have working video all the way from installation to using applications, while sound is an afterthought to the PC architecture that has to squeeze itself into whatever address, IRQ, and DMA resources are available. The hardware configuration of your sound device may be controlled by settings in the BIOS or even jumpers or switches on the sound card.

Similarly, sound systems have multiple connections for inputs and outputs that must electrically match the source of the sound and your speaker system. Once the hardware is set up so that you can play sounds, Windows' sound support must have the proper drivers and codec (compression/decompression) features installed to support translation of bits and bytes into audible sound. Windows Media Player should decode most if not all typical (WAV, MID, and MP3) sound files, but you may need a third-party media player program such as RealPlayer, *http://www.real.com*, or WinAmp, *http://www.winamp.com*, to listen to sound files for Unix or other computer systems.

See Also

Microsoft devotes several articles to sound at MS KB 307918, "Resources for Troubleshooting Sound Problems in Windows XP," MS KB 81752, "Troubleshooting Media Player MIDI Sound Problems," and *http://www.microsoft.com/technet/prodtechnol/ winxppro/reskit/prdm_mtm_scit.asp*.

3.21   Troubleshooting Video Problems

Problems

- You suffer from one of the following issues:
- You receive the following error message:

    ```
    Display problems. This program can't continue.
    ```

- Your display flickers or is garbled.
- You are having a problem with the multiple-monitor feature.
- Videos or animations do not work correctly.
- You cannot set the video resolution above 640 × 480 or 800 × 600 with 16 colors.

Solution

Using a graphical user interface

1. If your video display is illegible when you start Windows normally, start up your PC in Safe Mode.
2. Click Start, navigate to Settings, and then select Control Panel.
3. Double-click System, click Hardware, and then click Device Manager.
4. Click the plus sign (+) to expand Display Adapters.
5. Double-click the listing for your video adapter driver.

6. Select the Driver tab, then click the appropriate button based on the action that you want to perform: (view) Driver Details, Update Driver, Roll Back Driver, Uninstall.

7. Typically you will need to select Update Driver and apply the correct video driver for the specific video adapter in your system, whether it be a built-in adapter on the motherboard or a plug-in (PCI or AGP) adapter.

Discussion

If Windows auto-detected the video adapter you have, or defaulted to Standard VGA Adapter and did not install the proper driver, your display capabilities will lack many features. It is rare that one generic video adapter driver will work for all implementations of a particular video chipset. An nVidia or ATI chip built into your motherboard will have different video BIOS and features and require a different driver than the same chip used on a plug-in video adapter. The wrong driver may not be able to support all of the video memory, scan rate, or color depth features the adapter is capable of. Installing the exact drivers for your video adapter will ensure all of its features and functions are available. Another hint: if the option is available, enable the IRQ for video setting in your system BIOS setup program—many video card features require an IRQ assignment to function properly.

3.22   Troubleshooting Video Monitor Problems

Problem

Your display flickers or is garbled and you want to fix it.

Solution

Using a graphical user interface

1. If your video display is illegible when you start Windows normally, start your PC in Safe mode.

2. Click Start, right-click My Computer, then select Properties.

3. Select the Hardware tab, then click Device Manager.

4. Click the plus sign (+) to expand Monitors.

5. Double-click the listing for your video monitor.

6. Select the Driver tab, then click the appropriate button based on the action that you want to perform: (view) Driver Details, Update Driver, Roll Back Driver, Uninstall.

7. Typically you will need to select Update Driver and apply the correct driver for your specific video monitor by make and model number. Check the manufacturer's web site for current drivers to be installed.

Discussion

If Windows cannot determine the specific make and model of your monitor it will assume a Plug and Play monitor (which, if it was truly Plug and Play would have provided specific make/model information to Windows) or one of many standard monitor types. Either of these may be inappropriate for your monitor and incapable of using all of its features. Monitors do not use drivers per se but display definition files that tell Windows which resolutions and video sync rates the monitor is capable of displaying. Video monitor files can usually be found on the manufacturer's web site. If your monitor is relabeled by your PC's manufacturer (like Dell, HP, Sony, etc.), you may be able to determine an exact manufacturer from a sticker on the back of the monitor, or you will need to visit the PC maker's web site to obtain the correct files for your monitor.

See Also

More information is available in MS KB 219404, "Monitor Detected as Generic Plug and Play," MS KB 162737, "No Plug and Play Detection for Non-DDC Monitors," and MS KB 309569, "You Cannot Select the Highest Monitor Graphics Modes."

3.23   Stopping LCD Monitor Resolution Messages

Problem

Your external LCD display shows a pop-up message indicating an optimal or preferred display resolution.

Solution

Using a graphical user interface

1. Right-click an empty area on your Windows desktop, then select Properties.
2. Select the Settings tab.
3. Under Screen Resolution, move the slider until the text beneath the slider shows the resolution values suggested by the monitor's pop-up message.

Using controls on the LCD display

Consult the manual to determine the sequence of steps necessary to access the monitor's on-screen display (OSD) and the selection for controlling the resolution message.

Discussion

LCD displays are designed for a minimum or optimal display resolution driven by the video adapter. Although low display resolutions may be visible, the image may appear blurry or blocky at less than optimal resolutions, which can be detected by the electronics in the display unit. The display manufacturer prefers to remind you of this fact through a built-in on-screen message, both to avoid tech support calls and to ensure you get the best image possible from the display.

See Also

Check the manual or manufacturer's web site for your monitor to learn if you can disable the resolution warnings and how to do it.

3.24   Interpreting Windows INF Files

Problem

You want to know what the parameters and data in INF files mean.

Solution

The different sections of device INF files and their significance to configuring device and driver installations are listed in brief excerpts from Microsoft's documentation below. The sections may appear in any order in an INF file.

Version
> This is a required section for every INF file and must contain a valid Signature entry for use with Windows XP.

SourceDisksNames
> This section identifies the individual source distribution disks or CD-ROM disks for the installation, and is required if a corresponding SourceDisksFiles section exists.

SourceDisksFiles
> This section identifies the locations of files to be installed.

ClassInstall32
> This section, required in any class installer INF file, initializes a device setup class. This section is not required in INF files that install devices and their drivers under any system-defined device class.

ClassInstall32.Services
> ClassInstall32.Services with an AddService directive control how and when the services of a particular device class are loaded.

DestinationDirs
> The DestinationDirs section specifies a default destination directory for files to be copied during installation.

ControlFlags

ControlFlags specify whether the Add Hardware Wizard will present a list of device make and model values. If the device being installed is a Plug and Play device, the wizard does not present a list.

Manufacturer

The Manufacturer section contains the list of device model information.

Models (per Manufacturer entry)

Models establishes a reference between the name of the device, device ID, and the related DDInstall section of the INF file.

DDInstall (per Models entry)

DDInstall indicates the driver to be installed.

DDInstall.Services

DDInstall.Services controls starting and establishes dependencies of services related to a device.

DDInstall.HW

DDInstall.HW adds or removes Registry entries related to a device.

DDInstall.CoInstallers

DDInstall.CoInstallers registers additional device installers related to a device.

DDInstall.FactDef

DDInstall.FactDef lists the default hardware configuration—I/O addressing, IRQ and DMA settings—for non-Plug and Play devices.

DDInstall.LogConfigOverride

DDInstall.LogConfigOverride provides an override to the default configuration of a Plug and Play device.

DDInstall.Interfaces

DDInstall.Interfaces indicates the export of functionality to other device classes.

InterfaceInstall32

InterfaceInstall32 establishes a set of device interfaces for a new device class.

DefaultInstall

This section is given control if you select Install after right-clicking an INF file.

DefaultInstall.Services

The DDInstall.Services section is related to the DefaultInstall section.

Strings

Strings supports localization of INF files.

[Version]

[Provider=%INF-creator%]

This is an optional entry used to indicate the source or author of the INF file.

AddReg and *DelReg*

These are used to specify Registry keys to be added or deleted.

CopyFiles

By reference to file-list-sections or to a single file, CopyFiles specifies copying a file or files from the installation media to a destination.

DelFiles

By reference to file-list-sections or to a single file, DelFiles specifies deleting a file or files from a specific location.

RenFiles

By reference to file-list-sections or to a single file, RenFiles specifies renaming a file or files from a specific location.

AddService

AddService references the service-install-section for adding services related to the item being installed.

DelService

DelService deletes a previously installed service.

AddInterface

AddInterface refers to AddReg entries for a device/driver or additional operations.

BitReg

BitReg refers to specific bit entries in Registry values to be modified.

LogConfig

LogConfig refers to bus configuration items supplied by Plug and Play devices or specific to non-Plug and Play devices.

UpdateInis

UpdateInis indicates specific changes to an associated INI file.

UpdateIniFields

This rarely used directive references one or more update-INI-fields-sections specifying modifications to be made on fields within the lines of an INI file.

Ini2Reg

This rarely used directive references one or more ini-to-registry-sections specifying lines or sections of an INI file to be written into the Registry.

Discussion

Working with INF files is seldom if ever addressed in the resolution of specific hardware problems, but if you are creating your own device drivers or troubleshooting an installation problem, knowing the meaning of INF file parameters and data variables can be quite valuable. If you are creating your own data CDs that you want to auto-run an installation script or auto-play a specific media file, you will want to become familiar with the simple constructs in AUTORUN.INF files, covered in Recipe 3.25.

See Also

A good layman's discussion of the AUTORUN.INF file can be found at *http://autorun. moonvalley.com/autoruninf.htm*, as well as at the official Microsoft developer references, *http://msdn.microsoft.com/library/en-us/shellcc/platform/shell/programmersguide/ shell_basics/shell_basics_extending/autorun/autoplay_cmds.asp*.

3.25 Figuring out AUTORUN.INF Files

Problem

You need to know which parameters and data values can be used in AUTORUN.INF files.

Solution

The possible key values and their parameters for creating AUTORUN.INF files are defined by Microsoft as follows:

Action

> The action entry, used only in Windows XP SP2, specifies the text that is used in the Autoplay dialog for the program named in the open or shellexecute entry in the Autorun.inf file. The value can be expressed simply as text or as a resource referenced in a binary file.
>
> Examples:
>
> ```
> action=ActionText
> action=@[filepath\]filename,-resourceID
> ```

Icon

> The icon entry specifies an icon to represent the AUTORUN.INF file in Windows Explorer.
>
> Example:
>
> ```
> icon=iconfilename[,index]
> ```

Label

> The label entry specifies a text label to represent the AUTORUN.INF file in Windows Explorer.
>
> Example:
>
> ```
> label=LabelText
> ```

Shellexecute

> The shellexecute entry specifies an application or data file that autorun will use to call ShellExecuteEx.
>
> Example:
>
> ```
> shellexecute=[filepath\]filename[param1, [param2]...]
> ```

Shell

> The shell entry specifies a default command for the drive's shortcut menu.
>
> Example:
>
> ```
> shell=verb
> ```

shell\verb

> The shell\verb entry adds a custom command to the drive's shortcut menu.
>
> Examples:
>
> ```
> shell\verb\command=Filename.exe
> shell\verb=MenuText
> ```

MenuText

> This parameter specifies the text that is displayed in the shortcut menu. If it is
> omitted, the text from verb (above) is displayed. The menu item behaves much
> like other Windows dialogs—the text can be mixed-case, can contain spaces,
> and may indicate a shortcut/hotkey by putting an ampersand (&) in front of the
> letter you want to use as the shortcut.

DriverPath

> This entry goes under the DeviceInstall section, which is supported only under
> Windows XP. It specifies a directory to search for driver files. This command is
> only used during a driver installation. It is recommended that you not hard-code
> drive letters in the directory path.

Discussion

The AUTORUN.INF file is a modest but powerful tool, commonly provided in the
root directory of CD-ROMs that store data and programs. AUTORUN.INF is used to
start installation programs, run demonstration slide shows, or launch multimedia
players.

Most AUTORUN.INF files are very simple, like the file in the root of the Windows
XP Professional CD-ROM shown below:

```
[AutoRun]
open=setup.exe
icon=setup.exe,0
```

The open= line indicates the program to be automatically run, and the icon= line indicates the icon embedded in the *setup.exe* file to display in Windows Explorer.

When creating your own multimedia presentation CDs you could specify a full command line to run a PowerPoint presentation or play an MPEG file, as shown below:

```
[AutoRun]
open=powerpoint.exe mypresentation.ppt
icon=powerpoint.exe,0
```

or

```
[AutoRun]
open=mplayer.exe mymovie.mpeg
icon=mplayer.exe,0
```

You can substitute the filename for an icon or your company logo in place of the default application icon.

You may need to modify the AUTORUN.INF file for a driver installation if you require drivers to be loaded from a specific drive/directory path, or the file provided with the drivers is hard-coded and you want to use a relative path instead.

See Also

MS KB 136214, "How to Test Autorun.inf Files"

3.26   Correcting Parameters in BIOS

Problem

Windows XP does not install correctly or you do not have access to all of your system board features and ports from within XP.

Solution

The typical types of values, and their settings, for most Plug and Play BIOS to get and keep Windows and your PC working well together and have access to all of your system hardware devices.

PNP OS Installed
> Windows XP supports Plug and Play (PnP), so this option should be set to Yes. Some say that it is best to leave this option set to No regardless of whether your OS is PNP-capable or not. When it is set to No, the BIOS will attempt to resolve any resource conflicts. If it is set to Yes, even if a conflict is detected, the BIOS will ignore it. Setting it to Yes provides a bit of a safety net, and it will not affect the ability of the OS to perform PNP on its own.

Reset Configuration Data (Force Update ESCD)
> Extended System Configuration Data (ESCD) is a feature of the Plug and Play BIOS that stores the IRQ, DMA, I/O, and memory configurations of all the ISA, PCI, and AGP cards in the system (PnP or otherwise).
>
> Normally, you should leave the setting as Disabled unless you encounter serious problems with the installation of a new PCI card. Setting this to Yes can help bail you out. If you set it to Yes, the next time the PC boots, the BIOS will reconfigure the settings for all PNP cards. The BIOS will automatically reset this setting to Disabled next time you boot.

Resources Controlled By

> Normally, the BIOS controls the IRQ and DMA assignments of all of the boot and PNP devices in the system. When this option is set to Auto, this is what happens, and the ESCD is the mechanism for doing it.

> If you set this option to Manual, you will be able to manually assign all IRQ and DMA information, usually via a subscreen of the BIOS that will enable if you set this option to Manual. Manual settings can be used to resolve device resource conflicts.

PCI/VGA Palette Snoop

> This option is only useful if you use an MPEG card or an add-on card that makes use of the graphics card's Feature Connector.

> It corrects incorrect color reproduction by "snooping" into the graphics card's framebuffer memory and modifying (synchronizing) the information delivered from the graphics card's Feature Connector to the MPEG or add-on card.

Assign IRQ for VGA

> Many high-end graphics accelerator cards now require an IRQ to function properly. Disabling this feature with such cards will cause improper operation and/or poor performance.

Assign IRQ for USB

> This assigns an IRQ to the USB controller. It enables or disables IRQ allocation for the USB. If you are using an AGP-based video adapter this should be enabled. If you are not, you can disable this to free up an IRQ.

Discussion

If the BIOS parameters or device information are incorrect, the operating system may not install or function properly. PC operating systems expect system BIOS to behave in specific ways and to provide specific information about system hardware, from the motherboard to attached peripherals. All current PC BIOS support Plug and Play, power management, and basic I/O device configuration. While no two BIOS are completely alike, BIOS must provide a core set of common, basic functions in order for PC hardware to behave like PC hardware. If you are having trouble installing or running Windows XP with your motherboard, resetting the BIOS to default or safe settings should give you a clean slate to work with.

See Also

For more information about BIOS issues, see *http://www.buildeasypc.com/sw/bios_setup.htm*, *http://www.pcbuyerbeware.co.uk/BIOS.htm* and *http://www.pcguide.com/proc/setup/biossafe-c.html*

3.27   Troubleshooting CD Autorun Software Installation Problems

Problem

The installation or setup program on a CD-ROM may not automatically run when inserted into a CD-ROM or the DVD-ROM drive.

Solution

Log on to Windows XP as either a power user or an administrator.

Check the properties of the CD-ROM drive to ensure autorun/autoplay is enabled with the following steps:

1. Double-click My Computer on the desktop, or go to Start then select My Computer.
2. Right-click the CD-ROM drive listed, then select Properties.
3. In the Properties dialog, select the AutoPlay tab.
4. The default may be set to Take No Action for one or more types of CD content. Select the action you want Windows to take when you insert a CD-ROM by specific type, such as music, data, or video.
5. Click OK to close the dialog and proceed.

Discussion

When a CD-ROM is detected and autorun/autoplay is enabled, Windows XP is notified that a new volume is available and the drive is then checked for the presence of an AUTORUN.INF file in the root directory of the CD-ROM.

Only users who are logged on to Windows XP with power user or administrator rights are allowed to install software. If you have only user-level rights, you will be prompted with an "Install Program as other user" message when the CD-ROM autorun is processed. This behavior is by design or may be controlled by user or group policies by your system administrator.

See Also

http://www.johncardinal.com/ss/seccd.htm

3.28 Troubleshooting CD-ROM and DVD-ROM Reading Problems

Problem

You receive any of a variety of error messages when reading a CD-ROM or DVD-ROM, similar to any of the following:

> *application name* is not a valid win32 application.

or

> A device attached to the system is not functioning.

or

> A required file kernl32.dll was not found.

or

> Not enough memory to run this application.

or

> Cannot find the file(s) needed to start this application.

or

> Error Reading From File [Installer Error 1305]

or

> Unable to find Setup.exe

or

> CDR-101

or

> Unable to read drive *drive letter:*

or

> Insufficient Memory

You receive an error message:

> Video cannot be shown on the computer monitor because of one of the following reasons:
> A) Low video memory. Please try using lower display resolution and/or colors.
> B) Another application is currently using the necessary display resources. Please ensure that no such application is running.
> C) The display adapter is incompatible with the DVD decoder. Please try to obtain a display driver update.
> Do you want to continue? Yes/No

You may also experience one of the following problems:

- No disk volume label appears in Windows Explorer.
- You cannot view the contents of the disk in Windows Explorer.
- The computer stops responding when you insert the disk in the drive or read a disk.
- You cannot eject the disk from the drive.
- It takes an exceptionally long time to read the disk contents.

Solution

Examine the disk
> If the disk is damaged, contact the manufacturer about a replacement CD. If you experience problems with a DVD disk, make sure that you insert the DVD into a DVD drive, not a CD-ROM drive.

Clean the disk
> To clean the CD-ROM or DVD-ROM, use a disk-cleaning kit, or gently wipe the silver/nonlabel side of the disk with a soft, lint-free cotton cloth. You may dampen the cloth with lightly soapy water, a 50/50 alchohol/water mixture to get the tough grime off the surface, then dry the disk thoroughly before you put it into the drive.

Test the disk in a different drive
> If your computer has multiple CD-ROM drives, CD-R drives, CD/RW drives, or DVD drives, test the disk in the other drive. For DVDs, make sure that the drive has a DVD logo on the front. If the disk works in another drive, the original drive may not be properly reading the disk. If the disk is clean and does not work in either drive, it is probably damaged and has to be replaced.

Clean the drive
> You can clean the disk drive by using a CD-ROM drive cleaning disk or DVD drive cleaning disk. These cleaning disks are available in most computer or home electronics stores.

Use only stick-on labels or CD marking pens to label CD and DVDs
> Believe it or not, the bottom or record/playback side of a CD-ROM or DVD is more resilient and abuse-resistant than the top or label side, and the use of sharp objects or bleeding-through of permanent marker ink can adversely affect the record- or play-ability of your disk. Record first, mark or label after.

Discussion

CD-ROM and DVD media are remarkable but not perfect nor do they last forever. Variations in manufacturing processes, materials, and of course day-to-day handling of CDs can affect their lifespan and performance. Placing dirty media into a drive will transfer some of the dirt to the drive's internal parts and reduce its life as well. Treat all media and drives with care.

Basic or low-performance video adapters may lack adequate internal RAM to support the high resolution of DVD movies. An error message may also appear if Microsoft NetMeeting is started, or even if the NetMeeting icon is on your Taskbar. NetMeeting and DVD playback both use the overlay mixer. Only one program at a time can gain access to the overlay mixer.

See Also

http://www.pcguide.com/ts/x/comp/cd/index-c.html, and MS KB 321641, "How to Troubleshoot Issues with Reading CD, CD-R, CD-RW, and DVD Disks"

3.29   Resolving DVD Reading and DVD Movie Problems

Problem

Attempts to play a DVD movie fail or you receive the following error message or experience specific problems:

```
DVD Player
Analog copy protection violation: Windows cannot play this copy-protected disk
because it cannot verify that the video outputs on your DVD and/or VGA cards support
copy protection.
```

Solution

To resolve this issue, install an updated driver or unplug any cables that are connected to the video outputs on your computer.

Discussion

Many video adapters help to decode DVDs, but that does not mean they can fully decode a DVD movie. This error message may occur if your DVD or video adapter driver does not fully support the capabilities of the adapter or your hardware does not support copy protection.

See Also

MS KB 249334, "Troubleshooting DVD Problems in Windows 2000," and *http://www.microsoft.com/windows/windowsmedia/windowsxp/dvdplay.aspx*

3.30   Restoring Access to CD-ROMs

Problem

You receive error code 19, 31, 32, or 39 when trying to access a CD-ROM, or you can no longer access a CD-ROM after you remove CD-burning software.

Solution

1. Go to Start, click Run, type in regedit, and click OK.
2. Navigate to and expand the HKEY_LOCAL_MACHINE\SYSTEM\Current ControlSet\ Control\Class\ sections.
3. Double-click the {4D36E965-E325-11CE-BFC1-08002BE10318} key.
4. In the right-pane locate and delete the UpperFilters and LowerFilters entries if they exist.

Discussion

The removal of CD-ROM burning software or a software malfunction can leave erroneous data in the Registry that prevents decoding of CD-ROM content. Removing the erroneous data allows Windows to use complete, correct references for CD-ROM decoding.

See Also

MS KB 314060, "CD-ROM Access Is Missing and Messages Cite Error Code 31, Code 32, Code 19, or Code 39 After You Remove Easy CD Creator in Windows XP." For more on PC hardware standards, configuration, and capabilities refer to these sources:

Advanced Graphics Port (AGP): *http://www.intel.com*

AT-Attachment (ATA, aka IDE): *http://www.t13.org*

IEEE-1394 (FireWire™): *http://www.ieee.org*

Peripheral Componenet Interconnect (PCI) and PCI Express: *http://www.pcisig.com*

Plug and Play: *http://www.microsoft.com/whdc/system/pnppwr/pnp/default.mspx*

Serial ATA: *http://www.serialata.org*

Univeral Serial Bus (USB): *http://www.usb.org*

Universal Plug and Play (UPnP): *http://www.upnp.org*

Video Electronics Standards Association (VESA): *http://www.vesa.org*

IRQ, DMA & I/O: Resolving and Preventing System Conflicts, Jim Aspinwall, Wiley, 1999

CHAPTER 4

Installing, Uninstalling, and Working with Applications

4.0 Introduction

An operating system is only as useful as the applications that run on top of it, and that's as true of XP as it is of any operating system. One of XP's greatest benefits is the astonishingly wide array of software that can run on it.

But the thousands of applications written to run on XP and on XP's Windows predecessors as well as on DOS are also the cause of problems and frustrations. There is no certification process an application has to go through when it's written for XP, and so there are quite a few applications that can cause problems with XP. (However if companies want to use the Designed for Windows logo on their packaging or advertising, they do have to go through a certification process. For more information, see *http://www.microsoft.com/windowsserver2003/partners/isvs/cfwfaq.mspx#EBAAA*.) In particular, when you install some applications, they leave bits of themselves behind, cause system conflicts, and take up precious resources and memory. In addition, you may have programs written for earlier versions of Windows, or for DOS, and have problems running them in XP.

In this chapter, you'll find recipes for troubleshooting applications, as well as for getting more out of your applications. So, for example, you'll learn how you can change the default installation location for all programs, as well as learning keyboard shortcuts that will help you use XP more effectively. In addition, you'll learn how to transfer application settings from an old computer to a new one and much more.

4.1 Uninstalling "Unremovable" Components

Problem

You have standard utilities on your PC, such as WordPad or Windows Messenger, that you want to uninstall because you never use them and you want to free up disk space. You can't remove them using the Control Panel's normal Add or Remove Programs applet because the utilities don't show up in the applet.

Solution

Using a graphical user interface

To remove built-in utilities and components, you normally choose Control Panel → Add or Remove Programs → Add/Remove Windows Components to get to the Windows Component Wizard, shown in Figure 4-1. To remove a component, click the checkbox, click Next, and follow the wizard's instructions for removing the component.

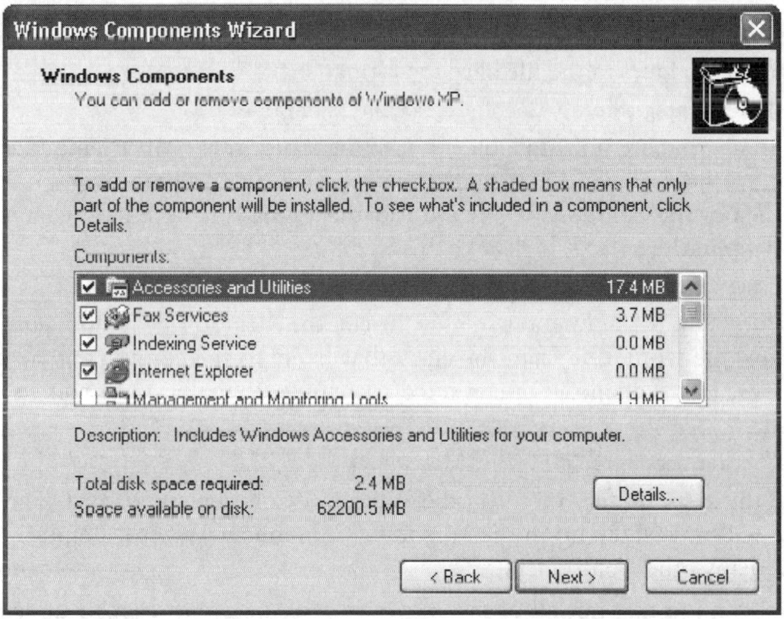

Figure 4-1. The Windows Component Wizard only lets you remove certain applications and utilities

But a number of Windows utilities and components, such as Windows Messenger and WordPad, don't show in the Windows Component Wizard, so there's no apparent way to uninstall them.

But you can, in fact, remove these components. To do it, you'll have to make the components show up in the Windows Component Wizard. Then you can remove them as you can any other file.

To force them to show up in the Windows Component Wizard, you edit the Setup Information file that controls what appears in the Windows Component Wizard:

1. Use Notepad or another text editor to open the Setup Information file, *sysoc.inf*, which is generally found in the *C:\WINDOWS\INF* folder. For safety's sake, make a backup of the file before editing it, so you can revert to it if you need to. And you should also set up a System Restore point before making the changes as well. To set up a System Restore point, see Recipe 19.5.

 C:\WINDOWS\INF is a hidden folder, so if you want to view its contents, you will first have to enable hidden folders by going into Windows Explorer and choosing Tools → Folder Options → View and choosing Show Hidden Files and Folders.

2. When you open the file, look for the line describing the program that you want to uninstall. Lines in the file have the format:

   ```
   program=program.dll,OcEntry,program.inf,,numeral
   ```

   Programs that are uninstallable all have the word hide or HIDE embedded in the string. When the word is included in the string, the program won't show up in the Windows Component Wizard. So the Pinball game entry, which doesn't show up in the wizard, looks like this:

   ```
   Pinball=ocgen.dll,OcEntry,pinball.inf,HIDE,7
   ```

3. To force the component to show up in the Windows Component Wizard, remove the word hide from the entry that refers to the component you want to remove. For example, if you wanted to remove Pinball, you'd edit its entry to this:

   ```
   Pinball=ocgen.dll,OcEntry,pinball.inf,,7
   ```

4. Save the *sysoc.inf* file, then run the Windows Component Wizard. The component will now show up in the Windows Component Wizard. Remove it as you would any other component.

   Keep in mind that not all of the entries in *sysoc.inf* are as easy to understand as Pinball and WordPad. For example, if you want to remove Windows Messenger, look for the entry that starts with the text msmsgs, and if you want to remove the Accessibility Wizard, look for the entry for AccessOpt. Table 4-1 lists the "uninstallable" programs and what their entries are in the *sysoc.inf* file.

Table 4-1. "Uninstallable" programs and their sysoc.inf entries

Entry	What entry refers to
AccessOpt	Accessibility Wizard
MultiM	Multimedia components, including Media Player, Volume Control, and Sound Recorder
CommApps	Communications components, including Chat, Hyperterminal, and Phone Dialer

Table 4-1. "Uninstallable" programs and their sysoc.inf entries (continued)

Entry	What entry refers to
AutoUpdate	Windows Automatic Update
TerminalServer	Terminal Server
Dtc	Distributed Transaction Coordinator
Dom	COM+
WBEM	Windows Management Instrumentation
Pinball	Pinball game
MSWordPad	WordPad
Msmsgs	Windows Messenger

Discussion

You can use this same technique in reverse to hide components you don't want to be accidentally uninstalled. Simply put the word HIDE in the proper place in the entry that you don't want to show up in the Windows Component Wizard. That way, the entry can't be accidentally deleted. For example, if you wanted to hide the uninstall entry for the fax utility, you'd edit its entry by changing:

```
Fax=fxsocm.dll,FaxOcmSetupProc,fxsocm.inf,,7
```

to:

```
Fax=fxsocm.dll,FaxOcmSetupProc,fxsocm.inf,HIDE,7
```

Also, you may run into a few problems when trying to remove "uninstallable" components. On some systems, you won't be able to remove Windows Messenger. Windows Messenger won't show up on the Windows Component Wizard even after you edit the *sysoc.inf* file. And some components, such as Terminal Server, will show up in the wizard if you edit the *sysoc.inf* file, but the wizard still won't let you uninstall them.

See Also

Recipe 4.2 for information about how to remove applications that leave bits of themselves behind even after uninstallation

4.2   Removing Unruly Applications

Problem

You want to uninstall an unruly application and make sure no remnants of the application are left behind.

Solution

Using a graphical user interface

Before uninstalling the application, look through your hard disk to see where the program stores its files and folders. Then choose Start → Control Panel → Add or Remove Programs, scroll to the program you want to uninstall, and click Change/Remove and follow the instructions. After you run the uninstallation routine, look for those files and folders, and delete them if they haven't been deleted. Often, this is in *C:\Program Files\<Publisher>\<Program Name>*.

Also, before you install the program, create a restore point so that you can restore your system to the state it was in before installation. That way, if you run the program and decide you don't want to use it any more, you can immediately revert to your system's pre-installation state. To set up a system restore point, see Recipe 19.5. Then, after you've installed the application and decided not to use it, revert to that restore point instead of using the uninstallation routine—it's more thorough.

> The restore point solution will only work if you use it directly after using the application for the first time, and if you make no other system changes. If you make system changes, after you install the software, and then revert to the restore point, you'll not only uninstall the program, but you'll also wipe out all the system changes that you made.

Using the Registry

After you've run the uninstallation routine, run the Registry Editor, search through the Registry for any keys and values the program left behind, and then delete them. Frequently, you can find the settings for the program at \HKEY_LOCAL_MACHINE\ SOFTWARE*<Publisher>**<Program Name>* where *<Publisher>* is the name of the software company that made the program and *<Program Name>* is the name of the software package (in the case of companies with multiple products like Symantec or Adobe).

You should also make sure that no parts of the program are still being run at startup. To do that, check the following two keys and delete any relevant entries:

```
HKEY_LOCAL_MACHINE\SOFTWARE\Microsoft\Windows\CurrentVersion\Run
HKEY_CURRENT_USER\Software\Microsoft\Windows\CurrentVersion\Run
```

Using downloadable software

RegSpy is shareware available from *http://www.utils32.com/regspy.htm* that tracks changes made to the Registry whenever a program installs and runs, and lets you roll back the changes the program makes. So run the program, and use the program's ability to build rollback scripts, which will let you review all Registry changes a program makes, step-by-step, and then roll them back. After you uninstall a program, run Reg-Spy and roll back any Registry changes the uninstallation program missed. RegSpy is shareware, and free to try, but costs $19.95 if you continue to use it.

Discussion

Unruly applications can cause a variety of problems. They might leave behind DLLs that load every time you start Windows, even though the original program is gone, which takes up memory and can cause system conflicts. They may also leave behind Registry entries, which cause similar problems. In both instances, your system performance takes a hit loading resources for programs that no longer exist. The programs also might leave behind unnecessary files and folders, which takes up hard disk space.

See Also

Registry First Aid is an excellent tool for checking for Registry entries that have been left behind by unruly programs. It will also check for other Registry problems, such as incorrect and outdated entries. You can get it from *http://www.rosecitysoftware. com/reg1aid/*. It's shareware and if you continue to use it after 30 days, you're required to pay a $21 registration fee.

4.3 Removing Stubborn Uninstall Entries from Already Uninstalled Programs

Problem

You've uninstalled a program, but its entry still remains listed in the Add or Remove Programs dialog box. You want to remove the entry.

Solution

Using the Registry

Run the Registry Editor and open \HKEY_LOCAL_MACHINE\SOFTWARE\Microsoft\Windows\ CurrentVersion\Uninstall. Look for the entry of the uninstalled program (it will be the program name) and delete it. In some instances, instead of the program name, you'll see an entry like this: {3075C5C3-0807-4924-AF8F-FF27052C12AE}. In that case, open the DisplayName subkey in that entry; it should have the name of the program: in this instance, Norton Antivirus 2002. When you find the proper entry, delete it.

Discussion

It's a good idea, before using the Registry Editor, to use the entry in the Add or Remove Programs dialog box as if the program were still installed on your PC. In some instances, pieces of the program were left behind, fooling Windows into thinking that the entire program is still there, and the Add or Remove Programs dialog box will uninstall those pieces. After it does that, the uninstall entry will be removed as well. However, this often doesn't work, and if it doesn't, you'll have to use the Registry to solve the problem.

See Also

Recipe 4.2 for information on how to remove applications that leave bits of themselves behind even after uninstallation

4.4   Changing the Default Location for Installing Applications

Problem

You want to change the default directory that programs are installed to—from the directory *C:\Program Files* to another directory or drive.

Solution

Using the Registry

Run the Registry Editor and go to HKEY_LOCAL_MACHINE\SOFTWARE\Microsoft\Windows\ CurrentVersion\ProgramFilesDir. By default, the value will be *C:\Program Files*. Edit the value to any valid drive or folder, and Windows will use that new location as the default installation directory for new programs. You'll have to reboot for the change to take effect.

Discussion

Changing the default location for installing applications will change the default location selected when you install an application and it prompts for the destination folder. Make sure that you have a good reason for changing the default location of the default installation folder, because many programs expect to be in the Program Files folder. If you have a second or third drive on your PC and want programs to be installed into that drive, consider creating a Program Files folder on that drive, and using that as the default installation folder.

See Also

MS KB 175037, "How to Change the Default Location of Mail and News Folders"

4.5   Launching Applications with Keyboard Shortcuts

Problem

You want to launch an application quickly using a keyboard shortcut rather than having to hunt down icons and click them.

Solution

Using a graphical user interface

1. Right-click on the desktop and choose New → Shortcut.

2. Enter or browse to the filename of the application for which you want to create a shortcut, including its path, and surrounding it by quotation marks, such as "C:\ Program Files\MusicMatch\MusicMatch Jukebox\mmjb.exe".

3. Click Next, then select a name for the shortcut box, type in the name of your new shortcut, and click Finish. You've now created a shortcut for launching the application. But you still need to create a keyboard shortcut that will launch the application.

4. Right-click on the shortcut you just created and choose Properties. In the Shortcut tab, pictured in Figure 4-2, put your cursor in the Shortcut keys box and press the key combination you want to use to start the program. It has to be a combination of Ctrl-Alt, Shift-Alt, or Shift-Ctrl, plus a letter key, such as Ctrl-Alt-A or Shift-Alt-A, or Shift-Ctrl-A. (Note: Any quick key combo that you use will overshadow any local application use of the combo.)

5. Click OK. The program will now launch whenever you press the shortcut key combination.

Discussion

Note that there are entries on the Shortcut tab that let you customize how the program launches when you use the shortcut. The Run drop-down list lets you start the program minimized, maximized, or in a normal window. The Start in box lets you determine the start location for the application. And you can even customize the ScreenTip that appears when you hover the mouse over the shortcut. In the Comment box, type in the text that you want to appear as a ScreenTip. Figure 4-3 shows how such a customized ScreenTip looks like when a mouse hovers over it.

Also, make sure you choose a unique shortcut key sequence that isn't used to launch another application or that you use inside another application. Otherwise either or both of the shortcut keys might not work.

Figure 4-2. The Shortcut Properties dialog box lets you create a shortcut key to launch programs, and customize how the program launches

Figure 4-3. The Shortcut Properties dialog box lets you create a customized ScreenTip, like this one, that appears when you hover your mouse over the shortcut's desktop icon

See Also

Recipe 4.6 shows you how you can use keyboard shortcuts in concert with command-line switches and parameters.

4.6   Customizing the Way Applications Open Using Switches and Parameters

Problem

You want to customize the way you open an application. For example, you might want Microsoft Word to run a specific macro when it first starts.

Solution

Using a graphical user interface

When you use a shortcut to launch a program, as outlined in Recipe 4.5, you can use parameters and switches that let you customize the way it runs. These switches and parameters are usually specific to each individual program, although some work on many or all programs.

For example, you can launch any Microsoft Office application and have it automatically open a specific document by using the right syntax in the Target box. For example, if you wanted to launch Microsoft Word and have it automatically open a file called *Chapter 9.doc* in the *C:\Power Tools Book* directory, you'd put this in the Target box (make sure to include the quotes):

```
"C:\Program Files\Microsoft Office\Office11\WINWORD.EXE" "c:\Power Tools Book\
Chapter 9.doc"
```

In addition to launching individual files, you can use a variety of switches. For example, if you wanted to open Word without opening a document and not have previously opened documents show up in the Word File menu, you'd use the switch /n in the Target box:

```
"C:\Program Files\Microsoft Office\Office10\WINWORD.EXE" /n
```

And you can combine switches with opening individual files. So if you wanted to run Word and have it open a file called *Chapter 9.doc* in the *C:\Power Tools Book* directory, and have Word run a specific macro but not run any Autoexec macros, you'd use this syntax:

```
"C:\Program Files\Microsoft Office\Office11\WINWORD.EXE" /m "c:\Power Tools Book\
Chapter 9.doc"
```

Tables 4-2 through 4-5 list switches for Microsoft applications Word, Excel, Power-Point and Outlook.

Table 4-2. Switches for starting Word

Switch	What it does
/a	Stops add-ins and global templates, including the Normal template, from being loaded automatically. It also locks Word settings so that they cannot be read or modified.
/l *addinpath*	Loads a specific Word add-in.
/m	Starts a new instance of Word without running AutoExec macros.
/m *filen*	Opens the file specified by number on the File menu's Most Recently Used list.
/m *macroname*	Runs a specific macro and prevents Word from running any AutoExec macros.
/n	Starts a new instance of Word without opening a document. Documents opened will not appear as choices in the Window menu of other Word instances.
/t *templatename*	Starts Word with a new document based on the specified template.
/w	Starts a new instance of Word with a blank document. Documents opened will not appear as choices in the Window menu of other Word instances.
/r	Opens Word, reregisters it in the Registry, and quits. Use this switch if there have been problems with Word's settings and you want to reregister it.
/q	Starts Word without the splash screen.

Table 4-3. Switches for starting Excel

Switch	What it does
/r *workbook path/filename*	Opens the specified workbook as read-only.
/e	Opens Excel without a startup screen and without a new blank workbook.
/m	Opens Excel with a new workbook that contains a single macro sheet.
/p *workbook path*	Opens Excel and uses the specified path as the active path instead of the default path.
/o	Opens Excel and then reregisters it in the Registry. Use this switch if there have been problems with Excel's settings and you want to reregister it.
/regserver	Opens Excel, reregisters it, and quits.
/unregserver	Opens Excel, unregisters it, and quits.

Table 4-4. Startup switches for PowerPoint

Switch	What it does
/s	Opens a presentation into the slide show window.
/p	Prints the presentation.
/n *template_name*.pot	Creates a new presentation based on the specified template.

Table 4-5. Startup switches for Outlook

Switch	What it does
/safe:1	Starts Outlook with the Reading Pane off. (Only works with Outlook 2003.)
/safe:2	Starts Outlook without checking mail at start. (Only works with Outlook 2003.)
/select *foldername*	Opens the specified folder in a new window when Outlook starts.
/autorun *macroname*	Opens Outlook and runs the macro specified in macroname.

Using a command-line interface

You can use the same syntax, switches, and parameters at the command line as you can in the Target box when you create a shortcut. So you can launch applications using those parameters and switches straight from the command line.

 When you use the command line to launch programs, make sure you get to the command line by typing cmd.exe at the Run box, not command.exe. The command.exe command line doesn't support long folder names.

To launch a program at the command line, type in its full path and filename, then press Enter, like this. (Note that you won't have to type in the path, if the file can be found in your PATH.)

```
C:\Program Files\Microsoft Office\Office11\WINWORD.EXE
```

Add switches and parameters as outlined earlier in this recipe. For example:

```
C:\Program Files\Microsoft Office\Office11\WINWORD.EXE /n
```

Discussion

The true power of using switches and parameters for launching programs comes into play when you use them with shortcuts. If you have a particular customized way that you generally like to launch an application, create a shortcut for it with the right switches and parameter, and normally run it that way. But then, when you vary from your normal way of launching it—if you want to launch a specific file, for example —it'll be easier to use the command line.

Also, consider creating multiple shortcuts for each of your applications, so that you can launch different customized versions.

Remember when you use the command line that the command you type in doesn't include quotes around it, but when you use the Target box for creating shortcuts, you need to include the quotes. (On the command line, though, if you're using a path with any spaces, you need to include quotes.) Finally, keep in mind that many applications, not just Microsoft Office applications, include switches and parameters you can use to launch them, so check your documentation or the web site of the software make to find them.

See Also

Recipe 4.5 for help in creating keyboard shortcuts; MS KB 130510, "Command-Line Switches for Windows Explorer," and MS KB 296192, "OL2002: Additional Command-Line Switches"

4.7   Running Older Applications

Problem

You want to run applications written for versions of Windows previous to XP, but they don't run at all or have problems running in XP.

Solution

Using a graphical user interface

The Application Compatibility Wizard will fix most problems with running software written for older versions of Windows. To run the Compatibility Wizard, choose Start → Help and Support → Fixing a Problem → Application and software problems → Fix a problem → Getting older programs to run on XP, then scroll down and click Program Compatibility Wizard. (Note: You can also get to the Help and Support area by pressing F1 when you're on the desktop.)

You'll be prompted to choose the software you want to fix, and then asked a series of questions, including the operating system for which the software was written, or on which it last ran properly; and the screen resolutions recommended for the program. You can see the wizard in action in Figure 4-4. The wizard then applies those settings and tries to run the program. If the settings work, tell the wizard to always run the program using them. If they don't, try different settings until you get it working properly.

If you're not a fan of wizards, there's an easier way to set the program's compatibility settings. Right-click on the program's shortcut icon and choose Properties → Compatibility. You can then manually configure compatibility settings, as shown in Figure 4-5. You can change the same settings as you can using the wizard. You may have to try several different settings before you find one that works.

At the bottom of the Compatibility dialog box, you'll notice a setting that lets you turn off "advanced text services." That setting is applicable if you use speech recognition and text services. If you use these services, try turning them off to see whether that helps.

Discussion

If the Compatibility Wizard doesn't fix the problem, try these steps:

1. Check the software manufacturer's web site to see whether an update, patch, or fix is available.
2. Use Windows Update to see whether a fix is available. Get to Windows Update by choosing Start → Control Panel → Windows Update.

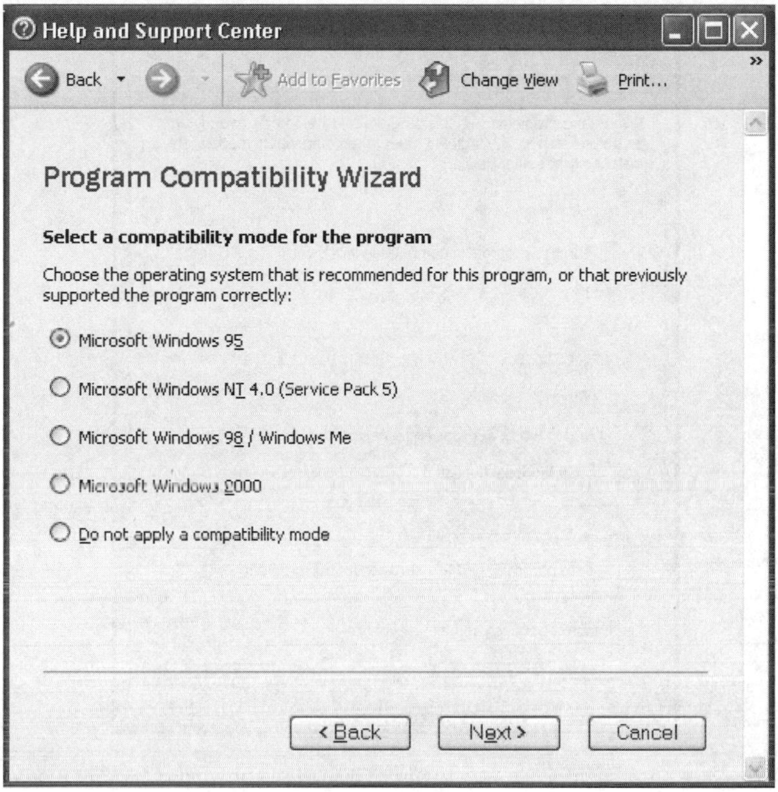

Figure 4-4. Selecting the operating system that the program was written for is key to helping make sure it runs in XP

3. Update your sound card and video card drivers by checking the manufacturer sites.

4. If the problem program is a game that uses DirectX, upgrade to the newest version of DirectX at *http://www.microsoft.com/windows/directx/downloads*.

There may be some instances in which a program won't even install on your system. In those instances, run the Compatibility Wizard on the installation or setup program, commonly *Setup.exe* or a similar filename.

See Also

Recipe 4.8 and Recipe 4.9 for more steps you can take to get older programs to run properly

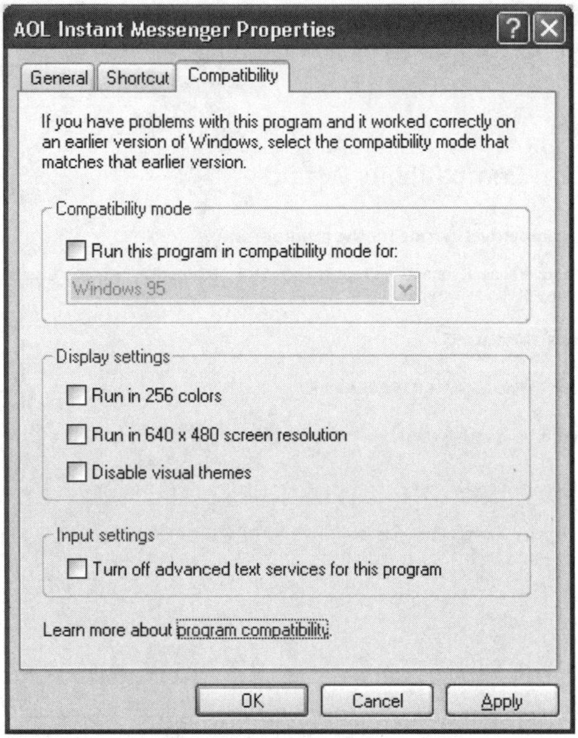

Figure 4-5. If you're not a fan of wizards, you can change the compatibility settings manually

4.8   Using the Application Compatibility Toolkit to Solve Compatibility Problems

Problem

You've used the Application Compatibility Wizard to try to get an older program to run under XP, but it still won't run, or it runs and has problems. You want to be able to run the program without problems.

Solution

Using downloadable software

A little-known downloadable program, the Application Compatibility Toolkit, free from Microsoft, can help you fine-tune the application environment for troublesome programs. Download it from *http://www.microsoft.com/windows/appexperience*. (Note: The latest version of the Appliation Compatibility Toolkit may not have the QFixApp program required for this recipe. Previous versions should have it, however.)

Most of the applications on the Toolkit are debugger tools aimed at developers. However, you can use the QFixApp program to ensure that problem programs run properly on XP. There are over 200 fixes in the application, and there is no room to cover them all here, but follow these steps for the best way to use the tool to fine-tune your problem program's application environment so that it runs properly:

1. Run *Qfixapp.exe*. Click on the Browse button to find the program you want.

2. In the Layers tab, choose the layer to apply to your application. A layer is a set of fixes that work best to fix certain problems, such as for programs that run in 256 colors, or were written for Windows 95, Windows 98, or Windows 2000.

3. After you choose the layer, click on the Fixes tab. You'll see that many fixes have already been chosen, depending on the layer that you've applied to your application. Figure 4-6 shows several of the fixes applied to a program written for Windows 95.

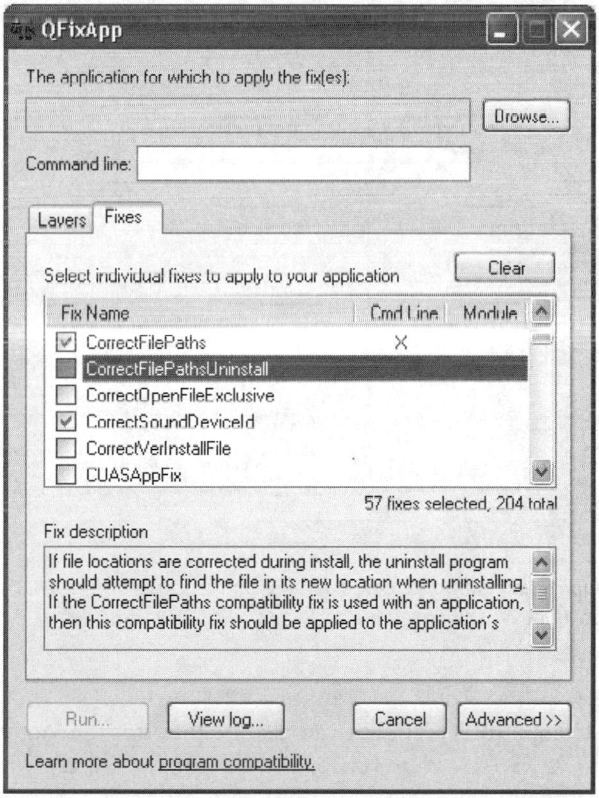

Figure 4-6. These are just two of the many fixes you can apply to fine-tune the application environment for problem applications

4. Add or remove fixes by checking or unchecking the box next to them. To learn more about any single fix, highlight it, and a description of the fix will appear in the lower pane.

You can use another component of the Application Compatibility Toolkit to help decide which fixes to apply. Run the Compatibility Administrator tool and choose System Database → Applications. You'll find a database of thousands of applications and specific fixes that should be applied to them, shown in Figure 4-7. Search through the database for your program, and when you find the fixes it requires, apply them using the QFixApp program, as outlined above. If your program isn't on the list, look for a program that is similar to it, and try applying its specific fixes to your program.

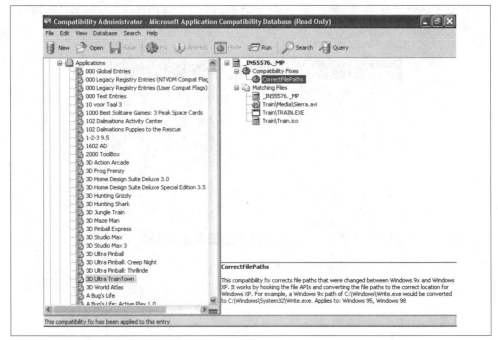

Figure 4-7. The Compatibility Administrator's database has records of fixes that should be applied to hundreds of applications

Discussion

The Application Compatibility Toolkit can also be found it the *\Support\Tools* directory of the Windows XP CD. New versions of the toolkit are always being released, so you are better off downloading it from the Microsoft site.

See Also

MS KB 294895, "How to Obtain the Windows Application Compatibility Toolkit," and MS KB 285909, "How to troubleshoot program compatibility issues in Windows XP"

4.9 Troubleshooting Application Compatibility

Problem

You want to run a legacy application, you've run the Application Compatibility Wizard, and you've tried the Application Compatibility Toolkit, but the program still is causing problems.

Solution

Try this series of troubleshooting tasks:

1. Check the software maker's web site for fixes. The maker may have posted patches that will solve the problem. Additionally, check the Microsoft Windows Update site at *http://windowsupdate.microsoft.com* to see whether Microsoft has issued a patch that fixes the problem

2. Uninstall the program and reinstall it using an administrator account. Older programs for Microsoft Windows 95, Microsoft Windows 98, Microsoft Windows 98 Second Edition, or Microsoft Windows Millennium Edition were written without recognizing that different types of accounts, including administrator's accounts and limited user accounts, might exist. Reinstalling the application using an administrator account may solve the problem. When doing this, make sure that you first log off all accounts except for the administrator account that will install the program.

3. Games may have a variety of problems and can require a variety of fixes. Try running the game with an administrator account rather than another type of account. Update your video driver by going to the web site of your video card manufacturer. If the game uses DirectX, you should get the newest version of DirectX from *http://www.microsoft.com/windows/directx*.

Discussion

Some older applications claim that they are compatible with Windows XP, and in most instances, they should run with no problem. However, you may you come across an application that doesn't run on your system even after you follow the steps in this and previous recipes. In that case, one problem might be that after you uninstalled the application before reinstalling it, it didn't completely uninstall. It could have left behind Registry keys or files and folders on your hard disk. Follow the advice in Recipe 4.2 after you uninstall the program to make sure that you've removed all its traces. Then reinstall the application.

See Also

MS KB 285909, "How to troubleshoot program compatibility issues in Windows XP"

4.10 Running DOS Programs in Their Own Optimized Environments

Problem

You have an older DOS-based application that you want to run, but it requires its own customized *Autoexec.bat* and *Config.sys* files.

Solution

The operating environment for DOS programs are set by the *Config.sys* and *Autoexec.bat* files. Windows lets you create fine-tuned, customized environments for each separate DOS program by building individual *Config.sys* and *Autoexec.bat* files for each. To do so:

1. Copy *Config.nt* and *Autoexec.nt* files to the directory of the DOS program you plan to run. Typically, the files are found in the *C:\Windows\System32* folder.

2. Rename the files and edit them to reflect the specific conditions that are best suited for the DOS program you're going to run.

3. Right-click on the icon of the DOS program, and select Properties → Program → Advanced. Fill in the names of the Autoexec and Config files, as shown in Figure 4-8. If they're outside your PATH, include the path names.

4. If the program performs actions based on the speed of the processor (such as certain games), check the Compatible timer hardware emulation box.

5. Click on OK. The DOS program will now run in its own customized environment.

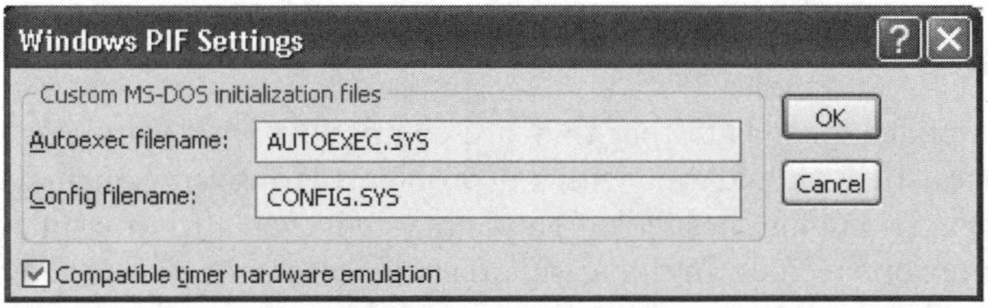

Figure 4-8. Edit a DOS file's PIF settings to create its ideal operating environment

Discussion

Config.sys and *Autoexec.bat* files are used to create customized environments for DOS programs to run. Typically, an *Autoexec.bat* file automatically runs a series of commands, while *Config.sys* sets environment variables, defines path, and contains other, similar settings, such as how to handle memory. For example, a *Config.sys* file might look like this:

```
DEVICE=C:\WINDOWS\HIMEM.SYS
DOS=HIGH,UMB
DEVICE=C:\WINDOWS\EMM386.EXE NOEMS
FILES=30
STACKS=0,0
BUFFERS=20
DEVICEHIGH=C:\WINDOWS\COMMAND\ANSI.SYS
DEVICEHIGH=C:\MTMCDAI.SYS /D:123
```

See Also

MS KB 314106, "Troubleshooting MS-DOS-based programs in Windows XP." For help in running DOS-based games on Windows XP, see *http://www.longhighway.com/sandbox/xp.html*.

4.11   Forcing Older Programs to Use Windows XP Common Controls

Problem

You want programs written for earlier versions of Windows to use the rounded, XP-type common graphical controls for things such as checkboxes and buttons. Normally, when you run an older program in XP, the operating system applies an XP-type frame around it, with rounded title bars. But the older program itself still uses its older style interface.

Solution

To force older programs to use XP-type common controls, you have to create a manifest file—a specifically formatted XML file—and place it in the same folder as the older program.

The manifest file should be almost exactly the same for each older program that you want to use XP common controls, changing only the name and description of the program itself.

Following is the code to put in your manifest file. Note that for "Description of Program" you should enter a description for the program, and for "Program Name" you should enter the name of the program.

To create the file, open Notepad, type the following text into it, and save it to the same folder as the executable file of the program you want to force to use XP common controls. Give it the same name as the program's executable file, but with an extension of *.manifest*. So, for example, if the program's executable file were named *oldprogram.exe*, you'd give the manifest file the name *oldprogram.exe.manifest*.

Use the following code to create a *.manifest* file to force an older program to use XP common controls:

```
<?xml version="1.0" encoding="UTF-8" standalone="yes"?>
<assembly xmlns="urn:schemas-microsoft-com:asm.v1" manifestVersion="1.0">
<assemblyIdentity
    version="1.0.0.0"
    processorArchitecture="X86"
    name="Program Name"
    type="win32"
/>
<description>Description of Program</description>
<dependency>
    <dependentAssembly>
        <assemblyIdentity
            type="win32"
            name="Microsoft.Windows.Common-Controls"
            version="6.0.0.0"
            processorArchitecture="X86"
            publicKeyToken="6595b64144ccf1df"
            language="*"
        />
    </dependentAssembly>
</dependency>
</assembly>
```

Discussion

When you create the manifest file, the program will not only use XP common controls in the older Windows application, but will also apply whatever current XP theme you're using. If you don't want to use the XP common controls any longer, delete the manifest file or rename it. Also, keep in mind that the manifest file will not necessarily work with every older Windows application, such as old versions of Microsoft Money.

See Also

If you want to force an older Windows program to use XP's common controls, but don't want to have to go through the trouble of creating a manifest file, you can download XPME for Windows from *http://www.tlhouse.co.uk/XPME.shtml*. Run it and select the program that you want to use common controls. The program automatically creates a manifest file for you. XPME is freeware.

4.12 Using Keyboard Application Shortcuts

Problem

You want to perform common tasks such as opening, closing, or printing a document, more quickly than you can by using the mouse and clicking menu items and dialog boxes.

Solution

List of keyboard shortcuts

Every application has its own set of keyboard shortcuts for performing common tasks,. But there are some shortcuts that tend to work for many different applications, not just one.

Table 4-6 lists the most common and useful keyboard shortcuts. Keep in mind that not all work with every application.

Table 4-6. Common keyboard application shortcuts

Key combination	What the combination does
Alt-F4	Closes the current window or file.
Ctrl-A	Selects the whole document.
Ctrl-B	Turns text bold.
Ctrl-C	Copies highlighted data to the Clipboard.
Ctrl-D	Displays a font dialog box, or switches between monospaced and proportional fonts.
Ctrl-E	Centers text or an object in the document.
Ctrl-F	Displays a Find or Search dialog box.
Ctrl-G	Displays a GoTo dialog box.
Ctrl-H	Displays a Replace dialog box.
Ctrl-I	Turns text italic.
Ctrl-J	Justifies text in the document.
Ctrl-L	Moves the text or object to the left part of the document.
Ctrl-N	Creates a new document.
Ctrl-O	Displays the Open dialog box.
Ctrl-P	Displays the Print dialog box.
Ctrl-Q	Exits the application.
Ctrl-R	Moves the text or object to the right part of the document.
Ctrl-S	Saves the document or opens a Save dialog box.
Ctrl-U	Underlines text.

Table 4-6. Common keyboard application shortcuts (continued)

Key combination	What the combination does
Ctrl-V	Pastes highlighted data from the Clipboard into the document.
Ctrl-X	Cuts the highlighted data and places it in the Clipboard.
Ctrl-Z	Undoes the last action.
Ctrl-Insert	Copies highlighted data to the Clipboard.
Shift-Insert	Pastes highlighted data from the Clipboard into the document.
Tab	Moves to the next cell in a table.
Shift-Tab	Moves to the previous cell in a table.
Ctrl-Arrow	Moves the cursor forward one word or object.
Ctrl-Back Arrow	Moves the cursor backwards one word or object.
Alt-Hyphen	Opens a menu that lets you restore, move, size, minimize, maximize, or close the current window.
Ctrl-Space Bar	Opens a menu that lets you restore, move, size, minimize, maximize, or close the current window.
Ctrl-End	Moves to the end of the document.
Ctrl-Home	Moves to the beginning of the document.
Ctrl-F6	Switches between documents.
Ctrl-F4	Closes the current window or file.

Discussion

Don't expect every one of these standard shortcuts to work for every Windows application, because they won't. But as a general rule, they'll work with most, especially with Microsoft Office applications. But even in Office, there are anomalies, and they can sometimes get you into trouble. In Outlook, for example, if you're reading an email, and use the Ctrl-F keyboard shortcut to find text in the email, you'll instead create a new email message, one that includes the existing email in it already. In Outlook, you use F4 to find text in an email message.

See Also

MS KB 301583, "List of the keyboard shortcuts that are available in Windows XP"; list of shortcuts for many Microsoft applications at *http://www.microsoft.com/enable/products/keyboard.aspx*; MSDN information about keyboard shortcuts at *http://msdn.microsoft.com/library/default.asp?url=/library/en-us/csui/html/csconKeyboardShortcuts.asp*; list of the Elder Geek's shortcuts for XP at *http://www.theeldergeek.com/keyboard_shortcuts_for_xp.htm*

4.13 Moving a New Microsoft Application to Another Windows XP System

Problem

You want to move a Microsoft application from one Windows XP system to another because you want to be able to reuse your settings on the new system. If you merely installed the application on the new system, you would lose all of your settings.

Solution

Using a graphical user interface

1. Install the software on your new PC.

2. Connect the old and the new PC, either over a network, or via a null modem serial cable, which you can find at computer stores or online retailers.

3. On the PC that has the settings you want to transfer, run the Files and Settings Transfer Wizard by choosing Start → All Programs → Accessories → System Tools → Files and Settings Transfer Wizard.

4. Click Next on the introductory screen, then from the following screen choose Old computer, and click Next.

5. On the Select a transfer method screen that appears, choose the method you're using to connect the two computers (direct cable, network, etc.). If you choose a network, or Other, select the folder location on your new PC where you want to transfer the settings. Click Next.

> In some instances, if you choose a network as the way to transfer your settings, the wizard will not be able to recognize the network. If that happens, choose Other. That will let you browse through your network for a location, even though the Network choice didn't recognize your network.

6. The "What do you want to transfer" screen appears next, as shown in Figure 4-9. You can choose to transfer settings, files, or both files and settings. Make your choice.

7. You now have to choose what settings to transfer. The default is settings for applications and Windows such as taskbar options and Outlook Express, specific folders such as Desktop, Fonts, My Documents, and My Pictures, and file type associations (what files open with what programs). To add or remove settings, select the "Let me select a custom of files and settings" checkbox, and then click Next.

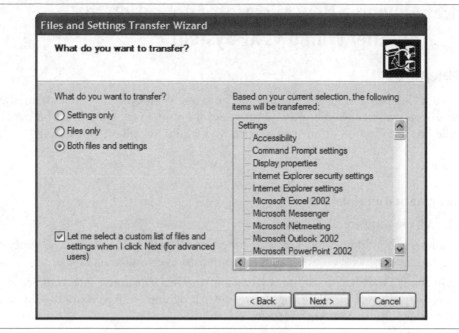

Figure 4-9. You can transfer all the files and settings found by the Files and Settings Transfer Wizard, or else select from a custom list of your own

8. From the screen that appears, add new files and settings, or remove existing ones. Click Next when you're done.

9. The wizard will gather the files and settings, and save them in the location you've chosen. Click Finish when you're done.

10. Go to the computer onto which you're going to transfer the settings. If you've copied the settings to a removable disk, put the removable disk in its drive.

11. Run the run the Files and Settings Transfer Wizard on the computer onto which you're transferring settings.

12. Click Next on the introductory screen, then from the following screen choose New computer, and click Next.

13. From the screen that appears, choose "I don't need the Wizard Disk. I have already collected my files and settings from my old computer." Click Next and Next again from the screen that appears.

14. From the screen that appears, choose the location where the wizard should look for your settings, for example, direct cable connection, floppy drive, or other. Use other if you've saved it to a removable drive, network drive, or to a location on your new PC. If you choose other, browse to the location of where you saved your settings. Select the folder where the data is stored.

15. Click Next. The wizard will gather your settings and apply them. When it's done, click Next and then Finish. Your settings are now transferred to your new computer.

Discussion

The wizard only transfers settings, not the application itself. So you have to remember to first install the application on the new computer before running the wizard. Simply copying the program's folders, files, and executables from your old computer to your new computer won't work, because there may be Registry settings the program requires, as well as DLLs and other files that it may have installed in folders that you don't know about.

Keep in mind that the File and Settings Transfer Wizard works with Microsoft applications, but with only a very few non-Microsoft applications. So don't count on using it if you want to transfer settings for any applications other than those written by Microsoft.

See Also

For more details about using the Files and Settings Transfer Wizard, see *http://www.microsoft.com/windowsxp/using/setup/expert/crawford_november12.mspx*

PCmover from LapLink (*http://www.laplink.com/products/pcmover/overview.asp*) will move entire applications and settings from one PC to another, as will Alohabob PC Relocator (*http://www.alohabob.com*).

4.14 Remotely Installing a Microsoft Application Using Group Policy

Problem

You want to remotely install a Microsoft application to users from a central server, using Group Policy.

Solution

Create a distribution point

You first need to create a distribution point for the software:

1. Log onto the server as an administrator.
2. Create a shared network folder where you'll put the Microsoft Software Installer (MSI) package that you're going to distribute.

3. Set permissions on the share to allow access to MSI package.

4. Copy or install the MSI package to the distribution point.

Create a Group Policy Object (GPO)

Once you've created a distribution point, you need to create a Group Policy Object (GPO), which will be used to distribute the software:

1. Run the Active Directory Users and Computers snap-in by choosing Start → Programs → Administrative Tools, and then choose Active Directory Users and Computers.

2. In the console tree, right-click your domain, choose Properties, click the Group Policy tab, and click New.

3. Type in the name that you'll call the policy and press Enter.

4. Click Properties and then click the Security tab.

5. Clear the Apply Group Policy checkbox for the security groups that you want to prevent from having this policy applied.

6. Select the Apply Group Policy checkbox for the groups to which you want to apply this policy.

7. Click OK.

Assign a package

Now you can install the software to the PCs, what's called "assigning" the package:

1. Run the Active Directory Users and Computers snap-in by choosing Start → Programs → Administrative Tools, and then choose Active Directory Users and Computers.

2. In the console tree, right-click your domain, choose Properties, click the Group Policy tab, select the Group Policy Object you've created for installing the software, and click Edit.

3. In Computer Configuration, expand Software Settings.

4. Right-click Software installation and choose New → Package.

5. In the Open dialog box enter full Universal Naming Convention (UNC) path to the shared folder that contains the MSI package that you're going to install, for example, *file server\share\filename.msi*. Make sure that you don't browse to the location. Instead, type in the UNC path to the shared folder.

6. Click Open, then click assigned and click OK. You'll see the package listed in the right pane of the Group Policy window.

7. Close the Group Policy snap-in, click OK, and then quit the Active Directory Users and Computers snap-in. When the computer onto which you've assigned the software starts, the software will be automatically installed.

Discussion

This technique is best used when you're installing Microsoft software to multiple machines, and you want to manage them from a central server. The technique is called assigning software. When you assign software with Group Policy, the software is installed when the user of the computer logs on. When the user runs the software for the first time, the installation is finalized.

You can, however, also "publish" software with Group Policy. When you do this, the software is not automatically installed when the user logs on. Instead, the software will be displayed in the Add/Remove Programs dialog box when the user first logs on. The user can then install the software from there. This choice gives the user the option of installing the software or not, while when you assign software, it is automatically installed. For details on how to publish software using Group Policy, see MS KB 314934.

See Also

Recipe 4.16 for remotely uninstalling a Microsoft application using Group Policy; Recipe 4.15 for remotely redeploying a Microsoft application using Group Policy; MS KB 314934, "Use Group Policy to Remotely Install Software in Windows 2000," and MS KB 304953, "How to deploy Office XP over a network"

4.15 Remotely Redeploying a Microsoft Application Using Group Policy

Problem

You want to remotely redeploy a Microsoft application using Group Policy, for example, if the application has been upgraded.

Solution

Using a graphical user interface

1. Run the Active Directory Users and Computers snap-in by choosing Start → All Programs → Administrative Tools, and then choose Active Directory Users and Computers.

2. In the console tree, right-click your domain, choose Properties, click the Group Policy tab, select the GPO you've created for installing the software, and click Edit.

3. Expand the Software Settings container that contains the software installation item that you used to deploy the package. Click the Software installation container that contains the package.

4. In the right pane of the Group Policy window, right-click the program, choose All Tasks, and click Redeploy application.

5. You'll see this message: "Redeploying this application will reinstall the application everywhere it is already installed. Do you want to continue?" Click Yes.

6. Quit the Group Policy snap-in, click OK, and then quit the Active Directory Users and Computers snap-in. The application will be redeployed.

Discussion

Use this recipe when a Microsoft application has been upgraded and you want to upgrade it on user machines. Before redeploying, you'll have to update the distribution point with the upgraded software.

See Also

Recipe 4.14 for installing a Microsoft application using Group Policy; Recipe 4.16 for uninstalling a Microsoft application using Group Policy; and MS KB 314934, "Use Group Policy to Remotely Install Software in Windows 2000"

4.16   Remotely Uninstalling a Microsoft Application Using Group Policy

You want to remotely uninstall a Microsoft application that you've installed to users from a central server, using Group Policy.

Solution

Using a graphical user interface

1. Run the Active Directory Users and Computers snap-in by choosing Start → All Programs → Administrative Tools, and then choose Active Directory Users and Computers.

2. In the console tree, right-click your domain, choose Properties, click the Group Policy tab, select the Group Policy Object you've created for installing the software, and click Edit.

3. Expand the Software Settings container that contains the software installation item that you used to deploy the package. Click the Software installation container that contains the package.

4. In the right pane of the Group Policy window, right-click the program, choose All Tasks, and then click Remove.

5. Select "Immediately uninstall the software from users and computers," and click OK.

6. Quit the Group Policy snap-in, click OK, and then quit the Active Directory Users and Computers snap-in. The application will be uninstalled on all users' machines.

Discussion

If you want, you can choose to allow users to keep using the software, but not allow any new users to install it. To do that, in step 5, choose "Allow users to continue to use the software, but prevent new installations," and then click OK.

See Also

Recipe 4.14 for installing a Microsoft application using Group Policy; Recipe 4.15 for redeploying a Microsoft application using Group Policy; and MS KB 314934, "Use Group Policy to Remotely Install Software in Windows 2000"

CHAPTER 5

Customizing the Interface

5.0   Introduction

Windows XP has the most distinctive user interface of any version of Windows that has yet been released. Its bright colors, rounded 3D windows, and slightly cartoonish look are only the beginning. The Start menu has been completely redone compared to earlier Windows versions as well, and you'll find changes throughout the entire operating system.

The interface, as shipped, is not to everyone's liking, though. You may want to change the way the Start menu works, or how Windows Explorer functions. You may want to change the icons displayed on the desktop, or make many other changes as well.

The obvious changes can be made easily, through the normal kinds of dialog boxes available throughout Windows XP. For example, to change your background or screensaver, the desktop resolution and so on, right-click on the desktop and choose Properties, and a variety of tabs will let you make the obvious changes.

But it's not as readily apparent how to make other changes. For example, there are a variety of desktop icons such as the Recycle Bin that can't be changed or deleted through any normal methods—what if you want to change that? How can you change the way the Start menu looks and functions? And what tools can you use to make a wide variety of interface changes?

We'll cover all that and more in the recipes in this chapter.

About the GUI

In this chapter, you'll find many recipes for changing various parts of the Windows XP GUI. The terminology that people use about the GUI may vary, so to be clear, following are the primary parts of the GUI we talk about in this chapter.

Desktop icons

The icons on XP's desktop run an application when double-clicked. An XP desktop, with its icons, is shown in Figure 5-1.

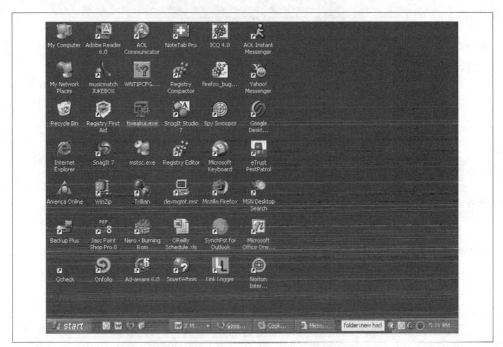

Figure 5-1. The XP desktop, with desktop icons

Balloon tips

Words in a "balloon" appear over an icon or some other part of XP when you hover your mouse over it. Figure 5-2 shows an example of a balloon tip.

Taskbar, Quick Launch, Address Bar, and Notification Area

The Taskbar, shown in Figure 5-3, is the bar across the bottom of the screen that has the Start button and icons that show most of the programs that are running. The Taskbar also has several important areas:

Quick Launch
    The area just to the right of the Start button. Icons stay there permanently; when clicked, they run a program.

Address Bar
    A bar that can be displayed, or turned off, that lets you type in a URL or a folder name and sends you straight to that web site or folder.

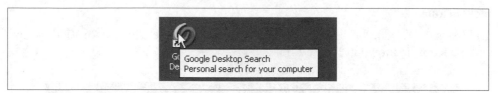

Figure 5-2. A balloon tip, appearing when the mouse is hovered over a desktop icon

Notification Area
> The area on the far right of the Taskbar which most of the programs that are running in the background, and in which notifications are displayed, such as that an update is ready to be downloaded or installed to XP.

Figure 5-3. The Taskbar, Quick Launch, Address Bar, and Notification Area (also called the System Tray)

Start menu, Frequently Used Programs List, and Pinned Programs List

The Start menu (Figure 5-4) appears when you click the Start button. There are a couple different areas of it:

Frequently Used Programs List
> This area just under the Pinned Programs List displays icons that, when clicked, run programs. Icons are automatically placed here and taken away from here by XP, depending on how often the programs are used.

Pinned Programs List
> This is the area on the left near the top, just under the icon for the currently logged-in user. It displays icons that, when clicked, run programs. These icons stay here permanently.

5.1   Getting Rid of Undeletable Desktop Icons

Problem

You want to delete "undeletable" desktop icons such as the Recycle Bin, Outlook, and Internet Explorer, but you can't delete them by highlighting them and pressing the Delete key. Unnecessary desktop icons take up screen real estate, clutter the interface, and use system RAM.

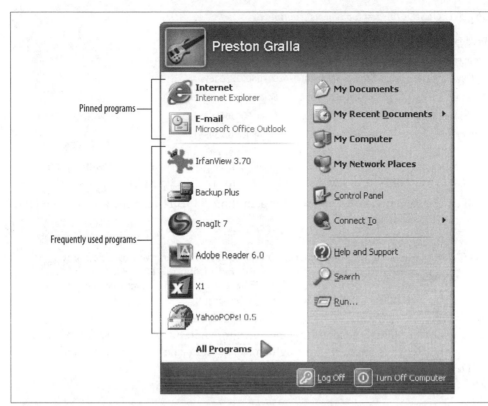

Figure 5-4. The Start menu, Frequently Used Programs List, and Pinned Programs List

Solution

Using the Registry

1. Open the Registry Editor and navigate to HKEY_LOCAL_MACHINE\SOFTWARE\ Microsoft\Windows\CurrentVersion\Explorer\Desktop\NameSpace. Here's where you'll find various special desktop icons, such as the Recycle Bin. They're not listed by name, but instead by class ID (CLSID), a unique identifier, such as {645FF040-5081-101B-9F08-00AA002F954E} for the Recycle Bin.

2. Find the CLSID of the desktop icon you want to delete. Use Table 5-1 to find it.

Table 5-1. CLSIDs for desktop objects

Desktop object	CLSID
My Computer	{20D04FE0-3AEA-1069-A2D8-08002B30309D}
Recycle Bin	{645FF040-5081-101B-9F08-00AA002F954E}
Microsoft Outlook	{00020D75-0000-0000-C000-000000000046}
Internet Explorer	{FBF23B42-E3F0-101B-8488-00AA003E56F8}

Table 5-1. CLSIDs for desktop objects (continued)

Desktop object	CLSID
The Internet	{3DC7A020-0ACD-11CF-A9BB-00AA004AE837}
My Network Places	{208D2C60-3AEA-1069-A2D7-08002B30309D}
Briefcase	{85BBD920-42A0-1069-A2E4-08002B30309D}
Dial-Up Networking	{992CFFA0-F557-101A-88EC-00DD010CCC48}
America Online	{955B7B84-5308-419c-8ED8-0B9CA3C56985}

3. Delete the key of the icon that you want gone from the desktop, such as {645FF040-5081-101B-9F08-00AA002F954E} for the Recycle Bin.

4. Exit the Registry, go to your desktop, and hit F5 to refresh the screen. The icon should now be gone.

 On some PCs the America Online icon can be removed by deleting it in the normal way—clicking on it and hitting the Delete key—while on others, it's "undeletable." The computer manufacturer decides whether to make the icon undeletable or not.

5. On some systems, the icons may not be immediately deleted. Instead, after making the Registry change, you might have to right-click on the icon and choose Delete.

6. If you want to restore the icon, re-create the key that you deleted.

Using downloadable software

TweakUI, one of a suite of free, unsupported utilities from Microsoft called Power-Toys for Windows XP, can also hide these undeletable icons. Get it from *http://www.microsoft.com/windowsxp/pro/downloads/powertoys.asp*. After you install it and run it, go to the Desktop section, and you'll see a list of icons that can't otherwise be deleted. Uncheck the box next to any that you don't want to show up on your desktop, as shown in Figure 5-5, and click on OK. The icons will be immediately removed. To make them appear again, check the box next to them.

Discussion

Some CLSIDs that you'll find in HKEY_LOCAL_MACHINE\SOFTWARE\Microsoft\Windows\CurrentVersion\Explorer\Desktop\NameSpace can be deleted from the desktop without having to edit the Registry, but when you try to delete them, they may give you a special warning message. For example, depending on your system, when you try to delete Microsoft Outlook from the desktop, you get the warning message "The Outlook Desktop icon provides special functionality and we recommend that you do not remove it." If you'd like, you can edit that message so that it displays whatever you

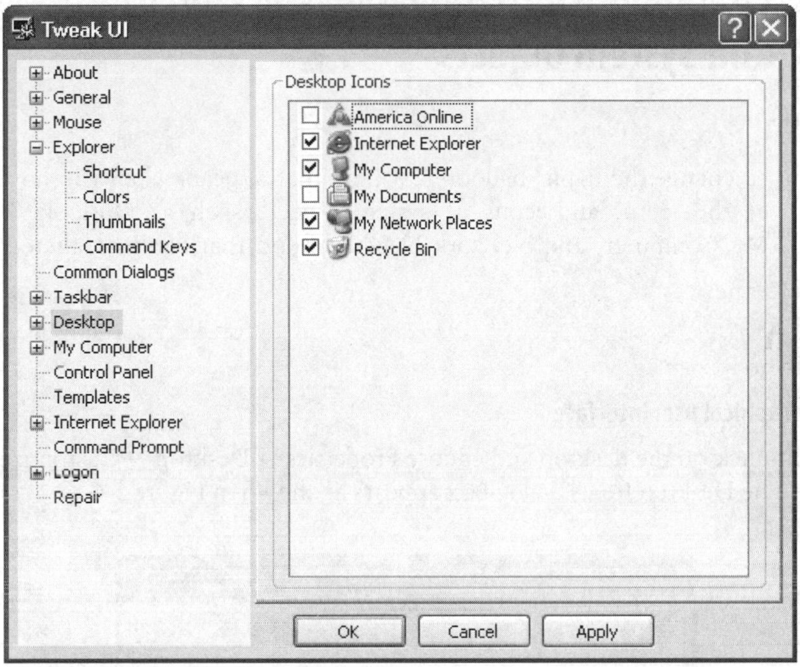

Figure 5-5. Uncheck the boxes of icons that you want to remove from the desktop; put a check next to them to make them appear again

want. In the CLSID's subkey, for example {00020D75-0000-0000-C000-000000000046} for Microsoft Outlook, you'll find the value Removal Message. Edit its value to whatever text you want, save it, and whenever someone tries to delete it, your warning message will appear.

Also, keep in mind that when you remove desktop icons, you're only removing icons, not the underlying feature or program. So, for example, the Recycle Bin still works even if you remove its icon. To open the Recycle Bin, go to C:\RECYCLER and open the folder inside it. To restore an item that's been deleted, right-click on it and choose Properties → Restore. You can delete items from the folder as you would any other item.

See Also

You may find yourself with the opposite problem of not being able to delete desktop icons—the Recycle Bin can, on occasion, vanish for no obvious reason. To fix the problem, see MS KB 810869, "Recycle Bin Does Not Appear on the Desktop." X-Setup Pro (*http://www.x-setup.net*) will solve the problem as well.

5.2 Changing "Unchangeable" Desktop Icons and System Objects

Problem

You want to change the name, balloon text (text that appears when you hover your mouse over the icon), and icons of system objects such as Outlook, Internet Explorer, My Computer, and Network Neighborhood that can't be altered in the normal way.

Solution

Using a graphical user interface

1. Right-click on the desktop and choose Properties → Desktop → Customize Desktop. The Desktop Items dialog box appears as shown in Figure 5-6.

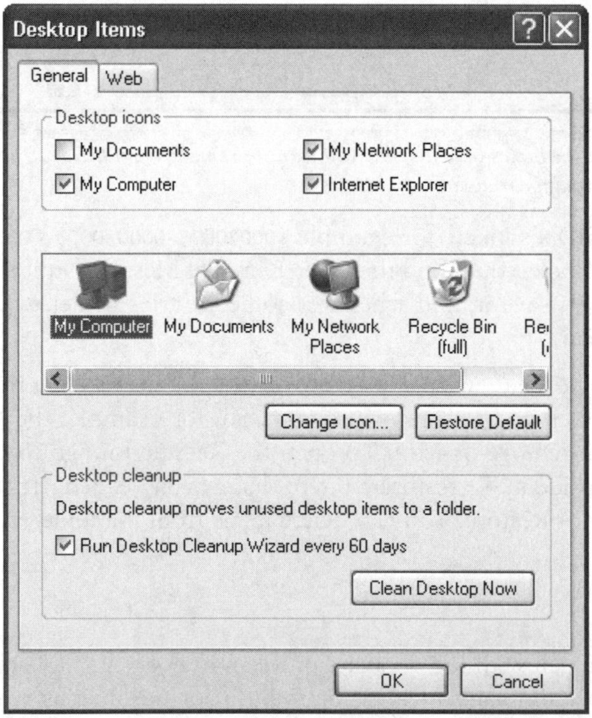

Figure 5-6. If you can't change a desktop icon in the normal way, the Desktop Items dialog box will let you do it

2. Click on the desktop item whose icon you want to change, such as My Computer.

3. Choose an icon from the group that appears and click on OK twice.

4. If you don't see an icon in the group that you want to use, click on the Browse button, navigate to the location of the icon you want to use, click on Open, and then click OK twice.

Using the Registry

1. Open the Registry Editor and go to `HKEY_CLASSES_ROOT\CLSID`, a key that lets you change characteristics of system objects.

2. Find the CLSID of the desktop icon whose properties you want to change. Use Table 5-1 to find the CLSID for the icon.

3. Highlight the CLSID whose name or balloon text you want to change. For example, for My Computer, highlight the subkey `HKEY_CLASSES_ROOT\CLSID\` `{20D04FE0-3AEA-1069-A2D8-08002B30309D}`. Keep in mind that `HKEY_CLASSES_ROOT\` `CLSID` has many CLSIDs listed under it, so it might take you a while to find the proper subkey.

4. Once you find the right subkey, if you want to edit the name of the object, open the `Default` value and type in the text that you want to appear underneath the object. If you want to edit the balloon text for the object, open the `InfoTip` value and type in the text that you want to appear as balloon text.

5. Save your work. Exit the Registry and reboot. You may also be able to force the changes to take effect without rebooting. After you exit the Registry, go to your desktop, and hit F5 to refresh the screen. The new names and balloon tips might now appear.

That will let you change the name or balloon text, but not the icon itself. To change the icon:

1. Open the Registry Editor and go to `HKEY_CLASSES_ROOT\CLSID`.

2. Find the CLSID of the desktop icon whose properties you want to change. Use Table 5-1 to find the CLSID for the icon.

3. Open the subkey and then the `DefaultIcon` subkey under that. For example, to change the icon for My Computer, open the subkey `HKEY_CLASSES_ROOT\CLSID\` `{20D04FE0-3AEA-1069-A2D8-08002B30309D}\DefaultIcon`.

4. Change the `Default` value to the path and name of the icon that you want displayed.

5. Exit the Registry. You may have to reboot in order for the new settings to take effect.

Some people aren't able to change their icons using this method. If you can't, try editing the key HKEY_CURRENT_USER\Software\Microsoft\ Windows\CurrentVersion\Explorer\CLSID\ using this method. It should do the trick.

Discussion

Most desktop objects, unlike Outlook, Internet Explorer, My Computer, and Network Neighborhood, and a few others, let you easily change all of their properties. First right-click on the icon and choose Properties. To change the name of the icon, choose the General tab and in the box at the top, type in the name that you want to appear beneath the icon. To change the balloon text, click on the Shortcut tab and in the Comment box type in the text that you want to appear. To change the icon, click on Change Icon, choose an icon from the group that appears, and click on OK. When you're ready to make the change—to the name, balloon text, or icon—click on OK again. The object's name, balloon text, and icon should now be changed.

But some desktop objects require special handling, so use Recipe 5.1 for changing them.

See Also

Windows XP doesn't normally allow you to change the icons for individual files. However, you can download a piece of shareware that will do it for you. Get IconChanger from Shell Labs at *http://www.shelllabs.com*.

5.3   Showing Your XP Version on Your Desktop

Problem

You want to be able to instantly know the exact XP version, including SP number and build number, directly on your desktop, or on the desktops of computers that you support.

Solution

Using the Registry

1. Open the Registry Editor and go to HKEY_CURRENT_USER\Control Panel\Desktop.
2. Find the DWORD value PaintDesktopVersion.
3. Change the value to 1.
4. Exit the Registry and reboot. You should see a box similar to that shown in Figure 5-7. To remove the version and build number from your desktop, change the value back to 0.

Figure 5-7. Use the Registry to show the precise XP build number and SP number on your desktop

Using downloadable software

TweakUI, one of a suite of free, unsupported utilities from Microsoft called Power-Toys, can also be used to display the XP version on your desktop. After you install it and run it, go to the General section and check Show windows version on desktop and click OK. After you reboot, the XP version will be displayed.

Discussion

If you don't put the precise XP build number and SP number on the desktop, you can still easily find that information for any computer. Right-click on My Computer and choose Properties → General.

5.4   Turning Off Balloon Tips

Problem

You want to turn off balloon tips, which frequently don't give any useful information, especially for experienced users, and are more distracting then they are useful, particularly when they show up in the Notification Area.

Solution

Using the Registry

1. Open the Registry Editor and go to `HKEY_CURRENT_USER\Software\Microsoft\Windows\CurrentVersion\Explorer\Advanced`.
2. Create a new DWORD value called `EnableBalloonTips`.
3. Give it a value of 0.
4. Exit the Registry and restart. Balloon tips will be turned off. To turn them on, either delete the DWORD value, or else give it a value of 1.

Using downloadable software

TweakUI, one of a suite of free, unsupported utilities from Microsoft called Power-Toys, can hide balloon tips. Get it from *http://www.microsoft.com/windowsxp/pro/downloads/powertoys.asp*. After you install it and run it, go to the Taskbar section and uncheck Enable Balloon Tips. Click on OK, and the balloon tips will vanish after you reboot.

Discussion

Although balloon tips can be distracting, they also serve a useful purpose, so make sure you want to turn them off before using this recipe. For example, when you hover your mouse over an item on the Taskbar showing an open window, the balloon tip will show you the filename or web location of the window.

See Also

MS KB 307729, "HOW TO: Disable Notification Area Balloon Tips in Windows XP"

5.5   Cleaning Your Desktop Automatically

Problem

You want to clean out all of your unused desktop icons automatically.

Solution

Using a graphical user interface

1. Right-click on the desktop and choose Properties → Desktop → Customize Desktop. The Desktop Items dialog box appears.
2. Click on Clean Desktop Now and click on OK. Icons that you haven't used for the past 60 days will be deleted from your desktop, although you can still run the programs in the normal way.
3. If you want to clean your desktop of unused icons every 60 days, check the box next to Run Desktop Cleanup Wizard every 60 days. From then on, every 60 days the wizard will appear, and you'll get a prompt asking you whether you want it to delete your unused icons.

Using the Registry

Run the Registry Editor and go to `HKEY_CURRENT_USER\Software\Microsoft\Windows\CurrentVersion\Explorer\Desktop\CleanupWiz`. Double-click the `NoRun` DWORD value, and edit its value to 0. Exit the Registry. The wizard will now run automatically every 60 days. If you want to change the interval at which it automatically cleans your desktop, double-click the `Days between clean up` DWORD value. Click Decimal, enter a number, click OK, and exit the Registry. The number will be the number of days between automated cleanups.

Discussion

Why clean out your desktop icons? Because your desktop can easily become cluttered with icons that you rarely, if ever use. That clutter means that it will be more difficult for you to find icons to programs that you want to use. You can always clean them out automatically by deleting each one, but that can be a time-consuming process, so the automated clean-up procedure can be a better way to go.

See Also

Recipe 5.1 if you want to delete icons that apparently can't be deleted and Recipe 5.2 to change desktop icons that appear unchangeable

5.6 Adding an Address Bar to the Taskbar

Problem

You want to be able to go to an Internet site without first having to open your browser and type in the URL.

Solution

You can add an Address Bar to the Taskbar that will let you type in a URL and go to the site using Internet Explorer.

Using a graphical user interface

1. Right-click on the Taskbar and from the menu that appears, make sure that there is no check next to Lock the Taskbar.
2. Right-click the Taskbar again. From the menu that appeared, choose Toolbars and put a check next to Address.
3. The word Address will appear on the Taskbar, just to the left of the Notification Area. To the left of the word Address will be a handle. Drag the handle to the left until a box for the Address Bar appears. You can now type in URLs. If you want to lock the Address Bar in that position, right-click on the Taskbar and put a check next to Lock the Taskbar.

Discussion

When you launch a URL in this way you will, of course, launch it in your default web browser. If you want to launch the URL in another browser, type in the executable filename in front of the URL, including the full path, like this:

```
C:\Program Files\Mozilla Firefox\Firefox.exe http://www.oreilly.com
```

See Also

MS KB 221754, "How to Search the Internet from the Address Bar in Internet Explorer"

5.7   Adding a Shortcut to a Disk, Folder, or Internet Address to the Taskbar

Problem

You want to add a shortcut to your Taskbar that, when clicked, will open to a specific folder, let you choose from any folder on a hard disk, or launch to an Internet address.

Solution

Using a graphical user interface

1. Right-click on the Toolbar and from the menu that appears, make sure that there is no check next to Lock the Taskbar.

2. From the menu that appears, choose Toolbars → New Toolbar.

3. Browse to the folder, disk, or object you want to add as a shortcut on the Taskbar. If you want to add it as an Internet address, type in the Internet address.

4. Click on OK.

5. If you're satisfied with the position of the new toolbar, and want to lock it in position, right-click on the Taskbar and put a check next to Lock the Taskbar. Otherwise, you can move its position by dragging the handle that appears to the left of the new toolbar.

See Also

Recipe 5.6 for information on how to add an Address Bar to the Taskbar

5.8   Hiding Specific Icons in the Notification Area

Problem

Many utilities and programs that run in the background, such as antivirus software, show their icons in the Notification Area (also called the System Tray) when they run. You want to hide these icons on a case-by-case basis.

Solution

Using a graphical user interface

1. Right-click on the Taskbar and choose Properties → Taskbar. The Taskbar and Start menu Properties dialog box appears.

2. In the Notification Area, select Hide inactive icons. When you choose this, a small arrow appears to the left of the System Tray. When the arrow is pointed to the left, inactive icons are hidden. Click it to display all icons in the System Tray. The arrow then points to the right. To hide the inactive icons, click on it again.

3. To customize which icons will be hidden and which won't be, click on Customize in the Notification Area of the Taskbar and Start menu Properties dialog box. The Customize Notifications dialog box appears, shown in Figure 5-8.

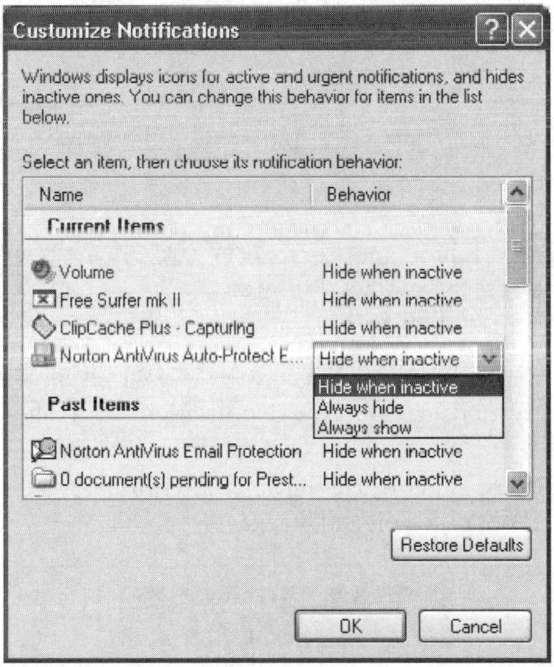

Figure 5-8. Choose whether the icons of background program should appear in the Notification Area

4. Click on the program's listing in the Behavior column, and choose from the drop-down menu whether to hide the icon always, never, or only when the program is inactive.

5. Click on OK twice.

Discussion

Keep in mind that hiding icons in the Notification Area won't actually stop any software from running—the software will run whether the icon is displayed or not. If you want to not just hide the icons, but also stop software from automatically running on startup, turn to Chapter 6.

See Also

Recipe 5.9 for information on how to hide all of the icons in the Taskbar

5.9   Hiding All Icons in the Notification Area

Problem

You want to hide all icons in the Notification Area, not just individual ones, so that you will only see the time and date in the Notification Area; no other icons will appear there.

Solution

Using the Registry

1. Open the Registry Editor and go to HKEY_CURRENT_USER/Software/Microsoft/ Windows/CurrentVersion/Policies/Explorer.
2. Create a new DWORD called NoTrayItemsDisplay.
3. Assign it a value of 1. (A value of 0 will keep the icons displayed.)
4. Exit the Registry and reboot. The Notification Area should appear as in Figure 5-9.
5. To display the icons, either delete the NoTrayItemsDisplay key or else change its value to 0 and reboot or log off and on again.

Figure 5-9. The Notification Area with no icons displayed

Discussion

One potential problem with hiding all icons from displaying in the Notification Area is that you won't be able to know at a glance which programs are running. This can cause problems because when you install some software, it always launches on startup, even if you don't want it to. If you hide all icons in the Notification Area, you won't know what software is automatically launching. So if you do hide all icons, remember to display them every once in a while, so you can know what's running on your system.

See Also

Recipe 5.8 for information on how to hide only specific the icons in the Notification Area

5.10 Controlling the Start Menu's Frequently Used Programs List

Problem

You want to customize the Most Frequently Used Programs list, which appears on the Start menu just above the All Programs link. You want control the number of programs that appear on that list, or change how programs appear there—and even stop the list from appearing altogether.

Solution

Using a graphical user interface

You can easily change the number of programs that appear on the list, delete programs from the list, rename them, and clear the list. Here's how:

1. Right-click on the Start button and choose Properties → Customize → General The Customize Start menu dialog box appears, shown in Figure 5-10.

2. To set the number of programs that will appear on the list, edit the Number of programs on Start menu box. You can choose any number up to 30, although obviously 30 programs will not be able to appear on the list, because there's not enough room.

3. If you want no programs to appear on the list, choose 0.

4. If you want to clear the current programs from the list, click on Clear List.

5. When you're finished making your changes, click on OK, and then click OK again.

You can also delete programs from the list manually by right-clicking on the shortcut to the program and selecting Remove from This List. To rename the shortcut, right-click on it and choose Rename. To add a program to the list, right-click on its icons from the desktop or from Windows Explorer and drag it to the Start button. The Start menu will pop up. Drag the icon to the location on the list where you want it to appear, and release the mouse button. The program will now appear on the list.

Figure 5-10. Customize the Start menu from this dialog box

Using the Registry

By default, a variety of programs do not appear on the Start menu's Frequently Used Programs list. If any of the following text is included in the program's shortcut name, the program will be excluded from the list:

- Documentation
- Help
- Install
- More Info
- Readme
- Read me
- Read First
- Setup
- Support
- What's New

Additionally, the following executables are excluded from the list:

- *Setup.exe*
- *Install.exe*
- *Isuninst.exe*
- *Unwise.exe*
- *Unwise32.exe*
- *St5unst.exe*
- *Rundll32.exe*
- *Explorer.exe*
- *Icwconn1.exe*
- *Inoculan.exe*
- *Mobsync.exe*
- *Navwnt.exe*
- *Realmon.exe*
- *Sndvol32.exe*

There may be other programs that you don't want to show up there, though. You can specify that certain applications never show up on the list by using the Registry. To do it:

1. Open the Registry Editor and go to `HKEY_CLASSES_ROOT\Applications`.
2. Look for a subkey that is the executable name of the application that you want to ban from the list—for example, `visio.exe`.
3. Create a new String value for that subkey, named `NoStartPage`. Leave the value blank.
4. Exit the Registry. You may have to reboot in order for the setting to take effect.
5. To allow the program to show up on the list, delete its `NoStartPage` subkey, and exit the Registry. You may have to reboot in order for the setting to take effect.

You can also use the Registry to stop all programs from showing up on the list:

1. Open the Registry Editor and go to `HKEY_CURRENT_USER\Software\Microsoft\Windows\CurrentVersion\Policies\Explorer`.
2. Create a new DWORD value of `NoStartMenuMFUprogramsList` and give it a value of 1.
3. Exit the Registry. You may need to reboot in order for the setting to take effect.
4. Delete `NoStartMenuMFUprogramsList` or enter a value of 0 to let programs start showing up on the list again. Exit the Registry. Reboot in order for the settings to take effect.

Discussion

The rules for what appears and doesn't appear on the Frequently Used Programs list are rather mysterious. Windows XP uses a counter of some kind, counts the number of times a program runs, and, based on that counter, displays programs on the list. So just clearing the list using the GUI will only temporarily stop a program from appearing there. If there's a program you don't want to ever show up, use the Registry, as outlined in this recipe, to ban the program from the list.

See Also

MS KB 282462, "Programs Removed from the Most Frequently Used Programs List Can Reappear," and MS KB 284198, "How To Prevent a Program from Being Displayed in the Most Frequently Used Programs List in Windows XP"

5.11 Customizing the Start Menu's Pinned Programs List

Problem

You want to change the programs that appear on the Pinned Programs List, just above the Frequently Used Programs List on the Start menu. But by default, Windows XP puts specific programs on the list, notably Internet Explorer and Outlook or Outlook Express. But you use a different browser or email program, so you want it to appear there, or want to put a different program altogether on the Pinned Programs List.

Solution

Using a graphical user interface

1. To add your email program or web browser to the list, right-click on the Start button and choose Properties → Start Menu → Customize → General.

2. In the Show on Start menu section, check the box next to Internet if you want to show your browser's icon to appear on the pinned items list, and check the box for email if you want to show your email program's icon on the pinned items list.

3. To choose which program's icon to use for each of the programs, choose the program from the drop-down box. Click OK and then click OK again.

To add other programs to the Pinned Programs List, right-click on their icons from the desktop or from Windows Explorer and drag it to the Start button. The Start menu will pop up. Drag the icon to the location on the Pinned Programs List where you want it to appear, and release the mouse button. The program will now appear on the list. To delete a program from the list, right-click on its icon and choose Unpin from Start menu. To rename a program on the list, right-click on it and choose Rename.

Using the Registry

You can use the Registry to stop any programs at all from showing up on the list at all:

1. Open the Registry Editor and go to HKEY_CURRENT_USER\Software\Microsoft\ Windows\CurrentVersion\Policies\Explorer.
2. Create a new DWORD value of NoStartMenuPinnedList and give it a value of 1.
3. Exit the Registry. You may need to reboot in order for the setting to take effect.
4. To let programs start showing up on the list again, delete NoStartMenuPinnedList or give a value of 0. Exit the Registry. You may need to reboot in order for the settings to take effect.

Discussion

The Pinned Programs List is much more useful than the Frequently Used Programs List, because you have absolute control over what shows up on it and what doesn't. Because of that, consider killing the Frequently Used Programs list entirely, as outlined in the previous recipe, which will make room for more programs on the Pinned Programs List.

See Also

MS KB 279767, "Description of the Start Menu in Windows XP"

5.12 Displaying Control Panel Applets in a Cascading Menu

Problem

You want to be able to quickly get to Control Panel applets without having to navigate numerous menus.

Solution

Using a graphical user interface

You can speed up the time it takes to get to Control Panel applets by forcing Windows XP to display them in a cascading menu when you choose Control Panel from the Start button, as shown in Figure 5-11.

Figure 5-11. To speed up access to Control Panel applets, force XP to display them as a cascading menu

Here's how:

1. Right-click on the Taskbar and choose Properties → Start Menu.
2. Click the Customize button and chose the Advanced tab.
3. In the Control Panel heading, choose Display as a menu.
4. Click OK twice.

Discussion

Displaying the Control Panel like this will make it easier to get to specific Control Panel applets quickly. But it won't reorganize the Control Panel for you. So the applets will still stay organized the way that XP organizes them by default. Some people may get more out of the Control Panel by hiding Control Panel applets altogether, or recategorizing them, as you'll see in the next recipe. And, in fact, combining this recipe with the next one may be the best solution for many to getting the Control Panel under control. If you hide and recategorize applets in the way shown in the next recipe, you'll only display those applets that you really use, and you'll have them displayed in the most organized way possible. Then if you display them in a cascading menu, your favorite ones will be within immediate reach.

See Also

Recipe 5.13 to hide and recategorize control panel applets

5.13 Hiding and Recategorizing Control Panel Applets

Problem

You want to be able to hide and recategorize Control Panel applets. There are some applets that you never use and that you want to hide or you would like to move applets from one category to another.

 When you hide an applet, you don't actually delete that applet. It is still available to be run. To run an applet that you've hidden, type its name into the Run box and press Enter. For example, to run the System Properties applet, type *sysdm.cpl* at the Run box and press Enter. For a list of executable names of Control Panel applets, see Table 5.2.

Solution

Using a graphical user interface

If you have Windows XP Professional, you can use the Group Policy Editor to hide unused Control Panel applets. The Group Policy Editor isn't available in the Home Edition. For more information about using the Group Policy Editor, see Recipe 5.19. Here's how to do it:

1. Run the Group Policy Editor by typing *gpedit.msc* at a command prompt or the Run box.
2. Go to User Configuration\Administrative Templates\Control Panel.
3. Right-click on Show only specified Control Panel applets, and choose Properties. You'll see the screen pictured in Figure 5-12.
4. On the Setting tab, click on the Enabled radio button. This will hide all of the applets on the Control Panel.
5. You'll want to display some applets on the Control Panel, so to add them, click on the Show button, and then click on Add from the Show Contents screen that appears.
6. For each item that you want to appear, type in its the Control Panel filename. Control Panel filenames end in *.cpl*—for example, *timedate.cpl* for the Date and Time applet. Table 5-2 lists the names of Control Panel applets and their corresponding filenames.
7. Click on OK and exit the Group Policy Editor. Only the items that you've chosen to display will be shown.

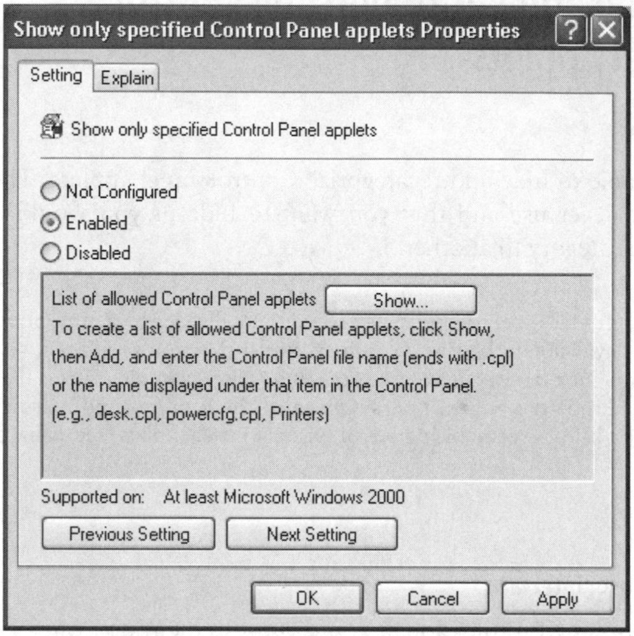

Figure 5-12. From this screen, you can hide all Control Panel applets, or decide to display them on a case-by-case basis

Table 5-2. Control Panel applets and their filenames

Applet	Filename
System Properties	*sysdm.cpl*
Display Properties	*desk.cpl*
Network Connections	*ncpa.cpl*
Accessibility Options	*access.cpl*
Add or Remove Programs	*appwiz.cpl*
Add Hardware Wizard	*hdwwiz.cpl*
Internet Properties	*Inetcpl.cpl*
Region and Language Options	*intl.cpl*
Game Controllers	*joy.cpl*
Mouse Properties	*main.cpl*
Sound and Audio Devices	*mmsys.cpl*
User Accounts	*nusrmgr.cpl*
ODBC Data Source Administrator	*odbccp32.cpl*
Power Options Properties	*powercfg.cpl*

Table 5-2. Control Panel applets and their filenames (continued)

Applet	Filename
Phone and Modem Options	*telephon.cpl*
Time and Date Properties	*timedate.cpl*
Speech Properties	*sapi.cpl*

Using the Registry

1. Open the Registry Editor and go to `HKEY_LOCAL_MACHINE\SOFTWARE\Microsoft\Windows\CurrentVersion\Control Panel\don't load`.

2. Create a new string value whose name is the filename of the applet that you want to hide. For example, to hide the Mouse Control dialog box, the string value would be *main.cpl*. See Table 5-2 for a list of Control Panel applets and their filenames.

3. Exit the Registry. The applet won't appear in the Control Panel.

Recategorize Control Panel Applets

Using the Registry

As mentioned previously, you aren't stuck with the way that XP organizes Control Panel applets into categories—you can put them anywhere you want. To do it, you need two pieces of information—the filename of the applet (for example, *main.cpl* for the Mouse Properties dialog box), and the Registry value for each different Control Panel category. For filenames of each applet, use Table 5-2. For the Registry value for each Control Panel category, use Table 5-3. With that information in hand, you can recategorize any or all Control Panel applets.

Table 5-3. Control Panel categories and their Registry value data

Control Panel category	Value data
Accessibility Options	0x00000007 (7)
Add or Remove Programs	0x00000008 (8)
Appearance and Themes	0x00000001 (1)
Date, Time, Language, and Regional Options	0x00000006 (6)
Network and Internet Connections	0x00000003 (3)
Other Control Panel Options	0x00000000 (0)
Performance and Maintenance	0x00000005 (5)
Printers and Other Hardware	0x00000002 (2)
Sounds, Speech, and Audio Devices	0x00000004 (4)
User Accounts	0x00000009 (9)
No Category	0xffffffff

To recategorize a Control Panel applet:

1. Open the Registry and go to `HKEY_LOCAL_MACHINE\SOFTWARE\Microsoft\Windows\CurrentVersion\Control Panel\Extended Properties\{305CA226-D286-468e-B848-2B2E8E697B74}2`.

2. Find the Registry key of the applet that you want to recategorize. The filename of the applet will appear on the end of the key—for example, `%SystemRoot%\system32\main.cpl` is the Mouse Properties dialog box.

3. Edit the DWORD value of the Control Panel category into which you want the applet to appear. For example, if you wanted the applet to appear in the Performance and Maintenance category, you would give it a value of 5. The value would then be displayed in the Registry as `0x00000005(5)`.

4. Exit the Registry. The applet will now appear in the new category.

Discussion

You'll find this recipe useful because the Control Panel is cluttered with so many applets, and you might never use many of them. For example, if you do not have disabilities, you may not need to ever use the Accessibility Options applet. Additionally, the Control Panel may categorize applets in a way that doesn't suit the way you work. You might, for example, want the Power Options Properties applet available from the Printers and Other Hardware section of the Control Panel instead of from the Performance and Maintenance section because if you have a laptop, you may want to make changes to the way you use power at the same time you make changes to the way you use a mouse. (The Mouse Properties applet is also available from the Printers and Other Hardware section of the Control Panel.)

See Also

MS KB 149648, "Description of Control Panel (*.cpl*) Files"

5.14   Customizing Right-Click Menu Choices in Windows Explorer

Problem

You want to customize the pop-up shortcut menu that appears when you right-click on a file in Windows Explorer. The pop-up menu differs according to the program that you right-click on. So if you right-click on a graphics file, for example, one set of programs will appear on the menu, and if you click on a text file, a different set of programs will appear on the menu. You want to be able to change the choices that appear for specific file types. And you want to add new choices to the pop-up menu, so that you can do things such as easily move and copy files between folders.

Solution

Using a graphical user interface

It's easy to add choices to the right-click pop-up menu for specific file types. Let's say that you want to add a shortcut menu item that would allow *.gif* files to be opened with the graphics viewer and editor IrfanView. Here's how to do it:

1. From Windows Explorer, choose Tools → Folder Options → File Types.
2. In the Registered File Types list, select the file type to which you want to add a new shortcut menu item. In our example, we'll choose a GIF file.
3. Choose Advanced → New. You'll see the New Action dialog box shown in Figure 5-13.
4. In the Action box, type in the text that you want to appear on the shortcut menu, for example, `Open with IrfanView`.
5. In the Application used to perform action box, enter the executable program you want to open the file with, including the full path. Surround it with quotation marks. Then leave a space and type in "%1". The "%1" is a placeholder for the name of the file on which you right-clicked. In our instance, the entire string would look like this: "*C:\Program Files\i_view32.exe*" "%1".
6. Click on OK. The change will take place immediately, and the new command will appear on the shortcut menu for the specified file type.

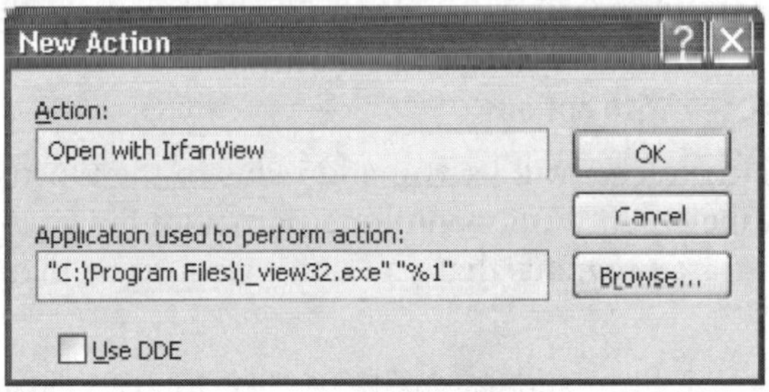

Figure 5-13. Use the New Action dialog box to add an item to a file's shortcut menu

Add and remove destinations for the Send To option

A particularly useful item on the right-click context menu is the Send To option, which allows you to send the file you've selected to anyone of a list of programs or locations, for example to a drive, folder, or program. When you install new programs, some install various options on this menu choice. You can, however, easily delete or add to options on the menu. In Windows Explorer go to *C:\Documents and Settings\<User Name>\SendTo*, where *<User Name>* is your user name. The folder will be filled with shortcuts to all the locations that you find on your Send To context menu. To remove an item from the Send To menu, delete the shortcut from the folder. To add an item to the menu, add a shortcut to the folder by highlighting the folder, choosing File → New → Shortcut, and following the instructions for creating a shortcut. The new setting will take effect immediately; you don't have to exit Windows Explorer for it to go into effect.

Using the Registry

You can use the graphical user interface to add a menu choice to the Open With dialog box for specific file types. But if you want to add the same shortcut menu item to every type of file, you'll have to use the Registry. Here's how to do it:

1. Open the Registry Editor and go to HKEY_CLASSES_ROOT*.

2. Create a new subkey called Shell if it doesn't yet exist.

3. Create a new subkey under Shell and name it what your new command will be, for example, OpenWithIrfanView.

4. For the default value of the new subkey, type in the text that you want to appear on the shortcut menu, for example, Open with IrfanView.

5. Create a new subkey named Command under the subkey that you just created.

6. For the default value of the Command subkey, enter the command string that you want to be executed when the shortcut menu item is chosen, for example, *"C:\ Program Files\i_view32.exe" "%1"*.

7. Exit the Registry. The new shortcut menu item should be immediately available, although you may need to reboot in order for it to take effect.

Cleaning up Explorer's Open With options

The previous parts of the recipe will let you add items to the Open With menu. But what if you find that the Open With menu for a particular file type is filled with too many options, or there are programs that you don't want to be there? Use the Registry to clean it up:

1. Open the Registry Editor and go to HKEY_CURRENT_USER\Software\Microsoft\ Windows\CurrentVersion\Explorer\FileExts.

2. Look for the file extension whose Open With list you want to edit and find its OpenWithList subkey, for example, HKEY_CURRENT_USER\Software\Microsoft\ Windows\CurrentVersion\Explorer\FileExts\.bmp\OpenWithList.

3. The subkey will have an alphabetical list of string values. Open each value and examine the value data. It will be the name of one of the programs on the Open With list, such as *Winword.exe*.

4. Delete any entry that you don't want to appear. Be sure to delete the string listing itself. In other words, if in the a string value, the value data was *Winword.exe*, delete the entire a string listing and not just the value.

5. Go to `HKEY_CURRENT_USER\.bmp\OpenWithList` and `HKEY_CURRENT_USER\.bmp\ OpenWithProgids` and remove any offending entries.

6. Exit the Registry. The change will take effect immediately.

Add Copy To Folder and Move To Folder context menu options

A substantial amount of the time, when you open Windows Explorer, you're going to want to perform one of two functions: Move a file between folders or copy a file to another folder. But doing these two simple tasks requires a fair amount of dragging files, or manually copying and pasting them. However, you can use the Registry to add Copy To Folder and Move To Folder options to the right-click context menu. Then, when you right-click on a file, you can chose either option from the menu and you'll be able to browse to any place on your hard disk to copy or move the file to, and then send the file there. To do it:

1. Run the Registry Editor (see *Chapter 9*, Working with the Registry), and go to `HKEY_CLASSES_ROOT\AllFilesystemObjects\shellex\ContextMenuHandlers`.

2. Create a new key called `Copy To`. Set the value to `{C2FBB630-2971-11d1-A18C-00C04FD75D13}`.

3. Create another new key called `Move To`. Set the value to `{C2FBB631-2971-11d1-A18C-00C04FD75D13}`.

4. Exit the Registry. The changes should take effect immediately. The Copy To Folder and Move To Folder options will appear. When you right-click on a file and choose one of the options, you'll be able to move or copy the file using a dialog box like that shown in Figure 5-14.

Open the command prompt from the right-click menu

XP may be a GUI, but that doesn't mean that you don't need the command prompt at times. There may be times when you want to open the command prompt from the right-click menu. Frequently, when you use the command prompt, you're going to want to perform an action from your current folder, so it would be nice to be able to open the command prompt to the current folder. For example, if you were to right-click on the *C:\Current Work* folder, you could then choose to open a command prompt at *C:\Current Work*. To add an option to the right-click menu:

1. Run the Registry Editor (see *Chapter 9*, Working with the Registry), and go to `HKEY_LOCAL_MACHINE/Software/Classes/Folder/Shell`.

2. Create a new key called `Command Prompt`.

3. For the default value, enter whatever text you want to appear when you right-click on a folder; for example, Open Command Prompt.

4. Create a new key beneath the `Command Prompt` key called `Command`.

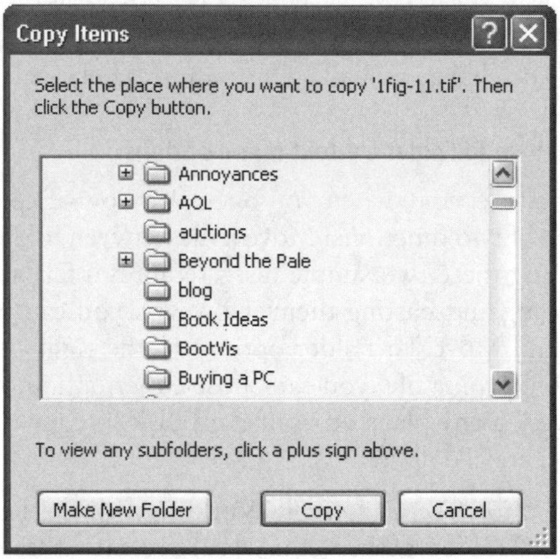

Figure 5-14. When you choose the Copy To Folder option on the right-click context menu, you'll use this dialog box to specify where you want the file copied

5. Set the default value to `Cmd.exe /k pushd %L`. That value will launch `Cmd.exe`, which is the XP command prompt. The `/k` switch puts the prompt into interactive mode—that is, it lets you issue commands from the command prompt; the command prompt isn't being used to issue only a single command and then exit. The `pushd` command stores the name of the current directory, and the `%L` uses the name of that stored directory to start the command prompt at it.

6. Exit the Registry. The new menu option will show up immediately. Note that it won't appear when you right-click on a file—it only shows up when you right-click on a folder.

Using downloadable software

Download and install a free copy of Microsoft's Open Command Window Here PowerToy from *http://www.microsoft.com/windowsxp/pro/downloads/powertoys.asp*. When you get to the page, look for the Open Command Window Here section. Click on the link next to `CmdHere.exe`. After you download it, run `CmdHere.exe`, and the option will be added to the right-click context menu.

Discussion

When you right-click on a file in Explorer, the shortcut menu that appears includes a list of programs with which you can open the file. To open the file with a given program, choose the program, and you'll be able to open the file with it. This pop-up menu differs according to the program that you right-click on. So if you right-click on a graphics file, for example, one set of programs will appear on the menu, and if you click on a text file, a different set of programs will appear on the menu.

Some programs, when you install them, automatically put themselves on that pop-up menu. But not all do. So this recipe lets you customize the pop-up menu so that certain programs appear on it for certain file types. It also lets some programs appear on *every* file type. And it allows you to remove some programs from appearing when you right-click on a file.

See Also

PC Magazine has an excellent utility, ContextMenu Plus, that makes it easy to edit, add, or remove menu commands from any Windows context menu. Get it at *http://www.pcmag.com/article2/0,1759,1554248,00.asp*. You can only download it if you're a subscriber to the *PC Magazine* utilities library; if you're a subscriber, it's free.

5.15 Changing the Resolution of Thumbnails in Windows Explorer

Problem

You can use Windows Explorer to display thumbnails of images in any folder, by choosing View → Thumbnails. By default, those thumbnails are 96 pixels and of a relatively high quality and resolution. But you want to change the size or resolution of the thumbnails, to make them larger so that they're easier to view, or to make them smaller and a lower resolution, because when you have large, high-quality thumbnails, you require more RAM to display them all.

Solution

Using the Registry

1. Open the Registry Editor and go to HKEY CURRENT USER\Software\Microsoft\ Windows\CurrentVersion\Explorer.

2. Create a new DWORD value called ThumbnailSize.

3. When you edit the value data, choose Hexadecimal as the base.

4. In the value data box, enter a number between 32 and 96. The larger the number, the higher the resolution, and the higher the quality of the thumbnails.

5. Exit the Registry Editor. The resolution of the thumbnails will change without your having to reboot. To change the actual size of the thumbnails, follow the next section of this recipe.

Using downloadable software

TweakUI, one of a suite of free, unsupported utilities from Microsoft called Power-Toys, can change not only the size of the thumbnails, but their image quality, so that you can have higher- or lower-quality images. Get it from *http://www.microsoft.com/ windowsxp/pro/downloads/powertoys.asp*. After you install it and run it, go to Explorer → Thumbnails and you'll see the screen shown in Figure 5-15. Move the slider Image Quality slider to the left to decrease the image quality of each thumbnail, and to the right to increase the image quality. To change the size of the thumbnails, choose a new size in the Thumbnail box.

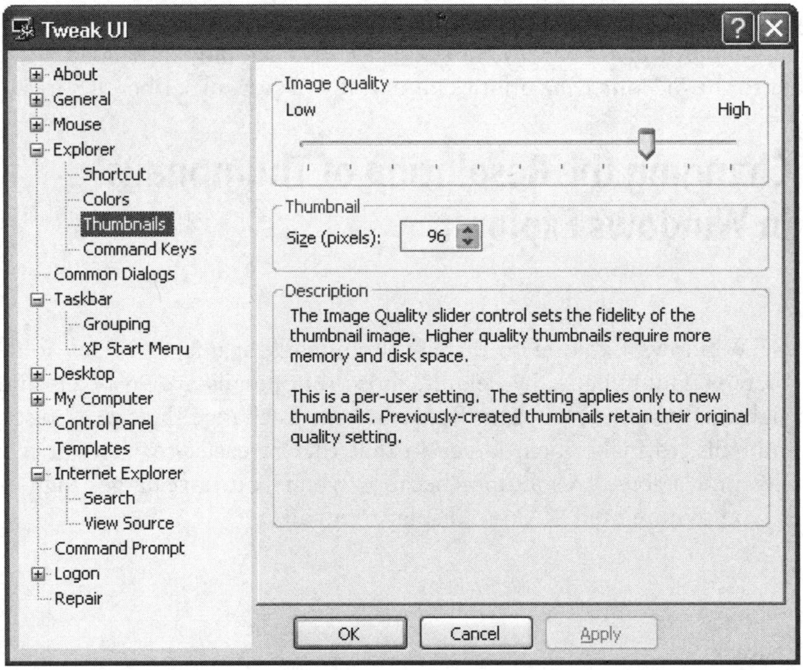

Figure 5-15. Changing the size and image quality of Windows Explorer thumbnails in Windows Explorer

 When you use TweakUI to change the size and quality of thumbnails, the change will apply only to new thumbnails. Any thumbnails already on your system will continue to be displayed with your old settings.

Discussion

Be careful before making your thumbnails larger, because doing so can slow down browsing through your system using Windows Explorer. Also, not all systems will allow you to display thumbnails larger than 96 pixels, so it may not work on yours. However, you should be able to make them smaller on any system.

See Also

There may be times when a thumbnail for a folder won't appear at all, or the wrong one is displayed. For information on how to fix the problem, see MS KB 813711, "Your view settings or customizations for a folder are lost or incorrect."

5.16 Improving Laptop and LCD Resolution with ClearType

Problem

You want to make it easier to read the type on laptop screens and LCD desktop screens.

Solution

Using a graphical user interface

1. Right-click on the Desktop and choose Properties → Appearance → Effects. The Effects dialog box appears.

2. Check the box next to Use the following method to smooth edges of screen fonts. Select ClearType from the drop-down box and click OK, then click OK again. ClearType will now be enabled.

 You can use ClearType on a normal PC monitor, but it often makes the text appear blurry. Additionally, people have complained that it gives them headaches.

3. ClearType will now be turned on, but you won't be able to fine-tune the way it looks on your screen—and because LCD screens are all different, you should fine-tune it. You'll have to download the free Microsoft PowerToy called the ClearType Tuning Control to improve how ClearType looks on your system. Download and install it from *http://www.microsoft.com/typography/ClearTypePowerToy.mspx*.

4. After it's installed, when the first screen appears, make sure the Turn on ClearType box is checked, then click Start Wizard.

5. You'll come to a page with two different samples of text. Click the one that looks best on your system, then click Next.

6. Now you'll come to a page that displays a block of text in six different ways. Click on the text that looks best and then click on Finish.

7. You'll come to a final page that displays text in four different fonts. If you're satisfied with the way that the text looks, click Finish; you're done. If you want to try a different setting, click Back, and you'll come to the page that displays a block of text in six ways. Choose a different text block, click Next, and if you're satisfied, click Finish. Otherwise, keep going back to the page with six blocks of text, until you choose one that's best for your system.

From now on, if you want to fine-tune ClearType again, choose Control Panel → Appearance and Themes → ClearType Tuning, and the ClearType Tuning Control will run.

Discussion

The laptop screen can be very hard on the eyes, especially because many laptops are designed to work at very high resolutions (for example, 1400 by 1050 pixels), so characters on them can be exceedingly small. As laptop screens get larger, resolutions increase, and type gets smaller. The problem isn't confined to laptops—increasingly popular LCD screens have the same problem.

When you turn on ClearType, it's only available after you log on to XP. So any fonts displayed before you log on won't benefit from ClearType. If you want those pre-logon fonts to use ClearType for display, you can use the Registry to force them to display. Open the Registry Editor and go to `HKEY_USERS\.DEFAULT\Control Panel\ Desktop`. Open the `FontSmoothingType` entry and change its value data to 2. (The default is 1, which means that font smoothing is enabled, but ClearType isn't. A value of 0 turns off both font smoothing and ClearType.) Exit the Registry Editor and reboot. ClearType will now be available before logon.

See Also

MS KB 306527, "HOW TO: Use ClearType to Enhance Screen Fonts in Windows XP," and MS KB 294847, "ClearType Does Not Work When Magnifier Is Enabled"

5.17   Converting to the Classic Windows Interface

Problem

You don't like the bright and cartoonish XP interface, with a new-style Start menu that takes up a significant amount of screen real estate. You want to use the previous lean-and-mean Windows interface, which is more staid and straightforward, with squared-off windows instead of rounded ones, and a Start menu that appears as a simple list.

Solution

Using a graphical user interface

There are two parts to reverting to the classic Windows interface. You'll have to change the Start menu, and then change the basic look and feel of XP. Here's how to do it:

1. To change the Start menu, first right-click on any blank space on the Taskbar and choose Properties → Start Menu.
2. Choose the button next to Classic Start Menu and click on OK. Your Start menu will now be of the classic Windows type—a single-width pop-up menu. Compare the Start menus in Figures 5-16 and 5-17 to see the difference.
3. Right-click on the desktop and choose Properties → Themes. Under Themes, select Windows Classic from the drop-down menu and click on OK. Your desktop will now have the old, familiar classic Windows look and feel, including squared-off windows and staid colors.

Figure 5-16. XP's interface features bright, cartoony colors, rounded windows, and a large new Start menu

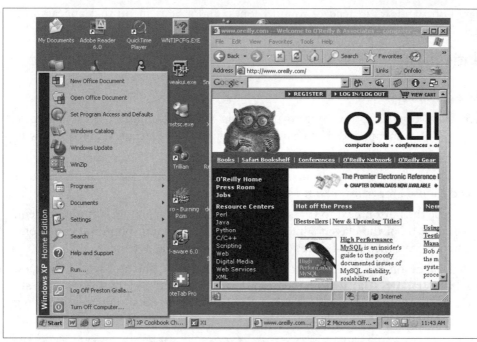

Figure 5-17. If you're a fan of the lean-and-mean look, you can easily convert to the classic Windows interface

Discussion

When you use the classic Start menu instead of the XP-style Start menu, you'll find that not as many features are within as easy reach, simply because you're devoting less real estate to the Start menu. You may not even know where to find some features. For example, in the classic Start menu there is no entry for the Control Panel. You can, however, get to it by choosing Settings; you'll find a link for the Control Panel directly from there.

You can also customize the classic Start menu by adding any items to it that you want, and deleting items from it that you don't want. When you choose Properties → Start Menu and select Classic Start Menu, a Customize button will appear. Click on it and you'll be able to add and remove items from the Start menu, as well as re-sort them.

See Also

If you want to "skin" XP so that you can change the style of title bars, buttons, the Start menu, toolbars, and more, get WindowsBlinds from *http://www.stardock.com/products/windowblinds*.

5.18   Using TweakUI

Problem

You want an easy way to make simple, useful changes to the user interface, without having to use the Registry or other complicated tools. You want to do it all from a single place, and you don't want to have to pay for the software.

Solution

Using downloadable software

TweakUI, one of a suite of free, unsupported utilities from Microsoft called Power-Toys, is the best job for the task. Get it from *http://www.microsoft.com/windowsxp/ pro/downloads/powertoys.asp*. After you install it and run it, simply scroll through the different major settings, and follow the directions for making changes. There is no logical rhyme or reason for which settings you can change with TweakUI—for example, in Windows Explorer you can change the color of different types of files (compressed, encrypted, and so on) displayed in folders, you can change how shortcuts will be displayed on the desktop (with an arrow, without an arrow, with a light arrow, or with a custom look); you can change the display of thumbnails, as described in Recipe 5.15, and other customizations. The best way to see what TweakUI can do is download it and give it a try.

Discussion

The latest version of TweakUI works only with versions of Windows XP with Service Pack 1 or higher, so if you don't have the service pack installed, you'll have to install it in order to use TweakUI. If you have an old version of TweakUI on your system, you have to uninstall it before installing the newest version.

See Also

Microsoft has a substantial number of free utilities available for download at *http:// www.microsoft.com/windowsxp/downloads/default.mspx*.

5.19   Using Group Policy Editor to Alter the Interface

Problem

As you've seen in the recipes in this chapter, there are many different ways to change the XP interface using a variety of different tools, including the Registry, menus and dialog boxes, and downloadable software. But it can be confusing to have to keep switching among all those different tools. You want a central way to alter many interface settings.

Solution

Using a graphical user interface

The Group Policy Editor, available only in Windows XP Professional, gives you literally dozens of ways to customize the interface. To run it, type *gpedit.msc* and press Enter. Once Group Policy Editor is running, go to *User Configuration\Administrative Templates*. Beneath it, you'll find a number of folders with different XP features you can change, including:

- Windows Components
- Start menu and Taskbar
- Desktop
- Control Panel
- Shared Folders
- Network
- System

Each of those folders may have subfolders beneath it—for example, Windows Components lists a number of components, including Internet Explorer, Windows Explorer, and NetMeeting.

The Start menu and Taskbar folder alone lets you change nearly four dozen separate settings, such as removing the Pinned Programs List from the Start menu, removing the My Documents icon from the Start menu, hiding the Notification Area (also called the System Tray) on the Taskbar, not showing the My Pictures icon, the Run menu, and the My Music icon on the Start menu, locking the Taskbar so that it can't be customized, and many others. To use the Group Policy Editor, first make sure that you click on the Extended tab at the bottom of the screen. When you do, you'll be shown a description of the setting, what the setting will change, and information about what changes you can make with the setting, as you can see in Figure 5-18.

To change a setting, double-click on it. As you can see in Figure 5-19, you'll have three choices: Not Configured, Enabled, or Disabled. Not Configured means that you aren't using the settings—you're letting XP handle it using XP's defaults, or using any changes to the defaults that you've made with the Registry, user interface, or other tool. To turn on the setting, choose Enabled; to turn off the setting, choose Disabled. Then click on OK and exit the Group Policy Editor.

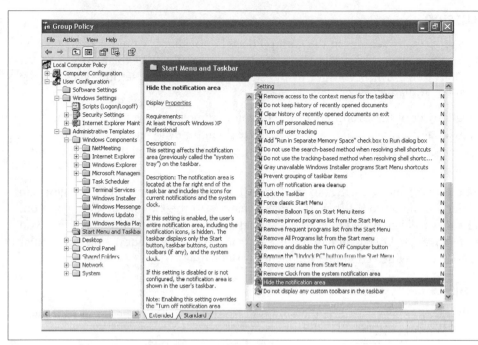

Figure 5-18. The Group Policy Editor lets you customize many aspects of the XP interface, including the Taskbar, Start menu, and Control Panel

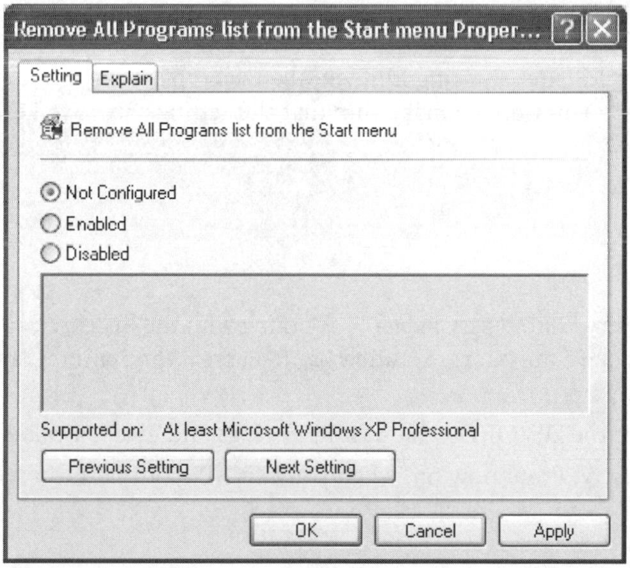

Figure 5-19. You can enable or disable settings from this screen; for more information about the settings, click on Explain

Discussion

There are so many settings in the Group Policy Editor that it would literally take an entire book to cover them all. The settings are generally self-explanatory, and for those that aren't, when you get to the screen to change the setting, click on the Explain tab and it will give you more details.

The real power of the Group Policy Editor comes in not when you make changes for an individual user, but rather when you make them for everyone who uses the same computer, or you apply them to someone on the network, no matter what computer they use.

There are two major branches to the Group Policy Editor: Computer Configuration and User Configuration. When you make changes to the Computer Configuration, the changes will be applied to everyone who uses the particular computer. When you make changes to User Configuration, the changes will be made to that particular user, no matter which computer on the network he uses.

See Also

MS KB 307882, "How To Use the Group Policy Editor to Manage Local Computer Policy in Windows XP"

5.20 Saving Your Desktop Settings

Problem

When you restart XP after shutting it down, the desktop settings from your last setting weren't saved. You want to make sure that the settings are saved every time you exit XP.

Solution

Using the Registry

1. Run the Registry Editor (see *Chapter 9*, Working with the Registry), and go to `HKEY_CURRENT_USER\Software\Microsoft\Windows NT\CurrentVersion\Program Manager\Restrictions`.
2. Create or edit the DWORD value `NoSaveSettings` and give it a value of 0.
3. Exit the Registry. From now on, when you exit XP, your desktop settings will be saved.

Discussion

Windows XP normally keeps track of your desktop settings, so that when you log out or shut down, it saves those settings so that they're in place the next time you log on. If you log off rather than restart, it will even keep track of open windows and their locations on your desktop. But if your Registry has been changed, perhaps by an application that you installed or for some other reason, the settings won't be saved unless you edit the Registry, as detailed in this recipe.

See Also

For advice on other shutdown problems, see "Windows XP Boot Problems & Edits" at *http://www.kellys-korner-xp.com/win_xp_restart.htm.*

5.21 Fixing the Start Shortcut Menu

Problem

When you right-click on at item on the Start menu, no shortcut menu appears, even though it is supposed to. You want the shortcut menu to start appearing again.

Solution

Using a graphical user interface

1. Right-click the Start button and choose Properties → Start Menu → Customize → Advanced.
2. In the Start menu items dialog box, select Enable Dragging and Dropping.
3. Click OK and then OK again.

Discussion

When you right-click on an item in the Start menu, the shortcut menu that is supposed to appear gives you a variety of options, including running the program or opening the file, removing it from the Start menu, copying or moving it to a folder, and so on. The exact menu will vary according to whether the item is a file or a folder.

There's no logical reason that turning off dragging and dropping should also turn off the shortcut menu for items on the Start menu, but it does. When dragging and dropping is turned off, you won't be able to drag items from one part of the Start menu to another—and as you can see in this recipe, it also kills the shortcut menu for Start items.

See Also

Sometimes the shortcuts and folders on the Start and Favorites menus may not be alphabetized, or new shortcuts may be added to the bottom of the menu. To fix the problem, see MS KB 177482, "Start Menu and Favorites Menu Are Not Listed in Alphabetical Order."

5.22   Troubleshooting My Recent Documents

Problem

Documents you've recently used are supposed to show up on the My Recent Documents list on the Start menu. They don't, so you want them to show up.

Solution

Using downloadable software

TweakUI, one of a suite of free, unsupported utilities from Microsoft called Power-Toys, can solve the problem. Get it from *http://www.microsoft.com/windowsxp/pro/ downloads/powertoys.asp*. After you install it and run it, click Explorer. In the Settings box, check the box next to Maintain document history (Figure 5-20), and click OK.

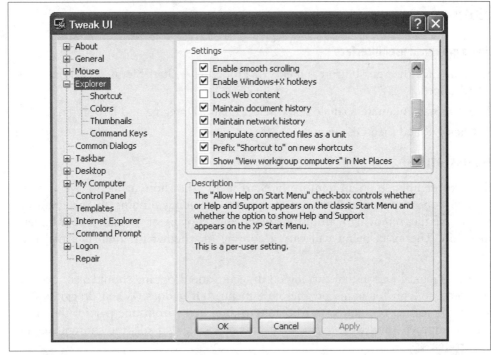

Figure 5-20. If documents aren't being added to My Recent Documents, make sure that Maintain document history is checked under Settings

Using a graphical user interface

If you have Windows XP Professional, you can use the Group Policy Editor to make sure that documents you've recently used show up in My Recent Documents. The

Group Policy Editor isn't available in the Home Edition. For more information about using the Group Policy Editor, see Recipe 5.19. Here's how to do it:

1. Run the Group Policy Editor by typing *gpedit.msc* at a command prompt or the Run box.

2. Go to User Configuration\Administrative Templates\Start Menu and Taskbar.

3. In the details pane, double-click on Do Not Keep History Of Recently Opened Documents. Select Disabled and click OK.

Discussion

If files aren't showing up in the My Recent Documents list, they most likely are not showing up in Microsoft Office documents as well. Normally, in Microsoft Office applications such as Word and Excel, the list of documents you've recently opened in each application shows up at the bottom of the File menu, but the same setting that controls My Recent Documents also controls whether files show up in Office applications. Additionally, if the files are now showing up in Office applications, the Options dialog box setting that controls how many should show up on the File menu won't appear as well. When you fix the problem with the My Recent Documents list, you'll also fix the problem with Office applications.

See Also

MS KB 307875, "How To Display, Use, and Clear 'My Recent Documents' on the Start Menu in Windows XP"

CHAPTER 6

System Properties, Startup, and Shutdown

6.0 Introduction

Starting up and shutting down a PC should be easy. Press a button and it turns on; click a few buttons and it turns off. The same holds true for your PC's system properties. There should be nothing complicated about doing things such as setting the system time or giving your computer a name.

But in computing, as in life, things are not always simple. And so things can get difficult and complicated. What if you sometimes want to start up your PC with debugging turned on, for example, or using safe mode, or using an entirely different operating system? What if you want to hunt down and kill programs and services that cause system conflicts? What if you want to change your boot screen or customize your system sounds?

You'll find recipes for doing all that and more in this chapter, so that you can take control of startup, shutdown, and setting your system's properties. For information about troubleshooting startup problems, turn to Chapter 20, Crashes and Errors.

6.1 Automatically Setting the Time on a Domain-Connected PC

Problem

You're on a PC connected to a domain, and you want the PC to have its clock set to the proper time automatically, without your intervention.

Solution

Using a graphical user interface

1. At the Run box, type `services.msc` and press Enter. This will run the services management module.

2. Scroll down to the Windows Time entry and double-click on it.

3. From the Startup type drop-down box, choose Automatic, as shown in **Figure 6-1**. Click OK. From now on, your PC will automatically synchronize its time with the domain controller every time the PC starts. (Note: This setting is turned on by default, but there is a chance that it has been turned off on your system, so it's a good idea to double-check.)

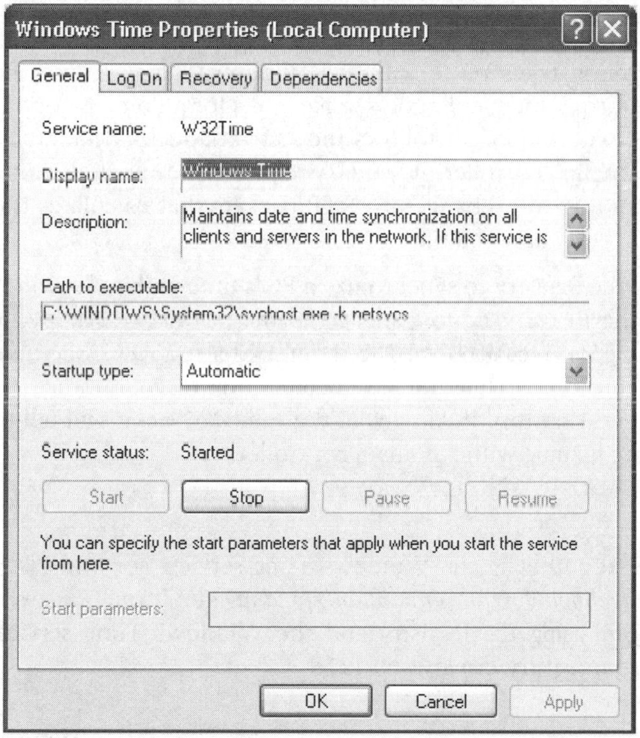

Figure 6-1. If you're connected to a domain, the Windows Time service will automatically connect to a domain controller to synchronize its clock

Using a command-line interface

At the command line, type net start w32time and press Enter. That will start the Windows Time service. To stop the service, at the command line type net stop w32time and press Enter. That will stop the Windows Time service. When you use the command line to start the Windows Time service, the service only runs for that single session. If you want the service to start every time you start XP you can use the service's management module, or you can use the *sc.exe* utility (run sc /config for more information).

Discussion

Only computers running Windows XP Professional can connect to domains, so XP Professional has Windows Time service, while the XP Home Edition does not. By default, the Windows Time service runs automatically on Windows XP Professional computers.

Time synchronization takes place with the Windows Time service during system startup. During startup, the Net Logon service looks for a domain controller that can synchronize time with the PC. It follows the Active Directory hierarchy. When the service finds a domain controller, it sends a request for time and waits for a reply. The communication is an exchange of SNTP packets that calculates the time offset and the roundtrip delay between the two computers.

You can also use the Registry to synchronize a PC's time with a domain controller on stsartup. Open the Registry Editor, and go to the key HKEY_LOCAL_MACHINE\SYSTEM\ CurrentControlSet\Services\W32Time\Parameters. Create a REG_SZ value called Type and give it the value Nt5DS. That will tell the computer to synchronize its time with a domain controller on startup. If you give it the value NoSync, it will tell the computer not to synchronize its time with a domain controller.

See Also

For more details about using the Windows Time service, see *http://www.microsoft. com/technet/prodtechnol/winxppro/maintain/xpmanaged/27_xpwts.mspx*. For more in-formation about using the Registry and the Windows Time service, see *http:// www.winguides.com/registry/display.php/1118*.

6.2 Automatically Setting the Time on a PC Not Connected to a Domain

Problem

You're on a PC that is not connected to a domain, and you want the PC to automatically have its clock set to the proper time without your intervention.

Solution

Using a graphical user interface

1. Double-click the time on the right side of the Taskbar.

2. From the Date and Time Properties dialog box that appears, click the Internet Time tab.

3. Check the box next to Automatically synchronize with an Internet time server (Figure 6-2). You can choose from a list of servers on the Server drop-down box. To synchronize the time immediately, click Update Now.

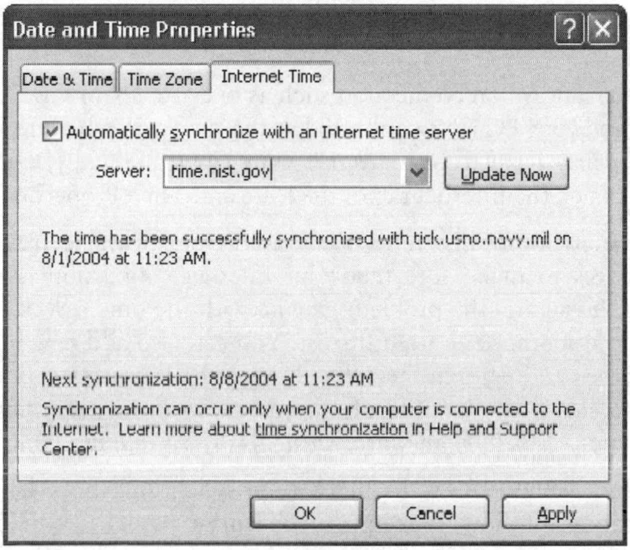

Figure 6-2. XP includes the built-in ability to automatically synchronize your clock with an Internet time server

4. Click OK. Your PC will now synchronize with a time server once a week.

Using the Registry

The default amount of time for synchronizing with a time server is once a week. But you can change that schedule to any you want, using the Registry. Open the Registry Editor, and go to HKEY_LOCAL_MACHINE\SYSTEM\CurrentControlSet\Services\W32Time\ TimeProviders\NtpClient\SpecialPollInterval. Open SpecialPollInterval by double-clicking it, then select Decimal. For the value data, give it the interval, in seconds, that you want your time to be automatically updated. The default is 604,800, which is the number of seconds in a week. There are 86,400 seconds in a day, so if you want your time to synchronized daily, enter that number. Click OK and then exit the Registry.

Using downloadable software

There are many pieces of software available that make it easier to automatically synchronize the time, or give you extra options for time synchronization. A very good free one is SymmTime, which runs as a separate applet. In addition to automatically synchronizing your PC time with Internet time servers, it lets you create separate clocks that each display the time in different parts of the world. It's particularly useful if you do business across time zones or countries. You can download and use it for free from *http://www.ntp-systems.com/symmtime.asp*.

Discussion

If you don't have an always-on connection such as over a LAN or via a cable modem or DSL modem, and your PC isn't connected at the time it is scheduled to do a synchronization, you may have to synchronize your clock manually, by clicking the Update Now button on the Internet tab of the Date and Time Properties dialog box.

Sometimes, synchronization fails. If so, there are several ways to troubleshoot the problem. First, check to make sure that your Internet connection is working and you're connected. If you are, the problem may be with the time server—it might not be available. Choose another one from the list. You can also add new time servers to the list by typing their addresses in the Server box on the Internet tab of the Date and Time Properties dialog box. For lists of servers, go to *http://www.boulder.nist.gov/ timefreq/service/time-servers.html* and *http://tycho.usno.navy.mil/ntp.html*.

Some personal and network firewalls block time synchronization. Check the firewall's documentation for how to allow synchronization. The Windows Firewall allows time synchronization, so if you're using that, you should not have a problem. Windows Time uses UDP port 123 to do its synchronization, so if your firewall is blocking it, open that port, and synchronization should work.

Finally, on the Date & Time tab of the Date and Time Properties dialog box, make sure that your computer is using the proper date. If your date is incorrect, your PC will not synchronize with Internet time servers.

See Also

MS KB 262680, "A List of the Simple Network Time Protocol Time Servers That Are Available on the Internet"

6.3 Changing the System Name

Problem

You want to change the name of your computer, or a computer on a domain on which you have administrative privileges.

Solution

Using a graphical user interface

1. Right-click My Computer, choose Properties, and click the Computer Name tab.
2. Click the Change button.
3. In the Computer Name Changes dialog box, shown in Figure 6-3, type in your new computer name in the Computer Name box. Click OK and then click OK again.

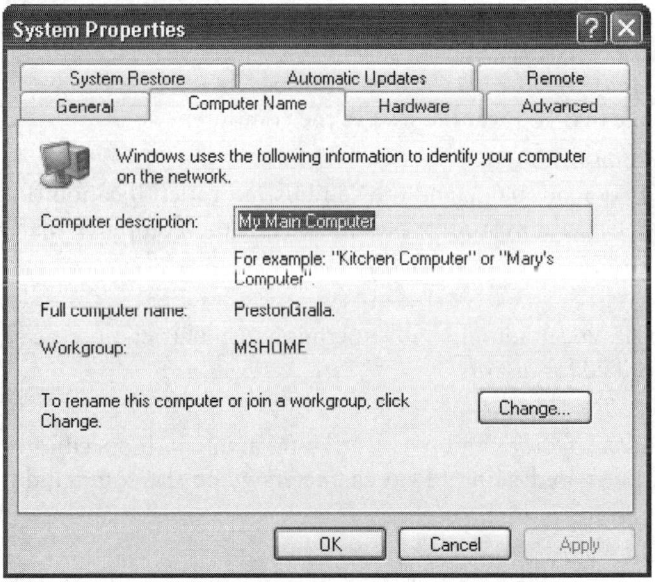

Figure 6-3. The Computer Name Changes dialog box

> You can only use this technique on your own computer, not on another computer in a domain to which you're attached.

Using a command-line interface

If you want to rename a computer that is a member of an Active Directory domain, you can use the `netdom` tool. You'll be able to rename not just the computer you're attached to, but others as well, as long as you have administrative permission to do so on the PC. You can do this only on Windows XP Professional, not on Home Edition.

To change a computer's name, do the following:

1. Install the Windows XP Support Tools from the *Support\Tools* folder on the Windows XP Professional CD.

2. At the command line, use the `netdom` command line tool to rename a computer, using this syntax:

```
> netdom renamecomputer machine /newname:new_computername /userd:domainname\
administrator_id /passwordd:* /usero:local_admin /passwordo:* /reboot:seconds
before automatic reboot
```

Following is an explanation of the syntax:

Machine
> The current name of the computer that you want to rename.

New_computername
> The new name that you want to give to the computer.

Domainname\administrator_id
> The NetBIOS domain name and the administrator identification (ID) of the user account that has administrative permissions to the computer that you want to rename.

Local_admin
> A user who has local administrative permissions. This can be the same account that you specified for */userd*.

The asterisk symbol (*)
> Used for the */passwordd:* and */passwordo:* parameters. It specifies that the password should be typed with hidden characters when the command is submitted, for security purposes.

Seconds before automatic reboot, in seconds
> The amount of time, in seconds, before the computer restarts after it is renamed. If you don't specify this parameter, the computer will have to be restarted manually.

/userd
> The user account used to make the connection with the domain specified by the */Domain* argument.

/usero
> The user account for making the connection with the trusting domain.

Discussion

Using a graphical user interface

When using the Computer Name tab, make sure you do not confuse the computer description with the computer name. The computer name is what will show up on a network and will be what your computer is called. The description allows you to provide more details about the computer, for example, "computer in the downstairs living room."

Using a command-line interface

When you use netdom to rename a computer, you may see the following, lengthy message: "This operation will rename the computer "Mycomputer" to "Yourcomputer." Certain services, such as certification authority, rely on a fixed computer name. If any services of this type are running on "Mycomputer", a computer name change would have an adverse impact." You'll then be prompted to proceed. If you don't want this warning to appear, and don't want to be prompted to proceed, use the /force switch when you enter the netdom command in addition to the other parameters you use.

See Also

MS KB 298593, "How To Use the Netdom.exe Utility to Rename a Computer in Windows XP"

6.4   Create a Multiboot Menu

Problem

You want to create a multiboot menu that will allow you choose from several different customized versions of Windows—for example, one without a boot screen, one that will automatically create a log about the boot process, and so on.

Solution

Using a graphical user interface

The *boot.ini* file, a plain text file found in your root C:\ folder, determines how XP starts up and controls a variety of startup options, including whether to use the XP splash screen when XP starts, whether to create a log file about the boot process, and so on.

You might not be able to see *boot.ini*, because it's a system file, and if you can see it, you might not be able to edit it, because it's a read-only file. To make it visible, launch Windows Explorer, and choose View → Tools → Folder Options → View and select the radio button "Show Hidden Files and Folders." To make it a file you can edit, right-click on it in Windows Explorer, choose Properties, uncheck the Read-Only box, and click on OK.

If you have only one operating system on your PC (XP), *boot.ini* will look something like this:

```
[boot loader]
timeout=30
default=multi(0)disk(0)rdisk(0)partition(2)\WINDOWS
[operating systems]
multi(0)disk(0)rdisk(0)partition(2)\WINDOWS="Microsoft Windows XP Home Edition"
/fastdetect
```

In this instance, your PC will boot straight into XP; no menu will be displayed to give you any other startup choices.

If you have more than one operating system on your PC, in the following instance XP Home Edition and Windows 2000 Professional, Windows *boot.ini* would look like this:

```
[boot loader]
timeout=30
default=multi(0)disk(0)rdisk(0)partition(1)\WINDOWS
[operating systems]
multi(0)disk(0)rdisk(0)partition(1)\WINDOWS="Microsoft Windows XP Home Edition"
/fastdetect
multi(0)disk(0)rdisk(0)partition(2)\WINNT="Windows 2000 Professional" /fastdetect
```

In this instance, when you boot your PC, a menu would be displayed, allowing you to choose between booting into XP Home Edition or Windows 2000 Professional.

Even if you have only one version of XP installed, though, you can create a multiboot menu that will let you choose to load XP with different parameters by editing the *boot.ini* file. For example, for menu choices, you might have your normal operating system; the operating system loading in a mode that lets you trace any startup problems; and the operating system loading in safe mode. To do it, create separate entries for each new operating system choice. For example, for the version of the operating system that traces potential startup problems, you could create this entry:

```
multi(0)disk(0)rdisk(0)partition(1)\WINDOWS="Trace Problems XP Home Edition"
/fastdetect /bootlog /sos
```

This entry creates a startup log and displays information about the drivers and other operating system information as it loads.

For the version of the operating system that loads in Safe Mode but that still allows networking, you could create this entry:

```
multi(0)disk(0)rdisk(0)partition(1)\WINDOWS="Safe Start XP Home Edition" /fastdetect
/safeboot:network
```

So the *boot.ini* file would look like this, assuming that you want the menu to display for 30 seconds, and you want normal XP startup to be the default:

```
[boot loader]
timeout=30
default=multi(0)disk(0)rdisk(0)partition(1)\WINDOWS
[operating systems]
multi(0)disk(0)rdisk(0)partition(1)\WINDOWS="Microsoft Windows XP Home Edition"
/fastdetect
multi(0)disk(0)rdisk(0)partition(1)\WINDOWS="Trace Problems XP Home Edition"
/fastdetect /bootlog /sos
multi(0)disk(0)rdisk(0)partition(1)\WINDOWS="Safe Start XP Home Edition" /fastdetect
/safeboot:network
```

To edit the file, open it with a text editor such as Notepad. Following is a typical *boot.ini* file for a PC that has two operating systems installed on it—Windows XP Home Edition and Windows Me:

```
[boot loader]
timeout=30
default=multi(0)disk(0)rdisk(0)partition(1)\WINDOWS
[operating systems]
multi(0)disk(0)rdisk(0)partition(1)\WINDOWS="Microsoft Windows XP Home Edition"
/fastdetect
multi(0)disk(0)rdisk(0)partition(2)\WINNT="Windows 2000 Professional" /fastdetect
```

As you can see, there are two sections in the file: [boot loader] and [operating systems]. To customize your menu and startup options, edit the entries in each section. Before editing *boot.ini*, make a copy of it and save it under a different name (such as *boot.ini.old*), so that you can revert to it if you cause problems when you edit the file.

Following are details about how to edit the entries in each section:

[boot loader]

This section controls how the boot process works; it specifies the default operating system, and how long a user has to make a selection from a boot menu if a boot menu has been enabled. The timeout value specifies, in seconds, how long to display the menu and wait for a selection before loading the default operating system; if you want a delay of 15 seconds, for example, enter 15 for the value. Use a value of 0 if you want the default operating system to immediately boot. If you want the menu to be displayed indefinitely and stay onscreen until a selection is made, use a value of –1. The default value specifies which entry in the [operating system] section is the default operating system. (It is used even if there is only one operating system in the [operating system] section.) To change the default operating system, edit the setting, in our example, to default=multi(0)disk(0)rdisk(0)partition(2)\WINNT.

So in our example, if you were going to change the menu settings so that the screen appeared for 10 seconds before loading the default operating system, and the default operating system is Windows 2000 Professional, the section would read:

```
[boot loader]
timeout=10
default=multi(0)disk(0)rdisk(0)partition(2)\WINNT
```

`[operating system]`

This section specifies which operating systems are present on the computer, and detailed options for each one. XP uses the Advanced RISC Computing (ARC) path to specify the location of the boot partition. In our example, the ARC path is:

```
multi(0)disk(0)rdisk(0)partition(2)\WINDOWS
```

The first parameter, which identifies the disk controller, should be 0. The second parameter, the disk parameter, should also be 0. The `rdisk` parameter specifies the disk number on the controller that has the boot partition. The numbers start at 0. So if you have three hard disks installed, and the second hard disk has the boot partition, the setting would be `rdisk(1)`. The `partition` parameter identifies the partition number of the boot partition. Partitions start with the number 1. The final section, which in our example is `\WINDOWS`, specifies the path to the folder where the operating system is installed.

To the right of the ARC path, in the example, is `="Microsoft Windows XP Home Edition" /fastdetect`. The words within quotes are what will appear on the boot menu next to the entry. You can change this to whatever you wish to customize the text on the menu; if you'd like, you can call it "My Favorite Operating System" or anything else you want. The `/fastdetect` switch disables the detection of serial and parallel devices, and so allows for faster booting. (The detection of these devices isn't normally required in XP, because the functions are performed by Plug and Play drivers, and so as a general rule, it's a good idea to use the `/fastdetect` switch. The `/fastdetect` switch is only one of many that can be used in the *boot.ini* file to customize how the operating system loads. Table 6-1 lists others you can use as well.

Table 6-1. Switches for boot.ini

Switch	What it does
/BASEVIDEO	Starts XP using the standard VGA driver. It's of most use if you can't boot normally because of a video driver problem.
/BOOTLOG	Logs information about the boot process to the file *ntbtlogl.txt* in the *C:\Windows* folder.
/CRASHDEBUG	Loads the debugger at boot, but the debugger remains inactive unless a crash occurs.
/DEBUG	Loads the debugger at boot and runs it.
/FASTDETECT	Disables the detection of serial and parallel devices.
MAXMEM:*n*	Specifies the maximum amount of RAM that XP can use.
/NOGUIBOOT	Does not allow the XP splash screen to load during boot.

Table 6-1. Switches for boot.ini (continued)

Switch	What it does
/NODEBUG	Stops the debugger from loading.
/SAFEBOOT: switch	Forces XP to boot into the safe mode specified by the `switch` parameter, which can be `minimal`, `network`, or `minimal(alternate shell)`. In minimal safe mode, only the minimum set of drivers are loaded necessary to start XP. In network-safe mode, the minimum set of drivers plus networking drivers are loaded. In `minimal(alternate shell)` the minimum set of drivers are loaded and XP boots into the command prompt.
/SOS	Displays the name of each driver as it loads and gives descriptions of what is occurring during the boot process. It also offers other information, including the XP build number, the service pack number, the number of processors on the system, and the amount of installed memory.

When you've finished editing the *boot.ini* file, save it. The next time you start your computer, its settings will go into effect.

So, in our example, if we wanted the menu to appear for 45 seconds, the default operating system to be Windows 2000, and the XP splash screen to be turned off when we choose to load XP, the *boot.ini* file would look like this:

```
[boot loader]
timeout=45
default=multi(0)disk(0)rdisk(0)partition(2)\WTNNT
[operating systems]
multi(0)disk(0)rdisk(0)partition(1)\WINDOWS="Microsoft Windows XP Home Edition" /
fastdetect /noguiboot
multi(0)disk(0)rdisk(0)partition(2)\WINNT="Windows 2000 Professional" /fastdetect
```

Discussion

If you've installed another operating system in addition to XP on your system, your PC automatically starts up with a multiboot menu, which allows you to choose which operating system you want to run. The menu stays live for 30 seconds, and a screen countdown tells you how long you have to make a choice from the menu. After the 30 seconds elapse, it boots into your default operating system, which is generally the last operating system that you installed. To change that menu and your startup options, edit *boot.ini*.

See Also

Advanced Startup Manager will let you create different profiles for starting XP. It's shareware; the registration fee is $19.95. Download it from *http://www.rayslab.com/startup_manager/startup_manager.html*. Also see MS KB 314081, "The purpose of the Boot.ini file in Windows XP."

6.5 Using Virtual PC to Run Multiple Operating Systems Simultaneously

Problem

You want to run multiple operating systems simultaneously on the same computer.

Solution

Using a graphical user interface

Microsoft's Virtual PC, available for between $100 and $120, will let you run multiple operating systems on the same computer; it can run all versions of Windows since Windows 95, as well as Linux, IBM OS/2, and others. This recipe cannot go into a full description of the entire configuration, installation, and use of Virtual PC, but here are the basics of how to install and use it:

1. Install Virtual PC from the CD. The first time you run the program, the New Virtual Machine Wizard will start. For each extra operating system you want to install, you need a virtual machine, so follow the wizard's instructions for creating a virtual machine.

    Before installing Virtual PC, make sure that you have enough physical RAM to run multiple operating systems on your PC. Microsoft offers these guidelines: Figure that you need 128MB for XP (either Professional or Home Edition) as a baseline, and then add the physical memory requirements of each additional operating system you want to add. Microsoft claims that Windows 95 requires 32MB; Windows 98 64MB; Windows ME 96MB; Windows NT 4 64MB; and Windows 2000 Professional 96MB. As a practical matter, though, those requirements are too slim. You should have at least 512MB of memory to run Virtual PC, and more than that if you plan to run more than two operating systems simultaneously.

2. If you aren't sure what operating system you plan to install on the virtual machine you create, choose "Use default settings to create a virtual machine" from the wizard. This will create a standard virtual machine that you can later customize, depending on the operating system you plan to install on the virtual machine.

3. If you know what operating system you plan to install on the virtual machine you create, choose "Create a virtual machine" from the wizard. That will let you customize the machine for the operating system. When you are prompted for the operating system you plan to install, choose it from the drop-down list.

4. Once you've installed a virtual machine and want to install a new operating system, run Virtual PC. The Virtual PC Console will display. Select the virtual machine onto which you want to install an operating system and choose Action → Start.

5. When you see the prompt to reboot and select a boot device or insert boot media, insert the startup or setup disk of the new operating system into the appropriate drive, and follow the instructions for installing the new operating system.

6. When you want to run the new operating system simultaneously with XP, start Virtual PC, and from the Virtual PC console, double-click the virtual machine that has the operating system you want to run in addition to XP.

Discussion

It can't be stressed enough how important it is to have enough memory on your system if you want to run multiple operating systems. Assume that you should have at least 512MB of memory, and preferably more. Virtual PC can support a total of up to 4GB for all operating systems, including the host. The maximum that any single operating system can use is 3.56GB.

When you run an operating system inside a virtual machine, the operating system must have the proper drivers in order to run. Windows XP drivers won't be used; instead the operating system drivers must be used. Make sure that in addition to the operating system, you have any necessary drivers as well. Each virtual machine can support up to four network adapters.

As a default, the operating systems are completely separate from one another. So, for example, you cannot cut and paste between them. However, you can install Virtual Machine Additions, which will allow for integration between operating systems, with features such as drag-and-drop and cut-and-paste between windows in different operating systems, and folder sharing. You'll need to install the Virtual Machine Additions on each operating system that you want to be used in this way. To do it, run Virtual PC and then run the virtual machine to whose operating system you want to add Virtual Machine Additions. Then from the Actions menu, choose Install or Update Virtual Machine Additions, and follow the Setup Wizard.

See Also

VMWare Workstation, available from *http://www.vmware.com* works like Virtual PC and lets you run multiple operating systems on the same computer. It requires XP Professional and won't work on the Home Edition.

MS KB 833506, "Virtual PC 2004 stops responding when it starts a virtual machine," and MS KB 833134, "The virtual machine networking settings in Virtual PC 2004"

6.6 Performing a Clean Boot

Problem

You want to perform a clean boot so that you can troubleshoot system problems and error messages when you cannot determine the cause of the problems. You then want to be able to track down the source of the problems.

Using a graphical user interface

1. Log on as an administrator.
2. In the Start menu or at the command line, type `msconfig` and press Enter. The System Configuration Utility runs.
3. On the General tab, click Selective Startup, and clear the Process System.ini File, Process Win.ini File, and Load Startup Items checkboxes.

You cannot clear the Use Original Boot.ini checkbox.

4. On the Services tab, select the Hide All Microsoft Services checkbox, and then click Disable All.
5. Click OK, and then click Restart. This will restart your computer. You'll now be able to see whether the symptoms still occur.
6. When Windows restarts, examine the General tab of the System Configuration Utility to see whether the checkboxes you've deselected are still cleared. If none are checked, you've done a clean boot. If your problems do not recur, you can now try to track down the source of the problem.
7. Run the System Configuration Utility again, and on the General tab check the box next to Process System.ini File, click OK, and then click Restart to restart XP. If the problem continues, the issue is with an entry in your *system.ini* file. If the problem does not recur, repeat this step for the Process Win.ini File, Load Startup Items, and Load System Services checkboxes until the problem occurs again. After the problem occurs, the last item that you selected is the item where the issue is occurring.

Discussion

If after you run the System Configuration Utility for the first time, your system reboots, none of the checkboxes are selected, and the issue is not resolved, repeat steps 2 through 5, except this time also clear the Load System Services checkbox on the General tab. This will temporarily disable XP services such as Networking, Plug and Play, Event Logging, and Error Reporting. After doing this, repeat steps 6 and 7.

Clearing the Load System Services checkbox permanently deletes all restore points used by the System Restore utility, so if you need to use restore points, don't clear the checkbox. Also, if you need to use an XP service to test the issue, don't clear the checkbox.

If you disable Load System Services, you might not be able to install a program, and may get the error message "The Windows Installer service could not be accessed. Contact your support personnel to verify that the Windows Installer service is properly registered." (Note: Windows Installer, as well as Add/Remove Programs, is not immediately available in Safe Mode and needs a manual start, as detailed in the next paragraph.)

To get around the problem, manually start the Windows Installer Service before installing any programs. To do it, right-click My Computer and select Manage. In the left-hand pane, click Services and Applications, and then click Services. After you do that, in the right pane, right-click Windows Installer, and click Start. The Windows Installer Service will run, so you should be able to install software.

See Also

MS KB 310353, "How to perform a clean boot in Windows XP," and MS KB 281770, "How to perform clean-boot troubleshooting for Windows 2000"

6.7 Shutting Down Unnecessary Programs and Services that Run on Startup

Problem

You want to stop unnecessary programs and services from running on startup, so that you can speed up the performance of your PC.

Solution

Stopping programs from running on startup

Stopping programs from running at startup is particularly difficult, because there is no single place you can go to stop them all. Some run because they're in the Startup folder, others because of Registry settings, and so on. So you'll have to combine several techniques to stop them from starting up automatically when you turn on or reboot your PC.

Using a graphical user interface

There are several techniques you can use with a graphical user interface to stop programs from running on startup. Again, you'll have to combine several, and not rely on a single one.

Clean out the Startup and Scheduled Tasks folders. The Startup folder contains shortcuts that each run a program whenever you start or reboot your PC, so you can halt a program from running on startup by deleting shortcuts found in it.

The Startup folder can be found in *C:\Documents and Settings\<User Name>\Start Menu\Programs\Startup*, where *<User Name>* is your Windows logon name. Delete the shortcuts of any programs you don't want to run on startup. As with any shortcuts, when you delete them, you're only deleting the shortcut, not the program itself. (You can also clear out the startup items by going to Start → Programs → Startup and right-clicking on items you want to remove.) Do the same for *C:\Documents and Settings\All Users\Start Menu\Programs\Startup* and *C:\Documents and Settings\ Default User\Start Menu\Programs\Startup*.

Next, clean out your Scheduled Tasks folder. Go to *C:\WINDOWS\Tasks*, and delete the shortcuts of any programs that you don't want to automatically run on a schedule.

 You can bypass all the programs in your Startup folder on an as-needed basis. To stop XP from loading any programs in the Startup folder, hold down the Shift key during boot-up. No programs in the Startup folder will be run, but the items will still remain there, so that they will start up as they would normally the next time you boot.

The System Configuration Utility. Deleting shortcuts out of the Startup and Schedule Tasks folders will stop many programs from running at startup, but it won't kill all of them. Probably the best all-around tool for keeping programs from running is the System Configuration Utility, shown in Figure 6-4. To run it, type `msconfig` at a command prompt and press Enter.

To stop a program from running at startup, click the Startup tab and uncheck the box next to it. It can sometimes be difficult to understand what programs are listed on the Startup tab. Some, such as America Online, are clearly labeled. But often, you'll see a phrase or collection of letters, such as *ctfmon*. In this case, *ctfmons.exe* is a program that activates Alternative User Input Text Input Processor (TIP) and the Microsoft Office Language Bar, which provides for text input services such as speech recognition and handwriting recognition. If you don't need those services, it's a good idea to stop this program from running on startup.

To get more information about a listing, expand the width of the Command column near the top of the Startup tab. Expand it enough and you'll see the startup command that the program issues, including its location, such as *C:\WINDOWS*

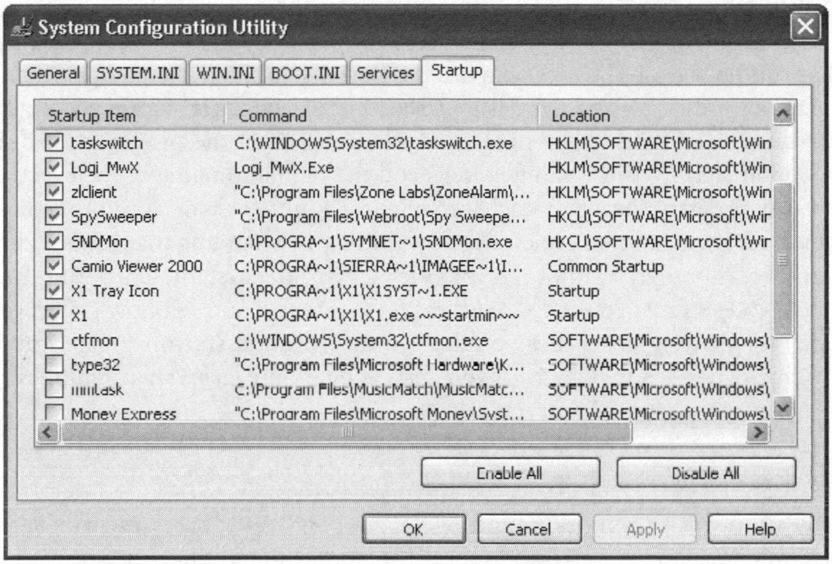

Figure 6-4. The Startup tab of the System Configuration Utility is the best place to halt programs from running on startup

System32\ctfmon.exe. The directory location should be another hint to help you know the name of the program.

That won't always help, though. To get more information about any particular program, do a Google search on its filename, and most of the time you'll get useful information about what it is, what it does, and whether you need it. You can also go to the WinTasks Process Library at *http://www.liutilities.com/products/wintaskspro/ processlibrary/*, which lists many programs that run on startup, and details what they are and whether they're necessary.

When stopping programs from running at startup, it's best to stop them one at a time rather than in groups. You want to make sure that you're not causing any system problems by stopping them. So stop one and restart your PC. If your PC runs fine, then stop another program and restart. Continue doing this until you've cleared all the programs you don't want to run automatically.

Each time you uncheck a box and restart your PC, you'll get a warning, telling you that you've used the System Configuration Utility to disable a program from starting automatically. If you don't want to see that warning appear, disable it by checking in the proper box in the dialog.

After you've used the System Configuration Utility to identify programs that run on startup, you may want to try disabling them from with the programs themselves. So run each program that starts automatically, and see if you can find a setting that will allow you to halt it from running on startup.

Using the Registry

The System Configuration Utility won't necessarily let you identify and kill all programs that run on startup, but you can use the Registry to find others. Open the Registry Editor, and go to `HKEY_CURRENT_USER\Software\Microsoft\Windows\CurrentVersion\Run`. Listed in the right pane will be some of the programs that automatically run at startup. The Data field tells you the path and name of the executable so that you can determine what each program is. Right-click on any program you don't want to run and choose Delete. That will kill any programs that run specific to your logon. To kill programs that run for every user of the system, go to `HKEY_LOCAL_MACHINE\SOFTWARE\Microsoft\Windows\CurrentVersion\Run` and follow the same instructions for deleting other files you don't want to run at startup. Again, for help deciding which to kill and which to run, try Google and *http://www.liutilities.com/products/wintaskspro/processlibrary*.

Disable services that run at startup

Constantly running in the background of XP are services—processes that help the operating system run or that provide support to applications. Many of these services launch automatically at startup. And while you need many of them, there are also many that aren't required and that can slow your system down while they run in the background. Here's how to stop unnecessary ones from running.

Using a graphical user interface

There are several techniques you can use with a graphical user interface to stop services from running on startup. You should combine several, and not rely on a single one.

The System Configuration Utility. You can disable services at startup by using the System Configuration Utility, in a similar way that you halt programs from running at startup, except that you use the Services tab instead of the Startup tab. Other than that, you use the utility the same, as outlined previously in this recipe.

The Services Computer Management Console. When you disable a service through System Configuration Utility, there's often no way to know what it does. So an even better way of disabling services at startup is via the Services Computer Management Console, shown in Figure 6-5. Run it by typing `services.msc` at the command prompt. The Services Computer Management Console includes a description of all services, so that you can know ahead of time whether it's one you want to turn off. It also lets you pause the service, so that you can test out your machine with the service off, to see whether it's needed or not.

After you run the console, click the Extended tab. This view will show you a description of each service in the left-hand pane when you highlight the service. The Startup

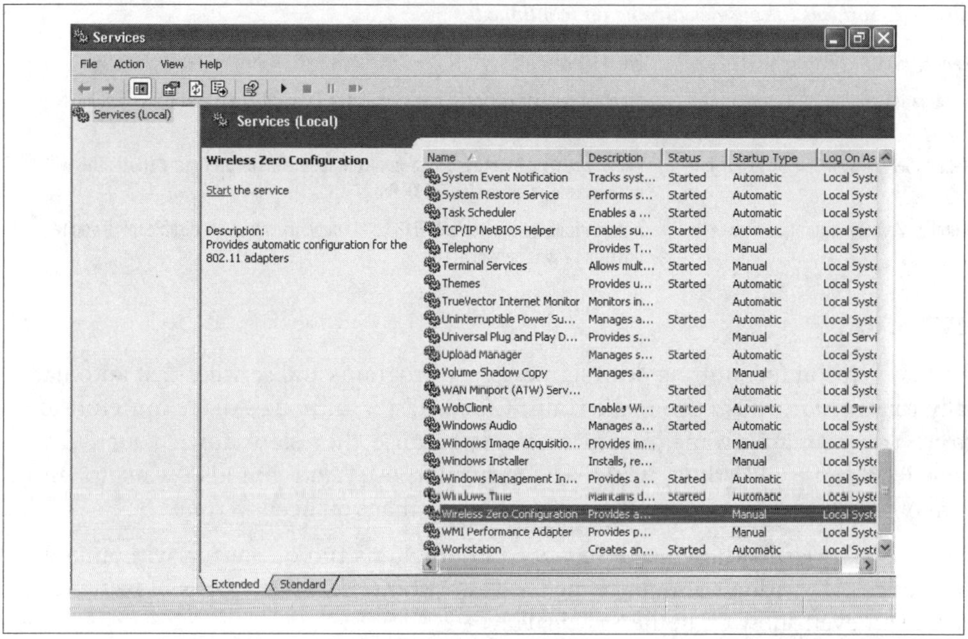

Figure 6-5. The Services Computer Management Console is a better tool than the System Configuration Utility for halting services that run on startup, because it includes descriptions of each service and an easy way to stop them from running on startup

Type column shows you which services launch on startup—any services with an Automatic in that column launch on startup. Click that column to sort together all the services that automatically launch on startup. Then highlight each of those services, and read the descriptions.

When you find a service you want to disable, right-click it and choose Properties. In the Properties dialog box that appears, chose Manual from the Startup type drop-down list. The service won't start automatically from now on, but you can start it manually via the console. If you want the service disabled so that it can't be run, choose Disabled. To test the effects of turning off the service, turn off any services that you don't want to run by clicking "Stop the service" in the left pane, or by right-clicking on the service and choosing Stop.

Table 6-2 lists common services you might want to halt from running at startup.

Table 6-2. Services to consider turning off

Service	What it does
Portable Media Serial Number	Retrieves the serial number of a portable music player attached to your PC.
Task Scheduler	Schedules unattended tasks to be run. If you don't schedule any unattended tasks, turn it off.
Uninterruptible Power Supply	Manages an Uninterruptible Power Supply (UPS) connected to your PC.

Table 6-2. Services to consider turning off (continued)

Service	What it does
Automatic Updates	Automatically checks for Windows updates. (You can check manually by going to *http://windowsupdate.microsoft.com*.)
Telnet (Service available on XP Pro only)	Allows a remote user to log in to your computer and run programs. (Note: This will not be found on all versions of XP Pro.)
Wireless Zero Configuration Service	Automatically configures a WiFi (802.11) network card. Only disable this if you're not using a WiFi network card.

Discussion

The main reason for shutting down unnecessary programs and services that automatically run on startup isn't to make your PC boot faster, although that's a useful side effect. You primarily want to turn them off because they slow down your PC by using RAM and CPU time, while serving no purpose. And you also want to turn them off because they may conflict with programs that you need to run.

You'd be surprised at how many services and programs run on startup without your knowledge. Many don't announce themselves or show any visible signs of being run; they won't even show up in the System Tray.

Some programs, of course, such as antivirus software, should run automatically at startup and always run on your computer. But many other programs, such as instant messenger software, serve no purpose by being run at startup. And while you need a variety of background services running on your PC in order for XP to function, there are many unnecessary services that run on startup—for example, on many systems, the Wireless Zero Configuration Service runs to automatically configure a WiFi (802. 11) network card, even though no such card is present in the system. You can also turn off Simple Service Discovery Protocol (SSDP) and Universal Plug and Play (UPnP).

See Also

WinTasks Standard and WinTasks Professional will both help you find out what programs and processes automatically load on startup, and then shut them down for you. The Standard version costs $29.95, and the Professional version costs $69.95. The Professional version includes many extra features, such as logging, a scripting language, the ability to list information about DLLs, and more. For information, go to *http://www.liutilities.com*. You can try them before buying them.

An excellent program for managing all phases of startup is Autoruns, available at *http://www.sysinternals.com/ntw2k/freeware/autoruns.shtml*.

6.8   Speeding Up Shutdown Time

Problem

Windows XP takes what seems an inordinate amount of time to shut down, and you want to speed up your shutdown time.

Solution

If shutting down XP takes what seems to be an inordinate amount of time, there are steps you can take to speed up the shutdown process.

Using a graphical user interface

Don't have XP clear your paging file at shutdown

For security reasons, you can have XP clear your paging file of its contents whenever you shut down. But if extreme security isn't a high priority, doing this can significantly slow shutdown times. To shut down XP without clearing your page file, run the Registry Editor and go to `HKEY_LOCAL_MACHINE\SYSTEM\CurrentControlSet\Control\Session Manager\Memory Management`. Change the value of `ClearPageFileAtShutdown` to 0. Close the Registry and restart your computer. Now, whenever you turn off XP, the paging file won't be cleared, and you should be able to shut down more quickly.

Turn off unnecessary services

Services take time to shut down, so the fewer you run, the faster you can shut down. Run the Services snap in to the Microsoft Management Console (MMC) by typing `services.msc` at a command prompt or the run box, and use it to see what services are running and to disable any unnecessary ones from running on startup. Consider shutting down the Nvidia driver helper service, the Indexing service, and the Machine Debug Manager. And if you are using a computer that doesn't use wireless networking, turn off Zero Wireless Configuration.

Discussion

Running unnecessary services is frequently the main cause of slow shutdown times, but running unnecessary software can cause problems as well. Make sure to close all of your programs before shutting down XP.

Not having your paging file cleared at shutdown will generally not be a security problem. It's very unlikely someone will manage to get access to the paging file, more unlikely that they'll look there for sensitive data, and even more unlikely that any sensitive data will be found there.

See Also

When you shut down XP, each running process is given 20 seconds to shut down; if it doesn't shut down in that time, you get a "Wait, End Task, or Cancel" dialog box, which prompts you to wait for another 20 seconds, stop the process, or cancel the shutdown process. If you find that some processes need more time to shut down, you can give them more than 20 seconds. For information on how to do this, see MS KB 305788, "How To Increase Shutdown Time So That Processes Can Quit Properly in Windows XP"

6.9   Changing Your Boot Screen

Problem

You want to change the screen that you see when XP boots.

Solution

Using downloadable software

The best tool for changing your startup screen is BootXP, shareware available from *http://www.bootxp.net*. (You can try it out for free, but if you continue to use it, there's a $7.95 registration fee.) To use it:

1. Download, install, and run the program. When you first run it, it asks where you want to store your boot screens. The default is *C:\WINDOWS\Resources\Bootscreens*. Unless you can think of a better place to keep them, use this folder. The software will create it for you.

2. Select the Your Boot Screens tab. If you have any graphics or boot screens in *C:\WINDOWS\Resources\Bootscreens*, the program displays a list of them.

3. If you don't have any boot screens stored, click the Get Boot Screens button to have BootXP search several web sites that have downloadable boot screens. (If you find any you like, download them to the folder where you've chosen to store your boot screens, such as *C:\Windows\Resources\Bootscreens*.)

> You can also create boot screens from an existing graphic. Put the graphic in *C:\Windows\Resources\Bootscreens*, so that, when you open them in BootXP and click Convert To Boot Screen, BootXP will convert them to the format Windows XP requires for boot screens: 640 × 480 pixels and 16-color. Once you have them in the right format, use BootXP to select any as your boot screen.

4. To choose a new boot screen, click the file in the list, and click OK. The program shows the graphic you've chosen on the left side of the screen, and how it looks as a boot screen on the right.

5. To confirm this is the boot screen you want, click the "Set As Your Boot Screen" button.

6. The next time you start XP, your new boot screen will be used.

Discussion

Be careful when going straight to Internet sites to download boot screens for your XP system. There are quite a few sites that specialize in boot screens, but when you install boot screens that you download from them, you may find that spyware rides on the back of the screens. If you download a boot screen and it includes an installation program, be wary, because the installation program often also installs spyware on your system.

If you decide to make your own boot screens using a graphics program, make sure they are 640 × 480 pixels and 16-color.

See Also

Another good program for selecting boot screen is ChangerXP, which is shareware available from *http://www.nihuo.com/changerxp.html*. In addition to changing boot screens, it also will change your wallpaper and Internet Explorer background.

6.10 Personalizing Your PC's Sounds

Problem

You want to personalize the sounds your PC makes for various system events, including recording new sounds of your own.

Solution

Using a graphical user interface

1. If a microphone didn't come with your PC, buy one and plug it into the microphone jack.

2. Open the Sound Recorder (Figure 6-6) by choosing Start → All Programs → Accessories → Sound Recorder, or typing *mmsys.cpl* at the Run box or command line and pressing Enter.

3. Click the Record button, record your sound clip, and when you're done, click the Stop button. When you record, speak in a normal tone of voice, about six

Figure 6-6. When you're recording with the Sound Recorder, Windows tells you how many seconds the sound will last

inches from the microphone. Keep the clip short, because you don't want sounds to last too long. A few seconds is ideal.

4. Choose File → Save and save the file to a folder. Note the location and the file-name (it ends in *.wav*). Exit the Sound Recorder.

5. Now that you've recorded the sound, you need to tell XP to use it. Choose Start → Control Panel → Sounds, Speech, and Audio Devices → Sounds and Audio Devices. On the Sounds and Audio Devices Properties dialog box that appears (Figure 6-7), click the Sounds tab. In the Program events list, select the event you want to associate with your sound.

6. Click Browse and locate the *.wav* file you just recorded (or the existing file you want to use). Select it and click OK. When the Sounds and Audio Devices Properties dialog box appears again, click OK.

7. From now on, Windows will use your sound with the associated event.

Discussion

Don't expect to record high-quality sounds with an inexpensive microphone, so if sound quality is important, buy a more expensive one. You can use any *.wav* sound with a Windows event, not just ones you record. Make sure when choosing a *.wav* sound to associate with an event that the sound only lasts a few seconds—you don't want it lasting well beyond the start of the event.

Many people use sounds from TV shows, movies, or popular music to associate with Windows events. The law governing such use is murky at best. Some lawyers say such files violate copyright laws; others say that they are covered by the fair use pro-vision of copyright laws, and so are legal. So follow your own conscience.

See Also

If you're looking for a place with a big selection of *.wav* files you can use to associate with Windows events, go to *http://www.wavcentral.com*.

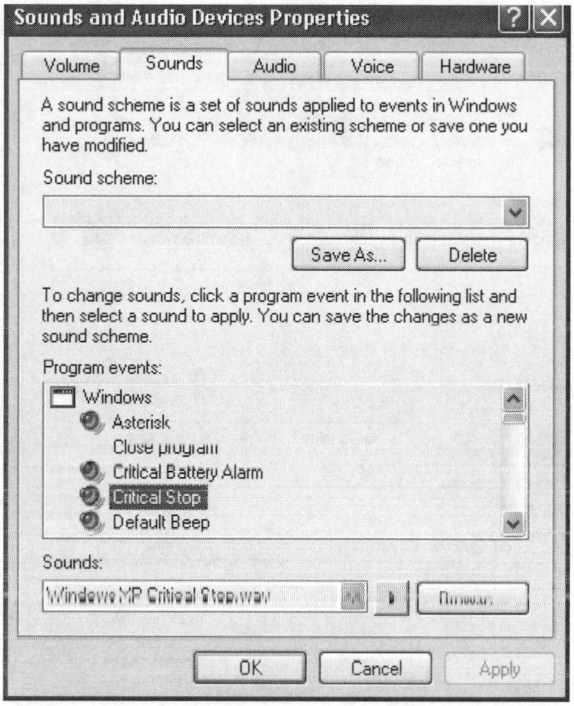

Figure 6-7. Choose the event you want to associate with a sound, and then click Browse to find the sound

6.11   Creating Power Schemes

Problem

You want to create different power schemes for your laptop—for example, one when it's plugged in at home, and another for maximum battery life when you're on an airplane on a cross-country trip.

Solution

Using a graphical user interface

1. Choose Control Panel → Performance and Maintenance → Power Options. The Power Options Properties dialog box appears.

2. Click the Power Schemes tab. This tab handles the most important power functions. It lets you customize how your laptop uses power when plugged in and when it runs on batteries. So you might have the laptop never turn off the power

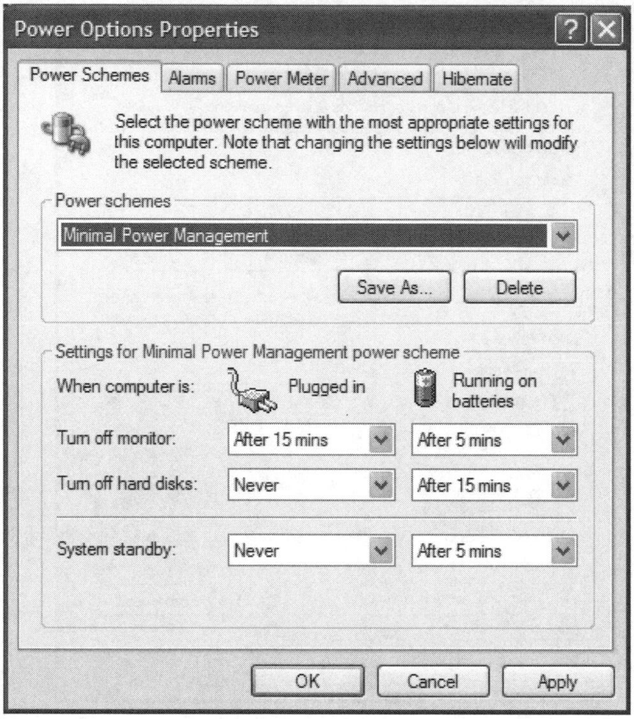

Power Options Properties ? X

Power Schemes | Alarms | Power Meter | Advanced | Hibernate

Select the power scheme with the most appropriate settings for this computer. Note that changing the settings below will modify the selected scheme.

Power schemes

Minimal Power Management

Save As... | Delete

Settings for Minimal Power Management power scheme

When computer is: Plugged in   Running on batteries

Turn off monitor: After 15 mins   After 5 mins

Turn off hard disks: Never   After 15 mins

System standby: Never   After 5 mins

OK | Cancel | Apply

Figure 6-8. One good way to save your batteries: Create separate power schemes for your laptop

to the LCD when it's plugged in, for example, and have it shut off the power to the LCD after 15 minutes when it runs on power.

3. To edit an existing scheme, choose your options from the drop-down boxes and click OK. For each scheme, you can choose options for when your laptop is running on batteries, and when it's plugged in. You choose when your system should turn off the monitor and hard disk after a specified time of inactivity. You also choose when your laptop should go into system standby. When your laptop goes into system standby, it goes into a very low power state, using only a few watts of power, just enough to retain the contents of RAM. Power is shut off to the hard drive, the LCD, the fan, and the CPU, so that it appears that the laptop is powered off. When you've made your choices, click OK.

4. To create an entirely new scheme, edit and existing scheme, choose Save As from the dialog box, and save it with a new name.

5. To use a power scheme, come back to the Power Options dialog box, choose the scheme you want to use from the drop-down list, and click OK.

Discussion

Your laptop will come configured with several different power schemes—for example, one that preserves the maximum amount of battery life, one that is used when the laptop is plugged in, one when you're making presentations on the road and so on. You may not need to change the power settings, but it's a good idea to look at them, in case you want to.

Using system standby

If you choose to use system standby, you can configure how it works by clicking on the Advanced tab of the Power Options Properties dialog box. It lets you decide whether to put the system into standby if you close the lid of the laptop, what to do when you press the laptop's power button, and what to do when you press the laptop's sleep button. Additionally, if you're worried about security, it lets you require that a password be used in order to wake up the laptop from standby. And it can put an icon that reports about your power on the Taskbar.

Setting power alarms

You can have your laptop alert you or take an action when it has little power left. To set alerts, click on the Alarms tab, and customize the settings for when to alert you—at what percent of battery life is left. There are two settings, one for lower battery alarm and one for a critical battery alarm. You can have the system alert you via text, via an audible alarm, or have it automatically go into standby or shut down. You can also have it automatically run a program when the batter reaches a certain level.

See Also

For more information about managing power on a laptop, see *http://www.microsoft.com/resources/documentation/windows/xp/all/proddocs/en-us/pwrmn_choose_power_scheme.mspx*.

6.12   Extending Battery Life on a Laptop

Problem

You want to extend the battery life of your laptop so that you can use it longer between recharges, for example on a cross-country plane flight.

Solution

Using a graphical user interface

- If you have a wireless network adapter and you're not using it, turn it off by right-clicking on its icon in the Notification Area and choosing Disable. Wireless and wired adapters can use a substantial amount of power—disabling yours could save you up to 20 minutes of battery life. If the wireless network adapter isn't built into your laptop but instead is a PC card, take the PC card out of the laptop.

- Lower the backlighting on your screen. Your screen takes up a substantial amount of electricity, and it most likely doesn't need to be lit up to its brightest level. Check your system documentation for how to change the lighting level.

- Use the right power scheme. XP includes a number of preset power schemes that you can use for various purposes. The schemes differ according to how long it takes for XP to shut off power to the monitor and hard disk when there is no system activity, or when the laptop should go into system standby. In system standby, power is cut to the hardware components you're not using, such as your monitor and your hard drive, but power is still supplied to your computer's memory so you don't lose your work. Get to the power schemes by choosing Control Panel → Performance and Maintenance → Power Options. For maximum battery life, choose Max Battery from the Power schemes drop-down list. Low Power Mode and Portable/Laptop are also good choices, although they don't preserve as much power as Max Battery. After you have selected your power scheme, click OK.

- Remove unused PCMCIA cards from your laptop, because they can use substantial amounts of power.

- Disconnect external drives, especially those that are USB-powered. External drives get power from your laptop and can be electricity hogs.

- Increase your RAM and decrease your swap file space to limit disk accesses. The fewer times you access your hard disk, the less power you'll use.

- Disable sounds. Each time a *.wav* file plays, you're using up juice unnecessarily.

Discussion

Take care when using laptop batteries that you fully discharge them before recharging them. Batteries have a "memory," so if you frequently use only half their power before recharging them, for example, you'll cut the amount of power that the battery retains.

There is at least one instance where trying to save power can interfere with the functioning of your PC. If you're using WiFi, don't use its power management feature, if it has one. You can lose your connection going into standby, and if you use EAP or other authentication methods, especially with separate secureID/cryptography devices, reconnecting can be very difficult.

See Also

For information about how to extend battery life by using standby and hibernate, see *http://www.microsoft.com/windows2000/techenthusiast/features/standby1127.asp*.

Many airplanes that make transcontinental flights have an Empower port, which can be used to power a laptop. You'll have to use a special adapter to connect your laptop to an Empower port. You can buy separate special adapters, or can instead buy a universal adapter that connects to Empower ports, AC power, and other power sources. Targus, among other hardware manufacturers, makes such a device.

6.13 Changing the Location of Your Startup Folders

Problem

You want to change the location of your startup folder to another drive or to another folder.

Solution

Using the Registry

You can turn any folder you want into the folder whose contents will be run on startup. To change the location of the current user's Startup folder, run the Registry Editor and then:

1. Go to `HKEY_CURRENT_USER\Software\Microsoft\Windows\CurrentVersion\Explorer\ User Shell Folders\Startup`.

2. The string value is `%USERPROFILE%\Start Menu\Programs\Startup`. `%USERPROFILE%\` refers to *C:\Documents and Settings\User* where *User* is the current user. Edit the string value to any folder on your hard disk. It doesn't have to be a subfolder of *C:\Documents and Settings\User*. For example, the location can be *C:\ YourStartup*.

3. Exit the Registry and reboot.

To change the location of the common Startup folder, go to `HKEY_LOCAL_MACHINE\ SOFTWARE\Microsoft\Windows\CurrentVersion\Explorer\User Shell Folders\Common Startup`. The string value will be `%ALLUSERSPROFILE%\Start Menu\Programs\Startup`. Change it to any folder you want, exit the Registry, and reboot.

Discussion

When you start XP, it automatically runs programs located in your system's Startup folders. There are more than one of these folders—one for each account, and one common one for all users. So when the system starts, it runs all programs in the account's Startup folder and the common Startup folder. The locations of the folders are:

- *C:\Documents and Settings\User\Start Menu\Programs\Startup* where *User* is the account of the current user
- *C:\Documents and Settings\All Users\Start Menu\Programs\Startup*

Shortcuts to any programs you put in either folder will be run at startup. To stop programs from running, remove their shortcuts from the folders.

 You can start XP without it running programs located in your Startup folders. You might want to do this if you're troubleshooting startup problems and want to see whether programs that automatically run at startup are causing the problems. To bypass the Startup folders, hold down the Shift key while you log on. When the logon dialog box appears, type in your user name and password, then hold down the Shift key and click on OK. Keep the Shift key depressed until the desktop appears.

6.14   Disabling Error Reporting

Problem

Whenever Windows encounters an unrecoverable error, it asks whether you want to report the error to Microsoft. You don't want to send information to Microsoft, and so want to disable the error reporting notice.

Solution

Using a graphical user interface

1. Right-click My Computer and choose Properties. The System Properties dialog box opens.
2. Click the Advanced tab.
3. Click the Error Reporting button.
4. Select the button next to Disable error reporting.
5. Check the box next to "But notify me when critical errors occur." That way, you'll still be notified when a critical error occurs, but you won't be prompted to send the error report to Microsoft.
6. Click OK.

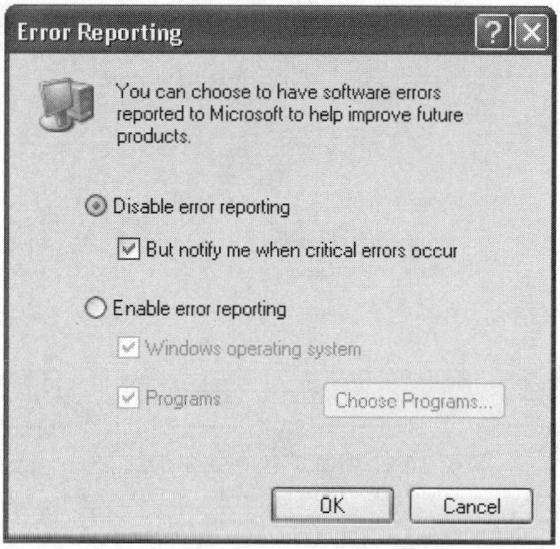

Figure 6-9. When turning off error reporting, make sure that you tell XP to notify you when critical errors occur, or else you might not know when applications crash or you run into other problems

If you'd like, you can enable error reporting for some applications and disable it for others. You can, for example, enable error reporting for critical errors having to do with XP itself but not applications, or you can enable error reporting for applications on a case-by-case basis. To do this, from the screen pictured in Figure 6-9:

1. Select the Enable error reporting button.

2. Check the box next to Windows operating system if you want to enable error reporting for XP itself. Check the box next to Programs if you want to enable error reporting for applications.

3. To turn error reporting on and off for individual applications, click Choose Programs. The Choose Programs dialog box, shown in Figure 6-10, appears. To specify programs for which you want to enable error reporting, click the Add button in the top pane and browse for the program. To specify programs for which you want to disable error reporting, click the Add button in the bottom pane and browse for the program. Click OK and then OK again.

Using the Registry

To disable error reporting, open the Registry Editor and go to HKEY_LOCAL_MACHINE\ SOFTWARE\Microsoft\PCHealth\ErrorReporting and edit the DoReport value to 0. Exit the Registry. You may need to reboot in order for the setting to take effect. Edit the value to 1 to enable error reporting.

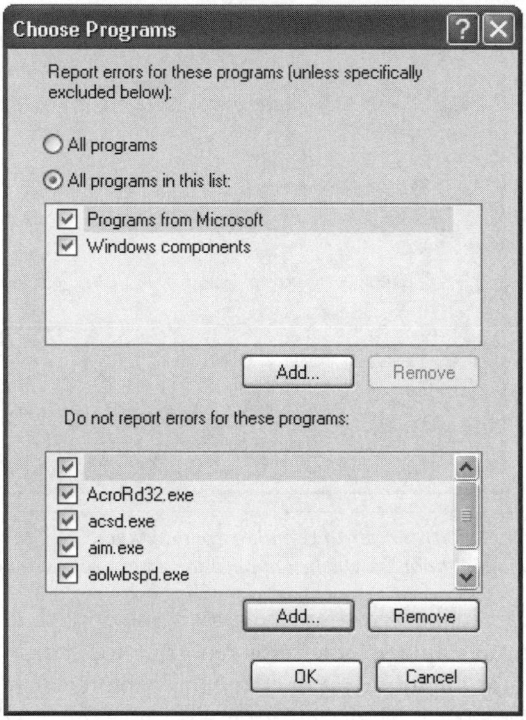

Figure 6-10. Select programs for which you want to enable and disable error reporting

You can also use the Registry to turn off error reporting for applications and XP itself on a case-by-case basis. Go to HKEY_LOCAL_MACHINE\SOFTWARE\Microsoft\PCHealth\ ErrorReporting. Then:

- To disable error reporting for Microsoft applications, edit the IncludeMicrosoftApps value to 0.

- To disable error reporting for Windows components, edit the IncludeWindowsApps value to 0.

- To exclude any individual application from error reporting, create a new DWORD value under HKEY_LOCAL_MACHINE\SOFTWARE\Microsoft\PCHealth\ ErrorReporting\ExclusionList, and give it the executable name of the application you want to exclude, for example, Notepad.exe. Don't include the path; just use the executable name.

- To use error reporting for any individual application, create a new DWORD value under HKEY_LOCAL_MACHINE\SOFTWARE\Microsoft\PCHealth\ErrorReporting\ InclusionList, and give it the executable name of the application that you want to use error reporting, for example, Notepad.exe. Don't include the path; just use the executable name.

- Exit the Registry. You may have to reboot in order for the changes to take effect.

Discussion

Windows Error Reporting (WER) is used to help Microsoft and other developers fix bugs in their programs. If you send an error report after a program crashes, you're essentially sending a snapshot of your system to Microsoft at the time of the crash. The information is incorporated into a database that includes all the other crash reports that Microsoft has received, and that information is then made available to developers.

By default, error reports don't contain any identifying information about you or your system, except for what might be inadvertently found on the stack, which is an area of memory used by executing programs and that is included in the crash reports. The stack can contain personal information, depending on what was being done on your computer at the time of the crash. For example, it could potentially reveal your credit card number, the web site you were visiting, and emails you've written. However, developers do not get your user name, machine name, or Registry information. Developers that use WER are legally bound to keep any information they find private.

If you're exceedingly worried about your privacy, you'll want to turn off error reporting, although no instances of private information being used from it have yet been found.

See Also

For an excellent discussion of error reporting, privacy issues, and an examination of exactly what information is sent in an error report, see the article "Windows Error Reporting Under the Covers," in WindowsDevCenter at *http://www.windowsdevcenter.com/pub/a/windows/2004/03/16/wer.html*.

6.15   Creating Environment Variables

Problem

You want to be able to add environment variables to XP, so that scripts and certain programs can operate properly.

Solution

Using a graphical user interface

1. Log in as an administrator (only system administrators can set environment variables).

2. Right-click My Computer and choose Properties.

3. Click the Advanced tab and click Environment variables. The environment variables dialog box, shown in Figure 6-11, appears.

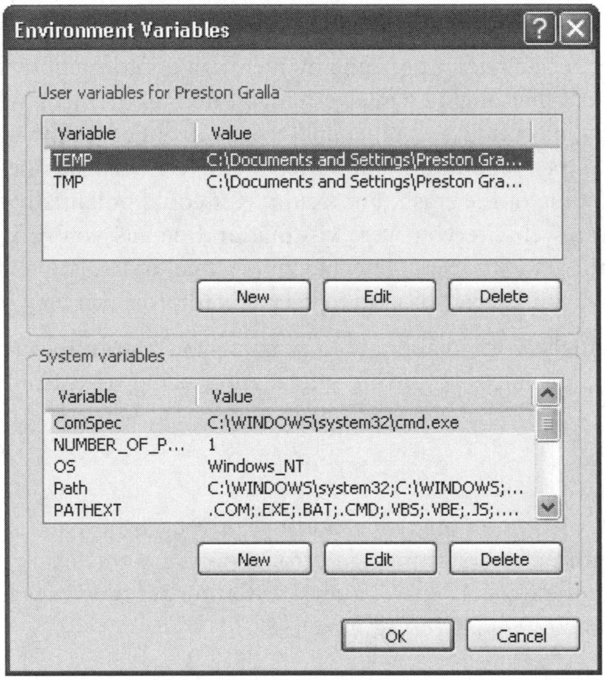

Figure 6-11. The Environment Variables dialog box lets you see what variable are already set, edit them, delete them, and add new ones

4. To add a new value, click New in the User variables or System variables area, depending on whether you're adding variables for all users of the system or just the logged-on user.

5. In the New User Variable dialog box that appears, type the name for the variable in the Variable name box, and the value for the variable in the Variable value box, for example, TMP for the variable name, and %USERPROFILE%\Local Settings\Temp.

6. Click OK until all boxes close.

7. To edit a value, highlight it, click Edit, change the variable name and value, and click OK until all boxes close. To delete a value, highlight it, click Delete, then click OK until all boxes close.

8. Usually, changes to values require that you restart your PC, so restart to make sure that the changes take effect.

Using a command-line interface

At the command prompt, use this syntax to set an environment variable:

```
> set variablename=variablevalue
```

For example, to set the variable ProgramFilesc to the value C:\Program Files, you'd type this at a command prompt and press Enter:

```
> set variablename=variablevalue
```

That will set the environment variable only temporarily, and only in the command prompt; it won't affect the rest of the system. To set permanent environment variables, use the GUI as detailed in the earlier part of this recipe.

Discussion

Environment variables that contain information about the environment for the system and/or for the currently logged on user are used for a wide variety of purposes—for example, to determine where to place files such as temporary files, what the root drive is, and where the Windows directory is. They're often used in scripting as well. Windows contains a variety of environment variables by default, such as defining the root directory and the Windows directory.

If you're at the command prompt and want to see the current environment variables, type set and press Enter. You'll see a list like this:

```
PATHEXT=.COM;.EXE;.BAT;.CMD;.VBS;.VBE;.JS;.JSE;.WSF;.WSH
PROCESSOR_ARCHITECTURE=x86
PROCESSOR_IDENTIFIER=x86 Family 15 Model 1 Stepping 2, GenuineIntel
PROCESSOR_LEVEL=15
PROCESSOR_REVISION=0102
ProgramFiles=C:\Program Files
PROMPT=$P$G
SESSIONNAME=Console
SystemDrive=C:
SystemRoot=C:\WINDOWS
TEMP=C:\DOCUME~1\PRESTO~1\LOCALS~1\Temp
TMP=C:\DOCUME~1\PRESTO~1\LOCALS~1\Temp
USERDOMAIN=PRESTONGRALLA
USERNAME=Preston Gralla
USERPROFILE=C:\Documents and Settings\Preston Gralla
windir=C:\WINDOWS
```

See Also

MS KB 310519, "How To Manage Environment Variables in Windows XP"

6.16   Creating a Reboot or Shutdown Shortcut

Problem

You want to reboot or shut down your PC quickly, and customize the way that it shuts down.

Solution

Using a graphical user interface

For a fast way to shut down or reboot your PC, create a shortcut on your desktop, and then double-click the shortcut.

To create the shortcut, right-click the desktop and select New → Shortcut. The Create Shortcut wizard appears. On the first screen, for the location of the item, type shutdown, followed by one of several switches, like this:

```
shutdown -r -t 01 -c "Rebooting your PC"
```

Click Next, and in the next screen, type in the name of the shortcut. This is what will appear on the shortcut on the desktop. Then click Finish. To shut down or reboot, double-click the shortcut.

The example above would create a shortcut that would reboot your PC after a one-second delay and display the message "Rebooting your PC." You can instead tell the PC to reboot or you can have it log you off instead of shutting down. Table 6-3 lists the switches you can use with shutdown.

Table 6-3. Switches you can use with shutdown

Switch	What it does
-s	Shuts down the PC
-l	Logs the current user off.
-t *nn*	Indicates the delay, in seconds, before performing the action.
-c "messagetext"	Displays a message in the System Shutdown window. A maximum of 127 characters can be used. The message must be enclosed in quotation marks.
-f	Forces any running applications to shut down.
-r	Restart the PC.

6.17 Scheduling a Reboot

Problem

You want reboot your PC automatically, on a schedule that you specify.

Solution

Using a graphical user interface

1. Create a shortcut to reboot your PC, as explained in Recipe 6.16. Use this syntax for creating it:

   ```
   shutdown -r -t 01 -c "Rebooting your PC"
   ```

2. From the Control Panel, open the Scheduled Tasks applet.
3. Double-click Add Scheduled Task.
4. Click Next.
5. In the screen that appears, click the Browse button, browse to *C:\Windows\ System32* and select *shutdown.exe*.
6. Type a name for the task (such as Reboot), select the frequency in which to run it, and click Next.
7. Enter the username and password of the user the task should run as and click Next.
8. If you want to go back and modify any of the settings for the task, check the box beside Open advanced properties and click Finish.

Discussion

Some people believe a periodic reboot is required to keep Windows snappy. Indeed, some updates for virus protection and security policies require a reboot to either take effect or poll network resources for updates and policy changes. So it's a good idea to reboot Windows every once in a while, even if it doesn't seem as if it's needed.

See Also

Recipe 10.12 for scheduling a task and Recipe 6.16 for creating a reboot or shutdown shortcut

6.18 Speeding Up System Startup

Problem

You want your system to start more quickly.

Solution

Perform a boot defragment

Doing a boot defragment will put all the boot files next to one another on your hard disk. When boot files are in close proximity to one another, your system will start faster. On most systems, boot defragment should be enabled by default, but it might not be on yours, or it might have been changed inadvertently. To make sure that boot defragment is enabled on your system, run the Registry Editor and go to `HKEY_LOCAL_MACHINE\SOFTWARE\Microsoft\Dfrg\BootOptimizeFunction`. Edit the Enable string value to Y if it is not already set to Y. Exit the Registry and reboot. The next time you reboot, you'll do a boot defragment.

Edit your BIOS

When you turn on your PC, it goes through a set of startup procedures in its BIOS before it starts XP. So, if you speed up those initial startup procedures, you'll make your system start faster.

You can speed up your startup procedures by changing the BIOS with the built-in setup utility. How you run this utility varies from PC to PC, but you typically get to it by pressing the Delete, F1, or F10 key. You'll come to a menu with a variety of choices. Here are the choices to make for faster system startups.

Quick Power-On Self Test (POST)
    When you choose this option, your system runs an abbreviated POST rather than the normal, lengthy one.

Boot-Up Floppy Seek
    Disable this option. When it's enabled, your system spends a few extra seconds looking for your floppy drive—a relatively pointless procedure, especially considering how infrequently you use your floppy drive.

Boot Delay
    Some systems let you delay booting after you turn on your PC so that your hard drive gets a chance to start spinning before bootup. Most likely, you don't need to have this boot delay, so turn it off. If you run into problems, you can turn it back on.

Clean out your Registry

Over time, your Registry can become bloated with unused entries, slowing down your system startup because your system loads them every time you start up your PC. Registry First Aid (*http://www.rosecitysoftware.com/Reg1Aid*) can help you delete unneeded Registry entries and speed up startup times. It combs your Registry for outdated and useless entries, and lets you choose which entries to delete and which to keep. It also creates a full Registry backup so that you can restore the Registry if you run into a problem.

See Also

Registry First Aid is shareware and free to try, but it costs $21 if you decide to keep using it. Download it from *http://www.rosecitysoftware.com/reg1aid*.

Stop unnecessary services that run on startup

Another cause of system slowdown is services that run on startup that you don't need—for example, the Wireless Zero Configuration Services running on a desktop computer that doesn't use a wireless adapter and is connected to a network via an Ethernet connection. For details, see Recipe 6.7.

CHAPTER 7

Disks, Drives, and Volumes

7.0 Introduction

Before you can start using a filesystem on a computer, you have to configure the disks, drives, and volumes. You have to split up the disks into volumes and assign drive letters to the volumes. You have to format a volume with a filesystem such as NTFS or FAT32. The filesystem you choose dictates the security, encryption, file storage efficiency, and performance of your file storage system.

Once you have usable volumes in place, there are many ongoing maintenance tasks you should do to keep your disks healthy. You'll want to periodically defragment your volumes so that new files aren't spread across many separate chunks, which decreases file access performance. You'll want to check your volumes for errors to ensure there aren't any bad sectors. And if you start running low on space, you may want to clean up a volume or see which users are using the most space. If disk space usage is a concern for you, you can implement the Windows quota feature that lets you limit the amount of space users' use. In this chapter we cover all of these tasks and more.

Using a Graphical User Interface

The two primary graphical interfaces for managing disks, drives, and volumes are Windows Explorer and the Disk Management MMC snap-in. With Windows Explorer, you can right-click a drive, select Properties, and perform functions such as enabling quotas, running disk cleanup, performing defragmentation, and running an error check of a volume.

The Disk Management snap-in lets you perform lower-level disk administration and volume management than Windows Explorer allows. With it you can create new volumes, assign drive letters, format volumes with a particular filesystem, and convert basic disks to dynamic disks. You can access this snap-in by opening the Computer Management snap-in in Administrative Tools and clicking on Disk Management in the left pane under Storage.

Using a Command-Line Interface

Several important new command-line utilities have been added to Windows XP to help with managing disks and volumes. *diskpart* and *fsutil* give you control over managing disks, drives, and volumes from the command line. These new tools also provide interfaces for running in batch mode, which make them easy to script.

Table 7-1 lists all the command-line tools used in this chapter.

Table 7-1. Command line tools used in Chapter 7

Tool	Location	Recipes
chkdsk	%SystemRoot%\system32	7.10
cleanmgr	%SystemRoot%\system32	7.7
compact	%SystemRoot%\system32	7.9
defrag	%SystemRoot%\system32	7.8
diruse	Windows Support Tools	7.14
diskpart	%SystemRoot%\system32	7.1–2, 7.5
diskperf	%SystemRoot%\system32	7.3
diskuse	Windows Resource Kit	7.14
format.com	%SystemRoot%\system32	7.4
fsutil	%SystemRoot%\system32	7.15–17
label	%SystemRoot%\system32	7.6
net	%SystemRoot%\system32	7.12
subst	%SystemRoot%\system32	7.13

Using Downloadable Software

Recipe 7.8 discusses a couple of third-party tools for defragmenting disks. Recipe 7.11 describes the free Joeware tool (i.e., *http://www.joeware.net*) called *writeprot*; with it you can make a disk read-only. Recipe 7.14 covers the DiskPie utility, which you can use to find large files and folders.

Using VBScript

Table 7-2 lists the WMI classes used in this chapter. The only WSH solution is the MapNetworkDrive method in Recipe 7.12.

Table 7-2. WMI classes used in Chapter 7

WMI class	Description	Recipes
CIM_Datafile	Enumerate and manage files.	7.14
Win32_Directory	Enumerate directories.	7.9
Win32_DiskDrive	Enumerate and manage physical disks.	7.1

Table 7-2. WMI classes used in Chapter 7 (continued)

WMI class	Description	Recipes
Win32_DiskQuota	Enumerate the quota usage for a particular user.	7.16–17
Win32_LogicalDisk	Enumerate and manage logical disks.	7.1, 7.10, 7.16–17
Win32_MappedLogicalDisk	Enumerate and manage mapped network drives.	7.1
Win32_QuotaSetting	Enumerate and manage disk quota settings on volumes.	7.15

7.1   Viewing the Disk, Drive, and Volume Layout

Problem

You want to see how the disks, drives, and volumes are laid out on a computer.

Solution

Using a graphical user interface

1. Open the Computer Management snap-in.
2. In the left pane, expand Storage and click on Disk Management. The right pane will display the disk, volumes, and drives.

Using a command-line interface

On Windows XP, you can use the *diskpart* utility to view the disk, drive, and volume configuration. First, get into interactive mode:

```
> diskpart
```

Next, to view the list of disks, run the following:

```
> list disk
```

Now, to see the list of volume and assigned drive letters, run the following:

```
> list vol
```

Using VBScript

```
' This code enumerates the physical and logical disks on a system.
' ------ SCRIPT CONFIGURATION ------
strComputer = "."
' ------ END CONFIGURATION ---------
WScript.Echo "Physical Disks:"
set objWMI = GetObject("winmgmts:\\" & strComputer & "\root\cimv2")
set colDisks = objWMI.ExecQuery("select * from Win32_DiskDrive")
for each objDisk in colDisks
    WScript.Echo " Caption: " & vbTab &  objDisk.Caption
    WScript.Echo " Device ID: " & vbTab &  objDisk.DeviceID
```

```
    WScript.Echo " Manufacturer: " & vbTab & objDisk.Manufacturer
    WScript.Echo " Media Type: " & vbTab &  objDisk.MediaType
    WScript.Echo " Model: " & vbTab &  objDisk.Model
    WScript.Echo " Name: " & vbTab &  objDisk.Name
    WScript.Echo " Partitions: " & vbTab & objDisk.Partitions
    WScript.Echo " Size: " & vbTab &  objDisk.Size
    WScript.Echo " Status: " & vbTab &  objDisk.Status
    WScript.Echo
next

WScript.Echo
WScript.Echo "Logical Disks:"
set colDisks = objWMI.ExecQuery("select * from Win32_LogicalDisk")
for each objDisk in colDisks
    WScript.Echo " DeviceID: " & objDisk.DeviceID
    WScript.Echo " Description: " & objDisk.Description
    WScript.Echo " VolumeName: " & objDisk.VolumeName
    WScript.Echo " DriveType: " & objDisk.DriveType
    WScript.Echo " FileSystem: " & objDisk.FileSystem
    WScript.Echo " FreeSpace: " & objDisk.FreeSpace
    WScript.Echo " MediaType: " & objDisk.MediaType
    WScript.Echo " Name: " & objDisk.Name
    WScript.Echo " Size: " & objDisk.Size
    WScript.Echo
next
```

Discussion

The solutions show how to enumerate all the disks and volumes on a computer, but
if you have any mapped drives, it won't show those. The easiest way to see mapped
drives is to open Windows Explorer and look at My Computer or run net use from a
command line. From VBScript, you can use the Win32_MappedLogicalDisk WMI class,
which is new to Windows XP. Here is some sample code:

```
strComputer = "."
set objWMI = GetObject("winmgmts:\\" & strComputer & "\root\cimv2")
set colDrives = objWMI.ExecQuery("select * from Win32_MappedLogicalDisk")
WScript.Echo "Mapped Drives:"
for each objDrive in colDrives
    WScript.Echo " Device ID: " & objDrive.DeviceID
    WScript.Echo " Volume Name: " & objDrive.VolumeName
    WScript.Echo " Session ID: " & objDrive.SessionID
    WScript.Echo " Size: " & objDrive.Size
    WScript.Echo
next
```

See Also

Recipe 7.12 for mapping a network drive

7.2 Converting a Basic Disk to Dynamic

Problem

You want to convert a basic disk to a dynamic disk.

Solution

Using a graphical user interface

1. Open the Computer Management snap-in.
2. In the left pane, expand Storage and click on Disk Management.
3. In the lower-right pane, right-click the disk you want to convert and select Convert to Dynamic Disk.
4. Check the box beside the disk(s) you want to convert and click OK.
5. Click Convert and click Yes to confirm the conversion.

Using a command-line interface

You can use the *diskpart* utility to convert a disk to dynamic. First, run diskpart to enter interactive mode:

```
> diskpart
```

You need to get a list of disks so you can select the one you want to convert:

```
> list disk
```

In the following example, we'll select disk 0:

```
> select disk 0
```

Now, run the following command to convert the disk:

```
> convert dynamic
```

You may be asked to reboot for the change to take effect.

Using VBScript

None of the WMI classes support converting a disk to a dynamic disk.

Discussion

By default, disks are initialized as basic on both Windows 2000 and Windows XP. You can convert a disk to dynamic to take advantage of features such as the ability to dynamically extend partitions. Some additional benefits of dynamic disks include the following:

- You can perform disk and volume management without needing to restart the operating system.

- You can organize dynamic disks into disk groups. Configuration information for all disks in a group is shared and kept up-to-date even if a dynamic disk fails or is moved to another system.

- You have more options for configuring volumes. Dynamic disks support the following dynamic volumes: simple volumes, spanned volumes, striped volumes, mirrored volumes, and RAID-5 volumes.

- You are not limited on the number of volumes you can create on a dynamic disk. With a basic disk you can create up to four primary partitions or three primary partitions and one extended partition.

 Once you convert a disk to dynamic, you cannot convert it back to basic unless you delete all of the dynamic volumes on the disk.

See Also

MS KB 175761, "Dynamic vs. Basic Storage in Windows 2000," MS KB 309044, "How To Convert to Basic and Dynamic Disks in Windows XP Professional," MS KB 254105, "Dynamic Disk Hardware Limitations," and MS KB 314343, "Basic Storage Versus Dynamic Storage in Windows XP"

7.3 Enabling Disk Performance Statistics

Problem

You want to monitor disk performance and you need to enable performance statistics.

Solution

On Windows 2000, run the following command and then reboot:

```
> diskperf -y
```

On Windows XP, all disk performance statistics are enabled by default.

Discussion

With Windows NT, both logical and physical disk performance counters were disabled by default. With Windows 2000, physical disk counters were enabled and logical disk counters were disabled. With Windows XP, both logical and physical disk counters are enabled. Logical and physical disk counters were disabled by default in previous versions of the OS because of the concern that the impact to performance would be too great to have them on all the time. As disk access times have steadily improved over the years, the performance hit has become negligible. Now, you can safely have both physical and logical disk counters enabled on either Windows 2000 or Windows XP.

 Within Performance Monitor, the LogicalDisk and PhysicalDisk objects contain the counters that are available when disk performance statistics are enabled.

See Also

MS KB 253251, "Using Diskperf in Windows 2000"

7.4 Formatting a Volume

Problem

You want to reformat an existing volume or initialize a new one.

Solution

Using a graphical user interface

1. Open Windows Explorer.
2. Right-click on the drive letter for the volume you want to format and select Format.
3. Leave NTFS selected for File system unless you have a very good reason to use FAT32. The same goes for the Allocation unit size; use the default selected unless you have a good reason.
4. Type a description under Volume label.
5. Check the box beside Quick Format if you've previously formatted the volume with the same filesystem and just want to delete the file table (i.e., links to all the files and folders).
6. Check the box beside Enable Compression if you want to compress the contents of the volume.
7. Click Start.

Using a command-line interface

The following command formats the D drive using NTFS and sets the volume label to Data:

```
> format D: /fs:ntfs /v:Data
```

You will be prompted to enter the current label of the D drive. Type it in and press Enter. Then you'll be asked for confirmation; continue by typing Y and pressing Enter.

Add the /q option to the previous command line to perform a quick format and add the /c option to enable compression on the volume. You can use the /x option to force a dismount in case someone has a handle open on the volume.

Discussion

Before you can use a volume, you first need to format it with a filesystem. On Windows 2000 and Windows XP, you can format a volume with FAT, FAT32, or NTFS. Unless you have a good reason, you should use NTFS due to its increased security features.

Another choice you will have to make when formatting a volume is whether to perform a quick format or normal format. Both options erase the table that tracks file locations on the filesystem. A normal format will scan the entire volume for bad sectors. This scan is responsible for most of the time required to do a format. A quick format bypasses this, so you should only use it when the volume has been previously formatted with a filesystem and you are confident the disk isn't damaged.

You can also enable compression on a newly formatted volume. See Recipe 7.9 for more on the effects of compression.

See Also

MS KB 140365, "Default Cluster Size for FAT and NTFS," and MS KB 313348, "How to partition and format a hard disk in Windows XP"

7.5   Setting the Drive Letter of a Volume

Problem

You want to set the drive letter of a volume.

Solution

Using a graphical user interface

1. Open the Computer Management snap-in.
2. In the left pane under Storage, click on Disk Administrator.
3. In the bottom right pane, right-click the target volume or disk and select Change Drive Letter and Paths.
4. Click the Change button.
5. Beside Assign the following drive letter, select the new drive letter from the drop-down list and click OK.
6. Click Yes to confirm.

Using a command-line interface

The *diskpart* command lets you assign drive letters from the command line. First, start by running the command in interactive mode:

```
> diskpart
```

List the current volumes on the system:

```
DISKPART> list vol
```

From the output, select the volume in which you want to set the driver letter. In the following command, we're selecting volume 0:

```
DISKPART> select vol 0
```

Now, assign the drive letter you want. In the following example, we're assigning letter F:

```
DISKPART> assign letter=F
```

Discussion

When volumes are made active and removable media added to a system, they are automatically assigned the next available drive letter (in alphabetical order starting from C). It is a straightforward operation to change the drive letter of a drive, but you need to be sure nothing references the prior drive letter. If you attempt to assign a different drive letter to an existing drive that is currently in use, the system will let you do it and allow both the old drive letter and new drive letter to be used until the system is rebooted. After the system restarts, the old drive letter will go back into the pool of available drive letters.

 If you want to change the drive letter of the system drive, you have to follow special procedures. See MS KB 223188 for more information.

See Also

MS KB 234048, "How Windows 2000 Assigns, Reserves, and Stores Drive Letters," and MS KB 223188, "How To Restore the System/Boot Drive Letter in Windows"

7.6   Setting the Label of a Volume

Problem

You want to set the label of a volume.

Solution

Using a graphical user interface

1. Open Windows Explorer.
2. Right-click the drive you want to clean up and select Properties.
3. Click the General tab if it doesn't open by default.
4. The lone input box on this tab is the label for the volume. Modify it as necessary and click OK.

Using a command-line interface

Use the *label* command to set the label of a volume. The following example sets the label for the C drive to be System Volume:

```
> label c: System Volume
```

 Do not put quotes around multiword labels. The label command captures everything after the drive parameter so no quotes are necessary.

Discussion

The label of a volume is nothing more than a short description that is displayed in tools such as Windows Explorer when you view the list of drives. A label can contain up to 32 characters. You can use a mix of alphanumeric and special characters. Also, labels do not have to be unique across volumes, but it defeats the purpose of having labels in the first place if you configure multiple volumes with the same label. And unlike setting drive letters, you can modify the label of a volume regardless of whether the volume is the system volume or has files that are locked.

7.7   Cleaning Up a Volume

Problem

You want to clean up unused or unneeded files on a volume to reclaim space.

Solution

Using a graphical user interface

1. Open Windows Explorer.
2. Right-click the drive you want to clean up and select Properties.
3. Click the General tab if it doesn't open by default.

4. Click the Disk Cleanup button. Depending on the size of the volume you are scanning, cleanup can take a while to complete.

5. Under Files to delete, check the boxes beside the type of files you want to remove.

6. When you are done with your selections, click OK.

7. Click Yes to confirm that you want to delete the files.

Using a command-line interface

You can launch the Disk Cleanup tool from the command line by running the following command:

```
> cleanmgr
```

To target a specific drive, use the /d option:

```
> cleanmgr /d E:
```

You can automate the Disk Cleanup tool to run against all the drives on a system in a couple of steps. First, you need to configure the types of files you want to clean up. Run the `cleanmgr` utility with the `/sageset:` option followed by an integer. The integer represents a Disk Cleanup profile. In the following example, we'll use 1:

```
> cleanmgr /sageset:1
```

This opens the Disk Cleanup Settings property page. Under Files to delete, check the boxes beside the types of files you want to clean up. Click OK when you are done. Now, use the `/sagerun:` option followed by the same number we just used (in this case 1):

```
> cleanmgr /sagerun:1
```

This command enumerates all drives on the system and performs a disk cleanup according to the profile you just created.

Discussion

Disk Cleanup is a tool to help you remove unneeded files from your system, files that are doing nothing more than taking up space. It can find temporary files used by Internet Explorer and old setup files for applications such as Microsoft Office and let you delete them.

After you've analyzed a particular volume, you can click on a file type, such as Temporary Internet Files, and a description of that file type will appear at the bottom of the dialog box. As you check or uncheck boxes, you'll see the number beside Total amount of disk space you gain increase or decrease, respectively. Depending on the file type, a View Files button will be displayed, which when clicked opens a Windows Explorer window to the location of the files. The list of file types will vary depending on the volume you are looking at. Only file types that apply to a particular volume are displayed.

The Compress old files option is a good way to minimize disk bloat over time. When enabled, it will compress files that haven't been accessed in a certain number of days. It won't delete any files, just compress them. That means files you rarely access are compressed and the impact to the disk is minimized.

The More Options tab provides buttons for opening the Windows Components and Add/Remove Programs screens and a button for removing all but the most recent system restore point. Depending on how much space you need to reclaim, all three of these can be good sources for reclaiming unused or rarely used disk space.

See Also

MS KB 253597, "Automating Disk Cleanup Tool in Windows," and MS KB 310312, "Description of the Disk Cleanup Tool in Windows XP"

7.8   Defragmenting a Volume

Problem

You want to defragment a volume to improve disk access performance.

Solution

Using a graphical user interface

1. Open Windows Explorer.
2. Right-click the drive you want to defragment and select Properties.
3. Click the Tools tab.
4. Click the Defragment Now button. This launches the Disk Defragmenter application.
5. Click the Analyze button to find out how badly the volume is fragmented. After the analysis is complete, Windows will inform you whether it believes you should defragment the volume.
6. Click the View Report button to view statistics about fragmentation and to see the most fragmented files.
7. Click the Defragment button to proceed with defragmenting the volume.

Using a command-line interface

The *defrag* utility is the command-line version of the Disk Defragmenter application. Run the following command to perform an analysis of the D drive:

```
> defrag d: /a
```

Add the /v option to see similar information to the View Report button in Disk Defragmenter:

```
> defrag d: /a /v
```

Lastly, just include the drive and /v (for verbose output) to perform a defragmentation of the volume:

```
> defrag d: /v
```

You can force a defragmentation even if disk space is low by including the /f option.

Using a downloadable software

Diskeeper from *http://www.diskeeper.com* and PerfectDisk from *http://www.raxco.com* have options for defragmenting disks, including scheduling defragmenting, deploying on multiple machines, and defragmenting boot files. Diskeeper runs in the background and defrags files as they become fragmented, so your disks stay defragmented automatically. Both tools offer trial downloads, although if you keep using them, you'll have to pay.

Discussion

When you save a file on a volume, Windows tries to save the file in one contiguous section on the disk. However, as the disk becomes full, the largest available contiguous sections of the disk become smaller and smaller. New files eventually become spread over multiple sections of the disk; this is called fragmentation. Fragmentation leads to decreased disk access performance because Windows has to access multiple sections of the disk to piece together a single file.

The Windows defragmentation feature helps alleviate this problem by scanning a disk and attempting to combine the sections of files in larger contiguous portions. To perform a full defragmentation on a volume, the target volume needs to have at least 15% free space. This is necessary because Windows needs some space to store file fragments it is trying to piece together. If you have less than 15% available, you'll need to free up some space first. See Recipe 7.7 for more details.

You can determine how badly a volume is fragmented by analyzing the volume. All three solutions provide options for generating a report that provides details on the fragmentation level of a volume. The report will also recommend whether you should perform a defragmentation or not. This is useful only as a general guide because it may always recommend that you perform a defragmentation even after you've just run one.

You should consider performing periodic defragmentation on heavily used volumes that have become more than 50% utilized. As disk space decreases on a volume, the level of fragmentation generally increases because the number of contiguous sections of disk decrease. If you have really large disks that are rarely more than 25% used, performing a defragmentation will not likely be of much benefit.

Defragmenting a disk can take several minutes and even hours depending on the size of the disk and the level of fragmentation. Also, the disk will be continually busy during the defragmentation period, so do it during off-hours because disk access performance will definitely decrease.

See Also

Recipe 7.7 for cleaning up a volume; MS KB 283080, "Description of the New Command Line Defrag.exe Included with Windows XP," MS KB 305781, "How To Analyze and Defragment a Disk in Windows XP," and MS KB 312067, "Shadow copies may be lost when you defragment a volume"

7.9   Compressing a Volume

Problem

You want to compress a volume.

Solution

Using a graphical user interface

1. Open Windows Explorer.
2. Right-click the drive you want to compress and select Properties.
3. Click the General tab if it doesn't open by default.
4. Check the box beside Compress drive to save disk space and click OK.
5. Select the radio button beside the option for compressing only the files contained directly under C or compressing all subfolders and files on the drive.
6. Click OK.

Using a command-line interface

The following command causes files only at the root of drive D to be compressed:

```
> compact /c d:\
```

Add the /s option to compress all files and folders on drive D:

```
> compact /c /s d:\
```

Using VBScript

```
' This code compresses a volume.
' ------ SCRIPT CONFIGURATION ------
strComputer = "."
strDrive = "<Drive>"   ' e.g. D:
```

```
    boolRecursive = True
    ' ------ END CONFIGURATION ---------
    set objWMI = GetObject("winmgmts:\\" & strComputer & "\root\cimv2")
    set colFolder = objWMI.ExecQuery("select * from Win32_Directory " & _
                                     " where name = '" & strDrive & "\\'")

    if colFolder.Count <> 1 then
       WScript.Echo "Error: Volume not found."
    else
       for each objFolder in colFolder
          intRC = objFolder.CompressEx(strErrorFile,,boolRecursive)
          if intRC <> 0 then
             WScript.Echo "Error compressing volume: " & intRC
             WScript.Echo "Stopped on file: " & strErrorFile
          else
             WScript.Echo "Successfully compressed volume."
          end if
       next
    end if
```

Discussion

Compressing an entire volume is a good idea if disk space utilization is a concern and you have really fast disks and adequate processing resources. And since support for compression is built into the NTFS filesystem, compression and decompression of files happens automatically when applications attempt to open them. That makes the use of compression largely transparent. It will, however, have an impact on system load, since compressing and uncompressing files, especially large ones, can require significant processing cycles. These days, disk space is much cheaper than CPUs, so you are generally better off taking the hit in disk space than adding processing load.

If you plan on compressing a volume that has disk quotas enabled, be sure to read MS KB 320686 first. You might think that when you compress a volume, your users' quota usage would go down, but it doesn't work this way. Quotas are determined by allocated disk usage, which is the actual size of the files before compression. Due to how compressed files are stored, it is possible for users' quota usage to increase when you enable compression. Again, if this issue pertains to you, KB 320686 goes into a good amount of detail about why this happens.

Using VBScript

The `Win32_Directory` class has a `Compress` method in addition to the `CompressEx` method we used in this solution, but it does not provide a way to perform compression recursively. It simply allows you to compress an individual directory. With `CompressEx`, the third parameter is a Boolean that, when true, performs a recursive compression.

The first two parameters to `CompressEx` are the stop file and start file. The stop file will be populated if `CompressEx` encounters an error and will contain the filename where the error occurred. The start file parameter is the filename within the directory where

---

compression should start. This parameter is necessary only if you are attempting to catch failures from previous `CompressEx` calls. You'd pass the results from the stop file parameter you captured after the failure as the start file to the next iteration `CompressEx`. This is a little funky, but it does allow you to create a robust compression script.

See Also

Recipe 8.14 for more on compressing and uncompressing individual files; MS KB 153720, "Cannot Compress a Drive with Little Free Space," MS KB 251186, "Best practices for NTFS compression in Windows," MS KB 307987, "How To Use File Compression in Windows XP," and MS KB 320686, "Disk Quota Charges Increase If You Turn On the NTFS Compression Functionality"

7.10   Checking a Volume for Errors

Problem

You want to check a volume for errors.

Solution

Using a graphical user interface

1. Open Windows Explorer.
2. Right-click the drive you want to defragment and select Properties.
3. Click the Tools tab.
4. Under Error-checking, click the Check Now button.
5. If you want any filesystem errors that are found to be fixed, check the box beside Automatically fix filesystem errors. If you want to perform a thorough scan of the disk and check for bad sectors, check the box beside Scan for an attempt recovery of bad sectors.
6. Check the disk options you want and click Start.
7. Click OK when the check completes.

Using a command-line interface

The *chkdsk* utility can detect problems with a volume and attempt to fix them. Specify the name of the volume you want to check to run *chkdsk* in read-only mode:

```
> chkdsk D:
```

Use the /f option to have *chkdsk* attempt to fix any errors it finds:

```
> chkdsk D: /f
```

With the /f option, *chkdsk* will try to lock the drive, so if it is in use by another process, you will only be able to schedule it to run during the next reboot. You can include the /x option with /f to force the volume to be dismounted (for a nonsystem volume).

Using VBScript

```
' This code tries to perform a chkdsk on the specified volume.
' ------ SCRIPT CONFIGURATION ------
strComputer = "."
strDrive = "<Drive>" ' e.g. D:
boolFixErrors = True  ' True = chkdsk /f, False = chkdsk
' ------ END CONFIGURATION ---------
set objWMI = GetObject("winmgmts:\\" & strComputer & "\root\cimv2")
set objDisk = objWMI.Get("Win32_LogicalDisk.DeviceID='" & strDrive & "'")
intRC = objDisk.ChkDsk(boolFixErrors)
if intRC = 0 then
   WScript.Echo "Chkdsk completed successfully."
elseif intRC = 1 then
   WScript.Echo "Chkdsk scheduled on next reboot."
else
   WScript.Echo "Error running chkdsk: " & intRC
end if
```

Discussion

Running *chkdsk* on an active volume it may report transient errors that are due to the volume being in use. If you see any errors at all, you should run chkdsk /f to schedule the errors to be examined and fixed after the next reboot.

See Also

"Chkdsk Method of the Win32_LogicalDisk Class," MS KB 160963, "CHKNTFS. EXE: What You Can Use It For," MS KB 187941, "An explanation of CHKDSK and the new /C and /I switches," MS KB 191603, "Modifying the Autochk.exe Time-out Value," and MS KB 218461, "Description of Enhanced Chkdsk, Autochk, and Chkntfs Tools in Windows 2000"

7.11 Making a Disk or Volume Read-Only

Problem

You want to make a disk or volume read-only so that users or programs can't write to it.

Solution

Using downloadable software

The Joeware (*http://www.joeware.net*) tool, *writeprot*, allows you to make a disk or volume read-only as long as no files are locked on that volume. The following command lists the read/write state of all disks and volumes on a system:

```
> writeprot /mview
```

The following command attempts to make the D drive read-only:

```
> writeprot /vol d: /ro
```

The following command makes the D drive read-write:

```
> writeprot /vol d: /rw
```

The following command attempts to make all volumes on the basic disk represented by the D drive read-only:

```
> writeprot /vol d: /ro
```

Using VBScript

```
' This code makes a volume or disk read only (if possible)
' ------ SCRIPT CONFIGURATION ------
strDrive = "<Drive>"   ' e.g. e:

' This assumes writeprot is in your PATH, if not, fully qualify
' the path to the command (e.g. c:\bin\writeprot.exe)
strCommand = "writeprot /vol " & strDrive & " /ro"
' ------ END CONFIGURATION
set objWshShell = WScript.CreateObject("WScript.Shell")
intRC = objWshShell.Run(strCommand, 0, TRUE)
if intRC <> 0 then
    WScript.Echo "Error returned from running the command: " & intRC
    WScript.Echo "Command attempted: " & strCommand
else
    WScript.Echo "Command executed successfully."
end if
```

Discussion

Volumes on basic disks and dynamic disks are treated differently when it comes to enabling write protection. You can make individual volumes on a dynamic disk read-only, but for basic disks, you have to write-protect the entire disk, including all volumes. If you attempt to write-protect a single volume on a basic disk with multiple volumes using *writeprot*, an error will be returned. You'd need to run the same command with the –unsafe option to write-protect all volumes on the basic disk.

You cannot write protect any volume that has files locked for read or write access. Since files are always opened for reading on the system volume, you will not be able to write protect that volume.

 It was reported by some of the technical reviewers of this book that the third-party drivers do NOT properly support write protection.

See Also

Recipe 8.13 for making a file or folder read-only and Recipe 8.19 for finding open files

7.12 Mapping a Network Drive

Problem

You want to map a drive to a folder on a remote computer.

Solution

Using a graphical user interface

1. Open Windows Explorer.
2. From the menu, select Tools → Map Network Drive.
3. Beside Drive, select the drive letter you want to assign.
4. Beside Folder, enter the UNC path to the network share you want to map.
5. If you want the drive to be persistent, make sure the box beside Reconnect at logon is checked.
6. By default, your current credentials will be used to access the network share, if you want to use alternate credentials, click the different username link. Enter a username and password and click OK.
7. Click Finish.

Using a command-line interface

The following command maps a drive to a network share point:

```
> net use <Drive> <Share>
```

The following example maps \\rtp01\myshare to the N drive using your current credentials:

```
> net use N: \\rtp01\myshare
```

The following example maps a persistent drive using alternate credentials:

```
> net use N: \\rtp01\c$ /user:amer\rallen /savecred /persistent:yes
```

The following command lists all network connections including mapped drives:

```
> net use
```

The following command deletes the N network drive:

```
> net use N: /delete
```

Using VBScript

```
' This code creates a mapped drive to a network path.
' ------ SCRIPT CONFIGURATION ------
strDrive - "<Drive>" ' e.g. N:
strPath = "<Path>"    ' e.g. \\rtp01\c$\temp
strUser = "<User>"    ' e.g. AMER\rallen
strPassword = "<Password>"
boolPersistent - True  ' True = Persistent ; False = Not Persistent
' ------ END CONFIGURATION ---------
set objNetwork = WScript.CreateObject("WScript.Network")
objNetwork.MapNetworkDrive strDrive, strPath, boolPersistent, _
                          strUser, strPassword
WScript.Echo "Successfully mapped drive"
```

Discussion

Mapping a drive to a folder on a remote computer is primarily done for convenience. There is nothing you can do with a mapped drive that you can't also do with a UNC path (e.g., \\rtp01\myshare). However, some applications may not support accessing files via UNC path, so you might need to use a mapped drive instead. A mapped drive is more convenient if you access a remote computer frequently from a tool such as Windows Explorer. Instead of typing a long UNC path, you can simple type the drive letter and access the folder much quicker. And if you need to access the remote folder using alternate credentials, creating a mapped drive can save you even more time because you can store the credentials with the mapped drive so that when your computer starts up, the drive is automatically mapped using the alternate credentials. But be warned, this approach is also a great way to create account lockouts following password changes.

> You can't use the *cd* command within a CMD session to change directories into a UNC path. You can, however, use the *pushd* command, which creates a temporary drive for the UNC path (much as if you were mapping a drive) and *cd* into that drive. After you end the CMD session, the drive is dismounted and the previously assigned drive letter becomes available again.

See Also

MS KB 149861, "How Authentication Works for Net Use Command," and MS KB 308582, "How to connect and disconnect a network drive in Windows XP"

7.13 Creating a Virtual Drive to Another Drive or Folder

Problem

You want to make a folder the root of a drive or you want to use multiple drive letters for the same drive.

Solution

Using a command-line interface

Use the following command to create a new drive pointing to an existing path on the system:

```
> subst <Drive> <Path>
```

The following example creates an E drive pointing to *C:\scripts*:

```
> subst E: C:\scripts
```

The following example creates an F drive pointing to *C:*

```
> subst F: C:\
```

Using VBScript

There aren't any WMI or WSH interfaces for creating virtual drives, but you can shell out to the *subst* command if you really want to do it via a script.

```
' This code creates a virtual drive.
' ------ SCRIPT CONFIGURATION ------
strDrive = "<Drive>"  ' e.g. e:
strPath  = "<Path>"   ' e.g. c:\scripts

' This assumes subst is in your PATH, if not, fully qualify
' the path to the command here:
strCommand = "subst " & strDrive & " " & strPath
' ------ END CONFIGURATION ---------
set objWshShell = WScript.CreateObject("WScript.Shell")
intRC = objWshShell.Run(strCommand, 0, TRUE)
if intRC <> 0 then
    WScript.Echo "Error returned from running the command: " & intRC
    WScript.Echo "Command attempted: " & strCommand
```

```
else
    WScript.Echo "Command executed successfully."
end if
```

Discussion

The *subst* command is a useful utility for making folders on a volume appear as a drive. Let's say, for example, that you like to store files in your user profile (e.g., *C:\ Documents and Settings\rallen\My Documents\scripts*) and need to frequently access those files from a command line. You are starting to get carpal tunnel syndrome because even with tab-completion enabled, it takes a bit of wrist work to type out that path. You can use *subst* to create a drive that is mapped to that folder path and save yourself a lot of typing.

There are a few caveats to be aware of when using *subst*:

The drives are removed after reboot
    Perhaps the biggest drawback to virtual drives is that they are removed when a machine restarts. That means to create a persistent virtual drive you need to use a logon script.

Shadow copies are not created
    On Windows XP, shadow copies are created for all local volumes, but this doesn't apply to virtual drives created with *subst*. Since the virtual drive corresponds to a logical volume, a shadow copy is already created for its contents.

The drives cannot be used to set quotas
    Again, due to the fact the contents of a virtual drive are already part of a volume, which may already have quotas enabled, you cannot configure quotas.

Deleting the virtual drive deletes only the mapping, not the data
    If you delete a virtual drive using the /d option, only the drive mapping is deleted, not the underlying contents of the drive.

See Also

Recipe 7.12 for mapping a network drive; MS KB 218740, "Cannot Use Subst.exe with UNC Path," and MS KB 269163, "Drives Created with the Subst Command Are Not Connected"

7.14 Finding Large Files and Folders on a Volume

Problem

You want to find files or folders that exceed a certain size on a volume.

Solution

Using a graphical user interface

1. From the Start menu, select Search.
2. If you are presented with the options for what to search on, click All files and folders.
3. Click on What size is it?
4. Select the radio button beside Specify size and enter the size you want to search.
5. Select additional criteria if necessary and click Search.

Using a command-line interface

The following command finds folders that are greater than 100 MB in size on the D drive:

```
> diruse /s /m /q:100 /d d:
```

The /s option causes subdirectories to be searched, the /m option displays disk usage in megabytes, the /q:100 option causes folders that are greater than 100 MB to be marked, and the /d option displays only folders that exceed the threshold specified by /q.

Use the *diskuse* command to find files over a certain size. The following command displays files over 100 MB in size on the D drive:

```
> diskuse D: /x:104857600 /v /s
```

The /x:104857600 option causes files over 104,857,600 bytes to be displayed and is valid only if you include the /v option (verbose). The /s option means subdirectories from the specified path (in this case the D drive) are searched.

Using downloadable software

The DiskPie Pro utility from *PC Magazine* (*http://www.pcmag.com/article2/ 0,1759,1616002,00.asp*) can, among other things, display the largest files on a particular drive. Figure 7-1 shows an example of the largest files on the C drive.

DiskPie Pro is available for free to *PC Magazine* subscribers or can be purchased for $5.97 by itself. Other features include displaying the total size of files with a particular type and monitoring folders that exceed a certain size.

Using VBScript

```
' This code finds all files over a certain size.
' ------ SCRIPT CONFIGURATION ------
strComputer = "<ComputerName>"
intSizeBytes = 1024 * 1024 * 500  ' = 500 MB
' ------ END CONFIGURATION ---------
```

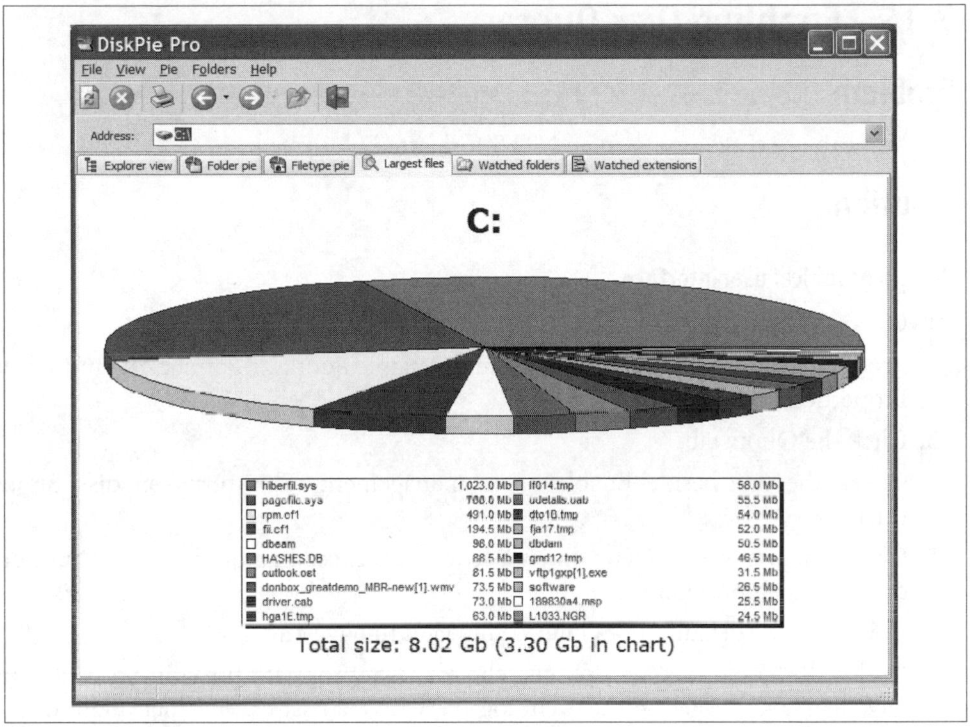

Figure 7-1. DiskPie Pro utility

```
set objWMI = GetObject("winmgmts:\\" & strComputer & "\root\cimv2")
set colFiles = objWMI.ExecQuery
    ("Select * from CIM_DataFile where FileSize > '" & intSizeBytes & "'")
for each objFile in colFiles
    Wscript.Echo objFile.Name & "  " & objFile.Filesize / 1024 / 1024 & "MB"
next
```

Discussion

If you find that you are running out of space on a volume and want to see what is consuming the most space, you are better off using the *diruse* command-line solution. With the other solutions, you could search for all files over 100 MB, for example, but a user could have created a bunch of 10 MB MPEG files. Unfortunately, you can't use the Search dialog box or VBScript to search on folder sizes, which leaves *diruse* as the most appropriate tool in this scenario.

See Also

Recipe 7.7 for cleaning up disk space and MSDN: CIM_DataFile

7.15 Enabling Disk Quotas

Problem

You want to use disk quotas on an NTFS-formatted file system.

Solution

Using a graphical user interface

1. Open Windows Explorer.
2. Browse to the drive on which you want to enable quotas, right-click it, and select Properties.
3. Click the Quota tab.
4. Check the box beside Enable quota management. This turns on disk quota tracking.
5. Check the box beside Deny disk space to users exceeding quota limit to turn on disk quota enforcement.
6. Configure the default quota limit if you want to have one.
7. Under the quota logging options, check the appropriate boxes if you want to have messages logged to the event log every time a user exceeds her quota warning or limit levels.
8. Click OK.
9. A dialog box will pop open that informs you the disk needs to be scanned to collect disk statistics. Click OK.

Using a command-line interface

The following command enables disk quota enforcement on drive D:

```
> fsutil quota enforce d:
```

The following command enables disk quota tracking on drive D:

```
> fsutil quota track d:
```

The following command disables disk quotas on drive D:

```
> fsutil quota disable d:
```

 You cannot modify the default limit and warning settings with *fsutil*.

Using VBScript

```
' This code enables disk quotas on a drive.
' ------ SCRIPT CONFIGURATION ------
strComputer = "."
strDrive = "<Drive>"  ' e.g. D:
intEnable = 2  ' 0 = Disabled, 1 = Tracked, 2 = Enforced
intDefaultLimit   = 1024 * 1024 * 500  ' 500 MB
intDefaultWarning = 1024 * 1024 * 400  ' 400 MB
' ------ END CONFIGURATION ---------
set objWMI = GetObject("winmgmts:\\" & strComputer & "\root\cimv2")
set objDisk = objWMI.Get("Win32_QuotaSetting.VolumePath='" & strDrive & "\\'")
objDisk.State = intEnable
objDisk.ExceededNotification = True
objDisk.WarningExceededNotification = True
objDisk.DefaultLimit = intDefaultLimit
objDisk.DefaultWarningLimit = intDefaultWarning
objDisk.Put_
WScript.Echo "Quotas enabled on " & objDisk.Caption
```

Discussion

NTFS disk quotas are based on the files a user owns on a volume, not where those files are located on a volume. Quotas are set on a per-volume basis so it doesn't matter where within a volume a user owns files; they all count against any configured quota for that volume. If you have multiple volumes you want quotas on, you have to configure each separately.

When you initially enable quotas, you have a choice between tracking quota usage and enforcing quota usage. Tracking quota usage means that a message will be written to the System event log when a user exceeds his warning or limit quota thresholds. The user isn't notified of this and can continue to exceed his quota limits. Enforcing quota usage means that when the user exceeds his quota limit and attempts to add more files to the volume, he receives an "insufficient disk space" error message. Events are still logged to the System event log just as with quota tracking.

There are two default settings that you can configure when quotas are enabled. The first is the default warning threshold. After a user exceeds this size, a message is logged to the event log. The default limit threshold is the maximum amount of storage that individual users can use. If you want to apply nondefault quota parameters to specific users or groups, see Recipe 7.16.

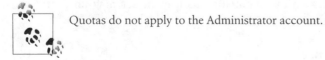 Quotas do not apply to the Administrator account.

You can also enable quotas using Group Policy if your computers are in an Active Directory domain. You can find the quota settings under Computer Configuration\ Administrative Templates\System\Disk Quotas. If your users have administrative rights over the machine you've enabled quotas on, those users can disable or modify the quota configuration. If you use Group Policy to configure quotas, users cannot change them even if they are administrators.

See Also

Recipe 7.16 for configuring disk quotas for users; MS KB 183322, "How to Enable Disk Quotas in Windows 2000," MS KB 307984, "HOW TO: Create Disk Quota Reports in Windows XP," MS KB 308664, "How To Export and Import Disk Quota Settings to Other Volumes in Windows XP," and MS KB 320686, "Disk Quota Charges Increase If You Turn On the NTFS Compression Functionality"

7.16   Limiting a User to a Specified Disk Quota

Problem

You want to configure disk quota limits for a particular user.

Solution

Using a graphical user interface

1. Open Windows Explorer.
2. Browse to the drive on which you want to enable quotas, right-click it, and select Properties.
3. Click the Quota tab.
4. If quotas are enabled, click the Quota Entries button. If quotas are not enabled, enable them as described in Recipe 7.15.
5. To configure a new quota entry for a user, select Quota → New Quota Entry from the menu.
6. Use the object picker to locate the target user and click OK. The Add New Quota Entry dialog will open.
7. If you've configured a default quota, that limit will be selected by default. You can disable disk quota enforcement for this user or set new limit and warning levels. After you are done, click OK.

Using a command-line interface

The following command configures a quota for a particular user:

```
> fsutil quota modify <Drive> <WarningBytes> <LimitBytes> <Domain\User>
```

The following example sets a quota for user AMER\rallen with a ~381 MB warning and ~476 MB limit:

```
> fsutil quota modify d: 400000000 500000000 AMER\rallen
```

Using VBScript

```
' This code configures a quota for a particular user.
' ------ SCRIPT CONFIGURATION ------
strComputer = "."
strUser = "<User>"                  ' e.g. rallen
strUserDomain = "<Domain>"          ' e.g. AMER
strDrive = "<Drive>"                ' e.g. D:
intLimit = 1024 * 1024 * 600    ' = 600 MB
intWarning - 1024 * 1024 * 350 ' = 350 MB
' ------ END CONFIGURATION ---------
set objWMI = GetObject("winmgmts:\\" & strComputer & "\root\cimv2")
set objDisk = objWMI.Get("Win32_LogicalDisk.DeviceID='" & strDrive & "'")
WScript.Echo "Found disk " & objDisk.Caption
set objUser = objWMI.Get("Win32_Account.Domain='" & strUserDomain & _
                          "',Name='" & strUser & "'")
WScript.Echo "Found user " & objUser.Name
set objQuota = objWMI.Get("Win32_DiskQuota.QuotaVolume=" & _
        "'Win32_LogicalDisk.DeviceID-""" & strDrive & """'," & _
        "User='Win32_Account.Domain=""" & strUserDomain & _
        """,Name=""" & strUser & """'")
objQuota.Limit = intLimit
objQuota.WarningLimit = intWarning
objQuota.Put_
WScript.Echo "Set quota for user " & objUser.Name
```

Discussion

If you decide that you want to delete a quota entry for a particular user, perhaps because you don't want to limit that user anymore, you have to first reassign ownership of all files owned by the user on the volume. Since quota usage is entirely determined by file ownership, you can't have files on a quota-enabled volume that belong to a user that doesn't have a quota entry. You must take ownership of the files yourself, move the files to another volume, or permanently delete the files before deleting the quota entry.

 If you don't want to go to all the trouble of transferring ownership of files, another option would be to simply set the quota for the user really high (like to the overall size of the volume).

See Also

Recipe 7.15 for enabling disk quotas; MS KB 183322, "How to Enable Disk Quotas in Windows 2000," MS KB 307984, "HOW TO: Create Disk Quota Reports in Windows

XP," and MS KB 308664, "How To Export and Import Disk Quota Settings to Other Volumes in Windows XP"

7.17   Viewing Disk Quota Usage

Problem

You want to view the quota usage for one or more users.

Solution

Using a graphical user interface

1. Open Windows Explorer.
2. Browse to the drive on which you want to enable quotas, right-click it, and select Properties.
3. Click the Quota tab.
4. If quotas are enabled, click the Quota Entries button. If quotas are not enabled, enable them as described in Recipe 7.15.
5. The Quota Entries application contains a listing of all users that have quotas configured along with their quota limit, warning limit, and amount used. You can sort this screen by select View → Arrange Items from the menu and choosing one of the options to sort by.

Using a command-line interface

Use the following command to view the quota usage for all users on drive D:

```
> fsutil quota query d:
```

Use the following command to search the event log for all users that are violating their quota:

```
> fsutil quota violations
```

 Before using the violations options of *fsutil*, be sure that you've enabled event logging of warning and limit errors (see Recipe 7.15).

Using VBScript

```
' This code displays the quota usage for users on a particular drive.
' ------ SCRIPT CONFIGURATION ------
strComputer = "."
strDrive = "<Drive>"  ' e.g. D:
' ------ END CONFIGURATION ---------
set objWMI = GetObject("winmgmts:\\" & strComputer & "\root\cimv2")
```

```
    set colQuotas = objWMI.ExecQuery("select * from Win32_DiskQuota " & _
        "where QuotaVolume = 'Win32_LogicalDisk.DeviceID=""" & strDrive & """'")
    for each objQuota in colQuotas
        WScript.Echo "User: "& objQuota.User
        WScript.Echo "  Volume: "& objQuota.QuotaVolume
        WScript.Echo "  Quota Limit: " & _
                         objQuota.Limit / 1024 / 1024 & "MB"
        WScript.Echo "  Warning Limit: " & _
                         objQuota.WarningLimit / 1024 / 1024 & "MB"
        WScript.Echo "  Disk Space Used: " & _
                         objQuota.DiskSpaceUsed / 1024 / 1024 & "MB"
        WScript.Echo ""
    next
```

Discussion

One of the nice features of the Quota Entries application is that you can drag-and-drop entries in it to a spreadsheet application like Excel. Simply highlight the entries you're interested in and drag them to Excel. You can also copy and paste them using Ctrl-C and Ctrl-V.

If you've enabled compression on a volume where quotas are also enabled, you may actually see quota usage increase compared to the same volume without compression.

See Also

Recipe 7.16 for enabling disk quotas for users; MS KB 307984, "HOW TO: Create Disk Quota Reports in Windows XP," MS KB 308664, "How To Export and Import Disk Quota Settings to Other Volumes in Windows XP," and MS KB 320686, "Disk Quota Charges Increase If You Turn On the NTFS Compression Functionality"

CHAPTER 8
Files, Folders, and Shares

8.0 Introduction

This chapter covers some of the common tasks facing administrators when it comes to managing the Windows filesystem. We'll not only touch on the really basic tasks such as creating, deleting, renaming, and moving files and folders, but more advanced topics such as viewing a list of all open files and identifying the process that has a file locked.

Using a Graphical User Interface

You are undoubtedly familiar with the all-purpose file, folder, and shared folder management tool, Windows Explorer. With it you can create, move, rename, and delete files and folders as well as hide, encrypt, and make them read-only. As you'll see, this is the most often used graphical tool in this chapter.

You are also probably familiar with the Shared Folder MMC snap-in (*fsmgmt.msc*), which is commonly seen as a part of the Computer Management tool. This snap-in allows you to do just about anything with shares (i.e., create, delete, see who is using them, etc.).

Using a Command-Line Interface

As you might expect, there are a host of command-line tools to manipulate files and folders on Windows XP. Table 8-1 lists the command-line tools used in this chapter and the recipes they are used in.

Table 8-1. Command-line tools used in Chapter 8

Tool	Location	Recipes
attrib	%SystemRoot%\system32	8.12, 8.13
auditpol	Windows 2000 Resource Kit	8.18
cipher	%SystemRoot%\system32	8.15

Table 8-1. Command-line tools used in Chapter 8 (continued)

Tool	Location	Recipes
compress	Windows Resource Kit	8.14
copy	CMD shell	8.10
creatfil	Windows Resource Kit	8.1
del	CMD shell	8.1
dir	CMD shell	8.5
fc	%SystemRoot%\system32	8.11
findstr	%SystemRoot%\system32	8.9
forfiles	Windows 2000 Resource Kit	8.22
inuse	Windows 2000 Resource Kit	8.16
linkd	Windows Resource Kit	8.7
mkdir	CMD shell	8.2
move	CMD shell	8.10
net file	%SystemRoot%\system32	8.19
net share	%SystemRoot%\system32	8.23, 8.24
openfiles	%SystemRoot%\system32	8.19
ren	CMD shell	8.10
rmdir	CMD shell	8.2
subinacl	Windows Resource Kit	8.17, 8.25
takeown	Windows 2000 Resource Kit	8.17
where	Windows 2000 Resource Kit	8.9

Using Downloadable Software

Sysinternals (*http://www.sysinternals.com*) produces several file-related utilities, and we use many of them in this chapter. They include File Monitor (Recipe 8.19) for monitoring file activity, Fundelete (Recipe 8.3) for replacing the recycle bin, Shareenum (Recipe 8.24), for enumerating share points on a network, Process Explorer and *handle* for listing all the file handles a particular process has open (Recipe 8.20), *junction* for creating junction points (Recipe 8.20), *sdelete* for securely deleting files (Recipe 8.4), and *strings* for searching for text strings in binary files (Recipe 8.9).

The other downloadable tools we describe in this chapter include PowerDesk Pro for managing files (Recipe 8.10), WinZip for compressing files (Recipe 8.14), PGP for encrypting files (Recipe 8.15), *setacl* for setting auditing on files (Recipe 8.18), and folders from the command line and *shortcut* for creating shortcuts from the command line (Recipe 8.6).

Using VBScript

Between WMI and WSH, you have the ability to automate reading, writing, and searching files and folders. Unfortunately, the WMI file and folder classes don't provide the capability to do basic manipulation, which is where WSH comes in. Table 8-2 lists all the WSH and WMI classes used in this chapter.

Table 8-2. WMI and WSH classes used in Chapter 8

WMI class	Description	Recipes
Cim_DataFile	Enumerate and manage files and folders. (Note that this class represents both files and folders, not just files.)	8.1, 8.5, 8.10, 8.14, 5,17, 8.22
Scripting.FileSystemObject	Read, write, and manipulate files and folders.	8.1, 8.2, 8.11, 8.12, 8.13
Win32_Directory	Enumerate folders.	8.5, 8.14
Win32_ShortcutFile	Enumerate and manage shortcut files (*.lnk*).	8.6
Win32_Share	Enumerate and manage share points.	8.23, 8.24

8.1   Creating and Deleting a File

Problem

You want to create or delete a file.

Solution

Using a graphical user interface

1. Open Windows Explorer.
2. In the left pane, browse to the folder where you want to create the file or that contains the file you want to delete. Click on the folder.
3. To create a new file, right-click in the right pane and select New and the type of file you want to create. To edit the file, double-click on it.
4. To delete a file, right-click the file in the right pane and select Delete. Click Yes to confirm. This moves the file to the recycle bin. You can also press Shift+Del to bypass the recycle bin and permanently delete the file.

Using a command-line interface

There aren't many options for creating files from the command line. You can create a simple text file by redirecting output from a command. Here is an example:

```
> echo hello > myfile.txt
```

One command you may not be familiar with is *creatfil.exe* from the Resource Kit. With it you can create files of arbitrary length. This is useful only if you need to create some files to test with or to test low disk space scenarios. The following command creates a 10 MB file named *foobar.txt*:

```
> creatfil foobar.txt 10240
```

To delete a file use the *del* command:

```
> del c:\scripts\foobar.vbs
```

If you want to delete a file on a remote system, you can use the *psexec* command (from Sysinternals):

```
> psexec \\<ComputerName> cmd.exe /c del c:\scripts\foobar.vbs
```

To provide alternate credentials with *psexec* use the /u and /p options to specify a username and password respectively.

Using VBScript

See Chapter 1 for examples of creating and appending to files using VBScript.

```
' This code deletes a file
' ------ SCRIPT CONFIGURATION ------
strFilePath = "<FilePath>" ' e.g. "d:\scripts\test.txt"
' ------ END CONFIGURATION ---------
set objFSO = CreateObject("Scripting.FileSystemObject")
objFSO.DeleteFile(strFilePath)
WScript.Echo "Successfully deleted file"


' This code deletes a file using WMI
' ------ SCRIPT CONFIGURATION ------
strComputer = "."
strFilePath = "<FilePath>" ' e.g. "d:\scripts\test.txt"
' ------ END CONFIGURATION ---------
set objFile = GetObject("winmgmts:\\"& strComputer & _
                        "\root\cimv2:CIM_Datafile.Name='" & strFilePath & "'")
objFile.Delete
WScript.Echo "Successfully deleted file"
```

8.2   Creating and Deleting a Folder

Problem

You want to create or delete a folder.

Solution

Using a graphical user interface

1. Open Windows Explorer.

2. In the left pane, browse to the folder where you want to create a folder or that contains the folder you want to delete. Click on the folder.

3. To create a new folder, right-click in the right pane and select New and the type of folder you want to create.

4. To delete a folder, right-click the folder in the right pane and select Delete. Click Yes to confirm. This moves the folder and its contents to the recycle bin.

Using a command-line interface

To create a folder, use the `mkdir` command (or `md` for short):

```
> mkdir c:\scripts
```

To remove a folder, use the `rmdir` command (or `rd` for short):

```
> rmdir c:\scripts
```

Use the `/s` option to remove a folder and all files and subfolders contained within it. Use the `/q` option to bypass the confirmation prompt when using `/s`.

To delete a folder on a remote system, use the *psexec* command (from Sysinternals):

```
> psexec \\<ComputerName> cmd.exe /c rmdir /s c:\temp
```

To provide alternate credentials with *psexec*, use the `/u` and `/p` options to specify a username and password respectively.

Using downloadable software

If you want a New Folder option when you right-click in the *left* pane of Windows Explorer, check out the following tool: *http://www.createwindow.com/freeware/newfold.htm*.

Using VBScript

```
' This code deletes a folder
' ------ SCRIPT CONFIGURATION ------
strFolderPath = "<FolderPath>" ' e.g. "d:\temp"
' ------ END CONFIGURATION ---------
set objFSO = CreateObject("Scripting.FileSystemObject")
objFSO.DeleteFolder(strFolderPath)
WScript.Echo "Successfully deleted folder"
```

8.3   Undeleting a File

Problem

You want to attempt to undelete a file that you previously deleted.

Solution

Using a graphical user interface

Files that you delete with Windows Explorer can be restored using the recycle bin:

1. Double-click the recycle bin icon on the desktop.
2. Right-click the file you want to undelete and select Restore.

This assumes that you didn't use the Shift+Del key combination to delete the file or haven't emptied the recycle bin since the file was deleted. One problem with this method is that the recycle bin captures only files deleted from Explorer. None of the files that are deleted over the network, via a command prompt, or with a script are sent to the recycle bin.

Using downloadable software

The Sysinternals Fundelete tool can be used as a replacement for the recycle bin. It works just like the recycle bin except it does more. The recycle bin icon on the desktop is replaced with a Fundelete Bin icon. The Fundelete Bin captures any type file deletion that occurs on the computer. And just as with the recycle bin, you can restore files contained in the Fundelete Bin.

Fundelete hasn't been updated since 2000, so if you are looking for something that is more recently updated, Executive Software makes a product that is similar to Fundelete with even more features, called Undelete. Unlike Fundelete, you have to pay for Undelete. For more information, visit: *http://www.undelete.com*.

See Also

MS KB 136517, "How the Recycle Bin Stores Files"

8.4   Securely Deleting a File

Problem

You want to delete a file so that it cannot be retrieved by undeleting it.

Solution

Using downloadable software

Use the Sysinternals `sdelete` command to securely delete files:

```
> sdelete <FileName>
```

Use the –p option to specify the number of passes to overwrite the disk segments. The more passes, the less likely the file can be recovered.

The –s option can be used to recursively delete everything within a folder:

```
> sdelete -p 4 -s c:\logs
```

Using VBScript

```
' This code runs the sdelete command
' ------ SCRIPT CONFIGURATION ------
strCommand = "sdelete -p 5 c:\logs\tue.log"
' ------ END CONFIGURATION ---------
set objWshShell = WScript.CreateObject("WScript.Shell")
intRC = objWshShell.Run(strCommand, 0, TRUE)
if intRC <> 0 then
   WScript.Echo "Error returned from running the command: " & intRC
else
   WScript.Echo "Command executed successfully"
end if
```

Discussion

When you delete a file through Windows Explorer, it is sent to the recycle bin. You can use the recycle bin to restore the file back to its original location or you can permanently delete the file by emptying the recycle bin. But wait a second—the file doesn't really get deleted when you empty the recycle bin. All that happens is that the link to the collection of bits on the hard disk that make up the file is deleted. The bits that make up the file are still present on the disk. And it stays like this until the file system overwrites those bits with a new file. That means that if a bad guy stole your computer, he could run a program to examine the hard drive and restore files that have been previously deleted and not overwritten. That is, unless you *securely* delete the file using the Sysinternals `sdelete` command. `sdelete` works by writing random characters to the bits that made up the file before. This prevents programs from piecing the file back together. This doesn't prevent someone from restoring a previous copy of the file from backup, but no one will be able to take the hard drive and restore a deleted file on which you used `sdelete`.

 You can also use the cipher tool to overwrite deleted data. See MS KB 814599 for more information.

See Also

MS KB 136517, "How the Recycle Bin Stores Files," and MS KB 814599, "HOW TO: Use Cipher.exe to Overwrite Deleted Data in Windows Server 2003"

8.5   Viewing the Properties of a File or Folder

Problem

You want to view the creation or last modification timestamp of a file or folder or determine whether it is encrypted, archived, compressed, and so on.

Solution

Using a graphical user interface

1. Open Windows Explorer.
2. In the left pane, browse to the parent folder of the file or folder you want to view properties for. Click on the parent folder. This displays the list of subfolders and files in the right pane.
3. In the right pane, right-click on the file or folder you want to view and select Properties.
4. Several properties are displayed in the General tab. Click the Advanced button to see additional attributes.

Using a command-line interface

The *dir* command can be run as part of a CMD session to display the last-modified time, size, and owner of a file or directory. Here is an example:

```
> dir /q <Path>
```

You can also display other attributes of a file or folder with the /A option. Run dir /? for a complete list of options and parameters.

One way to view the files on a remote system is to use a UNC path. This command displays the contents of the *c:\scripts* folder on the host *fs01*:

```
> dir /q \\fs01\c$\scripts
```

You can use the *runas* command to specify alternate credentials if needed or use the Sysinternals *psexec* command.

Using VBScript

```
' This code displays the properties and attributes of a file
' ------ SCRIPT CONFIGURATION ------
strFilePath = "d:\\myfile.txt"
```

```
strComputer = "."
' ------ END CONFIGURATION ---------
set objWMI = GetObject("winmgmts:\\" & strComputer & "\root\cimv2")
set objFile = objWMI.Get("CIM_Datafile=""" & strFilePath & """")
WScript.Echo objFile.Name

WScript.Echo " 8.3 Name: " & objFile.EightDotThreeFileName
WScript.Echo " Drive: " & objFile.Drive
WScript.Echo " FileName: " & objFile.FileName
WScript.Echo " Extension: " & objFile.Extension
WScript.Echo " FileType: " & objFile.FileType
WScript.Echo " Path: " & objFile.Path
WScript.Echo " InUse Counter: " & objFile.InUseCount

WScript.Echo " Creation Date: " & objFile.CreationDate
WScript.Echo " Last Accessed: " & objFile.LastAccessed
WScript.Echo " Last Modified: " & objFile.LastModified

WScript.Echo " Archive: " & objFile.Archive
WScript.Echo " Compressed: " & objFile.Compressed
WScript.Echo " Encrypted: " & objFile.Encrypted
WScript.Echo " System: " & objFile.System
WScript.Echo " Writeable: " & objFile.Writeable
WScript.Echo " Hidden: " & objFile.Hidden


' This code displays the properties and attributes of a folder
' ------ SCRIPT CONFIGURATION ------
strDirPath = "c:\\scripts"
strComputer = "."
' ------ END CONFIGURATION ---------

set objWMI = GetObject("winmgmts:\\" & strComputer & "\root\cimv2")
set objFile = objWMI.Get("Win32_Directory=""" & strDirPath & """")
WScript.Echo objFile.Name

WScript.Echo " 8.3 Name: " & objFile.EightDotThreeFileName
WScript.Echo " Drive: " & objFile.Drive
WScript.Echo " Folder Name: " & objFile.FileName
WScript.Echo " File Type: " & objFile.FileType
WScript.Echo " Path: " & objFile.Path
WScript.Echo " InUse Counter: " & objFile.InUseCount

WScript.Echo " Creation Date: " & objFile.CreationDate
WScript.Echo " Last Accessed: " & objFile.LastAccessed
WScript.Echo " Last Modified: " & objFile.LastModified

WScript.Echo " Archive: " & objFile.Archive
WScript.Echo " Compressed: " & objFile.Compressed
WScript.Echo " Encrypted: " & objFile.Encrypted
WScript.Echo " System: " & objFile.System
WScript.Echo " Writeable: " & objFile.Writeable
WScript.Echo " Hidden: " & objFile.Hidden
```

Discussion

Another useful tool for displaying file information is Visual File Information (*vfi.exe*) from the Resource Kit. It can display file information for several files on a single screen. You start by selecting a folder and from there it enumerates every file contained within that folder and all subfolders. You can then sort by creation or modification date, size, extension, and a number of other attributes. The tool is good at enumerating over hundreds or even thousands of files very quickly, so if you wanted to find the largest file on a disk or find the most recently modified file, this would be a great tool for the job.

Figure 8-1 shows sample output from VFI.

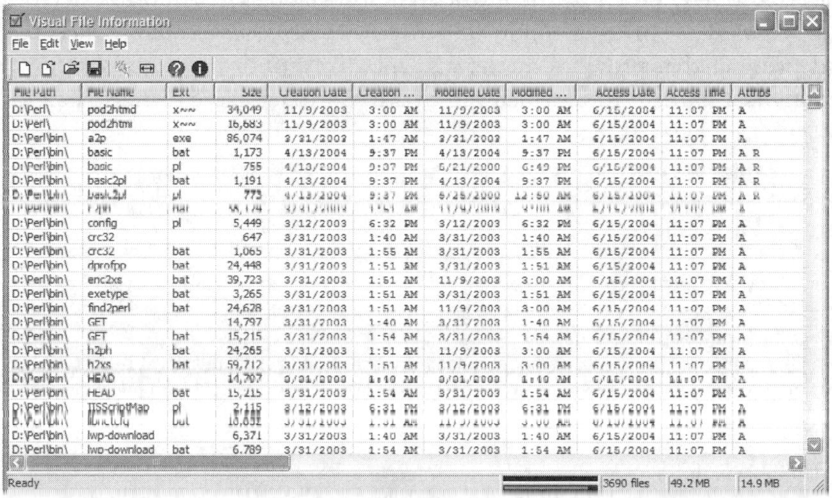

Figure 8-1. Visual File Information sample output

See Also

MS KB 320050, "HOW TO: Use the File Attribute Management Script (File-attributes.pl) in Windows 2000"

8.6   Creating a Shortcut

Problem

You want to create a shortcut to a file or folder. A shortcut is simply a file with a *.lnk* extension that redirects you to another file or folder when clicked on in Windows Explorer. You can also distinguish shortcut files from regular files by a small arrow in the bottom left side of their icons.

Solution

Using a graphical user interface

1. Open Windows Explorer.
2. Browse to the file or folder you want to create a shortcut for.
3. Right-click the file or folder and select Create Shortcut.
4. Move the shortcut file to desired location.

Using downloadable software

The Windows NT Resource Kit had a tool called *shortcut* that could be used to create shortcuts, but it isn't present in the Windows 2000 or Windows Server 2003 Resource Kits. The MKS Toolkit (*http://www.mkssoftware.com/products/tk/*), an excellent product that provides numerous Unix-like utilities for the Windows platform, contains a *shortcut* tool, which can create shortcuts. Here is the syntax for that tool:

```
> shortcut [-f dest-file] [-a arglist] [-w workdir] [-s show-keyword] [-i
iconpath[,iconindex]] [-d description] [-D] shortcut-file

-a arglist
defines any arguments to the executable file specified with the -f dest-file option.

-d description
specifies descriptive text to be embedded in the link file. description is only
displayed when you use the -p option to print the contents of the link file. If
description includes space, the text should be enclosed in double quotes (").

-D shortcut-file
specifies the shortcut-file is on the desktop.

-f dest-file
specifies the full path and file name of the executable file to be run when the link
file is double clicked.

-i iconpath[,iconindex]
specifies the icon to be displayed for the link file. If the specified icon contains
multiple images, determine which image is to be displayed by entering the appropriate
number for iconindex.

-p
displays the contents of the specified shortcut file.

-s show-keyword
specifies how the executable is displayed when invoked. show-keyword can be one of
the following:

SW_SHOW            starts the program in standard mode
SW_SHOWMAXIMIZED   starts the program in full screen mode
```

```
SW_SHOWMINIMIZED    starts the program minimized
SW_SHOWMINNOACTIVE  displays the program as an icon but does not start it

When this option is not specified, shortcut defaults to SW_SHOW.

-w workdir
specifies the working directory in which the program is started.
```

Here is an example:

```
> shortcut -f c:/perl/bin/perl.exe -a -L perl-link.lnk
```

> The MKS Toolkit isn't free and can be quite expensive, but there is
> another shortcut utility from the following site that is free: *http://www.optimumx.com*.

Using VBScript

```
' This code creates a shortcut.

set objWSHShell - CreateObject("WScript.Shell")

' Pass the path to the shortcut
set objSC = objWSHShell.CreateShortcut("d:\mylog.lnk")

' Description - Description of the shortcut
objSC.Description = "Shortcut to MyLog file"

' HotKey - hot key sequence to launch the shortcut
objSC.HotKey = "CTRL+ALT+SHIFT+X"

' IconLocation - Path of icon to use for the shortcut file
objSC.IconLocation = "notepad.exe, 0"   ' 0 is the index

' TargetPath = Path to source file or folder
objSC.TargetPath = "c:\windows\notepad.exe"

' Arguments - Any additional parameters to pass to TargetPath
objSC.Arguments = "c:\mylog.txt"

' WindowStyle - Type of window to create
objSC.WindowStyle = 1   ' 1 = normal; 3 = maximize window; 7 = minimize

' WorkingDirectory - Location of the working directory for the source app
objSC.WorkingDirectory = "c:\"
objSC.Save
WScript.Echo "Shortcut to mylog created"


' This code finds all shortcuts on a system.
' ------ SCRIPT CONFIGURATION ------
strComputer = "."
' ------ END CONFIGURATION ---------
```

```
set objWMI = GetObject("winmgmts:\\" & strComputer & "\root\cimv2")
set colSCs = objWMI.InstancesOf("Win32_ShortcutFile")
for each objSC in colSCs
    WScript.Echo "Name:   " & objSC.Name
    WScript.Echo "Target: " & objSC.Target
    WScript.Echo
    intCount = intCount + 1
next
WScript.Echo "Total shortcuts: " & intCount
```

Discussion

Shortcuts can be used to quickly access files and folders that are distributed across the filesystem or on remote systems. The problem with shortcuts is that they can quickly become out-of-date if not maintained. There is a tool in the Resource Kit to help identify dead shortcuts called *chklnks.exe*. It searches for all shortcuts whose target does not exist and displays them in a list. You can right-click on a shortcut to see the missing target location or delete selected dead shortcuts.

See Also

MS KB 140443, "How to Create a Shortcut on the Desktop"

8.7 Creating a Link or Junction Point

Problem

You want to create a link to a folder. This is sometimes referred to as a junction point. Links can be created only on NTFS file systems. Junction points are useful if you want to create a simplified path to a folder that is nested deeply in the filesystem.

Solution

Using a command-line interface

The *linkd.exe* command from the Resource Kit can create a link:

```
> linkd <LinkName> <Target>
```

This creates a link from folder *c:\program files\perl* to *c:\perl*:

```
> linkd c:\perl "c:\program files\perl"
```

This removes the link to *perl.exe*:

```
> linkd c:\perl /d
```

Using downloadable software

You can also use the Sysinternals *junction.exe* tool to create and delete links:

```
> junction c:\perl "c:\program files\perl"
> junction /d c:\perl
```

A cool thing about *junction.exe* is that you can also use it to search for links:

```
> junction /s c:\
```

If you are browsing the file system with Windows Explorer, you won't be able to differentiate links from normal files and folders, but in a CMD session you can. A link shows up as <JUNCTION>, as shown here:

```
> dir
 Volume in drive C is System
 Volume Serial Number is F0CE-2C6F

 Directory of C:\

01/02/2002  09:08 AM                 0 build.ini
10/06/2003  01:57 PM    <DIR>          Documents and Settings
11/02/2003  12:01 AM    <DIR>          Inetpub
11/18/2003  11:43 PM    <JUNCTION>     Perl
10/06/2003  02:14 PM    <DIR>          Program Files
11/16/2003  11:25 PM    <DIR>          scripts
12/04/2003  12:45 AM    <DIR>          WINDOWS
               6 File(s)    439,283,427 bytes
               7 Dir(s)   1,575,822,336 bytes free
```

Using VBScript

```
' This code creates a link by shelling out to the linkd command.
' ------ SCRIPT CONFIGURATION
strLink   = "c:\perl"
strTarget = "c:\program files\perl"
' ------ END CONFIGURATION ---------
strCommand = "linkd " & strLink & " " & strTarget
set objWshShell = WScript.CreateObject("WScript.Shell")
intRC = objWshShell.Run(strCommand, 0, TRUE)
if intRC <> 0 then
   WScript.Echo "Error returned from running the command: " & intRC
else
   WScript.Echo "Command executed successfully"
end if
```

Discussion

Links, or junction points, are different from shortcuts in that they are transparent to any process or application that accesses them. A shortcut is simply a file that redirects applications to a different location. A junction point is similar to a symbolic link in Unix. When you open a junction point, applications, such as Windows Explorer, behave as if you had opened the source folder. The only difference is that, if you delete the junction point in Windows Explorer, the source directory isn't deleted—only the junction point is deleted.

See Also

MS KB 205524, "How to create and manipulate NTFS junction points"

8.8   Creating a Program Alias

Problem

You want to create a program alias for an application or commonly accessed file. A program alias is a little different from a shortcut or link. It is similar in function to the *alias* command common on most Unix platforms. The alias name can be used as an alternative to typing the full program name. For example, let's say you use the Computer Management snap-in a lot and instead of going to Start menu → Administrative Tools → Computer Management, you prefer to type compmgmt.msc from the Run dialog or from the command line. You could create a program alias called *cmp* that points to compmgmt.msc, which reduces the number of characters you have to type by nine.

Solution

Here is how you'd create the *cmp* alias I just described.

Create a new subkey under the following key:

```
HKEY_LOCAL_MACHINE\SOFTWARE\Microsoft\Windows\CurrentVersion\App Paths
```

The name of the subkey should be the alias name. So you don't have to type an extension when using the alias, put *.exe* at the end of the name. In this case, the subkey name would be *cmp.exe*. You can, in fact, call the alias anything you want, but if the alias extension is not an executable extension such as *.exe*, you'll have to type the complete alias name when calling it. So it is perfectly fine to name the subkey *cmp.abc*, but you'd have to type **cmp.abc** instead of just **cmp** when typing it in the Run dialog.

Next, modify the default value under the new subkey; it shows up with the name (Default) in Registry Editor. Enter the full path to the program you are creating an alias for, which in this example would be *C:\Windows\system32\compmgmt.msc*. Actually, if the program is in your path, you only need to put the name of program and the system will find it for you, but you are probably better off entering the complete path so there is no mistake which program you want to run.

Now you'll be able to run *cmp* from the Run dialog. From a command prompt, you can't just type *cmp* and have it launch the program. Instead you need to type *start cmp*, which will do the trick.

Discussion

There are a couple of things to keep in mind when entering the path to the program in the value under the subkey:

- Don't use environment variables like *%SystemRoot%*. It won't work.
- Passing parameters to the program (which would have made aliases even more useful) also doesn't seem to work.

You can force the program to start in a particular directory by creating a Path value under the alias subkey. Create a REG_SZ value entry named Path and for its value put the full path to the directory where the program should start in.

8.9   Searching for Files or Folders

Problem

You want to find the files or folders that match certain criteria.

Solution

Using a graphical user interface

1. Select Search from the Start menu and click All files and folders if you are presented with an option for the types of files to search.
2. Now you'll be able to search for a particular file or folder name (use * as the wildcard) or enter one or more words to search within text-based files.
3. Select the drive, drives or folder you want to search in.
4. Click the Search button.
5. Below the search button you can select additional advanced search options, which allows you to search based on file timestamp, file size, and various file attributes.

Using a command-line interface

The where.exe utility searches the files in your path that match a pattern. This command finds all files that begin with *net* and have a *.exe* extension:

```
> where net*.exe
```

You can also use *where* to find files in a specific folder or tree of folders. This command finds all *.vbs* scripts whose names contain the letters *foo*:

```
> where /r c:\scripts *foo*.vbs
```

Windows comes with two other tools you can use to search for files that contain a certain string: find.exe and findstr.exe. The latter is more robust. If you only need to find the files in the current directory that contain the letters log, you can use this command:

```
> findstr log *
```

This next command performs a case-insensitive search (/i) for all nonbinary files (/p) on the *d:* drive (/s) that contain the text "confidential" (/c):

```
> findstr /s /p /i /c:"confidential" d:\*
```

findstr includes some regular expression support. For a list of all the features, look at the command help information (findstr /?).

Using downloadable software

With the introduction of Google Desktop search (*http://desktop.google.com*) in 2004, providing robust search capability for local files became a hot topic. Before long, both Yahoo (*http://desktop.yahoo.com*) and Microsoft (*http://beta.toolbar.msn.com*) released similar tools. All are free and provide roughly the same features. Take a look at each tool's web site for more information about the types of files that are indexed and can be searched.

If you want to search for strings within binary files, take a look at the Sysinternals strings.exe command. The following command displays any text strings contained in binary files within the *Program Files* directory:

```
> strings -s "c:\program files"
```

See Also

MS KB 185476, "HOWTO: Search Directories to Find or List Files," and "Inside Secrets of MSN Desktop Search" at *http://www.windowsdevcenter.com/pub/a/ windows/2004/12/21/msd_desktop_search.html*

8.10   Copying, Moving, or Renaming a File or Folder

Problem

You want to copy or move a set of files or folders to another location on the file system or to another computer.

Solution

Using a graphical user interface

1. Open Windows Explorer.

2. In the left pane, browse to the parent folder of the file or folder you want to copy, move, or rename.

3. In the right pane, right-click the file or folder.

    a. To rename, select Rename, enter the new name, and hit Enter.

    b. To move or copy, select Cut or Copy, respectively. Browse to the new location, right-click in the folder, and select Paste.

Using a command-line interface

Moving, copying, and renaming files is pretty straightforward from the command line:

```
> move <Source> <Destination>
> copy <Source> <Destination>
> ren <Source> <Destination>
```

Using downloadable software

PowerDesk Pro from VCOM (*http://www.v-com.com/product/PowerDesk_Pro_Home.html*) has extensive file management and organization features in an easy to use interface. You can use PowerDesk Pro to completely replace Windows Explorer. In addition to the standard edit, move, delete, and search features, PowerDesk Pro comes with an FTP Manager, Sync Manager (for comparing and syncing two folders), Size Manager (for monitoring drive space), and Archive Manager (for compressing and expanding files).

You can download a trial version of PowerDesk Pro called PowerDesk Express for free. You can purchase PowerDesk Pro for $49.99.

Using VBScript

```
' This code shows how to rename (same as move in WMI) and copy a file
' or folder.
' ------ SCRIPT CONFIGURATION ------
strComputer = "."
strCurrentFile = "<CurrentFilePath>"  ' Path to existing file or folder
strNewFile     = "<NewFilePath>"      ' New path of file or folder
' ------ END CONFIGURATION ---------
set objWMI = GetObject("winmgmts:\\" & strComputer & "\root\cimv2")
set objFile = objWMI.Get("Cim_Datafile='" & strCurrentFile & "'")
WScript.Echo "Renaming " & strCurrentFile & " to " & strNewFile
intRC = objFile.Rename(strNewFile)
if intRC <> 0 then
    WScript.Echo "There was an error renaming the file: " & intRC
else
    WScript.Echo "File rename successful"
end if
```

```
' ------ SCRIPT CONFIGURATION ------
strComputer = "."
strCurrentFile = "<CurrentFilePath>" ' Path to existing file or folder
strNewFile     = "<NewFilePath>"     ' Path to copy file or folder
' ------ END CONFIGURATION ---------
set objWMI = GetObject("winmgmts:\\" & strComputer & "\root\cimv2")
set objFile = objWMI.Get("Cim_Datafile='" & strCurrentFile & "'")
WScript.Echo "Copying " & strCurrentFile & " to " & strNewFile
intRC = objFile.Copy(strNewFile)
if intRC <> 0 then
   WScript.Echo "There was an error copying the file: " & intRC
else
   WScript.Echo "File copy successful"
end if
```

8.11   Comparing Files or Folders

Problem

You want to compare the contents of two files or two folders to determine the differences.

Solution

Using a graphical user interface

1. Open the WinDiff application (`windiff.exe`) from the Resource Kit.
2. To compare two files, select File → Compare Files from the menu. To compare two directories, select File → Compare Directories.

Using a command-line interface

The `fc.exe` command compares two or more files:

```
> fc <File1Path> <File2Path>
```

Here is an example:

```
> fc c:\netdiag.log c:\old\netdiag.log
```

To compare two binary files include the /b option in the previous command.

Using VBScript

```
' This code compares the contents of two text-based files.
' ------ SCRIPT CONFIGURATION ------
strFile1 = "<FilePath1>" ' e.g. c:\scripts\test1.vbs
strFile2 = "<FilePath2>" ' e.g. c:\scripts\test2.vbs
' ------ END CONFIGURATION ---------
set objFSO = CreateObject("Scripting.FilesystemObject")
set objFile1 = objFSO.opentextfile(strFile1,1)
```

```
set objFile2 = objFSO.opentextfile(strFile2,1)
arrFile1 = split(objFile1.ReadAll,vbNewLine)
arrFile2 = split(objFile2.ReadAll,vbNewLine)
objFile1.close
objFile2.close

if ubound(arrFile1) < ubound(arrFile2) then
   intLineCount = ubound(arrFile1)
   strError = strFile2 & " is bigger than " & strFile1
elseif ubound(arrFile1) > ubound(arrFile2) then
   intLineCount = ubound(arrFile2)
   strError = strFile2 & " is bigger than " & strFile1
else
   intLineCount = ubound(arrFile2)
end if

for i = 0 to intLineCount
   if not arrFile1(i) = arrFile2(i) then
      exit for
   end if
next

if i < (intLineCount + 1) then
   WScript.Echo "Line " & (i+1) & " not equal"
   WScript.Echo strError
elseif strError <> "" then
   WScript.Echo strError
else
   WScript.Echo "Files are identical."
end if
```

Discussion

Out of all of the methods we described, Windiff is by far the smartest in terms identifying when lines have been added to a file or a section of text has been moved around. By comparison, the VBScript isn't nearly as robust. It simply checks line by line to determine if two text files are identical.

See Also

MS KB 159214, "How to Use the Windiff.exe Utility"

8.12   Hiding a File or Folder

Problem

You want to hide a file or folder from view within Windows Explorer.

Solution

Using a graphical user interface

1. Open Windows Explorer.
2. Browse to the file or folder you want to hide.
3. Right-click the file or folder and select Properties.
4. Check the box beside Hidden (to hide) or uncheck the box (to unhide).
5. Click OK.

Using a command-line interface

To hide a file, use the `attrib.exe` command:

```
> attrib +H <Path>
```

Here is an example:

```
> attrib +H d:\mysecretscript.vbs
```

To unhide a file, use the –H option:

```
> attrib -H <Path>
```

Here is an example:

```
> attrib -H d:\mysecretscript.vbs
```

Using VBScript

```
' This code hides or unhides a file.
' ------ SCRIPT CONFIGURATION ------
strFile = "<FilePath>"  ' e.g. d:\mysecretscript.vbs
boolHide = True          ' True to hide, False to unhide
' ------ END CONFIGURATION ---------
set objFSO = CreateObject("Scripting.FileSystemObject")

' Change this to GetFolder to hide/unhide a folder
set objFile = objFSO.GetFile(strFile)

if boolHide = True then
   if objFile.Attributes AND 2 then
      WScript.Echo "File already hidden"
   else
      objFile.Attributes = objFile.Attributes + 2
      WScript.Echo "File is now hidden"
   end if
else
   if objFile.Attributes AND 2 then
      objFile.Attributes = objFile.Attributes - 2
      WScript.Echo "File is not hidden"
```

```
        else
            WScript.Echo "File is already not hidden"
        end if
    end if
```

Discussion

There are many operating system files that are hidden by default. Microsoft did this so you don't get yourself into trouble by accidentally editing or deleting important system files. You also may want to do this if you don't want users to see certain files or folders. The files and folders will still be accessible if the users know the full path; they just won't be visible by default in Windows Explorer. That, however, can be easily circumvented. Windows Explorer provides an option to make all hidden files and folders viewable. From the menu, select Tools → Folder Options. Click the View tab. You just need to select Show hidden files and folders and you'll be able to see them. If you truly don't want users to be able to access certain files or folders, your best bet is to restrict access to them via NTFS permissions.

See Also

MS KB 141276, "How to View System and Hidden Files in Windows"

8.13 Making a File or Folder Read-Only

Problem

You want to prevent a file or folder from being updated by making it read-only.

Solution

Using a graphical user interface

1. Open Windows Explorer.
2. Browse to the file or folder you want to hide.
3. Right-click the file or folder and select Properties.
4. Check the box beside Read-only.
5. Click OK.

Using a command-line interface

To make a file read-only, use the attrib.exe command:

```
> attrib +R <Path>
```

Here is an example:

```
> attrib +R d:\mysecretscript.vbs
```

To make a file available for reading and writing, use the –R option:

```
> attrib -R <Path>
```

Here is an example:

```
> attrib -R d:\mysecretscript.vbs
```

Using VBScript

```
' This code enables or disables the read-only attribute of a file.
' ------ SCRIPT CONFIGURATION ------
strFile = "<FilePath>"   ' e.g. d:\mysecretscript.vbs
boolReadOnly = True      ' True = read-only, False = not read-only
' ------ END CONFIGURATION ---------
set objFSO = CreateObject("Scripting.FileSystemObject")

' Change this to GetFolder to hide/unhide a folder
set objFile = objFSO.GetFile(strFile)

if boolReadOnly = True then
   if objFile.Attributes AND 1 then
      WScript.Echo "File already read-only"
   else
      objFile.Attributes = objFile.Attributes + 1
      WScript.Echo "File is now read-only"
   end if
else
   if objFile.Attributes AND 1 then
      objFile.Attributes = objFile.Attributes - 1
      WScript.Echo "File is not read-only"
   else
      WScript.Echo "File is already not read-only"
   end if
end if
```

8.14   Compressing a File or Folder

Problem

You want to regain some space on the hard disk by compressing files or folders.

Solution

Using a graphical user interface

1. Open Windows Explorer.
2. In the left pane, browse to the parent folder of the file or folder you want to compress. Click on the parent folder. This displays the list of subfolders and files in the right pane.
3. In the right pane, right-click on the target file or folder and select Properties.

---

4. Click the Advanced button.

5. Check the box beside Compress contents to save disk space.

6. Click OK and Apply.

Using a command-line interface

The compact command can compress and decompress files similar to Windows Explorer. The following command compresses all files in the current directory (/c option) and all subdirectories (/s option):

```
> compact /c /s
```

This command also causes all future files added anywhere under the current directory to be compressed.

To decompress all the files in the current directory and cause all future files to not be compressed, use the /u option with /s:

```
> compact /u /s
```

The following command compresses all of the files with the *.doc* extension (i.e., Word documents) in the *c:\docs* directory:

```
> compact /c /s:c:\docs *.doc
```

The *compress.exe* utility works a little bit differently from compact. It doesn't compress files transparently within in the file system using NTFS compression. Instead it creates a compressed copy of a file. Here is an example:

```
> compress largetextfile.txt compressedfile.txt
```

The source file (*largetextfile.txt*) remains unchanged and the target file (*compressed file.txt*) is a compressed version of that file. To compress all of the files in a directory, use this command:

```
> compress -R *.*
```

This creates compressed versions of each file and names them by replacing the last character of the source file with an underscore. For example, the compressed version of *test.txt* would be named *test.tx_*.

 To decompress files that you compressed with the compress command, you must use the extract command.

Using downloadable software

One of the most well-known third-party tools, which most Windows users have used at one point or another deals with compressing files. WinZip (*http://winzip.com/*) is a simple tool that lets you create compressed archives of files and folders.

You can download an evaluation version of WinZip that is good for 21 days. After 21 days, you must purchase a license for $29 to continue to use the tool.

Using VBScript

```
' This code compresses a folder and its contents using NTFS compression
' ------ SCRIPT CONFIGURATION ------
strComputer = "."
strFile     = "<FilePath>" ' e.g. d:\scripts\test.vbs
' ------ END CONFIGURATION ---------
set objWMI = GetObject("winmgmts:\\" & strComputer & "\root\cimv2")
set objFile = objWMI.Get("Cim_Datafile='" & strFile & "'")
WScript.Echo objFile.Name
intRC = objFile.Compress ' To uncompress change this to objFile.Uncompress
if intRC <> 0 then
    WScript.Echo "There was an error compressing the file: " & intRC
else
    WScript.Echo "File compression successful"
end if


' This code compresses a folder and its contents using NTFS compression
' ------ SCRIPT CONFIGURATION ------
strComputer = "."
strFolder   = "<FolderPath>" ' e.g. d:\scripts
' ------ END CONFIGURATION ---------
set objWMI = GetObject("winmgmts:\\" & strComputer & "\root\cimv2")
set objFolder = objWMI.Get("Win32_Directory='" & strFolder & "'")
intRC = objFolder.Compress   ' To uncompress change this to objFolder.Uncompress
if intRC <> 0 then
    WScript.Echo "There was an error compressing the folder: " & intRC
else
    WScript.Echo "Folder compression successful"
end if
```

Discussion

NTFS compression is a great feature because once you compress a file, NTFS handles decompressing it for you automatically when you attempt to view it, copy it, or move it to another folder. However, you shouldn't start using compression everywhere. Decompressing and compressing files is CPU intensive. Be very careful when enabling compression on frequently accessed or modified files because it can have an adverse impact on performance.

NTFS compression works only on partitions that were formatted using a 4 KB cluster size (the default) or smaller. See MS KB 171892 for more information.

Compressing files and folders with WinZip is a little different than using NTFS compression. If you want to send several large files to a colleague, your best option is to create a WinZip archive of the files and send the archive, not the individual files. This reduces the overall footprint of the files (assuming they are not already compressed).

See Also

MS KB 171892, "Err Msg: The File System Does Not Support Compression," MS KB 198038, "INFO: Useful Tools for Package and Deployment Issues," MS KB 251186, "Best Practices for NTFS Compression in Windows," MS KB 307987, "HOW TO: Use File Compression in Windows XP," MS KB 314958, "How To Use the COMPRESS, COMPACT, and EXPAND Commands to Compress and Expand Files and Folders in Windows 2000," and MS KB 323425, "HOW TO: Use the COMPACT Command to Compress and Uncompress Files and Folders in Windows Server 2003"

8.15 Encrypting a File or Folder

Problem

You want to encrypt a file or folder so that other users cannot read its contents.

Solution

Using a graphical user interface

1. Open Windows Explorer.
2. In the left pane, browse to the parent folder of the file or folder you want to compress. Click on the parent folder. This displays the list of subfolders and files in the right pane.
3. In the right pane, right-click on the target file or folder and select Properties.
4. Click the Advanced button.
5. Check the box beside Encrypt contents to secure data.
6. Click OK and Apply.

Using a command-line interface

With the cipher.exe command you can encyrpt and decrypt files and folders. Running it without any options lists the files in the current directory with a flag indicating which ones are encrypted (U = unencrypted, E = encrypted):

```
> cipher
```

The following command encrypts a single file:

```
> cipher /e /a <FileName>
```

Here is an example:

```
> cipher /e /a mysecretfile.doc
```

The following command causes any new file added to the scripts directory to get encrypted. Existing files are not encrypted:

```
> cipher /e d:\scripts
```

The following command encrypts all files in a directory and any subdirectories:

```
> cipher /e /f /a /s:d:\scripts
```

This is the same command, with /e replaced by /d, which causes everything within the *d:\scripts* directory to become unencrypted:

```
> cipher /d /f /a /s:d:\scripts
```

Using downloadable software

A non-native, but standardized approach to encrypting files is to use Pretty Good Privacy (PGP). With PGP, not only can you encrypt local files, but you can also integrate it with your email client to securely send email. PGP is available for free from *http://web.mit.edu/network/pgp.html*. The commercial version can be purchased from *http://www.pgp.com/*.

Discussion

NTFS supports the Encrypting File System (EFS) for encrypting the contents of files. Similar to compression, EFS is built into the file system so encryption and decryption of EFS-enabled files and folders is seamless to the end-user. And just like compression, enabling EFS should only be done after much thought about its impact. EFS can have a significant hit on the performance of a computer and the access times for files.

For more on how to use EFS, including the recovery mechanisms built-in to EFS, see MS KB 324897.

See Also

MS KB 230520, "HOW TO: Encrypt Data Using EFS in Windows 2000," MS KB 298009, "Cipher.exe Security Tool for the Encrypting File System," and MS KB 324897, "HOW TO: Manage the Encrypting File System in Windows Server 2003 Enterprise Server"

8.16   Replacing a File That Is in Use

Problem

You want to replace a file that is currently locked by a process.

Solution

Using a command-line interface

You can use the *inuse* command to replace a file that is locked by a process. You need to reboot after running the command for the change to take effect.

```
> inuse c:\foo.dll c:\windows\system32\foo.dll
```

In this example, the file *c:\windows\system32\foo.dll* will be replaced by *c:\foo.dll* after the system reboots.

Using VBScript

```
' This code executes the inuse command to replace a file.
' ------ SCRIPT CONFIGURATION ------
' Modify the command string as necessary
strCmdString = "inuse.exe c:\foo.dll c:\windows\system32\foo.dll"
' ------ END CONFIGURATION ---------
set objWshShell = CreateObject("WScript.Shell")
set objExec = objWshShell.Exec(strCmdString)
do while not objExec.StdErr.AtEndOfStream
    WScript.Echo objExec.StdErr.ReadLine()
loop
do while not objExec.StdOut.AtEndOfStream
    WScript.Echo objExec.StdOut.ReadLine()
loop
```

Discussion

Ever needed to replace a DLL or other file, but couldn't because the system said it was in use? With the *inuse* utility, you can replace files that are currently locked. Simply pass *inuse* the location of the new version of the file and the location of the currently locked file, and on reboot, the file will be overwritten. *Inuse* works by setting a Registry value that Windows looks at when booting up to determine if there are any pending file renames. For more information on the specific key and value, see MS KB 181345.

On Windows 2000 and Windows XP, *inuse* is a Resource Kit tool and therefore not officially supported by Microsoft, so use it at your own risk. On Windows Server 2003, the command is part of the default installation and is supported. Also keep in mind that there is no "undo" function. So once you've overwritten a file, unless you made a copy of the original previously, you won't be able to revert back to it.

See Also

Recipe 8.20 for more on finding the process that has a file open; MS KB 181345, "How to replace in-use files at Windows restart," and MS KB 228930, "How to replace currently locked files with Inuse.exe"

8.17   Taking Ownership of a File or Folder

Problem

You want to take ownership of a file or folder. This may be necessary if you find that NTFS permissions have you locked out of a file or folder. As long as you are an administrator of the system, you should be able to take control of it and reset permissions as necessary.

Solution

Using a graphical user interface

1. Open Windows Explorer.
2. In the left pane, browse to the parent folder of the file or folder you want to take ownership for. Click on the parent folder. This displays the list of subfolders and files in the right pane.
3. In the right pane, right-click on the target file or folder and select Properties.
4. Select the Security tab.
5. Click the Advanced button.
6. Select the Owner tab.
7. Under the Change owner to heading select the new owner and click Apply.

Using a command-line interface

Use the following command to attempt to take ownership of a file:

```
> takeown <FileName>
```

For example:

```
> takeown d:\iwanna.exe
```

If you want to grant ownership to someone else, use the subinacl.exe command:

```
> subinacl /file <FilePath> /setowner=<User>
```

For example:

```
> subinacl /file \\rallen-svr1\docs\guide.doc /setowner=AMER\rallen
```

Or you can even grant ownership to a user over all the files in a directory:

```
> subinacl /subdirectories \\rallen-svr1\docs\* /setowner=AMER\rallen
```

Using VBScript

```
' This code transfers ownership of the specified file to the
' user running the script.  If strFile is set to a folder path
' then ownership of all files within the folder will be changed.
```

```
' ------ SCRIPT CONFIGURATION ------
strFile = "<FilePath>"          ' e.g. d:\scripts
strComputer = "<ComputerName>" ' e.g. rallen-svr1 or . for local system
' ------ END CONFIGURATION ---------
set objWMI = GetObject("winmgmts:\\" & strComputer & "\root\cimv2")
set objFile = objWMI.Get("CIM_DataFile.Name='" & strFile & "'")
intRC = objFile.TakeOwnership
if intRC = 0 then
   WScript.Echo "File ownership successfully changed"
else
   WScript.Echo "Error transferring file ownership: " & intRC
end if
```

Discussion

If you are taking ownership of a file or folder because you were locked out of it, even after you take ownership you still have to go in and grant yourself the necessary NTFS permissions to access and manipulate the file or folder. With Windows Explorer on Windows XP, you can only assign one of the members of the local administrators group as an owner of a file or folder. With Windows Server 2003, there is a new button called Other Users or Groups that lets you use the object picker to select any user as an owner.

See Also

MS KB 268019, "HOW TO: Take Ownership of Files," and MS KB 320046, "HOW TO: Use the File Ownership Script Tool (Fileowners.pl) in Windows 2000"

8.18 Finding Out Who Opened or Modified a File Last

Problem

You want to find out who opened or modified a file last.

Solution

To find who opened or modified a file last, you have to enable auditing on that file. To enable auditing, you have to enable auditing at the system level and then enable auditing on the particular object (in this case a file) in which you are interested.

Using a graphical user interface

Do the following to enable auditing at the system level:

1. From Administrative Tools, open the Local Security Policy snap-in (*secpol.msc*).
2. In the left pane, expand Local Policies and click on Audit Policy.

3. In the right pane, double-click Audit object access.

4. Check the boxes beside Success or Failure (as needed).

5. Click OK.

Now you need to enable auditing on the target file(s) or folder(s):

1. Open Windows Explorer.

2. In the left pane, browse to the parent folder of the file or folder on which you want to enable auditing. Click on the parent folder. This displays the list of sub-folders and files in the right pane.

3. In the right pane, right-click on the target file or folder and select Properties.

4. Select the Security tab.

5. Click the Advanced button.

6. Select the Auditing tab.

7. Click the Add button.

8. Enter the user or group you want to audit access for (use the Everyone principal to audit all access) and click OK.

9. In the Auditing Entry dialog box, select the types of access you want to audit. You have to select Success events separately from Failure events. Click OK when you are done.

10. Click Apply.

Using a command-line interface

Use the *auditpol* command to enable auditing at the system level:

```
> auditpol \\<ComputerName> /enable /object:all
```

Microsoft doesn't provide a tool to configure the audit settings of files. However, you can do this with the *setacl.exe* tool. It is available for download from SourceForge at *http://setacl.sourceforge.net/*. Here is an example of setting an audit entry on the file *d:\myimportantfile.txt* for all failed access attempts by the Everyone principal:

```
> setacl -on "d:\myimportantfile.txt" -ot file -actn ace -ace
"n:everyone;p:full;m:aud_fail;w:sacl"
```

Discussion

Be careful when enabling auditing on a frequently accessed set of files or folders. The number of audit messages in the Security event log can grow quickly with just a few accesses of the file. Monitor the Security event log closely after initially enabling auditing just to make sure you don't flood it.

See Also

Recipe 17.2 for more on auditing

8.19   Finding Open Files

Problem

You want to find the open files on a system.

Solution

There are two different categories of open files on a system. Since the days of Windows NT, the operating system has supported the capability to view the files that are open from shared folders. This is useful when you want to see who is accessing files on a file server, especially if you need to take the system down for maintenance and you want to notify the impacted users.

First seen in Windows XP and supported in Windows Server 2003 is the ability to view all open files on a system (not just shared folders). To use this feature, you first have to enable support for it. The reason this isn't enabled by default is because there is a slight systemwide performance impact when tracking all open files. To enable support for it, run the following command:

```
> openfiles /local on
```

Using a graphical user interface

None of the standard graphical tools provide a list of the open files on a system. The closest thing to it would be the Sysinternals File Monitor tool. For more information see Recipe 8.21.

To view the open files from shared folders, do the following:

1. From the Administrative Tools, open the Computer Management snap-in.
2. In the left pane, expand System Tools → Shared Folders → Open Files.
3. To close an open file, right-click on it in the right pane and select Close Open File.

Using a command-line interface

To view the open files from shared folders, run this command:

```
> net file
```

The output from that command displays open files and their associated ID. Using this ID you can close a specific file:

```
> net file <ID> /close
```

You'll need to reboot the system before this setting takes effect. At point you can see open files using this command:

```
> openfiles
```

Use the /s *<ComputerName>* option to target a remote system. As with the `net file` command, you can close any open file by running this command:

```
> openfiles /disconnect /id <ID>
```

You can also disconnect all the files open by a particular user:

```
> openfiles /disconnect /a <UserName>
```

See Also

Recipe 8.21 for viewing file activity

8.20   Finding the Process That Has a File Open

Problem

You want to find the process or processes that have a file open. This is often necessary if you want to delete or modify a file but are getting errors telling you it is in use by another process.

Solution

Using downloadable software

One option is to use the Sysinternals Process Explorer:

1. Open Process Explorer (*procexp.exe*).
2. Click the Find icon (binoculars) or select Search → Find from the menu.
3. Beside Handle substring, enter the name of the file and click Search.

Alternatively, you can use the Sysinternals `handle` command to view the processes that have a lock on a file:

```
> handle <FileName>
```

This example command shows all the processes that have a handle to the *personal. pst* file:

```
> handle personal.pst
```

Using VBScript

```
' This code prints the output from the handle.exe command
' ------ SCRIPT CONFIGURATION ------
strFilePattern = "<FileName>" ' e.g. personal.pst
strHandleExec = "handle.exe"  ' If handle.exe isn't in your PATH, you will
                              ' need to specify the full path.
' ------ END CONFIGURATION ---------
set objWshShell = CreateObject("WScript.Shell")
set objExec = objWshShell.Exec(strHandleExec & " " & strFilePattern)
```

```
do while not objExec.StdOut.AtEndOfStream
    WScript.Echo objExec.StdOut.ReadLine( )
loop
```

Discussion

Processes running on your system are constantly opening and closing files (see Recipe 8.21 for more on how to see this activity). When a process accesses a file, the process is said to have a *handle* to the file. Processes can also have handles to other system resources, such as Registry keys and values. For certain types of file accesses, a process may obtain an exclusive lock on the file (such as when it needs to write to the file), which means no other processes can modify the file; you may still be able to read the file, but you won't be able to overwrite it, move it, or delete it.

This may be a bit annoying if there is a file you need to do something with. You have a couple of options. First, if you determine the process that has a handle to the file is not important, you could try to kill it (see Recipe 10.5). This will often remove the lock on the file, but this isn't the most graceful approach. If you just want to replace the file, another option entails following the instructions in Recipe 8.16, which will replace a file after the next reboot.

See Also

Recipe 10.5 for more on how to kill a process; Recipe 8.16 for more on how to replace a file that is in use; Recipe 8.21 for more on viewing file activity; and MS KB 242131, "How to: Display a List of Processes That Have Files Open"

8.21   Viewing File Activity

Problem

You want to view the file activity on a system.

Solution

Using downloadable software

Open the Sysinternals File Monitor (*filemon.exe*). It automatically starts logging all file activity when it is opened.

To stop capturing file activity, click the Capture icon (magnifying glass), select File → Capture Events from the menu, or type CTRL+E.

To search the captured data, click the Find icon (binoculars), select Edit → Find from the menu, or type CTRL+F. The text you enter will be matched against any part of the captured data (index, time, process name, request, and file path).

To filter the captured data so that only the entries that match your filter are displayed, click the Filter icon, select Options → Filter/Hightlight from the menu, or type CTRL+L.

If you double-click a particular entry in File Monitor, it will open a Windows Explorer window to the directory containing the target file.

Discussion

Ever hear your hard disks spinning or seen the disk indicator light flashing, but you don't know why? You may not appear to have any applications open or running, but something is still accessing the hard disks. The Sysinternals File Monitor utility lets you see what processes are reading or writing files. It has some robust filter and search capability as well, which is helpful considering the fact that File Monitor can capture thousands of operations in a matter of minutes. Figure 8-2 shows sample output from File Monitor.

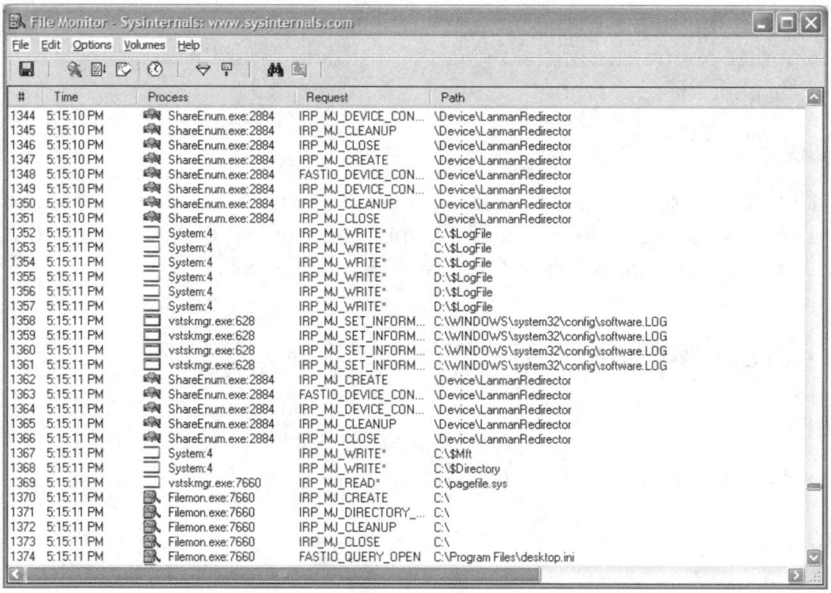

Figure 8-2. File Monitor screen

8.22 Performing an Action on Several Files at Once

Problem

You want to perform an action on several files at once.

Solution

Using a command-line interface

The `forfiles.exe` utility is a handy tool that lets you search and iterate over a group of files and perform an action against them. For example, this command searches the *d:* drive for all files with a *.zip* extension and prints out the name of each file and its size:

```
> forfiles -pd:\ -s -m*.zip -c"cmd /c echo @FILE : @FSIZE"
```

Here is another example that opens everything that ends in *.txt* with notepad. It performs a check to make sure only files are opened, not directories (`@ISDIR==FALSE`):

```
> forfiles -m*.txt -c"cmd /c if @ISDIR==FALSE notepad.exe @FILE"
```

For more information about the command line options `forfiles` supports, run `forfiles -h` for the Windows 2000 version (used above) and `forfiles /h` for the Windows Server 2003 version. The two versions vary slightly.

Using VBScript

```
' This code shows how to iterate over all the zip files on a system
' ------ SCRIPT CONFIGURATION ------
strComputer  = "."
strExtension = "zip"
' ------ END CONFIGURATION ---------
set objWMI = GetObject("winmgmts:\\" & strComputer & "\root\cimv2")
set colFiles = objWMI.ExecQuery("select * from Cim_DataFile " & _
                         " where extension = '" & strExtension & "'")
WScript.Echo "Files with a ." & strExtension & " extension:"
intCount = 0
for each objFile in colFiles
   WScript.Echo "   " & objFile.Name

   ' Do some action here

   intCount = intCount + 1
next
WScript.Echo "Total: " & intCount
```

Discussion

If you aren't familiar with the `forfiles` command, we highly recommend that you check it out. We don't know how many times we've had to write a script or piece together a long command line to iterate over a series of files and perform some action. Forfiles makes the process much easier.

8.23 Creating and Deleting Shares

Problem

You want to create or delete a shared folder.

Solution

Using a graphical user interface

1. Open Windows Explorer.
2. In the left pane, browse to the folder you want to start or stop sharing.
3. Right-click folder and select Sharing and Security.
4. To stop sharing the folder, select Do not share this folder.
5. To share the folder, select Share this folder. Enter the Share name, enter a description for the share in the Comment field, and specify the User limit.
6. Click OK to close the dialog box.

Using a command-line interface

The following command creates a share called `Perl Libs`:

```
> net share "Perl Libs"=d:\perl\lib /unlimited /remark:"Core Perl modules"
```

The /unlimited option means that an unlimited number of users can access the share simultaneously. You can limit the number of simultaneous users by using the */users: <Number>* option instead.

This command deletes a share:

```
> net share "Perl Libs" /delete
```

Using VBScript

```
' This code creates a share.
' ------ SCRIPT CONFIGURATION ------
strComputer   = "."
strPath       = "d:\perl\lib"
strName       = "Perl Libs"
intType       = 0 ' share a disk drive resource
intMaxAllowed = 10
strDescr      = "Core Perl modules"
' ------ END CONFIGURATION ---------
set objWMI = GetObject("winmgmts:\\" & strComputer & "\root\cimv2")
set objShare = objWMI.Get("Win32_Share")
intRC = objShare.Create(strPath, strName, intType, intMaxAllowed, strDescr)
if intRC <> 0 then
    WScript.Echo "Error creating share: " & intRC
else
```

```
      WScript.Echo "Successfully created share"
end if


' This code deletes a share.
' ------ SCRIPT CONFIGURATION ------
strComputer   = "."
strName       = "Perl Libs"
' ------ END CONFIGURATION ---------
set objWMI = GetObject("winmgmts:\\" & strComputer & "\root\cimv2")
set objShare = objWMI.Get("Win32_Share.Name='" & strName & "'")
intRC = objShare.Delete
if intRC <> 0 then
   WScript.Echo "Error deleted share: " & intRC
else
   WScript.Echo "Successfully deleted share"
end if
```

Discussion

After you create a share, you need to modify the access control list (ACL) to include the users and groups that can access the contents of the share (see Recipe 8.25 for more on this).

If you want to create a hidden share, simply append $ to the end of the share name. The only thing different about a hidden share is that it won't be directly viewable when listing the shared folders on a system. Hiding shares is kind of like hiding files (Recipe 8.12)—it is up to the application to display them or not. So hidden shares are not truly hidden, but they will not be visible to the casual user.

See Also

MS KB 324267, "HOW TO: Share Files and Folders over the Network in a Windows Server 2003 Domain Environment"

8.24   Viewing Shares

Problem

You want to view the list of shares on a system.

Solution

Using a graphical user interface

1. Open the Computer Management snap-in.
2. In the left pane, expand System Tools → Shared Folders → Shared Folders.
3. To view the properties of a share, double-click on it in the right pane. To disable a share, right-click on it and select Stop Sharing.

Using a command-line interface

The following command displays administrative and nonadministrative shares:

```
> net share
```

To view the list of shares on a remote system, use the Sysinternals *psexec* utility to run the net share command against the system:

```
> psexec \\<ComputerName> -u <User> net share
```

For example:

```
> psexec \\srv01 -u administrator net share
```

You can also view all of the nonadministrative shares on a remote system using this command:

```
> net view \\<ComputerName>
```

Using VBScript

```
' This code displays all of the shares on a system.
' ------ SCRIPT CONFIGURATION ------
strComputer = "."
' ------ END CONFIGURATION ---------
set objWMI = GetObject("winmgmts:\\" & strComputer & "\root\cimv2")
set colShares = objWMI.InstancesOf("Win32_Share")
for each objShare in colShares
   WScript.Echo objShare.Name
   WScript.Echo "  Path:        " & objShare.Path
   WScript.Echo "  Allow Max:   " & objShare.AllowMaximum
   WScript.Echo "  Caption:     " & objShare.Caption
   WScript.Echo "  Max Allowed: " & objShare.MaximumAllowed
   WScript.Echo "  Type:        " & objShare.Type
   WScript.Echo
next
```

Discussion

The Sysinternals Shareenum program is another tool that you can use for viewing shares. It lists the shared folders on all hosts in a particular domain. Depending on the number of hosts in the domain, it can take a while to complete. It is interesting to see the output and discover what types of shared folders users have created. You may even want to periodically check the security on these shared folders to ensure that users are following your documented policies for shared folder security.

8.25   Restricting Access to a Share

Problem

You want to restrict access to a share.

Solution

There are two ways to restrict access to a share; you can set share permissions or NTFS permissions. I'm going to describe how to set share permissions, but see the Discussion section for more on NTFS permissions, the preferred method.

Using a graphical user interface

1. Open Windows Explorer.
2. In the left pane, browse to the shared folder.
3. Right-click the folder and select Sharing and Security.
4. Select the Sharing tab.
5. Click the Permissions button.
6. From here, you can grant users or groups Full Control, Read, or Change access to the share.

Using a command-line interface

This command grants the AMER\rallen user with Full Control over the Perl Libs share:

```
> subinacl /share "Perl Libs" /grant=amer\rallen=F
```

This command revokes the permission:

```
> subinacl /share "Perl Libs" /revoke=amer\rallen
```

Discussion

The generally accepted way to manage share permissions is not to actually manage permissions on the shares themselves, but on the underlying files and folders using NTFS permissions. With Windows 2000, this is pretty straightforward. By default, share and NTFS permissions are both set to allow Everyone Full Control. So you create a share and just modify the NTFS permissions to include the user or groups that should have access and remove the Everyone entry.

With Windows XP, it isn't as straightforward. In an effort to make things more secure, Microsoft changed the default share permissions when creating a new share to allow Everyone only Read access. That means that, regardless whether the underlying NTFS permissions grant Write access to a group, members of that group won't be able to write to the share until you also grant Change (or more appropriately, remove the Read restriction) on the share permissions. I said that this is the generally accepted way to manage permissions because you may find some people prefer to rely on share permissions. In my mind, using share permissions makes things a little more complicated, but to each his own.

See Also

MS KB 301195, "HOW TO: Configure Security for Files and Folders on a Network (Domain) in Windows 2000," and MS KB 324267, "HOW TO: Share Files and Folders over the Network in a Windows Server 2003 Domain Environment"

8.26   Enabling Web Sharing

Problem

You want to enable web sharing for a folder. This allows users from non-Windows-based PCs to view the contents of a share using the web.

Solution

Using a graphical user interface

1. Open Windows Explorer.
2. In the left pane, browse to the folder you want to share.
3. Right-click folder and select Sharing and Security.
4. Select the Web Sharing tab.
5. Select Share this folder.
6. A dialog box appears with the settings you can configure for the web share. Click OK when you are done.
7. Click OK to close the dialog box.

Discussion

To use web sharing, you must have IIS installed and running. When you create a web share, you are doing nothing more than creating a virtual directory in IIS.

The security for a web share is a little different from that of a regular share: you have to select the access permissions and application permissions you want to use. Here is a list of access permissions:

Read
    Allows web users to read files in the folder
Write
    Allows web users to write files in the folder
Script source access
    Allows web users to view the source code of scripts in the folder
Directory browsing
    Allows web users to browse the folder contents

And here are the application permissions:

None
> Does not allow the execution of scripts or programs

Scripts
> Allows the execution of scripts, but not programs

Execute
> Allows the execution of both scripts and programs

Keep in mind that NTFS and web server permissions also apply to web shares. If the user is accessing the share without authenticating, the permissions will be based on the IUSR account IIS is running under (normally IUSER_*<computername>*). If the user authenticates, permissions will be based on his or her credentials.

See Also

Recipe 12.5 in *Windows Server Cookbook* for more on creating virtual directories in IIS

8.27 Publishing a Share in Active Directory

Problem

You want to publish a share in Active Directory so that other users can find it.

Solution

Using a graphical user interface

1. Open the Active Directory Users and Computers (ADUC) snap-in.
2. In the left pane, browse to the organizational unit (OU) in which you want to publish the share.
3. Right-click the OU and select New → Shared Folder (if you don't see the New heading then you don't have permission to create objects in the OU).
4. For Name, enter the name of the share as you want it displayed to users.
5. For UNC Path, enter the network path of the share (e.g., *fs01\myshare*).
6. Click OK.

Using VBScript

```
' This code publishes a share in AD.
' ------ SCRIPT CONFIGURATION ------
strComputer = "ad-01"  ' name of a domain controller
strShareName = "Perl Libraries"
strSharePath = "\\fs01\perl-libs"
strShareDescr = "Core Perl libraries"
```

```
set objRootDSE = GetObject("LDAP://" & strComputer & "/RootDSE")
strParentDN = "/OU=SharedFolders," & objRootDSE.Get("defaultNamingContext")
' ------ END CONFIGURATION ---------
set objOU = GetObject("LDAP://" & strComputer & strParentDN)
set objVol = objOU.Create("volume", "cn=" & strShareName)
objVol.Put "uncName", strSharePath
objVol.Put "Description", strShareDescr
objVol.SetInfo
WScript.Echo "Successfully created object: " & objVol.Name
```

Discussion

After you've created a shared folder, your users may not be able to find it or even know about it. One way to make available shared folders more accessible to users is by publishing them to Active Directory. Shared folders are represented by the volume object class in Active Directory. The main pieces of information you need in order to create a volume object are the share name, the share UNC path, and a share description.

Users can search shared folders in Active Directory using the Find Users, Contacts, and Groups dialog box. You can get to this box by going to My Network Places and clicking Search Active Directory in the left pane, or by running the Active Directory Users and Computers snap-in, right-clicking the target domain in the left pane, and selecting Find. After the box is displayed, select Shared Folders beside Find, enter your search criteria, and click Find Now.

The one major downside to publishing shares in Active Directory is the maintenance overhead. Unlike printer publishing in Active Directory, there is no automatic pruning or maintenance process that will clean up volume objects for shares that no longer exist. Unless you create a process to update Active Directory whenever a share is created, moved, or deleted, Active Directory will eventually become out-of-date and ultimately be an unreliable source of shared folder information.

 Another way to solve this problem is to use DFS, whereby you have a single directory tree of shared folders, but that is beyond the scope of this chapter.

See Also

MS KB 234582, "Publishing a Shared Folder in Windows 2000 Active Directory"

CHAPTER 9

The Registry

9.0 Introduction

The Registry is the primary repository for system, application, and user profile configuration information for the Windows operating system. It is a hierarchical database that is structured and used much like a filesystem. The operating system uses the Registry to store information as static as environment variables and as dynamic as performance data. The Registry is constantly being used by the OS and applications to read, write, and query configuration settings.

Don't Be Scared of the Registry

You have probably seen this warning or one similar to it in an article, book, or Microsoft KB article:

WARNING: If you use Registry Editor incorrectly, you may cause serious problems that may require you to reinstall your operating system. Microsoft cannot guarantee that you can solve problems that result from using Registry Editor incorrectly. Use Registry Editor at your own risk.

We think this type of warning has made some people overly cautious about modifying or even browsing the Registry. We're here to say that it doesn't have to be that way. Sure, you can muck up the Registry, just like you can muck up the operating system or just about any application if you haphazardly delete or modify things. But you are a reasonable person who won't go around making changes on a production system unless you know the impact, so let's put concerns about modifying the Registry behind us and move forward. Use the Registry as a great source of configuration information and as a tool for customizing the operating system.

Using a Graphical User Interface

Windows 2000 came with two graphical Registry editors that had different benefits. The first (*regedit.exe*) was more user-friendly, had better search capabilities, and was easy to work with while the other (*regedt32.exe*) was much more powerful. In Windows XP, most of the features of these two tools were combined into a single tool. Now, Registry Editor has the same look and feel as the user-friendly version in Windows 2000 (*regedit.exe*), but also incorporates some important features such as permission editing from *regedt32.exe*. If you run either *regedit.exe* or *regedt32.exe*, you'll bring up the same tool.

Using a Command-Line Interface

The one command-line tool we use extensively throughout this chapter is *reg.exe*. It comes installed by default with Windows XP. With it, you can:

- Search the Registry
- Add, modify, and delete Registry keys and values
- Import, export, and compare Registry files

Using Group Policy

You can use Group Policy to manipulate the Registry using predefined Group Policy settings that correspond to Registry values or by creating a custom template that contains any keys and values you want to configure. See Recipe 9.3 for more information.

Using Downloadable Software

A graphical downloadable tool you should be familiar with is Registry Monitor (*regmon.exe*) from Sysinternals (*http://www.sysinternals.com*). With it, you can view all of the Registry activity on a system in real time. You can restrict the output to a certain key, and limit the type of activity (read, write, etc.). We cover Registry Monitor in more detail in Recipes 9.11 and 9.12.

To create Registry links, we use the `regln` tool as described in Recipe 9.10. You can download `regln` from the following location: *http://www.ntinternals.net/regln/*.

Using VBScript

WMI has a single class called `StdRegProv` that provides most of the functions you'll need to programmatically manage the Registry. Table 9-1 contains the methods available with this class. This class is a little different from most others in that it doesn't contain properties for object instances (keys, values, etc.). To obtain information about a Registry key or value, you have to use one of the methods shown in Table 9-1.

Table 9-1. StdRegProv methods

Method	Description
CheckAccess	Determines if a user has the specified permissions on a Registry key.
CreateKey	Create a key
DeleteKey	Delete a key
DeleteValue	Delete a value
EnumKey	Enumerates the subkeys of a key
EnumValues	Enumerates the values of a key
GetBinaryValue	Retrieves data from REG_BINARY value
GetDWORDValue	Retrieves data from REG_DWORD value
GetExpandedStringValue	Retrieves data from REG_EXPAND_SZ value
GetMultiStringValue	Retrieves data from REG_MULTI_SZ value
GetStringValue	Retrieves data from REG_SZ value
SetBinaryValue	Sets data for REG_BINARY value
SetDWORDValue	Sets data for REG_DWORD value
SetExpandedStringValue	Sets data for REG_EXPAND_SZ value
SetMultiStringValue	Sets data for REG_MULTI_SZ value
SetStringValue	Sets data for REG_SZ value

9.1   Creating and Deleting a Key

Problem

You want to create or delete a Registry key.

Solution

Using a graphical user interface

1. Open the Registry Editor (*regedit.exe*).
2. Browse to the location where you want to create or delete a key.
3. To create a key:
    a. Right-click the parent key and select New → Key.
    b. Type the name of the key and hit Enter.
4. To delete a key:
    a. Right-click the key you want to delete and select Delete.
    b. Click Yes to confirm.

Using a command-line interface

The following command creates a Registry key in the HKLM hive called `Rallencorp`:

```
> reg add \\<ComputerName>\HKLM\Software\Rallencorp
```

The following command deletes the same Registry key:

```
> reg delete \\<ComputerName>\HKLM\Software\Rallencorp
```

You will be prompted to confirm the deletion. Use the /f option to delete the key and bypass the confirmation prompt.

If you have a Registry file (i.e., a file with a *.reg* extension), you can also import it using regedit:

```
> regedit /s <Filename>
```

The /s option suppresses all windows and dialog boxes. See MS KB 310516 for more on creating Registry files.

Using VBScript

```
' This code creates a Registry key.
' ------ SCRIPT CONFIGURATION ------
const HKLM = &H80000002
strKeyPath = "<RegKey>"        ' e.g. Software\Rallencorp
strComputer = "<ComputerName>" ' e.g. wks01 (use "." for local computer)
' ------ END CONFIGURATION ---------
set objReg = GetObject("winmgmts:\\" & strComputer & "\root\default:StdRegProv")
intRC = objReg.CreateKey(HKLM, strKeyPath)
if intRC <> 0 then
   WScript.Echo "Error creating key: " & intRC
else
   WScript.Echo "Successfully created key " & strKeyPath
end if


' This code deletes a Registry key.
' ------ SCRIPT CONFIGURATION ------
const HKLM = &H80000002
strKeyPath = "<RegKey>"        ' e.g. Software\Rallencorp
strComputer = "<ComputerName>" ' e.g. wks01 (use "." for local computer)
' ------ END CONFIGURATION ---------
set objReg = GetObject("winmgmts:\\" & strComputer & "\root\default:StdRegProv")
intRC = objReg.DeleteKey(HKLM, strKeyPath)
if intRC <> 0 then
   WScript.Echo "Error deleting key: " & intRC
else
   WScript.Echo "Successfully deleted key " & strKeyPath
end if
```

Discussion

A Registry key is nothing more than a container of other keys and Registry values. There are six root keys that are used to logically group similar Registry data. Table 9-2 contains a list of each of the root keys and describes their purpose.

Table 9-2. The six root keys of the Registry

Root Key	Description
HKEY_LOCAL_MACHINE	This is the most important root key. It is where most system and application configuration data is stored. It is abbreviated HKLM.
HKEY_CURRENT_USER	This is actually a link to the subkey under HKEY_USERS for the currently logged on user. This is useful because it allows applications to access a single Registry path to get any configuration information for the currently logged on user. It is abbreviated HKCU.
HKEY_CURRENT_CONFIG	This is also a link that points under HKLM to hardware information for the current hardware profile. Since you can have different hardware profiles (as you can user profiles), this allows applications to access the one that is currently in use. It is abbreviated HKCC.
HKEY_CLASSES_ROOT	The subkeys under this key map file extensions to the applications that own them. It is abbreviated HKCR and is a link to HKLM\Software\Classes.
HKEY_PERFORMANCE_DATA	This key is used by applications that want to access performance data. It doesn't actually store the performance data, but serves as an interface to the data. It is abbreviated HKPD.
HKEY_USERS	This key stores profile information for all users of the system. It contains things such as environment variable values and user-specific customization settings. It is abbreviated HKU.

See Also

Recipe 9.2 for setting a value; MS KB 310516, "How to back up, edit, and restore the Registry in Windows XP and Windows Server 2003," MS KB 82821, "Registration Info Editor (REGEDIT) Command-Line Switches," and MS KB 310516, "How To Add, Modify, or Delete Registry Subkeys and Values by Using a Registration Entries (.reg) File"

9.2 Setting a Value

Problem

You want to create, modify, or delete a Registry value.

Solution

Using a graphical user interface

1. Open the Registry Editor (*regedit.exe*).
2. Browse to the parent key of the value you want to set or delete.

3. To create a value:

   a. Right-click on the parent key, select New and the type of value you want to create.

   b. Type the name of the value and hit enter twice. This should cause the Edit dialog box to open.

   c. Type the value for the value and click OK.

4. To modify a value:

   a. In the right pane, right-click on the value and select Modify.

   b. Enter the new data for the value and click OK.

5. To delete a value:

   a. In the right pane, right-click on the value and select Delete.

   b. Click Yes to confirm.

Using a command-line interface

The following command sets a Registry value:

```
> reg add \\<ComputerName>\<Key> /v <ValueName> /t <ValueType> /d <ValueData>
```

For example:

```
> reg add \\fs01\HKLM\Software\Rallencorp /v Version /t REG_SZ /d "1.2"
> reg add \\.\HKLM\Software\Rallencorp /v Setting1 /t REG_DWORD /d 1024
```

One nice thing about the reg add command is that it automatically creates the Rallencorp subkey if it doesn't already exist.

This command deletes a Registry value:

```
> reg delete \\<ComputerName>\<Key> /v <ValueName>
```

For example:

```
> reg delete \\fs01\HKLM\Software\Rallencorp /v Version
```

Using VBScript

```
' This code sets a Registry string value
' ------ SCRIPT CONFIGURATION ------
const HKLM = &H80000002
strKeyPath = "<RegKey>"              ' e.g. Software\Rallencorp
strStringValueName = "<ValueName>"   ' e.g. Version
strStringValue = "<ValueData>"       ' e.g. 1.2
strComputer = "<ComputerName>"       ' e.g. wks01 (use "." for local computer)
' ------ END CONFIGURATION ---------
set objReg = GetObject("winmgmts:\\" & strComputer & "\root\default:StdRegProv")
intRC = objReg.SetStringValue(HKLM, strKeyPath, strStringValueName, _
                          strStringValue)
if intRC <> 0 then
   WScript.Echo "Error setting value: " & intRC
```

```
else
    WScript.Echo "Successfully set value: " & strStringValueName
end if
```

 WMI has different methods for setting each of the Registry value datatypes. For example, to set a DWORD, you must use SetDWORDValue, not SetStringValue. See Table 9-1 for the complete list of methods.

```
' This code deletes a Registry value
' ------ SCRIPT CONFIGURATION ------
const HKLM = &H80000002
strKeyPath = "<RegKey>"                ' e.g. Software\Rallencorp
strStringValueName = "<ValueName>"  ' e.g. Version
strComputer = "<ComputerName>"         ' e.g. wks01 (use "." for local computer)
' ------ END CONFIGURATION ---------
set objReg = GetObject("winmgmts:\\" & strComputer & "\root\default:StdRegProv")
intRC = objReg.DeleteValue(HKLM, strKeyPath, strStringValueName)
if intRC <> 0 then
    WScript.Echo "Error deleting value: " & intRC
else
    WScript.Echo "Successfully deleted value: " & strStringValueName
end if
```

Discussion

Registry keys are used to structure the Registry. Registry values are to files what Registry keys are to folders. This simple analogy helps describe the purpose of Registry values: to store data. Values are made up of three elements: value name, value datatype, and value data. The datatype defines the type of data the value can contain. There are 11 total datatypes; I have listed the six most common in Table 9-3. If you want to see the more obscure datatypes, see MS KB 256986.

Table 9-3. Most common Registry datatypes

Datatype	Description
REG_DWORD	A double word (DWORD). A single word is a 16-bit number, so a double word is a 32-bit number (range from 0-4,294,967,296). Often, this datatype is used when a Boolean value is called for (0 or 1).
REG_SZ	An ASCII or Unicode string. This is another popular datatype, which is frequently used to store names, descriptions, and other text-based data.
REG_MULTI_SZ	Stores multiple independent ASCII or Unicode strings. Each string is null-terminated.
REG_EXPAND_SZ	An ASCII or Unicode string that contains one or more environment variables. This is essentially the same as REG_SZ, except that the embedded environment variables should be evaluated when the data is retrieved by the calling application.
REG_BINARY	Binary data. Avoid storing large binary blobs in the Registry with this type so you don't exceed the maximum size of the Registry or impact query performance.
REG_LINK	Similar to creating a shortcut on the filesystem, except that a REG_LINK creates a shortcut or link from one section of the Registry to another. See Recipe 9.10 for more on creating a REG_LINK.

See Also

Recipe 9.3 for setting the Registry with Group Policy; and MS KB 256986, "Description of the Microsoft Windows Registry"

9.3 Setting Keys or Values Using Group Policy

Problem

You want to set Registry keys or values on client computers using Group Policy. If you need to configure certain Registry settings on a large number of hosts, Group Policy can help you get the job done.

Solution

Using a graphical user interface

1. Open the Group Policy Management Console (*gpmc.msc*).
2. In the left pane, browse to the Group Policy object you want to modify.
3. Right-click on the Group Policy object and select Edit. This will launch the Group Policy Object Editor.
4. Set the predefined Registry values, which are contained under Administrative Templates, under the User Configuration and Computer Configuration sections.

If you want to configure Registry values that aren't contained in the User Configuration and Computer Configuration sections, you can create a custom administrative template and apply it to a Group Policy object. For more on how to do that, see the following whitepaper: *http://www.microsoft.com/WINDOWS2000/techinfo/howitworks/management/rbppaper.asp*

Discussion

Unfortunately, the Group Policy Object Editor doesn't show you the corresponding Registry path for each setting under Administrative Templates. To get that or to see the complete list of Registry settings supported in Group Policy on Windows Server 2003, Windows 2000, and Windows XP, check out the following whitepaper: *http://www.microsoft.com/downloads/details.aspx?FamilyId=7821C32F-DA15-438D-8E48-45915CD2BC14*.

> If you need to manage a lot of Registry settings via Group Policy, you might want to evaluate AutoProf Policy Maker Registry Extension, which can greatly simplify the task: *http://www.autoprof.com/policy/registry.html*.

9.4 Exporting Registry Files

Problem

You want to export part of the Registry to a Registry (*.reg*) file.

Solution

Using a graphical user interface

1. Open the Registry Editor (*regedit.exe*).
2. In the left pane, browse to the key you want to export.
3. Right-click on the key and select Export.
4. Enter a filename to save the export to and click Save.

Using a command-line interface

The following command exports part of the Registry to a file:

```
> regedit /e <FilePath> <RegKey>
```

For example:

```
> regedit /e c:\rallencorp.reg HKEY_LOCAL_MACHINE\Software\Rallencorp
```

Using VBScript

```
' This code exports the contents of a key to a Registry file.
' Since there are no scripting functions to do this, I simply
' shell out to the regedit tool to do it.

' strCommand = "regedit /e <FilePath> <RegKey>"
strCommand = "regedit /e c:\rallencorp.reg HKEY_LOCAL_MACHINE\Software\Rallencorp"
set objWshShell = WScript.CreateObject("WScript.Shell")
intRC = objWshShell.Run(strCommand, 0, TRUE)
if intRC <> 0 then
    WScript.Echo "Error returned from exporting Registry: " & intRC
else
    WScript.Echo "No errors returned from exporting the Registry file"
end if
```

Discussion

The Registry Editor allows you to export parts of the Registry to a text-based file. You can then modify the file and import it back into the Registry (perhaps on another host) using Registry Editor (see Recipe 9.5). These Registry files have an extension of *.reg*. Windows recognizes this extension so that if you double-click on a *.reg* file, you will automatically be prompted to import its contents into the Registry.

The format for this file is pretty easy to follow. Here is an example Registry file containing the contents of the HKLM\Software\Google key:

```
Windows Registry Editor Version 5.00

[HKEY_LOCAL_MACHINE\Software\Google]
"DesktopBarAdminInstall"=dword:00000001

[HKEY_LOCAL_MACHINE\Software\Google\CustomSearch]

[HKEY_LOCAL_MACHINE\Software\Google\Deskbar]
"path"="C:\\PROGRA~1\\Google\\GGTASK~1.DLL"
"Version"=dword:00000051

[HKEY_LOCAL_MACHINE\Software\Google\Miniviewer]
"path"="C:\\Program Files\\Google\\ggviewer81-47.exe"
"Version"=dword:00000051

[HKEY_LOCAL_MACHINE\Software\Google\NavClient]
"test"="41"
"brand"="GGLD"
"installtime"="1068347808"
"sent"=dword:00000001

[HKEY_LOCAL_MACHINE\Software\Google\NavClient\Obsolete]

[HKEY_LOCAL_MACHINE\Software\Google\Verscheck]
"path"="C:\\Program Files\\Google\\ggverscheck81-47.exe"
"Version"=dword:00000051
```

Exporting the Registry is useful if you need to implement a significant change to a system. A Registry export can act both as a backup in case things go wrong and as a change log to help you determine what was modified after the change.

9.5   Importing Registry Files

Problem

You want to import changes to the Registry using a Registry (*.reg*) file.

Solution

Using a graphical user interface

1. Open an Explorer (*explorer.exe*) window.
2. Browse to the *.reg* file you want to import.
3. Double-click on the file.
4. Click Yes to confirm the import.

5. You can accomplish the same thing within Registry Editor by going to File →
Import.

Using a command-line interface

The following command imports a Registry key or subkey:

```
> regedit /s <FilePath>
```

For example:

```
> regedit /s c:\rallencorp.reg
```

Using VBScript

```
' This code imports the contents of a Registry file.
' Since there are no scripting functions to do this, I simply
' shell out to the regedit tool to do it.

' strCommand = "regedit /s <FilePath>"
strCommand = "regedit /s c:\rallencorp.reg"
set objWshShell = WScript.CreateObject("WScript.Shell")
intRC = objWshShell.Run(strCommand, 0, TRUE)
if intRC <> 0 then
   WScript.Echo "Error returned from importing registry: " & intRC
else
   WScript.Echo "No errors returned from importing the registry file"
end if
```

Discussion

Importing a Registry file is as easy as double-clicking it, but this is where the danger
lies. Be careful anytime you import a Registry file; make sure it contains exactly what
you want to import. If you accidentally import the wrong file, it can overwrite values
you didn't intend to overwrite. Since Registry files are text-based, open a file in a text
editor such as Notepad to see what it contains.

9.6   Searching the Registry

Problem

You want to search the Registry for the occurrence of a string or number.

Solution

Using a graphical user interface

1. Open the Registry Editor (*regedit.exe*).
2. In the left pane, browse to the key you want to begin the search. If you want to
   search the entire Registry, click on My Computer at the top.

3. From the menu, select Edit → Find.

4. Enter the string you want to search with and select whether you want to search keys, values, or data.

5. Click the Find Next button.

6. If you want to continue searching after a match is found, either select Edit → Find Next from the menu or press the F3 key.

Using a command-line interface

You can use the `regfind` utility from the Windows 2000 Resource Kit to search for certain values under a given key. Here is the syntax:

```
> regfind -m \\<ComputerName> -p <RegKey> -n "<ValueName>"
```

For example:

```
> regfind -m \\wks01 -p HKEY_LOCAL_MACHINE\Software\Microsoft -n "Run"
```

See the `regfind` command line help to view all supported search options.

Using VBScript

Unfortunately, the `StdRegProv` WMI Provider doesn't support searching the Registry. Your only options to search the Registry via VBScript would be to enumerate over all the keys and values you want to search against (very inefficient), shell out to a command-line utility such as reg (see Recipe 9.5 for an example of how to do this), or find a third-party ActiveX control that implements a Registry search interface that can be used by scripting languages.

Discussion

The Registry contains a significant amount of data. Don't be surprised if your initial search matches a lot of different keys or values that you weren't intending. This is especially true if you search across a whole hive or all of the hives. Try to restrict your search to a specific key when possible.

9.7   Comparing the Registry

Problem

You want to compare the Registry on two hosts or compare the Registry on the same host after you've installed an application or made other modifications to the Registry.

Solution

Using a graphical user interface

1. Use the Registry Editor (*regedit.exe*) to export part of the Registry you want to compare for the two target computers (or before and after changes are made on the same computer). See Recipe 9.4 for more information on exporting Registry files.

2. Open the WinDiff program (*windiff.exe*).

3. From the menu select File → Compare Files.

4. Select the exported Registry files you created in step 1.

5. Select View → Expand or View → Outline from the menu to see the differences.

Discussion

When you export the Registry, you are simply exporting the contents of the Registry to a text-based file, which you can use to compare against other export files. Windiff is just one example tool that can compare text files and show the differences. Some text editors can do the same (e.g., Textpad is a favorite of mine).

If you only want to see the changes that an application makes during installation, another option is to use the Sysinternals Registry Monitor tool. You can configure Registry Monitor to display only write events for a certain key. For more information on Registry Monitor, see Recipe 9.12.

See Also

MS KB 171780, "How to Use WinDiff to Compare Registry Files"

9.8   Restricting Access to the Registry

Problem

You want to restrict access to a certain Registry key or value. This may be necessary if you need to store sensitive data in the Registry and want to prevent normal users from seeing it.

Solution

Using a graphical user interface

1. Open the Registry Editor (*regedit.exe*).

2. In the left pane, browse to the key on which you want to set permissions.

3. Right-click the key and select Permissions.

4. To add a new permission click the Add button. This launches the Object Picker dialog box. Select the user or group you want to add permissions for and click OK. The default permission granted to this user or group is Read Access.

   a. To delete a permission select the user or group you want to remove under Group or user names and click the Remove button. Click OK.

   b. To modify a permission, click the Advanced button. Select the permission you want to modify under Permission entries and click the Edit button. Check the boxes corresponding to the permissions you want to grant. Click OK until all dialog boxes are closed.

 You can also configure Registry permissions with Group Policy. In the left pane of the Group Policy Object Editor, navigate to \Windows Settings\Security Settings\Registry in either the Computer Configuration or the User Configuration section. Right-click on Registry and select Add Key. This will allow you to select a target Registry key and configure the permissions you want on that key.

Using a command-line interface

Use the *subinacl* command to grant access to a Registry key. This grants full control for the specified user over a key:

```
> subinacl /verbose=1 /keyreg \\<ComputerName>\<KeyPath> /grant=<UserOrGroup>
```

For example:

```
> subinacl /verbose=1 /keyreg \\fs01\HKEY_LOCAL_MACHINE\Software\Rallencorp
/grant=AMER\rallen
```

You can also revoke access to a key using the next command. The following command revokes members of the users group from being able to access the specified Registry key:

```
> subinacl /verbose=1 /keyreg \\<ComputerName>\<KeyPath> /revoke=<UserOrGroup>
```

For example:

```
> subinacl /verbose=1 /keyreg \\.\HKEY_LOCAL_MACHINE\Software\Rallencorp
/revoke=Users
```

Lastly, you can view what users and groups have access on a Registry key using the /display option with *subinacl* as shown here:

```
> subinacl /verbose=1 /keyreg \\<ComputerName>\<KeyPath> /display
```

For example:

```
> subinacl /verbose=1 /keyreg \\fs01\HKEY_LOCAL_MACHINE\Software\Rallencorp /display
```

Discussion

Another useful feature of the permissions function in Registry Editor is Effective Permissions. With it, you can select a user or group and determine what rights it has over a key.

9.9   Backing Up and Restoring the Registry

Problem

You want to back up or restore the Registry on a computer.

Solution

With the NT Backup utility (*ntbackup.exe*) you can back up the Registry by backing up the System State. The System State includes such things as the files necessary to boot the system, the Active Directory database, and the Registry. To restore the Registry, you have to restore the System State from a previous backup.

Using a graphical user interface

Do the following to back up the System State:

1. Open the NT Backup utility (*ntbackup.exe*) from the Start menu by selecting Programs → Accessories → System Tools → Backup.
2. Click the Advanced Mode link to configure backup settings manually or click Next to use the wizard interface.
3. Make sure Back up files and settings is selected and click Next.
4. To only back up the System State, select Let me choose what to back up and click Next.
5. Expand My Computer, check the box beside System State and click Next.
6. Click the Browse button to browse to the location you want to save the backup file to and click Next.
7. Click Finish to start the backup.

Do the following to restore the System State:

1. Browse to the backup file containing the System State you want to restore and double-click the file. This launches the NT Backup utility (*ntbackup.exe*).
2. Click Next.
3. Select Restore files and settings and click Next.
4. Under Items to restore, check the box beside System State and click Next.
5. Click Finish to start the restore.

You may see on the final screen that it states that existing files will not be replaced. This doesn't apply to the System State. Any time the System State is restored, all System State components are overwritten with the backup version.

Using a command-line interface

The following command backs up the system state to a file:

```
> ntbackup backup systemstate /j "<Description>" /f "<FilePath>"
> ntbackup backup systemstate /j "System State Backup 1" /f "c:\sysstate.bkf"
```

You can't use ntbackup from the command line to restore files.

Another option for backing up the Registry is to use the *regedit* command to back up specific Registry hives to a file. The following command backs up the HKLM hive to a file called *hklm.hiv*:

```
> regedit /e hklm.hiv hkey_local_machine
```

To restore the hive, use the following command:

```
regedit /s hklm.hiv
```

You can use the reg command to copy specific subkeys if you don't want to back up an entire hive. For example:

```
> reg save HKLM\Software\Microsoft c:\backup\hklm-sw-ms.hiv
```

To restore the backup back to the Registry, use the same syntax except replace "save" with "restore":

```
> reg restore <Key> <Filename>
```

Discussion

If you ever run into the case where you have a corrupt Registry or you perhaps accidentally deleted a section of the Registry you shouldn't have, the best solution is to restore from your last good backup of the system. You have to be careful though; restoring the system state restores more than just the Registry and system boot files. It also restores the NTDS database for a domain controller.

See Also

MS KB 318149, "How to Maintain Current Registry Backups in Windows NT 4.0 and Windows 2000," MS KB 322755, "HOW TO: Backup, Edit, and Restore the Registry in Windows 2000," and MS KB 322756, "HOW TO: Back Up, Edit, and Restore the Registry in Windows XP and Windows Server 2003"

9.10 Creating a Registry Link

Problem

You want to create a link from one Registry key to another. Registry links are used extensively by the operating system, but most people aren't aware that they exist or that they can be created manually.

Solution

Using a command-line interface

Registry links have never been a highly publicized feature and as a result there are very few tools that can create them. You can download a tool called regln from *http://www.ntinternals.net/regln/* to do the job. This is how you create a Registry link with it:

```
> regln  <LinkKeyName> <CurrentKeyName>
```

For example:

```
> regln HKLM\SOFTWARE\LinkToMS HKLM\Software\Microsoft
```

Use the –d switch to delete a Registry link:

```
> regln -d <LinkKeyName>
```

For example:

```
> regln -d HKLM\SOFTWARE\LinkToMS
```

Using VBScript

The StdRegProv WMI Provider does not support creating Registry links, so you'll need to shell out to regln if you want to create them in a script.

Discussion

You have undoubtedly created a shortcut to a file or folder, perhaps on your desktop, at one point or another. Shortcuts are useful if you have a file that is nested deeply within the filesystem and you don't want to navigate to it each time to access it. Think of Registry links in the same way. If there are Registry keys you need to access on a regular basis, but they are nested deeply, you can use Registry links to make them easier to get to.

Let's say there are a bunch of keys I access frequently that are contained somewhere under the HKEY_LOCAL_MACHINE\Software key. What I could do is create a key called HKEY_LOCAL_MACHINE\Software\Rallencorp and then put all of my Registry links under that key. Here is an example of creating a link to the Run key:

```
regln HKLM\Software\Rallencorp\Run HKLM\SOFTWARE\Microsoft\Windows\CurrentVersion\Run
```

See Also

More information about the *regln* command can be found at the following web site: *http://www.tenox.tc/out/regln.txt.*

9.11   Monitoring Registry Activity

Problem

You want to monitor Registry accesses. This could involve anything from watching what processes are using the Registry to monitoring what a specific user is doing with the Registry.

Solution

There are two ways to monitor Registry activity. You can view real-time access to the Registry with the Sysinternals Registry Monitor (*regmon.exe*) tool. With it you can view the process name, the PID, and the operation performed (e.g., QueryKey, EnumerateValue, SetValue, etc.) for all the processes that have a key or value open. Figure 9-1 shows this tool.

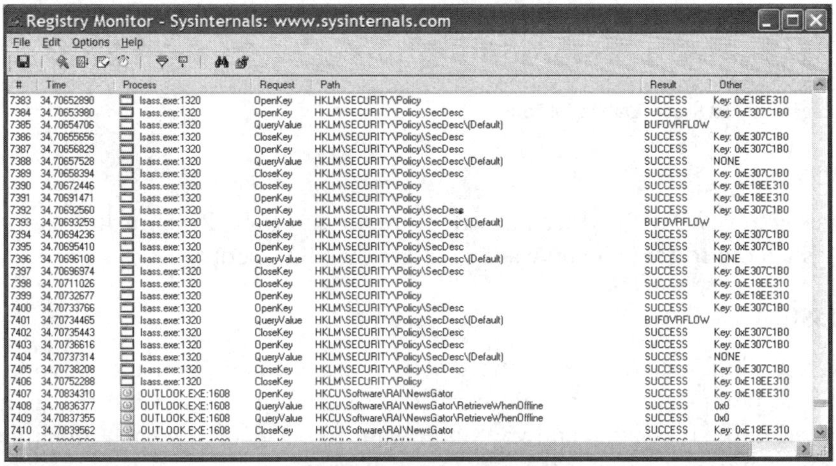

Figure 9-1. Sysinternals Registry Monitor

If you want to monitor Registry activity over a long period of time or cannot keep a copy of Registry Monitor open at all times, another option is to enable Registry auditing. With Registry auditing enabled, you can get detailed information in the Security event log about the successful or failed attempts a particular user or group of users make to the Registry. Here is how you set that up:

1. Open the Registry Editor (*regedit.exe*).

2. In the left pane, browse to the key you want to audit. (You can't audit individual Registry values.)

3. Right-click on the key and select Permissions.

4. Click the Advanced button.

5. Click the Auditing tab.

6. Click the Add button.

7. Use the Object Picker to find the user or group for whom you want to audit access.

8. In the Auditing Entry box, select the types of things you want to audit. Success is audited separately from Failure, so be sure to check all the types you want to audit.

9. Click OK until all windows are closed.

10. Open the Local Security Policy snap-in (available from Administrative Tools).

11. In the left pane, expand Local Policies and click on Audit Policy.

12. In the right pane, double-click on Audit object access.

13. Check the box beside Success to audit successful actions.

14. Check the box beside Failure to audit failed actions.

15. Click OK.

Discussion

To enable auditing in the Registry, you have to complete two steps. The first consists of configuring what you want to audit in the Registry, which you can do with the Registry Editor. See Table 9-4 for the complete list of audit options. After you've completed this, auditing isn't turned on yet. To do that, you have to go to the Local Policies snap-in (or Group Policy Object Editor in a domain environment) and enable auditing as described above. At this point, any Registry access to the keys you configured should be logged to the Security event log.

Table 9-4. Registry audit options

Audit name	Description
Create Link	Any attempt to create a symbolic link in a particular key.
Create Subkey	Any attempt to create subkeys on a selected Registry key.
Delete	Any attempt to delete a key.
Enumerate Subkeys	Any attempt to list the subkeys of a key.
Notify	Any notification events from a key in the Registry.
Query Value	Any attempt to read a value from a key.

Table 9-4. Registry audit options (continued)

Audit name	Description
Read Control	Any attempt to open the discretionary access control list on a key.
Set Value	Any attempt to set a value in a key.
Write DAC	Any attempt to write a discretionary access control list on a key.
Write Owner	Any attempt to change the owner of a key.

 It is always a good idea to monitor your event logs closely after you enable auditing. You don't want fill up your Security log unnecessarily because you are auditing too much.

See Also

MS KB 315416, "HOW TO: Use Group Policy to Audit Registry Keys in Windows 2000"

9.12   Viewing Processes That Have a Registry Key Open

Problem

You want to view the processes that have a Registry key open. If a process has a key open, you may not be able to modify or delete that key or its values.

Solution

Using a graphical user interface

Open the Sysinternals Registry Monitor (*regmon.exe*) tool. By default, the Registry Monitor shows all processes that have a handle to a Registry key or value. You have two options for finding a specific key or value:

- From the menu, select Edit → Find. Enter the some part of the Registry key or value you want to search against. Make sure Direction is selected correctly (by default Down is selected, but if you want to search Up).

- The second option consists of filtering the output. Select Options → Filter/ Highlight from the menu. In the Include text box, enter the key or value you want to view. Click OK and then Yes to confirm.

You can also use the Sysinternals Process Explorer (*procexp.exe*) tool to search for Registry handles.

Using a command-line interface

With the Sysinternals handle command, you can find a process that has a Registry key open. Simply specify the —a switch and some part of the key path or value name you want to search on. Since the search is fuzzy, there is a chance it might match things other than Registry access (e.g., an open file), but if your search string is specific enough, you should be able to narrow it down. For example, the following command finds all processes that have a handle to something containing RunOnce in the name (often a Registry key):

```
> handle -a RunOnce
```

You can also use handle to view all processes that are accessing a key under HKLM\Software:

```
> handle -a HKLM\Software
```

CHAPTER 10

Processes, Tasks, and Services

10.0 Introduction

Processes are a fundamental component of the Windows XP operating system. For anything you do on a system, whether it is deleting a file, starting a service, or writing text in Notepad, there is a process behind it. Since processes are so important, it is critical that you understand how to manage, monitor, and troubleshoot them.

Processes use system resources, such as CPU and memory, in order to run. But not all processes are created equal. Some use more resources than others and often you'll run into situations where you need to identify processes that are using more resources than they should, which may make it difficult for other processes to work. Processes also frequently open files, DLLs, and Registry keys and values. These resources are known as handles, and often when a process has one open, no other process can modify or delete it. This can make it problematic, for example, if you need to rename a file that a process has a lock on.

There are several processes that start by default whenever a Windows server boots up. Any applications you've installed that run at system startup will also have one or more processes running, all without you doing a thing. It is for this reason that you need to be able to create, query, suspend, and terminate processes on demand, otherwise it is very easy to lose control over how your system performs.

A task is simply a program, application, command, or script that does something useful. In the Windows environment, you need to know how to run tasks with alternate credentials, so you don't always have to be logged on to your workstation with administrator credentials. You also need to know how to run tasks against remote servers or workstations, which enables you to do daily administration tasks without ever leaving the comfort (and security) of your workstation. Often it can be beneficial to have tasks run as soon as someone logs into a system, and there are several ways you can set this up. Finally, if you are trying to automate certain tasks (as all good system administrators should), you'll need to schedule various tasks to run at certain times of the day or night.

Windows services are nothing more than continually running processes that are controlled by the Service Control Manager (SCM). Instead of directly creating a service process, you (or the system itself) send a start or stop message to SCM, which takes care of starting or stopping the associated process. The DHCP Client provided with the Windows operating system is an example of a service. It is responsible for requesting and renewing DHCP requests (i.e., obtaining an IP address dynamically). After the system begins the boot up process, SCM starts the DHCP Client service, which kicks off a process that runs in the background to handle DHCP requests. You can stop the DHCP Client service via the Services snap-in, which causes SCM to terminate the underlying DHCP Client process. If you start the service, SCM starts the process.

Each service has a corresponding key in the Registry contained under HKEY_LOCAL_MACHINE\SYSTEM\CurrentControlSet\Services. This stores basic configuration information about the service, including service dependencies, the command line to execute to start the service, and startup type. For more information on some the service-specific Registry values, take a look at MS KB 103000, "CurrentControlSet\Services Subkey Entries."

One of the knocks Windows 2000 received when it debuted was that it had too many services enabled by default. This was both a good and a bad thing, however. On the one hand, it meant that a lot of functionality was turned on out of the box. On the other hand, many of the default services, such as IIS, had security issues, so *all* default installations were vulnerable. As a result, Microsoft changed their stance in Windows XP and Windows Server 2003, opting for a more secure route. Many of the services that were started up by default in Windows 2000 are now disabled at startup in Windows Server 2003. For a list of the changes in the default startup mode, see MS KB 812519, "Services That Are Turned Off by Default in Windows Server 2003."

10.1 Viewing the Running Processes

Problem

You want to see all processes that are currently running on a system.

Solution

Using a graphical user interface

1. Open the Windows Task Manager (*taskmgr.exe*).
2. Click on the Processes tab.

Using a command-line interface

Use *tasklist.exe* to view all processes (use the /S option to target a remote system):

```
> tasklist
```

tasklist has several options for searching processes. This command searches for all iexplore (Internet Explorer) processes being run by the Administrator user:

```
> tasklist /FI "IMAGENAME eq iexplore*"  /FI "USERNAME eq Administrator"
```

You can also use tasklist to perform searches based on PID, memory usage, CPU time, and other attributes. This command finds all processes running on host dhcp01 that are consuming more than 10 MB of memory:

```
> tasklist /S dhcp01 /FI "MEMUSAGE gt 10240
```

Another Windows XP tool you can use to get a process list is *wmic* as shown here (use the /node: option to target a remote system):

```
> wmic process list brief
```

Using downloadable software

The Sysinternals Process Explorer (*procexp.exe*) tool can be used to view and search for processes. Sysinternals also has a command-line tool called pslist.exe that can list processes.

Using VBScript

```
' This code displays the running processes on the target computer.
' ------ SCRIPT CONFIGURATION ------
strComputer = "."  ' Can be a hostname or "." to target local host
' ------ END CONFIGURATION ---------
set objWMI = GetObject("winmgmts:\\" & strComputer & "\root\cimv2")
set colProcesses = objWMI.InstancesOf("Win32_Process")
for each objProcess In colProcesses
    WScript.Echo objProcess.Name & " (" & objProcess.ProcessID & ")"
next


' This code finds the processes that have a memory usage greater
' than the specified amount.  To search on different criteria,
' modify the WQL used in the ExecQuery call.
' ------ SCRIPT CONFIGURATION ------
strComputer = "."
intMaxMemKB = 1024 * 10000
' ------ END CONFIGURATION ---------
set objWMI = GetObject("winmgmts:\\" & strComputer & "\root\cimv2")
set colProcesses = objWMI.ExecQuery("Select * from Win32_Process " & _
                            " Where workingsetsize > " & intMaxMemKB )
WScript.Echo "Process, Size (in KB)"
for each objProcess in colProcesses
   WScript.Echo objProcess.Name & ", " & objProcess.WorkingSetSize / 1024
next
```

Discussion

Sometimes it is difficult to associate an application (e.g., Internet Explorer) with its underlying process (e.g., *iexpore.exe*). In each of the command-line solutions, only the process name will be shown, and it may be completely different from the name of the application. With Internet Explorer, it is pretty easy to figure out that *iexplore.exe* is probably the underlying process, but how can you tell for sure? One way is to look at Sysinternals Process Explorer. It displays a Description field that contains the application name of the process. Alternatively, you can specify the /v option with the *tasklist* command, which displays a Window Title field for each process. This typically includes the name of the application. Here is an example command you can run:

```
> tasklist /v /fo list
```

Unfortunately, you can't programmatically retrieve the Window Title using the `Win32_Process` class.

10.2   Viewing the Properties of a Process

Problem

You want to view the properties of a process. This includes the process executable path, command line, current working directory, parent process (if any), owner, and startup timestamp.

Solution

Using downloadable software

1. Open the Sysinternals Process Explorer tool (*procexp.exe*).
2. Double-click the process you want to view.
3. View the Image tab, which contains the process properties.

Some of this information can also be viewed using Windows Task Manager (*taskmgr.exe*). After starting *taskmgr.exe*, click on the Processes tab. Select View → Select Columns from the menu and check the boxes beside the properties you want to see.

Using a command-line interface

The `tasklist.exe` command can display a subset of the properties described in the Problem section:

```
> tasklist /v /FI "IMAGENAME eq <ProcessName>" /FO list
```

Using VBScript

```
' This code displays the properties of a process.
' ------ SCRIPT CONFIGURATION ------
intPID = 3280    ' PID of the target process
strComputer = "."
' ------ END CONFIGURATION ---------
WScript.Echo "Process PID: " & intPID
set objWMIProcess = GetObject("winmgmts:\\" & strComputer & _
                    "\root\cimv2:Win32_Process.Handle='" & intPID & "'")
WScript.Echo "Name: " & objWMIProcess.Name
WScript.Echo "Command line: " & ObjWMIProcess.CommandLine
WScript.Echo "Startup date: " & ObjWMIProcess.CreationDate
WScript.Echo "Description: " & ObjWMIProcess.Description
WScript.Echo "Exe Path: " & ObjWMIProcess.ExecutablePath
WScript.Echo "Parent Process ID: " & ObjWMIProcess.ParentProcessId
objWMIProcess.GetOwner strUser,strDomain
WScript.Echo "Owner: " & strDomain & "\" & strUser
```

Discussion

Another option from the command line is to use `wmic` to harness the power of WMI. You can retrieve all of the properties defined by the `Win32_Process` class (see Table 7-3) by running this simple command:

```
> wmic process list full
```

And if you want to limit your retrieval to just a single process, use this command:

```
> wmic process where name="snmp.exe" get /format:list
```

10.3   Viewing the Resources a Process Is Using

Problem

You want to view the memory, I/O, and CPU statistics of a process along with any handles, DLLs, and network connections it has open. If you find that you are running low on memory on a particular system, this can often be attributed to a single process that has consumed a large amount of memory. If you can terminate that particular process, the system should go back to a stable state.

Finding the DLLs a process is using can be handy if you need to update a DLL and want to find out which programs are actively using it, or if you are trying to delete a DLL, but cannot do so due to a lock on the file by a process that is using it.

You may also want to see other handles, such as Registry keys or files, that a process has open and potentially locked, which may prevent you from modifying or deleting them.

Solution

Using a graphical user interface

To view the performance statistics of a process, do the following:

1. Open the Sysinternals Process Explorer tool (*procexp.exe*).

2. Double-click the process you want to view.

3. View the Performance tab, which contains the process properties.

 This information can also be viewed using Windows Task Manager (*taskmgr.exe*). After starting *taskmgr.exe*, click on the Processes tab. Select View → Select Columns from the menu and check the boxes beside the properties you want to see.

To view the DLLs being used by a process, do the following:

1. Open the Sysinternals Process Explorer tool (*procexp.exe*).

2. From the menu, select View → Lower Pane View → DLLs.

3. Click on the process you want to view. In the bottom window, the list of DLLs being used by that process is displayed.

To view the processes using a specific DLL, do the following:

1. Open the Sysinternals Process Explorer tool (*procexp.exe*).

2. From the menu, select Find → Find DLLs.

3. Type the name of the DLL (partial string accepted) and click the Search button.

To view the handles being used by a process, do the following:

1. Open the Sysinternals Process Explorer tool (*procexp.exe*).

2. From the menu select View → View Handles.

3. Click on the process you want to view. In the bottom window, the list of handles being used by that process will be displayed.

To view the network connections that a process has open, do the following:

1. Open the Sysinternals TCPView tool (*tcpview.exe*).

2. View the complete list of processes and associated ports, which are displayed by default. New connections show up in green and terminating connections show up in red.

Using a command-line interface

The Sysinternal's `pslist` command displays all of the performance metrics for a process:

```
> pslist -x <ProcessName>
```

In place of `<ProcessName>`, put the name of the process without its extension. For example:

```
> pslist -x iexplore
```

To view the DLLs being used by a process, use the `listdll` command available from Sysinternals:

```
> listdlls <ProcessName>
```

To view the processes using a specific DLL, use the following command:

```
> listdlls -d <DLLName>
```

To view all of the handles a process has open, use the following command:

```
> handle -a -p <ProcessName>
```

You can also search for a specific handle using the following command:

```
> handle <HandleName>
```

For example, if you want to find all processes that have the *c:\test* directory open, you would replace *<HandleName>* with *c:\test*.

The following command displays the open ports and the process ID of the process associated with the port. The –o option is new to *netstat.exe* in Windows XP:

```
> netstat -o
```

The Sysinternals *netstatp.exe* command is similar to *netstat.exe*, except it displays the process name associated with each port (not just the PID):

```
> netstatp
```

And for yet another extremely useful port querying tool, check out *portqry.exe* (see MS KB 310099 for more information). With `portqry` you can get even more information than with `netstatp`. Run this command to output all of the ports and their associated processes:

```
> portqry -local
```

This command also breaks port usage down by service (e.g., DnsCache). You can watch the port usage for a particular PID and log it to a file. The following command does this for PID 1234:

```
> portqry -wpid 1234 -wt 5 -l portoutput.txt -v
```

The –wt defines the watch time, which is how long `portqry` waits before examining the process again (the default is 60 seconds). The –v option is for verbose output.

Using VBScript

There are no APIs available to VBScript to query the DLLs, which handles, and which network connections a process is using, but you can use WMI to retrieve memory and CPU usage as shown here:

```
' This code displays the performance stats of a process.
' ------ SCRIPT CONFIGURATION ------
intPID = 3280  ' PID of target process
strComputer = "."
' ------ END CONFIGURATION ---------
WScript.Echo "Process PID: " & intPID
set objWMIProcess = GetObject("winmgmts:\\" & strComputer & _
                    "\root\cimv2:Win32_Process.Handle='" & intPID & "'")
arrProps = Array("Name", "KernelModeTime", "UserModeTime", _
            "MaximumWorkingSetSize", "MinimumWorkingSetSize", _
            "PageFaults", "PageFileUsage", "VirtualSize", _
            "WorkingSetSize", "PeakPageFileUsage", "PeakVirtualSize", _
            "PeakWorkingSetSize", "PrivatePageCount", _
            "QuotaNonPagedPoolUsage", "QuotaPagedPoolUsage", _
            "QuotaPeakNonPagedPoolUsage", "QuotaPeakPagedPoolUsage", _
            "ThreadCount")
for each strProp in arrProps
   WScript.Echo strProp & ": " & objWMIProcess.Properties_(strProp)
next
```

Discussion

If you need to get serious about analyzing performance statistics for one or more processes, you should consider using Performance Monitor (*perfmon.exe*). With the Process performance object (click the little + icon in the System Monitor and select Process under Performance object), you can graph a variety of metrics for individual processes or for all of them together using the _Total instance. Even if you don't want to use Performance Monitor to monitor processes, it can still be useful if you have a question about what a particular metric, such as Working Set, really means. Click the Explain button when you view the Process performance object, which will cause another dialog to appear that contains additional information about what each counter means. These counters are mostly the same ones you'll find in Task Manager, pslist, and the Win32_Process class.

See Also

MS KB 137984, "TCP Connection States and Netstat Output," and MS KB 310099, "Description of the Portqry.exe Command-Line Utility"

10.4   Suspending a Process

Problem

You want to suspend a process from running. This is helpful if you want to temporarily stop an application, perhaps due to high CPU consumption, but you don't want to kill it. This can give you an opportunity to launch further diagnostics utilities to troubleshoot the process.

Solution

Using downloadable software

1. Open the Sysinternals Process Explorer tool (*procexp.exe*).
2. To suspend a process, right-click on the target process and select Suspend.
3. To resume a process, right-click on the target process and select Resume.

Sysinternals also has a command-line tool to suspend processes:

```
> pssuspend <PID>
```

And this resumes a process:

```
> pssuspend –r <PID>
```

Using VBScript

Currently, no scripting API supports suspending processes. However, if you are so inclined, you can use the SuspendThread and ResumeThread functions that are defined in *kernel.lib* with a language like Visual Basic.

Discussion

Applications are much better behaved these days than they were a few years ago, but that still doesn't mean you won't see one peg the CPU on a system and render it virtually useless from time to time.

You can specify alternate credentials with the pssuspend command using the –u (user) and –p (password) options. If you specify –u without –p, it will prompt you to enter the password (this is the more secure way to do it). Here is an example command line:

```
> pssuspend \\jamison –u rallen notepad.exe
```

10.5   Killing a Process

Problem

You want to terminate a process. Even though Windows has come a long way in the last 10 years, the operating system can't prevent buggy or poorly written applications from becoming unresponsive, which means you may need to manually terminate processes from time to time.

Solution

Using a graphical user interface

1. Open the Windows Task Manager (*taskmgr.exe*).
2. Click on the Processes tab.
3. If you do not see the process you want to set, be sure the box beside Show processes from all users is checked.
4. Right click on the target process, select End Process, and select the desired priority.
5. You can also accomplish the same task using the Sysinternals Process Explorer (*procexp.exe*) tool. Right-click the process and select Kill Process.

Using a command-line interface

This command kills a process by PID:

```
> taskkill -pid <PID>
```

And this kills a process by name:

```
> taskkill  -im <ProcessName>
```

Use the /f option to forcefully kill the process.

Using downloadable software

The pskill.exe utility works in a very similar manner to taskkill. You can specify the PID to kill:

```
> pskill <PID>
```

Or the process name:

```
> pskill <ProcessName>
```

Using VBScript

```
' This code terminates the specified process.
' ------ SCRIPT CONFIGURATION ------
intPID = 2560    ' PID of the process to terminate
```

```
strComputer = "."
' ------ END CONFIGURATION ---------
WScript.Echo "Process PID: " & intPID
set objWMIProcess = GetObject("winmgmts:\\" & strComputer & _
                    "\root\cimv2:Win32_Process.Handle='" & intPID & "'")
WScript.Echo "Process name: " & objWMIProcess.Name
intRC = objWMIProcess.Terminate( )
if intRC = 0 Then
    Wscript.Echo "Successfully killed process."
else
    Wscript.Echo "Could not kill process. Error code: " & intRC
end if
```

Discussion

Manually killing processes is not good practice, but it is a necessary evil. Be selective about forcibly killing a process, because this will also terminate any child processes in an ungraceful manner and can leave lingering remnants of the process in memory, which may cause problems if you attempt to restart the process later.

10.6 Running a Task with Alternate Credentials

Problem

You want to run a task using a username and password other than the one you are currently logged in with.

Solution

Using a graphical user interface

1. Open the Start Menu.
2. Browse to the application you want to open and right-click it.
3. Select Run As.
4. When prompted, enter the username, password, and domain of the user being authenticated.

Using a command-line interface

The runas.exe command allows you to run a command as an alternate user:

> runas /user:<User> "<ExectuablePath>"

Here is an example:

> runas /user:AMER\rallen.adm "mmc.exe"

If you want to authenticate using credentials of a user who does not have logon privileges to the local machine, you'll also need to specify the /netonly option.

Using VBScript

```
' This code shows how to use alternate credentials using WMI
' Note that you cannot use this to connect to the local machine.
' ------ SCRIPT CONFIGURATION ------
strServer = "<HostName>"  ' e.g. wks01
strUser = "<User>"        ' e.g. AMER\rallen.adm
strPasswd = "<Password>"
' ------ END CONFIGURATION ---------
on error resume next
set objLocator = CreateObject("WbemScripting.SWbemLocator")
set objWMI = objLocator.ConnectServer(strServer, "root\cimv2", _
                                      strUser, strPasswd)
if Err.Number <> 0 then
   WScript.Echo "Authentication failed: " & Err.Description
end if

' Now you can use the objWMI object to get an instance of a class
' or perform a WQL query.  Here is an example:
colDisks = objWMI.InstancesOf("Win32_LogicalDisk")
```

Discussion

A best practice system administrators should follow is to log on to desktop systems using a normal user account that has no administrator level privileges outside of that system. This has three distinct advantages:

- It reduces the impact a virus can have on your network if your machine becomes infected.
- It reduces the chance of accidentally deleting important files and folders or making administrative changes unknowingly.
- It ensures that the network remains secure even if someone gains physical access to your workstation while you are logged in.

If you need to access a network resource with administrator privileges, you should do so using alternate credentials as we showed in the solutions. This is also necessary if you want to access a resource on a machine in an untrusted domain, different from the one your account resides in. If you have some test systems in a lab that are not part of your domain, you'll have to use alternate credentials to access them.

Using a graphical user interface

If you need to run several different programs at the same time as an alternate user, it can be annoying to have to follow the graphical or command-line solution for each one. In this case, you'd probably be better off just using a remote desktop client to log on to the machine as the target user.

Using a command-line interface

One problem with runas is that you cannot specify the password for the user on the command line, even by piping it in. That means runas must always prompt you to enter a password. Some may argue that this is intentional because it is insecure to specify passwords on the command line; however, passing a password on the command line can be useful in situations where you need runas capability in a batch file. Fortunately, an alternative exists in the form of the Joeware *cpau.exe* utility. It works like the runas /netonly command, but you can specify the –p option to pass in a password:

```
> cpau -u <User> -p <Password> -ex "<ExectuablePath>"
```

This utility also has a more secure option. You can create an encrypted "job" file that contains the command to run and the password to use. If you open a job file, all you'll see is a string of letters and numbers. This prevents people from casually reading a password in a batch file.

To use this feature, you must first create the job file:

```
> cpau -u <User> -p <Password> -ex "<ExecutablePath>" -enc -file <JobFile>
```

Then to execute a job file, use the following command:

```
> cpau -dec -file <JobFile>
```

If you don't want to have to type a runas or cpau command every time you open a certain tool, consider creating a shortcut that automatically does this for you. For more on creating shortcuts, see Recipe 8.6.

Using VBScript

Obviously, hardcoding passwords within a script is not the most secure practice. There are a few alternatives, however. You can invoke a script as you would any other command-line tool using runas or cpau. Also, if you want to schedule the script to run periodically, you can specify credentials when you create the scheduled task.

See Also

MS KB 225035, "Secondary Logon (Run As): Starting Programs and Tools in Local Administrative Context"

10.7 Running a Task on a Remote System

Problem

You want to run a task on a remote system. By this we don't mean run a task against a remote system, but rather that the command or script will actually run on the remote system. This is useful if the tool you want to use can only be run locally on a system, or if it generates a lot of network traffic and could work more efficiently if run locally.

Solution

Using a graphical user interface

To run a command or utility on a remote computer via a graphical interface, you'll need to use a remote desktop application such as Remote Desktop.

Using downloadable software

The following Sysinternals utility executes the diruse command on the host fs01 to find directories that contain more than 100 MB of data:

```
> psexec \\fs01 c:\tools\diruse.exe /s /m /d /q:100 c:\
```

This assumes that *c:\tools\diruse.exe* exists on fs01. You can also have psexec copy the command you want to run from the local system to the target system by specifying the –c option. The following command executes the same one as before, except the diruse utility is copied to the target system:

```
> psexec \\fs01 -c diruse.exe /s /m /d /q:100 c:\
```

As with other Sysinternals tools, you can specify alternate credentials with psexec using the –u option. Here is an example:

```
> psexec \\fs01 -u CORP\rallen -c c:\diruse.exe /s /m /d /q:100 c:\
```

Using VBScript

```
' This code shows how to run a task on a system.
' ------ SCRIPT CONFIGURATION ------
strComputer = "<HostName>"
strCommand  = "cscript.exe c:\scripts\dircheck.vbs"
' ------ END CONFIGURATION ---------
set objController = WScript.CreateObject("WSHController")
set objRemoteScript = objController.CreateScript(strCommand, strComputer)
WScript.ConnectObject objRemoteScript, "remote_"
objRemoteScript.Execute
do While objRemoteScript.Status <> 2
    WScript.Sleep 100
loop
WScript.DisconnectObject objRemoteScript
```

Discussion

If you want to use psexec to run a CMD command (e.g., *dir*, *date*, *set*, etc.), you can use either the /c or /k option available with cmd.exe. The following command simply lists the contents of the C drive on fs01:

```
> psexec \\fs01 cmd /c dir c:\
```

Occasionally, we have seen situations where a command such as `dir` will not display any results when run with psexec. If you encounter this, you can create an interactive CMD session on the remote system using the `/k` option. Here is an example:

```
> psexec \\fs01 cmd /k dir c:\
```

This will print the results of *dir*, but also leave you at a command prompt on the remote system, thereby allowing you to run additional command-line utilities without calling psexec again.

10.8 Running a Task Automatically via the Registry

Problem

You want to run a task when a user logs on to a system.

Solution

There are four avenues you can use to make tasks run automatically after a user logs on: the Registry, startup folders, login scripts, and Group Policy. We explain how to use login scripts in Recipe 10.9 and Group Policy in Recipe 10.10. Here we'll describe the Registry and startup folder options.

Registry

There are four Registry keys that you can use to run tasks automatically. To use any of the keys, simply create a value entry of type REG_SZ under the key. Give the value any name you want and specify the full path to the program or script and any parameters as the value data. See Figure 10-1 for some example entries.

Values defined under the following key cause tasks to run for every user that logs into the system:

```
HKEY_LOCAL_MACHINE\Software\Microsoft\Windows\CurrentVersion\Run
```

Values defined under the following key cause tasks to run whenever the user who is currently logged on logs on to the system:

```
HKEY_CURRENT_USER\Software\Microsoft\Windows\CurrentVersion\Run
```

Values defined under the following key cause a task to run the next time any user logs into the system (and not after that):

```
HKEY_LOCAL_MACHINE\Software\Microsoft\Windows\CurrentVersion\RunOnce
```

Values defined under the following key cause a task to run the next time the current user logs into the system:

```
HKEY_CURRENT_USER\Software\Microsoft\Windows\CurrentVersion\RunOnce
```

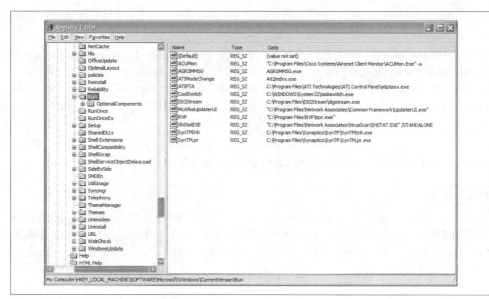

Figure 10-1. Sample Registry Run key values

The values under the RunOnce keys are deleted once the tasks start.

Startup Folders

Similar to the Run and RunOnce Registry keys, programs contained in the startup folders run after a user logs in. Generally, shortcut files (*.lnk* files), not the actual programs, are placed in the startup folders, but you can do it either way.

Programs placed in the following folder are run after any user logs into the system:

    %ALLUSERSPROFILE%\Start Menu\Programs\Startup

Programs placed in this folder are run for a specific user:

    %USERPROFILE%\Start Menu\Programs\Startup

Discussion

By default, tasks defined under the Run and RunOnce keys are not executed if the system is booted into Safe mode. You can force tasks defined under the RunOnce keys to execute even if the system is booted into Safe mode by prefixing the value names under the RunOnce key with an asterisk (*).

RunOnce value entries may also be prefixed with an exclamation point (!), which causes the associated task not to be deleted until after the program completes. Without this, each value entry is deleted before each task is executed. If there is a failure in the task, it may result in the task not completing successfully.

Multiple value entries under the Run or RunOnce keys and multiple programs in the *Startup* folders are loaded in an indeterminate order, so you can't assume one will run before another. If this is an issue for you, you could create a batch file that calls the programs in a particular order and put only the batch file in the Run or RunOnce key.

There are several other Registry keys that can cause tasks to run automatically. For a complete list of all of these Registry keys, see Recipe 10.11.

See Also

Recipe 10.11 for more on viewing all automatic tasks; MS KB 137367, "Definition of the RunOnce Keys in the Registry," MS KB 179365, "INFO: Run, RunOnce, RunServices, RunServicesOnce and Startup," and MB KB 314866, "A Definition of the Run Keys in the Windows XP Registry"

10.9   Running a Task Automatically via Login Scripts

Problem

You want to set the login script for a local or domain user account.

Solution

The following solutions describe how to set the login script for a local user account on a system.

Using a graphical user interface

1. Open the Computer Management snap-in (*compmgmt.msc*).
2. In the left pane under System Tools, expand Local Users and Groups.
3. Click the Users folder.
4. In the right pane, double-click the user you want to set the login script for.
5. Select the Profile tab.
6. Beside Logon script, enter the relative path (from the NETLOGON share) of the login script (e.g., *myscript.vbs*).
7. Click OK.

Using a command-line interface

The following command sets the login script for a local user:

```
> net user <UserName> /scriptpath:<ScriptName>
```

<ScriptName> should be the relative path of the script from the NETLOGON share.

Using VBScript

```
' This code sets the login script for a local user
' ------ SCRIPT CONFIGURATION ------
strComputer = "<HostName>"
strUser = "<UserName>"          ' e.g. administrator
strLoginScript = "<ScriptName>" ' e.g. login.vbs
' ------ END CONFIGURATION ---------
set objUser = GetObject("WinNT://" & strComputer & "/" & strUser & ",user")
objUser.LoginScript = strLoginScript
objUser.SetInfo
WScript.Echo "Set login script for " & objuser.Name
```

The following solutions describe how to set the login script for a domain user account.

Using a graphical user interface

1. Open the Active Directory Users and Computers snap-in (*dsa.msc*).
2. In the left pane, connect to the domain that contains the user you want to set the login script for.
3. Browse to the container the user account is located in.
4. In the right pane, right-click the user and select Properties.
5. Select the Profile tab.
6. Beside Logon script, enter the relative path (from the NETLOGON share on the DCs) of the login script.
7. Click OK.

Using a command-line interface

The following command sets the login script for a domain user:

```
> net user <UserName> /domain /scriptpath:<ScriptName>
```

The following command can also set the login script for a domain user:

```
> dsmod user "<UserDN>" -loscr <ScriptName>
```

<ScriptName> should be the relative path of the script from the NETLOGON share on the DCs.

Using VBScript

```
' This code sets the login script for a domain user
' ------ SCRIPT CONFIGURATION ------
strUserDN = "<UserDN>" ' e.g. cn=administrator,cn=users,dc=rallencorp,dc=com
strScriptPath = "<ScriptName>" ' e.g. login.vbs
' ------ END CONFIGURATION ---------
set objUser = GetObject("LDAP://" & strUserDN)
objUser.Put "scriptPath", strScriptPath
objUser.SetInfo
WScript.Echo "Login script set for " & objUser.Name
```

Discussion

A login script can be a Windows batch file (*.bat* extension) or anything supported by Windows Scripting Host on the system that runs the script. By default, this includes VBScript and JScript.

The login script setting you configure in a user's profile must contain the name of the script and the relative path from the NETLOGON share. When a user (with a local user account) logs into a system, a check is done to see if there is a login script defined for that user—let's say that *login.vbs* has been configured. The system then attempts to run *\\localhost\NETLOGON\login.vbs*. By default, the NETLOGON share does not exist on Windows XP systems. See Recipe 8.23 for more on how to create a share. You can point the NETLOGON share to any directory on the system.

You can also use subdirectories under the NETLOGON share. If the NETLOGON share is pointing to *c:\Scripts* and we created a subdirectory under that called *Local*, then we'd need to configure my local user's login script setting to *Local\login.vbs*.

See Also

MS KB 258286, "HOW TO: Assign a Logon Script to a Profile for a Local User in Windows 2000," and MS KB 315245, "How to Assign a Logon Script to a Profile for a Local User"

10.10 Running a Task via Group Policy

Problem

You want to configure Group Policy in an Active Directory environment so that a task runs at system startup or shutdown or when a user logs on or off.

Solution

Using a graphical user interface

1. Open the Group Policy Management Console (*gpmc.msc*).
2. In the left pane, browse to the Group Policy Object you want to edit.

3. Right-click on it and select Edit. This will launch the Group Policy Object Editor.

4. If you want a task to run during user logon or logoff:

   a. Expand User Configuration → Windows Settings and click on the Scripts icon.

   b. In the right pane, double-click on Logon to configure a script to run at user logon or Logoff to configure a script to run at user logoff.

   If you want a task to run during system startup or shutdown:

   c. Expand Computer Configuration → Windows Settings and click on the Scripts icon.

   d. In the right pane, double-click on Startup to configure a script to run at system start or Shutdown to configure a script to run at system shut down.

5. Click the Add button.

6. Fill in Script Name and Script Parameters and click OK.

7. Click OK.

Discussion

You have two options for storing the scripts or commands you run via Group Policy. One option is to specify a UNC path to the script (this could reference a remote file server), in the Script Name field. The key here is that all users that the Group Policy applies to must have at least read-only access to the script with their domain account. The second method is to copy the script to the folder within the Group Policy template on the file system of a domain controller (you can see this by clicking Browse on the Add screen). If you do this, the script will be copied automatically via the File Replication Service (FRS) to all domain controllers in the domain. This is the more efficient option in terms of client performance. If you use a UNC path, the client has to access the file on a remote server that may not be geographically close to it.

And just as we described in Recipe 6.4, scripts specified in Group Policy can be a Windows batch file (*.bat* extension) or anything supported by Windows Scripting Host on the system that runs the script. By default, this includes VBScript and JScript.

See Also

MS KB 198642, "Overview of Logon, Logoff, Startup, and Shutdown Scripts in Windows 2000," and MS KB 322241, "HOW TO: Assign Scripts in Windows 2000"

10.11 Viewing All Automatic Tasks

Problem

You want to find the tasks that run during system startup or after a user logs on. This is good to check after you've installed new software, to determine if any new tasks or applications are started automatically. This helps identify applications that have been configured to run automatically without your knowledge (e.g., spyware).

Solution

Using downloadable software

The Sysinternals *Autoruns* utility displays all Registry- and file-based entries that cause tasks to be run at system startup or after a user logs on.

You can open Registry Editor or Windows Explorer to the specific location that defines a task by right-clicking the task and selecting Jump To. You can delete a task by right-clicking it and selecting Delete.

Discussion

In Recipe 10.8, we described some of the Registry keys you can configure to make tasks run at user log on, but as you can see with the Autoruns output, there are many more keys do the same thing. Figure 10-2 shows a sample Autoruns screen. With it you can view the complete list of all Registry keys, files, and folders that could cause a task to run automatically by selecting View → Show All Locations from the menu.

10.12 Scheduling a Task

Problem

You want to schedule a task to run at a certain time or periodically.

Solution

Using a graphical user interface

1. From the Control Panel, open the Scheduled Tasks applet.
2. Double-click Add Scheduled Task.
3. Click Next.
4. Select the program you want to schedule to run.
5. Type a name for the task, select the frequency in which to run it, and click Next.

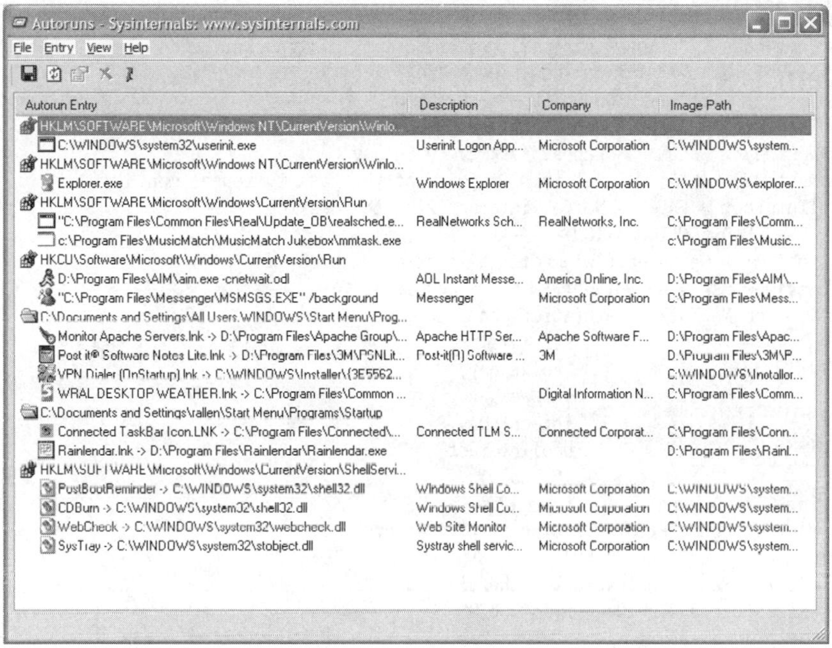

Figure 10-2. Sysinternals Autoruns utility

6. Enter the username and password of the user the task should run as and click Next.

7. If you want to go back and modify any of the settings for the task, check the box beside Open advanced properties and click Finish.

Using a command-line interface

Use the schtasks.exe command to schedule a task. The following command creates a task to run weekly at 1:00 A.M.:

```
> schtasks /create /SC WEEKLY /TN "Disk Space Checker" /TR "c:\perl\bin\perl.exe c:\
scripts\diskchecker.pl" /ST 01:00
```

Using VBScript

```
' This code schedules a task to run every Sunday at 1:30AM.

const MON = 1
const TUE = 2
const WED = 4
const THU = 8
const FRI = 16
const SAT = 32
const SUN = 64
```

```
' ------ SCRIPT CONFIGURATION ------
strComputer  = "."
strCommand   = "c:\perl\bin\perl.exe c:\scripts\diskchecker.pl"
strStartTime = "*******013000.000000-240"  ' 01:30 EDT
               'YYYYMMDDHHMMSS.MMMMMM-/+TZO
boolRepeat   = TRUE  ' Repeat the task periodically
intWeekDay   = SUN   ' Repeat task every Sunday
intMonthDay  = ""    ' Set this if you want the task to repeat monthly
boolInteract = FALSE ' Do not interact with the desktop
' ------ END CONFIGURATION ---------
set objWMI = GetObject("winmgmts:\\" & strComputer & "")
set objNewTask = objWMI.Get("Win32_ScheduledJob")
intRC = objNewTask.Create(strCommand,   _
                          strstartTime, _
                          boolRepeat,   _
                          intWeekDay,   _
                          intMonthDay,  _
                          boolInteract, _
                          intJobID)
if intRC <> 0 then
   Wscript.Echo "Error creating task: " & intRC
else
   WScript.Echo "Successfully scheduled task."
   WScript.Echo "JobID: " & intJobID
end if
```

Discussion

In Recipes 10.8 through 10.10, we described how to set up tasks to run when a user logs on or off, or the system starts up or shuts down, but if you want to schedule a job to run at a specific time, you'll need use the Task Scheduler service. The Task Scheduler service is similar to cron on Unix; it allows to you schedule jobs using a variety of time-based criteria. You can run a job only once, once a week, every Monday and Tuesday night, etc.

The Task Scheduler service runs under the LocalSystem account by default. That means that scheduled tasks will have full access to the local system. But if any jobs need to access any network resources, they won't have sufficient permissions. In this case, you can do one of two things. You can either run the Task Scheduler service under a different set of credentials (see Recipe 10.19) or set a user account and password the task should run as. The Scheduled Tasks applet lets you set the user account and password by entering the account name beside the Run as field and clicking the Set Password button. You can do the same thing using the *schtasks.exe* utility by specifying the /RP and /RU options. You can get more information on this by running schtasks /create /? from a command line.

Often we find that after we create a new scheduled task we want to run it once to make sure it does what we expect. You can force a scheduled task to run immediately in the Scheduled Tasks applet by right-clicking the task and selecting Run.

Likewise, with the *schtasks* utility you can do the same using the /Run option. Here is an example:

```
> schtasks /Run /TN "Disk Space Checker"
```

With Windows 2000 and earlier, you could schedule jobs only with the *at.exe* command. AT jobs are a little different and less flexible than the ones you can create using schtasks or the Scheduled Tasks applet. You cannot create a task using *at* that relies on alternate credentials like you can one that uses schtasks. Also, scheduled tasks created using schtasks cannot be displayed or modified using *at*. Another difference is that *at* tasks are represented by a number (id) that is automatically generated when you create the task, whereas with schtasks you can assign a name to a given task.

The Win32_ScheduledJob class represents *at* jobs, so it is not possible to set alternate credentials when creating a new task with it. And if you query for all Win32_ScheduledJob objects, you are going to get only the jobs created with the at command or Win32_ScheduledJob class, which isn't necessarily all the schedules tasks.

See Also

Recipe 10.14 for deleting a scheduled task; Recipe 10.13 for listing the schedules tasks; and Recipe 10.19 for setting the user account of a service

10.13 Viewing Scheduled Tasks

Problem

You want to view the list of scheduled tasks on a system.

Solution

Using a graphical user interface

From the Control Panel, open the Scheduled Task applet.

Using a command-line interface

The following command lists the scheduled tasks:

```
> schtasks /query
```

To get detailed information about each task, run the following command:

```
> schtasks /query /v /fo list
```

Using VBScript

```
' This code lists the scheduled AT tasks on a computer.
' ------ SCRIPT CONFIGURATION ------
strComputer = "<HostName>"
' ------ END CONFIGURATION ---------
set objWMI = GetObject("winmgmts:\\" & strComputer & "\root\cimv2")
set colScheduledJobs = objWMI.ExecQuery("Select * from Win32_ScheduledJob")
for each objJob in colScheduledJobs
   WScript.Echo "Job ID: " & objJob.JobID
   for each objProp in objJob.Properties_
       WScript.Echo "   " & objProp.Name & ": " & objProp.Value
   next
next
```

Discussion

Another quick way to view the scheduled tasks on a system is to simply browse the Scheduled Tasks share point on the system (\\<HostName>\Scheduled Tasks). When you create a scheduled task, a job file is created that contains the settings for the task, which is placed in %SystemRoot%\Tasks. This directory is shared out as Scheduled Tasks. Unfortunately, the job files are stored in a binary format, so you cannot simply create or modify them with a text editor. You can, however, copy and paste jobs between machines. If you want to copy a job from HostA to HostB, open the Scheduled Tasks share point on both servers, right-click on the target job on HostA and select Copy, then paste the copy into the Scheduled Tasks share of HostB. Make sure any localized settings in the task are modified on HostB after the copy is complete.

See Also

Recipe 10.12 for creating a scheduled task; Recipe 10.14 for deleting a scheduled task; MS KB 310424, "HOW TO: Work with Scheduled Tasks on Remote Computers in Windows XP"

10.14 Deleting a Scheduled Task

Problem

You want to delete a scheduled task.

Solution

Using a graphical user interface

1. From the Control Panel, open the Scheduled Task applet.
2. Right click on the target task and select Delete.
3. Click Yes to confirm.

Using a command-line interface

You can use the schtasks.exe command to delete a task. The following command deletes the task named Job1:

```
> schtasks /delete /tn Job1
```

Using Group Policy

You can't delete a task with Group Policy, but you can prevent it from being deleted. Here is where you can find that setting:

```
\Computer Configuration\
    Administrative Templates\Windows Components\Task Scheduler
\User Configuration\
    Administrative Templates\Windows Components\Task Scheduler

Prohibit Task Deletion
```

Using VBScript

```
' This code deletes a scheduled AT task.
' ------ SCRIPT CONFIGURATION ------
intJobID = <JID>                    ' e.g. 1452
strComputer = "<HostName>"   ' e.g. dns01
' ------ END CONFIGURATION ---------
set objWMI = GetObject("winmgmts:\\" & strComputer & "\root\cimv2")
Set objInstance = objWMI.Get("Win32_ScheduledJob.JobID=" & intJobID)
intRC = objInstance.Delete
if intRC <> 0 then
   Wscript.Echo "Failure deleting task id: " & intJobID
else
   Wscript.Echo "Sucessfully deleted task id: " & intJobID
end if
```

Discussion

Using a graphical user interface

You can't use the applet to delete a task on a remote system. However, there is another option. By default, a Scheduled Tasks share is created on Windows XP, which contains the job files for each scheduled task. Simply browse to \\<HostName>\ Scheduled Tasks and you should see the list of scheduled tasks on that system (if you have administrator privileges). From here you can right-click a task and select Delete.

Using a command-line interface

To delete a task from the command line, you need to know the task name. Unless you know it off the top of your head, you'll need to query the current scheduled tasks to find the name of the one you want to delete. See Recipe 10.13 for more on how to do that.

See Also

Recipe 10.9 for creating a scheduled task; Recipe 10.13 for listing the scheduled tasks; and MS KB 310424, "HOW TO: Work with Scheduled Tasks on Remote Computers in Windows XP"

10.15 Troubleshooting Scheduled Tasks

Problem

You want to determine why a scheduled task is not running.

Solution

There are three places you can check to help determine why a task is not running:

1. Open the Scheduled Tasks applet. By default, the applet displays columns for Next Run Time, Last Run Time, Status, and Last Result for each scheduled task. Here you can see when the task was last run and if it generated an error. If there is anything other than 0 x 0 for Last Result, an error of some type occurred. This doesn't necessarily mean the task didn't complete, but some error was identified.

2. Ensure that the Task Scheduler Service is running. You can do this by opening the Services snap-in (*services.msc*) and looking at the Status column for Task Scheduler. It should have a status of Started. Alternatively, you can run the following command:

   ```
   > sc query schedule
   ```

3. Open the Scheduled Tasks log file located at *%SystemRoot%\Schedlgu.txt*. This log file is written to every time a scheduled task starts and finishes. It can provide useful information about when a task was run and what errors there were, if any. This is helpful because, unlike the Scheduled Tasks applet, this shows the start and finish times every time the task was run, instead of just the most recent time.

Discussion

A good test of the configuration of a task is to run it once manually. You can do this by right-clicking the task in the Scheduled Tasks applet and selecting Run. If everything works ok, make sure the task is enabled by double-clicking the task and making sure the checkbox beside Enabled is checked. If it is checked, make sure the time in the Next Run Time column in the Scheduled Tasks applet is what you think it should be.

One thing to note about the *Schedlgu.txt* log file is that by default it will only grow to 32 KB in size. Once it reaches that size, it will start overwriting the beginning of the file. You can increase the max size by setting the following Registry value:

```
Key: HKEY_LOCAL_MACHINE\Software\Microsoft\SchedulingAgent
Value Name: MaxLogSizeKB
Value Type: REG_DWORD
Value Data: <SizeInKiloBytes>
```

Replace *<SizeInKiloBytes>* with the maximum size you want the log file to grow to. The default value is 32. Restart the Task Scheduler service after setting the value.

See Also

MS KB 169443, "How to Limit the Maximum Size of the Scheduled Tasks Log File," and MS KB 308558, "HOW TO: Troubleshoot Scheduled Tasks in Windows XP"

10.16 Starting and Stopping a Service

Problem

You want to start or stop a service.

Solution

Using a graphical user interface

1. Open the Services snap-in.
2. In the left pane, right-click on the service and select Start or Stop.

Using a command-line interface

Run any of the following commands to start a service:

```
> psservice start <ServiceName>
> sc start <ServiceName>
> wmic service <ServiceName> call StartService
> net start <ServiceName>
```

Run any of the following commands to stop a service:

```
> psservice stop <ServiceName>
> sc stop <ServiceName>
> wmic service <ServiceName> call StopService
> net stop <ServiceName>
```

Using VBScript

```
' This code stops and starts (effectively restarts) a service.
' ------ SCRIPT CONFIGURATION ------
strComputer   = "<HostName>"   ' e.g. fs-rtp01 (use . for local system)
```

```
strSvcName    = "<ServiceName>"  ' e.g. dnscache
' ------ END CONFIGURATION ---------
set objWMI = GetObject("winmgmts:\\" & strComputer & "\root\cimv2")
set objService = objWMI.Get("Win32_Service.Name='" & strSvcName & "'")

intRC = objService.StopService
if intRC > 0 then
   WScript.Echo "Error stopping service: " & intRC
else
   WScript.Echo "Successfully stopped service"
end if

intRC = objService.StartService
if intRC > 0 then
   WScript.Echo "Error starting service: " & intRC
else
   WScript.Echo "Successfully started service"
end if
```

Discussion

Starting and stopping a service is a straightforward procedure that everyone has to do at one point or another. The only potentially tricky thing you need to be aware of is when you need to stop a service that has dependencies. For example, if ServiceA depends on ServiceB and both services are currently running, you can't stop ServiceB unless you stop ServiceA (the service that is dependent on it) first. If you are using the Services snap-in, it will stop all dependent services if there are any. From the command line, the process is more manual. You need first to look up the dependent services and stop them. The same applies to the scripting solution. You will receive an error when you use the StopService method on a service that has dependencies. See Recipe 10.21 for more on how to find service dependencies from the command line and VBScript.

See Also

MSDN: StartService Method of the Win32_Service Class, and MSDN: StopService Method of the Win32_Service Class

10.17 Running Any Program or Script as a Service

Problem

You want to run a program or script as a service. This is useful whether you want a program to run continuously regardless of whether someone is logged in.

Solution

The following solutions install the Perl script *monitor.pl* as a service named MyMonitor.

Using a graphical user interface

1. Open the Service Creation Wizard (*srvinstw.exe*).
2. Select Install a service and click Next.
3. Select the target machine to install the service on and click Next.
4. Enter MyMonitor for the service name and click Next.
5. Enter the path of the *srvany.exe* executable and click Next.
6. Select Service is its own process and click Next.
7. Select the account to run the service under and click Next.
8. Select the service startup type and click Next.
9. Click Finish.
10. Open the Registry Editor (*regedit.exe*).
11. In the left pane, browse to the service's Registry key by opening `HKEY_LOCAL_MACHINE` → `SYSTEM` → `CurrentControlSet` → `Services` → `MyMonitor`.
12. Right-click on MyMonitor and select New → Key.
13. Enter Parameters and press Enter.
14. Right-click on Parameters and select New → String Value.
15. Enter Application and press Enter twice.
16. Enter the path to the Perl executable (e.g., *c:\perl\bin\perl.exe*) and click OK.
17. Right-click on Parameters and select New → String Value.
18. Enter AppParameters and hit Enter twice.
19. Enter the path to the Perl script (e.g., *c:\scripts\monitor.pl*) and click OK.
20. Open the Services snap-in.
21. In the left pane, right-click on MyMonitor and select Start.

Using a command-line interface

```
> instsrv MyMonitor "C:\Windows Resource Kits\Tools\srvany.exe"
> reg add HKLM\System\CurrentControlSet\Services\MyMonitor\Parameters
/v Application /d "c:\perl\bin\perl.exe"
> reg add HKLM\System\CurrentControlSet\Services\MyMonitor\Parameters
/v AppParameters /d "C:\scripts\monitor.pl"
> sc start MyMonitor
```

Using VBScript

```
' This code creates and starts the MyMonitor Perl service
' ------ SCRIPT CONFIGURATION ------
strComputer   = "."
strSvcName    = "MyMonitor"
strSrvAnyPath = "c:\Windows Resource Kits\Tools\srvany.exe"
strPerlPath   = "c:\perl\bin\perl.exe"
```

```
strPerlScript = "c:\scripts\monitor.pl"
' ------ END CONFIGURATION ---------
const HKLM = &H80000002

' Service Type
Const KERNEL_DRIVER        = 1
Const FS_DRIVER            = 2
Const ADAPTER             = 4
Const RECOGNIZER_DRIVER    = 8
Const OWN_PROCESS         = 16
Const SHARE_PROCESS        = 32
Const INTERACTIVE_PROCESS = 256

INTERACT_WITH_DESKTOP = FALSE

' Error Control
Const NOT_NOTIFIED      = 0
Const USER_NOTIFIED     = 1
Const SYSTEM_RESTARTED = 2
Const SYSTEM_STARTS     = 3

set objWMI = GetObject("winmgmts:\\" & strComputer & "\root\cimv2")
set objService = objWMI.Get("Win32_Service")
intRC = objService.Create(strSvcName, _
                          strSvcName, _
                          strSrvAnyPath, _
                          OWN_PROCESS, _
                          NOT_NOTIFED, _
                          "Automatic", _
                          INTERACT_WITH_DESKTOP, _
                          "NT AUTHORITY\LocalService",_
                          "")
if intRC > 0 then
   WScript.Echo "Error creating service: " & intRC
   WScript.Quit
else
   WScript.Echo "Successfully created service"
end if

strKeyPath = "SYSTEM\CurrentControlSet\Services\" & _
             strSvcName & "\Parameters"
set objReg = GetObject("winmgmts:\\" & _
                       strComputer & "\root\default:StdRegProv")
objReg.CreateKey HKLM,strKeyPath
objReg.SetStringValue HKLM,strKeyPath,"Application",strPerlPath
objReg.SetStringValue HKLM,strKeyPath,"AppParameters",strPerlScript
WScript.Echo "Created registry values"

set objService = objWMI.Get("Win32_Service.Name='" & strSvcName & "'")
intRC = objService.StartService
if intRC > 0 then
   WScript.Echo "Error starting service: " & intRC
```

```
    else
        WScript.Echo "Successfully started service"
    end if
```

Discussion

Do you have a cool script or executable that you'd like to run continuously? You
could use Task Scheduler to periodically run the job, but that doesn't give you a lot
of flexibility over stopping, starting, or monitoring the job. Another option is to turn
the program into a service as we outlined in the solutions. By doing this, the program will run continuously and no one needs to be logged in for it to run.

To turn a script or executable into a service, you need the help of another program
called *srvany.exe* from the Resource Kit. SrvAny acts as a wrapper around your script
or executable by handling all the service control messages (e.g., stop, start, pause).

Creating a service consists of setting a few Registry keys and values under the HKLM\
SYSTEM\CurrentControlSet\Services\ key. For a SrvAny service, you need to configure several values under the new service's Parameter key. The Application value
should contain the path to the script or executable you want to run. In this case,
since we're using Perl, we set the Application value to the Perl executable. And since
we need to pass the name of the Perl script to the executable, we create an
AppParameters key, which contains any parameters (in this case the script path) to the
executable.

See Also

MS KB 137890, "HOWTO: Create a User-Defined Service," MS KB 821794, "INFO:
Best Practices When You Create Windows Services," and MSDN: Create Method of
the Win32_Service Class

10.18 Setting the Startup Type of a Service

Problem

You want to configure the startup type (automatic, manual, or disabled) for a service.

Solution

Using a graphical user interface

1. Open the Services snap-in.
2. In the left pane, double-click on the service you want to configure.
3. Choose the startup type under the General tab.
4. Click OK.

Using a command-line interface

```
> sc config <ServiceName> start= [boot | system | auto | demand | disabled]
```

The following command disables the Messenger service:

```
> sc config Messenger start= disabled
```

Note that the space after start= is required.

Using VBScript

```
' This code sets the startup type for a service.
' ------ SCRIPT CONFIGURATION ------
strSvcName     = "MyMonitor"
strStartupType = "Automatic"  ' can be "Automatic", "Manual", or "Disabled"
strComputer    = "."
' ------ END CONFIGURATION ---------
set objWMI = GetObject("winmgmts:\\" & strComputer & "\root\cimv2")
set objService = objWMI.Get("Win32_Service.Name='" & strSvcName & "'")
intRC = objService.Change(,,,,strStartupType)
' can alternatively use objService.ChangeStartup(strStartupType) method
if intRC > 0 then
   WScript.Echo "Error setting service startup type: " & intRC
else
   WScript.Echo "Successfully set service startup type"
end if
```

Discussion

The startup type of a service determines whether the service starts when the system boots and whether it can be started at all. The Automatic startup type causes the service to automatically start at system boot up. The Manual startup type means the service will not be started automatically at system boot up, but can be started later manually. The Disabled startup type means that the service is not started at system boot up and cannot be manually started. You have to change the startup type to either Manual or Automatic before you can start a service that is set to Disabled.

You may have noticed that there are two other startup options you can configure with the *sc* utility. These additional startup options are in fact available with the scripting solution as well. They are, however, not applicable to system services. They are used for starting device drivers and can only be configured for drivers. The Boot startup type indicates that the driver is started by the operating system loader. The System startup type means that the driver will be started by the IoInitSystem method (if you are a driver programmer you know what this is).

See Also

MSDN: Change Method of the Win32_Service Class

10.19 Setting the Account and Password of a Service

Problem

You want to configure the account and password used by a service.

Solution

Using a graphical user interface

1. Open the Services snap-in.
2. In the left pane, double-click on the service you want to configure.
3. Click the Log On tab.
4. Select This Account.
5. Enter the domain and username of the account or click Browse to find it.
6. Enter and confirm the account's password.
7. Click OK.

Using a command-line interface

```
> sc config <ServiceName> obj= <Domain>\<Username> password= <Password>
```

The following command configures the MyMonitor service to use the local administrator account.

```
> sc config MyMonitor obj= RALLEN-WXP\administrator password= foobar
```

Using VBScript

```
' This code configures the service account
' ------ SCRIPT CONFIGURATION ------
strUser     = "<Domain>\<Username>" ' e.g. FS-RTP01\administration
strPassword = "<Password>"          ' e.g. foobar
strSvcName  = "<ServiceName>"       ' e.g. MyMonitor
strComputer = "<HostName>"          ' e.g. rallen-wxp (use . for local system)
' ------ END CONFIGURATION ---------
set objWMI = GetObject("winmgmts:\\" & strComputer & "\root\cimv2")
set objService = objWMI.Get("Win32_Service.Name='" & strSvcName & "'")
intRC = objService.Change(,,,,,,strUser,strPassword)
if intRC > 0 then
   WScript.Echo "Error setting service account: " & intRC
else
   WScript.Echo "Successfully set service account"
end if
```

Discussion

If you need to configure a user account to run a service under, make sure the account has *Log on as service* right on the system. Without this, the service will not start up correctly. The Services snap-in will automatically grant this right when you configure the log on account for a service. However, neither the command line nor scripting solutions do this. From the command line, you can use the *ntrights.exe* utility from the Resource Kit:

```
> ntrights +r SeServiceLogonRight -u <User>
```

Here is an example:

```
> ntrights +r SeServiceLogonRight -u RALLENCORP\rallen
```

Unfortunately, WMI doesn't support setting user rights, so if you need to do it programmatically, you'll have to shell out to the ntrights command.

There are a couple issues you need to be aware of if you configure a local or domain account to run a service under. If have a password policy enabled in your domain that forces users to change their password after a period of time, make sure any service accounts you are using are configured to have nonexpiring passwords. If a service account has an expired password, it will cause the service to fail when starting. The same is true for accounts that are locked out.

To avoid these problems, you can use local system accounts that don't have a password in the traditional sense. Here is an overview of these accounts:

Local System
> This account has full access to the underlying system. It has similar rights to the Administrator account. On a domain controller, it has administrator-level access to all objects in the domain. Be careful when using this account for a service.

Local Service
> This account is similar to an authenticated user that is a member of the local Users group on the computer. It has anonymous access to network resources. This account is new in Windows XP.

Network Service
> Like the Local Service account, this account has similar access to an authenticated user that is a member of the local Users group. The main difference with this account is that it accesses network resources using the credentials of the computer account. This account is new in Windows XP.

See Also

MS KB 279664, "How to Set Logon User Rights with the Ntrights.exe Utility," and MSDN: Change Method of the Win32_Service Class

10.20 Performing an Action Automatically When a Service Fails

Problem

You want to perform an action automatically when a service fails.

Solution

Using a graphical user interface

1. Open the Services snap-in.
2. In the left pane, double-click on the service you want to configure.
3. Click the Recovery tab.
4. Configure the failure options you want and click OK.

Using a command-line interface

The following command causes the MyMonitor service to be automatically restarted after two failures and then reboots on the third failure. Each failure can be up to 5 seconds apart:

```
> sc failure MyMonitor reset= 3600 reboot="Restarting do to repeated MyMonitor
failure" actions= restart/5000/restart/5000/reboot/5000
```

Using VBScript

The Win32_Service class does not support setting the recovery options for a service.

Discussion

Windows 2000 added a new capability that was sorely missing in previous versions: the ability to automatically perform an action when a service fails. You can configure an action to occur after the first failure, second failure, or subsequent failures. The actions you can take include no action (the default), restarting the service, running a program, or restarting the computer.

You can also reset the failure count after a certain number of days. So let's say that you want to have a service restart itself after a failure, but no more than once a day. You would configure the first failure action to restart the service and set the reset fail count to one day.

You can also combine multiple actions by choosing to run a program after service failure. You can create a simple batch file that restarts the service and emails you a report. This gives you a lot of flexibility in how you handle service failures.

10.21 Viewing the Antecedent and Dependent Services for a Service

Problem

You want to view the services that a particular service depends on (i.e., antecedent services) and services that are dependent on that service. This is helpful to know when you want to stop a service and determine the impact it would have on other services.

Solution

Using a graphical user interface

1. Open the Services snap-in.
2. In the left pane, double-click on the service you want to view
3. Click the Dependencies tab.

Using a command-line interface

The following command displays the services that depend on a service:

```
> sc enumdepend <ServiceName>
```

The following command displays the services that a service depends on:

```
> sc qc <ServiceName>
```

Using downloadable software

You can also use the Sysinternals psservice command to enumerate dependencies:

```
> psservice <ServiceName> depend
```

Using VBScript

```
' This code lists the antecedent and dependent services for a service
' ------ SCRIPT CONFIGURATION ------
strService = "<ServiceName>"  ' e.g. TapiSrv
strComputer = "<HostName>"     ' e.g. wks01 (use . for local system)
' ------ END CONFIGURATION ---------
set objWMI = GetObject("winmgmts:\\" & strComputer & "\root\cimv2")
set colServices = objWMI.ExecQuery("Associators of " _
                   & "{Win32_Service.Name='" & strService & "'} Where " _
                   & "AssocClass=Win32_DependentService Role=Antecedent" )
WScript.Echo "Antecedent services for " & strService & ":"
for each objService in colServices
    Wscript.Echo vbTab & objService.DisplayName
next
WScript.Echo
```

```
set colServices = objWMI.ExecQuery("Associators of " _
                 & "{Win32_Service.Name='" & strService & "'} Where " _
                 & "AssocClass=Win32_DependentService Role=Dependent" )
WScript.Echo "Dependent services for " & strService & ":"
for each objService in colServices
   Wscript.Echo vbTab & objService.DisplayName
next
```

A practical use of enumerating dependencies is for programmatically restarting a service. You could just call the Stop and Start methods on a service as we showed in Recipe 10.16, but if you tried to restart a service that had a dependency, the restart would fail. An alternative is to write a bit of code that can handle restarting services, regardless of dependencies. Here is that code:

```
' This code restarts a service by first stopping all
' dependent services before stopping the target service.
' Then the target service is started and all dependent
' services are started.

Option Explicit

' ------ SCRIPT CONFIGURATION ------
Dim strComputer : strComputer = "."        ' e.g. fs-rtp01
Dim strSvcName  : strSvcName  = "Alerter"  ' e.g. dnscache
' ------ END CONFIGURATION ---------
Dim objWMI : set objWMI = GetObject("winmgmts:\\" & strComputer & _
                          "\root\cimv2")
Dim objService: set objService = objWMI.Get("Win32_Service.Name='" & _
                          strSvcName & "'")

WScript.Echo "Restarting " & objService.Name & "..."
RecursiveServiceStop  objService
RecursiveServiceStart objService
WScript.Echo "Successfully restarted service"

Function RecursiveServiceStop ( objSvc )

   Dim colServices : set colServices = objWMI.ExecQuery("Associators of " _
             & "{Win32_Service.Name='" & objSvc.Name & "'} Where " _
             & "AssocClass=Win32_DependentService Role=Antecedent" )
   Dim objS
   for each objS in colServices
      RecursiveServiceStop objS
   next

   Dim intRC : intRC = objSvc.StopService
   if intRC > 0 then
      WScript.Echo " Error stopping service: " & objSvc.Name
      WScript.Quit
   else
      WScript.Echo " Successfully stopped service: " & objSvc.Name
   end if
End Function
```

```
Function RecursiveServiceStart ( objSvc )

   Dim intRC : intRC = objSvc.StartService
   if intRC > 0 then
      WScript.Echo " Error starting service: " & objSvc.Name
      WScript.Quit
   else
      WScript.Echo " Successfully started service: " & objSvc.Name
   end if

   Dim colServices : set colServices = objWMI.ExecQuery("Associators of " _
              & "{Win32_Service.Name='" & objSvc.Name & "'} Where " _
              & "AssocClass=Win32_DependentService Role=Antecedent" )
   Dim objS
   for each objS in colServices
      RecursiveServiceStart objS
   next

End Function
```

Discussion

Service dependencies play a role in how you can stop a service. For example, if ServiceA depends on ServiceB, then ServiceB must be running before ServiceA can start. Similarly, ServiceB cannot be stopped until ServiceA is stopped due to the dependency. A good practical example of this is the Logical Disk Manager Administrative service. It depends on the Logical Disk Manager service. It wouldn't make a lot of sense for the administrative service to be running, while the underlying disk manager service (the thing it manages) was not.

Service dependences are configured in each service's Registry entry. In the case of the Logical Disk Manager Administrative service, you can find its Registry entry in the following key:

    HKEY_LOCAL_MACHINE\SYSTEM\CurrentControlSet\Services\dmadmin

If you open Registry Editor (*regedit.exe*) and look at that key, you'll see a DependOnService value. The data for this REG_MULTI_SZ value is a list of the services it depends on. One of them is dmserver, which corresponds to the Logical Disk Manager service.

You may also see a DependOnGroup value under a service's Registry key. This is similar to DependOnService except that DependOnGroup corresponds to a group of services. For more on service groups, check out Recipe 10.22.

Using VBScript

To enumerate dependencies, we need to use something called a WMI associator. The Associators of clause in a WQL query is similar to a table join in a relational database. It allows you to relate two different types of classes. For services, WMI supports a class called Win32_DependentService, which defines the service dependencies for a given service. The first query finds all of the antecedent services (those that depend on the target service). Here is the query:

```
"Associators of {Win32_Service.Name='" & strService & "'} Where " _
    "AssocClass=Win32_DependentService Role=Antecedent"
```

The `Associators of` clause tells WMI we are going to associate or join another class to the one specified within the curly braces. We set `Win32_Service.Name` equal to the target service. The `Where` clause then has two parts. The first sets the associated class, which in this case is `Win32_DependentService`; the second part (`Role=Antecedent`) limits the dependent services that are returned to just antecedent services, or ones that depend on the target service. The only difference with the second query is that the query sets `Role=Dependent`, which returns all of the dependent services of the target service.

In the service restart example, you have to stop all services that are dependent on the service and then stop the service itself. Then to start the service, you have to start the service followed by all dependent services. And that is exactly what that code does. It makes use of a couple of recursive functions that walk through all of the dependent services.

10.22 Viewing the Service Load Order

Problem

You want to view the order in which services load during system startup. You typically don't need to worry about the service load order, but it can be helpful if you are experiencing problems with services that are not starting correctly after reboot. Something else to note is that device drivers are treated like services. So by viewing the service load order, you can see the device driver load order as well.

Solution

Using downloadable software

Open the Sysinternals LoadOrd (*loadord.exe*) utility. See Figure 10-3 for an example of the output.

Discussion

As we described in Recipe 10.21, Windows supports the concept of service dependencies whereby a service cannot start until the services it depends on have started successfully. Windows also supports the notion of a service load order so that services and groups of services start in a particular order.

A service group is a collection of services that are loaded together at system startup. For example, Figure 10-3 shows particular service groups listed under the Group

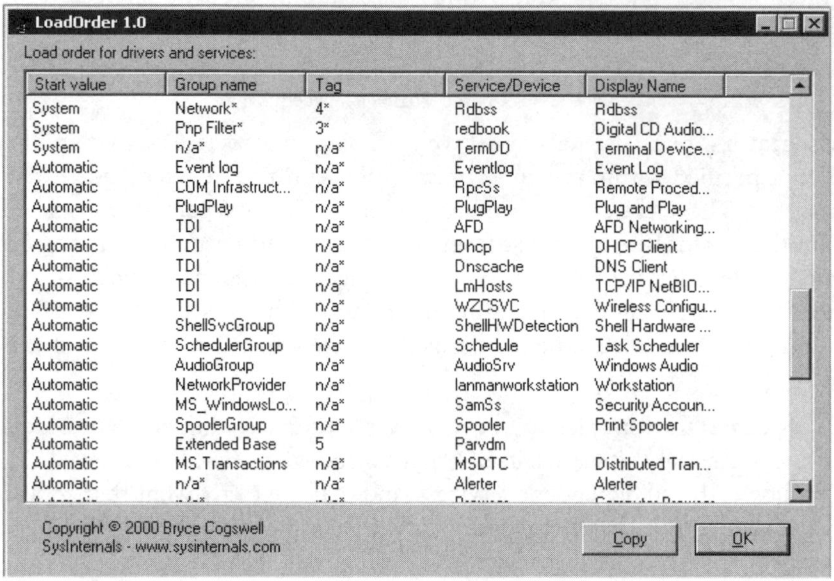

Figure 10-3. LoadOrd utility

Name column. The complete list of service groups can be found in the Registry under the following key:

```
HKEY_LOCAL_MACHINE\SYSTEM\CurrentControlSet\Control\GroupOrderList
```

Not all services are part of a group, and the ones that are load before the ones that aren't. The following Registry value contains a list of service groups in the order of how they are loaded:

```
HKEY_LOCAL_MACHINE\SYSTEM\CurrentControlSet\Control\ServiceGroupOrder\List
```

Each service has Registry values under its specific Registry key (HKEY_LOCAL_MACHINE\SYSTEM\CurrentControlSet\System\Services\<*ServiceName*>) that determine which group it is a member of (if any) and its dependencies. Here is a list of them:

Group
: REG_SZ value that contains the service group name the service belongs to

Tag
: REG_DWORD value that contains a number that dictates the relative order the service starts within a service group

DependOnGroup
: REG_MULTI_SZ value that contains the service groups that must load successfully before this service can start

DependOnService
: REG_MULTI_SZ value that contains the services that must load successfully before this service can start

See Also

MS KB 115486, "HOWTO: Control Device Driver Load Order," and MS KB 193888, "How to Delay Loading of Specific Services"

10.23 Viewing the Startup History of a Service

Problem

You want to view the startup history of a service to determine whether it has had problems starting successfully.

Solution

Every time a service is started or stopped a message is logged to the Application event log.

Using a graphical user interface

1. Open the EventCombMT utility (*eventcombmt.exe*).
2. Right-click on the Select To Search/Right To Add box and select Add Single Server.
3. Enter the server name, click Add Server, and click Close.
4. Highlight the server by clicking on it.
5. Under Choose Log Files to search, be sure that System is selected.
6. Under Event Types, select only Informational.
7. Beside Event IDs, enter 7035 7036
8. Beside Text, enter the display name of the service (e.g., The Windows Installer service).
9. Click the Search button.
10. A Windows Explorer window should pop up containing a file with the output of the search. Double-click on the file to view the results.

Using a command-line interface

The following command displays all the 7035 and 7036 events that pertain to a particular service. This isn't very efficient because all 7035 and 7036 events are retrieved and piped to a second qgrep command to only display the ones we are interested in. Unfortunately, you cannot perform pattern matching of the event message with the eventquery command.

```
> eventquery /v /L system /FI "ID eq 7036 or ID eq 7035" | qgrep -e "The
<ServiceDisplayName> service"
```

Using downloadable software

You can accomplish something similar with the Sysinternals psloglist command, but you need to do it in two steps to retrieve the two different event IDs:

```
> psloglist -s -i 7035 system | qgrep -e "The <ServiceDisplayName> service"
```

Here is an example:

```
> psloglist -s -i 7036 system | qgrep -e "The DNS Client service"
```

Using VBScript

```
' This code displays the startup history of a service
' ------ SCRIPT CONFIGURATION ------
strService = "<ServiceDisplayName>" ' e.g. Windows Installer
strLog = "<EventLogName>"           ' e.g. System
strComputer = "<HostName>"          ' e.g. fs-rtp01 (use . for local system)
' ------ END CONFIGURATION ---------
set objWMI = GetObject("winmgmts:\\" & strComputer & "\root\cimv2")
set colEvents = objWMI.ExecQuery _
             ("Select * from Win32_NTLogEvent " & _
              " Where Logfile = '" & strLog & "' " & _
              "   and ( EventCode = '7036' or EventCode = '7035' ) " & _
              "   and Message like 'The " & strService & " service %'")
set objDate = CreateObject("WbemScripting.SWbemDateTime")
for each objEvent in colEvents
   objDate.Value = objEvent.TimeWritten
   Wscript.Echo objDate.GetVarDate & ":" & objEvent.Message
next
```

Discussion

In the command line and VBScript solutions, you need to know the service display name in order to find the start and stop events. To get that, you can view it either in the Services snap-in or by running the sc query command.

10.24 Granting Permissions to Manage One or More Services

Problem

You want to grant a user the right to manage (stop and start) a particular service.

Solution

Using a command-line interface

The following command grants full control of a service to a user:

```
> subinacl /service \\<HostName>\<ServiceName> /grant=<User>
```

The following example grants full control of the `Messenger` service on system `wks01` to the `AMER\rallen` user:

```
> subinacl /service \\wks01\Messenger /grant=AMER\rallen
```

Use this command to view the users that have been granted access to manage a particular service:

```
> subinacl /verbose=1 /service \\<HostName>\<ServiceName>
```

Here is an example:

```
> subinacl /verbose=1 /service \\wks01\Messenger
```

To revoke access to a service, use this command:

```
> subinacl /service \\<HostName>\<ServiceName> /revoke=<UserName>
```

This next command grants the `AMER\rallen` user control over all services on the system `wks01` and saves the output to *out.txt*:

```
> for /f "tokens=2,*" %s in ( '"psservice.exe | findstr SERVICE_NAME"' ) do subinacl
/verbose=1 /service \\wks01\%s /grant=AMER\rallen >> out.txt
```

 Be sure to download the latest version of subinacl from *http://download.microsoft.com*. Older versions work in unexpected ways. Another alternative you can also use is the setacl command, which is similar in functionality to subinacl but has even more options. setacl is available under the GNU Public License from the following web site: *http://setacl.sourceforge.net*.

Using Group Policy

You can use Group Policy to control who can manage a service. You'll find a list of services in the following location within a Group Policy object:

```
\Computer Configuration\Windows Settings\System Services
```

In the right pane of the Group Policy Object Editor, double-click the service you want to configure. Check the box beside Define this policy setting, select the appropriate startup type, and click the Edit Security button. This will launch the ACL Editor from which you can select the users or groups that should have specific permissions on the service.

Discussion

The access control list (ACL) for a service is stored in the Registry under the service's Security key, such as `HKLM\System\CurrentControlSet\Services\<ServiceName>\Security`. If you misconfigure the permissions on a service or just want to start over, delete the service's Security key. It will get automatically recreated with the default security.

See Also

For more on service permissions, visit *http://www.microsoft.com/technet/prodtechnol/windowsserver2003/proddocs/entserver/sys_srv_permissions.asp.*

CHAPTER 11

Digital Media

11.0 Introduction

Before Windows XP, Windows wasn't thought of as being particularly friendly to digital media—to using and creating videos, music, and graphics files. But Windows XP is the most media-friendly version of Windows yet released, and so a variety of multimedia is now easily available to Windows users. It includes a variety of built-in tools, such as Windows Media Player and Windows Movie Maker.

In this chapter, you'll find recipes for handling a variety of media—everything from copying digital music to your PC, to making music CDs, recording video, making DVDs, and handling and converting graphics.

11.1 Ripping Digital Music

Problem

You want to rip music from an audio CD to your computer's hard disk—in other words, copy it to your PC in a digital format, so that you can listen to it on your PC, or on a portable MP3 player.

Solution

Using a graphical user interface

Windows Media Player offers built-in tools for ripping music and storing it in a variety of formats, including MP3 and WMA. (Note: versions of Windows Media Player older than version 10 cannot rip music into the MP3 format, without buying extra software.) Here's how to do it:

1. Run Windows Media Player by choosing Start → All Programs → Accessories → Entertainment → Windows Media Player.

2. Click the Rip button.

3. Insert the CD whose music you want to rip into your CD drive.

4. Windows Media Player will show a list of all the tracks on the CD, but there may be no information associated with each track. To have Windows Media Player search the Internet for information about the CD and each track, click Find Album Info.

5. Windows Media Player will display the name of your album. If the information is correct, click Finish. If it's not, click Search to see if it can find the information in your existing music database, or else click Edit, and you can manually enter information about the album and each track.

 This recipe shows you how to rip music with version 10 of Windows Media Player, which offers more features, and a simpler interface than earlier versions. If you have a version earlier than 10, you should upgrade by visiting the Windows Update site at *http://windowsupdate. microsoft.com*.

6. Depending on the information that Windows Media Player finds, it may not find all the information about each track. After it populates the information, you can edit any track by right-clicking it, choosing Edit, and typing in the new information.

7. Put a check box next to each track that you want to rip, and uncheck the box next to each that you don't want to rip.

8. Before ripping your music, choose the audio format, and the quality of the files that you will rip. Choose Tools → Options → Rip Music, and from the Format drop-down box, choose an audio format, either MP3, or one of several WMA formats. Then choose the audio quality by moving the slider under Audio quality to the left for less quality, and to the right for higher quality. Generally, a rate of 128 Kbps is considered almost CD quality, while bit rates above that provide higher quality. The higher the quality, the larger each file.

9. When you've chosen audio quality and format, and checked all the tracks you want to rip, click Rip Music. As you can see in Figure 11-1, Windows Media Player will show you its overall progress, as well as its progress of ripping each track.

10. When you're done, you can play your music by clicking the Library button. Your new tracks will appear there. To play any one, double-click it.

Discussion

Keep in mind before ripping music that copyright laws limit what you can do with the digital music files that you rip. You're only allowed to use them for your own personal use—you're not allowed to share them with others.

Figure 11-1. Windows Media Player ripping music from an audio CD

You may not be able to rip digital music from every CD that you buy. Music companies have been using a variety of ways to fight piracy, and have used techniques on some CDs that don't let you rip music from them, or that limit what you can do with that ripped music, for example, by not letting you copy it to an MP3 player.

You may run into another problem with Windows Media Player—when you rip music from a CD, and transfer the digital files to your portable MP3 player, those files may not work on the player. If that happens, a likely culprit is that when you ripped the music, you left on CD copy protection. An option in Windows Media Player will copy-protect any music you rip so that it cannot be played on any device except your PC, and also won't allow others to listen to the music. You can easily solve the problem, though, by turning off automatic copy protection. In Window Media Player, choose Tools → Options → Privacy, uncheck the box next to Acquire licenses automatically for protected content, and click OK. You'll have to rerip all of your music.

If the music still doesn't play in the portable MP3 player, you may have used a format that the player won't recognize. All portable MP3 players will play MP3s, but not all will play other formats, such as WMA. So if you're planning to transfer files to a portable player, first check what file formats it recognizes.

When ripping music, a major issue you face is what format and audio quality to choose. MP3 files are more widely used than WMA, and more players support the

MP3 format. But WMA files generally offer higher quality at smaller bit rates. So you'll have to make decisions based on that. As to what bit rate to use, 128 Kbps is generally considered near-CD quality, and is suitable for most kinds of listening. Depending on the quality of your speakers, headphones, or MP3 player, you may or may not be able to recognize much of a difference between music ripped at 128 Kbps and 192 Kbps. If you have high-quality speakers, headphones, and an MP3 player, you'll notice the higher quality, but if you don't, you may not be able to tell the difference. But you most likely won't be able to tell a difference in quality of files ripped at 192 Kbps and files ripped at rates above that. Keep in mind that the higher the bit rate, the larger the file size. Table 11-1 shows you how much disk space a typical CD takes up when ripped at varying bit rates in the MP3 and WMA formats: you'll notice that WMA is listed with more bit rates than MP3 files. That's because Windows Media Player gives you a wider choice of bit rates when recording WMAs rather than MP3s. That has nothing to do with the underlying MP3 or WMA technology—WMA is a Microsoft format, and the company has chosen to give you more choices when recording in that format. Other software that rips digital music gives you equal choices between the MP3 and WMA formats.

Table 11-1. Bit rate and file size for MP3s and WMAs

File type	Bit rate	MBs per entire CD
MP3	128 Kbps	57 MB
MP3	192 Kbps	86 MB
MP3	256 Kbps	115 MB
MP3	320 Kbps	144 MB
WMA	48 Kbps	22 MB
WMA	64 Kbps	28 MB
WMA	96 Kbps	42 MB
WMA	128 Kbps	56 MB
WMA	160 Kbps	69 MB
WMA	192 Kbps	86 MB

See Also

There are many pieces of software, in addition to Windows Media Player, that can rip music. Many are for pay, but there are free ones as well. An excellent free one is MusicMatch Jukebox, available from *http://www.musicmatch.com*. Note that there are both for-pay and free versions of the software, so be careful which version you download.

11.2 Creating a Playlist

Problem

You want to create a playlist in Windows Media Player so that you can listen to a set of songs.

Solution

Using a graphical user interface

1. Click the Library button at the top of the screen so that you are in your library area.

2. Tell Windows Media Player to display the Playlist pane by choosing View → Now Playing Options → Show Playlist. On the right side of the screen a pane will appear, with Now Playing List at the top.

3. Choose Now Playing List → New List → Playlist.

4. Drag files from the Library onto the Playlist pane. You drag multiple files at once. To select adjacent items, press and hold the Shift key while you select files. To select nonadjacent items, press and hold the Ctrl key while you select files. The result will look like Figure 11-2.

Figure 11-2. Create a playlist by dragging music from your library to the Playlist pane

5. Select New Playlist → Save Playlist As, name it and click Save.

6. To play your current playlist, highlight the first file in it and click the Play button at the bottom of the screen. Your playlist will now play all the files in it, one after another. If you want to start in the middle of the playlist, highlight the file where you want to begin, and click the Play button.

7. To play a different playlist, scroll to the My Playlists area of the Contents pane on the far right side of Windows Media Player, and double-click the list you want to play. Its contents will appear in the library area and in the Playlist pane, and the list will begin playing.

Discussion

Playlists are at the core of using Windows Media Player. In addition to using them to create songs that play automatically, one after another, you create playlists when you want to burn CDs.

By default, when you save a playlist, it is saved with a *.wpl* extension in the *My Playlists* folder, which is usually located in the *My Music* folder. You can also save playlists with the other extensions: *.m3u*, *.asx*, *.wax*, or *.wvx*. And you can save them in any folder that you like.

See Also

You can create a playlist in Windows Media Player, and then use that playlist to play in the background during a Microsoft PowerPoint presentation. For details, see *http://support.microsoft.com/default.aspx?scid=kb;en-us;555066*.

11.3   Burning a CD

Problem

You want to burn music to an audio CD so that you can play it in a CD player. Burning means copying digital music from your PC to a blank CD and turning the CD into an audio CD.

Solution

Using a graphical user interface

1. Record any music you want to put onto your CD using Windows Media Player. To learn how to record music onto your PC, see Recipe 11.1.

2. Create a playlist that contains all the music you want to put on your CD. To learn how to create a playlist, see Recipe 11.2.

3. Click the Burn button at the top of the screen. (Note, you can also choose File → CDs and Devices → Burn Audio CD.) The Burn pane appears on the left side of your screen.

4. Click the drop-down button underneath Start Burn, and choose the playlist that you want to burn onto CD. The playlist will appear, with checkboxes next to each track. If you don't want certain tracks to be burned onto CD, uncheck the boxes next to them.

5. If you want to add tracks to the list of files that will be burned to your CD, click Edit Playlist and add the tracks.

6. If you want to move around the order of the tracks before burning, drag them to the new positions you want them to be in on the burned CD.

7. Insert a blank, recordable CD into your CD drive.

8. Click the Start Burn button. Each track will first be converted to a burnable format, and then all will be copied to the CD, as shown in Figure 11-3. This will take several minutes. After the files are burned onto the CD, the CD will be ejected. You can now play it in a CD player.

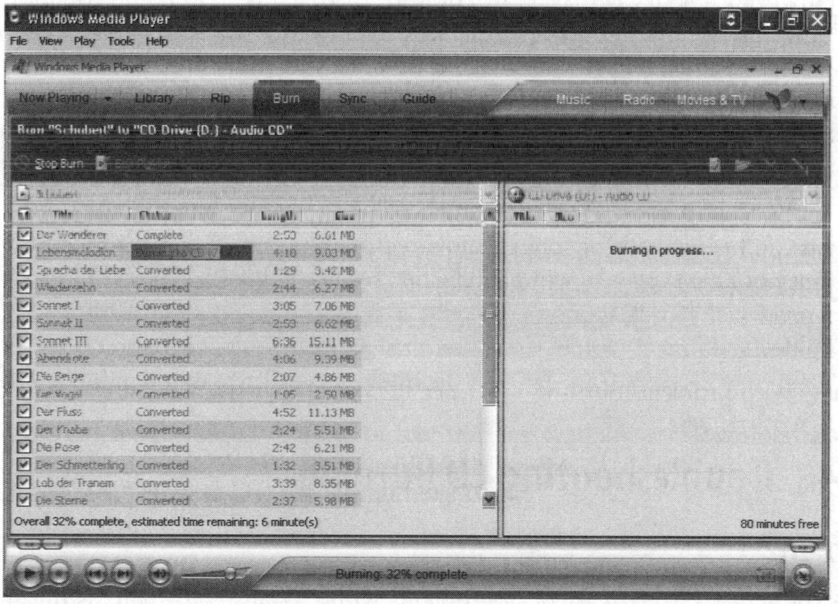

Figure 11-3. When you burn a CD, the Windows Media Player first converts each file to a format that can be burned onto a CD, and then copies each track to the CD

Discussion

In order to burn music, you must have a recordable CD drive, not one that can only play CDs. If you have a recordable DVD drive, almost all will be able to burn CDs as well as DVDs.

When burning a CD, you can use two types of blank disks: a CD-R, or a CD-RW. Blank CD-R disks are less expensive than CD-RWs, but you can only record to them once. You can record to CD-RWs many times.

If you burn to a CD-R, you can't burn any additional tracks onto the CD after you've started the first burn. If you are using a CD-RW, you can record to it many times. If you have a CD-RW and you want to delete the existing music on it before burning to it, click the Erase button, and all the music on the CR-RW will be erased.

This recipe shows how to create an audio CD, but you can also create a CD with music on it that is not in audio CD format, but instead contains digital files—in other words, you can copy the digital music files from your PC directly to the CD. Some CD players can play MP3 files, so if you insert the CD into a CD player, the player will be able to play the music, even though the CD is not in the audio CD format. However, not all CD players will do this. Also, many CD players will play music in MP3 format, but not in other formats, such as WMA. To copy music files directly from Windows Media Player to a CD, follow the directions in this recipe, with one exception. Before you click the Start Burn button, click the drop-down list on the right side of the screen and choose Data CD. Your files will be copied onto the CD.

You can fit many more files onto a CD if you copy digital files directly, rather than burn them as an audio CD. Depending on the bit rate at which you recorded each file, you can fit hundreds of songs, compared to about two dozen, at most, for audio CDs. But not all CD players will play digital files like MP3s.

See Also

For help with problems burning a CD, see Recipe 11.4.

11.4   Troubleshooting CD Burning

Problem

You experience any of a variety of problems with CD burning, such, as burning not completing, CD player not playing the finished audio CD, or the music skips, pops, or has some other audio problem.

Solution

There are many different problems that occur when burning CDs, but here are some of the most common problems and solutions.

Windows Media Player is unable to burn the music onto the CD
This happens more frequently on older CD drives than on newer ones. The most common cause of this problem is that your CD drive cannot record to the specific brand of CD-Rs or CD-RWs you've bought. This usually happens more frequently with no-name CD-Rs or CD-RWs than with brand names. Also, make sure that you have a recordable CD drive, not just a drive that plays CDs.

All of the music won't fit onto the CD
Some tracks may not burn onto the CD because there isn't room on the CD for them. In this case, "Will not fit" will appear next to the items that won't be burned because there's not enough free disk space left. Be aware that there are two size formats for CDs 74 minutes and 80 minutes—so you may have bought a CD with the lesser number of minutes. Also, even if the total time of the tracks you've selected matches the CD length exactly, all the tracks might not fit. Windows Media Player inserts two seconds between every track on the CD you burn, so count in the extra seconds between tracks when figuring how many tracks you can burn onto a CD.

Solving ripping problems

The problem with your music may not be the burning process, but instead with the ripping process that recorded the audio files. The audio files, when you play them on your PC, may skip and pop, and so any CD you burn from them will skip and pop as well.

One cause of the problem may be dirt and grime on the original CD. So wipe the bottom of the CD clean—the problem may have been dust and dirt. Also, the bottom of the CD may be scratched, and that can cause problems as well. In that instance, you can try some of the CD cleaning devices sold at music stores and computer stores. Also make sure that no one stomps around during recording. With enough movement, CD drives can skip just like turntables.

 If the ripping software you're using allows it, try slowing down the speed at which you rip your music. Windows Media Player doesn't allow this, but other ripping software, such as MusicMatch Jukebox, available at *http://www.musicmatch.com*, does.

If that doesn't work, try ripping it at a lower bit rate, which sometimes works. Also, try not running any other software when you're ripping (or burning), which also might solve the problem.

Finally, if you have a very old CD drive, the drive itself may be a problem—with some older, slower drives, when you rip music, you'll frequently get skips. If that's your problem, the only solution will be to buy a newer drive.

Solving burning problems

Sometimes your source and the digital music files will be free of skips, but when you burn a CD, the resulting CD skips. Slowing down the speed at which you burn a CD sometimes solves the problem. Most burning software will let you adjust your burning speed. In Windows Media Player, choose Tools → Options → Devices, and highlight your CD drive. Then click Properties, and choose the Recording tab, as shown in Figure 11-4.

From the Select a write speed drop-down box, choose a slower speed than the fastest. Also, close all other programs when you're burning a CD so that CPU, RAM, and system resources are all devoted to CD burning.

Another common problem with burning is buffer overrun, when the source of the material is not filling the recording buffer fast enough. If you get a buffer overrun error message, close other applications to give yourself plenty of memory, and disable virus scanning.

If that doesn't solve the problem, try using analog rather than digital CD writing. Choose Tools → Options → Devices, highlight the CD drive that you want to use analog playback, click Properties, and go to the Audio tab. From the Copy section, choose Analog. If that still doesn't work, go back to the same tab and choose "Use error correction." This will slow down the CD burning process even further, but may solve the problem.

Discussion

Tracking down the source of skipping and popping on burned CDs can be very difficult. But if you're recording from old LPs, the problem is most likely that the vinyl on the LP has been damaged, and so the resulting digital music suffers from skips and pops. You can solve the problem by cleaning up the skips and pops using downloadable software.

WaveCorrector, available from *http://www.wavecor.co.uk*, and WAVClean, available from *http://www.excla.com/WAVclean/English*, will both eliminate pops, skips, crackles, hisses, and similar noises from music that you record from old LPs. Both programs require a several-step process. First, record the digital music using Windows Media Player or similar ripping software. You'll have to record in *.wav* format, because that's the only format these programs handle. Next, clean up the *.wav* files with the programs. Which one you use depends on whether you want to automate the clean-up, or take a hands-on approach, and on how bad the problems are that you want to correct. WAVClean is the more automated of the two—load the *.wav*

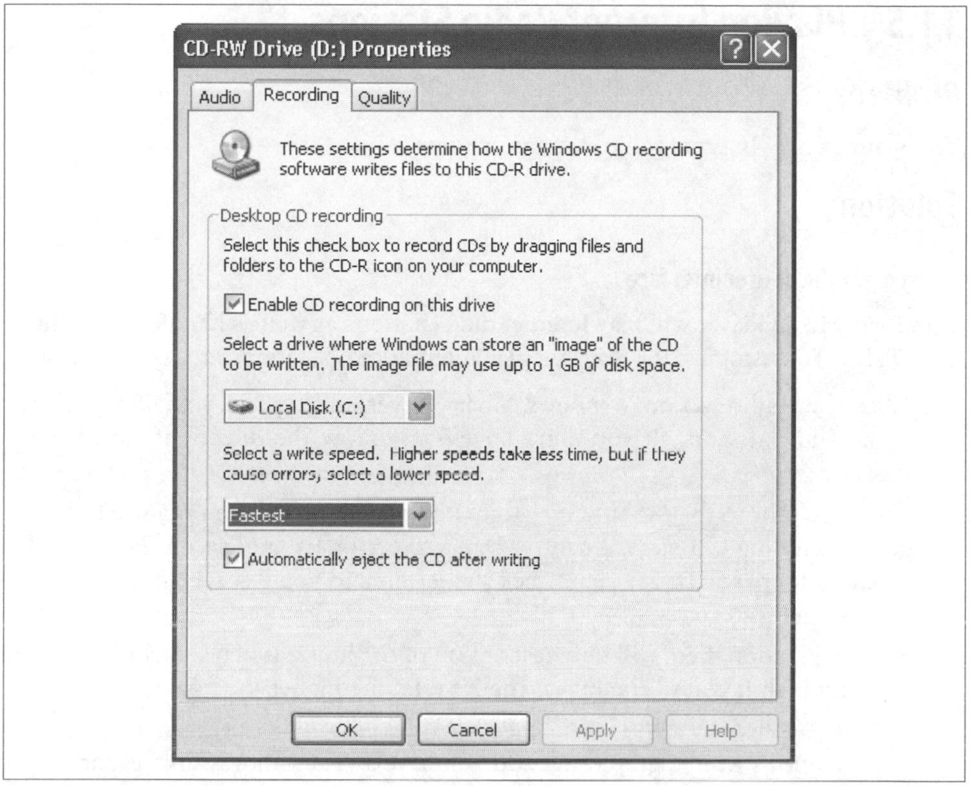

Figure 11-4. Slowing down CD burning in Windows Media Player may help eliminate skips in music CDs

file, select Scrub, and choose from basic settings, and it eliminates hisses and crackles. It won't, however, clean up deeper scratches, so it's best for recordings that suffer from just hissing and crackling. With WaveCorrector, on the other hand, you see an actual oscilloscope view of the music files, with pops and similar problems highlighted in blue. You can either have the program make the edits to the file itself, or you can preview the edits and do correcting yourself. WaveCorrector also includes a recording feature, so that you don't have to use Media Player or other ripping software, such as MusicMatch Jukebox. Once you've cleaned up the music, you can either convert them to *.mp3* or *.wma* digital music to save on your hard disk using Windows Media Player, or you can burn directly from a *.wav* file to a CD.

Both programs are shareware and free to try, but you are expected to pay if you continue using them. WaveCorrector costs $45 to register, and WAVClean costs $30.

See Also

For more advice on solving CD burning problems, see *http://www.epinions.com/content_1041473668*.

11.5   Playing Internet Radio Stations

Problem

You want to play Internet radio stations on your PC.

Solution

Using a graphical user interface

Windows Media Player will play Internet radio stations as well as handle digital music and DVDs. To customize the way you play Internet radio stations, do the following:

1. Click the Radio tab on Windows Media Player and type in your Passport user name and password. If you don't have one, follow the directions for getting a Passport.

2. You'll be sent to the MSN Radio page. Radio stations will be organized by category, including Classical, Country, Dance/Electronica, and so on. Next to each category there will be a + sign. Click the + sign and you'll see a list of all the stations in that category.

3. For each station there will be a description of the music it plays, including the bit rate at which it plays. The higher the bit rate, the higher the quality of the radio stream. To play a station, click the play button to its left.

4. Some stations will be grayed-out and will have a "learn more" link as part of the description. Those are for-pay stations, and you can only listen to them if you subscribe to MSN Radio. To subscribe, click the "learn more" link and follow the subscription directions.

5. To make it easier to return to your favorite stations, you can use the My Stations feature. To add a station to your My Stations list, click the + sign to the right of the station description.

6. When you click the + sign, the station will be put at the top of the page, underneath the heading My Stations. The station you just added will be at the top of the list. That station will always appear at the top of the list until you add another station, or until you remove the station from the list. To remove a station from the list, click the – sign to its right.

Discussion

There are generally two kinds of Internet radio stations—normal, broadcast stations that also stream their signal over the Internet, and Internet-only stations. There's no difference in the way you play each.

The sound quality of the music you listen to over Internet radio varies widely. It's dependent on many factors, including the bandwidth of your connection, whether there is any Internet congestion, and the bit rate of the radio stream. In most instances, the quality isn't nearly up to FM standards, and often is quite below that. Not uncommonly, the stream will be interrupted by short breaks in the transmission, primarily due to Internet congestion.

See Also

Windows Media Player is only one of many ways to play Internet radio stations. You can also listen to stations by going directly to their home pages, and clicking on a link that will play the music. You can also go to web sites that include links to Internet radio stations, and that often let you play the radio station without having to visit the station's home page, and just by clicking on a link. Among the sites that have links to radio stations are *http://www.live365.com/index.live*, and *http://www.radio-locator.com*.

Also, other music-playing software, in addition to Windows Media Player, will let you tune into radio stations. A good one is MusicMatch, available at *http://www.musicmatch.com*.

11.6 Protecting Your Privacy in Windows Media Player

Problem

You want to make sure that your privacy isn't violated when using Windows Media Player.

Solution

Using a graphical user interface

There is some controversy over whether the normal use of Windows Media Player may violate your privacy by reporting on what CDs you listen to and DVDs you view, and by the use of cookies which may allow web sites to learn that information. If you are worried, you can take these steps:

1. In Windows Media Player, choose File → Work Offline. When you do that, Windows Media Player won't automatically connect to Microsoft servers, and potentially exchange information about your CD and DVD use.

2. Choose Tools → Options → Privacy to get to the Privacy options dialog box, shown in Figure 11-5. Uncheck the box next to Send unique Player ID to content providers. If this box is checked, your PC can be identified on web sites through the use of a special cookie put on your hard disk by Windows Media Player.

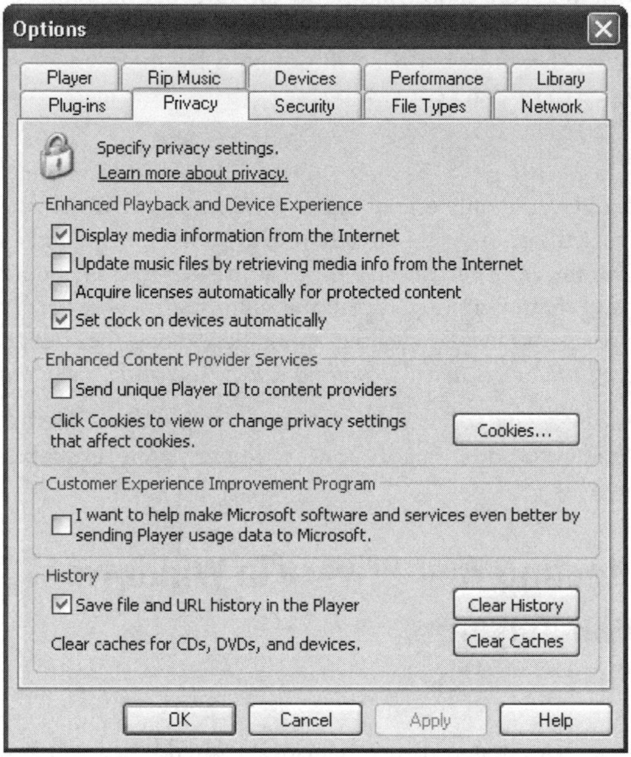

Figure 11-5. If you want to protect your privacy when using Windows Media Player, here's where to go to change your options

3. Uncheck the box in the Customer Experience Improvement Program area if you don't want information about the CDs and DVDs you have played to be reported to Microsoft.

4. Click the Clear Caches button if you want to delete from your cache information about what CDs and DVDs you have played. Some web sites may be able to look into your cache.

5. Uncheck the box next to Save file and URL history in the Player, if you don't want the history and file information saved inside the player itself.

6. Click OK when you're done.

Discussion

There is a great deal of controversy over whether Windows Media Player violates your privacy, with some privacy advocates claiming that it represents a potential threat, and Microsoft saying that there are no privacy problems with it.

The discussion centers in large part around problems that could theoretically allow Microsoft to track what DVDs you play, and could allow for the creation of a "super-cookie" on your PC that can let web sites exchange information about you.

When you use Windows Media Player to play DVD movies, each time a new DVD is played, Media Player contacts a Microsoft server and gets the DVD's title and chapter information. The server, in turn, identifies your specific version of Media Player, uses a cookie to identify the DVD that you're watching, and then records information about the DVDs you watch onto a database on your hard disk in *C:\Documents and Settings\All Users\Application Data\Microsoft\Media Index*.

Microsoft claims that the cookie used is an anonymous one and you can't be personally identified. The company also says that it does not keep track of what DVDs individuals watch, and that the database created on your PC is never accessed from the Internet. Instead, the company says, it's used only by your own computer—the next time you put a DVD in your drive that you've played before, Media Player will get information from that database instead of getting it from a Microsoft web server. This speeds up getting the information.

The so-called supercookie that Windows Media Player creates is a unique ID number in the form of a 128-bit GUID (Globally Unique Identifier) assigned to your player and stored in the Registry. You can find it in HKEY_CURRENT_USER\Software\Microsoft\Windows Media\WMSDK\General\UniqueID. This ID number can be retrieved by any web site through the use of JavaScript. The ID number is called a super-cookie because it can be retrieved by *any* web site. Normally, web sites can retrieve only cookies that they create and put on your PC, and so it becomes difficult for web sites to share information about you. However, this supercookie can be retrieved by any site to track you, and web sites can share this information with each other, allowing them to create a sophisticated profile about your Internet usage. Additionally, cookie blockers can't block its use.

Again, Microsoft claims that the supercookie does not invade your privacy because all it can do is identify your computer to web sites.

The Customer Experience Improvement Program can also be problematic for those who worry about privacy. When you check boxes in that area, Windows Media Player will report on your music and movie use to Microsoft.

See Also

For a full report on potential privacy problems with Windows Media Player, see articles by privacy expert Richard Smith at *http://www.computerbytesman.com/privacy/supercookie.htm* and *http://www.computerbytesman.com/privacy/wmp8dvd.htm*. Note that the article was written about Windows Media Player 8, but the issues remain the same. For Microsoft's response to Mr. Smith, see *http://www.computerbytesman.com/privacy/wmp8response.htm*.

11.7 Searching Through Digital Media Collections Using Metadata

Problem

You have many digital media files on your PC, including music, video, and graphics, and want to be able to easily find the file you want quickly.

Solution

The problem with searching through media files is that they are made up of pictures, animations, and sounds, not text. So you can't easily find the exact file you want by searching through the text in the files, because they don't contain text.

For example, let's say you're looking to find an MP3 recording by the mezzo-soprano Cecilia Bartoli of "Là ci darem la mano," from Mozart's opera *Don Giovanni*. You don't remember the filename, and you don't remember where it's stored. Since the recording doesn't contain any text, how do you find it?

You find it by using a little-known feature of the Windows Search Companion that looks not only for filenames, but also for details embedded in a media file known as *metadata*. Metadata is descriptive information about a file, and it varies according to the type of file. For example, metadata for music files in WMA and MP3 formats can include the artist's name, the album title, the musical genre, and even the lyrics. (Metadata for graphics files doesn't offer as much descriptive information, but does include the file's resolution and if you've taken the photo with a digital camera, will even include the camera model.)

 For MP3 files, metadata is also called ID3 information.

Metadata is added to a file when it's created, so how much information appears mostly depends on what information was grabbed at that time. For example, if you've recorded an MP3 file from a CD, the metadata for the MP3 includes whatever information your music recording software copied from the CD, such as the kind of music it is, the CD title, and the song title.

You don't have to do anything special to tell XP to search through metadata—the Search Companion does it automatically. You just need to know what kind of metadata you can look for.

To see the metadata for any media file, right-click the file, and choose Properties-Summary. (Sometimes you have to choose Properties → Summary → Advanced.) The metadata for music files often contains a great deal of hidden information, including its genre, the CD title, song title, track number, the year it was recorded, and comments inserted by the person who recorded the track. Usually, not all the metadata fields contain information. What's available depends on the software used to record the music—or what someone added later. Figure 11-6 shows the metadata associated with an MP3 recording by the mezzo-soprano Cecilia Bartoli of "Là ci darem la mano," from Mozart's opera *Don Giovanni*.

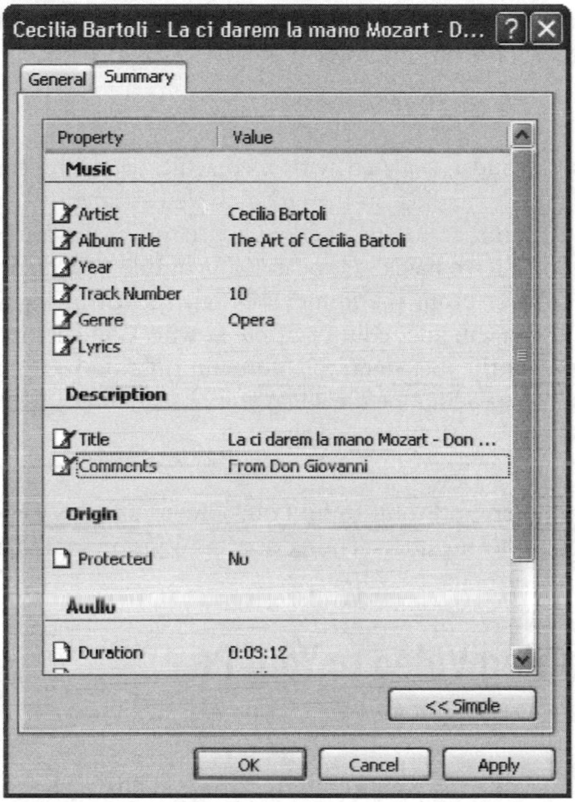

Figure 11-6. Metadata for a music file

Examine the media files on your hard disk, to see the variety of fields in metadata. The exact fields vary not only according to the type of file, but even the exact program that created the file. To search through metadata, first launch the Windows Search Companion in any of these four ways:

- Choose Start → Search.
- Press the Windows Key-F.
- Press F3 in a Windows Explorer Window.
- Choose Search in a Windows Explorer Window.

When the Search Companion launches, go to the box that says "A word or part of the filename," and type whatever you want to find. For example, if you type *Classical*, the Search Companion looks for any music in that genre, and typing *Mozart* or *Don Giovanni* narrows the field.

Graphics files don't contain as much information, but you can search for the resolution of the file. For example, type "800 × 600" in the box that says "A word or part of the filename." If you've taken a picture with your digital camera, you can type in the camera name. This will only work if your camera was smart enough to put this metadata in the file. Some do, and some don't.

Discussion

The metadata you'll find associated with media files is very inconsistent, and will vary from file to file, depending on the software that created or recorded the media file. That doesn't mean that you're stuck with what the software puts in, though. If your media files don't have metadata, or if it's incomplete or incorrect, you can edit or add to what's there. From the Summaries tab shown in Figure 11-6, click any metadata field and you can add, edit, or delete at will. While it can be time-consuming and tedious to edit the metadata, the more information you put in the metadata, the easier you'll be able to find the file when you're searching.

See Also

If you're a programmer, and want to find out how to use the Windows Media Format SDK to access the metadata embedded in Windows Media files, see *http://blogs.msdn.com/tims/articles/100730.aspx*.

11.8 Capturing Video to Your PC

Problem

You want to capture video to your PC so that you can edit it there or view it on your computer.

Solution

Windows Movie Maker, built into Windows XP, will let you record and edit videos and create DVDs from them. To run it, choose Start → All Programs → Accessories → Windows Movie Maker.

Follow this advice for capturing video:

Using an analog camera or videotape

- If you have an analog video camera or videotape, you need some way of turning those analog signals into digital data that can be stored on your PC. You can do this via a video capture board or by using a device you can attach to your FireWire™ or USB port. If you're going the route of a video capture board, make sure the board has XP-certified drivers, or else you may run into trouble. To find out whether a board has XP-certified drivers, go to the Windows Compatibility List at *http://www.microsoft.com/windows/catalog* and do a search.

- If you have a USB port, you can import analog video via your USB port, with DVD Express, or InstantDVD, or Instant DVD+DV, available from *http://www.adstech.com*. They're hardware/software combinations—to get the video into your PC, connect the analog video device to DVD Express, InstantDVD, or Instant DVD+DV, and then connect a USB cable from it to the USB port on your PC. (A similar set of products, called the Dazzle Digital Video Creators, will do the same thing. For details, go to *http://www.dazzle.com*.)

- Check your system documentation to see what type of USB port you have. If you have a USB 1.1 port, you won't be able to import high-quality video, and you'd be better off installing a video capture card. USB 2.0 will work fine, though.

- If you have a FireWire™-enabled PC, you're also in luck, because its high-speed capacity is also suitable for importing video. You'll have to buy extra hardware, such as the DAC-100 FireWire™ Digital/Analog Video Capture-Converter. Plug your RCA cable or S-Video cable into it, and then plug a FireWire™ cable from it into your FireWire™ port, and you'll be able to send video to your PC. For information, go to *http://www.synchrotech.com/product-1394/analog-dv-converter_02.html*.

- Once you've gotten the hardware and your camera set up, recording the video is easy. Open Windows Movie Maker, choose File → Record, start the camera or video, and click Record.

Capturing video with a digital video camera

If you have a digital video camera, you shouldn't need any extra hardware in order to capture video from it, as long as you have a FireWire™ port (or a USB 2.0 port) on your PC. These devices generally include built-in FireWire™ ports (note that the cameras might call the port an IEEE 1394 or an i.Link™ port) or USB 2.0 ports. If you don't have a FireWire™ port on your PC, you can install a FireWire™ port card. These generally cost well under $100. Make sure that the card is OHCI (Open Host Controller Interface)-compliant.

When you plug your digital camera into a FireWire™ port and turn it on, Windows will ask you what you want to do with the camera. Tell it that you want to record in Movie Maker and Record in Movie Maker, and it will launch Movie Maker to the Record dialog box, with a video showing in the preview window.

Best settings for recording video

Before you start recording, you'll see a preview of your movie in the Record dialog box, shown in Figure 11-7. Before you begin recording, choose your video settings here.

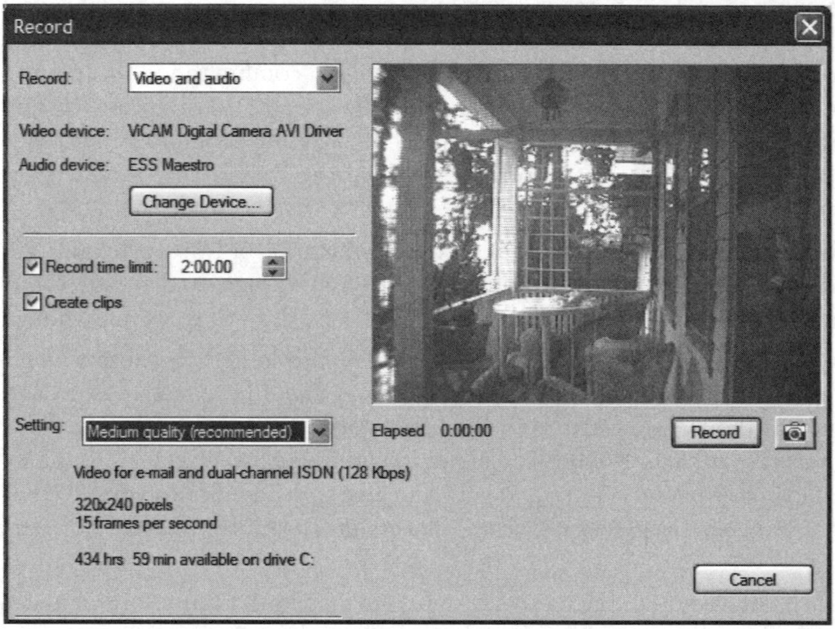

Figure 11-7. Before recording your video, choose the best settings for video capture

From the Setting drop-down box, choose the quality of the final video that you'll capture. Movie Maker comes with a number of preset profiles, including three basic ones, High, Medium, and Low quality. When you make a choice of your profile, Movie Maker tells you how many hours and minutes of recording time you have, based on your disk space, and the disk requirements of the profile. So, for example, you might have 193 hours of recording time based on the High setting, but 1630 hours based on the low setting.

These preset settings will be dependent on the input source—if you're using a digital camera, for example, you can record at a higher quality than an analog camera, and so you'll have a wider range of options.

Those three basic profiles of High, Medium and Low quality aren't your only choices of profiles. You can choose from a much wider variety of profiles, based on what you plan to do with the eventual video. Do you plan to post the video on the Web? Just play it back at home? Run in on a personal digital assistant? You'll find profiles designed for specific purposes like that.

To select the profile, choose Other in the Setting drop-down list. Underneath it a new drop-down list appears, with a range of profiles from which you can choose. They're prebuilt for specific uses, for example, recording video to post on the Web, for color PDA devices, and for broadband NTSC (National Television Standards Committee), which is standard TV.

Whenever you choose a profile, you'll see underneath it the frame size of the video, the frames per second, and if you choose a profile from Other, you'll also see the video bit rate. Here's what the settings mean:

Video display size
> The size of the video, in pixels, for example, 740 × 480, or 320 × 240.

Frames per second
> The number of frames captured per second. For smooth video, you need 30 frames per second, which is the High quality setting. The Medium and Low quality settings record at 15 frames per second.

Video bit rate
> The bit rate of the recorded video—the higher the bit rate, the greater the quality.

Audio bit rate and properties
> These settings aren't shown in the Windows Movie settings, but they vary according to which profile you choose. Audio properties are measured in kilohertz (khz); the higher the greater the quality. Audio bit rate measures the bit rate, and again, the higher the bit rate, the greater the quality.

To help you make the best choice among profiles, Table 11-2 shows the settings for every one of the Movie Maker profiles.

Table 11-2. Settings for Movie Maker profiles

Profile name	Video display size	Video bit rate	Audio properties	Audio bit rate
Video for Web servers (28.8 Kbps)	160x120 pixels	20 kilobits per second (Kbps)	8 kilohertz (kHz)	8 Kbps
Video for Web servers (56 Kbps)	176x144 pixels	30 Kbps	11 kHz	10 Kbps
Video for single-channel ISDN (64 Kbps)	240x176 pixels	50 Kbps	11 kHz	10 Kbps
Video for e-mail and dual-channel ISDN (128 Kbps)	320x240 pixels	100 Kbps	16 kHz	16 Kbps
Video for broadband NTSC (256 Kbps)	320x240 pixels	225 Kbps	32 kHz	32 Kbps
Video for broadband NTSC (384 Kbps)	320x240 pixels	350 Kbps	32 kHz	32 Kbps
Video for broadband NTSC (768 Kbps)	320x240 pixels	700 Kbps	44 kHz	64 Kbps
Video for broadband NTSC (1500 Kbps total)	640x480 pixels	1,368 Kbps	44 kHz	128 Kbps
Video for broadband NTSC (2 Mbps total)	640x480 pixels	1,868 Kbps	44 kHz	128 Kbps
Video for broadband film content (768 Kbps)	640x480 pixels	568 Kbps	44 kHz	128 Kbps
Video for broadband film content (1500 Kbps total)	640x480 pixels	1,368 Kbps	44 kHz	128 Kbps

Table 11-2. Settings for Movie Maker profiles (continued)

Profile name	Video display size	Video bit rate	Audio properties	Audio bit rate
Video for color PDA devices (150 Kbps)	208x160 pixels	111 Kbps	22 kHz	32 Kbps
Video for color PDA devices (225 Kbps)	208x160 pixels	186 Kbps	22 kHz	32 Kbps
DV-AVI (25 Mbps)	720x480 pixels (NTSC) 720x525 pixels (PAL)	1,411 Kbps	48 kHz	16 Kbps

After you make your choices, click Record, and record your video. When you're done, click Stop. The recording will be saved to your hard disk, where you can open it and edit it with Windows Movie Maker or other video editing software.

Discussion

Be aware that videos can take up a significant amount of hard disk space, so make sure that you have a very large disk before recording any videos. Also, you should have as fast a PC as possible, and should not be using the computer for any other purposes during video capture. You can also capture video directly from TV, if you have a capture board.

See Also

For excellent advice about capturing video, and creating videos, see *http://www.eicsoftware.com/PapaJohn/MM2/MM2.html*.

11.9   Making Your Own DVDs

Problem

You want to create the best possible DVDs when you burn them using Windows Movie Maker.

Solution

If you use Movie Maker to make or copy your own videos and burn them to DVDs, consider these tips and advice:

- The USB 1.0 standard is not fast enough to connect a camera or other video input to your PC. Its throughput of 11 Mbps isn't fast enough for capturing high-quality video, which is 30 frames per second with 24-bit color at a resolution of 640 × 480, and requires speeds of at least 210 Mbps. USB 2.0, which has a speed of 480 Mbps, and FireWire™, which has a speed of 400 Mbps, will work, however.

- Make sure that you have a substantial amount of free hard disk space if you're going to burn your videos onto DVDs. The video will be cached onto your hard disk before it's burned onto CDs, and so you'll typically need several free gigabytes of disk space.

- Defragment your hard drive before creating and burning DVDs for best performance. If you have a second hard drive, use that rather than your primary one for DVD creation. No matter the speed of your CPU, turn off any background applications that are running when you import video and create your DVD.

- If you're burning high-quality video onto a DVD, figure that you'll be able to fit about an hour's worth onto a single DVD. At a lower quality (lower bit rate), you can fit up to about two hours onto a DVD. Keep in mind, though, that if you write at the lower bit rate, the DVD might not be able to be played on a set-top DVD player, although it will work on your PC's DVD player.

- There's no single, accepted standard for DVD burning, and so not all DVD disks that you burn will work on all set-top DVD players. Generally, most set-top DVD players will play DVD-R disks, but may not play DVD-RW or DVD+RW disks. Manufacturer information can't always be trusted, but check the web sites for the latest details.

- After you've created your video, and you're ready to burn it onto a DVD, set aside plenty of time. It can take up to two hours to burn a one hour DVD, depending on your CPU and drive speed.

Discussion

If you don't have a PC that runs at least at 1 GHz or faster, and 512 MB of RAM, don't try to burn DVDs—your PC simply won't be able to handle it. Also, keep in mind that blank DVDs are more expensive than blank CDs, and typically cost between $2 and $4.

See Also

If you want features beyond those offered by Windows Movie Maker, try Ulead DVD Movie Factory. In addition to basic video editing tools, it lets you use transitions, add special effects and menus, and includes backgrounds, preset layouts and music you can add to your videos. In addition, it will burn to DVD, VCD, and SVCD, and can save files in a variety of video formats. It's shareware and available to try for free, but if you keep using it, you're expected to pay $44.95. It's available from Internet download sites, as well as from *http://www.ulead.com*. And for more advice about burning DVDs, see the *PC World* article, Step-By-Step: Burn Your Own DVDs for Backup or Video Playback at *http://www.pcworld.com/howto/article/0,aid,113461,00.asp*.

11.10 Converting Images Easily Between Graphics Formats

Problem

You want to convert a file from one image format to another, for example, so that you can take a file in TIFF format and convert it to JPEG so that it can be posted on the Web.

Solution

Using downloadable software

IrfanView is the best tool for doing image conversion. It's free, easy to use, gives you a wide variety of formats among which you can convert, and will do batch conversions as well as conversions of individual files.

Download the program from *http://www.irfanview.com*. If you're going to convert only a single file, follow these steps:

1. Run IrfanView and open the file you want to convert by choosing File → Open, browsing to the file you want to open, and then choosing it.

2. Choose File → Save As. From the "Save As type" drop-down box, choose the format you want to convert the file to.

3. Click the Options button to choose any special options for the file you're saving. The options available to you will differ according to the file type you're converting to. For example, if you're converting to a JPEG, you can choose how high quality an image to save, whether to save the file as a grayscale file, and so on, as shown in Figure 11-8.

4. Click OK when you've chosen your options, and then click Save.

5. Choose where to save the file and what name to give it and click OK. Your image will now be converted.

To batch-convert files:

1. Run IrfanView and choose File → Batch Conversion.

2. In the Batch Conversion dialog box that appears, shown in Figure 11-9, browse to the directory that has the files you want to convert, and select them.

3. From the Output format dialog box, choose the format to which you want to convert the files.

4. Click the Options button to choose any special options for the files. Again, these will vary according to the file format to which you're converting the files.

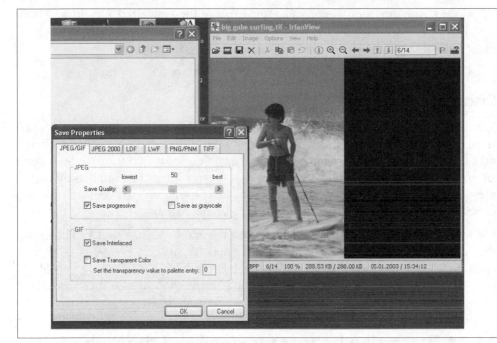

Figure 11-8. Saving at different quality levels in IrfanView

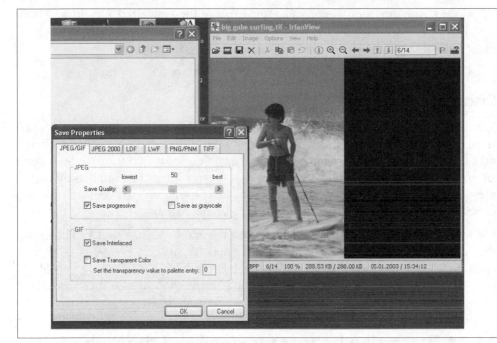

Figure 11-9. Batch conversion in IrfanView

5. Choose the directory where you want to store the converted files (the Output directory box).

6. Click the Add button

7. Click Start. IrfanView will convert all your files in a batch.

Discussion

You may be tempted to try to use XP's built-in Paint program to do image conversion, but don't bother, because it can't really do the trick. It can only convert a handful of graphics formats (for example, it can't handle *.pcx* or *.ico* format), and won't let you customize the graphic; for example, you can't alter the compression of *.jpg* files to make them smaller. And it can't do batch conversions—to convert a file you have to open it, and then save it in a different graphics format.

For image conversion you don't need a full-blown graphics program like Photoshop that carries a full-blown price tag of up to $600 (Photoshop Elements is another alternative, but that's not free either). A freebie like IrfanView does a great job. In fact, IrfanView does a lot more than just image conversion. It also includes editing tools.

11.11 Processing Images for Email and the Web

Problem

You want to use images on a web site, or to send via email, but the images are so large that they would make a web page load very slowly, or would take too long to send via email.

Solution

Using downloadable software

ImageConverter.EXE (available from *http://www.stintercorp.com/genx/imageconverter. php*) is a great tool for converting files for use on the Web, because it shows you a side-by-side comparison of the before-and-after images, before you do the actual conversion, and also displays the size of each image. That way, before you do the conversion, you can keep tweaking it until you have it at the size and quality you want. To convert an image:

1. Click the Open button, browse to the file you want to convert, and click Open. The graphic will be displayed in two panes—the left-hand pane, which shows you the original graphic, and the right-hand pane, which shows you how the graphic will look after it's converted. Note that underneath each picture, you will see the file size.

2. In the Conversion Settings section, choose the file type to which you want to convert the file. If you're going to post the graphic on the Web, you should choose JPEG, GIF, or PNG.

3. In the Bits per Pixel box, choose 1, 4, 8, or 24. The more bits per pixel, the higher the image quality, but the larger the picture. As you choose different image qualities, the preview picture will alter, and the preview size will change.

4. If you want to add special effects to the picture, choose them from the Effect section. As you choose them, the effects will be added to the preview picture, and its preview size will change as well.

5. When you're satisfied with balance between file size and image quality, click the Convert button. The file will be converted to the new format.

Figure 11-10 shows an example of the program converting a TIFF file to a JPEG file, and shrinking the file size—not its dimensions, but the total number of bytes. The image has been shrunk from 295 K down to 10 K, yet the image quality is not dramatically different.

Figure 11-10. Doing a side-by-side comparison of image quality and size before doing the conversion will help you determine what image quality to choose, and find out the resulting file size

Discussion

ImageConverter.EXE is shareware, and is free to try, but you're expected to pay $35 if you keep using it. So why bother with software that costs money instead of a piece of freeware like IrfanView? IrfanView can't display before-and-after pictures of the graphic you're converting. So you can't, for example, preview what the converted picture will look like after it is converted. This can make image conversion a hit-or-miss affair: you'll first have to choose your conversion options, then convert the image, and then finally look at the output. If you're not happy with the results, you have to start back at the beginning, choose different options, and hope this one works.

ImageConverter.EXE does batch conversions, as well as letting you convert files one at a time. It also lets you edit and add a wide variety of special effects when you convert, such as changing the color depth and contrast, adding a motion blur, posterizing the image and more.

See Also

Paint Shop Pro (*http://www.paintshoppro.com*) is an excellent all-around graphics program that also does image conversion, including batch image conversion. It's shareware and free to try, but has a registration fee of $99.

CHAPTER 12

Network Configuration

12.0 Introduction

In this chapter, we'll cover many of the configuration tasks needed to get a Windows XP system up on the network and how to troubleshoot network issues. Some topics include the configuration of an IP address, configuring DNS, and viewing network activity. For more on wireless networking, see Chapter 14.

Using a Graphical User Interface

The Network Connections applet hasn't changed significantly since Windows NT, with the exception of adding a few more tabs and buttons. You can do most network configuration tasks with it, but it is not a very efficient or intuitive interface.

For viewing current network activity, we talk about the Sysinternals TCPView (Recipe 12.9) later in the chapter, which is invaluable for troubleshooting network connectivity issues. Get familiar with it if you haven't already.

Using a Command-Line Interface

Table 12-1 contains all of the command-line tools we use in this chapter.

Table 12-1. Command-line tools used in Chapter 12

Tool	Location	Recipes
devcon	MS KB 311272	12.2
ipconfig	%SystemRoot%\system32	12.1, 12.4, 12.6
linkspeed	Windows Server 2003 Resource Kit	12.12
netdiag	Windows Server 2003 Support Tools	12.11
netsh	%SystemRoot%\system32	12.1, 12.3, 12.5, 12.13
netstat	%SystemRoot%\system32	12.9
netstatp	Sysinternals	12.9
nltest	Windows Server 2003 Support Tools	12.7

Table 12-1. Command-line tools used in Chapter 12 (continued)

Tool	Location	Recipes
ping	%SystemRoot%\system32	12.11
reg	%SystemRoot%\system32	12.7, 12.11
route	%SystemRoot%\system32	12.8
tracert	%SystemRoot%\system32	12.11
wmic	%SystemRoot%\system32\wbem	12.1, 12.11

Using VBScript

Table 12-2 contains the list of WMI classes we use throughout this chapter, including the recipe numbers where each was used.

Table 12-2. WMI classes used in Chapter 12

WMI Class	Description	Recipes
SNMP_RFC1213_MIB_tcpConnTable	Represents the current TCP connections on a system.	12.9
SNMP_RFC1213_MIB_udpTable	Represents the current UDP connections on a system.	12.9
Win32_IP4RouteTable	Represents the routing table of a network adapter. This class is new to Windows XP.	12.8
Win32_NetworkAdapter	Represents network adapters installed in the computer. This class has several read-only properties that describe the manufacturer hardware and software settings.	12.1, 12.3, 12.4, 12.8, 12.12
Win32_NetworkAdapterConfiguration	Represents the network configuration of network adapters. This class has several properties for reading network configuration information and numerous methods for modifying various settings.	12.1, 12.3, 12.4

12.1   Viewing the Network Configuration

Problem

You want to view the network configuration of a computer, including a list of all installed network adapters.

Solution

Using a graphical user interface

1. From the Control Panel, open the Network Connections applet.
2. Open the network connection for which you want to view the settings.
3. Click the Properties button.
4. Click the Configure button to view network adapter properties. Or double-click Internet Protocol (TCP/IP) to view network configuration settings.

Using a command-line interface

To view the list of connections and network configuration on the local system, run the following command:

```
> ipconfig /all
```

To view this information on a remote system, use the Sysinternals *psexec* command:

```
> psexec \\<ComputerName> -u administrator -p MyPass ipconfig /all
```

Another command you can use to view network configuration information is *netsh*, as shown here:

```
> netsh int ip show config
```

Using VBScript

```
' This code displays the network configuration for all connections.
' ------ SCRIPT CONFIGURATION ------
strComputer = "."
' ------ END CONFIGURATION ---------
set objWMI = GetObject("winmgmts:\\" & strComputer & "\root\cimv2")
set colNAs = objWMI.InstancesOf("Win32_NetworkAdapter")
for each objNA in colNAs
    Wscript.Echo objNA.Name
    Wscript.Echo "  Description:   " & objNA.Description
    Wscript.Echo "  Product Name:  " & objNA.ProductName
    Wscript.Echo "  Manufacturer:  " & objNA.Manufacturer
    Wscript.Echo "  Adapter Type:  " & objNA.AdapterType
    Wscript.Echo "  AutoSense:     " & objNA.AutoSense
    Wscript.Echo "  MAC Address:   " & objNA.MACAddress
    Wscript.Echo "  Maximum Speed:" & objNA.MaxSpeed
    Wscript.Echo "  Conn Status:   " & objNA.NetConnectionStatus
    Wscript.Echo "  Service Name:  " & objNA.ServiceName
    Wscript.Echo "  Speed:         " & objNA.Speed

    set colNACs = objWMI.ExecQuery(" select * from " & _
                          " Win32_NetworkAdapterConfiguration " & _
                          "  where Index = " & objNA.Index)
    ' There should only be one item in colNACs
    for each objNAC in colNACs
        if IsArray(objNAC.IPAddress) then
            for each strAddress in objNAC.IPAddress
                Wscript.Echo "  Network Addr: " & strAddress
            next
        end if
        Wscript.Echo "  IP Metric:    " & objNAC.IPConnectionMetric
        Wscript.Echo "  IP Enabled:   " & objNAC.IPEnabled
        Wscript.Echo "  Filter:       " & objNAC.IPFilterSecurityEnabled
        Wscript.Echo "  Port Security:" & objNAC.IPPortSecurityEnabled
        if IsArray(objNAC.IPSubnet) then
            for each strAddress in objNAC.IPSubnet
                Wscript.Echo "  Subnet Mask:  " & strAddress
            next
        end if
```

```
        if IsArray(objNAC.DefaultIPGateway) then
            for each strAddress in objNAC.DefaultIPGateway
                Wscript.Echo "  Gateway Addr: " & strAddress
            next
        end if
        Wscript.Echo "  Database Path:" & objNAC.DatabasePath
        Wscript.Echo "  DHCP Enabled: " & objNAC.DHCPEnabled
        Wscript.Echo "  Lease Expires:" & objNAC.DHCPLeaseExpires
        Wscript.Echo "  Lease Obtained: " & objNAC.DHCPLeaseObtained
        Wscript.Echo "  DHCP Server:  " & objNAC.DHCPServer
        Wscript.Echo "  DNS Domain:   " & objNAC.DNSDomain
        Wscript.Echo "  DNS For WINS: " & objNAC.DNSEnabledForWINSResolution
        Wscript.Echo "  DNS Host Name:" & objNAC.DNSHostName
        if IsArray(objNAC.DNSDomainSuffixSearchorder) then
            for each strName in objNAC.DNSDomainSuffixSearchOrder
                Wscript.Echo "  DNS Suffix Search Order: " & strName
            next
        end if
        if IsArray(objNAC.DNSServerSearchOrder) then
            for each strName in objNAC.DNSServerSearchOrder
                Wscript.Echo "  DNS Server Search Order: " & strName
            next
        end if
        Wscript.Echo "  Domain DNS Reg Enabled: " & _
                        objNAC.DomainDNSRegistrationEnabled
        Wscript.Echo "  Full DNS Reg Enabled: " & _
                        objNAC.FullDNSRegistrationEnabled
        Wscript.Echo "  LMHosts Lookup:    " & objNAC.WINSEnableLMHostsLookup
        Wscript.Echo "  WINS Lookup File:  " & objNAC.WINSHostLookupFile
        Wscript.Echo "  WINS Scope ID:     " & objNAC.WINSScopeID
        Wscript.Echo "  WINS Primary Server: " & objNAC.WINSPrimaryServer
        Wscript.Echo "  WINS Secondary:    " & objNAC.WINSSecondaryServer
    next

    WScript.Echo
next
```

Discussion

There are several different ways to get at the network configuration of a host, as we
showed in the Solution section. And since the scripting solution used WMI, there is
yet another way using *wmic*. Here are two commands that display some of the properties of the Win32_NetworkAdapter and Win32_NetworkAdapterConfiguration WMI
classes, respectively:

```
> wmic nic list brief
> wmic nicconfig list brief
```

To view all available properties for those classes, replace brief with full in both
commands.

12.2   Disabling a Connection

Problem

You want to disable a network connection for either a virtual interface or a network adapter.

Solution

Using a graphical user interface

1. From the Control Panel open the Network Connections applet.
2. Right-click the network connection you want to disable and select Disable.

Using a command-line interface

You would think that it would be straightforward to disable a connection from the command line, but unfortunately that is not the case. In fact, the *netsh* command supports disabling connections, but only non-LAN interfaces, which is very disappointing.

But all is not lost! There is an alternative if you really must have a way to disable connections from the command line. The *devcon.exe* tool is the command-line alternative to the Device Manager interface and comes with the Driver Development Kit (DDK). You can download it separately by viewing MS KB 311272 (*http://support.microsoft.com/ default.aspx?scid=311272*).

Once you have it downloaded, run this command to get a list of all network devices:

```
> devcon listclass net
```

This displays the list of devices in two columns. The left column contains the hardware ID for each device, and the right column contains the description for the device.

After you've found the device you want to disable, run the following command:

```
> devcon disable =net <HardwareID>
```

For example:

```
> devcon disable =net PCI\VEN_14B9^&DEV_A504^&SUBSYS_500014B9^&REV_00
```

There are a couple of important things we need to point out. First, if the hardware ID contains any ampersands (&), you have to escape them using a caret (^). Otherwise, the CMD session will interpret everything after the first & as another command and *devcon* will attempt to match any hardware ID that matches the string up until the first &. This can be dangerous because it can cause you to disable devices you didn't intend to.

Second, if the hardware ID contains two backslashes, remove the second backslash and everything following it. For example, if the `listall` command returned this for a device we wanted to disable:

```
PCI\VEN_14B9&DEV_A504&SUBSYS_500014B9&REV_00\4&39A85202&0&10F0: Cisco Systems PC I
Wireless LAN Adapter
```

then we would need to use this as the hardware ID (including the carets):

```
PCI\VEN_14B9^&DEV_A504^&SUBSYS_500014B9^&REV_00
```

Using VBScript

If you thought the command line way to disable connections was painful, we won't even begin to describe how it can be done via a script. There is a way, but it essentially involves simulating the steps in the graphical solution. Because the script is a major hack and not very reliable, we won't include it here. We will make it available on the book's website (*http://www.rallenhome.com/*) in case you are still interested.

A somewhat viable mechanism for using VBScript is to shell out to the *devcon.exe* tool to accomplish your objectives. Don't forget the escaping!

Discussion

Some workstations come with two network adapters installed to avoid a single point of failure with the network connection. Generally, you'll only want one connection to be active and use the other as a back up. There are a couple of ways to do this. One is to simply disable one of the connections and manually enable it if the primary fails. Since you probably won't have network connectivity after the primary adapter fails, you'll need another way to access the server, such as an out-of-band console connection of some type.

Another way to do this is to use a feature that many hardware vendors support now called *teaming*. With teaming, both adapters are used to form a virtual adapter. If the primary adapter becomes unavailable, the backup takes over automatically. (See your hardware vendor for more details.) The problem with teaming is that, depending on the implementation, it can be unreliable and ultimately cause more configuration headache than it is worth. We recommend testing teaming configurations thoroughly before implementing them in production.

See Also

MS KB 262265, "Error Message When You Use Netsh.exe to Enable or Disable a Network Adapter"

12.3   Configuring an IP Address

Problem

You want to configure a static IP address or DHCP for a connection.

Solution

Using a graphical user interface

1. From the Control Panel open the Network Connections applet.
2. Double-click the connection you want to configure.
3. Click the Properties button.
4. Double-click Internet Protocol (TCP/IP).
5. To enable DHCP, select Obtain an IP address automatically. To use a static address, select Use the following IP address. Then configure the IP address, subnet mask, and default gateway.
6. Click OK until all windows are closed.

Using a command-line interface

The following command configures DHCP for a connection:

```
> netsh int ip set address name="<ConnectionName>" source=dhcp
```

Here is an example for configuring the connection named "Local Area Connection" to use DHCP:

```
> netsh int ip set address name="Local Area Connection" source=dhcp
```

This configures a connection with a static IP and default gateway:

```
> netsh int ip set address name="<ConnectionName>" source=static <IP> <Mask>
<GateWayIP> <Metric>
```

This example configures a static IP address for "Local Area Connection":

```
> netsh int ip set address name="Local Area Connection" source=static 10.3.53.3
255.255.255.0 10.3.53.1 1
```

Using VBScript

```
' This code enables DHCP for the specified connection.
' ------ SCRIPT CONFIGURATION ------
strComputer = "."
strConnection = "Local Area Connection"
' ------ END CONFIGURATION ---------
set objWMI = GetObject("winmgmts:\\" & strComputer & "\root\cimv2")
set colNA = objWMI.ExecQuery("select * " & _
                       " from Win32_NetworkAdapter " & _
                       " where NetConnectionID = '" & strConnection & "'" )
```

```
        for each objNA in colNA
            set colNAConfig = objWMI.ExecQuery _
                ("ASSOCIATORS OF {Win32_NetworkAdapter.DeviceID='" & _
                    objNA.DeviceID & "'} " & _
                " WHERE resultClass = win32_NetworkAdapterConfiguration ")
            for each objNAConfig in colNAConfig
                if objNAConfig.DHCPEnabled = True then
                    WScript.Echo "DHCP already enabled for " & strConnection
                else
                    intRC = objNAConfig.EnableDHCP( )
                    if intRC = 0 then
                        WScript.Echo "DHCP Enabled for " & strConnection
                    elseif intRC = 1 then
                        WScript.Echo "You must reboot to start using DHCP for " & _

                    else
                        WScript.Echo "There was an error enabling DHCP for " & _
                                    strconnection & ": " & intRC
                    end if
                end if
            next
        next


' This code configures an IP address, subnet mask and default gateway
' for the specified connection.
' ------ SCRIPT CONFIGURATION ------
strComputer = "."
strConnection = "Local Area Connection"
strIP = Array("1.22.2.2")
strMask = Array("255.255.255.0")
strGatewayIP = Array("1.2.3.3")
' ------ END CONFIGURATION ---------
set objWMI = GetObject("winmgmts:\\" & strComputer & "\root\cimv2")
set colNA = objWMI.ExecQuery("select * " & _
                        " from Win32_NetworkAdapter " & _
                        " where NetConnectionID = '" & strConnection & "'" )
for each objNA in colNA
    set colNAConfig = objWMI.ExecQuery _
        ("ASSOCIATORS OF {Win32_NetworkAdapter.DeviceID='" & _
            objNA.DeviceID & "'} " & _
        " WHERE resultClass = win32_NetworkAdapterConfiguration ")
    for each objNAConfig in colNAConfig
        intRC = objNAConfig.EnableStatic(strIP,strMask)
        intRC2 = objNAConfig.SetGateways(strGatewayIP)
        if intRC = 0 and intRC2 = 0 then
            WScript.Echo "IP address configured for " & strConnection
        elseif intRC = 1 or intRC2 = 1 then
            WScript.Echo "You must reboot for the changes to take effect for " & _
                        strConnection
        else
            WScript.Echo "There was an error configuring IP for " & _
                        strconnection & ": " & intRC & " and " & intRC2
```

```
        end if
    next
next
```

Discussion

If you use static IP addresses, any time you add a new computer to the network, you have to configure an IP address on that computer. However, there is no reason why you can't automate the process using either the *netsh* command we showed in the command line solution or with WMI. You still have to find an available IP address, which may not be easy to automate depending on your environment, but at least you can provision the IP address in an automated fashion.

12.4   Renewing or Releasing a DHCP IP Address

Problem

You want to release or renew an IP address obtained via DHCP.

Solution

Using a graphical user interface

1. From the Control Panel, open the Network Connections applet.
2. Right-click the DHCP-enabled network connection you want to renew and select Repair. This will automatically attempt to renew the connection's IP address.

Using a command-line interface

The following commands renew and release a DHCP IP address, respectively:

```
> ipconfig /renew
> ipconfig /release
```

With either of these commands you can specify a pattern to match if you want to affect only a subset of adapters. The following command would release the IP address for any adapter that had "Con" (e.g., Local Area Connection 1) in its name:

```
> ipconfig /renew *Con*
```

Using VBScript

```
' This code releases all DHCP IP addresses.
' ------ SCRIPT CONFIGURATION ------
strComputer = "."
' ------ END CONFIGURATION ---------
set objWMI = GetObject("winmgmts:\\" & strComputer & "\root\cimv2")
set objAdapterConfig = objWMI.Get("Win32_NetworkAdapterConfiguration")
intRC = objAdapterConfig.ReleaseDHCPLeaseAll( )
if intRC = 0 then
```

```
      WScript.Echo "Released all DHCP IP addresses"
elseif intRC = 1 then
      WScript.Echo "You must reboot to release all DHCP IP addresses"
else
      WScript.Echo "There was an error releasing all DHCP IP addresses: " & intRC
end if


' This code shows performs the same function as the previous example
' but it performs a query for all DHCP enabled IP addresses.  Use this
' if you don't want to release all IP addresses.  Modify the WQL statement
' based on the criteria you need.
' ------ SCRIPT CONFIGURATION ------
strComputer = "."
' ------ END CONFIGURATION ---------
set objWMI = GetObject("winmgmts:\\" & strComputer & "\root\cimv2")
set colNetworkAdapters = objWMI.ExecQuery _
      ("Select * From Win32_NetworkAdapterConfiguration Where DHCPEnabled = True")
for each objNetworkConfig in colNetworkAdapters
      intRC = objNetworkConfig.ReleaseDHCPLease( )
      if intRC = 0 then
         WScript.Echo "Released IP address for " & objNetworkConfig.Description
      elseif intRC = 1 then
         WScript.Echo "You must reboot to release the IP address for " & _
                     objNetworkConfig.Description
      else
         WScript.Echo "There was an error releasing the IP address for " & _
                     objNetworkConfig.Description & ": " & intRC
      end if
next


' This code renews all DHCP IP addresses.
' ------ SCRIPT CONFIGURATION ------
strComputer = "."
' ------ END CONFIGURATION ---------
set objWMI = GetObject("winmgmts:\\" & strComputer & "\root\cimv2")
set objAdapterConfig = objWMI.Get("Win32_NetworkAdapterConfiguration")
intRC = objAdapterConfig.RenewDHCPLeaseAll( )
if intRC = 0 then
      WScript.Echo "Renewed all DHCP IP addresses"
elseif intRC = 1 then
      WScript.Echo "You must reboot to renew all DHCP IP addresses"
else
      WScript.Echo "There was an error renewing all DHCP IP addresses: " & intRC
end if


' This code renews all adapters made by Intel that are installed on the system.
' ------ SCRIPT CONFIGURATION ------
strComputer = "."
' ------ END CONFIGURATION ---------
```

```
set objWMI = GetObject("winmgmts:\\" & strComputer & "\root\cimv2")
set colNAs = objWMI.ExecQuery("select * " & _
                              " from Win32_NetworkAdapter    " & _
                              " where manufacturer = 'Intel' " )
for each objNA in colNAs
    set colSubNAConfig = objWMI.ExecQuery _
        ("ASSOCIATORS OF {Win32_NetworkAdapter.DeviceID='" & _
          objNA.DeviceID & "'} " & _
        " WHERE resultClass = win32_NetworkAdapterConfiguration ")

    for each objNAConfig in colSubNAConfig
        if objNAConfig.DHCPEnabled = True then
            intRC = objNAConfig.RenewDHCPLease( )
            if intRC = 0 then
                WScript.Echo "Renewed IP address for " & objNA.Name
            elseif intRC = 1 then
                WScript.Echo "You must reboot to renew the IP address for " & _
                        objNA.Name
            else
                WScript.Echo "There was an error renewing the IP address for " & _
                        objNA.Name & ": " & intRC
            end if
        end if
    next
next
```

Discussion

Fortunately, the whole DHCP release/renew process is automatic and not something
you have to do manually. When a client receives a DHCP lease for an IP address, it
will automatically attempt to renew that address after 50% of the lease duration. The
DHCP Server can grant the renewal, after which the client restarts its lease timer. If
the server doesn't respond, the client tries again after 87.5% of the lease duration
and then attempts to contact other DHCP Servers.

Even though this process is automatic, there may be times when you need to initiate
it yourself—especially if you've made network configuration changes. For example,
let's say you configured a reservation on your DHCP Server for a particular host. If
that host already has an IP address, you'll need to release the current lease and run
the renew command to get the new address.

12.5 Configuring DNS Settings

Problem

You want to configure the DNS settings on a system.

Solution

Using a graphical user interface

To configure the DNS suffix, do the following:

1. From the Control Panel, open the System applet.
2. Select the Computer Name tab.
3. Click the Change button.
4. Click the More button.
5. Enter the suffix under the Primary DNS suffix of this computer heading.
6. Check the box beside Change primary DNS suffix when domain membership changes if you want the suffix to change to the name of the Active Directory domain the computer joins.
7. Click OK until all the windows are closed. You will be prompted to reboot for the changes to take effect.

To modify the list of DNS servers used during name resolution, configure how unqualified names are resolved, and configure DNS dynamic registration, do the following:

1. From the Control Panel, open the Network Connections applet.
2. Double-click the connection you want to modify.
3. Choose the Internet Protocol (TCP/IP) item in the list.
4. From this screen you can configure whether to use the DNS servers obtained through DHCP or to manually enter them. In the latter case, you can enter preferred and alternate DNS servers.
5. To configure the other DNS settings, click the Advanced button.
6. Select the DNS tab.
7. From this screen you can configure additional DNS servers to use during resolution, configure how unqualified names are handled, set a DNS suffix for this connection, and configure DNS registration for this connection.
8. When you are done, click OK until all screens are closed.

Using a command-line interface

To view the current DNS configuration for all connections on the local system, run this command:

```
> netsh int ip show dns
```

To make a connection use DHCP-specified DNS settings, use this command:

```
> netsh int ip set dns "<ConnectionName>" dhcp
```

Here is an example:

```
> netsh int ip set dns "Local Area Connection" dhcp
```

To make a connection use a specified DNS server for name resolution, use this command:

```
> netsh int ip set dns "Local Area Connection" static <IPAddress>
```

Here is an example:

```
> netsh int ip set dns "Local Area Connection" static 10.0.0.1
```

This command allows you to specify only one DNS server for name resolution.

With the same command, you can also configure whether the connection registers the host's name under the primary DNS suffix or the connection-specific suffix. To register just the primary DNS suffix, append "primary" to the end of the command. To register both, append "both." To register nothing, append "none." Here is an example:

```
> netsh int ip set dns "Local Area Connection" static 10.0.0.1 primary
```

Discussion

With Windows Server 2003 Active Directory, you can set most Windows XP DNS client settings via Group Policy.

You can configure the DNS suffix, dynamic updates settings, search list, and DNS servers used for name resolution among many other settings. These settings can be found by navigating the following path of a Group Policy Object: Computer Configuration → Administrative Templates → Network → DNS Client.

 Be careful with this setting, as users that use their laptops to connect to third-party ISPs end up inheriting your company's DNS settings and their third party connections may not work.

See Also

MS KB 178277, "INFO: Setting DNS Domain Suffix Search Order During an Unattended Installation," MS KB 246804, "How to enable or disable dynamic DNS registrations in Windows 2000 and in Windows Server 2003," and MS KB 275553, "How to Configure a Domain Suffix Search List on the Domain Name System Clients"

12.6 Registering DNS Records or Flushing the DN Cache

Problem

You want to register a system's DNS records dynamically or flush the local DNS cache.

Solution

Using a command-line interface

The following command displays the contents of the local DNS cache:

```
> ipconfig /displaydns
```

And this clears that cache:

```
> ipconfig /flushdns
```

The following command causes the local host to re-register its DNS records via dynamic DNS:

```
> ipconfig /registerdns
```

Using VBScript

```
' This code flushes the local DNS cache.  There are no scripting
' interfaces designed to do this so I have to shell out and run
' the ipconfig /flushdns command.
strCommand = "ipconfig /flushdns"
set objWshShell = WScript.CreateObject("WScript.Shell")
intRC = objWshShell.Run(strCommand, 0, TRUE)
if intRC <> 0 then
   WScript.Echo "Error returned from running the command: " & intRC
else
   WScript.Echo "Command executed successfully"
end if


' This code registers DNS records for the local host.  There are
' no scripting interfaces designed to do this so I have to shell
' out and run the ipconfig /registerhdns command.
strCommand = "ipconfig /registerdns"
set objWshShell = WScript.CreateObject("WScript.Shell")
intRC = objWshShell.Run(strCommand, 0, TRUE)
if intRC <> 0 then
   WScript.Echo "Error returned from running the command: " & intRC
else
   WScript.Echo "Command executed successfully"
end if
```

Discussion

The Windows operating system maintains a name resolution cache of DNS records that the system has queried. This cache is maintained in memory and speeds up future requests for the same record. Each record has an associated time-to-live value. This setting informs clients of the maximum amount of time to cache that particular record. After the time-to-live period expires, Windows removes the record from its cache.

The Windows name resolution cache is maintained by the DNS Cache (DnsCache) service. You can prevent records from being cached by stopping this service (and disabling it if you never want records to be cached again). If you are getting strange results when querying DNS, you may want to view the local DNS cache just to see if you are accessing locally cached records instead of what is current on the DNS Server.

The /registerdns option of ipconfig attempts to dynamically re-register DNS records for all IP addresses configured on the system. The DHCP Client (Dhcp) service does the DNS re-registration, so if that service is disabled, the /registerdns option won't work (even if all addresses are statically configured).

See Also

MS KB 245437, "How to Disable Client-Side DNS Caching in Windows," MS KB 264539, "Dynamic DNS Updates Do Not Work if the DHCP Client Service Stops," and MS KB 318803, "How to Disable Client-Side DNS Caching in Windows XP and Windows Server 2003"

12.7 Finding a Computer's Active Directory Site

Problem

You want to find the Active Directory site a computer is part of, which is based on the IP address of the computer.

Solution

Using a command-line interface

In the following command replace *<HostName>* with the name of the host you want to find the site for.

```
> nltest /server:<HostName> /DsGetSite
```

To force a computer to use a particular site, modify the Registry as follows:

```
> reg add HKLM\System\CurrentControlSet\Services\Netlogon\Parameters /v SiteName /t
REG_SZ /d <SiteName>
```

Using VBScript

Although you cannot use it directly from a scripting language such as VBScript, Microsoft provides a DsGetSiteName method that can be used by languages such as Visual Basic and C++ to retrieve site coverage information. In fact, the nltest command shown in the CLI solution is a wrapper around this method.

The IADsTools interface provides a wrapper around this method:

```
set objIadsTools = CreateObject("IADsTools.DCFunctions")
strSite = objIadsTools.DsGetSiteName("<HostName>")
Wscript.Echo "Site: " & strSite
```

```
' This code forces the host the script is run on to use a particular site
' ------ SCRIPT CONFIGURATION ------
strSite = "<SiteName>"    ' e.g. Raleigh
' ------ END CONFIGURATION ---------
strNetlogonReg = "SYSTEM\CurrentControlSet\Services\Netlogon\Parameters"
const HKLM = &H80000002
set objReg = GetObject("winmgmts:root\default:StdRegProv")
objReg.SetStringValue HKLM, strNetlogonReg, "SiteName", strSite
WScript.Echo "Set SiteName to " & strSite
```

Discussion

Each domain controller has a server object that is contained within a site. Clients are different—they are associated with a site based on their IP address, and the corresponding subnet that it matches is in the Subnets container. The client site information is important because it determines which domain controller it will authenticate against. If the client's IP address does not match a subnet range of any of the subnets stored in Active Directory, it will randomly pick a site to use, which means it could authenticate against any domain controller in the domain.

Finding the site that contains a client is an important first step when troubleshooting authentication delays or errors. If a client is experiencing significant delays, it could be that the client is authenticating with a random site because it is on a new subnet that has yet to be added to Active Directory. This may also result in a client authenticating over a slow WAN link.

You can bypass the part of the DC Locator process that determines a client's site by hard-coding it in the Registry. This is generally not recommended and should primarily be used as a troubleshooting tool. If a client is experiencing authentication delays due to a misconfigured site or subnet object, you can hard-code its site so they temporarily point to a more optimal location (and domain controller).

See Also

MS KB 247811, "How Domain Controllers Are Located in Windows," and MSDN: DsGetSiteName

---

12.8 Managing Routes

Problem

You want to view the routing table on a system or possibly configure static routes. Configuring static routes generally isn't needed with today's networks, but it can be necessary especially when working in restricted lab environments that are not fully routed.

Solution

Using a command-line interface

The following command displays all the static and dynamic routes on a system:

```
> route print
```

 For a good overview of what each column represents in the route print output, see MS KB 140859.

This command only shows routes that start with 64:

```
> route print 64.*
```

To add a temporary route (one that is erased after the system reboots), use this command:

```
> route ADD <Network> MASK <Mask> <Gateway> METRIC <Metric> IF <Interface#>
```

Example:

```
> route ADD 157.0.0.0 MASK 255.0.0.0  157.55.80.1 METRIC 3 IF 2
```

To add a permanent route, use the same command as before except include the –p switch. To delete a route, use this command:

```
> route DELETE <Network>
```

Example:

```
> route DELETE 157.0.0.0
```

Using VBScript

```
' This code prints similar information to the "route print" command.
' ------ SCRIPT CONFIGURATION ------
strComputer = "."
' ------ END CONFIGURATION ---------
set objWMI = GetObject("winmgmts:\\" & strComputer & "\root\cimv2")
set colRoutes = objWMI.InstancesOf("Win32_IP4RouteTable")
for each objRoute in colRoutes
```

```
        WScript.Echo "Network:    " & objRoute.Destination
        WScript.Echo "NetMask:    " & objRoute.Mask
        WScript.Echo "Gateway:    " & objRoute.NextHop
        WScript.Echo "Metric:     " & objRoute.Metric1

        ' Other properties you can display:
        ' WScript.Echo "Age: " & objRoute.Age
        ' WScript.Echo "Description: " & objRoute.Description
        ' WScript.Echo "Information: " & objRoute.Information
        ' WScript.Echo "Interface Index: " & objRoute.InterfaceIndex
        ' WScript.Echo "Metric 2: " & objRoute.Metric2
        ' WScript.Echo "Metric 3: " & objRoute.Metric3
        ' WScript.Echo "Metric 4: " & objRoute.Metric4
        ' WScript.Echo "Metric 5: " & objRoute.Metric5
        ' WScript.Echo "Name: " & objRoute.Name
        ' WScript.Echo "Protocol: " & objRoute.Protocol
        ' WScript.Echo "Status: " & objRoute.Status
        ' WScript.Echo "Type: " & objRoute.Type

        WScript.Echo
next


        ' This code shows how to add a route.
        ' ------ SCRIPT CONFIGURATION ------
        strComputer = "."
        ' ------ END CONFIGURATION ---------
        set objLocator = CreateObject("WbemScripting.SWbemLocator")
        set objWMI = objLocator.ConnectServer(strComputer, "root/CIMv2")

        set objR = objWMI.get("Win32_IP4RouteTable").SpawnInstance_()
        objR.Destination = "64.0.0.0"
        objR.NextHop = "64.102.57.1"
        objR.Mask = "255.0.0.0"
        objR.InterfaceIndex = 65539
        objR.Metric1 = 22
        objR.Protocol = 1
        objR.Type = 4
        objR.Put_()
        Wscript.Echo "Successfully created route"
```

Discussion

If networks are designed properly, you shouldn't have to worry much about how
traffic is being routed. Nevertheless, in certain situations where the network is not
fully routed or you are experiencing routing issues, you may need to dig into a system's routing tables a bit. You can also add static routes to temporarily get traffic
flowing the way you want to or force it to go a certain way. However, we do not recommend configuring permanent static routes if you can avoid it. This type of manual configuration if often overlooked or forgotten about and can be a headache to
track down later unless the configuration changes are well known by all who are
maintaining the system.

See Also

MS KB 140859, "TCP/IP Routing Basics for Windows NT," and MS KB 157025, "Default Gateway Configuration for Multihomed Computers"

12.9 Viewing the Open Ports and Connections

Problem

You want to view the open ports and connections on a system.

Solution

Using downloadable software

The Sysinternals TCPView tool is a graphical interface that displays all of the active connections on a host. It displays all of the connection information you might need, including process name and ID, protocol, local address and port, and remote address and port. It is a real-time tool, so it shows connections that are terminating in red, and new connections in green. You can close a connection by right clicking it and selecting Close Connection. You can also kill the associated process by selecting End Process. See Figure 12-1 for a screenshot of TCPView.

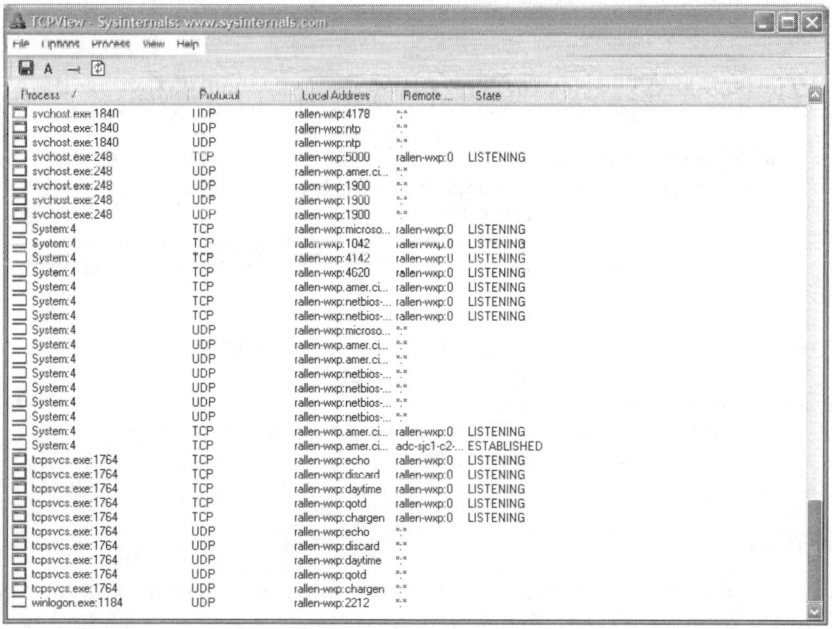

Figure 12-1. Sysinternals TCPView screenshot

Using a command-line interface

The *netstat* command displays all established connections on a host:

```
> netstat
```

Use the –a option to view all open ports, regardless if they are active. With the Windows XP version of *netstat*, you can view the process ID associated with connections by specifying the –o option.

The Sysinternals *netstatp* utility is the command line version of TCPView. It displays similar information to *netstat*, but it shows the process name and ID associated with the connection by default:

```
> netstatp
```

Using VBScript

```
' This code produces output very similar to the 'netstat -an' command.
' It requires that the target system have SNMP and the WMI SNMP
' Provider installed.
' ------ SCRIPT CONFIGURATION ------
strComputerIP = "127.0.0.1"
' ------ END CONFIGURATION ---------
set objLocator = CreateObject("WbemScripting.SWbemLocator")
set objWMI = objLocator.ConnectServer("", "root/snmp/localhost")
set objNamedValueSet = CreateObject("WbemScripting.SWbemNamedValueSet")
objNamedValueSet.Add "AgentAddress", strComputerIP
objNamedValueSet.Add "AgentReadCommunityName", "public"
objNamedValueSet.Add "AgentWriteCommunityName", "public"

WScript.Echo " Proto  Local Address    Foreign Address        State"
set colTCPConns = objWMI.Instancesof("SNMP_RFC1213_MIB_tcpConnTable",, _
                                     objNamedValueSet )
for each objConn in colTCPConns
       WScript.echo "  TCP    " & objConn.tcpConnLocalAddress & ":" & _
                    objConn.tcpConnLocalPort & _
                    "          " & objConn.tcpConnRemAddress & ":" & _
                    objConn.tcpConnRemPort & "         " & objConn.tcpConnState
next

set colUDPConns = objWMI.Instancesof("SNMP_RFC1213_MIB_udpTable",, _
                                     objNamedValueSet )
for each objConn in colUDPConns
       WScript.echo "  UDP    " & objConn.udpLocalAddress & ":" & _
                    objConn.udpLocalPort & "         *:*"
next
```

Discussion

When you take a look at the list of open connections on a system, you may be surprised to see so many. Unless the system is extremely busy, most should be in the Listening state, which simply means the port is open and waiting for a connection. For more on the various states that a connection may be in, see MS KB 137984.

See Also

MS KB 137984, "TCP Connection States and Netstat Output," and MS KB 281336, "How to determine which program uses or blocks specific transmission control protocol ports in Windows"

12.10 Troubleshooting Network Connectivity Problems

Problem

You want to troubleshoot network connectivity problems. This is often necessary if a client is experiencing slow logins or network-based failures when accessing resources.

Solution

First and above all else, make sure your network adapter is working. Generally there should be a flashing green light to indicate the adapter is connected and transmitting data.

After you've checked the hardware, you can run several command line tools to aid in troubleshooting connectivity issues. A good first step is to ping the target host, which can tell you if the remote host is reachable and how long it takes to reach it:

```
> ping <HostNameOrIP>
```

Here are some of the status messages you can receive from *ping*:

Reply
> The host was reachable.

Request timed out
> The target host either did not respond or there is no host configured with the corresponding IP address. You may also see this message if there is a lot of network latency between the two endpoints. You can work around this by using the –w option with ping and specify the number of milliseconds to wait for each reply.

Unknown host
> If you used a DNS name in the ping command, this indicates that the DNS name was not resolvable by the DNS client.

Destination unreachable
> The ICMP traffic could not reach the network of the target host. This is often due to a routing problem on an intermediate router, a router being down, or a firewall blocking ICMP.

If you've pinged a host and the request timed out or the host was unreachable, a good tool to try next is *tracert*, which attempts to trace a route from the source computer to the destination computer.

```
> tracert <HostNameOrIP>
```

This command shows you the path your data takes to get to the destination. If there are connectivity problems with a remote host, this command shows where along the path to the host the problem occurs.

If everything checks out, next run the *netdiag* command on the target system. *netdiag* provides a wealth of information about various network settings configured on the system along with information about DNS, Kerberos, and Active Directory connectivity. Use the /debug option to view detailed output. If you suspect authentication (Kerberos) to be a potential issue, run the *kerbtray* utility to ensure you have functioning Kerberos tickets.

If you are still having network problems, a good last step is to look at the network traffic to see if you can spot any obvious errors being transmitted. See Recipe 12.11 for more information.

See Also

MS KB 169790, "How to Troubleshoot Basic TCP/IP Problems," MS KB 321708, "HOW TO: Use the Network Diagnostics Tool (Netdiag.exe) in Windows 2000," MS KB 219289, "Description of the Netdiag/fix Switch," MS KB 314067, "How to troubleshoot TCP/IP connectivity with Windows XP," and MS KB 325487, "How to troubleshoot network connectivity problems"

12.11 Configuring TCP/IP Filtering

Problem

You want to configure TCP/IP filtering either to prevent a system from responding to certain protocols or ports, or to allow it to respond only to certain protocols or ports. This filtering is applied to inbound traffic and does not affect outbound traffic.

Solution

Using a graphical user interface

1. Open the Control Panel.
2. From the Network Connections applet, open the connection you want to configure.
3. Click the Properties button.
4. Select Internet Protocol (TCP/IP).

5. Click the Properties button.

6. Click the Advanced button.

7. Click the Options tab.

8. Select TCP/IP filtering.

9. Click the Properties button.

10. Check the box beside Enable TCP/IP Filtering.

11. Select Permit Only for TCP Ports, UDP Ports, and/or IP Protocols.

12. Click the Add button.

13. Enter the port or protocol number and click OK.

14. Repeat the last three steps until you've entered all desired ports and protocols.

15. After you are done, close all the dialog screens by clicking either OK or Close.

16. You will be prompted to reboot for the changes to take effect.

Using a command-line interface

The following command enables TCP/IP filtering:

```
> reg add HKLM\SYSTEM\CurrentControlSet\Services\Tcpip\Parameters /v
EnableSecurityFilters /t REG_DWORD /d 1
```

You must reboot for the changes to take effect. To disable filtering, change /d 1 to /d 0.

Next, configure the protocols and ports you want to filter. This must be done on a per-interface basis. To configure this using the Registry, you need to know the GUID assigned to the interface you want to modify. This is a sample interface entry:

```
HKLM\SYSTEM\CurrentControlSet\Services\Tcpip\Parameters\Interfaces\{07383FC4-FF4D-
4E16-9DD6-C27061719D76}
```

To find out what adapter that corresponds to, you can use this command (on Windows XP):

```
> wmic nicconfig get caption,settingid
```

Once you know the GUID of the interface, you can use the reg add command to modify the RawIPAllowedProtocols, TCPAllowedPorts, or UDPAllowedPorts values to filter what you want. Each of those values is of type REG_MULTI_SZ. Here is an example of setting protocols 25 and 80:

```
reg add HKLM\SYSTEM\CurrentControlSet\Services\Tcpip\Parameters\Interfaces\{07383FC4-
FF4D-4E16-9DD6-C27061719D76} /v RawIPAllowedProtocols /t REG_MULTI_SZ /d 25\080
```

You can also use WMIC utility to configure TCP/IP filtering. These two commands show you how:

```
> wmic /node:"<ServerName>" nicconfig call EnableIPFilterSec(1)
> wmic /node:"<ServerName>" nicconfig where ipenabled=True call EnableIPSec
(<TCPPortList>),(<UDPPortList>),(<ProtoList>)
```

This command allows all TCP and UDP ports, but allows only protocols 80 (http) and 25 (smtp):

```
> wmic nicconfig where ipenabled=True call EnableIPSec (80,25),(0),(0)
```

Using VBScript

```
' This code enables IP Filtering for all adapters and configures
' filtering for all IP-enabled adapters.
' ------ SCRIPT CONFIGURATION ------
strComputer = "."
arrTCPPorts = Array ( 0 )        ' Allow all TCP ports
arrUDPPorts = Array ( 0 )        ' Allow all UDP ports
arrProtos   = Array ( 80, 25 )  ' Allow only HTTP and SMTP
' ------ END CONFIGURATION ---------
set objWMI = GetObject("winmgmts:\\" & strComputer & "\root\cimv2")
set objAdapterConfig = objWMI.Get("Win32_NetworkAdapterConfiguration")
intRC = objAdapterConfig.EnableIPFilterSec( True )
if intRC = 0 then
   WScript.Echo "IP Filtering for all adapters enabled"
elseif intRC = 1 then
   WScript.Echo "IP Filtering enabled for all adapters, " & _
                "but you must reboot for the changes to take effect"
else
   WScript.Echo "There was an error enabling IP Filtering for all " & _
                "adapters: " & intRC
end if

set colNAConfigs = objWMI.ExecQuery( _
                         "select * " & _
                         " from Win32_NetworkAdapterConfiguration " & _
                         " where IPEnabled = True" )
for each objNAConfig in colNAConfigs
   intRC = objNAConfig.EnableIPSec( arrTCPPorts, arrUDPPorts, arrProtos )
   if intRC = 0 then
      WScript.Echo "IP Filtering configured for '" & _
                   objNAConfig.Description & "'"
   elseif intRC = 1 then
      WScript.Echo "IP Filtering configured for '" & objNAConfig.Description & _
                   "', but you must reboot for the changes to take effect"
   else
      WScript.Echo "There was an error configuring IP Filtering for '" & _
                   objNAConfig.Description & "': " & intRC
   end if
next
```

Discussion

Filtering by port or protocol can be useful in certain situations, but be aware of the limitations. A good example of when you might want to configure filtering is for external web servers. If your web server is running on the default HTTP port (80) and it is running no other networked application, then you only really need port 80 open. But allowing only port 80 traffic, you also prevent the system from acting as a member in an Active Directory domain (which requires several ports to be open) and it makes remote administration difficult because you won't be able to connect using the Terminal Services client. Obviously you can add these ports to the list you allow, but it is good to keep in mind that if you go down the road of port/protocol filtering, be sure you have the ports/protocols open that are needed to support the system (see Recipe 12.9 for more on how to get the list of open ports on a system).

See Also

For the list of pre-assigned port numbers, see the following site: *http://www.iana.org/ assignments/port-numbers*, MS KB 289892, "Internet Protocol Numbers," and MS KB 309798, "HOW TO: Configure TCP/IP Filtering in Windows 2000)"

12.12 Measuring Link Speed and Latency Between Two Hosts

Problem

You want to measure the link speed between two hosts.

Solution

Using a command-line interface

The Windows Server 2003 Resource Kit includes a new tool called *linkspeed*, which measures the connectivity between two hosts. You run the command from one system and target a remote system:

```
> linkspeed /s \\<ServerName>
> linkspeed /s <ServerDNSName>
```

Alternatively, you can specify the /dc switch to have it test the system's current domain controller:

```
> linkspeed /dc
```

Discussion

Finding the link speed between two hosts is often useful when troubleshooting network connectivity problems. For example, if a client is having problems authenticating to Active Directory, you should find out the link speed between the client and the domain controller with which it is authenticating. A slow speed, perhaps due to congestion, could be the cause. If you want to determine the average link speed between two hosts, you should run the *linkspeed* command several times over multiple days. The results for any particular run of *linkspeed* could vary significantly depending on what is happening in the network at that time.

12.13 Installing the IPv6 Stack

Problem

You want to install and configure the IPv6 stack on a system.

Solution

Using a graphical user interface

1. Open the Control Panel.
2. From the Network Connections applet, double-click the connection you want to install IPv6 for.
3. Click the Properties button.
4. Click the Install button.
5. Select Protocol and click the Add button.
6. Select Microsoft TCP/IP version 6 and click OK.
7. Click Close.

Using a command-line interface

The following command installs the IPv6 stack. It must be run directly on the target system:

```
> netsh interface ipv6 install
```

If you need to run the command remotely, you can use the *psexec* command:

```
> psexec \\server01 netsh interface ipv6 install
```

Using VBScript

There is no scripting interface to install the stack, but you can shell out and run the *netsh* command as in the following example:

```
' This code installs the IPv6 on the computer the script is run from.
strCommand = "netsh interface ipv6 install"
set objWshShell = WScript.CreateObject("WScript.Shell")
intRC = objWshShell.Run(strCommand, 0, TRUE)
if intRC <> 0 then
    WScript.Echo "Error returned from running the command: " & intRC
else
    WScript.Echo "Command executed successfully"
end if
```

Discussion

Windows XP provides native support for IPv6, which is the next generation TCP/IP protocol suite intended to replace IPv4. Adoption of IPv6 has been slow, but seems to be steadily gaining momentum. Fortunately, Windows XP provides better support for IPv6 than did Windows 2000. For a good overview of IPv6 and how to configure the Windows client, see the following site: *http://www.microsoft.com/ipv6*.

IPv6 has caused some XP systems to hang, so if you experience problems after installing IPv6, try uninstalling it:

1. Log onto XP using an administrator's account.

2. Right-click My Network Places, and choose Properties.

3. Right-click your Internet connection and choose Properties and click the General tab.

4. Select IPv6 Protocol and click the Uninstall button. Follow the directions and restart your PC.

5. After your computer restarts, log on as an administrator.

6. Type services.msc at the Run box or command prompt to run the Microsoft Management Console.

7. In the Services area to the right, right-click IPv6, choose Properties, and in the Startup type box choose Disabled from the drop-down menu. Note: IPv6 may not show up in the Microsoft Management Console; if it doesn't, don't worry—that means your problem has been solved.

For more details refer to MS KB 555059.

See Also

MS KB 325449, "HOW TO: Install and Configure IP Version 6 in Windows Server 2003 Enterprise Server"

CHAPTER 13
The Internet

13.0 Introduction

Increasingly, what people do when they use their computers is use the Internet. It's become an absolutely integral part of the way that people compute—and the way that they live.

That means it's vital that people get more out of their use of the Internet, improving their productivity and making their computing lives easier and more pleasant. So this chapter includes a variety of recipes for doing that and more.

You'll find recipes here for speeding up Internet access, troubleshooting DNS problems, getting more out of hosting a web site using Internet Information Services (IIS), customizing Internet Explorer, and many safety tips, such as protecting yourself from spyware and spam, using firewalls, and much more.

Using a Command-Line Interface

You'll use several command-line tools in this chapter, including *ipconfig* for checking your Internet and network configuration, *ping* for troubleshooting DNS problems, and the tlntadmn Telnet administrator command for managing Telnet.

Using Downloadable Software

You'll use a wide variety of downloadable software in this chapter, including EMS Free Surfer mk II (Recipe 13.8) to protect you against pop-up ads; Cookie Pal (Recipe 13.9) for managing cookies; Ad-Aware, Spybot Search & Destroy, Microsoft Windows AntiSpyware, and Webroot Spy Sweeper (Recipe 13.10) for protecting you against spyware; and the ZoneAlarm firewall (Recipes 13.10 and 13.14) for Internet protection, among others.

13.1   Using a *HOSTS* File to Speed Up Web Access

Problem

You want to increase the speed at which you connect to web sites.

Solution

The *HOSTS* file is a plain text file that you can create or edit with a text editor like Notepad, and that resolves hostnames with their corresponding IP addresses, without having to go out to a DNS server. To use it to speed up web access:

1. Run a text editor like Notepad or Wordpad.

2. In your text editor, open the file called *HOSTS* in *%SystemRoot%\System32\ Drivers\Etc\HOSTS*. The file has no extension; it is named only *HOSTS*. If the file doesn't exist, create it.

3. Enter the IP addresses and hostnames of your commonly visited web sites. Each entry in the file should be on one line. The IP address should be in the first column, and the corresponding hostname in the next column. At least one space should separate the two columns. It should look like this:

        208.201.239.37   oreilly.com
        216.92131.107   simtel.net

4. If you'd like, add comments to the file by preceding the line with a #, in which case the entire line will be ignored by the file, or by putting a # after the hostname, in which case only the comment after will be ignored. You might want to comment on individual entries—for example:

        130.94.155.164   gralla.com   #still in beta

5. When you're finished editing the file, save it to its existing location.

Discussion

One of the causes of slowdowns in accessing web pages is the way that your PC uses the Domain Name System (DNS). The Internet can't understand plain English words that you use to visit a web site, such as *http://www.oreilly.com*. Instead, it needs to know the numeric IP address. So whenever you type in a hostname, such as *http:// www.oreilly.com*, that address needs to be resolved to its IP address, such as 208.201. 239.37. DNS servers automatically provide that name resolution.

It takes time to send your request to a DNS server, have the server resolve the IP address, and then send the IP address back to your PC. You can speed up the process by creating or editing a local *HOSTS* file on your own PC that contains hostnames and their corresponding IP addresses. When you create one, XP will first look into the *HOSTS* file to see if there's an entry for the hostname, and, if it finds it, it will resolve the address itself. That way, you won't have to go out to a DNS server and wait for the response before visiting a web site.

You'll frequently come across software on the web that promises to speed up Internet access by changing a variety of "hidden" settings on your PC. It's questionable whether changing these settings has much of an effect on Internet speed, especially if you have broadband, such as a cable modem or DSL modem. And many of these programs also make changes to your *HOSTS* file, which, as this recipe shows, you can do yourself. So be wary of paying for Internet speed-up programs, because it's not clear that they actually have much of an effect.

If you use this recipe to edit your *HOSTS* file, make sure that you check the file regularly and keep it up to date, or else you may deny yourself access to certain web sites. For example, if the *http://www.gralla.com* web site were to change its IP address, but your *HOSTS* file kept the old, incorrect address, your browser would not be able to find the site, because it would be given the wrong addressing information.

See Also

For information about how you can use the *HOSTS* file to block ads on the Internet, see the O'Reilly WindowsDevCenter article "Kill Internet Ads with HOSTS and PAC Files" at *http://www.windowsdevcenter.com/pub/a/windows/2004/03/30/hosts.html*.

13.2   Troubleshooting DNS Problems

Problem

You can't connect to web sites because of DNS issues.

Solution

Sometimes when you can't connect to a web site, the cause is a DNS problem. While there is no single way to fix the problem, here are steps you should take.

First, find out whether the issue is with the web site itself, not with DNS. To find out if a web site is live, issue the ping command at the command prompt or Run box, like this:

```
ping www.zdnet.com
```

If the site is live, you'll get an answer like this:

```
Pinging www.zdnet.com [206.16.6.252] with 32 bytes of data:

Reply from 206.16.6.252: bytes=32 time=119ms TTL=242
Reply from 206.16.6.252: bytes=32 time=79ms TTL=242
Reply from 206.16.6.252: bytes=32 time=80ms TTL=242
Reply from 206.16.6.252: bytes=32 time=101ms TTL=242

Ping statistics for 206.16.6.252:
    Packets: Sent = 4, Received = 4, Lost = 0 (0% loss),
Approximate round trip times in milli-seconds:
    Minimum = 79ms, Maximum = 119ms, Average = 94ms
```

If it's not, you'll get a response like this:

```
Ping request could not find host. Please check the name and try again.
```

If you ping a site and it's live, but you can't connect to it with your browser, a DNS problem might be the reason. If you suspect you're having a DNS problem, take the following actions.

Check your HOSTS file

If your *HOSTS* file contains an incorrect or outdated listing, you won't be able to connect. Even if you don't recall adding listings to a *HOSTS* file, it still may contain listings, because some Internet accelerator utilities edit them without telling you. Open your *HOSTS* file with Notepad and see if the site you can't connect to is listed there. If it is, delete the entry, and you should be able to connect. For more details, see Recipe 13.1, "Using a *HOSTS* File to Speed Up Web Access."

Check your DNS settings

Make sure your DNS settings are correct for your ISP or network and use them on your system. To do it:

1. Call the technical support department of your ISP, or ask your network administrator, and find out the proper DNS settings.
2. Double-click the problem connection in the Network Connections folder.
3. Choose Support → Details, and look at the bottom of the tab to find your DNS servers.
4. If they don't match what your ISP or network administrator gave to you, right-click the problem connection and choose Properties. Then, highlight Internet Protocol (TCP/IP) and choose Properties.
5. Change the DNS servers to the proper ones, or choose Obtain DNS server address automatically if your ISP or network administrator tells you to use that setting.

The problem may be related to your DNS cache. Your PC keeps a cache of DNS information about recent sites you've visited. When you type in a URL to visit, your PC first checks this cache before going out to a DNS server, and if it finds the entry in the cache, it uses that entry. So if your DNS cache has outdated information, you won't be able to connect to the web site. The best solution is to flush the DNS cache. Do it by typing `ipconfig /flushdns` at a command prompt.

If you know the address of DNS servers, ping them. If you can't reach them, the problem may be with your router, or with your DSL or cable modem.

Find out if your ISP is having DNS problems

The problem may be caused by your ISP—perhaps its DNS servers are down. Ping each of your ISP's DNS servers and, if any of them don't respond, remove them from your DNS list, as outlined earlier in this recipe.

Adjust XP's DNS cache settings

The problem may be caused by your DNS cache settings. As a way of speeding up DNS, when you visit a site, XP puts the DNS information into a local DNS cache on your PC. So, when you want to go to a site, XP first looks in its local DNS cache, called the *resolve cache*, to see whether the DNS information is contained there. That way, if it finds the information locally, it doesn't have to query a remote DNS server to find IP information. The cache is made up of recently queried names and entries taken from your *HOSTS* file.

The cache contains both negative and positive entries. Positive entries are those in which the DNS lookup succeeded, and you were able to connect to the web site. When XP looks in the cache, if it finds a positive entry, it immediately uses that DNS information and sends you to the requested web site.

Negative entries are those in which no match was found, and you end up getting a "Cannot find server or DNS Error" in your browser. Similarly, when XP looks in the cache and finds a negative entry, it gives you the error message without bothering to go out to the site.

Negative entries can lead to problems. When you try to make a connection to a site that has a negative entry in your cache, you'll get an error message, even if the site's problems have been resolved and it's now reachable.

You can solve this problem, though, by changing a Registry setting. By default, XP caches negative entries for five minutes. After five minutes, they're cleared from your cache. But if you'd like, you can force XP not to cache these negative entries, so that you'll never run into this problem. To do it:

1. Run the Registry Editor and go to HKEY_LOCAL_MACHINE\SYSTEM\CurrentControlSet\ Services\Dnscache\Parameters.

2. Create a new DWORD value with the name NegativeCacheTime and give it a value of 0. (The value may already exist. If it does, edit the value to 0.) The DWORD determines how much time, in seconds, to keep negative entries in the DNS cache. If you like, you can have the entries stay alive for one second by giving it a value of 1.

3. After you're done editing, exit the Registry. To make the change take effect, restart your computer.

4. After you edit the Registry change, you can also make the change take effect by issuing the command ipconfig /flushdns at a command prompt. This command

will flush your DNS cache—all the entries, both positive and negative—and your cache will remain empty until you start visiting web sites again. Negative entries, however, will not be added to the cache if you've given the DWORD a value of 0.

Discussion

You can also use the Registry to control the amount of time that positive entries are kept in the DNS cache. By default, they are kept for 24 hours. To change the default, go to HKEY_LOCAL_MACHINE\SYSTEM\CurrentControlSet\Services\Dnscache\Parameters again and create a DWORD value called MaxCacheEntryTtlLimit. (If it's already present, just edit the value.) For the value, enter the amount of time you want the entry to remain, in seconds, making sure to use decimal as the base.

Also, you can sometimes fix DNS cache problems without having to edit the Registry. First try flushing the DNS cache by issuing the command ipconfig /flushdns at a command prompt. That often solves the problem, and you won't have to resort to Registry editing.

See Also

The *http://www.seoconsultants.com/tools/dns.asp* site provides a variety of DNS troubleshooting tips. It can also generate a DNS report for a domain and detail any DNS problems it finds.

13.3   Installing Internet Information Services (IIS)

Problem

You want to install Internet Information Services (IIS) so you can create and maintain a web site.

Solution

IIS isn't installed by default in XP Professional. To install it take these steps:

1. From the Control Panel, select Add or Remove Programs and click Add/Remove Windows Components.

2. From the Windows Component wizard that appears, highlight Internet Information Services (IIS) and click on Details. Check all those you want to install. Table 13-1 describes the purpose of each component.

3. Click on OK. Depending on your setup, you may be prompted to insert your XP Professional disk.

Table 13-1. IIS components

Component	What it does
Common Files	These files are required by other components. Don't clear this checkbox—if these files aren't installed, other IIS components won't work.
Documentation	Provides help for IIS components. The files are installed in the *C:\Windows\Help\ lishelp* folder.
File Transfer Protocol (FTP) Service	Lets you host an FTP server.
FrontPage 2000 Server Extensions	These server-side programs let you use Microsoft's FrontPage Web authoring tool to add features to your web site such as forms, hit counters, discussions, and full-text search.
Internet Information Services Snap-In	This snap-in lets you use the Microsoft Management Console (MMC) to administer IIS. You should make sure to install this, or else you'll have to use scripts to manage your servers.
SMTP Service	Lets you provide SMTP mail services, although it is not a full-blown SMTP server.
World Wide Web Service	Lets you host web pages. If you install IIS, you must install this component, or else other components won't work. There are optional subcomponents you can install; to see them, highlight this component and click on Details.

Discussion

IIS comes only with Windows XP Professional, not the Home, Edition. IIS lets you host web sites and FTP sites, and run a Simple Mail Transfer Protocol (SMTP) service for sending email.

The XP version of IIS is a stripped-down version of the Windows Server editions, so don't expect a full-blown Internet server. It's best suited for relatively small sites that don't require a great deal of functionality. It has the following features—and drawbacks—for each type of server it lets you host:

Web sites

You can only host one web site with the version of IIS that ships with XP Professional. And that site can only support a maximum of 10 simultaneous TCP connections. Web pages not uncommonly require more than one connection, so that means that usually fewer than 10 people will be able to be on your web site at a given time. This means that it's not really practical to use IIS to host a public web site, unless you don't publicize it and only tell close friends and family members about it. However, for internal purposes on a company intranet, it can be useful. And you can use the server as a "staging server" to test out sites before publicly posting them on a different server.

FTP sites

FTP sites have the same limitations as web sites—you can host only one FTP site, and that site cannot have more than 10 simultaneous connections. For similar reasons, that means it's not practical to host a public FTP site, although it will work fine as a file repository within a small business or for friends and family members.

SMTP service

This isn't a full-blown mail server, and you can only use it to relay mail. So it can collect email information and then forward it to another SMTP server that will send the mail.

See Also

Excellent sites for getting help with IIS are the IIS FAQ site at *http://www.iisfaq.com*, and IIS-Reources.com at *http://www.iis-resources.com*.

Recipe 13.4 for using the IIS MMC snap-in to manage Internet servers.

13.4   Using the IIS MMC Snap-in to Manage Your Internet Servers

Problem

You want to manage the configuration of your IIS Internet servers.

Solution

You administer your web site by using the Microsoft Management Console (MMC) IIS snap-in. To run it, from the Control Panel go to Administrative Tools and double-click Internet Information Services. The Console tree, shown in Figure 13-1, shows the structure of your web and FTP sites and gives you control over those sites.

To rename your web and FTP sites and to customize other aspects of the site, double-click on the site name (for example, Default Web Site), choose Properties, and then choose the tab that corresponds to what you want to customize. For example, to change the web site's name, IP address, and enable logging and several other features, choose the Web Site tab, shown in Figure 13-2, and make your new choices.

You can perform actions on any component of your web site listed in the snap-in in the same way: right-click on it, choose Properties, choose the proper tab, and fill in the form to perform an action. For example, to change the name of the home page for your site, right-click on Default Web Page, choose Documents, and edit the name on the screen.

Discussion

IIS automatically creates default web and FTP sites and default locations. The web site is located at *C:\Inetpub\Wwwroot* and the FTP site is located at *C:\Inetpub\Ftproot*. The default names are, not surprisingly, Default Web Site and Default FTP Site.

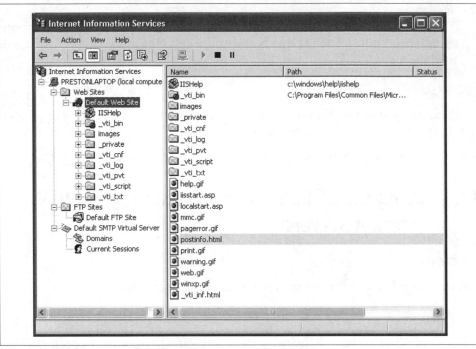

Figure 13-1. The IIS snap-in for MMC displays the structure of your Internet sites and gives you the tools to manage them

The folder structure shown by the IIS snap-in includes both real and virtual folders (the snap-in refers to folders by their older name, directories). You can tell virtual from real directories in the snap-in by looking in the right pane at the path listing. Virtual directories will have a path listed, because the path will be different from the name of the directory. You can also right-click on a directory and choose Properties to see whether it's virtual or not—virtual directories include a Virtual Directory tab, while real directories have a Directory tab.

Keep in mind that managing IIS from an XP workstation has many limitations.

See Also

Recipe 13.3 for installing IIS. Excellent sites for getting help with IIS are the IIS FAQ site at *http://www.iisfaq.com*, and IIS-Reources.com at *http://www.iis-resources.com*

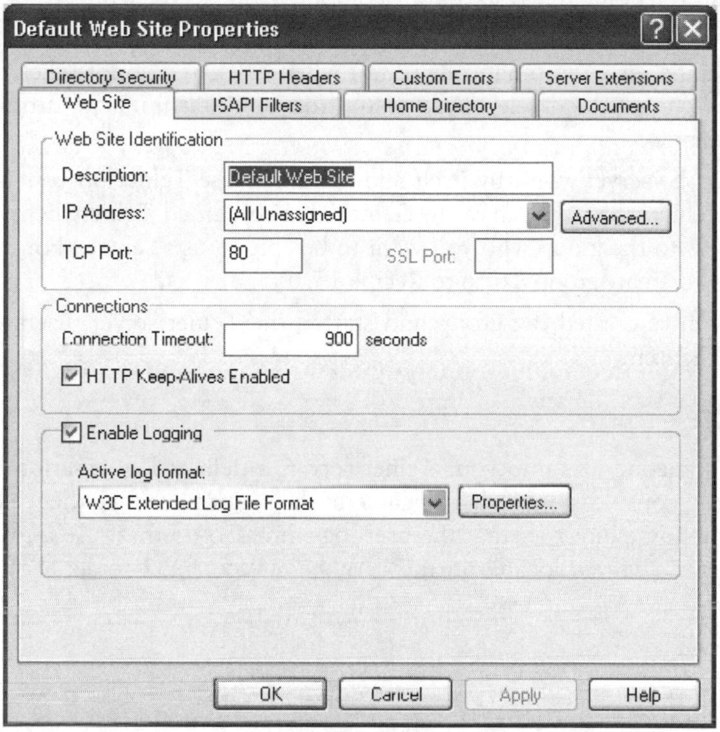

Figure 13-2. Use this tab to customize your web site name, its IP address, and many other site functions and features

13.5   Setting Up and Configuring a Telnet Server

Problem

You want to set up a Telnet server to allow Telnet access into a machine.

Solution

When you install XP Professional, it installs a Telnet server. The server is not part of IIS, though, and you don't administer it using IIS. Although the Telnet server is installed, by default it is not enabled. To enable the server:

1. From the Control Panel, select Administrative Tools → Services, to run the Services console.

2. Find the Telnet service in the list and click the Start button on the toolbar. That will enable it, and you can now use it.

3. At whatever point you restart your computer, the server won't restart by itself. You'll have to configure it to start whenever XP starts.

4. To have the server automatically restart when XP starts, double-click on it in the Services console, and select Automatic from the Startup Type drop-down list. Then click OK.

5. Starting the server won't by itself allow users to use Telnet on your system. To allow Telnet access, you have to create a group named TelnetClients, and then add users to the group who you want to be able to use Telnet. (For information on how to create groups, turn to Recipe 15.10.)

6. Once you've created the group and started the Telnet server, users can Telnet into the system.

Discussion

Whenever someone logs into your Telnet server, a default logon script is run after the command console is opened. You can edit the script to change the welcome message and the home directory that the user logs into. To do that, use a text editor to open the file *Login.cmd* located in the *C:\Windows\System32* folder. Following is a default script:

```
@echo off
rem
rem  Default global login script for the Telnet Server
rem
rem  In the default setup, this command script is executed when the
rem  initial command shell is invoked.  It, in turn, will try to invoke
rem  the individual user's login script.
rem

echo *=================================================================
echo Welcome to Microsoft Telnet Server.
echo *=================================================================

cd /d %HOMEDRIVE%\%HOMEPATH%
```

The text to the right of each line next to *echo* is displayed to the user when she logs in, so change it to whatever welcome message you want, such as:

```
echo *=================================================================
echo Welcome to Preston's Telnet Server. You're welcome to use any of
echo my resources, but please take care in what you do!
echo *=================================================================
```

The bottom part of the default script places users in their home directories—the script replaces the *%HOMEDRIVE%* and *%HOMEPATH%* with the variables of the home directory of the user logging in. The */d* switch allows the drive to be changed if necessary.

If you want, you can force all Telnet users into the same directory by editing the last line of the file. For example, if you wanted all Telnet users to have their command consoles opened in the *C:\Telnet* directory, the last line of the script would be *cd C:\Telnet*.

Note: The Telnet server comes only with the XP Professional, not the Home Edition.

See Also

Recipe 13.6 for using the Telnet Administrator to manage a Telnet server

13.6   Use the Telnet Administrator to Manage a Telnet Server

Problem

You want to manage your Telnet server.

Solution

You administer your Telnet server using the tlntadmn Telnet Administrator command-line tool. You can change Telnet settings with it, find out information about sessions, disconnect a session or sessions, and send a message to a remote user.

To see your basic settings, type tlntadmn at a command prompt. You'll see something like this:

```
The following are the settings on localhost

Alt Key Mapped to 'CTRL+A'   :   YES
Idle session timeout         :   1 hours
Max connections              :   2
Telnet port                  :   23
Max failed login attempts    :   3
End tasks on disconnect      :   NO
Mode of Operation            :   Console
Authentication Mechanism     :   NTLM, Password
Default Domain               :   PRESTONLAPTOP
State                        :   Stopped
```

To change your settings, use the syntax tlntadmn config followed by the configuration option. For example, to set the maximum number of connections to 8, you would issue this command:

```
tlntadmn config maxconn = 8
```

Table 13-2 lists common tlntadmn configuration commands and what they do.

Table 13-2. Common tlntadmn configuration commands

Configuration command	What it does
Tlntadmn config ctrlakeymap = yes	Maps the Alt key to Ctrl-A; the Telnet server will interpret Ctrl-A as pressing the Alt key
Tlntadmn config timeout = *hh:mm:ss*	Specifies the amount of time that a session is allowed to be idle before it is disconnected, for example, 2:30:30 for two hours, thirty minutes and thirty seconds.
Tlntadmn config timeoutactive = *yes* or *no*	Specifies whether idle users should be disconnected when the session timeout is reached.
Tlntadmn config maxfail = *n*	Specifies the number of login failures before the server disconnects the session with the user. The default is three.
Tlntadmn config maxcon = *n*	Sets the maximum number of concurrent connections.
Tlntadmn config port = *n*	Sets the port to be used by Telnet. The default is port 23.

Discussion

You can also use tlntadmn to disconnect a session, or to send a user a message. To do that, you first need to know what sessions are active, and you need to find the session ID for each session. Issue the command tlntadmn -s all and you'll be shown each session. The session ID is the number in the first column, for example, 366 or 924. To kill a session, issue the command tlntadmn -k ID, for example, tlntadmn -k 366. To send a message to a user, use the command:

```
Tlntadmn -m ID Your message
```

For example:

```
Tlntadmn -m 366 I'm about to bring the system down.
```

See Also

Recipe 13.5 for setting up and configuring a Telnet server

13.7 Customizing Internet Explorer's Logo and Titlebar

Problem

You want to customize Internet Explorer by putting your company brand or name in it rather than the default name and logo.

Solution

You can put your company name or logo into Internet Explorer in two separate locations—in the logo in the upper-right corner of the Internet Explorer screen or in the name in the title bar. This recipe will show you how to do both.

Change the Internet Explorer logo. Internet Explorer has both a static and an animated logo. The static logo displays when the browser is inactive, while the animated logo displays when the browser is locating a site, connecting, and actively downloading pages or images from the web. Because you have the choice of displaying large or small icons on the Internet Explorer toolbar, there are two sizes of both the static and animated logos.

Before you begin, you'll need to create new logos to replace the existing ones. You'll have to create two sets of icons in *.bmp* format: one set for the smaller logo and another set for the larger logo. Each set will have a static logo and an animated logo. The static logos should be 22 × 22 pixels for the smaller size and 38 × 38 pixels for the larger size. The animated logos have to be animated bitmaps, each of which should have a total of 10 frames in it. So, the smaller animated bitmap should be 22 pixels wide by 220 pixels high, and the larger animated bitmap should be 38 pixels wide by 380 pixels high.

Create the static bitmaps with any graphics program. You can also use special icon-creation programs to create your icons, such as Microangelo, available from *http://www.microangelo.us/*. (Make sure when using Microangelo to choose Tools → New Image format, which will let you create the icons with the proper pixel dimensions, as explained in the previous paragraph.)

To create the animated bitmaps, you'll need special tools. Microangelo does a great job of creating them, and that's your best bet. If you prefer, though, you can create the 10 separate frames for the animated bitmaps in a graphics program such as Paint and then stitch the 10 separate frames together using the Animated Bitmap Creator (*http://jsanjuan.tripod.com/download.html*), a free command-line program.

To change Internet Explorer's static logos to your new ones, run the Registry Editor and navigate to:

```
HKEY_LOCAL_MACHINE\SOFTWARE\Microsoft\Internet Explorer\Main
```

Create two string values named SmallBitmap and BigBitmap and give them each the value of their filename and location, including the full path—for example, *C:\Windows\IEbiglogo.bmp* and *C:\Windows\IEsmalllogo.bmp*. As you might guess, the SmallBitmap value points to the smaller logo, and the BigBitmap value points to the larger logo.

To use your new animated logos, go to:

```
HKEY_LOCAL_MACHINE\SOFTWARE\Microsoft\Internet Explorer\Toolbar
```

Create two string values named SmBrandBitmap and BrandBitmap and give them each the value of their filename and location—for example, *C:\Windows\IEbiganimatelogo.bmp* and *C:\Windows\IEsmallanimatelogo.bmp*. Once again, as you might guess, SmBrandBitmap is for the smaller animated logo and BrandBitmap is for the larger logo.

Exit the Registry and close Internet Explorer. When you next start up Internet Explorer, it should display your new logos. To revert to the default logos, delete the values you've created.

Change the text of Internet Explorer's titlebar. Internet Explorer's titlebar displays the text "Microsoft Internet Explorer," along with the title of the page you're currently visiting. However, you can change the "Microsoft Internet Explorer" text to any text you want. Run the Registry Editor and go to:

```
HKEY_CURRENT_USER\Software\Microsoft\Internet Explorer\Main
```

Add a new string value named `Window Title` and give it a value of whatever text you want displayed in the titlebar. Exit the Registry and close Internet Explorer if it's open. The next time you open Internet Explorer, the titlebar will have your new text.

If you want your titlebar to have no text in it, aside from the title of the page you're currently visiting, create the `Window Title` string value but leave the value field empty.

Discussion

You can also change the background of the Internet Explorer toolbar if you'd like, and place any graphic you want there. Just make sure, though, that the graphic is in *.bmp* format, that it's light enough to show black text, and it's not so busy that you can't read the menu text that will be on top of it. If you create or use a file that's too small, Internet Explorer will tile it for you. However, don't use a bitmap smaller than 10×10 pixels because all the work Internet Explorer has to do to tile images that small will slow down your web browsing.

You can make the graphic the background by using TweakUI, one of a suite of free, unsupported utilities from Microsoft called XP Power Toys. Get it from *http://www.microsoft.com/windowsxp/pro/downloads/powertoys.asp*. After you download it and run it, run TweakUI, click Internet Explorer, and click the box next to "Use custom background for Internet Explorer toolbar." Then click the Change button and choose the file you want to use as the background. You'll see a sample of how the toolbar will look, so change the file until you find one you want to use. When you find it, click OK, close Internet Explorer, and restart it. The new toolbar will be there.

See Also

For a variety of other ways to customize Internet Explorer, see *http://www.mvps.org/winhelp2002/ietips.htm*.

13.8   Blocking Pop Ups

Problem

You want to block pop-up ads when you browse the Web.

Solution

Using a graphical user interface

Windows XP SP2 includes an excellent built-in pop-up blocker that does an exceptional job of blocking pop ups, and it lets you allow pop ups from some sites while banning those from all others.

The pop-up blocker should be turned on by default. If it's not, choose Tools → Pop-up Blocker → Pop-up Blocker Settings, check the box next to Show Information Bar when a pop-up is blocked, and click Close.

With the pop-up blocker turned on when you visit a site that delivers a pop-up ad, the blocker will block the ad and then tell you that it has blocked the ad in the Information Bar, just below the Address Bar.

If it's the first time you've used the pop-up blocker, you'll get a warning in the middle of the screen, telling you to look at the Information Bar. Turn it off by selecting Do not show this message again and click OK.

In some cases, pop ups are useful—they may deliver more information in a small window, for example. If you want to allow pop ups from the site, click the Information Bar, and you'll see the screen shown in Figure 13-3.

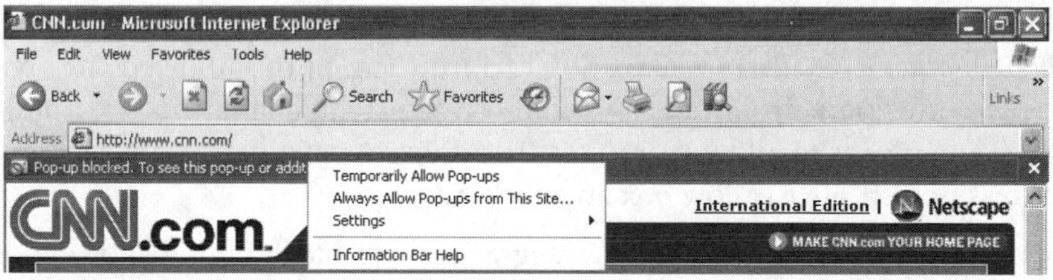

Figure 13-3. Choosing to allow pop ups

Choose Temporarily Allow Pop-ups to allow pop ups from the site on just this visit, and choose Always Allow Pop-ups from This Site if you want to always let pop ups from the site through. Whichever you choose, the pop up will be let through immediately.

If you want to turn off the pop-up blocker altogether, choose Settings → Turn Off Pop-up Blocker. And if you'd like to turn off the Information Bar so that it doesn't appear when a pop up is blocked, choose Settings and select Show Information Bar for Pop-ups to remove the check next to it.

If you've chosen to permanently allow pop ups from a site and later decide you no longer want to let them through, choose Tools → Pop-up Blocker → Pop-up Blocker Settings. The Pop-up Blocker Settings dialog appears, as shown in Figure 13-4.

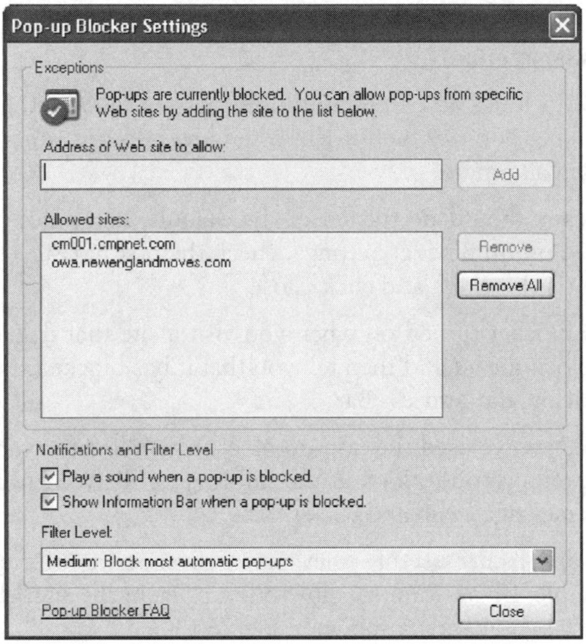

Figure 13-4. Customizing your pop-up settings

All the sites you've decided to allow pop ups from are in the Allowed sites box. To no longer allow pop ups from any of those sites, highlight the sites and click Remove. If you want to allow more sites than those shown here, type each site into the Address of web site to allow box and click Add.

You can also tell Internet Explorer how aggressively to block pop ups, by choosing a different filter level from the Filter Level drop-down box. There are three levels you can choose.

Low

> Allows pop ups from secure sites—that is, sites that use SSL encryption, such as banking sites. You'll know you're at a secure site if its URL begins with *https://*.

Medium

> The default level, which blocks most pop ups. It will allow a few pop ups, through—notably, if it detects that the pop up is one you might want to be allowed. What kind of pop up might that be? In some cases, a site might include

a link that, when clicked, initiates a pop up—for example, launching a small map in a pop-up window. At the medium level, that pop up will get through.

High

Blocks all pop ups of any type, even if you've clicked a link to initiate them.

Finally, the screen lets you choose to play a sound when a pop up is blocked. It also gives you the option of displaying the Information Bar when a pop up is blocked.

Using downloadable software

If you don't have SP2 and want to block pop ups, you can use any one of several pop-up blockers, many of which are free. EMS Free Surfer mk II (*http://www.kolumbus.fi/eero.muhonen/FS/fs.htm*) lets you set several levels of pop-up protection—you can block all pop ups or only those that appear to be unwanted—and you can turn it on and off with a click. It has other helpful tools as well, such as letting you shut every open instance of Internet Explorer with a single click, and it includes an add-in that will clean out your system cache and list of recently visited sites. (Don't confuse the program with a related product, EMS Free Surfer Companion, which offers more features than the free version and costs $20.)

Another good pop-up blocker is Pop-Up No-No! (*http://www.popupnono.com*). It blocks Flash animation ads, as well as pop ups. The Google Toolbar (*http://toolbar.google.com/googlebar.html*) also blocks pop ups, although it only works with Internet Explorer and no other browsers.

Discussion

An even more annoying form of pop ups are those that aren't connected to a browser, that appear even when you're not surfing the web, and that show up in a text-message window for no apparent reason. You've taken no conceivable action that could have caused them to appear, such as visiting a web site, but they still appear.

These text pop ups use XP's Messenger service, which was designed for sending notifications over internal LANs—for example, when a network administrator wants to notify network users that a server is about to go down, or when you're notified that a printer has completed a job of yours.

Spammers, though, have used the technology to send text pop ups to IP addresses across the Internet. To kill these pop ups, disable the Messenger service. Run the Services Microsoft Management Console by typing services.msc at a command prompt or the Run box and pressing Enter. Double-click the entry for Messenger, choose Disabled as the Startup type from the screen that appears, and click OK. Pop ups will no longer get through. Unfortunately, neither will any network messages from administrators if you're on a LAN. If you install SP2, it automatically turns off Messenger Service pop ups.

Browsers other than Internet Explorer include built-in pop-up killers:

Opera

Download Opera from *http://www.opera.com*. To enable its pop-up killer, choose File → Preferences → Refuse pop-up windows. You can also have the program open pop-up windows in the background instead of on top of your browser.

Mozilla

Download Mozilla from *http://www.mozilla.org*. To enable its pop-up killer, choose Edit → Preferences → Privacy & Security → Pop-ups, and check Reject pop-up windows.

Firefox

Download Firefox from *http://www.mozilla.org/products/firefox*. To enable its pop-up killer, choose Tools → Options and check the box next to Block Popup Windows.

See Also

O'Reilly's *Internet Annoyances* includes more information about how to kill pop ups and related annoyances.

13.9 Protecting Your Privacy by Handling Cookies Properly

Problem

You want to protect your privacy when surfing the web by handling cookies properly.

Solution

Using a graphical user interface

To customize your cookie settings in Internet Explorer, choose Tools → Internet Options → Privacy. Under Settings, move the slider to your desired level. Table 13-3 shows how each setting affects Internet Explorer's cookie-handling.

Table 13-3. Internet Explorer's privacy settings and your privacy

Setting	How the setting affects your privacy
Block All Cookies	Blocks all cookies, without exception.
	Does not allow web sites to read existing cookies.
High	Blocks cookies from all web sites that don't have a compact privacy policy.
	Blocks all cookies that use personally identifiable information without your explicit consent.

Setting	How the setting affects your privacy
Medium High	Blocks third-party cookies from sites that don't have a compact privacy policy.
	Blocks third-party cookies that use personally identifiable information without your explicit consent.
	Blocks first-party cookies that use personally identifiable information without your implicit consent.
Medium (Default)	Blocks third-party cookies from sites that don't have a compact privacy policy.
	Blocks third-party cookies that use personally identifiable information without your implicit consent.
	Accepts first-party cookies that use personally identifiable information without your implicit consent, but deletes them when you close Internet Explorer.
Low	Blocks third-party cookies from sites that don't have a compact privacy policy.
	Accepts third-party cookies that use personally identifiable information without your implicit consent, but deletes them when you close Internet Explorer.
Accept All Cookies	Accepts all cookies, without exception.
	Allows web sites to read existing cookies.

Customizing IE cookie-handling. You're not locked into IE's preset levels of cookie-handling. If you like, you can customize how it handles cookies so that you can, for example, accept or reject cookies from individual sites, or accept or reject all first-party and third-party cookies.

To accept or reject all cookies from a specific site, choose Tools ▸ Internet Options → Privacy → Sites. You'll see the Per Site Privacy Actions dialog box. Type in the name of the site you want to accept or block cookies from, and click either Block or Allow.

To customize how you handle first-party and third-party cookies, choose Tools → Internet Options → Privacy → Advanced. Check the Override automatic cookie handling box. You can accept or reject all first-party or third-party cookies, or be prompted whether to accept them. You can also decide to always allow *session cookies*: cookies that last only as long as you're on a specific web site and are deleted once you leave the site.

Using downloadable software

The tools built into XP for managing cookies are reasonable, but for the most flexibility in handling cookies you should get a third-party cookie manager. The best is Cookie Pal, available at *http://www.kburra.com*. It's shareware; it's free to try, but $15 if you use it beyond 15 days. It lets you easily customize which sites you'll allow to put cookies on your PC, and it includes a cookie manager that lets you read and delete cookies. It also lets you accept or reject cookies on a case-by-case basis as you browse the web. If you use browsers other than IE, you might be out of luck, though. As of this writing, Cookie Pal works only with Versions 3 and 4 of Netscape Navigator and Versions 4, 5, and 6 of Opera. (Mozilla, Firefox, and later Netscape versions have similarly good managers built in, as mentioned earlier.)

Discussion

Cookies can be used to track your online activities and identify you to advertising networks and web sites. Information about you, based on what cookies gather, can be put in a database, and profiles of you and your surfing habits can be created.

Not all cookies are privacy-invaders, though, and some can be used for useful purposes, such as logging you into web sites, and customizing web sites.

Internet Explorer lets you customize your use of cookies according to the level of privacy you want. You can choose from six levels of privacy settings, from Accept All Cookies to Block All Cookies. When choosing, keep in mind that some sites won't function well or at all at the higher privacy settings, particularly if you choose to reject all cookies. I generally find that Medium High is a good compromise between protecting privacy and still being able to personalize web sites.

Cookies have gotten a lot of press—most of it bad—but the truth is, not all cookie use is bad. As a means of site customization, they're a great way of helping you get the most out of the Web. They can also carry information about log-in names and passwords, which is a timesaver, since you won't have to log into each site every time you visit.

 Cookies can be security holes. If you use them to log you into a site automatically, anyone who uses your computer will be able to log into those sites with your username and password.

To help you better decide how to use this recipe for handling cookies, you should understand three cookie-related terms.

First-party cookie
> A cookie created by the site you're currently visiting. These cookies are often used by sites to let you log on automatically—without having to type in your username and password—and customize how you use the site. Typically, these kinds of cookies are not invasive.

Third-party cookie
> A cookie created by a site other than the one you're currently visiting. Frequently, third-party cookies are used by advertisers or advertising networks. Some people (including me) consider these kinds of cookies invasive.

Compact privacy statement
> A publicly posted policy that describes the details of how cookies are used on a site—for example, detailing the purpose of cookies, how they're used, their source, and how long they will stay on your PC. (Some cookies are automatically deleted when you leave a web site, while others stay valid until a specified date.)

You also need to know the difference between implicit consent and explicit consent. *Explicit consent* means you have specifically told a site it can use personally identifiable information about you. It's the same as *opting in*. *Implicit consent* means you haven't specifically told a site not to use personally identifiable information. It's the same as not having *opted out*, or specifically requesting to be taken off a list.

Export, import, or back up your cookies

Although some cookies can be intrusive, some can be helpful. They can log you into web sites automatically and customize the way you use and view the site. So, when you buy a new PC, you might want to export cookies from an older computer to it. If you have more than one PC, you might want all of them to have the same cookies. And you might want to back up your cookies for safe-keeping in case you accidentally delete the wrong ones.

To export or back up cookies from IE, choose File → Import and Export. The Import/Export wizard will launch. Choose Export Cookies and follow the directions. A single text file containing all your cookies will be created in My Documents, though you can choose a different location for them. To import cookies, launch the Import/Export wizard, choose Import Cookies, and browse to the location where the cookie file has been stored.

Examine and delete cookies manually

You can't examine and delete your cookies from within Internet Explorer. However, because XP stores each IE cookie as an individual text file, you can read them and delete them just as you would any other text file. Go to *C:\Documents and Settings\ <Your Name>\Cookies* in Windows Explorer, and you'll see a list of individual cookies in a format like this:

```
your name@abcnews.com[1].txt
```

As a general rule, the name of the web site or ad network will be after the @, but not always—sometimes it will merely be a number. Open the file as you would any other text file (in Notepad, WordPad, or another text editor). Usually, there will be a list of numbers and letters inside, though you might find other useful information in there—for example, your username and password for the web site. If you don't want the cookie on your hard disk, simply delete it as you would any other text file.

Netscape Navigator and Mozilla handle cookies differently than Internet Explorer. They store all cookies in a single file, *cookies.txt*, typically found in *C:\Documents and Settings\<Your Name>\Application Data\Mozilla\Profiles\default********.slt*, where ******** is a random collection of numbers and letters. So, the directory might be *C:\ Documents and Settings\Name\Mozilla\Profiles\default\46yhu2ir.slt*. If you've set up different Netscape/Mozilla profiles (Tools → Switch Profile → Manage Profiles → Create Profile), *cookies.txt* won't be in the *default* subfolder, but under each profile's name. You can open the file and see each individual cookie. You can't however, delete individual entries from the file by editing this file. Instead, use Netscape's built-in Cookie Manager (at Tools → Cookie Manager → Manage Stored Cookies) to read and delete cookies.

In Firefox, you'll find the *cookies.txt* file in *C:\Documents and Settings<Your Name>\ Application Data\Mozilla\Firefox\Profiles\default.xxx*, where *xxx* is a random collection of three letters. Use Firefox's built-in Cookie Manager (Tools → Options → Privacy) to read and delete cookies.

See Also

For comprehensive information about cookies and how to handle them, see Cookie Central at *http://www.cookiecentral.com*. And for Microsoft's cookie FAQ, go to *http:// www.microsoft.com/info/cookies.mspx*.

13.10 Protecting Yourself Against Spyware

Problem

You want to protect yourself against spyware from spying on your Internet activities, delivering blizzards of pop-up ads, and hijacking your home page so that you're sent to a different home page than the one you've set—and you're hijacked even when you try to reset the home page.

Solution

Protecting yourself against spyware involves changing the way you use your PC, changing your security settings, and using antispyware software (for details on using antispyware software, see the Using downloadable software section later in this recipe).

Be careful about what you download

Before you download any file, know exactly what you're downloading. Do you know other people who have tried the program? Have they reported spyware problems? Who made the software—is it from a large, reputable company, or an unknown startup? Only download software from reputable companies that have no reported problems with spyware.

 Before you install any software, use System Restore to create a snapshot of your system. That way, if the software you download also includes spyware, you can use the restore point to restore your system to its previous spyware-free state. See Recipe 19.4 for information about System Restore.

Consider getting an alternative browser

Internet Explorer has more security holes than other browsers and is more closely tied to the operating system. This makes it easier to slip spyware onto your system using techniques such as drive-by downloads. Switch to an alternative browser, such as Firefox (*http://www.mozilla.org/products/firefox*), for better security.

Change your Internet Explorer security settings

If you want to keep Internet Explorer, change the security settings to prevent drive-by downloads and other dangers. You can turn off the automatic downloading of ActiveX controls and scripting, for example. For details, see Recipe 13.11 on handling Internet Explorer security settings.

Keep your system up to date

Spyware authors exploit loopholes in Windows and Internet Explorer in order to plant spyware on your system. But if you keep your system up to date, you'll close many of those loopholes and stave off infection. It is especially important to install Windows XP Service Pack 2 (SP2), because it closes many loopholes in Windows.

In addition to SP2, make sure you download and install the latest Microsoft security patches. Download them by going to Microsoft Update at *http://windowsupdate. microsoft.com/*, or by turning on Automatic Updates (see Recipe 2.16).

Kill pop ups

Spyware frequently spreads via pop ups. If you click a pop up, you may get infected by spyware. And, of course, spyware infestations can deliver more popups, sometimes in swarms. So killing pop ups will help keep you free from spyware. For details on how to do it, see Recipe 13.11.

Use a personal firewall

A personal firewall will protect you in two ways. Its inbound protection will help prevent spyware infections. But more importantly its outbound protection will stop spyware from "phoning home" and sending information about you to a web site. Unlike the firewall built into Windows XP, ZoneAlarm (*http://www.zonealarm.com*), McAfee Personal Firewall (*http://www.mcafee.com*), and Norton Personal Firewall (*http://www.symantec.com*) all provide outbound protection. Of the three, only ZoneAlarm includes a free version.

Using downloadable software

There are many pieces of antispyware software you can download, some of which are free. The two best free ones are Ad-Aware (*http://www.lavasoftusa.com/software/ adaware/*) and Spybot Search & Destroy (*http://www.spybot.info*). Both of them do a very good job of scanning your system for spyware, and then killing what they find.

But they both have a drawback—their free versions don't offer significant real-time protection. (Spybot offers some basic real-time protection.) So they can't stop you from becoming infected; they can only kill spyware after you've already gotten invaded by spyware. Ad-Aware has a for-pay version that offers real-time protection, and you can pay for that.

But a better bet is either Microsoft Windows AntiSpyware (*http://www.microsoft.com/athome/security/spyware*) or Webroot Spy Sweeper (*http://www.webroot.com*). Both offer real-time protection as well as spyware scanners and killers. As this book went to press, Microsoft Windows AntiSpyware was still in beta, and pricing was not set. So it may or may not be free. Spy Sweeper is free to try, but $29.95 if you decide to keep it.

No matter which spyware detector you use, though, you should use more than one. No single piece of antispyware software can detect and kill all spyware, so a combination of two or more is best.

Using a graphical user interface

Download Microsoft Windows AntiSpyware (*http://www.microsoft.com/athome/security/spyware*, and follow the installation instructions. The default settings as a general rule work fine, and so mostly they can be left as is. However, the software could end up changing your home page, your default search engine, and similar settings, without telling you, and so you should change that. (Note: the beta version of Microsoft AntiSpyware changed these settings, but there is a chance that the final version will not.)

The problem is caused by the software's feature that is designed to prevent home-page hijacking. When a piece of spyware tries to hijack your home page or search page, Microsoft AntiSpyware is designed to restore your home page or search page to your original settings. However, rather than restoring the setting to your home page, Microsoft AntiSpyware instead changes them to Microsoft's MSN.com page, and it similarly changes your search engine of choice to the MSN search engine.

To instead have Microsoft AntiSpyware use your own settings:

1. Run Microsoft AntiSpyware.
2. Click Advanced Tools.
3. Click Browser Hijack Restore.
4. From the list that appears, select Start Page and click Change restore setting to a new URL.
5. Type in your home page URL and click OK.
6. Select other pages that you want to keep as your own, instead of Microsoft's, such as Search Page, and follow steps 4 and 5.

Discussion

Spyware has become perhaps the most prevalent pest on the Internet. It can silently record all your Internet activity and report on your travels; hijack your home page and search engine; inundate you with swarms of popups; and much more, including installing so much junk that it can disable your computer. A related problem is adware, which is software that displays advertising on your PC. Some people consider adware a part of spyware, while others differentiate between the two pests.

Home-page hijackers have become increasingly common as well. This type of spyware hijacks your home page. When you start your browser, you're sent to an unfamiliar home page that usually includes a blizzard of popups.

Whether you call the pest spyware, adware, or a home-page hijacker, all have become serious problems. You fight adware and home-page hijackers in the same way you fight spyware.

Spyware can infect your PC in several ways. But it usually happens when a piece of spyware rides on the back of a free program you install. The Gator eWallet is notorious for the spyware it installs, and file-sharing software, especially Kazaa, can install spyware on your system as well.

Spyware can also be installed via drive-by downloads, in which a web site takes advantage of a security hole in Internet Explorer to download and install software onto your PC without your knowledge. They can also be installed via ActiveX downloads, when you approve the download of an ActiveX control before knowing what the download actually does. Spyware can also get on your system when you click a pop up—merely clicking on the pop up can initiate a download. And spyware can also infect you via email, when you open an infected attachment.

State and federal governments have proposed a variety of laws that claim to crack down on spyware, but the truth is, none of them can possibly eliminate the problem; the laws are weak and full of loopholes. So your best bet for protecting yourself is to follow the advice in this recipe.

See Also

Harvard researcher Ben Edelman maintains the best site (*http://www.benedelman.org*) on the Internet for finding out behind-the-scene and financial and legal aspects of spyware. SpywareInfo (*http://www.spywareinfo.com*) is a very useful site for general spyware information, and has a free spyware newsletter to which you can subscribe.

13.11 Customizing Internet Explorer Security Settings

Problem

You want to select more secure Internet Explorer security settings for ActiveX and Active Scripting.

Solution

Using a graphical user interface

1. In Internet Explorer, choose Tools → Internet Options, and click the Security tab. Click Internet, and then click Custom Level. The Security Settings screen shown in Figure 13-5 appears.

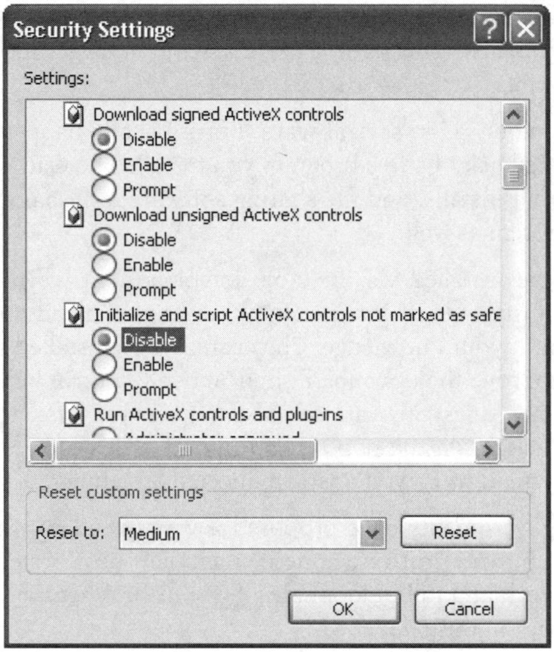

Figure 13-5. Controlling Internet Explorer security settings

2. Scroll to Download signed ActiveX Controls. A signed ActiveX control is one that has been guaranteed as having been created by a specific company. Because the company that created them is willing to be identified, signed controls are considered more secure than unsigned controls, but there's still no absolute guarantee that they're safe. Choose Disable if you want to completely stop ActiveX controls or choose Prompt if you want to receive a message before you download and run a signed ActiveX control. The message would let you download and run controls on a case-by-case basis. If you choose this setting, you might choose to run a control from a big, well-known company like Microsoft, but not run one from a smaller company that you never heard of.

3. In the Download unsigned ActiveX Controls, select Disable. Unsigned controls are a security risk, and you should never run them.

4. In the Initialize and script ActiveX Controls not marked as safe section, choose Disable. This will make sure that Internet Explorer doesn't run any controls that aren't safe.

 Some sites, like Microsoft Update, are designed to use ActiveX controls. So if you disable the controls, some sites might not work properly.

5. Scroll to the Java VM entry. This controls how Java applets are treated by Internet Explorer. Java applets are small programs downloaded to your computer from a web site, similar in some ways to ActiveX controls. Select High Safety. This will ensure that Java applets are isolated in what's called a sandbox so that they can't damage or attack your computer.

6. Scroll to Miscellaneous and select Disable for Access to data sources across domains. This will help avoid certain scripting attacks.

7. Click OK when you're done.

 For security, you may want to disable Microsoft's Java Virtual Machine (JVM), and instead install Sun's JRE. For details, see *http://java.sun.com/j2se/1.4.2/docs/guide/deployment/deployment-guide/upgrade-guide/*.

Using Group Policy

1. Run the Group Policy Editor by typing `gpedit.msc` at the command line and pressing Enter.
2. Select User Configuration → Internet Explorer Maintenance → Security.
3. Double-click Security Zones and Content Ratings.
4. In the Security Zones and Privacy section, select Import the current security zones and privacy settings, and click Modify Settings. The Internet Properties dialog box appears. Click Custom Level. The Security Settings screen shown in Figure 13-5 appears.
5. Follow the directions in steps 2 through 7 of the Using a GUI solution, above.
6. When you're done customizing the settings, you'll be returned to the Group Policy Editor. Click OK.

Discussion

ActiveX controls and scripting are two of the most glaring security holes in Internet Explorer, and are frequently exploited by malware authors to install spyware, homepage hijackers, and other dangerous software on your PC.

These security holes are a particular problem because Internet Explorer is tied directly into XP. That means that the malware won't just affect Internet Explorer—it can target the entire operating system. That's why it's particularly important to change you Internet Explorer security settings, as outlined in this recipe.

If you have ActiveX settings that prompt you before downloading and installing an ActiveX control, whenever you come across a web site that tries to download a control, you'll get a message asking if you want to install the control. Click Install if you want to install it, and Don't Install if you choose not to.

This message can get annoying, especially if you commonly download ActiveX controls from safe, well-known sites such as Microsoft or Symantec. You might be tempted to change your Internet Explorer settings to automatically download signed ActiveX controls. That's dangerous, so there's a better way to handle the problem. The next time you download an ActiveX control from a site, click More Options. If it's a site you trust, click Always install software, then click Install. From now on, ActiveX controls from that company will automatically install, and you won't be bothered again by a message. Similarly, if it's a site you don't trust, click Never install and then click Don't Install. From then on, the warning won't pop when you visit, and the ActiveX control won't be installed.

Another solution is to use an alternative browser, such as the free open-source browser Firefox (*http://www.mozilla.org/products/firefox*). Firefox doesn't have the same security holes as Internet Explorer. Additionally, it's not directly tied to the operating system, so that if Firefox is attacked, the entire operating system isn't imperiled.

If you use Firefox, though, some web sites may not work properly, because they require ActiveX controls.

See Also

You can get a free online checkup that examines Internet Explorer or another browser for security holes. Go to the Qualsys Browser Checkup (*http://browsercheck. qualys.com*).

13.12 Allowing Programs to Bypass the Windows Firewall

Problem

XP's built-in Windows Firewall is blocking programs from using the Internet, such as instant messaging programs or FTP software that you want to use.

Solution

1. Choose Control Panel → Security Center → Windows Firewall. This brings you to the Windows Firewall dialog box.

2. Click the Exceptions tab, shown in Figure 13-6. This tab lists all the programs for which the firewall will accept inbound connections. If a program is listed here but doesn't have a check next to it, it means the firewall blocks it. To tell the firewall to stop blocking inbound connections for the program, check the box next to it and click OK.

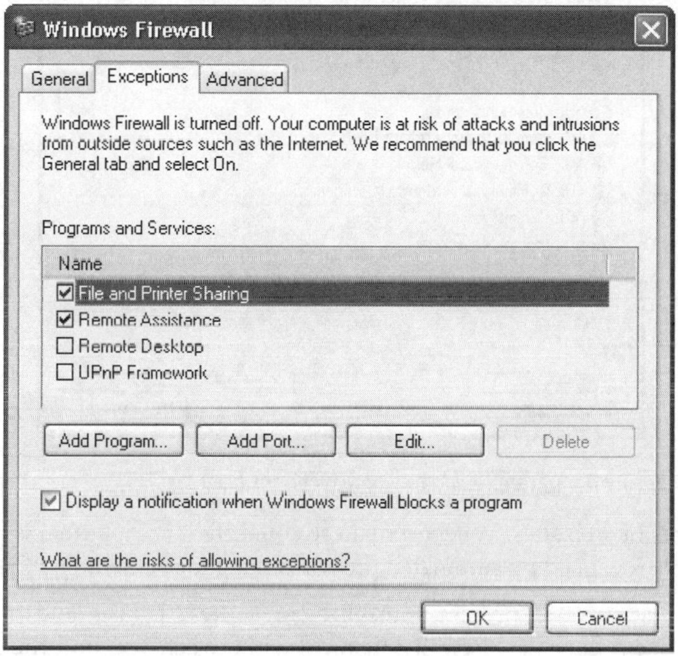

Figure 13-6. The Windows Firewall Exceptions tab

> When you get a warning from the Windows Firewall and click Ask Me Later, the program will be listed on the Exceptions tab, with no check next to it.

3. To add a new program to the exceptions list, click Add Program to bring up the window shown in Figure 13-7. Choose a program from the list and click OK, and then click OK again to add it to your list. If the program you want to add isn't listed in the Add a Program dialog box, click the Browse button to find it and then add it.

Discussion

The moment you connect to the Internet, you're in some danger of intrusion, especially if you have a broadband connection. PCs with broadband connections are tempting targets because their high-speed connections are ideal springboards for attacking

Add a Program

To allow communications with a program by adding it to the Exceptions list, select the program, or click Browse to search for one that is not listed.

Programs:

- Ad-Aware SE Personal
- Address Book Import Assistant
- America Online 7.0
- America Online 8.0
- America Online 9.0
- AOL Communicator
- AOL Communicator Address Book
- AOL Communicator Help
- AOL Communicator Identity Manager
- AOL Communicator Mail
- AOL Instant Messenger

Path: `C:\Program Files\Lavasoft\Ad-Aware SE Pers`   Browse...

Change scope...   OK   Cancel

Figure 13-7. Choosing a program to add to your exceptions list

other networks or web sites. Whenever you're connected, your system is among many constantly being scanned by automated probes looking for vulnerable PCs.

One of the best ways to protect yourself against these probes and more targeted attacks is to use a firewall. Firewall software sits between you and the Internet and acts as a gatekeeper of sorts, only allowing nonmalicious traffic through. In SP2, XP's firewall, called the Windows Firewall, is turned on by default.

 Before SP2, the firewall was called the Internet Connection Firewall (ICF). It was much the same as the Windows Firewall, although with some differences, notably in how you access the firewall and its features.

The Windows Firewall offers protection from inbound threats by blocking inbound connections. But a variety of software, such as instant messaging programs and FTP software, need to be able to accept inbound connections, and the firewall blocks them from working.

Usually, but not always, the first time you run one of these programs, you'll get a warning from the Windows Firewall. The warning will show you the name of the program and the publisher, and will ask if you want to keep blocking the program. If you'd like to allow the Windows Firewall to let the program use the Internet, click

Unblock. To keep blocking the program, click Keep Blocking. The Ask Me Later choice doesn't really ask you later, as it implies. Instead, it lets the program accept incoming connections for just this one time when you run it. After you exit, the next time you run the program, you'll get the same warning.

Unfortunately, though, the Windows Firewall does not always pop up this alert when it blocks an inbound connection. So, you might find that some programs inexplicably don't work with the firewall on, but you won't get a warning about them. In that case, you can manually tell the Windows Firewall to let it through by adding programs to its exceptions list, as explained in the recipe.

The Windows Firewall offers basic Internet security by stopping all unsolicited inbound traffic and connections to your PC and network, unless your PC or another PC on the network initially makes the request for the connection. However, it will not block outgoing requests and connections, so you can continue to use the Internet as you normally would for browsing the web, getting email, using FTP, or similar services.

The Windows Firewall has one serious drawback: it won't protect you against Trojans, such as the Back Orifice Trojan. Trojans let other users take complete control of your PC and its resources. For example, someone could use your PC as a launch pad for attacking web sites and it would appear you were the culprit, or he could copy all your files and find out personal information about you, such as your credit card numbers if you store them on your PC.

The Windows Firewall won't stop Trojans because it blocks only incoming traffic, and Trojans work by making outbound connections from your PC. To stop Trojans, get a third-party firewall. The best is ZoneAlarm—see Recipe 13.14, about configuring ZoneAlarm for details.

When you install XP SP2, you're automatically protected because it turns on the Windows Firewall. (It's not turned on by default in XP versions before SP2.) There's a chance, though, that the firewall has been turned off. To make sure it's turned on, click Security Center from the Control Panel. When the Security Center appears, there should be a green light next to the Firewall button, and it should say On. If it's not on, click the Windows Firewall icon at the bottom of the screen, click On, and then click OK. That will turn it on.

See Also

Recipe 13.13 on tracking your firewall activity with the Windows Firewall log; Recipe 13.14 on using the ZoneAlarm firewall; MS KB 875356, "How to configure the Windows Firewall feature in Windows XP Service Pac 2," and MS KB 875357, "Troubleshooting Windows Firewall settings in Windows XP Service Pack 2."

13.13 Tracking Firewall Activity with a Windows Firewall Log

Problem

You want to track all intrusion attempts that have been made against your PC.

Solution

Using a graphical user interface

1. From the Control Panel, choose Windows Firewall, click the Advanced tab, and click the Settings button in the Security Logging section. The dialog box shown in Figure 13-8 appears.

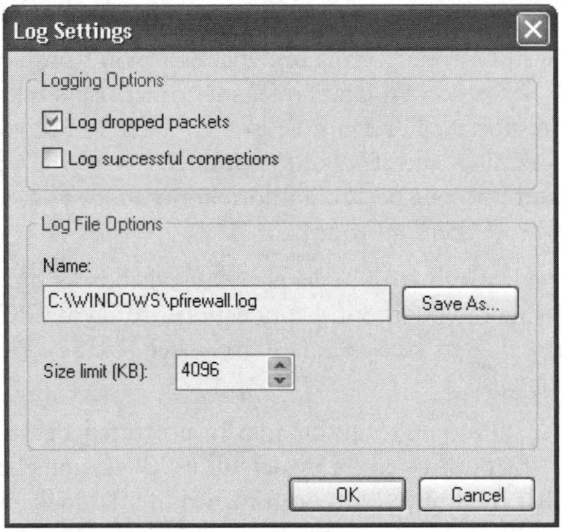

Figure 13-8. Creating a Windows Firewall log

2. Choose whether to log dropped packets, successful connections, or both. A dropped packet is a packet that the Windows Firewall has blocked. A successful connection doesn't mean an intruder has successfully connected to your PC; it refers to any connection *you* have made over the Internet, such as to web sites. Because of this, there's usually no reason for you to log successful connections. If you do log them, your log will become large quickly, and it will be more difficult to track only potentially dangerous activity. So, your best bet is to log only dropped packets.

3. After you've made your choices, choose a location for the log, set its maximum size, and click OK. I don't let my log get larger than 1 MB, but depending on

how much you care about disk space and how much you plan to use the log, you might want yours larger or smaller.

4. The log will be created in a W3C Extended Log format (*.log*) that you can examine with Notepad or another text editor or by using a log analysis program such as the free AWStats (*http://awstats.sourceforge.net*). Each log entry has a total of up to 16 pieces of information associated with each event, but the most important columns for each entry are the first eight.

 In a text editor, the names of the columns don't align over the data, but they will align in a log analyzer.

Discussion

When examining the logs, you need to keep in mind that the source IP address is the source of the attack. Keep in mind that most probes are automated and not targeted at your specific computer. The probes are sent out to thousands of IP addresses. You might notice the same source IP address continually cropping up; if so, you might be targeted by an intruder. It's also possible that the intruder is sending out automated probes to thousands of PCs across the Internet and your PC is not under direct attack. In either case, you can send the log information to your ISP and ask them to follow up by tracking down the source of the attempts. Either forward the entire log or cut and paste the relevant sections to a new file.

To help you better understand the logs, Table 13-4 describes the most important columns.

Table 13-4. The columns in the Windows Firewall log

Name	Description
Date	Date of occurrence, in *year-month-date* format
Time	Time of occurrence, In *hour:minute:second* format
Action	The operation that was logged by the firewall, such as DROP for dropping a connection, OPEN for opening a connection, and CLOSE for closing a connection
Protocol	The protocol used, such as TCP, UDP, or ICMP
Source IP (src-ip)	The IP address of the computer that started the connection
Destination IP (dst-ip)	The IP address of the computer to which the connection was attempted
Source Port (src-port)	The port number on the sending computer from which the connection was attempted
Destination Port (dst-port)	The port to which the sending computer was trying to make a connection
size	The packet size
tcpflags	Information about TCP control flags in TCP headers
tcpsyn	The TCP sequence of a packet
tcpack	The TCP acknowledgment number in the packet

Table 13-4. The columns in the Windows Firewall log (continued)

Name	Description
tcpwin	The TCP window size of the packet
icmtype	Information about the ICMP messages
icmcode	Information about the ICMP messages
Info	Information about an entry in the log

See Also

Recipe 13.12 setting up the Windows Firewall; Recipe 13.14 on using the ZoneAlarm firewall; MS KB 875356, "How to configure the Windows Firewall feature in Windows XP Service Pack 2," and MS KB 875357, "Troubleshooting Windows Firewall settings in Windows XP Service Pack 2"

13.14 Protecting Yourself with the ZoneAlarm Firewall

Problem

You want to protect yourself with a more capable firewall than XP's Windows Firewall.

Solution

Using downloadable software

The Windows Firewall doesn't provide outbound protection, but the ZoneAlarm firewall does. To use it, after you install ZoneAlarm, click Firewall in the left panel and you'll get to choose the level of protection (from Low to High) you want for the Internet Zone and the Trusted Security Zone (for computers on your network, or that you trust for some other reason). The settings are self-explanatory.

When you start using ZoneAlarm, alerts (such as the one shown in Figure 13-9) will start popping up every time a program attempts to make a connection to the Internet. It will most likely be a program you are familiar with, such as Internet Explorer, Outlook Express, or a similar program. If it's a program you're familiar with and you want the program to always be able to access the Internet, click the box that reads Remember this answer the next time I use this program, and then click Yes to let the program access the Internet.

If it's a program you're unfamiliar with, or if you have no idea why it would be connecting to the Internet, click More Info. You might be asked whether you want to allow your browser to access the Internet. Click Yes, and you'll be sent to ZoneAlarm's site, which will offer some basic information about the alert. The general

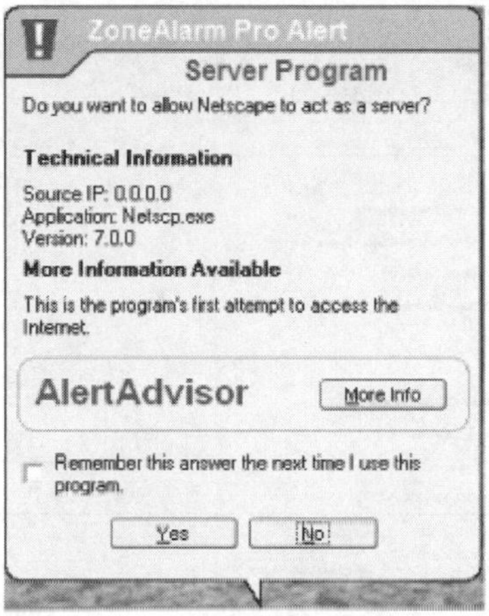

Figure 13-9. A ZoneAlarm warning

rule, though, is to allow only programs you are familiar with to access the Internet. If you've just launched a program that requires Internet access and you get the alert, let the program access the Internet. Or, you might want to let a program you've just installed contact the maker's web site for automatic updates and patches, if you like that sort of thing. But if the alert pops up for no reason at a random time and you're unfamiliar with the program, you should deny it access. You should also immediately run an antivirus program to see whether it can detect a Trojan.

If you allow the program to access the Internet, and you check the box so that you're not alerted next time, it will always be able to access the Internet. If you want to always be alerted when the program tries to access the Internet, don't check the box.

After you designate a program as always being allowed to access the Internet, it will be put onto a list that ZoneAlarm maintains about trusted programs. You can customize any program on that list, take programs off the list, or customize their security settings: click Program Control in ZoneAlarm's left panel, and click the Programs tab. You'll see a screen similar to Figure 13-10.

Use this screen to customize how you'll allow each program to access the Internet. By inserting a check mark in the appropriate column, you can choose whether to allow the program to access the Internet or Trusted Zone, whether you want it to act as a server in the Internet or Trusted Zone, and similar features. A check mark means the program is allowed to access the Internet; an X means it's not allowed to access the Internet; and a ? means it should ask before being allowed to access the Internet.

Discussion

XP's Windows Firewall has a serious deficiency: it can't monitor and block outbound traffic from your PC to the Internet. Many Trojans and other pests, including

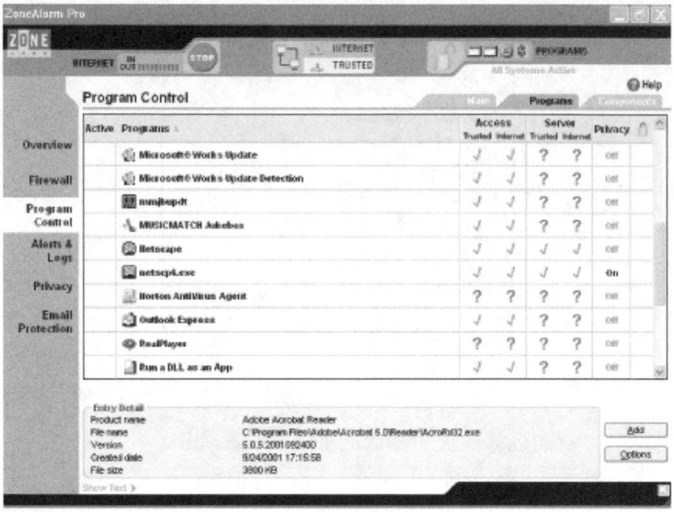

Figure 13-10. Customizing the way a program can access the Internet

spyware, do their damage by installing themselves on your system and then allowing others to take control of your PC or by using your PC to attack web sites, servers, and other computers. The Windows Firewall won't offer you protection against these types of Trojans; it won't be able to tell when a Trojan is making an outbound connection, so the Trojan will be able to do its damage without your knowledge.

Other firewalls, however, will offer that protection. ZoneAlarm (available from *http:// www.zonealarm.com*) offers a free version that provides excellent protection against inbound threats as well as against Trojans. It also tells you whenever someone is probing your computer for security holes and gives information about the prober, often including the IP address, and the nature of the probe.

The most important feature of ZoneAlarm is its ability to block outgoing traffic from your PC. That way, you can be sure a Trojan hasn't infected your PC and can't "call out" to make contact with someone malicious, or be used to attack others from your PC.

There are for-pay versions of ZoneAlarm, and there are other for-pay firewalls, such as the Norton Personal Firewall, and the McAfee Personal Firewall. The for-pay version of ZoneAlarm adds features such as virus protection and spam protection. But for basic firewall protection, the free version of ZoneAlarm is more than adequate.

See Also

Recipe 13.12 for setting up the Windows Firewall and Recipe 13.13 for using a Windows Firewall log

13.15 Surfing the Web Anonymously

Problem

You want to be completely anonymous when you surf the web.

Solution

Using a graphical user interface

To surf anonymously with an anonymous proxy server, follow these steps:

1. Find an anonymous proxy server. There are hundreds of free, public proxy servers available, but many frequently go offline or are very slow. To find the best one, go to *http://www.atomintersoft.com/products/alive-proxy/proxy-list*. The web site lists information about each server, including its average response time, uptime, and the last time the server was checked.

2. Find the server with the highest percentage of uptime and write down its IP address and the port it uses. For example, in the following listing 212.170.23.82:80, the IP address is 212.170.23.82, and the port number is 80.

3. In Internet Explorer, select Tools → Internet Options, click the Connections tab, and click the LAN Settings button.

4. Check the Use a proxy server for your LAN box. In the Address field, type in the IP address of the proxy server. In the Port field, type in its port number. Check the Bypass proxy server for local addresses box; you don't need to remain anonymous on your local network (see Figure 13-11).

5. Click OK and then OK again to close the dialog boxes.

Now when you surf the web, the proxy server will protect your privacy. Keep in mind that proxy servers can make surfing the web much slower.

Using downloadable software

You can also download a piece of software to automatically configure your browser to use anonymous proxy servers, and find the fastest one. GhostSurf (*http://www.tenebril.com/products/ghostsurf*) uses multiple anonymous proxy servers and always looks for the fastest one. The software costs $29.95, but you can download a free, 15-day trial.

Discussion

Simply browsing the web leaves you vulnerable to privacy invasions by web sites. They can track your online travels, know what operating system and browser you're running, peer into your clipboard, uncover the last sites you visited, examine your history list, delve into your browser cache, and examine your IP address to learn

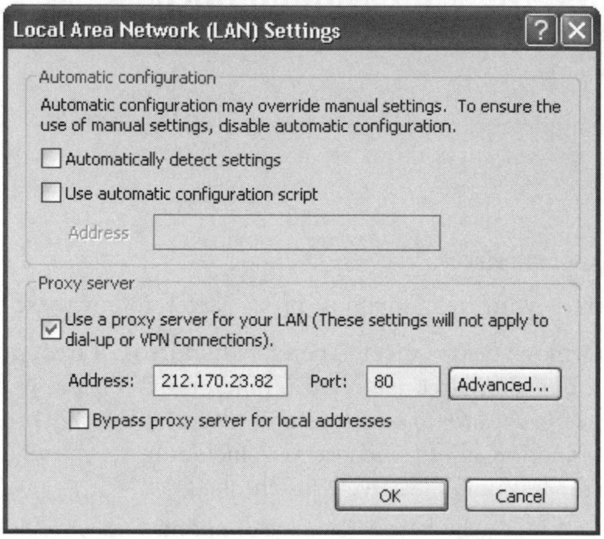

Figure 13-11. Configuring an anonymous proxy server

basic information about you, such as your geographic location, and more. In short, your life is an open book.

Using an anonymous proxy server can protect your privacy by hiding all these details and more from web sites. An anonymous proxy server sits between you and the web sites you visit. Instead of contacting a web site directly, your browser tells a proxy server which web site you want to visit. That way, the web site sees the proxy server, not your PC. It can't read your cookies, find out your IP address, see your history list, or examine your clipboard and cache. It can't probe your system at all because your PC is never in direct contact with it. You can surf anonymously, without a trace.

See Also

To see just a small portion of the kinds of information that sites can easily find out about you, go to *http://www.anonymizer.com* and click "Free Privacy Test."

13.16 Finding and Reading RSS Feeds

Problem

You want to find and read RSS (Really Simple Syndication) feeds on the Internet.

Solution

Using downloadable software

A variety of freeware and shareware will let you find and read RSS feeds:

- FeedDemon (*http://www.feeddemon.com*) RSS reader was awarded a *PC World*'s Editor's Pick award. Free to try; $29.95 if you decide to keep and use it.
- RssReader (*http://www.feeddemon.com*) Freeware.
- Gator (*http://www.newsgator.com*). NewsGator Outlook works from directly within Outlook and is free to try, $29 if you continue to use it. The Newsgator Online RSS reader is free and requires that you read RSS online, not in software on your PC.
- AmphetaDesk (*http://www.disobey.com/amphetadesk*) Freeware
- FeedReader (*http://www.feedreader.com*) Freeware
- Radio Userland (*http://www.radiouserland.com*)

Discussion

RSS and a competing format, Atom, allow web sites and blogs to syndicate news and information from their sites and feed them to anyone interested. RSS uses XML to create the feeds, and RSS readers are capable of reading that XML and displaying them as news feeds.

RSS readers include built-in ways to find RSS and Atom feeds using search tools, subscribe to them, and will then automatically grab those feeds and display them for easy reading. They'll also allow you to easily organize your feeds and search through them. You can also use the readers to unsubscribe as well.

When you come across an orange box on a web site with the letters "XML" on it, that means the site has an RSS feed. To subscribe to the feed, right-click it, and then either copy the link location and pop it into your RSS reader, or else choose an option that will automatically subscribe to it in your RSS reader. The exact way you do it varies from RSS reader to RSS reader.

See Also

Sites that will let you search through RSS feeds for ones you want include *http://www.syndic8.com*, *http://www.newsisfree.com/sources/bycat*, *http://www.rssreader.com/rssfeeds.htm*, and *http://www.feedster.com*.

CHAPTER 14
Wireless Networking

14.0 Introduction

Wireless networking has become nearly ubiquitous. Many laptops include wireless capabilities built directly into them, and wireless hardware, including both routers and network adapters, have become increasingly affordable. You can buy a router or network adapter for under $50.

Additionally, hotspots, public areas where you can connect to the Internet, have become increasingly popular as well. There are literally thousands of hotspots available, in airports, hotels, cafes, and even entire metropolitan neighborhoods.

XP has played a big part in making all this possible. It includes easy-to-use wireless networking built directly into it. That means that instead of wrestling with different types of software to make a wireless connection, there's a simple, standard way of connecting and setting up networks.

XP's Service Pack 2 (SP2) makes wireless networking even easier than earlier versions of XP. The client for making a connection to wireless networks is simpler, and it includes Wi-Fi Protected Access (WPA) encryption built into it.

In this chapter, you'll learn all about wireless and XP, everything from setting up wireless routers to installing wireless network adapters, protecting wireless networks, connecting to hotspots and more. Note that all recipes show how to use wireless networking with SP2.

14.1 Installing a Wireless Adapter

Problem

You want to install a wireless networking adapter so that you can use a laptop or desktop with one or more wireless networks.

Solution

You have several decisions to make when installing a wireless adapter. First is which wireless standard to use. There are two popular wireless standards (both called WiFi): 802.11b and 802.11g. They are compatible to a certain extent, but there are some anomalies you should know about before deciding which adapter to buy. Here's what you need to know about the two standards:

802.11b
> This is the older of the two standards and transfers data at a maximum rate of 11 Mbps. An 802.11b wireless adapter will typically sell for less than an 802.11g adapter, by at least $10 or more. If you're connecting your laptop or PC to an 802.11b router, then you should buy an 802.11b adapter, because the only way that you can get the higher 802.11g speeds is if all devices on the network are 802.11g. However, if you think that you might want to use your laptop or PC with an 802.11g network, you should buy an 802.11g adapter. An 802.11b adapter will work with an 802.11g network, but it will communicate at 11 Mbps, not the faster 802.11g. In fact, putting an 802.11b adapter on an 802.11g network will slow the entire network down to 802.11b.

802.11g
> This is the newer of the two standards and transfers data at a maximum rate of 54 Mbps. It sells for about $10 more than an 802.11 adapter. If you're connecting to an 802.11g router, buy an 802.11g adapter; an 802.11b adapter will slow the entire network down to 802.11b. If you're connecting to an 802.11b network, but think that you might at some point be connecting to an 802.11g network, it's a good idea to buy an 802.11g adapter. An 802.11g adapter will connect to an 802.11b network at the 802.11b standard of 11 Mbps.

Next, decide whether you want to buy a WiFi card, USB device, or PCI device. If you have a laptop, your best bet is a card, because it's the easiest to carry with you. For desktops, either a USB device or PCI device will do. USB devices are easier to install, because they don't require that you take off your system's case and use empty slots on the motherboard. If your PC only has a limited number of USB ports, though, they may be taken up by a printer, keyboard, mouse, or other devices. However, you can easily add extra USB ports to your PC by buying a USB hub, which connects to a USB port on your PC.

Once you've decided which to buy, here's how to install a WiFi adapter:

1. Physically install the adapter. How you do this varies according to whether you're installing a PC card, a USB device, or a PCI card. If you have a PC card, slip it into the card slot and push it in so that it's attached firmly, as shown in Figure 14-1. Don't force it, though, or else you could damage it. For a USB device, plug it into the USB port. For a PCI card, turn off your PC and unplug it. Then take off the case, and find an empty slot. Unscrew the backplate attached

Figure 14-1. To install a PC WiFi card, slip it into the card slot and make sure that the connection is secure

to the slot, and firmly seat the PCI card in the slot. Then attach the screw. Finally, put the case back on, attach the power cord, and turn on your PC.

2. The adapter may be automatically recognized by XP. If it is, you'll get a message in the Notification Area telling you that the adapter has been installed and is ready to use.

3. If the adapter is not automatically recognized by XP, the Add Hardware Wizard should appear, as shown in Figure 14-2. Click the Next button on it, and follow the simple directions for installing the hardware. If your adapter came with a disk that includes a driver, when the wizard asks for the location of the driver, insert the disk in your PC, and tell it to find the driver from that location.

4. If your adapter came with an installation disk, you may want to use that instead of the Add Hardware Wizard. If so, when the Add Hardware Wizard appears, click the Cancel button, insert the installation disk in your PC, and follow the installation instructions.

5. If the XP doesn't recognize your adapter, and the Add Hardware Wizard doesn't automatically appear, choose Start → Control Panel and choose Printers and Other Hardware. The Add Hardware Wizard should appear.

Figure 14-2. The Add Hardware Wizard

Discussion

If you're starting a network from scratch, your best bet is to buy 802.11g adapters and a router. They cost only a little more than 802.11b hardware, but offer a higher connection speed. Over time, manufacturers may stop selling 802.11b hardware as well.

The 802.11b and 802.11g standards aren't the only 802.11 standards, although they're the main ones used in homes and businesses. The 802.11a standard operates in the 5.15–5.35 Ghz bandwidth and so is less prone to interference than 802.11b and 802.11g, which operate in the 2.4 Ghz bandwidth used by portable phones. 802.11a, like 802.11g, has a maximum speed of 54 Mbps, although its range is smaller than 802.11g's.

See Also

For help in troubleshooting hardware installation problems, including for wireless adapters, see Chapter 3.

14.2   Installing a Wireless Router

Problem

You want to install a wireless router, so that you can set up a wireless network.

Solution

Before installation, you need to decide whether to buy an 802.11b or 802.11g network. 802.11g networks are only slightly more expensive than 802.11b networks but operate at much higher speeds, a maximum of 54 Mbps, compared to 11 Mbps for 802.11b.

How you set up a wireless router varies from manufacturer to manufacturer, and even among different models from the same manufacturer. Here's how to install a typical wireless router from Linksys. It assumes that you're installing it at home, to connect to a broadband Internet device, such as a cable modem, in order to share Internet access among all the computers on your network:

1. Connect one end of an Ethernet cable to the cable modem or DSL modem, and the other end to the router. The router will have multiple Ethernet ports, because wireless routers also let you connect PCs to it via Ethernet ports. You need to connect the cable from the broadband modem to a special port on the router—it will be labeled WAN or Internet. Different manufacturers may use different terminologies, so you should check for the right connection port.

 When you first connect the Ethernet cable to your router, don't turn on the router.

2. After you connect the Ethernet cable, turn off your broadband modem for five minutes. Then turn it back on again, plug in your router's powercord, and turn on the power switch if your router has a power switch. After several minutes, you should see green lights flashing on your router. Check your router's documentation for details of how your router looks when it is properly connected to the cable or DSL modem.

3. Go to the Setup screen. How you do this varies from router to router. Every manufacturer has a different setup screen, and the way that you get to that screen varies by manufacturer. For a Linksys router, for example, you open a browser, type *http://192.168.1.1* in the address bar, and press Enter. A login screen appears. Leave the username field blank; in the Password field, type admin and press Enter. You'll see a Setup screen like that shown in Figure 14-3.

4. You shouldn't need to change any of the basic setup options. If you're connecting to the Internet via DSL rather than by cable modem, in the Internet Connection type drop-down box, you may need to choose PPPoE. Check with your ISP for details.

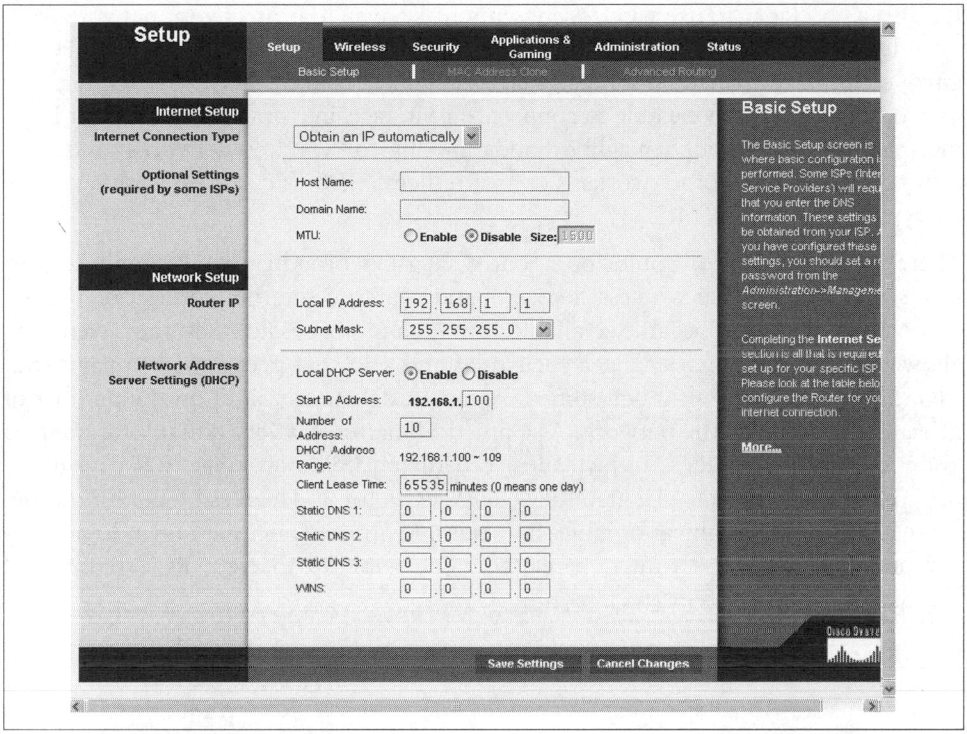

Setup

Setup　Wireless　Security　Applications & Gaming　Administration　Status

Basic Setup | MAC Address Clone | Advanced Routing

Internet Setup

Internet Connection Type　Obtain an IP automatically ▾

Optional Settings
(required by some ISPs)
Host Name: _____
Domain Name: _____
MTU:　○ Enable　◉ Disable　Size: 1500

Network Setup

Router IP
Local IP Address:　192 . 168 . 1 . 1
Subnet Mask:　255 . 255 . 255 . 0 ▾

Network Address
Server Settings (DHCP)
Local DHCP Server:　◉ Enable　○ Disable
Start IP Address:　192.168.1. 100
Number of Address:　10
DHCP Address Range:　192.168.1.100 ~ 109
Client Lease Time:　65535 minutes (0 means one day)
Static DNS 1:　0 . 0 . 0 . 0
Static DNS 2:　0 . 0 . 0 . 0
Static DNS 3:　0 . 0 . 0 . 0
WINS:　0 . 0 . 0 . 0

Save Settings　Cancel Changes

Basic Setup

The Basic Setup screen is where basic configuration is performed. Some ISPs (Internet Service Providers) will require that you enter the DNS information. These settings will be obtained from your ISP. After you have configured these settings, you should set a new password from the *Administration->Management* screen.

Completing the **Internet Setup** section is all that is required to set up for your specific ISP. Please look at the table below to configure the Router for your Internet connection.

More...

Cisco Systems

Figure 14-3. A Linksys router Setup screen

5. Click the Wireless tab to get to the basic wireless settings. Next to Wireless, choose Enabled. In the Wireless Network Name (SSID), type in a name to give your network. That is the name that will be broadcast to any PCs that want to connect to it.

6. Click Save Settings when you're done.

7. Your router may not yet be able to connect to the Internet. Depending on your ISP, you might have to call it in order to enable Internet access. Some ISPs require that you give them the router's MAC address, a number such as 00-90-4B-0E-3F-BD, that uniquely identifies a piece of hardware such as a router or a network card. If your ISP requires it, call the technical support line and give them the MAC address. After a few minutes, your router will be connected to the Internet.

Discussion

It's good practice, when setting up a wireless router, to choose a new network name (SSID) rather than use the default. If you use the default, it's easier for passersby to try and connect to your network. You should also set the router so that it does not broadcast its SSID. Check your router manual for details.

It's also a good idea to use wireless encryption as a way to protect your network from intruders. Your network is available wirelessly not just to your PCs, but to the PCs of anyone within range, which can be as far as 300 feet. That means that neighbors and anyone passing by may be able to connect to it. In fact, in a practice called War Driving, people drive through neighborhoods looking for wireless networks, and even create and post maps of networks, along with their SSIDS. (For details on how to use encryption, see Recipe 14.7.)

There is a great deal of confusion about what rules broadband ISPs apply toward those who want to use wireless networks and share an Internet connection. When home networks first became available, broadband ISPs said that they were not allowed to be used, then changed their rules and said that people had to pay extra. That no longer holds, although some ISPs may say there is a limit on the number of PCs allowed to be on the network. As a practical matter it is very difficult for them to know the number of PCs. In fact, most broadband ISPs now offer to set up home networks for customers, although they charge extra for it. The fees range from somewhat high, to downright affordable. For example, in the Cincinnati area, RoadRunner provides a wireless router, wireless adapters for up to eight PCs, setup, and technical support, for $4 extra a month.

See Also

For information about speeding up a wireless network, see Recipe 14.5.

14.3   Connecting to Your Wireless Network

Problem

You've set up a WiFi router and installed WiFi adapter cards, and you want to connect a WiFi-enabled PC to the WiFi network.

Solution

When you turn on a WiFi-enabled PC that is within the transmission range of a WiFi router, it should automatically find the network and make a connection. You'll know a connection has been made by looking in the Notification Area for the wireless icon, as shown in Figure 14-4.

Figure 14-4. The wireless icon in the Notification Area at the right of the Taskbar

If the wireless icon looks different than the one pictured here, for example if it has an X over it or it appears to be blinking, then for some reason you haven't been able to automatically connect to the network. To make the connection, click the icon, then click View Wireless Networks. If your wireless network shows up on the Wireless Network Connection screen, but the screen shows that you're not connected, double-click the entry for the network, and you should connect to it. When you make a successful connection, you'll see a screen like that pictured in Figure 14-5.

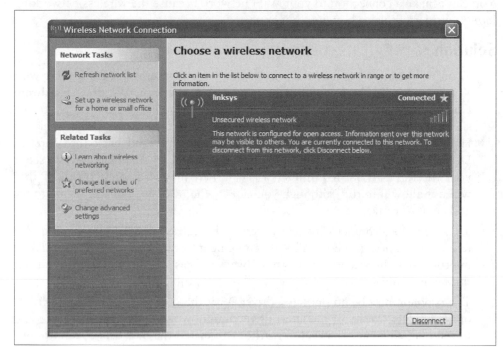

Figure 14-5. A successful connection to a wireless network

If the screen doesn't show any wireless networks, click the Refresh network list underneath Network Tasks on the left-hand part of the screen. After a few moments, you will see your wireless network. Double-click it to connect.

Discussion

Making a simple wireless connection, as outlined in this recipe, usually goes smoothly. In this recipe, though, no encryption is being used, and setting up encryption can be difficult. If it is not done correctly, it won't allow you to connect to the network.

It's a good idea, though, to use encryption. If you don't, anyone passing by can easily connect to your wireless network. For details on how to use encryption to keep your wireless network safe, see Recipe 14.7.

See Also

For information about troubleshooting wireless connection problems, see Recipe 14.4.

14.4 Troubleshooting WiFi Network Connections

Problem

You can't make a connection to your WiFi network because the wireless networking icon or properties dialog box does not appear.

Solution

- Your problem may be that your wireless network adapter is not compatible with Windows XP. To check whether it is compatible, check the Windows Hardware Compatibility List (HCL) at *http://www.microsoft.com/hcl*. When you get to the site, click See the Windows Catalog, then from the page that appears, click the Hardware tab. Next click Networking and Modems, and click the Wireless Devices link. Browse the list, which is alphabetized by manufacturer, to see if your wireless card is listed. If it's not listed, there may be a conflict with XP that will not allow it to run, although you can try the next steps in this recipe to try and get it to work.

- There may be a conflict between routers and wireless adapters bought from different companies. In theory, all WiFi equipment, regardless of vendor, should be interoperable. In practice, that is not always the case. Buying all hardware from the same manufacturer lessens the likelihood of problems.

- The problem may be an outdated driver. Visit the web site of the manufacturer of the adapter, check for the latest driver, and download and install it according to the manufacturer's instructions. After you install the new driver, restart your PC and see if it can now make the connection.

- In order for your PC to automatically connect to a wireless network, the Wireless Zero Configuration service must be running. If it's not enabled, XP won't automatically make the connection. To make sure that it is, select Start → Run and in the Open box, type services.msc at a command line and press Enter. This runs the Services Microsoft Management Console. Scroll down until you see the Wireless Zero Configuration entry. The status should be Started. If it's not, right-click it, choose Start, and exit the console. XP should now automatically search for and connect to your wireless network.

- Your driver, for some reason, may not recognize the Wireless Zero Configuration service. To see if it does, right-click My Network Places (visible usually on the Start menu, or as a desktop icon) and choose Properties. This opens the Network Connections folder. You should see an icon for a Wireless Network connection, as shown in Figure 14-6. If you don't see an icon, you have a problem with your driver, and you'll need to find out whether it's installed correctly or has a conflict with another device. For details on how to do that, see Chapter 3.

Figure 14-6. The Network Connections folder

- If the icon is visible, right-click the icon and choose Properties. If you don't see a Wireless Network tab, the problem is that your wireless network adapter doesn't fully support the Wireless Zero Configuration service. You'll have to manually create a fully working network connection. To do it:

  1. In the Network Connections folder, right-click Wireless Connection, and then choose Properties. On the General tab, click configure. Click the Advanced tab, and then select the right configuration options for your network. The available options on this tab and the option names will vary depending on the manufacturer of your wireless adapter. However, here are some basic configuration options you may come across:

  Service Set Identifier (SSID)
  > Type in the name of your SSID, which is your network name. For details, see Recipe 14.2 in this chapter.

  Wireless Equivalent Protocol (WEP), Wi-Fi Protected Access (WPA),
  or Encryption
  > This encrypts data so that only those who have the right encryption key can access your network. For now, disable encryption for troubleshooting purposes. After you get the connection working, you can enable encryption, as outlined in Recipe 14.2.

Mode or Network Type

There are two choices here: Infrastructure or Ad-Hoc. Infrastructure means that you're connecting to a WiFi router; Ad-Hoc means you're directly connecting to another PC with a WiFi card in it. Since you're trying to connect to a WiFi network, choose Infrastructure.

Data Rate

Set this option to Auto or to 11 Mbps if it's an 802.11b network, or 54 Mbps if it's an 802.11g network.

Power Save

For troubleshooting purposes, set Power Save to Off or to Disabled. After you get the connection working correctly, you can change this setting to save power.

2. After you configure these options, click OK.

3. Restart your computer. It should now recognize your network. If a red X appears over the connection icon in the Network Connections folder or if you cannot connect, try turning off the Wireless Zero Configuration service. Because you've manually changed the settings, you won't need the service to run in order to connect to the network.

4. To turn Wireless Zero Configuration off, follow the directions outlined in this recipe. When you right-click Wireless Zero Configuration, choose Stop. Restart your PC. You should now be able to connect.

- If, when you right-clicked the Wireless Connection and chose Properties, the Wireless Networks tab was visible, the Wireless Zero Configuration service recognizes your driver. But if you can't make the connection, you need to configure your adapter for your network. Here's how to do it:

1. Click the Wireless Networks tab, highlight your network, and click Properties.

2. Click the Association tab. In the Network name (SSID) box, type in the name of your network. From the Data encryption drop-down box, choose Disabled. (After you get your connection working, you can enable encryption.)

3. Click the Connection tab. Make sure the box is checked next to Connect when this network is in range. Click OK.

4. You'll be sent back to the Wireless Network connections tab, with your network highlighted. Click Advanced. Select either Access point (infrastructure) networks only or Any available network (access point preferred). Click Close and then OK.

5. You may need to restart your PC. You should be able to connect to the wireless network.

Discussion

The Wireless Zero Configuration service represents a major jump over previous versions of Windows when it comes to making a wireless connection. When possible, you should use it to manage your wireless connections, rather than turning it off. Some manufacturers of wireless cards have their own software for managing the wireless connection, but you'll usually run into fewer problems if you instead let XP handle the connection with the Wireless Zero Configuration service.

Troubleshooting wireless connections can be one of the more difficult tasks you'll ever encounter. Problems may be caused by drivers or the Wireless Zero Configuration service, and in those cases, this recipe should solve the problem. However, general TCP/IP and Internet connectivity problems may have nothing to do with the wireless connection—they may be related to general Internet connectivity. And they may also be caused by interference. Turn to Chapter 13 for more details. Other factors may be causing you to have wireless connectivity problems. The problem may be TCP/IP related. For details on how to troubleshoot it, see MS KB 314067. You may also have problems with interference. For details, and how to troubleshoot, see Recipe 14.5.

See Also

MS KB 870702 for troubleshooting wireless connections in SP2, and MS KB 314067 for troubleshooting pre-SP2 connections

14.5   Speeding Up a WiFi Network

Problem

Your wireless network is sluggish, and you want to improve its speed.

Solution

WiFi networks are notorious for sometimes sluggish connections, because of potential interference from devices like cordless phones, and from walls, furniture, and other objects. Additionally, wireless networks rarely deliver data at their rated bandwidth speed. You often will get only half the rated speed, even in the best of conditions.

Interference from other devices and the layout of your house or office can affect network speed as well. So here's what you can do to get more throughput throughout your home or office.

Put your wireless router in a central location
> If you tuck your router in a corner of the house or office, PCs near it may get high throughput, but for others, speed may drop significantly.

Install a booster or extender antenna

You can buy a variety of devices that can extend the range of your network and can help speed up its speed at the edge of its transmission distance. For example, the Linksys HGA7T high-gain antenna kit includes antennas that can replace the existing antennas in Linksys routers and extend the range of a Linksys wireless network. And wireless repeaters such as the D-Link DWL-800AP+ Wireless Range Extender can strengthen a weak signal to extend the range of a network.

Point the router's antennas vertically

As a general rule, transmission is best when antennas are vertically oriented rather than horizontally. However, wireless transmissions are notoriously eccentric, so experiment at your home or office for best results.

Point the antennas of your wireless PCs in the direction of the router

If your WiFi adapter has an external, adjustable antenna, point it at the router. For PC Card WiFi adapters that don't have external antennas, orient your PC or laptop until you get the best signal strength.

Don't place your router next to an outside wall

Putting an access point next to an outside wall will broadcast signals to the outside, not the inside.

Don't place routers or wireless PCs near filing cabinets and other large metal objects

They often cause significant interference and can cut throughput dramatically. Also, remove any metal objects in the path from the router to the client, or else reposition them so that no metal objects are in between. Filing cabinets, water pipes, electrical wires, and even coat hangers and metal beads under drywall surfaces can cause problems.

Set your router to use "b" mode only

Some "g" mode protocols can cause interference problems, so if you tell your router to only use "b" mode, you'll cut down on interference.

Discussion

Trying to track down the source of interference or slowdowns on WiFi networks can be maddening, because so many objects and devices can cause interference. On some days, there might be interference, and on other days, there may be none.

Making matters worse is that common household devices interfere with WiFi networks. Portable phones and microwave ovens both operate in the 2.4 Ghz spectrum, the same as WiFi. Both 802.11b and 802.11g WiFi networks operate in that spectrum. The rarely used 802.11a standard instead operates in the 5 Ghz band. So if you're running into problems, try turning off portable phones, and see if any other household appliances might be causing problems. Baby monitors, wireless cameras, and X-10 home-automation devices are notorious for causing problems.

The problem may also be caused by another nearby WiFi network. To see if any are nearby, click the wireless network icon and from the screen that appears, choose View Wireless Networks. You'll see any nearby networks that might be causing problems. If that's an issue, you can cut down or eliminate interference by using a different channel than the nearby network. Some wireless adapters include software that will tell you which channels each wireless network uses. Set your network so that it is not in the same channel to your neighbor's.

See Also

Check out Chapter 5, "Configuring Wireless Access Points," in *Windows XP Unwired*, by Wei-Meng Lee, from O'Reilly, for more information about interference problems that you might encounter, and how to solve them.

14.6   Keeping Your WiFi Network Secure

Problem

You want to protect your WiFi network from intruders.

Solution

No single fix will keep you protected, so you'll have to combine a variety of security measures:

- Stop broadcasting your network's SSID (its network name). Your router normally sends out its SSID, which makes it easier for intruders to find it and connect to it. You can, however, tell it not to broadcast its SSID. Someone needs to know its SSID in order to connect to it. How you stop it from broadcasting varies from manufacturer to manufacturer, and even from model to model from the same manufacturer. But for many models of Linksys routers, here's how to do it:

  1. Log into the setup screen by opening your browser and going to *http://192.168.1.1*. When the login screen appears, leave the username blank. In the password section, type admin and press Enter. (Note: if you've changed the login name and password from the default, use that instead.)

  2. Click the Wireless tab. Select Disabled for Wireless SSID Broadcast and click Save Settings. (Note: on older Linksys routers, stay on the Setup tab, go to the ESSID box, type in a new name for your network, and click the Apply button.)

  3. After you change your network name, reconnect each WiFi computer to the network, using the new network name. To reconnect, right-click the small wireless icon in the Windows Notification Area, and from the screen that appears, click Change advanced settings, then click the Wireless Networks

tab. Click the Add button in the Preferred network section, type in the network name, and click OK, and OK again.

 In addition to stopping broadcasting your SSID, you should also change your SSID so that it's not the default as shipped by the manufacturer, because snoopers know default names and can look for WiFi networks using default names. How you change the name varies according to router manufacturer and model. In many Linksys routers, you change it on the same screen on which you tell the router to stop broadcasting your SSID. In the Wireless Network Name (SSID) box, type in the new name, then click Save Settings.

• Regularly change the channel your router transmits over. That way, if someone has tapped into it before, he won't know on which channel it's now broadcasting. Again, how you do this varies by manufacturer and model. To do it, first log onto your router's setup screen. In a Linksys router, after you log in, click the Wireless tab, and choose a new wireless channel from the Wireless Channel drop-down list.

• Limit the number of IP addresses your DHCP server allows on your network to the number of computers that you actually have. That way, no one else will be able to be get an IP address from your network's DHCP server because your PCs will use up all the available IP addresses. Your router's built-in DHCP server hands out IP addresses whenever a computer needs to use the network, and the router lets you set the maximum number of IP addresses it hands out. To limit the number on a Linksys router, go to the Setup screen and scroll to the bottom. In the Number of addresses box, shown in Figure 14-7, type in the number of computers that will use your network, and click Save Settings. If you add another computer to your network, make sure you go back to the screen and increase the number of DHCP users by one.

• Filter out MAC addresses. You can tell your network to allow in only network adapters with specific MAC addresses. That way, only hardware that you specify can use your network. (Note that not all routers have this capability, although Linksys routers do.) A MAC address is a number that uniquely identifies a network adapter or other piece of communications hardware. There are several ways to find out the MAC address of a network adapter. One simple way is to go to a command prompt, type ipconfig /all, and press Enter. In the results you get, look for the numbers next to Physical Address, such as 00-08-A1-00-9F-32. That's the MAC address. Find out the MAC addresses of all the network adapters that you're giving network access to. Then, on a Linksys router, log into the Setup screen and click Security. Click Edit MAC Filter Settings, and from the screen that appears, type in the MAC address for each of your PCs on a separate line next to Mac 1, Mac 2, and so on. Click Apply, and

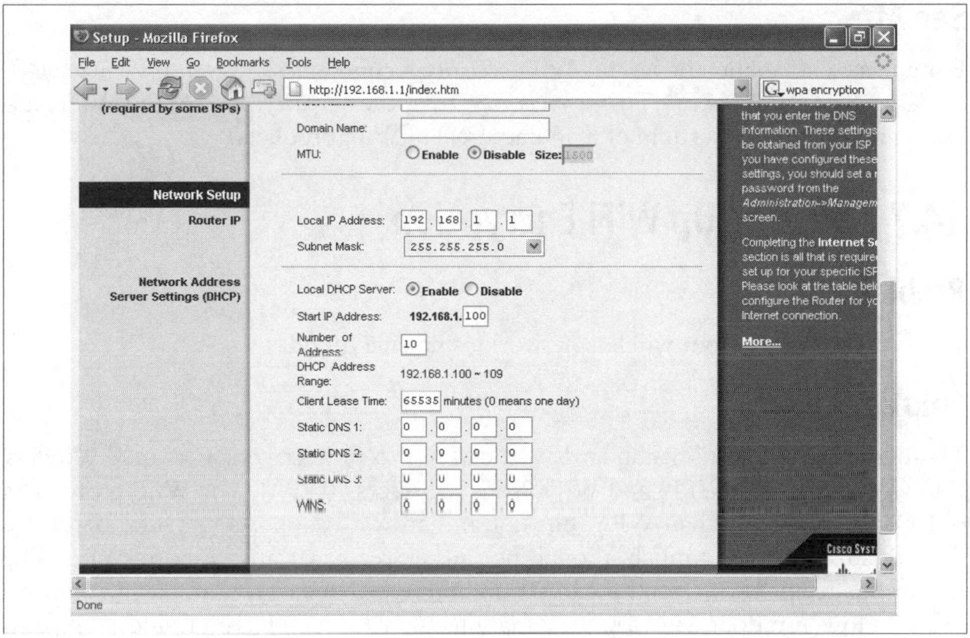

Figure 14-7. Limiting the number of IP addresses your DHCP server hands out

then click Save Settings. Whenever you add a new PC to your network, make sure to add its MAC address.

- Use encryption. Use either WEP encryption or WPA encryption. (WPA is newer and more secure.) For details, see Recipe 14.7.

Discussion

If you use a home network, it's unlikely that you'll be specifically targeted by intruders. Someone may accidentally discover your network when war-driving, or a neighbor may accidentally discover it when she connects to her own network. In some neighborhoods, you're more likely than others to face intruders. For example, if you live in a neighborhood that has many student houses and apartments, you're more likely to face intruders. When students share a house or apartment, they frequently use WiFi networks as a way to give everyone Internet access, so there are many people who have PCs with wireless cards.

Corporate wireless networks, on the other hand, are more likely to be targeted and need to be more vigilant about security. So they should frequently change their SSIDs and channels on which they broadcast, and use the strongest possible encryption. Additionally, they should use other normal network security features, such as firewalls and authentication.

See Also

For a basic explanation of various WiFi security technologies, go to *http://www.wi-fi.org/OpenSection/secure.asp?TID=2#security_tech*, the security page of the WiFi Alliance, an industry consortium of manufacturers of WiFi products.

14.7   Setting Up WiFi Encryption

Problem

You want to protect your wireless network using encryption.

Solution

There are two encryption standards you can use to protect your network: Wireless Equivalent Protocol (WEP) and WiFi Protected Access (WPA). The WEP protocol is older and less secure than WPA, but not all hardware supports it. Older hardware doesn't support it, and much, though not all, newer hardware supports WPA. The rest of this recipe shows you how to set up both types of encryption, using a Linksys router. How you do it will vary from manufacturer to manufacturer, and even from model to model from the same manufacturer. It will also vary depending on your wireless adapter, but will generally follow these steps.

Setting up WEP encryption

1. Go to the Setup screen of your router. For a Linksys router, open a browser, type *http://192.168.1.1* in the address bar, and press Enter. A login screen appears. Leave the username field blank; in the Password field, type admin and press Enter. If you've changed the user name and password, use those instead.

2. Click Wireless, and then Wireless Security.

3. Select Enable next to Wireless Security.

4. Select WEP from the Security Mode drop-down list.

5. In the Default Key section, choose any key from one through four. (It doesn't matter which you choose.)

6. Next, select the wireless encryption level you want to use. From the Wireless Encryption Level drop-down box, choose either 64 bits 10 hex digits or 128 bits 26 hex digits. Using 128-bit encryption is more secure but will slow down your wireless network slightly more than does 64-bit encryption.

7. If you chose 64-bit encryption, type in a phrase in the Passphrase box, shown in Figure 14-8, and click Generate. That will generate the WEP key that you'll use on your router, and each PC on the network. Four keys will be created in the WEP Key boxes. You'll only use one of these keys at a time, but you generate four of them because you can manually switch between them at regular intervals,

for added security. You don't have to generate your keys this way—you can create them yourself and type them in manually, but chances are the ones you write will be far easier to crack than keys randomly generated by the router's software.

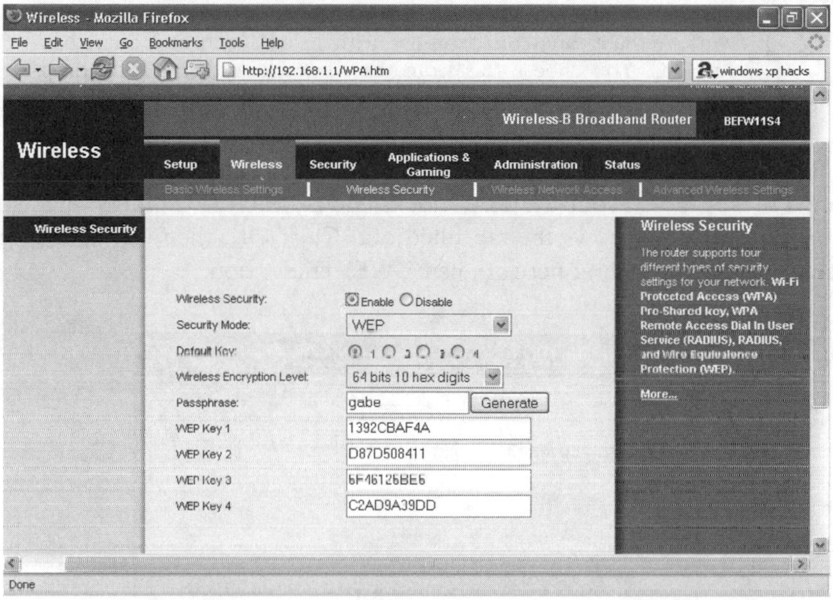

Figure 14-8. Enabling 64-bit WEP encryption

8. If you instead selected 128 bit encryption, you'll be sent to a new screen. In the Passphrase box, type in a phrase and click Generate. This will generate a 128-bit encryption key.

9. Whether you created a 64-bit key, or a 128-bit key, copy down the key (or keys, in the case of 64-bit) on a piece of paper. You'll use this key for each PC that is going to access the network.

> Not all adapters and routers handle alphanumeric keys well. If you run into a problem, use the Hex digits instead.

10. Click Save Settings. That applies the key to your network. Now only PCs that use WEP encryption and the key you just generated will be able to get onto your network.

11. Now you have to configure each wireless computer on your network to use WEP and the key you just generated. On each PC, click the wireless connection icon in the Notification Area, click Properties, click the Wireless Network tab, highlight your network, click Properties, and then click the Association tab.

12. In the Network Authentication drop-down box, select Shared. In the data encryption dialog box, choose WEP. When you do that, the "The key is provided for me automatically" box is checked. Uncheck this box.

 If you can't get WEP to work, it may be due to problems with Network Authentication. Experiment with using Open and Shared on each PC. You choose this from the Network Authentication drop-down box.

13. Enter your WEP key in the Network key box, and type it again in the Confirm network key box. From the Key Index, choose the key number that you are using. Figure 14-9 shows the tab filled out. Click OK, then OK again. The PC can now connect to your network using WEP encryption.

Figure 14-9. Using 64-bit WEP encryption

14. For added security, on a regular basis, go into each PC, and change the key number and associated network key. You shouldn't need to change the number on your router, because it will recognize all of the keys you generated. If you use 128-bit encryption, you'll only have one key to use.

Setting up WPA encryption

1. Install the WPA software. WPA is available in SP2, but not earlier versions of XP. If you don't have SP2, download it by visiting *http://windowsupdate.microsoft.com*.

2. Update your router's and network cards' firmware. Your hardware may not take advantage of WPA. Check with the relevant manufacturers and see if a firmware update will do the job. If so, download and install the firmware. Remember: you'll have to upgrade your router and wireless networking adapters, not just a few components. Also download the latest driver for your network adapters.

3. Go to the Setup screen of your router. For a Linksys router, open a browser, type *http://192.168.1.1* in the address bar, and press Enter. A login screen appears. Leave the User name field blank; in the Password field, type admin and press Enter. If you've changed the user name and password, use those instead.

4. Click Wireless, and then Wireless Security.

5. Select Enable next to Wireless Security.

6. Select WPA Pre-Shared Key from the Security Mode drop-down list.

7. In the WPA Algorithms drop-down list, choose TKIP, which is the approved, certified algorithm for WPA. Some products support Advanced Encryption System (AES), but that hasn't been certified for interoperability among different vendors' hardware.

8. In the WPA Shared Key box, type in a key between eight and 63 characters in length. The longer it is, and the more random the characters, the more secure it will be. Write down the key. You'll need to use this on each wireless PC on your network.

9. Leave the Group Key Renewal row at 3600. Figure 14-10 shows the screen properly filled in.

10. Click Save Settings. That applies the key to your network. Now only PCs that use WPA encryption and the key you just generated will be able to get onto your network.

11. Now you have to configure each wireless computer on your network to use WEP and the key you just generated. On each PC, click the wireless connection icon in the Notification Area, click Properties, click the Wireless Network tab, highlight your network, click Properties, and then click the Association tab.

12. In the Network Authentication drop-down box, select WPA-PSK. In the data encryption dialog box, choose TKIP. When you do that, the The key is provided for me automatically box is checked. Uncheck this box.

13. Enter your WPA key in the Network key box, and type it again in the Confirm network key box. Click OK, then OK again. The PC can now connect to your network using WPA encryption.

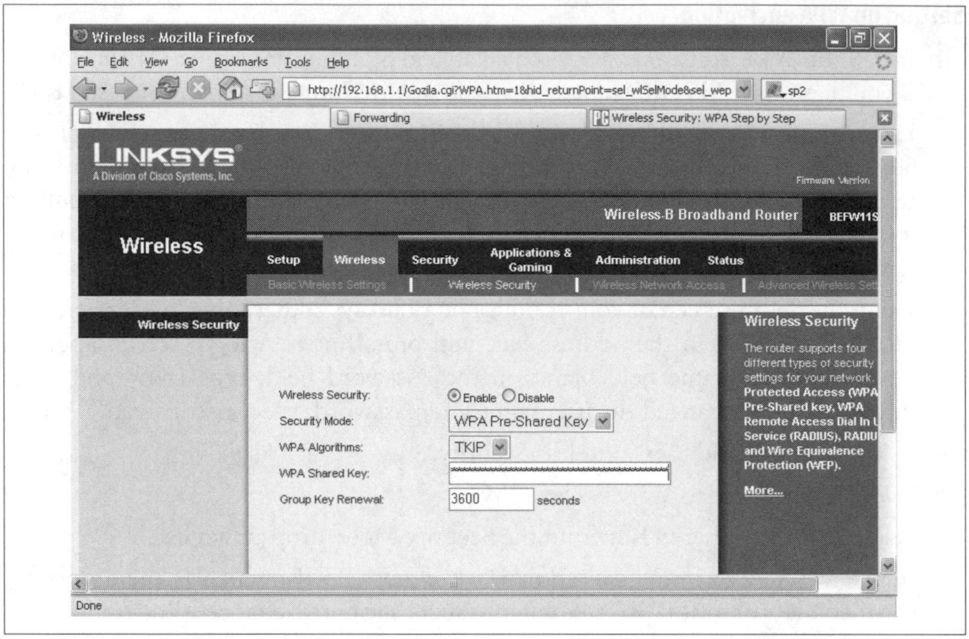

Figure 14-10. Using WPA encryption

Discussion

WEP has gotten a bad name among security experts because it isn't as secure as WPA, but for most home networks, it's perfectly suitable. As a general rule, home networks are not targeted by serious, dedicated intruders, and so WEP is perfectly suitable for keeping out passersby. Using 128-bit encryption will make it even more secure. However, for the most security, use WPA, even in home networks. Business networks, however, should use WPA encryption, at a minimum, if their hardware is capable of handling it. For even more safety, they should use private key methods such as those provided in Windows servers or third-party products.

It's a good idea to regularly change your key, because if someone monitors your network and captures network packets for long enough, they may be able to crack your encryption. So if you regularly change your key, it will be much harder for them to crack the encryption because they'll have less time and data for doing so.

You may come across some confusing and apparently misleading information when choosing WEP encryption. Some hardware manufacturers give you the choice of 40-bit or 104-bit encryption, rather than 64-bit and 128-bit encryption. In fact, 40-bit WEP encryption and 64-bit WEP encryption are two terms for the same thing, and 104-bit and 128-bit WEP encryption are similarly terms for the same thing. WEP uses a 24-bit "initialization vector," which means you don't control that part of the key. So some manufacturers refer to the standard as 40 bit or 104 bit, and others call it 64 bit or 128 bit.

See Also

For more detailed instructions on using WPA on your network, see the *PC Magazine* article "Wireless Security: WPA Step by Step" at *www.pcmag.com/print_article/0,3048,a=107756,00.asp*. MS KB 815485.

14.8   Mixing 802.11b and 802.11g Devices

Problem

You want to use 802.11b and 802.11g devices on the same network.

Solution

If you have an 802.11b router, you can connect 802.11g devices to it, and if you have an 802.11g router, you can connect 802.11b devices to it. But 802.11g devices can only connect to an 802.11b router at 802.11b speeds of a maximum of 11 Mbps, not at 802.11g speeds of 54 Mbps.

On a network with an 802.11g router, if you include any 802.11b devices, then all the devices on the network, including 802.11g devices, will slow down to 802.11b speeds. However, some products include a g-only mode that won't allow 802.11b clients to access the network, and so the network can operate at 802.11g speeds. You can turn the mode on when you want to get higher speeds from 802.11g devices, and off when you need 802.11b devices to access the network.

How you enable g-only mode varies from device to device, but here's how to do it on a Linksys router:

1. Log into the screen by opening your browser and going to *http://192.168.1.1*. When the login screen appears, leave the user name blank, and in the password section, type admin, and press Enter.

 If you've changed the default username and password, use that instead of admin.

2. Click the Wireless tab.
3. From the Wireless Network Mode drop-down box, select G-Only.
4. Click Save Settings.

With this setting in place, only 802.11g devices will be able to connect to the network, and so you'll get 802.11g speeds. When you want 802.11b devices to be able to connect to the network, choose Mixed from the Wireless Network Mode drop-down box, and click Save Settings.

Discussion

If you have an 802.11g router and only connect 802.11g devices to it, there's no need to go through the steps of forcing the router into g-only mode—the network will work at the higher speeds if only 802.11g devices are present.

There is also some controversy about how useful g-only mode is. *PC Magazine* ran tests and found that g-only mode works well and produces 802.11g network speeds. However, the Tom's Networking site also ran tests and found that g-only mode does not boost network speed if there are 802.11b devices nearby.

It's most likely that results vary according to both specific makes and models of routers, and specific network configurations, so it's worth trying g-only mode for yourself.

See Also

For the results of Tom's Networking testing of g-only mode, head to *http://www. tomsnetworking.com/Sections-article43-page8.php*. To see the *PC Magazine* tests, go to *http://www.pcmag.com/article2/0,1759,1245923,00.asp*.

14.9   Setting Up an Ad Hoc Wireless Network

Problem

You want to set up an ad hoc wireless network, in which you don't need a router to connect PCs—they can connect to one another directly.

Solution

When you create an ad hoc network, WiFi-enabled PCs within range of each other communicate with each other in a peer-to-peer fashion. To create an ad hoc wireless network, first install wireless cards in all the computers to be networked, and then do the following:

1. On one of the PCs that you want to be part of the ad hoc network, click the wireless icon in the Notification Area, choose Properties, and click the Wireless Networks tab.

2. Click the Add button to get to the screen shown in Figure 14-11. In the Network name (SSID) box, fill in your network name. Check the box next to This is a computer-to-computer (ad hoc) network; wireless access points are not used. Other wirelessly equipped PCs will connect using the network name you've just chosen. Don't use encryption or authentication at this point. If you want to use it, you can set it up later, following the steps in Recipe 14.7. Click OK.

3. The ad hoc network you just set up will now appear in the Preferred networks portion of the Wireless Networks tab. It will be displayed with a PC card icon next to it, to denote that it is an ad hoc network. (Networks that use access point

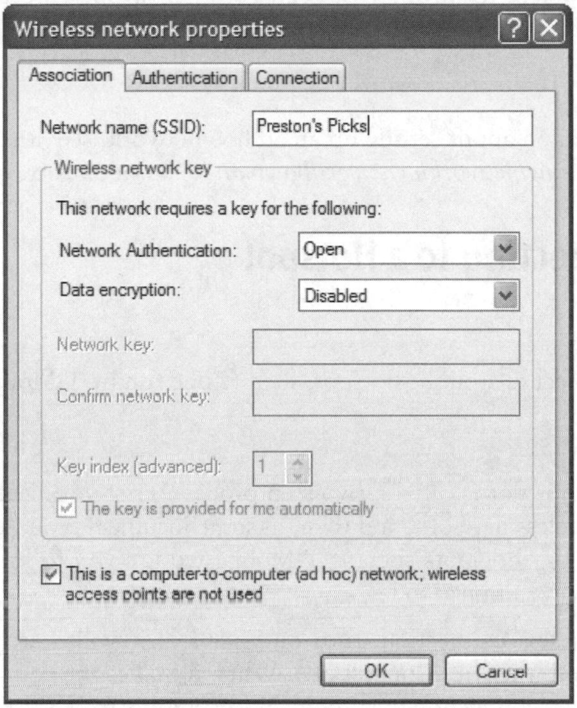

Figure 14-11. Naming your ad hoc network

show up with an icon of a small transmitter next to them.) It will also have a small red X on the icon to show that there are no current ad hoc network connections.

4. On another computer that you want to be part of the ad hoc network, click the wireless network icon. Click View Wireless Networks. If the ad hoc network shows up there, highlight it and click the Connect button. If it doesn't show up, click Refresh network list. When the network shows up, highlight it and click Connect.

5. Follow the same steps for any other PC you want to add to the ad hoc network.

Discussion

The first PC that you configure for the ad hoc network serves as the network's host. So if you're planning to use the network as a way to share a single Internet connection, make sure that you choose the one with the highest-speed Internet connection as the host.

Wireless routers are so inexpensive that there is no economic reason for setting up an ad hoc network. Ad hoc networks are best used when you need to transfer files between two PCs and there is no router available. Ad hoc networking without security puts your PCs at considerable risk, because providing file sharing over ad hoc opens your file system to anyone who can get a signal. Be sure to disable ad hoc mode as soon as you are done using it.

See Also

For more information about setting up an ad hoc network, see *http://www.microsoft.com/windowsxp/using/networking/expert/bowman_02april08.mspx*.

14.10 Connecting to a Hotspot

Problem

You want to connect to a public hotspot, such as one run by T-Mobile or Boingo.

Solution

Connecting to a hotspot is often a two-step process. First you need to make a connection to the wireless network, and then, in some instances, you need to enter login information. For-pay hotspots such as T-Mobile require you to log in, but at many free hotspots, you won't need to log in.

To make the wireless connection, turn on your PC; it will search for any nearby hotspots and connect to the strongest one. When it makes the connection, you'll see the familiar wireless connection icon in the Notification Area.

However, you won't automatically connect to the hotspot in all instances. Sometimes, XP may not find the connection, or it may attempt to connect to a hotspot that you've previously visited. If you can't make the connection, click the wireless icon, and then click View Wireless Networks. If you see the hotspot on the screen that appears, as shown in Figure 14-12, highlight it and click Connect. If you don't see the hotspot, click Refresh Network list, and it will search for any nearby hotspots.

In some instances, the hotspot may have turned off SSID broadcast. In that case, you'll have to ask at the hotspot for the SSID and use that information to connect.

If you're visiting a free hotspot, you may not need to do anything else; you'll be connected. But even some free hotspots require login information; if so, get it from the hotspot owner. If you're visiting a for-pay hotspot, or a free one that requires that you log in, launch your web browser. You'll see a login screen. The one pictured in Figure 14-13 is typical. If it's the first time you've logged in, you'll have to enter payment information, and get a user name and password, so click on the applicable link. If you're previously logged in to the hotspot, use your existing user name and password. Once you do that, you'll be able to use the hotspot.

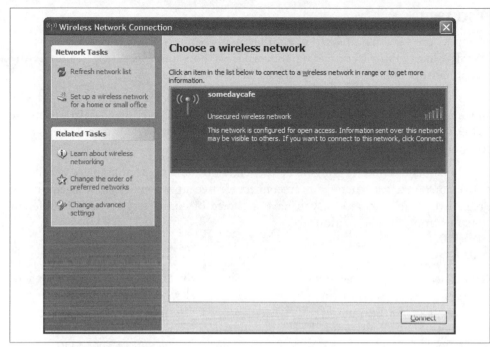

Figure 14-12. The first step in connecting to a hotspot

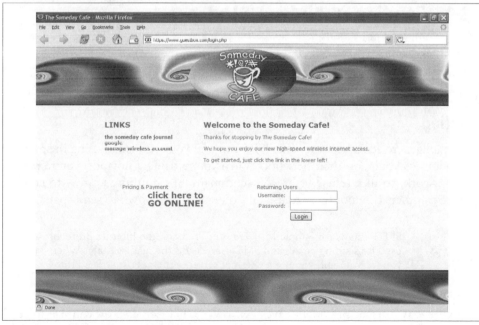

Figure 14-13. The login screen of a for-pay hotspot

Discussion

Hotspots are becoming nearly ubiquitous, with wireless Internet Service Providers (WISPs) like T-Mobile providing thousands of hotspots across the country. Any major metropolitan area typically has dozens or more hotspots.

For-pay hotspots are typically available on a per-hour, per-day, and per-month basis. In some cases, you can get them at a reduced rate, if you use other services from the WISP. For example, if you're a T-Mobile phone subscriber, you'll be able to sign up for monthly hotspot access at a reduced rate.

Free hotspots have been springing up as well, with some metropolitan areas building entire hotspot zones, where you can connect for free anywhere within a several-block area. In fact, in some areas, you have a choice of connecting to several different hotspots from a single location.

See Also

If you're planning on accessing hotspots when you travel, it's a good idea to search for them ahead of time. Several web sites let you do this, including *http://www.wi-fihotspotlist.com*, *http://www.wifinder.com*, *http://www.wifimaps.com*, or *http://www.jiwire.com*. They'll help you find free as well as for-pay hotspots. If you're looking for only free hotspots, head to *http://www.wififreespot.com*.

14.11 Sending Email from a Hotspot

Problem

You want to send email while you're connected to a hotspot, but whenever you try to send email, it's rejected by your SMTP server, so the messages can't get sent.

Solution

Your mail gets rejected because some ISPs won't let you send email using their SMTP servers unless you're on their network. When you're using a hotspot, you're not on their network, so they refuse to let you send mail. ISPs do this as a way to combat spam: Spammers commonly try to use ISPs other than their own to send spam.

 SMTP stands for Simple Mail Transfer Protocol, the Internet protocol used for sending email, and SMTP servers do the mail sending. When you receive mail, you use a different server, either a Post Office Protocol (POP3) or an Internet Message Access Protocol (IMAP) server.

Large, for-pay hotspot providers have their own SMTP servers you can use to send mail. So when you're at a hotspot, change your email account settings to use their

SMTP servers to send mail. You'll still be able to use your normal POP3 or IMAP servers to receive mail.

SMTP server settings for the major hotspot providers are:

T-Mobile
> myemail.t-mobile.com

Boingo
> mail.boingo.com

Wayport
> mail.wayport.net

Surf and Sip
> mail.surfandsip.net

You can also pay to use an SMTP relay service so that you'll be able to send mail from any hotspot, even if the hotspot provider doesn't have an SMTP server. The site *http://www.smtp.com* charges $49.99 per year for its service, unless you send more than 50 emails a day using it, in which case the price goes up, according to how many you send. And the site *http://www.authsmtp.com* lets you send up to 1,000 emails a month, for a fee of $25 a year. If you send more email than that, you can pay for higher-priced, and higher-volume, plans.

To take advantage of the SMTP services, you'll need to configure your email software to use the hotspot's SMTP server. To do it in Outlook 2003:

1. Choose Tools → E-mail Account → View or change existing email accounts and select the email account you plan to use at the hotspot.
2. Click the Change button.
3. In the Outgoing mail server (SMTP) box, enter the name of the hotspot's SMTP server, as shown in Figure 14-14.
4. Click Next, and then Finish.
5. You should now be able to send email while connected to the hotspot.

To do it in Outlook Express:

1. Choose Tools → Accounts, select the Mail tab, highlight your mail account, click the Properties button, and then click the Servers tab.
2. In the Outgoing mail (SMTP) box, enter the name of the hotspot's SMTP server.
3. Click OK, then OK again, and then Close.
4. You should now be able to send email when you're connected to the hotspot.

Discussion

The spam scourge has gotten so bad that most ISPs don't allow you to send mail using their SMTP server unless you're connected to their network. That means that

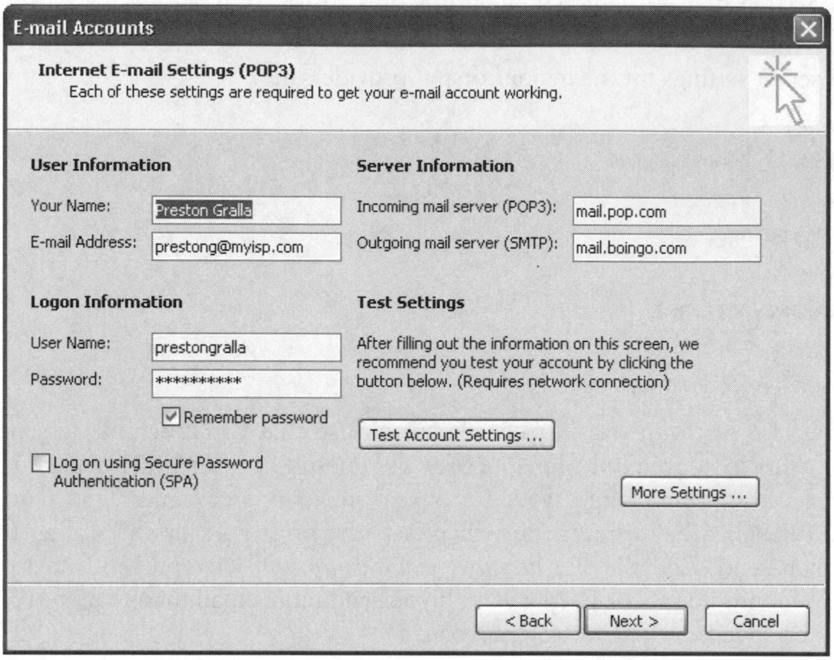

Figure 14-14. Configuring Outlook to use a hotspot SMTP server

frequently, you won't be able to use your ISP's SMTP server when you're at a hotspot.

If you have email provided by a web site provider, rather than an ISP, you may run into similar problems. For example, if you own your own domain, or have a web site, you may have the web site provider handle your email as well. Some of these providers will not let you send mail unless you've recently used their POP3 servers to receive mail. The idea behind this is that if you're receiving mail, you're not an outside spammer. But as a practical matter, this service doesn't always work—one of the authors of this book frequently cannot send mail from a hotspot using his normal SMTP server, so he has to use either the hotspot's SMTP server or a for-pay SMTP service.

Another solution to the problem is to check whether your mail provider has web-based access to email. In that case, you'll be able to send email from the web interface, but you won't be able to use your email client to do it.

14.12 Stopping Hotspot "Stuttering"

Problem

When you connect to a hotspot located near other hotspots, your connection "stutters" by dropping your hotspot connection, making a connection to another hotspot, dropping that one, then connecting to the first one, and so on.

Solution

Hotspots sometimes stutter if several of them are located near one another and you're connecting to one with a weak signal. The problem is caused by the Wireless Zero Configuration service, which runs when you start XP and looks for a wireless connection every three minutes. If your current hotspot connection is weak, when it looks for a hotspot to connect to, it may connect to a nearby hotspot instead—and you get the stuttering effect.

The fix is to disable WZC after you've made your connection—that way, it'll stay with your one connection, even as it fades out and fades in. But you'll want to enable WZC again after you're done, so that the next time you want to connect to a hotspot or your home WiFi network, it will do its job for you.

To temporarily disable WZC:

1. Select Start → Run and in the Open box, type **services.msc** at a command line and press Enter. This runs the Services Microsoft Management Console.

2. Scroll down until you see the Wireless Zero Configuration entry. Right-click it, and choose Stop, as shown in Figure 14-15. That will turn the service off; you'll stop the stuttering and jumping.

3. When you're done at the hotspot, repeat steps 1 and 2, except you should choose Start after you right-click the Wireless Zero Configuration entry.

> Remember that you should turn off Wireless Zero Configuration only after you've made your hotspot connection, or else you won't be able to connect to it. And make sure to turn Wireless Zero Configuration back on after you disconnect from the hotspot.

Discussion

The Wireless Zero Configuration service sits between XP and your wireless hardware, serving as a mediator. It's one of the main reasons that XP is so WiFi-friendly—before XP, wireless connections were usually handled by each different manufacturer's software, leading to compatibility problems and a great deal of confusion when trying to make a connection.

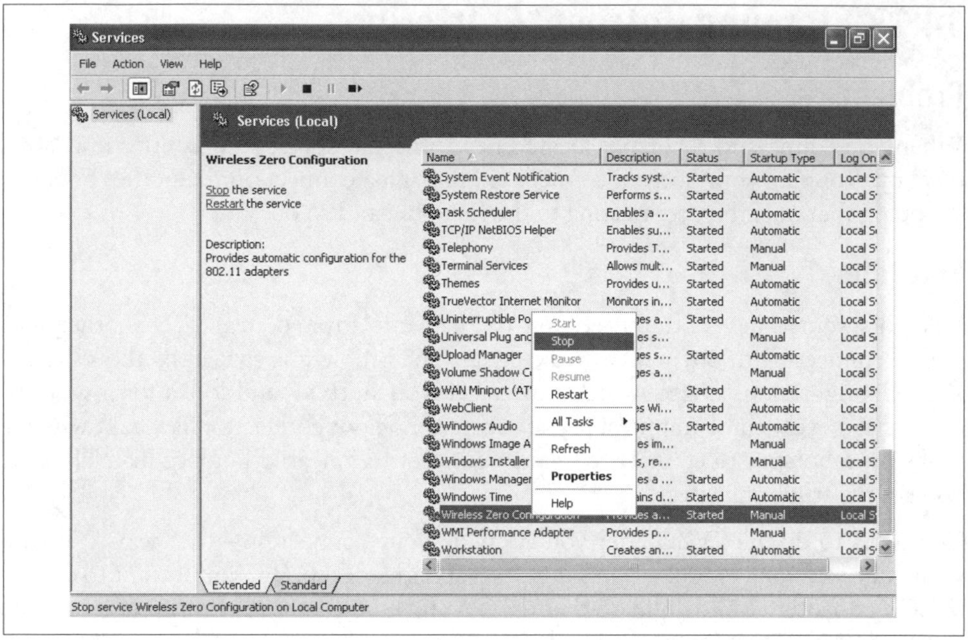

Figure 14-15. Turning off Wireless Zero Configuration

You can also use the service to help solve an occasional problem that WiFi users sometimes face—even though they maintain a strong connection to a WiFi router, they have no Internet connectivity. If you have ever used a WiFi network and seen the WiFi icon that shows a connection, but you can't actually connect to the Internet, you've had this problem. Sometimes, you can use the Wireless Zero Configuration service to solve the problem. Turn off the service, as described in this recipe, and then turn it back on. At times, that will jump-start your connection.

See Also

For more information about troubleshooting WiFi connections, see Recipe 14.5.

14.13 Protecting Yourself at Hotspots

Problem

You want to protect yourself at public hotspots from snoopers and hackers.

Solution

Hotspots don't use encryption, which means that when you visit one, you're open to other hotspot users who may steal your passwords or private information that you send over the Internet. Additionally, when you're on a hotspot, you're on the same network with other hotspot users, and they may be able to exploit vulnerabilities to break into your PC.

But there's a lot you can do to keep yourself safe:

Use a wireless Virtual Private Network (VPN)
> A wireless VPN will encrypt all the information you send and receive when you're online, so you'll be free from snoopers. An excellent one is HotSpotVPN (*http://www.hotspotvpn.com*). It's a breeze to set up and use; you won't even need to download any extra software, because you'll use it along with XP's built-in VPN software. The service isn't free, though; you'll have to pay $8.88 a month for it.

Use a personal firewall
> This will protect you from anyone trying to connect to your PC without your knowledge. XP's built-in firewall is a reasonable choice, although not the best. A better bet is the free Zone Alarm (*http://www.zonealarm.com*).

Turn off file sharing
> When you're on your home network, you might have enabled file sharing. Turn it off before logging onto a hotspot, unless you want the tattooed lad slurping high-octane double espresso to get access to all of the files on your system. Turn it off by running Windows Explorer, right-clicking the drive or folders you normally share, choosing Sharing and Security, and unchecking the box next to Share this folder on the network.

Avoid ad hoc mode
> When you use wireless ad hoc mode, someone can connect directly to your PC without your knowledge and browse your hard disk if you've enabled network file sharing. When you connect to a hotspot, there's no need to have ad hoc mode enabled, because hotspots work in infrastructure mode. So you should disable ad hoc mode before connecting to a hotspot. If you have SP2, to disable ad hoc mode, first click on the wireless connection icon in the Notification Area, then click the Properties button. Then click the Wireless Networks tab. In the Preferred Networks section of the screen, highlight your hotspot connection and click Properties. At the bottom of the Association tab, make sure the This is a computer-to-computer (ad hoc) network; wireless access points are not used box is unchecked.

Discussion

When you connect to a hotspot, you're joining a network that includes everyone else connecting to that hotspot. Normally, networks, such as WiFi home networks, include only people that you can trust. But when you're at a public network, you're joined in a network with people you don't trust. That's why you need to take extra precautions when you connect to hotspots. If your business has a VPN, then there's no need to use HotSpotVPN, because you should be able to use that VPN for security at hotspots.

Companies that run hotspots have started to recognize that security has become a problem, and some are doing something about it. The Boingo network of hotspots, for example, now incorporates security measures such as a VPN and WPA encryption. T-Mobile, as of this writing, says it will follow suit, but has yet to implement it.

See Also

For more information about potential dangers at hotspots, and how to protect yourself, see the *PC Magazine* article "HotSpot Hazards" at *http://www.pcmag.com/article2/0,4149,1277570,00.asp*.

CHAPTER 15

User, Group, and Computer Accounts

15.0 Introduction

When dealing with Windows XP systems, there are three types of accounts you'll work with most often. These include user, group, and computer accounts. You create user accounts to represent the employees, customers, or students in your environment. User accounts represent the virtual identity of the user in the system. It is important to understand how to properly configure and automate the management of user accounts so you cut down on many of the day-to-day tasks required to support them. We'll include a lot of scripts in this chapter to show you how to do this.

As far as Active Directory is concerned, computers are very similar to users. In fact, computer accounts have all of the same attributes as user accounts. Computers need to be represented in Active Directory for many of the same reasons users do, including the need to access resources securely, to use Group Policy objects (GPOs), and to have permissions granted or restricted on them.

To participate in a domain, computers need a secure channel to a domain controller. A secure channel is an authenticated connection that can transmit encrypted data. To set up the secure channel, a computer has to present a password to a domain controller. The domain controller then verifies that password against the password stored in Active Directory with the computer's account. Without the computer account, and subsequently the password stored within it, there would be no way for the domain controller to verify a computer is what it claims to be.

A group is a simple concept that has been used in many different types of systems over the years. In generic terms, a group is just a collection of things. Groups are used most frequently in a security context whereby you set up a group of users and apply certain permissions or rights to that group. Using a group is much easier when applying file permissions, for example, than using individual users, because you have to apply the permissions only once for the group instead of once per user.

In an Active Directory environment, groups are flexible objects that can contain virtually any other type of object as a member. Active Directory groups can be used for many different purposes including controlling access to resources, defining a filter for the application of group policies, and as an email distribution list. The scope and type of a group defines how the group can be used in a forest. The type of a group can be either security or distribution. Security groups can be used to restrict access to resources whereas distribution groups can be used only as a simple grouping mechanism. Both group types can be used as email lists. The scope of a group determines where members of the group can be located in the forest and where in the forest you can use the group in access control lists (ACLs). The supported group scopes include universal, global, and domain local. Universal groups and domain local groups can have members that are part of any domain in the forest. Global groups can only have members that are part of the same domain the group is in.

As is evident by this introduction, this chapter will include information on both local accounts—those that reside on an individual Windows XP system, and accounts stored in Active Directory—also called domain accounts. In a small office/home office environment, you may only use local accounts. If you have more than ten systems, it is likely you'll want to centralize account management using Active Directory. Most recipes in this chapter cover both types of accounts.

Using a Graphical User Interface

There are two primary graphical interfaces for managing accounts. For local system accounts, there is the Computer Management snap-in. Within this snap-in under the Local Users and Groups folder, you have options for creating and managing users and groups. This tool is available by default in the Administrative Tools applet of the Control Panel.

For Active Directory user, group and computer accounts, you'll need to use the Active Directory Users and Computers snap-in. You can install this snap-in along with several other Active Directory tools by installing the Active Directory Administrative Pack at the following URL: *http://www.microsoft.com/downloads/details. aspx?FamilyID=C16AE515-C8F4-47EF-A1E4-A8DCBACFF8E3&displaylang=en*.

Using a Command-Line Interface

Microsoft does not provide many good tools for managing local accounts via the command-line. The net user command allows you to create and modify local user accounts, but not group accounts.

There is no shortage of tools for managing Active Directory accounts. With the release of Windows Server 2003, Microsoft released several command-line utilities (e.g., *dsadd* and *dsmod*), which can be run on Windows XP, to manage user, group and computer accounts. See the AD Administrative Pack URL in the previous section for more details.

Using Downloadable Software

Joe Richards has authored numerous command-line tools for managing local accounts and we will use many of his tools in this chapter. You can download all of Joe's tools (referred to as Joeware) from the following URL: *http://www.joeware.net/*.

Using VBScript

With VBScript you can manage both local and Active Directory accounts using Active Directory Service Interfaces (ADSI). ADSI supports several providers that allow you to manage information in repositories such as the System Account Manager (SAM), Active Directory, and the IIS Metabase to name a few all using the same interfaces and methods. For local accounts, you use the WinNT provider. For Active Directory, you use the LDAP provider. You'll see numerous examples of both throughout this chapter.

15.1 Creating a User Account

Problem

You want to create a user account.

Solution

Using a graphical user interface

To create a local user account, do the following:

1. Open the Computer Management snap-in (*compmgmt.msc*).
2. In the left pane, expand Local Users and Groups.
3. Right-click on Users and select New User.
4. Enter a user name, full name, description, and password.
5. Check or uncheck any account option boxes as necessary.
6. Click Create.
7. Click Close when you are done.

To create a user account in Active Directory, do the following:

1. Open the Active Directory Users and Computers (ADUC) snap-in (*dsa.msc*).
2. If you need to change domains, right-click on Active Directory Users and Computers in the left pane, select Connect to Domain, enter the domain name and click OK.
3. In the left pane, browse to the parent container of the new user, right-click on it, and select New → User.

4. Enter the values for the first name, last name, full name, and user logon name fields as appropriate and click Next.

5. Enter and confirm the password, set any of the password flags, and click Next.

6. Click Finish.

Using a command-line interface

Use the following command to create a local user:

```
> net user <UserName> <UserPasswd> /add
```

For example:

```
> net user rallen MyPassword /add
```

You can set additional properties for local users with this command including the description (/comment) and full name (/fullname) among others. Search on "net user" in the Help and Support Center for the complete list of options.

You can create new user accounts in Active Directory with the *dsadd* command as shown here:

```
> dsadd user "<UserDN>" -upn "<UserUPN>" -fn "<UserFirstName>" -ln "<UserLastName>"
-display "<UserDisplayName>" -pwd "<UserPasswd>"
```

For example:

```
> dsadd user "cn=rallen,cn=users,dc=rallencorp,dc=com" -upn "rallen@rallencorp.com"
-fn "Robbie" -ln "Allen" -display "Robbie Allen" -pwd "MyPassword!"
```

Using VBScript

```
' This code creates a local user account
' ------ SCRIPT CONFIGURATION ------
strUserName = "<UserName>" ' e.g. rallen
strFullName = "<FullName>" ' e.g. Robbie Allen
strDescr = "<Description>" ' e.g. Employee account
strPassword = "<Password>"
strComputer = "<ComputerName>"
' ------ END CONFIGURATION ---------
set objSystem = GetObject("WinNT://" & strComputer)
set objUser = objSystem.Create("user", strUserName)
objUser.FullName = strFullName
objUser.Description = strDescr
objUser.SetPassword strPassword
objUser.SetInfo
WScript.Echo objUser.Name & " created"


' This code creates a user and sets several attributes in Active Directory.
set objParent = GetObject("LDAP://<ParentDN>") ' e.g. cn=users,dc=rallencorp,dc=com
set objUser   = objParent.Create("user", "cn=<UserName>") ' e.g. joes
objUser.Put "sAMAccountName", "<UserName>"   ' e.g. joes
objUser.Put "userPrincipalName", "<UserUPN>" ' e.g. joes@rallencorp.com
```

```
objUser.Put "givenName", "<UserFirstName>"    ' e.g. Joe
objUser.Put "sn", "<UserLastName>"            ' e.g. Smith
objUser.Put "displayName", "<UserFirstName> <UserLastName>" ' e.g. Joe Smith
objUser.SetInfo
objUser.SetPassword("<Password>")
objUser.AccountDisabled = FALSE
objUser.SetInfo
```

Discussion

Local user accounts are different from Active Directory user accounts in terms of the data you can store with them. With local accounts, the data fields are pretty limited. You can configure a user name, full name, description, and some basic profile attributes. With Active Directory, your options are virtually limitless. There are dozens of default attributes that let you store everything from telephone numbers to department names. You can also extend Active Directory to include additional attributes of your making. With local accounts, you are forced to use what the system gives you.

In Windows 2000 Active Directory, the only mandatory attribute that must be set when creating a user is sAMAccountName, which is the account name that is used to interoperate with down-level domains. For Windows Server 2003, if you don't specify a value for sAMAccountName, it will be auto-populated for you. The userPrincipalName attribute should be set to an email address-style string and is most often populated with a user's actual email address.

Using a graphical user interface

With ADUC, you can set additional attributes of a user by double-clicking on the user account after it has been created. There are several tabs to choose from that contain attributes that are grouped together based on function (e.g. Profile).

Using a command-line interface

Several additional attributes can be set with the dsadd user command. Run dsadd user /? for the complete list.

Using VBScript

Take a look at Recipe 15.7 for more information on the userAccountControl attribute and the various flags that can be set for it.

15.2   Unlocking a User

Problem

You want to unlock a locked-out user.

Solution

Using a graphical user interface

For a local account, do the following:

1. Open the Computer Management snap-in (*compmgmt.msc*).
2. In the left pane, expand Local Users and Groups and click on Users.
3. In the right pane, double-click the account you want to unlock.
4. If the account is locked, the box beside Account is locked out will be checked. Uncheck it and click OK.

For a domain account, do the following:

1. Open the Active Directory Users and Computers (ADUC) snap-in (*dsa.msc*).
2. In the left pane, right-click on the domain and select Find.
3. Select the appropriate domain beside In.
4. Type the name of the user beside Name and click Find Now.
5. In the Search Results, right-click on the user and select Unlock.
6. Click OK.

Using downloadable software

Joe Richards has written a tool called *unlock* that lets you find locked out users in a domain and unlock them in one shot. The following command displays all locked out accounts on the default domain controller:

```
> unlock . * -view
```

The following command unlocks the user rallen on dc01:

```
> unlock dc01 rallen
```

This command unlocks all locked users on the default domain controller:

```
> unlock . *
```

You can download *unlock* from *http://www.joeware.net/win/free/tools/unlock.htm*.

You can unlock also local user accounts with the *cusrmgr* tool in the Windows 2000 Resource Kit. Here is an example:

```
> cusrmgr  -S AccountLockout -u rallen
```

Using VBScript

```
' This code unlocks a locked user.
' ------ SCRIPT CONFIGURATION ------
strUsername = "<UserName>"          ' e.g. jsmith
strDomain = "<DomainOrComputerName>" ' e.g. RALLENCORP or rallen-winxp
' ------ END CONFIGURATION ---------
```

```
set objUser = GetObject("WinNT://" & strDomain & "/" & strUsername)
if objUser.IsAccountLocked = TRUE then
   objUser.IsAccountLocked = FALSE
   objUser.SetInfo
   WScript.Echo "Account unlocked"
else
   WScript.Echo "Account not locked"
end if
```

Discussion

If you've enabled account lockouts in a domain (see Recipe 15.4), users will inevitably get locked out. A user can get locked out for a number of reasons, but generally it is either because he mistypes his password a number of times (because he forgot it) or changes his password and does not log off and log on again.

Using VBScript

You can use ADSI's IADsUser::IsAccountLocked method to determine if a user is locked out. You can set IsAccountLocked to FALSE to unlock a user. Unfortunately there is a bug with the LDAP provider version of this method, so you have to use the WinNT provider instead even when unlocking Active Directory accounts. See MS KB 250873 for more information on this bug.

See Also

Recipe 15.4 for viewing the account lockout policy, MS KB 250873 (Programmatically Changing the Lockout Flag in Windows 2000), and MSDN: Account Lockout

15.3   Troubleshooting Account Lockout Problems

Problem

A user is having account lockout problems and you need to determine where it is getting locked from and how it is getting locked out.

Solution

Using a graphical user interface

LockoutStatus is a tool available for Active Directory that can help identify which domain controllers users are getting locked on. It works by querying the lockout status of a user against all domain controllers in the user's domain.

To determine the lockout status of a user, open *LockoutStatus* and select File → Select Target from the menu. Enter the target username and the domain of the user. Click OK. At this point, each domain controller in the domain will be queried and the results will be displayed.

Discussion

The *Lockoutstatus.exe* tool is just one of many that are available in the "Account Lockout and Management" tool set provided by Microsoft. These new lockout tools are intended to help administrators with account lockout problems that are very difficult to troubleshoot. Along with the tool mentioned in the Solution, here are a few others that are included in the set:

ALockout.dll
> Scripts can use this DLL to enable logging of application authentication, which can point out if an application is using bad credentials that cause account lockouts.

ALoInfo.exe
> Displays services and shares that are using a particular account name. It can also print all the users and their password age.

NLParse.exe
> Filter tool for the *netlogon.log* files. You can use it to extract just the lines that relate to account lockout information.

All of the new Account Lockout tools can be downloaded from the following location: *http://microsoft.com/downloads/details.aspx?familyid=7AF2E69C-91F3-4E63-8629-B999ADDE0B9E&displaylang=en*

See Also

MS KB 813500 (Support WebCast: Microsoft Windows 2000 Server and Windows Server 2003: Password and Account Lockout Features)

15.4   Viewing and Modifying the Account Lockout and Password Policies

Problem

You want to view or modify the account lockout and password policies for an Active Directory domain.

Solution

Using a graphical user interface

1. Open the Default Domain Policy console (under Administrative Tools on a domain controller).
2. In the left menu, expand Default Domain Policy → Computer Configuration → Windows Settings → Security Settings → Account Policies.

3. Click on Password Policy or Account Lockout Policy and double-click the property you want to set or view in the right frame.

Using a command-line interface

You can use the *enumprop* command from the Windows 2000 Resource Kit to review the account lockout and password policy settings in Active Directory. The following example queries the rallencorp.com domain:

```
> enumprop /ATTR:
lockoutduration,lockoutthreshold,lockoutobservationwindow,maxpwdage,minpwdage,minpwdl
ength,pwdhistorylength,pwdproperties "LDAP://dc=rallencorp,dc=com"
```

Using VBScript

```
' This code displays the current settings for the password
' and account lockout policies.
' ------ SCRIPT CONFIGURATION ------
strDomain = "<DomainName>"    ' e.g. rallencorp.com
' ------ END CONFIGURATION ---------
set objRootDSE = GetObject("LDAP://" & strDomain & "/RootDSE")
set objDomain  = GetObject("LDAP://" & objRootDSE.Get("defaultNamingContext"))

' Hash containing the domain password and lockout policy attributes
' as keys and the units (e.g. minutes) as the values
set objDomAttrHash = CreateObject("Scripting.Dictionary")
objDomAttrHash.Add "lockoutDuration", "minutes"
objDomAttrHash.Add "lockoutThreshold", "attempts"
objDomAttrHash.Add "lockoutObservationWindow", "minutes"
objDomAttrHash.Add "maxPwdAge", "minutes"
objDomAttrHash.Add "minPwdAge", "minutes"
objDomAttrHash.Add "minPwdLength", "characters"
objDomAttrHash.Add "pwdHistoryLength", "remembered"
objDomAttrHash.Add "pwdProperties", " "

' Iterate over each attribute and print it
for each strAttr in objDomAttrHash.Keys
    if IsObject( objDomain.Get(strAttr) ) then
        set objLargeInt = objDomain.Get(strAttr)
        if objLargeInt.LowPart = 0 then
           value = 0
        else
           value = Abs(objLargeInt.HighPart * 2^32 + objLargeInt.LowPart)
           value = int ( value / 10000000 )
           value = int ( value / 60 )
        end if
    else
        value = objDomain.Get(strAttr)
    end if
    WScript.Echo strAttr & " = " & value & " " & objDomAttrHash(strAttr)
next
```

```
'Constants from DOMAIN_PASSWORD_INFORMATION
Set objDomPassHash = CreateObject("Scripting.Dictionary")
objDomPassHash.Add "DOMAIN_PASSWORD_COMPLEX", &h1
objDomPassHash.Add "DOMAIN_PASSWORD_NO_ANON_CHANGE", &h2
objDomPassHash.Add "DOMAIN_PASSWORD_NO_CLEAR_CHANGE", &h4
objDomPassHash.Add "DOMAIN_LOCKOUT_ADMINS", &h8
objDomPassHash.Add "DOMAIN_PASSWORD_STORE_CLEARTEXT", &h16
objDomPassHash.Add "DOMAIN_REFUSE_PASSWORD_CHANGE", &h32

' The PwdProperties attribute requires special processing because
' it is a flag that holds multiple settings.
for each strFlag In objDomPassHash.Keys
  if objDomPassHash(strFlag) and objDomain.Get("PwdProperties") then
    WScript.Echo "  " & strFlag & " is enabled"
  else
    WScript.Echo "  " & strFlag & " is disabled"
  end If
next
```

Discussion

You can set several parameters to control account lockout and password complexity on the Default Domain Group Policy object. These settings are applied domain-wide and cannot be set on a per-organizational unit basis.

The properties that can be set for the Account Lockout Policy include:

Account lockout duration
Number of minutes an account will be locked before being automatically unlocked. A value of 0 indicates accounts will be locked out indefinitely, i.e. until an administrator manually unlocks them.

Account lockout threshold
Number of failed logon attempts after which an account will be locked.

Reset account lockout counter after
Number of minutes after a failed logon attempt that the failed logon counter for an account will be reset to 0.

The properties that can be set for the Password Policy include:

Enforce password history
Number of passwords to remember before a user can reuse a previous password.

Maximum password age
Maximum number of days a password can be used before a user must change it.

Minimum password age
Minimum number of days a password must be used before it can be changed.

Minimum password length
Minimum number of characters a password must be.

Password must meet complexity requirements

If enabled, passwords must meet all of the following criteria:

- Not contain all or part of the user's account name
- Be at least six characters in length
- Contain characters from three of the following four categories:
    1. English uppercase characters (A through Z)
    2. English lowercase characters (a through z)
    3. Base 10 digits (0 through 9)
    4. Nonalphanumeric characters (e.g., !, $, #, %)

Store passwords using reversible encryption

If enabled, passwords are stored in such a way that they can be retrieved and decrypted. This is essentially the same as storing passwords in plain text.

Using a graphical user interface

On a domain controller or machine that has *adminpak.msi* installed, the Default Domain Policy snap-in is present from the Start menu under Administrative Tools. On a member server, you need to open the GPO snap-in and locate the Default Domain policy.

Using a command-line interface

There is no standard CLI that can be used to modify a GPO, but you can use *enumprop* to view each of the attributes on the domain object that make up the account lockout and password policy settings.

Using VBScript

The VBScript solution required quite a bit of code to perform a simple task: printing out the account lockout and password policy settings. First, we created a Dictionary object with each of the 6 attributes as the keys and the unit's designation for each key (e.g. minutes) as the value. We then iterated over each key, printing it along with the value retrieved from the domain object.

Some additional code was necessary to distinguish between the values returned from some of the attributes. In the case of the time based attributes, such as lockoutDuration, an IADsLargeInteger object was returned from the Get method instead of a pure integer or string value. IADsLargeInteger objects represent 64-bit, also known as Integer8, numbers. 32-bit systems, which make up the majority of systems today, have to break 64-bit numbers into 2 parts (a high and low part) in order to store them. Unfortunately, VBScript cannot natively handle a 64-bit number and stores it as a double precision. To convert a 64-bit number into something VBScript can handle, we have to first multiply the high part by 4,294,967,296 (2^{32}) and then add the low part to the result:

```
value = Abs(objLargeInt.HighPart * 2^32 + objLargeInt.LowPart)
```

Then we divide by 10,000,000 or 10^7, which represents the number of 100 nanosecond intervals per second:

```
value = int ( value / 10000000 )
```

Next we use the `int` function to discard any remainder and finally divided the result by 60 (number of seconds).

```
value = int ( value / 60 )
```

Note that the result is only an approximation in minutes and can be off by several minutes, hours or even days depending on the original value.

The last part of the code iterates over another Dictionary object that contains constants representing various flags that can be set as part of the `pwdProperties` attribute.

See Also

MS KB 221930 (Domain Security Policy in Windows 2000), MS KB 255550 (Configuring Account Policies in Active Directory), MSDN: IADsLargeInteger, and MSDN: DOMAIN_PASSWORD_INFORMATION

15.5   Enabling and Disabling a User Account

Problem

You want to enable or disable a user.

Solution

Using a graphical user interface

For a local account, do the following:

1. Open the Computer Management snap-in (*compmgmt.msc*).
2. In the left pane, expand Local Users and Groups and click on Users.
3. In the right pane, double-click the account you want to enable/disable.
4. To disable the user, check the box beside Account is disabled. To enable the account, uncheck the box.
5. Click OK.

For a domain account, do the following:

1. Open the Active Directory Users and Computers snap-in (*dsa.msc*).

2. In the left pane, right-click on the domain and select Find.

3. Select the appropriate domain beside In.

4. Type the name of the user beside Name and click Find Now.

5. In the Search Results, right-click on the user and select Enable Account to enable or Disable Account to disable.

6. Click OK.

Using a command-line interface

Use the net user command to enable or disable local users. The following command enables a user:

```
> net user <UserName> /active:y
```

The following command disables the rallen user:

```
> net user rallen /active:n
```

To enable a user in Active Directory, use the following command:

```
> dsmod user <UserDN> -disabled no
```

For example:

```
> dsmod user cn=rallen,cn=users,dc=rallencorp,dc=com -disabled no
```

To disable a user in Active Directory, use the following command:

```
> dsmod user <UserDN> -disabled yes
```

Using VBScript

```
' This code enables or disables a user on a computer.
' ------ SCRIPT CONFIGURATION ------
' Set to FALSE to disable account or TRUE to enable account
strDisableAccount = FALSE
strUserName = "<UserName>" ' e.g. rallen
strComputer = "<ComputerName>"
' ------ END CONFIGURATION ---------
set objUser = GetObject("WinNT://" & strComputer & "/" & strUserName)
if objUser.AccountDisabled = TRUE then
   WScript.Echo "Account for " & objUser.Name & " currently disabled"
   if strDisableAccount = FALSE then
      objUser.AccountDisabled = strDisableAccount
      objUser.SetInfo
      WScript.Echo "Account enabled"
   end if
else
   WScript.Echo "Account currently enabled"
   if strDisableAccount = TRUE then
      objUser.AccountDisabled = strDisableAccount
      objUser.SetInfo
```

```
        WScript.Echo "Account disabled"
      end if
  end if

' This code enables or disables a user in Active Directory.
' ------ SCRIPT CONFIGURATION ------
' Set to FALSE to disable account or TRUE to enable account
strDisableAccount = FALSE
strUserDN = "<UserDN>" ' e.g. cn=jsmith,cn=Users,dc=rallencorp,dc=com
' ------ END CONFIGURATION ---------
set objUser = GetObject("LDAP://" & strUserDN)
if objUser.AccountDisabled = TRUE then
   WScript.Echo "Account for " & objUser.Get("cn") & " currently disabled"
   if strDisableAccount = FALSE then
      objUser.AccountDisabled = strDisableAccount
      objUser.SetInfo
      WScript.Echo "Account enabled"
   end if
else
   WScript.Echo "Account currently enabled"
   if strDisableAccount = TRUE then
      objUser.AccountDisabled = strDisableAccount
      objUser.SetInfo
      WScript.Echo "Account disabled"
   end if
end if
```

Discussion

A user's account status dictates whether she can log on to a system. When an
account is disabled, the user is not allowed to log on to a workstation or access
Active Directory controlled resources. Much like the lockout status, the account status for Active Directory accounts is stored as a flag in the userAccountControl
attribute (see Recipe 15.7).

Using VBScript

There is an IADsUser::AccountDisabled property that allows you to determine and
change the account status of a user. Set the method to FALSE to enable an account
or to TRUE to disable it.

See Also

Recipe 15.7 for more on the userAccountControl attribute

15.6   Setting a User's Password

Problem

You want to set a password for a user.

Solution

Using a graphical user interface

For a local account, do the following:

1. Open the Computer Management snap-in (*compmgmt.msc*).
2. In the left pane, expand Local Users and Groups and click on Users.
3. In the right pane, right-click the account you want to set and select Set Password.
4. Click Proceed after reading the warning dialog.
5. Enter and confirm the new password.
6. Click OK.

For a domain account, do the following:

1. Open the Active Directory Users and Computers snap-in (*dsa.msc*).
2. In the left pane, right-click on the domain and select Find.
3. Select the appropriate domain beside In.
4. Type the name of the user beside Name and click Find Now.
5. In the Search Results, right-click on the user and select Reset Password.
6. Enter and confirm the new password.
7. Click OK.

Using a command-line interface

There are several options for setting a password for a user from the command-line. You can use the built-in net user command as shown here:

```
> net user <UserName> <Password>
```

For example:

```
> net user rallen TheBestPassword!
```

Use the *changepw* utility from Joeware.net to set either local or domain password. The following command sets the password for a user on the local system:

```
> changepw /u:<UserName> /p:<Password>
```

You can also specify a target computer name. The following command sets the password for user rallen on a remote system:

```
> changepw /s:xp01 /u:rallen /p:TheBestPassword!
```

To change a user's password in the domain AMER, use the following command:

```
> changepw /d:AMER /u:rallen /p:TheBestPassword!
```

You can also use the *dsmod* utility to change the password for a domain user. Using * after the –pwd option causes you to be prompted you for the new password. You can replace * with the password you want to set, but it is not a good security practice, because other users that are logged into the machine may be able to see it.

```
> dsmod user <UserDN> -pwd *
```

For example:

```
> dsmod user cn=rallen,cn=users,dc=rallencorp,dc=com -pwd *
```

Using VBScript

```
' This code sets the password for a local user.
' ------ SCRIPT CONFIGURATION ------
strUserName = "<UserName>"   ' e.g. jsmith
strNewPasswd = "<Password>"
strComputer = "<ComputerName>"
' ------ END CONFIGURATION ---------
set objUser = GetObject("WinNT://" & strComputer & "/" & strUserName)
objUser.SetPassword(strNewPasswd)
Wscript.Echo "Password set for " & objUser.Name


' This code sets the password for a domain user.
' ------ SCRIPT CONFIGURATION ------
strUserDN = "<UserDN>"    ' e.g. cn=jsmith,cn=Users,dc=rallencorp,dc=com
strNewPasswd = "NewPassword"
' ------ END CONFIGURATION ---------
set objUser = GetObject("LDAP://" & strUserDN)
objUser.SetPassword(strNewPasswd)
Wscript.Echo "Password set for " & objUser.Get("cn")
```

Discussion

The password for a local user is stored in the SAM database and in the unicodePwd attribute for domain accounts. You cannot directly modify that attribute in Active Directory, so you have to use one of the supported APIs. With the VBScript solution you can use the IADsUser::SetPassword method as shown or IADsUser:: ChangePassword. The latter requires the existing password to be passed in as a parameter. This is the method you'd want to use if you've created a web page that requires the previous password before allowing a user to change it.

See Also

MS KB 225511 (New Password Change and Conflict Resolution Functionality in Windows), MS KB 264480 (Description of Password-Change Protocols in Windows 2000), MSDN: IADsUser::SetPassword, and MSDN: IADsUser::ChangePassword

15.7 Setting a Domain User's Account Options

Problem

You want to view or update the userAccountControl attribute for a domain user. This attribute controls various account options, such as when the user must change his password at next logon and whether the account is disabled.

Solution

Using a graphical user interface

1. Open the Active Directory Users and Computers snap-in (*dsa.msc*).
2. In the left pane, right-click on the domain and select Find.
3. Select the appropriate domain beside In.
4. Beside Name, type the name of the user and click Find Now.
5. In the Search Results, double-click on the user.
6. Select the Account tab.
7. Many of the userAccountControl flags can be set under Account options.
8. Click OK after you're done.

Using a command-line interface

The dsmod user command has several options for setting various userAccountControl flags as shown in Table 15-1. Each switch accepts yes or no as a parameter to either enable or disable the setting.

Using VBScript

```
' This code enables or disables a bit value in the userAccountControl attr.
' ------ SCRIPT CONFIGURATION ------
strUserDN = "<UserDN>"      ' e.g. cn=rallen,ou=Sales,dc=rallencorp,dc=com
intBit = <BitValue>         ' e.g. 65536
boolEnable = <TrueOrFalse> ' e.g. TRUE
' ------ END CONFIGURATION ---------
strAttr = "userAccountControl"
set objUser = GetObject("LDAP://" & strUserDN)
intBitsOrig = objUser.Get(strAttr)
intBitsCalc = CalcBit(intBitsOrig, intBit, boolEnable)
if intBitsOrig <> intBitsCalc then
    objUser.Put strAttr, intBitsCalc
    objUser.SetInfo
    WScript.Echo "Changed " & strAttr & " from " & _
                intBitsOrig & " to " & intBitsCalc
```

```
      else
         WScript.Echo "Did not need to change " & strAttr & " (" & _
                    intBitsOrig & ")"
      end if

      Function CalcBit(intValue, intBit, boolEnable)
         CalcBit = intValue
         if boolEnable = TRUE then
            CalcBit = intValue Or intBit
         else
            if intValue And intBit then
               CalcBit = intValue Xor intBit
            end if
         end if
      End Function
```

Discussion

The userAccountControl attribute on user (and computer) accounts could be considered the kitchen sink of miscellaneous and sometimes completely unrelated user account properties. If you have to do much creating and managing user accounts, you'll need to become intimately familiar with this attribute.

The userAccountControl attribute is a bit flag, which means you have to take a couple extra steps to search against it or modify it. For more on searching and modifying a bit flag attribute, see Recipes 4.10 and 4.13 in *Active Directory Cookbook*.

The dsmod user command can be used to modify a subset of userAccountControl properties as shown in Table 15-1. Table 15-2 contains the complete list userAccountControl properties as defined in the ADS_USER_FLAG_ENUM enumeration.

Table 15-1. dsmod user options for setting userAccountControl

dsmod user switch	Description
-mustchpwd	Sets whether the user must change password at next logon.
-canchpwd	Sets whether the user can change his password.
-disabled	Set account status to enabled or disabled.
-reversiblepwd	Sets whether the user's password is stored using reversible encryption.
-pwdneverexpires	Sets whether the user's password never expires.

Table 15-2. ADS_USER_FLAG_ENUM values

Name	Value	Description
ADS_UF_SCRIPT	1	Logon script is executed
ADS_UF_ACCOUNTDISABLE	2	Account is disabled
ADS_UF_HOMEDIR_REQUIRED	8	Home Directory is required
ADS_UF_LOCKOUT	16	Account is locked out
ADS_UF_PASSWD_NOTREQD	32	A password is not required

Table 15-2. ADS_USER_FLAG_ENUM values (continued)

Name	Value	Description
ADS_UF_PASSWD_CANT_CHANGE	64	Read-only flag that indicates if the user cannot change his password
ADS_UF_ENCRYPTED_TEXT_PASSWORD_ALLOWED	128	Store password using reversible encryption
ADS_UF_TEMP_DUPLICATE_ACCOUNT	256	Account provides access to the domain, but not to any other domain that trusts the domain
ADS_UF_NORMAL_ACCOUNT	512	Enabled user account
ADS_UF_INTERDOMAIN_TRUST_ACCOUNT	2048	A permit to trust account for a system domain that trusts other domains
ADS_UF_WORKSTATION_TRUST_ACCOUNT	4096	Enabled computer account
ADS_UF_SERVER_TRUST_ACCOUNT	8192	Computer account for backup domain controller.
ADS_UF_DONT_EXPIRE_PASSWD	65536	Password will not expire
ADS_UF_MNS_LOGON_ACCOUNT	131072	MNS logon account.
ADS_UF_SMARTCARD_REQUIRED	262144	Smart card is required for logon
ADS_UF_TRUSTED_FOR_DELEGATION	524288	Allow Kerberos delegation
ADS_UF_NOT_DELEGATED	1048576	Do not allow Kerberos delegation even if ADS_UF_TRUSTED_FOR_DELETATION is enabled
ADS_UF_USE_DES_KEY_ONLY	2097152	Requires DES encryption for keys
ADS_UF_DONT_REQUIRE_PREAUTH	4194304	Account does not require Kerberos pre-authentication for logon
ADS_UF_PASSWORD_EXPIRED	8388608	Read-only flag indicating account's password has expired. Used only with the WinNT provider
ADS_UF_TRUSTED_TO_AUTHENTICATE_FOR_DELEGATION	16777216	Account is enabled for delegation

See Also

Go to MSDN (*http://msdn.microsoft.com*) and search for "ADS_USER_FLAG_ENUM enumeration"

15.8 Setting a Domain User's Profile Attributes

Problem

You want to set one or more of the profile attributes for a domain user account.

Solution

Using a graphical user interface

1. Open the Active Directory Users and Computers snap-in (*dsa.msc*).
2. In the left pane, right-click on the domain and select Find.

3. Select the appropriate domain beside In.

4. Beside Name, type the name of the user and click Find Now.

5. In the Search Results, double-click on the user.

6. Click the Profile tab.

7. Modify the various profile settings as necessary.

8. Click OK.

Using a command-line interface

Use the *dsmod* command to set the various profile attributes:

```
> dsmod user "<UserDN>" -loscr ScriptPath -profile ProfilePath -hmdir HomeDir -hmdrv
DriveLetter
```

Using VBScript

```
' This code sets the various profile related attributes for a user.
strUserDN = "<UserDN>"    ' e.g. cn=jsmith,cn=Users,dc=rallencorp,dc=com
set objUser = GetObject("LDAP://" & strUserDN)
objUser.Put "homeDirectory", "\\fileserver\" & objUser.Get("sAMAccountName")
objUser.Put "homeDrive", "z:"
objUser.Put "profilePath", "\\fileserver\" & _
            objUser.Get("sAMAccountName") & "\profile"
objUser.Put "scriptPath", "login.vbs"
objUser.SetInfo
Wscript.Echo "Profile info for " & objUser.Get("sAMAccountName") & " updated"
```

Discussion

The four attributes that make up a user's profile settings in Active Directory include the following:

homeDirectory
>   UNC path to home directory

homeDrive
>   drive letter (e.g. z:) to map home directory

profilePath
>   UNC path to profile directory

scriptPath
>   path to logon script

When you set the homeDirectory attribute, the folder being referenced needs to already exist. For an example on creating shares for users, see MS KB 234746.

See Also

MS KB 234746 (How to Create User Shares for All Users in a Domain with ADSI), MS KB 271657 (Scripted Home Directory Paths Require That Folders Exist), and MS KB 320043 (HOW TO: Assign a Home Directory to a User)

15.9 Finding a Domain User's Last Logon Time

Problem

You want to determine the last time a user logged in to a domain. This recipe requires that your Active Directory forest is at the Windows Server 2003 forest functional level.

Solution

Using a graphical user interface

If you install the *AcctInfo.dll* extension to Active Directory Users and Computers, you can view the last logon timestamp:

1. Open the Active Directory Users and Computers snap-in (*dsa.msc*).
2. In the left pane, right-click on the domain and select Find.
3. Select the appropriate domain beside In.
4. Beside Name, type the name of the user you want to modify and click Find Now.
5. In the Search Results, double-click on the user.
6. Click the Additional Account Info tab.
7. View the value for Last-Logon-Timestamp.

 AcctInfo.dll can be downloaded from the Microsoft download site: *http://microsoft.com/downloads/details.aspx?FamilyId=7AF2E69C-91F3-4E63-8629-B999ADDE0B9E&displaylang=en*

Using VBScript

```
' This code prints the last logon timestamp for a domain user.
' ------ SCRIPT CONFIGURATION ------
strUserDN = "<UserDN>"  ' e.g. cn=rallen,ou=Sales,dc=rallencorp,dc=com
' ------ END CONFIGURATION ---------
set objUser = GetObject("LDAP://" & strUserDN)
set objLogon = objUser.Get("lastLogonTimestamp")
intLogonTime = objLogon.HighPart * (2^32) + objLogon.LowPart
intLogonTime = intLogonTime / (60 * 10000000)
intLogonTime = intLogonTime / 1440
WScript.Echo "Approx last logon timestamp: " & intLogonTime + #1/1/1601#
```

Discussion

Trying to determine when a user last logged on has always been a challenge in the Microsoft NOS environment. In Windows NT, you could retrieve a user's last logon timestamp from a PDC or BDC, but this timestamp was the last time the user logged on to the PDC or BDC. That means in order to determine the actual last logon, you'd have to query every domain controller in the domain. In large environments this wasn't practical. With Windows 2000 Active Directory, things did not improve much. A lastLogon attribute is used to store the last logon timestamp, but unfortunately this attribute isn't replicated. So again, to get an accurate picture, you'd have to query every domain controller in the domain for the user's last logon attribute and keep track of the most recent one.

Now with Windows Server 2003 we finally have a viable solution. A new attribute was added to the schema for user accounts called lastLogonTimestamp. This attribute is similar to the lastLogon attribute that was available previously, with two distinct differences. First, and most importantly, this attribute is replicated. That means when a user logs in, the lastLogonTimestamp attribute gets populated and then replicates to all domain controllers in the domain.

The second difference is that since lastLogonTimestamp is replicated, Microsoft needed to put in special safeguards to ensure that a user can repeatedly login over a short period of time, without any impact on replication. For this reason, the lastLogonTimestamp is updated only if the last update occurred a week or more ago. This means that the lastLogonTimestamp attribute could be up to a week off in terms of accuracy with a user's actual last logon. Ultimately this shouldn't be a problem for most situations because lastLogonTimestamp is intended to address the common problem where administrators want to run a query and determine which users have not logged in over the past month, or more.

See Also

Recipe 6.28 of *Active Directory Cookbook* (O'Reilly) for finding users that have not logged on recently in a domain

15.10 Creating a Group Account

Problem

You want to create a group account.

Solution

Using a graphical user interface

The following creates a local group:

1. Open the Computer Management snap-in (*compmgmt.msc*).
2. In the left pane, expand Local Users and Groups.
3. Right-click Groups and select New Group.
4. Enter a group name and description. Then click the Add button to populate the group with members.
5. Click the Create button to create the group.

The following creates a domain group:

1. Open the Active Directory Users and Computers snap-in (*dsa.msc*).
2. If you need to change domains, right-click on Active Directory Users and Computers in the left pane, select Connect to Domain, enter the domain name, and click OK.
3. In the left pane, browse to the parent container of the new group, right-click on it, and select New → Group.
4. Enter the name of the group and select the group scope (global, domain local or universal) and group type (security or distribution).
5. Click OK.

Using a command-line interface

The *lg* tool from Joeware.net can be used to create local groups. Here is the generic syntax:

```
> lg <GroupName> -addgroup
```

You can set the comment for the group when you create it. Here is an example:

```
> lg TestGroup -addgroup -setcomment "This is a test"
```

To create a local group on a remote machine, prefix the group name with the target computer. For example:

```
> lg \\winxp1\TestGroup -addgroup -setcomment "This is a test"
```

You can use the *dsadd* command to create a group in Active Directory. *<GroupDN>* should be replaced with the distinguished name of the group account to create, *<GroupScope>* should be l, g, or u for domain local group, global group, or universal group, respectively, and -secgroup should be set to yes if the group is a security group or no otherwise. Another recommended option to set is –desc to specify a description of the group.

```
> dsadd group "<GroupDN>" -scope <GroupScope> -secgrp yes|no -desc "<GroupDesc>"
```

Here is an example:

```
> dsadd group "cn=mygroup,cn=users,dc=rallencorp,dc=com" -scope g -secgrp yes -desc
"A test group"
```

Using VBScript

```
' This code creates a local group on a computer.
strGroupName  = "<GroupName>" ' e.g. ExecAdminsSales
strGroupDescr = "<GroupDesc>" ' e.g. Executive Admins for Sales group
strComputer = "<ComputerName>" ' e.g. winxp01

set objSystem = GetObject("WinNT://" & strComputer)
set objGrp = objSystem.Create("group", strGroupName)
objGrp.Description = strGroupDescr
objGrp.SetInfo
WScript.Echo objGrp.Name & " created successfully"


' This code creates a global security group in Active Directory.
' ------ SCRIPT CONFIGURATION ------
strGroupParentDN = "<GroupParentDN>" ' e.g. ou=Groups,dc=rallencorp,dc=com
strGroupName     = "<GroupName>"     ' e.g. ExecAdminsSales
strGroupDescr    = "<GroupDesc>"     ' e.g. Executive Admins for Sales group
' ------ END CONFIGURATION ---------
' Constants taken from ADS_GROUP_TYPE_ENUM
Const ADS_GROUP_TYPE_DOMAIN_LOCAL_GROUP = 4
Const ADS_GROUP_TYPE_GLOBAL_GROUP       = 2
Const ADS_GROUP_TYPE_LOCAL_GROUP        = 4
Const ADS_GROUP_TYPE_SECURITY_ENABLED   = -2147483648
Const ADS_GROUP_TYPE_UNIVERSAL_GROUP    = 8

set objOU = GetObject("LDAP://" & strGroupParentDN)
set objGroup = objDomain.Create("group","cn=" & strGroupName)
objGroup.Put "groupType", ADS_GROUP_TYPE_GLOBAL_GROUP _
                      Or ADS_GROUP_TYPE_SECURITY_ENABLED
objGroup.Put "description", strGroupDescr
objGroup.SetInfo
```

Discussion

In each solution, a group was created with no members. For more information on
how to add and remove group members, see Recipe 15.13.

See Also

MS KB 231273 (Group Type and Scope Usage in Windows), MS KB 232241 (Group
Management with ADSI in Windows 2000), MS KB 320054 (HOW TO: Manage
Groups in Active Directory in Windows 2000), and MSDN: ADS_GROUP_TYPE_
ENUM

15.11 Viewing the Members of a Group

Problem

You want to view the members of a group.

Solution

Using a graphical user interface

The following lets you view the members of a local group:

1. Open the Computer Management snap-in (*compmgmt.msc*).
2. In the left pane, expand Local Users and Groups → Groups.
3. In the right pane, double-click the group you want to view. The list of members will be displayed in the Properties dialog box.

The following lets you view the members of a group in Active Directory:

1. Open the Active Directory Users and Computers snap-in (*dsa.msc*).
2. If you need to change domains, right-click on Active Directory Users and Computers in the left pane, select Connect to Domain, enter the domain name, and click OK.
3. In the left pane, right-click on the domain and select Find.
4. Enter the name of the group and click Find Now.
5. Double-click on the group in the bottom results pane.
6. Click the Members tab.

Using a command-line interface

Use the *lg* command from Joeware.net to display the members of a local group:

```
> lg Administrators
```

The following *dsget* command displays the direct members of a group in Active Directory:

```
> dsget group "<GroupDN>" -members
```

Add the –expand option to enumerate all nested group members in Active Directory:

```
> dsget group "<GroupDN>" -members -expand
```

Using VBScript

```
' This code prints the members of a local group.
' ------ SCRIPT CONFIGURATION ------
strGroup = "<GroupName>" ' e.g. Administrators
strComputer = "<ComputerName>"
' ------ END CONFIGURATION ---------
```

```
set objGroup = GetObject("WinNT://" & strComputer & "/" & strGroup)
Wscript.Echo "Members of " & objGroup.Name & ":"
for each objMember in objGroup.Members
    Wscript.Echo objMember.Name
next
WScript.Echo "Done"


' This code prints the direct members of an Active Directory group.
' ------ SCRIPT CONFIGURATION ------
strGroupDN = "<GroupDN>" ' e.g. cn=SalesGroup,ou=Groups,dc=rallencorp,dc=com
' ------ END CONFIGURATION ---------
set objGroup = GetObject("LDAP://" & strGroupDN)
Wscript.Echo "Members of " & objGroup.Name & ":"
for each objMember in objGroup.Members
    Wscript.Echo objMember.Name
next
WScript.Echo "Done"


' This code prints the nested membership of an Active Directory group.
' ------ SCRIPT CONFIGURATION ------
strGroupDN = "<GroupDN>"  ' e.g. cn=SalesGroup,ou=Grps,dc=rallencorp,dc=com
' ------ END CONFIGURATION ---------
strSpaces = " "
set dicSeenGroupMember = CreateObject("Scripting.Dictionary")
Wscript.Echo "Members of " & strGroupDN & ":"
DisplayMembers "LDAP://" & strGroupDN, strSpaces, dicSeenGroupMember
WScript.Echo "Done"

Function DisplayMembers ( strGroupADsPath, strSpaces, dicSeenGroupMember)

    set objGroup = GetObject(strGroupADsPath)
    for each objMember In objGroup.Members
        Wscript.Echo strSpaces & objMember.Name
        if objMember.Class = "group" then
            if dicSeenGroupMember.Exists(objMember.ADsPath) then
                Wscript.Echo strSpaces & "   ^ already seen group member " & _
                                        "(stopping to avoid loop)"
            else
                dicSeenGroupMember.Add objMember.ADsPath, 1
                DisplayMembers objMember.ADsPath, strSpaces & " ", _
                            dicSeenGroupMember
            end if
        end if
    next

End Function
```

Discussion

Using VBScript

For the Active Directory examples, the member attribute of a group accounts contains the distinguished names of the direct members of the group. By direct members, we mean the members that have been directly added to the group. This is in contrast to indirect group members, which are members of the group due to nested group membership. To view the complete group membership, you have to recurse through each group's members.

In the second VBScript example, we used a dictionary object to ensure we did not get in an infinite loop. The dictionary object stores each group member; before the DisplayMembers function is called a check is performed to determine if the group has already been evaluated. If so, a message is displayed indicating the group will not be processed again. If this type of checking was not employed and you had a situation where group A was a member of group B, group B was a member of group C, and group C was a member of group A, the loop would repeat without terminating.

See Also

MSDN: IADsMember

15.12 Viewing a User's Group Membership

Problem

You want to view the group membership of an Active Directory user.

Solution

Using a graphical user interface

1. Open the Active Directory Users and Computers snap-in (*compmgmt.msc*).
2. In the left pane, right-click on the domain and select Find.
3. Select the appropriate domain beside In.
4. Type the name of the user beside Name and click Find Now.
5. In the Search Results, double-click on the user.
6. Click the Member Of tab.
7. To view all indirect group membership (from nested groups), you'll need to double-click on each group.

Using a command-line interface

The net user command can display a user's group membership. The following displays the group membership for the local administrator account:

```
> net user administrator
```

This command displays the group membership of a domain account named rallen:

```
> net user rallen /domain
```

You can also use dsget user to display domain group membership. The following command displays the groups that the rallen user is a member of in Active directory. Use the -expand switch to list nested group membership as well:

```
> dsget user cn=rallen,cn=users,dc=rallencorp,dc=com -memberof -expand
```

Using VBScript

```
' This code displays the group membership of a user.
' It avoids infinite loops due to circular group nesting by
' keeping track of the groups that have already been seen.
' ------ SCRIPT CONFIGURATION ------
strUserDN = "<UserDN>"   ' e.g. cn=jsmith,cn=Users,dc=rallencorp,dc=com
' ------ END CONFIGURATION ---------
set objUser = GetObject("LDAP://" & strUserDN)
Wscript.Echo "Group membership for " & objUser.Get("cn") & ":"
strSpaces = ""
set dicSeenGroup = CreateObject("Scripting.Dictionary")
DisplayGroups "LDAP://" & strUserDN, strSpaces, dicSeenGroup

Function DisplayGroups ( strObjectADsPath, strSpaces, dicSeenGroup)

    set objObject = GetObject(strObjectADsPath)
    WScript.Echo strSpaces & objObject.Name
    on error resume next ' Doing this to avoid an error when memberOf is empty
    if IsArray( objObject.Get("memberOf") ) then
       colGroups = objObject.Get("memberOf")
    else
       colGroups = Array( objObject.Get("memberOf") )
    end if

    for each strGroupDN In colGroups
       if Not dicSeenGroup.Exists(strGroupDN) then
          dicSeenGroup.Add strGroupDN, 1
          DisplayGroups "LDAP://" & strGroupDN, strSpaces & " ", dicSeenGroup
       end if
    next

End Function
```

Discussion

The memberOf attribute on domain accounts is multivalued and contains the list of distinguished names for the groups of which the user is a member. memberOf is actually linked with the member attribute on group accounts, which holds the distinguished names of its members. For this reason, you cannot directly modify the memberOf attribute; you must instead modify the member attribute on the group.

See Also

Recipe 15.11 for more on viewing the members of a group

15.13 Adding and Removing Members of a Group

Problem

You want to add or remove members of a group.

Solution

Using a graphical user interface

1. Follow the same steps as in Recipe 15.11 to view the members of the group.
2. To remove a member, click on the member name, click the Remove button, click Yes, and click OK.
3. To add a member, click on the Add button, enter the name of the member, and click OK twice.

Using a command-line interface

Use the *lg* tool from Joeware.net to add and remove members for local groups. The following command adds a user to a group:

```
> lg <GroupName> <UserName1> <UserName2> ... /add
```

For example:

```
> lg TestGroup rallen gralla /add
```

The following command removes a user from a local group:

```
> lg TestGroup rallen /remove
```

For Active Directory, the –addmbr option of *dsmod* adds a member to a group:

```
> dsmod group "<GroupDN>" -addmbr "<MemberDN>"
```

For example:

```
> dsmod group "cn=administrators,cn=user,dc=rallencorp,dc=com" -addmbr
"cn=rallen,cn=users,dc=rallencorp,dc=com"
```

The –rmmbr option removes a member from a group:

```
> dsmod group "<GroupDN>" -rmmbr "<MemberDN>"
```

The –chmbr option replaces the complete membership list:

```
> dsmod group "<GroupDN>" -chmbr "<Member1DN Member2DN ...>"
```

Using VBScript

```
' This code adds a member to a local group.
' ------ SCRIPT CONFIGURATION ------
strGroupName = "<GroupName>"  ' e.g. Administrators
strUserName = "<UserName>" ' e.g. rallen
strComputer = "<ComputerName>"
' ------ END CONFIGURATION ---------
set objGroup = GetObject("WinNT://" & strComputer & "/" & strGroupName)
objGroup.Add("WinNT://" & strComputer & "/" & strUserName)
WScript.Echo "Done"


' This code removes a member from a local group.
' ------ SCRIPT CONFIGURATION ------
strGroupName = "<GroupName>"  ' e.g. Administrators
strUserName = "<UserName>" ' e.g. rallen
strComputer = "<ComputerName>"
' ------ END CONFIGURATION ---------
set objGroup = GetObject("WinNT://" & strComputer & "/" & strGroupName)
objGroup.Remove("WinNT://" & strComputer & "/" & strUserName)
WScript.Echo "Done"


' This code adds a member to an Active Directory group.
' ------ SCRIPT CONFIGURATION ------
strGroupDN = "<GroupDN>"  ' e.g. cn=SalesGroup,ou=Groups,dc=rallencorp,dc=com
strMemberDN = "<MemberDN>" ' e.g. cn=jsmith,cn=users,dc=rallencorp,dc=com
' ------ END CONFIGURATION ---------
set objGroup = GetObject("LDAP://" & strGroupDN)
objGroup.Add("LDAP://" & strMemberDN)
WScript.Echo "Done"


' This code removes a member from an Active Directory group.
' ------ SCRIPT CONFIGURATION ------
strGroupDN = "<GroupDN>"  ' e.g. cn=SalesGroup,ou=Groups,dc=rallencorp,dc=com
strMemberDN = "<MemberDN>" ' e.g. cn=jsmith,cn=users,dc=rallencorp,dc=com
' ------ END CONFIGURATION ---------
set objGroup = GetObject("LDAP://" & strGroupDN)
objGroup.Remove("LDAP://" & strMemberDN)
WScript.Echo "Done"
```

Discussion

Using VBScript

For Active Directory, there are no restrictions on what distinguished names you put in the member attribute, so you can essentially have any type of object as a member of a group. While Organizational Units (OUs) are typically used to structure objects that share certain criteria, group accounts can be used to create loose collections of objects.

The benefit of using group accounts as a collection mechanism is that the same object can be a member of multiple groups whereas an object can only be a part of a single OU. Another key difference is that you can assign permissions on resources to groups because they are considered security principals in Active Directory, whereas OUs are not. This is different from some other directories, such as Novell Netware, where OUs act more like security principals.

See Also

Recipe 15.11 for viewing group membership, MSDN: IADsGroup::Add, and MSDN: IADsGroup::Remove.

15.14 Creating a Computer Account

Problem

You want to create a computer account in Active Directory.

Solution

Using a graphical user interface

1. Open the Active Directory Users and Computers snap-in (*dsa.msc*).
2. If you need to change domains, right-click on Active Directory Users and Computers in the left pane, select Connect to Domain, enter the domain name and click OK.
3. In the left pane, browse to the parent container for the computer, right-click on it, and select New → Computer.
4. Enter the name of the computer and click OK.

Using a command-line interface

Use the following command to create a computer account in Active Directory:

```
> dsadd computer "<ComputerDN>" -desc "<Description>"
```

For example:

```
> dsadd computer "cn=rallen-wxp,ou=my computers,dc=rallencorp,dc=com" -desc "Computer
owned by Robbie Allen"
```

You can also use the *netdom* utility to create a computer account. Here is the basic syntax:

```
> netdom add <ComputerName> /Domain:<DomainName> /OU:"<OrgUnitDN>"
```

For example:

```
> netdom add rallen-wxp /Domain:rallencorp.com /OU:"ou=my
computers,dc=rallencorp,dc=com"
```

If the /OU parameter is not specified, the computer will be created under the default computer's container (cn=computers).

Using VBScript

```
' This code creates a computer account in Active Directory.
' ------ SCRIPT CONFIGURATION ------
strBase = "<ParentComputerDN>"  ' e.g. cn=Computers,dc=rallencorp,dc=com
strComp = "<ComputerName>"      ' e.g. joe-xp
strDescr = "<Description>"       ' e.g. Joe's Windows XP workstation
' ------ END CONFIGURATION ---------

' ADS_USER_FLAG_ENUM
Const ADS_UF_WORKSTATION_TRUST_ACCOUNT = &h1000

set objCont = GetObject("LDAP://" & strBase)
set objComp = objCont.Create("computer", "cn=" & strComp)
objComp.Put "sAMAccountName", strComp & "$"
objComp.Put "description", strDesc
objComp.Put "userAccountControl", ADS_UF_WORKSTATION_TRUST_ACCOUNT
objComp.SetInfo
Wscript.Echo "Computer account for " & strComp & " created"
```

Discussion

Creating a computer account in Active Directory is not much different from creating a user account. In the CLI and API solutions, we set the description attribute, but it is not mandatory. The only mandatory attribute for computer accounts is sAMAccountName, which should be set to the name of the computer with $ appended (e.g., joe-wxp$).

These solutions simply create a computer account. You'll still need to join a computer with the same name as the computer account to a domain as we describe in Recipe 15.15.

See Also

MS KB 222525 (Automating the Creation of Computer Accounts), MS KB 283771 (HOW TO: Pre-stage Windows 2000 Computers in Active Directory), MS KB 315273 (Automating the Creation of Computer Accounts), MS KB 320187 (HOW TO: Manage Computer Accounts in Active Directory in Windows 2000), and MSDN: ADS_USER_FLAG_ENUM

15.15 Joining a Computer to a Domain

Problem

You want to join a computer to a domain after the computer account has already been created in Active Directory.

Solution

Using a graphical user interface

1. Log onto the computer you want to join and open the Control Panel.
2. Open the System applet.
3. Click the Computer Name tab.
4. Click the Change button.
5. Under Member of, select Domain.
6. Enter the domain you want to join and click OK.
7. You may be prompted to enter credentials of a user that has permission to join the computer.
8. Reboot the computer.
9. Note that the tab names in the System applet vary between Windows 2000, Windows XP and Windows Server 2003.

Using a command-line interface

Run the following command to join a computer to a domain:

```
> netdom join <ComputerName> /Domain <DomainName> /UserD <DomainUserUPN> /PasswordD *
/UserO <ComputerAdminUser> /PasswordO * /Reboot
```

Using VBScript

```
' This code joins a computer to a domain.
' The JoinDomainOrWorkGroup( ) method was introduced in Windows XP
' so this code works only against Windows XP and Windows Server 2003.
' ------ SCRIPT CONFIGURATION ------
strComputer      = "<ComputerName>"        ' e.g. joe-xp
strDomain        = "<DomainName>"          ' e.g. rallencorp.com
strDomainUser    = "<DomainUserUPN>"       ' e.g. administrator@rallencorp.com
strDomainPasswd  = "<DomainUserPasswd>"
strLocalUser     = "<ComputerAdminUser>"   ' e.g. administrator
strLocalPasswd   = "<ComputerUserPasswd>"
' ------ END CONFIGURATION ---------
```

```
'#########################
' Constants
'#########################
Const JOIN_DOMAIN              = 1
Const ACCT_CREATE             = 2
Const ACCT_DELETE             = 4
Const WIN9X_UPGRADE           = 16
Const DOMAIN_JOIN_IF_JOINED   = 32
Const JOIN_UNSECURE           = 64
Const MACHINE_PASSWORD_PASSED = 128
Const DEFERRED_SPN_SET        = 256
Const INSTALL_INVOCATION      = 262144


'###########################
' Connect to Computer
'###########################
set objWMILocator = CreateObject("WbemScripting.SWbemLocator")
objWMILocator.Security_.AuthenticationLevel = 6
set objWMIComputer = objWMILocator.ConnectServer(strComputer, _
                                     "root\cimv2", _
                                              strLocalUser, _
                                              strLocalPasswd)
set objWMIComputerSystem = objWMIComputer.Get( _
                              "Win32_ComputerSystem.Name='" & _
                              strComputer & "'")


'###########################
' Join Computer
'###########################
rc = objWMIComputerSystem.JoinDomainOrWorkGroup(strDomain, _
                                    strDomainPasswd, _
                                    strDomainUser, _
                                    vbNullString, _
                                    JOIN_DOMAIN)
if rc <> 0 then
    WScript.Echo "Join failed with error: " & rc
else
    WScript.Echo "Successfully joined " & strComputer & " to " & strDomain
end if
```

Discussion

Before you can join a computer to Active Directory, you must first create a computer account for it as described in Recipe 15.14. At that point you can join the computer to the domain.

Using a graphical user interface

If you have the correct permissions in Active Directory, you can actually create a computer account at the same time as you join it to a domain via the instructions described in the GUI solution. Since the System applet doesn't let you specify an organizational unit for the computer account, if it needs to create a computer account it will do so in the default Computers container (cn=computers).

Using a command-line interface

The *netdom* command attempts to create a computer account for the computer during the join operation if one does not already exist. An optional /OU switch can be included to specify the organizational unit in which to create the computer account. To do so you'll need to have permission to create and manage computer accounts in the OU.

There are some restrictions on running the netdom join command against a remote computer. If a Windows XP machine has the ForceGuest security policy setting enabled, you cannot join it remotely. Running the *netdom* command directly on the machine works regardless of the ForceGuest setting.

Using VBScript

In order for the Win32_ComputerSystem::JoinDomainOrWorkGroup method to work remotely, you have to use an AuthenticationLevel equal to 6 so that the traffic between the two machines (namely the passwords) is encrypted. You can also create computer accounts using JoinDomainOrWorkGroup by including the ACCT_CREATE flag in combination with JOIN_DOMAIN.

Just like with the *netdom* utility, you cannot run this script against a remote computer if that computer has the ForceGuest setting enabled.

See Also

More information on the ForceGuest setting can be found here: *http://www.microsoft. com/technet/prodtechnol/winxppro/reskit/prde_ffs_ypuh.asp*, MS KB 238793 (Enhanced Security Joining or Resetting Machine Account in Windows 2000 Domain), MS KB 251335 (Domain Users Cannot Join Workstation or Server to a Domain), MS KB 290403 (How to Set Security in Windows XP Professional That Is Installed in a Workgroup), MSDN: Win32_ComputerSystem::JoinDomainOrWorkgroup, and MSDN: NetJoinDomain

15.16 Renaming a Computer

Problem

You want to rename a computer.

Solution

Using a graphical user interface

1. Log on to the computer either directly or with a remote console application such as Terminal Services.

2. Open the Control Panel and double-click on the System Applet.

3. Select the Computer Name tab and click the Change button.

4. Under Computer Name, type the new name of the computer and click OK until you've closed all of the System applet screens.

5. Reboot the machine.

Using a command-line interface

The following command renames a computer and renames the corresponding Active Directory computer account:

```
> netdom renamecomputer <ComputerName> /NewName <NewComputerName> /UserD
<DomainUserUPN> /PasswordD * /UserO <ComputerAdminUser> /PasswordO * /Reboot
```

The renamecomputer option is only available in Windows XP and Windows Server 2003 (not Windows 2000).

Using VBScript

```
' This code renames a computer in AD and on the host itself.
' The Rename( ) method was introduced in Windows XP so this code works
' only against Windows XP and Windows Server 2003.
' ------ SCRIPT CONFIGURATION ------
strComputer      = "<ComputerName>"        e.g. joe-xp
strNewComputer   = "<NewComputerName>"     e.g. joe-pc
strDomainUser    = "<DomainUserUPN>"       e.g. administrator@rallencorp.com
strDomainPasswd  = "<DomainUserPasswd>"
strLocalUser     = "<ComputerAdminUser>"   e.g. joe-xp\administrator
strLocalPasswd   = "<ComputerAdminPasswd>"
' ------ END CONFIGURATION ---------

'###########################
' Connect to Computer
'###########################
set objWMILocator = CreateObject("WbemScripting.SWbemLocator")
objWMILocator.Security_.AuthenticationLevel = 6
set objWMIComputer = objWMILocator.ConnectServer(strComputer, _
                                       "root\cimv2", _
                                            strLocalUser, _
                                            strLocalPasswd)
set objWMIComputerSystem = objWMIComputer.Get( _
                            "Win32_ComputerSystem.Name='" & _
                            strComputer & "'")
```

```
'############################
' Rename Computer
'############################
rc = objWMIComputerSystem.Rename(strNewComputer, _
                                 strDomainPasswd, _
                                 strDomainUser)

if rc <> 0 then
    WScript.Echo "Rename failed with error: " & rc
else
    WScript.Echo "Successfully renamed " & strComputer & " to " & _
             strNewComputer
end if

WScript.Echo "Rebooting..."
set objWSHShell = WScript.CreateObject("WScript.Shell")
objWSHShell.Run "rundll32 shell32.dll,SHExitWindowsEx 2"
```

Discussion

Renaming a computer consists of two operations: renaming the computer account in
Active Directory and renaming the hostname on the machine itself. To do it in one
step, which each of the three solutions do, you must have permission in Active Directory to rename the account and administrator permissions on the target machine.
For the rename operation to be complete, you must reboot the computer.

 In some cases, renaming a computer can adversely affect services running on the computer. For example, you cannot rename a machine
that is a Windows 2000 domain controller or a Windows Certificate
Authority without first removing those services (which may have negative consequences). It also requires significant additional effort to
rename a server running either SQL Server or Exchange Server.

Using a graphical user interface

After you rename the computer you will be prompted to reboot the machine. You
can cancel out if necessary, but you'll need to reboot at some point to complete the
rename operation.

Using a command-line interface

You can also have *netdom* reboot the machine by including a /Reboot switch, which
automatically reboots the computer after the rename is complete.

Using VBScript

The Win32_ComputerSystem::Rename method must be run on the local machine unless
the computer is a member of a domain. Unlike the GUI and CLI solutions, you cannot specify alternate credentials for the connection to the computer other than
domain credentials. For this reason, the username and password you use with the

Rename method must have administrative privileges on the target machine (i.e. part of the Administrators group) and on the computer account in Active Directory.

See Also

MS KB 228544 (Changing Computer Name in Windows 2000 Requires Restart), MS KB 238793 (Enhanced Security Joining or Resetting Machine Account in Windows 2000 Domain), MS KB 260575 (HOW TO: Use Netdom.exe to Reset Machine Account Passwords of a Windows 2000 Domain Controller), MS KB 325354 (HOW TO: Use the Netdom.exe Utility to Rename a Computer in Windows Server 2003), and MSDN: Win32_ComputerSystem::Rename

15.17 Resetting a Computer Account

Problem

You want to test the secure channel of a computer and reset the computer account if it is failing.

Solution

Use the following command to test a secure channel for a computer:

```
> nltest /server:<ComputerName> /sc_query:<DomainName>
```

If this command returns errors, such as ERROR_NO_LOGON_SERVERS, try resetting the secure channel using the following command:

```
> nltest /server:<ComputerName> /sc_reset
```

If that doesn't help, you'll need to reset the computer account as described next.

Using a graphical user interface

1. Open the Active Directory Users and Computers snap-in (*dsa.msc*).
2. If you need to change domains, right-click on Active Directory Users and Computers in the left pane, select Connect to Domain, enter the domain name, and click OK.
3. In the left pane, right-click on the domain and select Find.
4. Beside Find, select Computers.
5. Type the name of the computer and click Find Now.
6. In the Search Results pane, right-click on the computer and select Reset Account.
7. Click Yes to verify.
8. Click OK.
9. Rejoin the computer to the domain (Recipe 15.15).

Using a command-line interface

You can use the *dsmod* utility to reset a computer's password. You will need to rejoin the computer to the domain after doing this:

```
> dsmod computer  "<ComputerDN>" -reset
> dsmod computer "cn=rallen-wxp,cn=computers,dc=rallencorp,dc=com" -reset
```

Another option is to use the *netdom* command, which can reset the computer so that you do not need to rejoin it to the domain:

```
> netdom reset <ComputerName> /Domain <DomainName> /UserO <UserUPN> /PasswordO *
> netdom reset rallen-wxp /Domain rallencorp.com /UserO rallen@rallencorp.com /
PasswordO *
```

Using VBScript

```
' This resets an existing computer account's password to the initial default.
' You'll need to rejoin the computer to the domain after doing this.
set objComputer = GetObject("LDAP://<ComputerDN>")
objComputer.SetPassword "<ComputerName>"
```

Discussion

Every member computer in an Active Directory domain establishes a secure channel with a domain controller. The computer's password is stored locally in the form of an LSA secret and in Active Directory. This password is used by the NetLogon service to establish the secure channel with a domain controller. If for some reason the LSA secret and computer password become out of sync, the computer will no longer be able to authenticate in the domain. The nltest /sc_query command can query a computer to verify its secure channel is working. Here is sample output from the command when things are working:

```
Flags: 30 HAS_IP  HAS_TIMESERV
Trusted DC Name \\dc1.rallencorp.com
Trusted DC Connection Status Status = 0 0x0 NERR_Success
The command completed successfully
```

Here is sample output when things are not working:

```
Flags: 0
Trusted DC Name
Trusted DC Connection Status Status = 1311 0x51f ERROR_NO_LOGON_SERVERS
The command completed successfully
```

When you've identified that a computer's secure channel has failed, you'll need to reset the computer, which consists of setting the computer account password to the name of the computer. This is the default initial password for new computers. Every 30 days Windows 2000 and newer systems automatically change their passwords in the domain. After you've set the password, you'll need to rejoin the computer to the domain since it will no longer be able to communicate with a domain controller due to unsynchronized passwords (the domain controller doesn't know the password has been reset). However, if you use the `netdom reset` command, it tries to reset the password on both the computer and in Active Directory, which if successful means you do not need to rejoin it to the domain.

See Also

Recipe 15.15 for joining a computer to a domain, MS KB 216393 (Resetting Computer Accounts in Windows 2000 and Windows XP), and MS KB 325850 (HOW TO: Use Netdom.exe to Reset Machine Account Passwords of a Windows Server 2003 Domain Controller)

CHAPTER 16

Event Logs and Log Files

16.0 Introduction

Event logs provide a standard way for the operating system, services, and applications to record important actions (e.g., application failures), report status messages, keep track of security events, and log boot up messages. In this way, event logs are similar to the syslog facility on UNIX and Linux platforms. They can be an extremely useful resource when you need to troubleshoot specific issues and are often the first places we look when trying to diagnose a problem. In fact, it is good to periodically check your event logs to find any application or system components that are failing without you knowing.

In addition to the event logs, Windows XP also has several log files that you can use to monitor and troubleshoot specific problems. The last few recipes we cover in this chapter describe how to enable some of the more important log files and in what situations you might want to use them.

Using a Graphical User Interface

There are two graphical tools that you should be familiar with for querying and viewing event log messages. Event Viewer (*eventvwr.msc*) has been around since the early days of Windows NT and is provided out of the box under Administrative Tools. It is a simple MMC snap-in that lets you view and filter messages in the event logs. You can also view the event logs on a remote machine with it, but depending on the size of the logs on the remote system and the network connection in between, this can be a painfully slow process.

As part of the Windows Server 2003 Resource Kit, Microsoft made the Event Comb utility (*eventcombmt.exe*) publicly available. Event Comb is a powerful utility that lets you search the event logs across multiple systems at once. With it, you can restrict your search by event ID, source, type, log, and event description. Event Comb is multi-threaded, so it can run against multiple machines simultaneously and you can configure the number of threads that can run at once.

Using a Command-Line interface

The event log command-line tools available for Windows 2000 are pretty limited in functionality. With Windows XP, three new tools were added to the default installation that provide many more features in terms of searching (*eventquery.vbs*) and creating events (*eventcreate.exe*), and configuring event triggers (*eventtriggers.exe*). You can see examples of these tools in action in Recipe 16.1, Recipe 16.2, and Recipe 16.13.

Using the Registry

Each event log is represented in the Registry with a subkey under the following key:

```
HKEY_LOCAL_MACHINE\SYSTEM\CurrentControlSet\Services\Eventlog
```

The name of each subkey is the same as the name of the event log (e.g., Application). The values under this subkey control settings such as the maximum size of the event log (Recipe 16.5), retention policy (Recipe 16.6), event log file location, and access control restrictions (Recipe 16.8).

Using Group Policy

The Group Policy settings that you can configure for event logs are available in the following location:

```
\Computer Configuration\Windows Settings\Security Settings\Event Log
```

Here you can configure the same settings as we just described with the Registry.

Using Downloadable Software

There are two downloadable tools that we use in this chapter. The first one comes from Sysinternals (*http://www.sysinternals.com*) and is named *psloglist.exe*. It is a command-line tool that is part of the PS Toolset. It allows you to query and enumerate events in an event log locally or on a remote machine (see Recipe 16.2 for an example).

The second downloadable tool we use comes from the Microsoft download website (*http://download.microsoft.com*). The *nlparse.exe* utility is part of the Account Lockout and Management Tools. It allows you to extract certain events from a *netlogon.log* file (see Recipe 16.17 for more information).

Using VBScript

There are two WMI classes that we use throughout this chapter. The Win32_NTLogEvent class represents individual event log messages, and Win32_NTEventlogFile represents the underlying file that contains event log messages. These two classes provide most of the functionality you'll need to retrieve, search, and configure event logs, except for one thing: neither class supports the ability to create event log messages. In Recipe 16.1, we show how to do this using the Windows Scripting Host LogEvent method.

16.1 Creating an Event

Problem

You want to write an event to an event log. This can be useful if you want to document certain actions you've performed on a workstation.

Solution

Using a command-line interface

The following command writes an event to the Application event log with event ID 999 and source SysAdmin:

```
> eventcreate /T <EventType> /ID <EventID> /L <LogName> /SO <EventSource> /D
"<EventDescr>"
```

For example:

```
> eventcreate /T INFORMATION /ID 999 /L Application /SO SysAdmin /D "Restarting
system after service pack install"
```

Using VBScript

```
' This code creates an event in the Application event log.
' ------ SCRIPT CONFIGURATION ------
strComputer = "\\<ComputerName>" ' e.g. wks01
strDescr = "<EventDescr>"      ' e.g. Restarting computer after installing SP2
'        END CONFIGURATION
Const EVENT_SUCCESS = 0
Const EVENT_ERROR   = 1
Const EVENT_WARNING = 3
Const EVENT_INFO    = 4

set objWSHShell = Wscript.CreateObject("Wscript.Shell")
boolRC = objWSHShell.LogEvent(EVENT_INFO, strDescr, strComputer)

if boolRC = TRUE then
   WScript.Echo "Successfully created event."
else
   WScript.Echo "Failed to create event."
end if
```

Discussion

Using a graphical user interface

None of the graphical tools (e.g., Event Viewer snap-in) allow you to create a custom event log message.

Using a command-line interface

To create an event on a remote machine, specify the /S option followed by the host name for *eventcreate*. Use /U and /P, respectively, to specify an alternate user account and password with *eventcreate*.

Using VBScript

With WSH, you can create an event only in the Application log. The WMI Event Log classes do not support creating custom event log messages.

See Also

MS KB 324145, "HOW TO: Create Custom Events"

16.2 Viewing Events

Problem

You want to view events in an event log.

Solution

Using a graphical user interface

1. Open the Event Viewer (*eventvwr.msc*). To connect to a remote computer, in the left pane right-click the Event Viewer icon and select Connect to another computer.
2. In the left pane, click on the event log containing the events you want to view.
3. Double-click on an event you want to view in the right pane.

Using a command-line interface

You can use the following command to list the events in an event log. In this example, the last ten records from the Application log are displayed. Both commands have numerous other options to view events, so look at the help information for more.

```
> eventquery.vbs /s <ComputerName> /l <LogName> /R <MaxEvents>
```

For example:

```
> eventquery.vbs /s wks01 /l Application /R 10
```

Using downloadable software

The Sysinternals *psloglist* utility is similar to *eventquery.vbs*. Here is the basic syntax:

```
> psloglist \\<ComputerName> -n <MaxEvents> <LogName>
```

This example is functionally equivalent to the previous *eventquery.vbs* example:

```
> psloglist \\wks01 -n 10 Application
```

 Both *psloglist* and *eventquery.vbs* have numerous other command line options. Check each command's Help information for the complete syntax.

Using VBScript

```
' This code displays events in an Event Log.
' ------ SCRIPT CONFIGURATION ------
strLog = "<LogName>"         ' e.g. Application
intNum = <intMax>            ' e.g. 10  (Max number of events to display)
strComputer = "<ComputerName>" ' e.g. wks01 (use "." for local machine)
' ------ END CONFIGURATION ---------
set objWMI = GetObject("winmgmts:\\" & strComputer & "\root\cimv2")
set colLogs = objWMI.ExecQuery("Select * from Win32_NTEventlogFile " & _
                               " Where Logfilename = '" & strLog & "'")
if colLogs.Count > 1 then
    WScript.Echo "Fatal error.  Number of logs found: " & colLogs.Count
    WScript.Quit
end if
for each objLog in colLogs
    intLogMax = objLog.NumberofRecords
next

if intLogMax > intNum then
    intNum = intLogMax - intNum
else
    intNum   intLogMax
end if

set colEvents = objWMI.ExecQuery("Select * from Win32_NTLogEvent " &
                "Where Logfile = '" & strLog & "' and RecordNumber >= " & intNum)
for each objEvent in colEvents
    Wscript.Echo "Date: " & objEvent.TimeWritten
    Wscript.Echo "Source: " & objEvent.SourceName
    Wscript.Echo "Category: " & objEvent.Category
    Wscript.Echo "Type: " & objEvent.Type
    Wscript.Echo "Event Code: " & objEvent.EventCode
    Wscript.Echo "User: " & objEvent.User
    Wscript.Echo "Computer: " & objEvent.ComputerName
    Wscript.Echo "Message: " & objEvent.Message
    WScript.Echo "------"
next
```

Discussion

An event log message is composed of several fields. Here is an explanation of each field:

Date
> Date the event occurred. Example: 3/15/2005

Time
> Time the event occurred. Example: 12:09:23A.M.

Type
> Information, Warning, or Error.

User
> User account that caused the event to be generated (if applicable). Example: AMER\rallen

Computer
> Computer the event was generated on. Example: RALLEN-WXP

Source
> Application or process that generated the event. Example: Automatic Updates

Category
> Used to classify events within a source. Example: Download

Event ID
> Number that identifies the event within the source and category. Example: 2512

Description
> Contents of the event message.

See Also

Recipe 16.10 for searching for events, and Recipe 16.12 for finding more information about a particular event

16.3   Creating a New Event Log

Problem

You want to create a custom event log. This can be useful if you are developing an application or script that needs to write a bunch of events to the event log, and you do not want to clutter one of the default logs.

Solution

Using the Registry

To create a new event log, all you have to do is create a subkey under the Eventlog services key. Replace *<LogName>* with the name you want to give the event log:

```
Key: HKEY_CURRENT_USER\SYSTEM\CurrentControlSet\Services\Eventlog\
Subkey: <LogName>
```

Using VBScript

```
' This code creates a new event log.
' ------ SCRIPT CONFIGURATION ------
strNewLog - "<LogName>"        ' e.g. MyLog
strComputer = "<ComputerName>"   ' e.g. wks01 (use "." for local machine)
' ------ END CONFIGURATION ---------
const HKLM = &H80000002
strKeyPath = "SYSTEM\CurrentControlSet\Services\EventLog\" & strNewLog
set objReg = GetObject("winmgmts:\\" & strComputer & "\root\default:StdRegProv")
objReg.CreateKey HKLM, strKeyPath
WScript.Echo "Created Event log " & strNewLog
```

Discussion

When you view events in the event log using a tool such as Event Viewer, you are actually interacting with the Event Log service. It is this service that applications interface with to write and retrieve events in event logs.

Each event log is defined as a subkey under the HKLM\SYSTEM\CurrentControlSet\ Services\Eventlog key. The name of the subkey is the name of the event log. The Event Log service constantly monitors this key for the creation of new subkeys. When it finds a new one, it creates a new event log. After it finds a new subkey, the Event Log service creates a file under the *%SystemRoot%\System32\config* directory to contain the event log messages. If you named the subkey Test, the file name would be *Test.evt*. You can then configure the new event log like you would one of the defaults (setting the maximum size, retention period, etc.).

See Also

MS KB 216169, "How to Change the Default Event Viewer Log File Location," and MS KB 315417, "HOW TO: Move Event Viewer Log Files to Another Location in Windows 2000"

16.4   Viewing the Size of an Event Log

Problem

You want to find the size of an event log. This can help you determine how large an event log is and if you are close to reaching the maximum size (and therefore will start dropping events).

Solution

Using a graphical user interface

1. Open the Event Viewer (*eventvwr.msc*).
2. In the left pane, right-click on the Target Event Log and select Properties.
3. The Size field contains the size of the event log in kilobytes and bytes.

Using a command-line interface

This command displays the file size for all of the event logs that are stored in the default location on the file system:

```
> dir %systemroot%\system32\config\*evt
```

Using VBScript

```
' This code displays the size of the specified event log in KB
' ------ SCRIPT CONFIGURATION ------
strLog = "<LogName>"          ' e.g. Security
strComputer = "<ComputerName>"  ' e.g. wks01 (use "." for local machine)
' ------ END CONFIGURATION ---------
set objWMI = GetObject("winmgmts:\\" & strComputer & "\root\cimv2")
set colLogs = objWMI.ExecQuery("Select * from Win32_NTEventlogFile Where " & _
                               Logfilename = '" & strLog & "'")
if colLogs.Count > 1 then
   WScript.Echo "Fatal error.  Number of logs found: " & colLogs.Count
   WScript.Quit
end if
for each objLog in colLogs
   WScript.Echo strLog & " size: " & objLog.FileSize / 1024 & "KB"
next
```

Discussion

Each event log has a corresponding event log file, which contains all of the event log messages. The size of an event log is determined by viewing the size of its event log file. By default, the *%systemroot%\system32\config* directory contains these files. Each file name directly corresponds to the name of the event log that uses it with an *.evt* extension (e.g., *Application.evt*).

See Also

Recipe 16.5 for setting the maximum size of an event log

16.5   Setting the Maximum Size of an Event Log

Problem

You want to set the maximum event log size. You need to make sure you size the event logs properly so they do not consume more disk space than necessary.

Solution

Using a graphical user interface

1. Open the Event Viewer (*eventvwr.msc*).

2. In the left pane, right-click on the Target Event Log and select Properties.

3. Beside Maximum Log Size, enter the maximum size in kilobytes that the event log can grow to.

4. Click OK.

Using the Registry

To configure the maximum size of an event log, set the following Registry value:

```
Key: HKEY_CURRENT_USER\SYSTEM\CurrentControlSet\Services\Eventlog\<LogName>
Value Name: MaxSize
Value Type: REG_DWORD
Value Data: <SizeInBytes>
```

Replace *<LogName>* with the name of the event log you want to configure (e.g., Application) and *<SizeInBytes>* with the maximum size the event log can grow to in bytes.

Using Group Policy

You can set the maximum event log size for the three default event logs using Group Policy as well:

```
\Computer Configuration\Windows Settings\Security Settings\Event Log\
Maximum application log file size
Maximum security log file size
Maximum system log file size
```

Using VBScript

```
' This code sets the maximum size for an event log.
' ------ SCRIPT CONFIGURATION ------
strLog = "<LogName>"            ' e.g. Application
intSizeBytes = <SizeInBytes>    ' e.g. 1024 * 512  (512KB)
```

```
strComputer = "<ComputerName>"    ' e.g. wks01 (use "." for local machine)
' ------ END CONFIGURATION ---------
set objWMI = GetObject("winmgmts:\\" & strComputer & "\root\cimv2")
set colLogs = objWMI.ExecQuery("Select * from Win32_NTEventlogFile Where " & _
                               "Logfilename = '" & strLog & "'")
if colLogs.Count <> 1 then
   WScript.Echo "Fatal error.  Number of logs found: " & colLogs.Count
   WScript.Quit
end if
for each objLog in colLogs
   objLog.MaxFileSize = intSizeBytes
   objLog.Put_
   WScript.Echo strLog & " max size set to " & intSizeBytes
next
```

Discussion

The default maximum size of each event log is 512 kilobytes. Depending on how busy your computer is and how many services and applications are running, this size may not be sufficient to store all the events that are generated. With disk space being really cheap, consider increasing the maximum limit to several megabytes. Ultimately, the maximum size of each of your event logs should be large enough to accommodate the number of events that are generated over the retention period (see Recipe 16.6). After you've hit the maximum size, each new event will cause the oldest event to be purged.

See Also

MS KB 216169, "How to Change the Default Event Viewer Log File Location," and MS KB 315417, "HOW TO: Move Event Viewer Log Files to Another Location in Windows 2000"

16.6   Setting the Event Log Retention Policy

Problem

You want to set the retention policy for events. This is necessary to prevent events from accumulating without bound and eventually filling up the hard disk.

Solution

Using a graphical user interface

1. Open the Event Viewer (*eventvwr.msc*).
2. In the left pane, right-click on the Target Event Log and select Properties.
3. You can select one of three options under When Maximum Log Size Is Reached.
4. Click OK.

Using the Registry

To configure the maximum size of an event log, set the following Registry value:

```
Key: HKEY_CURRENT_USER\SYSTEM\CurrentControlSet\Services\Eventlog\<LogName>
Value Name: Retention
Value Type: REG_DWORD
Value Data: <TimeInSeconds>
```

Replace *<LogName>* with the name of the event log you want to configure (e.g., Application) and *<TimeinSeconds>* with the number of seconds to keep events. Two special values you can set for *<TimeInSeconds>* are 0, to have events overwrite as needed, and 4294967295 (hexadecimal: ffffffff) to never overwrite events.

Using Group Policy

You can set the retention policy for the three default event logs using these Group Policy settings:

```
\Computer Configuration\Windows Settings\Security Settings\Event Log\
Retain application log
Retain security log
Retain system log
Retention method for application log
Retention method for security log
Retention method for system log
```

Using VBScript

```
' This code sets the number of days events are kept for an event log.
' ------ SCRIPT CONFIGURATION ------
strLog = "<LogName>"          ' e.g. Application
intDays = <NumDays>           ' e.g. 14   (number of days to keep events)
strComputer = "<ComputerName>"  ' e.g. wks01 (use "." for local machine)
' ------ END CONFIGURATION ---------
set objWMI = GetObject("winmgmts:\\" & strComputer & "\root\cimv2")
set colLogs = objWMI.ExecQuery("Select * from Win32_NTEventlogFile Where " & _
                               "Logfilename = '" & strLog & "'")
if colLogs.Count <> 1 then
   WScript.Echo "Fatal error.  Number of logs found: " & colLogs.Count
   WScript.Quit
end if
for each objLog in colLogs
   objLog.OverwriteOutdated = intDays
   objLog.Put_
   WScript.Echo strLog & " retention set to " & intDays
next
```

Discussion

There are three basic retention options for event logs:

Overwrite events as needed
> Once the maximum event log size is reached, the oldest events get overwritten with new events.

Overwrite events older than a certain number of days
> Once the maximum event log size is reached, overwrite only those events that are older than the specified number of days. If there are no events older than the specified day, the event won't be written.

Do not overwrite events
> Once the maximum event log size is reached, no events are written.

With the last two options, it is possible for events to not be written to the log because the event log reached its maximum size. In this case, you'd need to implement a process to archive and then clear the event log after a period. If you do this, be sure to set the maximum size so there is ample space.

See Also

Recipe 16.7 for clearing an event log, and Recipe 16.11 for archiving an event log

16.7   Clearing the Events in an Event Log

Problem

You want to clear all of the events in an event log.

Solution

Using a graphical user interface

1. Open the Event Viewer (*eventvwr.msc*).
2. In the left pane, right-click on the Target Event Log and select Clear all Events.
3. You then have an option to save the log before clearing it. Click Yes to save it, or No to not save it.

Using a command-line interface

The following command clears an event log:

```
> wmic /node:"<ComputerName>" nteventlog where "Logfilename = '<LogName>'" Call
ClearEventLog
```

Here is an example that clears the Application log on computer *wks01*:

```
> wmic /node:"wks01" nteventlog where "Logfilename = 'Application'" Call
ClearEventLog
```

Using VBScript

```
' This code clears all events from the specified event log.
' ------ SCRIPT CONFIGURATION ------
strLog = "<LogName>"         ' e.g. Application
strComputer = "<ComputerName>"  ' e.g. wks01 (use "." for local machine)
' ------ END CONFIGURATION ---------
set objWMI = GetObject("winmgmts:\\" & strComputer & "\root\cimv2")
set colLogs = objWMI.ExecQuery("Select * from Win32_NTEventlogFile Where " & _
                               "Logfilename = '" & strLog & "'")
if colLogs.Count <> 1 then
   WScript.Echo "Fatal error.  Number of logs found: " & colLogs.Count
   WScript.Quit
end if
for each objLog in colLogs
   objLog.ClearEventLog
   WScript.Echo strLog & " cleared"
next
```

Discussion

Typically, you do not want to clear an event log unless you've backed up or archived the log. Clearing an event log without saving the events makes it very difficult to later track down and troubleshoot problems.

If you clear the Security event log, event 517 will be automatically generated in the Security log. This event indicates the log was cleared and is important from an auditing perspective. Without event 517, you wouldn't have an idea if the security log had previously been cleared. This doesn't occur for the other logs.

See Also

MS KB 315147, "HOW TO: Clear the Event Logs in Windows 2000"

16.8   Restricting Access to an Event Log

Problem

You want to restrict who can view the event logs on a system.

Solution

The default behavior on Windows 2000 is that virtually anyone can view the event logs (including the Guest account and users connecting with null connections). To restrict this, you need to create the following Registry value: HKEY_LOCAL_MACHINE\ SYSTEM\CurrentControlSet\Services\EventLog\<LogName>\RestrictGuestAccess where <LogName> is the name of the event log (e.g., Application) you want to restrict. The value should be of type REG_DWORD with the value data set to 1. This limits access to members of the local Administrators group alone. You can also configure this in Group Policy. There are three settings that correspond to restricting access to the application, system, and security logs. These settings can be found under `Computer Configuration\Windows Settings\Security Settings\Event Log\`.

With Windows XP, things have changed. The `RestrictGuestAccess` Registry value is no longer used. It has been replaced with a `CustomSD` value (in the same Registry location) that contains a Security Descriptor string (SDDL) that determines what users have access to the event logs. Unfortunately, at the time of this writing, Microsoft has not provided a graphical interface or even a command line interface for abstracting away the messy details of SDDL. That means if you want to restrict access, you need to learn a little something about SDDL. For a good description of how you can accomplish this, read MS KB 323076, "HOW TO: Set Event Log Security Locally or by Using Group Policy in Windows Server 2003."

Discussion

If you are security conscious, as all good system administrators should be these days, you should be concerned that event logs (except the Security log) on your systems are world-readable by default. The event logs are a feeding ground of important information for potential attackers. Fortunately, the Security event log is treated differently and not viewable by non-administrators.

Restricting access to the event logs is not as easy as you might hope. In fact, on Windows XP you have to construct a SDDL string to do it, which can be a little complicated. See the following sites for more information:

http://msdn.microsoft.com/library/en-us/debug/base/event_logging_security.asp

http://msdn.microsoft.com/library/en-us/security/security/security_descriptor_string_format.asp

See Also

MS KB 323076, "HOW TO: Set Event Log Security Locally or by Using Group Policy in Windows Server 2003"

16.9   Searching an Event Log

Problem

You want to search for events in a specific event log.

Solution

Using a graphical user interface

1. Open the Event Viewer (*eventvwr.msc*).
2. In the left pane, right-click on the event log you want to search and select Properties.

---

3. Click the Filter tab.

4. Enter the search criteria and click OK.

 Another alternative for searching the event logs on a single host is the Eventcomb utility, which is covered in Recipe 16.10.

Using a command-line interface

You can use the *eventquery.vbs* command on Windows XP to search the event log of the local system or a remote machine. The following command displays the last 10 events with event ID 105 on the host fs01:

```
> eventquery.vbs /S fs01 /R 10 /L Application /FI "ID eq 105"
```

Using VBScript

```
' This code searches for events matching the specified criteria.
' ------ SCRIPT CONFIGURATION ------
intEventCode = <EventID>            ' Event ID to match; e.g. 105
strLog      = "<EventLogName>"      ' Event log name; e.g. Application
intMaxNum   = <MaxNumberOfEvents>   ' Max events to return (0 for all)
strComputer = "<ComputerName>"      ' Use "." for local system
' ------ END CONFIGURATION ---------
set objWMI = GetObject("winmgmts:\\" & strComputer & "\root\cimv2")
set colEvents = objWMI.ExecQuery("Select * from Win32_NTLogEvent " & _
                        " Where logfile = '" & strLog & "'" & _
                        " and EventCode = " & intEventCode)
count = 0
for each objEvent in colEvents
   Wscript.Echo "Date: " & objEvent.TimeWritten
   Wscript.Echo "Source: " & objEvent.SourceName
   Wscript.Echo "Category: " & objEvent.Category
   Wscript.Echo "Type: " & objEvent.Type
   Wscript.Echo "Event Code: " & objEvent.EventCode
   Wscript.Echo "User: " & objEvent.User
   Wscript.Echo "Computer: " & objEvent.ComputerName
   Wscript.Echo "Message: " & objEvent.Message
   WScript.Echo "------"
   WScript.Echo
   count = count + 1
   if intMaxNum > 0 and count >= intMaxNum then
      WScript.Echo "Reached maximum threshold...exiting"
      exit for
   end if
next
```

Discussion

The solutions in this recipe describe how to search events on a single machine. If you want to search for events across multiple systems at the same time, look at Recipe 16.10.

16.10 Searching the Event Logs on Multiple Systems

Problem

You want to search for events across multiple computers.

Solution

Using a graphical user interface

1. Open the Event Comb utility (*eventcombmt.exe*). When you first start the tool, it launches a Simple Instructions dialog box that contains the following directions:
2. Verify the Domain box shows the domain for which you want to search.
3. Right-click the box labeled Select to Search/Right Click To Add. Add the computers you want to search, e.g., All the DCs or individual computers.
4. Choose the log files you want to search, e.g., System, Application.
5. Select the event type you would like to search for, e.g., Error, Warning.
6. Enter the event IDs you would like to search for, e.g., 6005, in the Event IDs text box.
7. Click Search to start your search.

Using a command-line interface

None of the standard command-line tools support searching the event logs across multiple computers. You can however use a *for* command to run a query against several computers at once. Here is an example:

```
> for /D %i in ("wks01","wks02") do eventquery.vbs /S %i /R 10 /L Application /FI "ID
eq 105"
```

Using VBScript

```
' This code searches for events that match the specified criteria
' across several computers.
' ------ SCRIPT CONFIGURATION ------
intEventCode = <EventID>              ' Event ID to match; e.g. 105
strLog       = "<EventLogName>"       ' Event log name; e.g. Application
intMaxNum    = <MaxNumberOfEvents>    ' Max events to return (0 for all)
arrComputers = Array("wks01","wks02")
```

```
' ------ END CONFIGURATION ---------
for each strComputer in arrComputers
   WScript.Echo vbCrLf & vbCrLf
   WScript.Echo "Searching " & strComputer & "...." & vbCrLf
   set objWMI = GetObject("winmgmts:\\" & strComputer & "\root\cimv2")
   set colEvents = objWMI.ExecQuery("Select * from Win32_NTLogEvent " & _
                        " Where Logfile = '" & strLog & "'" & _
                        " and EventCode = " & intEventCode)
   count = 0
   for each objEvent in colEvents
      Wscript.Echo "Date: " & objEvent.TimeWritten
      Wscript.Echo "Source: " & objEvent.SourceName
      Wscript.Echo "Category: " & objEvent.Category
      Wscript.Echo "Type: " & objEvent.Type
      Wscript.Echo "Event Code: " & objEvent.EventCode
      Wscript.Echo "User: " & objEvent.User
      Wscript.Echo "Computer: " & objEvent.ComputerName
      Wscript.Echo "Message: " & objEvent.Message
      WScript.Echo "------"
      WScript.Echo
      count = count + 1
      if intMaxNum > 0 and count >= intMaxNum then
         WScript.Echo "Reached maximum threshold...exiting"
         exit for
      end if
   next
next
```

Discussion

The Event Comb utility is an extremely useful and powerful tool to have in your arsenal. Microsoft initially developed it for Windows 2000, but gave it out only to customers experiencing specific issues that required the ability to search the event logs on multiple computers. After the release of Windows Server 2003, Microsoft made it generally available as part of the Account Lockout toolset (*http://www.microsoft.com/downloads/details. aspx?displaylang=en&familyid=7af2e69c-91f3-4e63-8629-b999adde0b9e*) and also in the Windows Server 2003 Resource Kit.

See Also

MS KB 824209, "How to Use the EventcombMT Utility to Search Event Logs for Account Lockouts"

16.11 Archiving an Event Log

Problem

You want to archive your event logs so you can retrieve them later if necessary.

Solution

Using a graphical user interface

1. Open the Event Viewer (*eventvwr.msc*).
2. In the left pane, right-click on the Target Event Log and select Save Log File As.
3. Browse to the location to save the file, enter a name for the file, and click Save.

Using a command-line interface

Using the *wmic* utility, you can call the BackupEventLog method that is available with the Win32_NTEventlogfile class:

```
> wmic /node:"<ComputerName>" nteventlog where "Logfilename = '<LogName>'" Call
BackupEventLog "<FilePath>"
```

Here is an example of backing up the Application event log:

```
> wmic /node:"fs01" nteventlog where "Logfilename = 'Application'" Call
BackupEventLog "E:\app_back.evt"
```

Using VBScript

```
' This code archives an event log to the specified file.
' ------ SCRIPT CONFIGURATION ------
strLog = "<LogName>"                    ' e.g. Application
strBackupFile = "<FileNameAndPath>"  ' e.g. c:\app_back.evt
strComputer = "<ComputerName>"       ' e.g. wks1 (use "." for local system)
' ------ END CONFIGURATION ---------
set objWMI = GetObject(_
              "winmgmts:{impersonationLevel=impersonate,(Backup)}!\\" & _
              strComputer & "\root\cimv2")
set colLogs = objWMI.ExecQuery("Select * from Win32_NTEventlogFile Where " & _
                               " Logfilename = '" & strLog & "'")
if colLogs.Count <> 1 then
   WScript.Echo "Fatal error.  Number of logs found: " & colLogs.Count
   WScript.Quit
end if
for each objLog in colLogs
   objLog.BackupEventLog strBackupFile
   WScript.Echo strLog & " backed up to " & strBackupFile
next
```

Discussion

You might want to consider archiving your event logs on a periodic basis. If nothing else, archive your Security logs so that you can retrieve them if you need to go back and look for suspicious activity. Instead of backing up the log files on the local system, you can also specify a UNC path to a remote file server. If the event logs are using a lot of disk space, you might even want to create a simple batch script to archive the event logs and then clear them (see Recipe 16.7). If you are backing up your whole workstation, you probably don't need to archive the event logs individually.

16.12 Finding More Information about an Event

Problem

You want to find additional information about the cause or purpose of an event. Often, the information contained in an event is not sufficient to accurately assess or troubleshoot the issue that resulted in it being created.

Solution

You have a few options for finding additional information about a particular event.

When you view the details of an event in the Event Viewer under Windows XP, you will see a link at the bottom of the description for the event. If you click on that link, it will open the Help and Support Center and dynamically query the Microsoft web site to find if any more information is available for that event. We've tested this with quite a few events and so far, most have come back with no additional information. We assume that this will improve over time as Microsoft has a chance to update the site. You can also search for information about events on Microsoft's support web site (*http://support.microsoft.com/*).

A better source of information about events than the Microsoft Help and Support Center is the EventID web site (*http://www.eventid.net/*). There, they have been building a knowledge base about events since 2001. They have over 2800 events in their database that numerous contributors have commented on.

Another option is to search the news group archives. People like to include event log messages in news group posts when they are trying to troubleshoot a problem. It is possible that someone has posted a question about your event. The best source for searching news groups is the Google Groups web site (*http://groups.google.com*).

16.13 Triggering an Action When an Event Occurs

Problem

You want to launch a program or script when a particular event occurs. For example, you may want to send yourself an email when the event occurs or write another event to the event log.

Solution

Using a graphical user interface

Event Viewer doesn't support creating triggers.

Using a command-line interface

Windows XP comes with a new tool called *eventtriggers* that allows you to configure event log triggers:

```
> eventtriggers /Create /TR "<TriggerName>" /L <LogName> /EID <EventID> /TK <Command>
```

Example:

```
> eventtriggers /Create /TR "Email Trigger" /L Application /EID 177 /TK "cscript c:\
scripts\email.vbs"
```

To view the list of event log triggers configured on a system, run this command:

```
> eventtriggers /query /s <ComputerName>
```

To delete a trigger with ID 1, run this command:

```
> eventtriggers /delete /s <ComputerName> /TID 1
```

To get a list of configured triggers, run this command:

```
> eventtriggers /query /s <ComputerName>
```

Using VBScript

The event log WMI classes do not yet support creating triggers.

Discussion

The *eventtriggers* utility is a powerful new tool that can run on or against a Windows XP or Windows Server 2003 computer, and that runs a command when a specific even occurs. There are really no limitations on the type of commands or scripts you can use in a trigger. You can write your own custom script to send email or you can pipe several different commands together.

The *eventtriggers* command has three main options for managing event triggers: /Create, /Delete, and /Query. Here is the syntax for the eventtriggers /Create option:

```
Parameter List:
    /S      system          Specifies the remote system to connect to.

    /U      [domain\]user   Specifies the user context under which the
                            command should execute.

    /P      [password]      Specifies the password for the given user
                            context. Prompts for input if omitted.

    /TR     triggername     Specifies a friendly name to associate with
```

the Event Trigger.

/L	log	Specifies the NT Event Log(s) to monitor events from. Valid types include: Application, System, Security, DNS Server Log and Directory Log. The wildcard "*" may be used and the default value is "*".
/EID	id	Specifies a specific Event ID the Event Trigger should monitor for.
/T	type	Specifies an Event Type that the trigger should monitor for. Valid values include: "ERROR", "INFORMATION", "WARNING", "SUCCESSAUDIT" and "FAILUREAUDIT".
/SO	source	Specifies a specific Event Source the Event Trigger should monitor for.
/D	description	Specifies the description of the Event Trigger.
/TK	taskname	Specifies the task to execute when the Event Trigger conditions are met.
/RU	username	Specifies the user account (user context) under which the task runs. For the system account value must be "".
/RP	password	Specifies the password for the user. To prompt for the password, the value must be either "*" or none. Password will not effect for the "SYSTEM" account.

16.14 Troubleshooting a Corrupt Event Log

Problem

You have a corrupt event log that prevents you from viewing events. You may be seeing Dr. Watson errors after starting Event Viewer.

Solution

The following steps describe how to remove a corrupted event log:

1. Open the Services snap-in (*services.msc*).
2. In the right pane, double-click the Event Log service.
3. Beside Startup type, select Disabled, and click OK.

4. Reboot the computer. After the system restarts, you may see various error messages about some services failing to start.

5. Log in and delete the event log file (located under *%SystemRoot%\System32\Config*) that corresponds to the event log that is corrupted.

6. Open the Services snap-in (*services.msc*).

7. In the right pane, double-click the Event Log service.

8. Beside Startup type, select Automatic, and click OK.

9. Reboot the computer.

Discussion

The only way to get a corrupted event log working again is to delete it. Because the Event Log service always has the event log files (*%SystemRoot%\System32\Config*.evt*) open, you can't simply just delete them and be done. You need to first stop the Event Log service, but you can't even do that initially. Other services, such as Windows Management Instrumentation, depend on the Event Log service, so it cannot be stopped or paused. The only workaround is to set the Event Log service startup type to Disabled and reboot the computer. When the computer boots up, it will not start the service or any services that depend on it. This gives you an opportunity to log in and delete the corrupted files. After you are done with that, be sure to set the Event Log service back to Automatic and restart the computer. When the system restarts, the Event Log service will automatically create new files for any event logs that don't have one.

If your event log had important information that you don't want to lose, another option would be to restore the event log files from backup. You would follow the same procedure as the one just outlined, but instead of deleting the files, you would restore them from a good backup. Obviously, you will lose any events that were generated after the backup was taken, but at least you won't lose them all.

See Also

MS KB 172156, "How to Delete Corrupt Event Viewer Log Files"

16.15 Enabling Boot Logging

Problem

You are experiencing problems during system startup and you want to enable logging to determine what drivers and services are being loaded.

Solution

Restart your computer and press the F8 key until you see the Windows Advanced Options menu as shown in Figure 16-1.

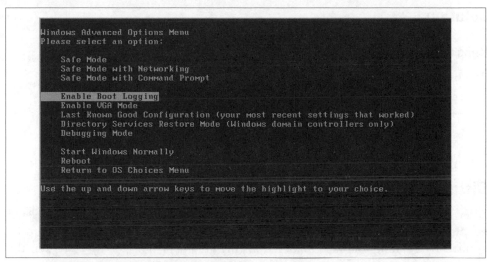

Figure 16-1. Windows Advanced Options menu

You can enable boot logging by selecting Safe Mode, Safe Mode with Networking, Safe Mode with Command Prompt, or Enable Boot Logging.

After the system boots up, you can log in and view the log file located at *%SystemRoot%\Ntbtlog.txt* using a tool such as Notepad.

Discussion

Boot logging can assist you in spotting drivers or services that may be preventing the system from starting up correctly. The system writes out the *ntbtlog.txt* log file after you see the Preparing network connections screen. If your system isn't making it that far in the boot process, check out MS KB 275735 for more troubleshooting tips.

See Also

MS KB 275735, "Ntbtlog.txt File Not Written When Boot Logging Is Enabled," and MS KB 315222, "A Description of the Safe Mode Boot Options in Windows XP"

16.16 Enabling User Environment Logging

Problem

You want to troubleshoot issues with a user's profile or the processing of system policy and Group Policy by enabling verbose user environment logging.

Solution

Using the Registry

To enable verbose user environment logging, set the following Registry value:

```
Key: HKEY_LOCAL_MACHINE\Software\Microsoft\Windows NT\CurrentVersion\Winlogon
Value Name: UserEnvDebugLevel
Value Type: REG_DWORD
Value Data: 10002 (hexadecimal)
```

The log file is located at *%SystemRoot%\Debug\UserMode\Userenv.log*.

Discussion

After you modify the Registry, verbose logging will occur as soon as a profile related action occurs (e.g., Group Policy is processed). You can force Group Policy to be applied by running gpupdate /force from the command line, or by restarting the computer.

By default, the logging level is "normal," even if the Registry value we described does not exist. That's why the *Userenv.log* may already exist before you enable verbose logging. To disable verbose logging and go back to normal logging, you can either delete the Registry value or set it to 10001. It is a good idea to disable it when you aren't using it because the log file will continue to grow and consume disk space.

See Also

MS KB 221833, "How to Enable User Environment Debug Logging in Retail Builds of Windows"

16.17 Enabling NetLogon Logging

Problem

You want to troubleshoot domain membership, Group Policy, site location, or user account (lockout, password, expiration, etc.) issues by enabling NetLogon logging.

Solution

Using a command-line interface

The following command enables NetLogon logging:

```
> nltest /dbflag:0x2000ffff
```

Using the Registry

To enable NetLogon logging, set the following Registry value:

```
Key: HKEY_LOCAL_MACHINE\SYSTEM\CurrentControlSet\Services\Netlogon\Parameters
Value Name: Dbflag
Value Type: REG_SZ
Value Data: 0x2000ffff
```

For both solutions, logging will start immediately—you do not need to restart the computer or even the NetLogon service. The log file will be located at *%Systemroot%\debug\netlogon.log*.

Discussion

The NetLogon service is responsible for authenticating a user, applying Group Policy objects, and other domain-based activities. If you enable NetLogon logging, you can see very detailed information about the actions this service performs. It is extremely useful when troubleshooting account lockout problems. The log will indicate which domain controller is locking the user out, and contains information about the domain controller the computer is authenticating against.

In the solutions, we described how to enable logging at the most verbose level. You can actually log specific actions by modifying the value data. The complete list of logging options is described in MS 109626. Simply add together each action you want to log and use the result in place of 0x2000ffff. To disable logging, use 0x0 for the value.

If you leave logging enabled for a period of time, the *netlogon.log* file can grow quite large. If you enabled logging specifically to troubleshoot user account issues, you may want to download the Account Lockout and Management toolset from Microsoft (*http://www.microsoft.com/downloads/details.aspx?familyid=7AF2E69C-91F3-4E63-8629-B999ADDE0B9E*). Included is a tool called *nlparse.exe*. With it you can extract lines that have a particular status code (e.g., 0x0 Successful Login). We've included a screenshot of *nlparse* in Figure 16-2.

See Also

MS KB 109626, "Enabling Debug Logging for the Net Logon Service," and MS KB 314861, "How Domain Controllers Are Located in Windows XP"

16.18 Enabling Windows Installer Logging

Problem

You are experiencing installation problems with an application and want to troubleshoot the cause.

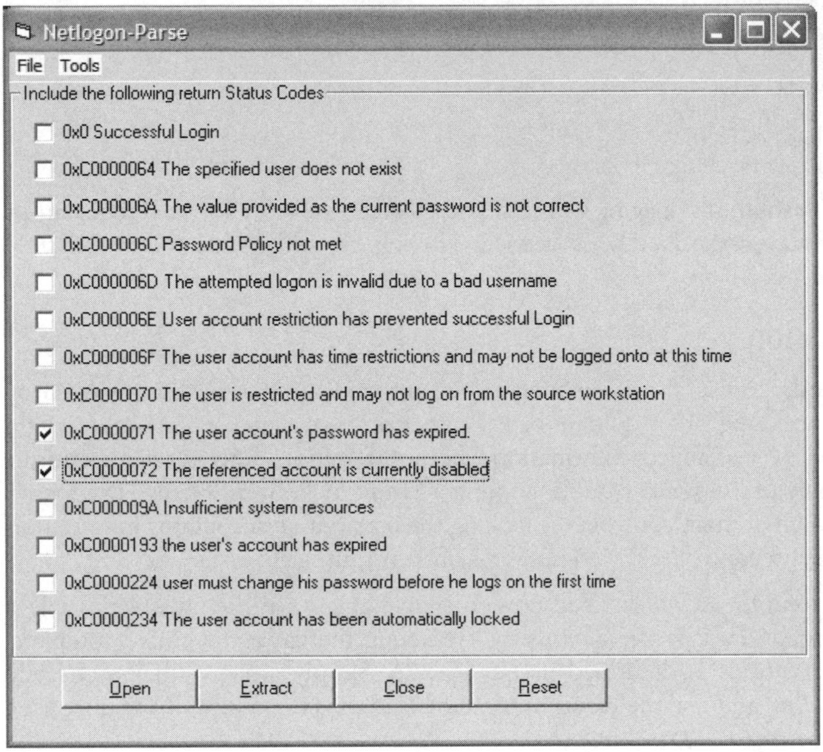

Figure 16-2. Nlparse utility

Solution

Using the Registry

To enable Windows Installer logging, set the following Registry value:

```
Key: HKEY_LOCAL_MACHINE\Software\Policies\Microsoft\Windows\Installer
Value Name: Logging
Value Type: REG_SZ
Value Data: voicewarmup
```

See the Discussion for more on what the value data means.

Using Group Policy

You can enable Windows Installer logging via Group Policy with the following setting:

```
\Computer Configuration\Administrative Templates\Windows Components\Windows
Installer\Logging
```

Discussion

If the installation program you are using is MSI-based (i.e., has a *.msi* extension), you can enable additional logging to troubleshoot issues during installation. After you enable logging, a log file is created each time you attempt a MSI installation in the *%temp%* directory (e.g., *C:\Documents and Settings\rallen\Local Settings\Temp*). These log files start with *msi* and have a *.log* extension. If there are multiple files like this in your temp directory, you may want to sort the output by timestamp to determine the most recent one.

 Disable Windows Installer logging when you no longer need it. Keeping it enabled causes a log file to be written every time an application is installed or uninstalled and may impact system performance.

The Registry value data that we showed you should enter was voicewarmup. This may have seemed like a strange thing to enter for logging options, but it is actually quite logical. Each letter in voicewarmup represents a particular type of event or action or information that Windows Installer will log. The combination of letters in voicewarmup represents all the options you can set. You can, of course, use a subset if you like. For example, you could just use the letters "cewp" if you wanted. How do you know what each letter represents? Table 16-1 has the complete listing.

Table 16-1. Logged events in Windows Installer

Option	Description
v	Log verbose output
o	Log out of disk space messages
i	Log status messages
c	Log initial UI parameters
e	Log all error messages
w	Log non-fatal warnings
a	Log start-up actions
r	Log action-specific records
m	Log out-of-memory or fatal exit information
u	Log user requests
p	Log terminal properties
+	Append to an exiting log file
!	Flush each line to the log as it is written

See Also

MS KB 314852, "How to Enable Windows Installer Logging in Windows XP"

16.19 Enabling Windows Time Service Logging

Problem

You are experiencing problems with your clock not being synchronized or being skewed from the actual time. By enabling logging of the Windows Time service you can see detailed information about interactions with the time server.

Solution

You need to set three Registry values to enable Windows Time service logging.

First, the following value configures the location of the log file:

```
Key: HKEY_LOCAL_MACHINE\SYSTEM\CurrentControlSet\Services\W32Time\Config
Value Name: FileLogName
Value Type: REG_SZ
Value Data: <LogFileName>
```

Replace *<LogFileName>* with the path to the log file (e.g., *c:\w32time.log*).

Second, the following value configures the maximum size you'll allow the log file to grow to:

```
Key: HKEY_LOCAL_MACHINE\SYSTEM\CurrentControlSet\Services\W32Time\Config
Value Name: FileLogSize
Value Type: REG_DWORD
Value Data: <SizeInBytes>
```

Replace *<SizeInBytes>* with the max size in bytes (e.g., 10485760 for 10 MB).

Last, the following value enables logging:

```
Key: HKEY_LOCAL_MACHINE\SYSTEM\CurrentControlSet\Services\W32Time\Config
Value Name: FileLogEntries
Value Type: REG_SZ
Value Data: 0-116
```

Enter the data exactly as shown (i.e., 0-116). You can enable verbose logging by entering 0-300.

You'll need to restart the Windows Time service for logging to begin:

```
> net stop w32time
> net start w32time
```

Discussion

Ever had a computer whose clock never kept the right time? It can be difficult to troubleshoot this problem, but enabling logging of the Windows Time service can usually pinpoint the problem. There may be a lot of text in the log file you don't understand, but look for lines that contain "Domain member syncing from," "Polling peer," or "Sending packet to." These lines will point out the time (NTP) server the machine is communicating with. Make sure that server has the correct time.

See Also

MS KB 816043, "HOW TO: Turn On Debug Logging in the Windows Time Service"

16.20 Enabling Outlook Logging

Problem

You want to troubleshoot some connection problems with Outlook. You can enable logging, which will show interactions between Outlook and any POP3, SMTP, or IMAP servers.

Solution

Use the following steps to enable Outlook logging:

1. Open Outlook.
2. From the Tools menu, select Options.
3. Click the Other tab.
4. Click the Advanced Options button.
5. Check the box beside Enable mail logging.
6. Click OK.
7. Restart Outlook for the logging to start.

Discussion

There are two locations for the log files that Outlook generates. For MAPI, POP3, and SMTP connections, Outlook writes out status information to the following file: *C:\Documents and Settings\\<Username>\Local Settings\temp\OPMLog.log*

For IMAP connections, Outlook writes out log files for each IMAP server you have configured. These log files are located in the following directory: *C:\Documents and Settings\\<Username>\Local Settings\temp\Outlook Logging\\<IMAPServerName>*

If you've enabled logging, restarted Outlook, and still don't see the logs, you may need to close Outlook before the log files are generated. Also remember to disable logging after you are done so the files don't take up disk space unnecessarily.

See Also

MS KB 300479, "How to Enable Transport Logging"

16.21 Troubleshooting Application Failures with the Dr. Watson Logs

Problem

You have an application that is failing and you want to find out why.

Solution

Whenever a program crashes, the Dr. Watson tool automatically appends a bunch of information to a log file located at *%SystemDrive%\Documents and Settings\All Users. WINDOWS\Application Data\Microsoft\Dr Watson\drwtsn32.log*. It writes things such as the application name, exception code, when the exception occurred, processes running at the time, DLLs loaded by the application, and a state dump of all threads. Depending on your level of technical sophistication, much of the log file may look indecipherable, but if the problem persists, you can provide this file to the technical support group of the application vendor and it will help them.

Discussion

Viewing log file with a text editor like Notepad can be a little cumbersome. You can use the Dr. Watson utility to select and view specific application failures. From a command line or the Start → Run menu, enter *drwtsn32.exe* and press Enter. You'll see a screen similar to that of Figure 16-3.

At the bottom under Application Errors, you can select from all of the previous application crashes and click View. This will launch a viewer that shows only the output related to that crash.

As you can see, this tool is useful for much more than viewing errors. You can also configure a variety of failure options. You can change the default log file path and also configure notification options.

 The Dr. Watson failure settings are stored in the Registry under the following key:

```
HKEY_LOCAL_MACHINE\SOFTWARE\Microsoft\DrWatson
```

See Also

MS KB 275481, "How to Troubleshoot Program Faults with Dr. Watson," and MS KB 308538, "Description of the Dr. Watson for Windows (Drwtsn32.exe) Tool"

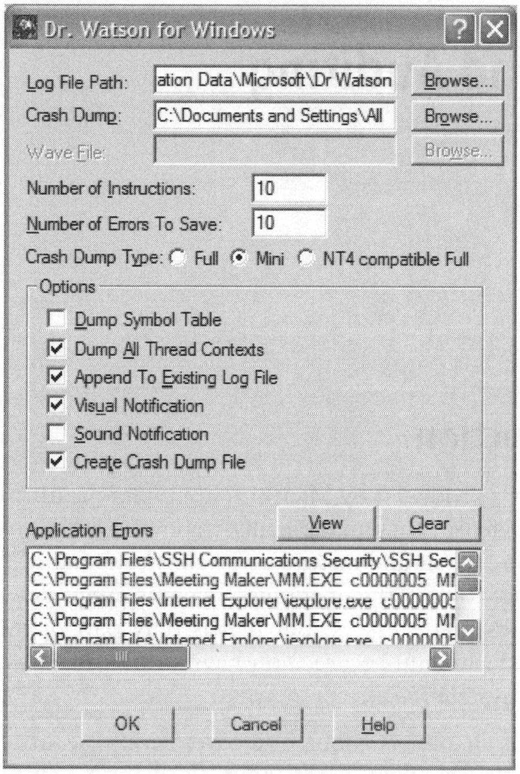

Figure 16-3. Dr. Watson utility

CHAPTER 17

Security and Auditing

17.0   Introduction

The operating systems produced by Microsoft are infamous for their lack of security, but in Microsoft's defense, they made many trade-offs early on to make Windows easier to use and "on by default" instead of "secure by default." With Windows XP, especially after Service Pack 2, the operating system is much more secure after installation compared to its predecessors. But that is only part of the story. Computers cannot lie in state and remain secure. You have to be proactive and play an active role in keeping your systems secure.

And that is what this chapter is about. We cover several security best practices that every user should consider when maintaining Windows XP systems. This chapter is by no means comprehensive, but it does cover many of the basic security precautions that all users should consider.

Basic Tips

Before we dive into recipes, we're going to review a few general security precautions. Again, this isn't a comprehensive list, but if you did these and nothing else, you would be doing better than most people.

Understand Microsoft's 10 immutable laws of security

Microsoft discusses 10 laws of security on the TechNet web site: *http://www.microsoft. com/technet/archive/community/columns/security/essays/10imlaws.mspx.*

Take some time to understand each law (if they aren't self-evident). These laws are some of the most basic tenants of computer security, especially when you are dealing with Microsoft technologies.

Protect physical access to computers

You could have the most hardened and locked-down system possible, but if an attacker can gain physical access to it, your efforts are for naught. Ensure that your computers are not left unattended.

Don't use administrative accounts during day-to-day use

In the Windows NT days, before Remote Desktop Connection and the runas command were available, it wasn't uncommon for administrators to have their own personal account as part of the Domain Admins group. Now, you shouldn't need to do this. Create alternate administrative accounts in Active Directory (e.g., *rallen* for my personal account and *rallen.adm* for my administrative account). Use Remote Desktop Connection or runas to run programs that need admin privileges. This will reduce the chance (however unlikely) that you accidentally perform a damaging action on your system. Using your normal user account will also reduce the damage a virus or worm can do if your computer becomes infected.

Keep virus and antispyware definitions up-to-date

One of the reasons viruses spread so fast is that virus definitions aren't up-to-date on computers. With many viruses and worms propagating at a blinding rate these days, you have to be on top of the latest definitions and able to push them out as quickly as you get them. The same goes for spyware, which is becoming an even larger problem today than viruses.

Make sure all critical patches are installed

Even if virus definitions aren't up-to-date, most viruses and worms would be struck dead in their tracks if everyone installed critical security updates when they came out. Granted, this wasn't as necessary with Windows NT and when Windows 2000 was first introduced, but now, if you don't update your systems within days (and sometimes minutes!) of new security updates becoming available, you are just asking to be hit with a new virus or worm. Here is a good site to bookmark and visit periodically to stay ahead of the curve with the latest Microsoft security issues:

http://www.microsoft.com/technet/security/current.aspx

Audit important activities

Windows provides the capability to log certain actions and activities that are performed on your systems. By logging important activities, such as the modification of particular files, you can maintain an audit trail for later reference in case incidents arise. For more information on auditing, see Recipe 17.2.

Check event logs regularly

The event logs can contain a wealth of important security-related information, but they are often overlooked. This is partly due to the amount of noise that is in the event logs in the form of unimportant event messages. Develop a process to centralize and analyze your event logs on a regular basis. Having a mechanism to scan your event logs on a regular basis will be even more critical if you are auditing important activities, as described previously.

Know what to do when you discover you've been attacked

Most people think it can never happen to them, but the sad truth is it can. In fact, most users don't have near as much security expertise as professional attackers. If a particular attacker (or worse, a group of attackers) takes a fancy to your organization, you'll have to be on top of your game to avoid some type of successful penetration. Some of the best in the business have been attacked. The moral of the story is that you should be prepared for the possibility of being attacked. What would you do? Here are a few good links that might help you develop an incident response plan:

http://www.cert.org/tech_tips/root_compromise.html
http://www.cert.org
http://www.securityfocus.com
http://microsoft.com/security

Maintain (and test!) backups

The worst case is that you have a system that gets successfully compromised. Unless you feel extremely confident that you know exactly what was compromised, your best bet would be to re-image the system and restore from a known good backup. That means you need good backups to start with. And if you are performing regular backups, we highly suggest performing a periodic test restore just to make sure the backups you have are good and can be used in case of an emergency. See Chapter 19 for more on performing backups of your system.

17.1   Analyzing Your Security Configuration

Problem

You want to analyze the security configuration of one or more systems to find any vulnerabilities or missing security updates.

Solution

The Microsoft Baseline Security Analyzer (MBSA) is a freely available tool from Microsoft that lets you scan computers for the latest security problems with Windows, along with numerous Microsoft products. Some of these include Office,

Exchange Server 2003, Microsoft Virtual Machine, and BizTalk. It can also check the configuration of Internet Configuration Firewall, Automatic Updates, and password settings.

MBSA has both a graphical and command-line interface. The MBSA graphical interface allows you to scan a single or multiple computers at one time (up to 10,000). Figure 17-1 shows the MBSA screen for selecting multiple computers. You can choose computers based on domain name and IP address range.

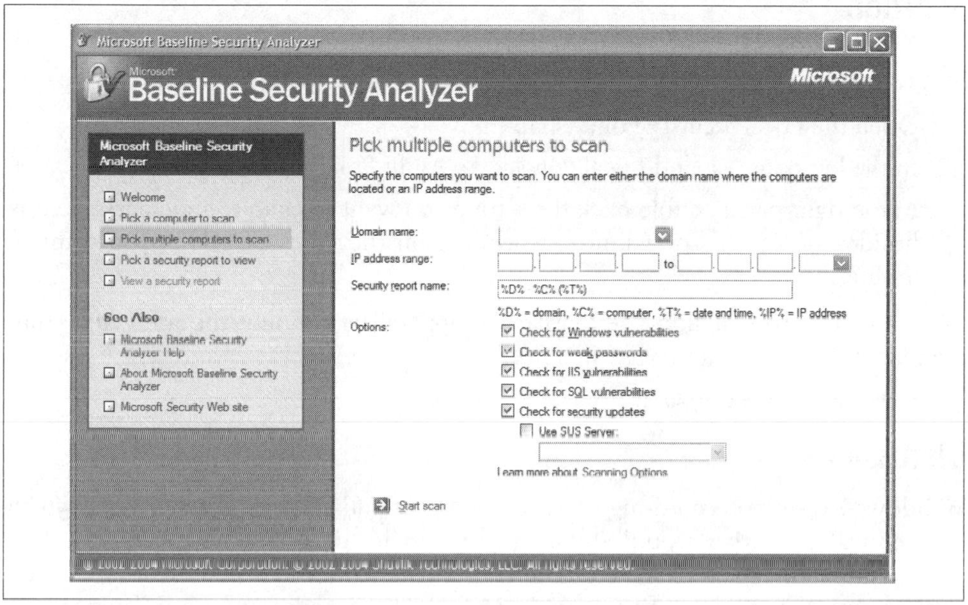

Figure 17-1. MBSA multiple computer selection screen

The MBSA command-line interface, *mbsacli.exe*, has the same functionality as the graphical interface. With it, you can easily automate periodic scans of your systems.

For more information on MBSA, including download instructions, see the following site: *http://www.microsoft.com/technet/security/tools/mbsahome.mspx*.

Discussion

MBSA keeps itself up-to-date with the latest vulnerabilities and security updates by automatically polling Microsoft when you start the program. As of version 1.2, you can alternately point MBSA at a SUS server to download the update catalog. This lets you determine what systems in your network are up-to-date according to your internal SUS server.

See Also

MS KB 320454, "Microsoft Baseline Security Analyzer (MBSA)"

17.2 Enabling Auditing

Problem

You want to enable auditing in order to track certain types of activity that can be useful in case you need to backtrack at a later point to determine the cause of security-related issues (e.g., user accidentally deleted, account being compromised, etc.).

Solution

Using a graphical user interface

1. Open the Local Security Policy snap-in.

2. In the left pane, expand Local Policies → Audit Policy.

3. In the right pane, double-click the setting you want to enable, and check the box beside Success and/or Failure, depending on the types of events you want to audit.

You can force new auditing settings to be applied by running the following command:

```
> gpupdate /target:computer
```

Discussion

Windows XP supports auditing of various account and system-related events, which can be invaluable when troubleshooting a security incident. You can enable auditing of nine different types of access on a local system. You can also configure these settings via an Active Directory Group Policy, which overrides any local settings that you've defined. After auditing has been configured, audit messages are created in the security event log.

The big question is: which audit settings should you enable? If you turned on everything, your system would start flooding your security event log and ultimately it wouldn't be very useful. In fact, there are no hard-and-fast rules for which settings you should enable.

All audit settings have three possible configurations: Not Configured, Success, and Failure. Not Configured means auditing isn't enabled for the setting, Success means log any applicable event that was successful, and Failure means log any applicable event that failed. Often, it is more useful to log Failure events, because you want to discover someone that is attempting to perform an activity surreptitiously, which may mean doing it several times until successful.

With some settings, simply enabling Success or Failure won't actually cause any events to be logged. You have to also enable auditing on specific objects, such as a particular file, before events will be audited. This is useful because in some cases, such as files and folders, you may only want to audit certain ones, not all of them. If auditing were enabled for all files, the amount of events would render auditing unfeasible.

We've listed each of the nine settings in Table 17-1, including information about what type of information is logged and my recommendation for whether you should consider enabling it.

 Be sure to thoroughly test any audit settings before implementing them in production. Even after implementing a change in production, periodically monitor the security event log to ensure the log isn't being flooded with events.

Table 17-1. Audit policy settings

Audit setting	Access type	Recommendation
Account Logon Events	User account log on and log off attempts that are validated by this system.	This setting is most often used on domain controllers, which are generally responsible for authenticating users in a domain environment. Be careful when enabling this because of the large number of events that might be logged.
Account Management	Creation, modification, and deletion of user, group, and computer accounts. Also includes password changes.	Consider enabling both Success and Failure auditing for this setting on member systems, which generally shouldn't have too much account management activity. For domain controllers, you may only want to enable Failure, due to the high number of account management activities.
Directory Service Access	Any type of read or write access to an object in Active Directory.	After enabling this setting, you must also modify the SACL of the object you want to audit. Be careful enabling this on a large container or commonly accessed object in the directory because it can generate a lot of events quickly.
Logon Events	User account log on and log off attempts, and the initiation of network connections.	Unlike the Account Logon Events setting, this setting logs the events on the computer that the request is being made on, not necessarily the computer that is validating the accounts involved. Depending on how busy your systems are, this setting may generate a large number of events.
Object Access	Any type of read or write access to an object on the system (file, folder, printer, Registry key, etc.).	After enabling this setting, you must also modify the SACL of the object you want to audit. Be careful enabling this on a frequently accessed object because it can generate a lot of events quickly.
Policy Change	Change to user right policies, audit policies, and trust policies.	Because the number of policy changes is generally low, you might want to consider enabling both Success and Failure auditing for this setting.

Table 17-1. Audit policy settings (continued)

Audit setting	Access type	Recommendation
Privilege Use	User exercising a user right (e.g., Act as part of the operating system, Access this computer from the network, Log on as a service, etc.).	Enabling either Success or Failure for this setting can generate a lot of events, so enable them only if explicitly needed.
Process Tracking	Process creation and termination, and other process-related activities.	Since processes are created and terminated very frequently, enabling Success or Failure for this setting can generate a lot of events. Enable it only if explicitly needed.
System Events	System restart or shutdown, and modifications to system security or the security event log.	Since the number of these type of events should be relatively low, consider enabling both Success and Failure.

See Also

MS KB 300549, "HOW TO: Enable and Apply Security Auditing in Windows 2000"

17.3   Renaming the Administrator and Guest Accounts

Problem

You want to rename the administrator and guest accounts on your systems. This is a good practice because these two default accounts are often the target of attackers.

Solution

Using a graphical user interface

To rename a domain administrator or guest account, do the following:

1. From Administrative Tools, open the Active Directory Users and Computers snap-in.
2. In the left pane, browse to the Users container and click on it.
3. In the right pane, right-click the administrator or guest account and select Rename.
4. Type the new name for the account and hit Enter.

To rename a local administrator or guest account, do the following:

1. From Administrative Tools, open the Computer Management snap-in.
2. In the left pane, expand System Tools → Local Users and Groups → Users.
3. In the right pane, right-click on either the Administrator or Guest account and select Rename.
4. Type the new name for the account and press Enter.

Using a command-line interface

To rename a domain administrator account, use the dsmove.exe command. The following shows the basic syntax:

```
> dsmove "cn=administrator,cn=users,<DomainDN>" -newname "<NewName>"
```

For example:

```
> dsmove "cn=administrator,cn=users,dc=rallencorp,dc=com" -newname "admn"
```

And this shows how to rename the domain guest account:

```
> dsmove "cn=guest,cn=users,dc=rallencorp,dc=com" -newname "noguest"
```

To rename local accounts, use the cusrmgr.exe utility from the Windows 2000 Resource Kit:

```
> cusrmgr -m \\<SystemName> -u admininstrator -r <NewName>
```

For example:

```
> cusrmgr -m \\srv01 -u admininstrator -r admn
```

And to rename the local guest account:

```
> cusrmgr  m \\<SystemName> -u guest -r <NewName>
```

For example:

```
> cusrmgr -m \\srv01 -u guest -r noguest
```

Using VBScript

```
' This code renames a domain account.
' ------ SCRIPT CONFIGURATION ------
strObjectOldName    = "<OldName>"         'e.g. administrator
strObjectNewName    = "<NewName>"         'e.g. RallencorpAdmin
strCurrentParentDN = "<CurrentParentDN>" 'e.g. cn=users,dc=rallencorp,dc=com
' ------ END CONFIGURATION ---------
set objCont = GetObject("LDAP://" & strCurrentParentDN)
objCont.MoveHere "LDAP://cn=" & strObjectOldName & "," & _
                 strCurrentParentDN, "cn=" & strObjectNewName
WScript.Echo strAccount & " successfully renamed"


' This code renames a local account.
' ------ SCRIPT CONFIGURATION ------
strComputer = "<SystemName>"   ' e.g. srv01
strOldName = "<OldName>"       ' e.g. Guest
strNewName = "<NewName>"       ' e.g. RallencorpGuest
' ------ END CONFIGURATION ---------
set objComp = GetObject("WinNT://" & strComputer)
set objUser = GetObject("WinNT://" & strComputer & "/" & strOldName & ",user")
set objNewUser = objComp.MoveHere(objUser.ADsPath, strNewName)
WScript.Echo "Successfully renamed account"
```

Discussion

You can also rename the administrator and guest accounts using Active Directory Group Policy or the Local Policy. To do so with Group Policy, do the following:

1. Edit the target GPO with the Group Policy Object Editor.
2. Navigate to Computer Configuration → Windows Settings → Security Settings → Local Policies → Security Options.
3. In the right pane, double-click either Accounts: Rename administrator account or Accounts: Rename guest account.
4. Check the box beside Define this policy setting and type in the new name for the account.
5. Click OK.

If you are worried about using an obscure name for your administrator account like vadar and forgetting what you used later, you can always discover the name by looking up the account by SID. And there is a Joeware tool called *sidtoname* to help do the job. Simply pass the SID of the account to the *sidtoname* command as shown here:

```
D:\>sidtoname S-1-5-21-1801674531-2025429265-839522115-500

SidToName V02.00.00cpp Joe Richards (joe@joeware.net) March 2003

[User]: RALLENCORP\Vadar

The command completed successfully.
```

You can get a complete list of the well-known accounts and their corresponding SIDs in MS KB 243330.

You may be wondering, since you can find out the actual administrator account name by looking up the SID, what the point is of renaming it. Ultimately, attackers can find out the name of well-known accounts, but there are still many viruses and worms that have attempted to access the administrator account by name. So this is still effective against less sophisticated attackers and viruses.

See Also

MS KB 243330, "Well Known Security Identifiers in Windows Server Operating Systems," and MS KB 320053, "HOW TO: Rename the Administrator and Guest Account in Windows 2000"

17.4 Disabling or Removing Unused Accounts, Services, and Software

Problem

You want to disable or remove anything that you don't explicitly need or use on a frequent basis on your system. The fewer things you have installed or active, the fewer potential vulnerabilities you have.

Solution

There is no one-size-fits-all rule for the accounts and services you should disable. It really depends on how you use your systems and what you use on them. As far as local accounts go, you should really only have a few on your system. The administrator and guest accounts are standard and you may also have built-in accounts for IIS or other applications. In the case of administrator and guest, you can't actually delete those accounts, but you can disable them. If nothing else, you should consider renaming them so that they aren't easy objects of attack (see Recipe 17.3 for more on this).

For services, you should review the services that are actively running and determine which ones you can safely disable. Again, there are no hard-and-fast rules here. Review the purpose of each service and determine whether it needs to be running. For example, if you aren't running any scheduled jobs and don't plan to do so, you don't really need the Task Scheduler service to run. Configure its startup type to Disabled. For some of the other services about which you aren't sure, don't just start disabling them on production systems. Test changes on a test system first.

Lastly, you'll want to make sure that all of the software that is installed on your systems is truly needed. Fortunately, Microsoft takes care of providing security updates for the default services that are installed on a system, but it is up to each application vendor to provide you with updates to their software when vulnerabilities are found. Don't forget about those.

See Also

Recipe 17.3 for more on renaming accounts

17.5 Enabling Screen Saver Locking

Problem

You want to enable screen saver locking to prevent an intruder from accessing an unattended system.

Solution

Using a graphical user interface

The following instructions enable screen saver locking for the currently logged on user:

1. Right-click the desktop background and select Properties.
2. Select the Screen Saver tab.
3. Select Blank for the screen saver, enter the number of minutes to wait before starting the screen saver, and check the box beside "On resume, password protect."
4. Click OK.

The following instructions enable screen saver locking using Group Policy:

1. Open the Group Policy Management Console (GPMC).
2. In the left pane, navigate to the target Group Policy, right-click it, and select edit. This will launch the Group Policy Object Editor.
3. In the left pane, expand User Configuration → Administrative Templates → Control Panel, and click on Display.
4. In the right pane, there are five settings you can modify to control screen saver behavior. These include the Hide Screen Saver tab, Activate screen saver, Screen saver executable name, Password protect the screen saver, and Screen Saver timeout.

Using a command-line interface

The following commands enable screen saver locking in the default user profile. Any user who logs in after these commands are run will use these settings. Any user who logged in before these commands are run will retain their original settings.

The following command configures the blank screen saver:

```
> reg add "\\<SystemName>\HKEY_USERS\.DEFAULT\Control Panel\Desktop" /v SCRNSAVE.EXE
/t R
EG_SZ /d scrnsave.scr
> reg add "\\<SystemName>\HKEY_USERS\.DEFAULT\Control Panel\Desktop" /v
ScreenSaveActive/t REG_SZ /d 1
```

The following command sets the screen saver timeout to 10 minutes (600 seconds):

```
> reg add "\\<SystemName>\HKEY_USERS\.DEFAULT\Control Panel\Desktop" /v
ScreenSaveTimeOut /t REG_SZ /d 600
```

The following command enables screen saver locking:

```
> reg add "\\<SystemName>\HKEY_USERS\.DEFAULT\Control Panel\Desktop" /v
ScreenSaverIsSecure /t REG_SZ /d 1
```

Using VBScript

```
' This code enables screen saver locking for all users that log on
' a system even if they've configured other screen saver settings previously.
' ------ SCRIPT CONFIGURATION ------
strComputer = "."
strScreenSaveActive    = "1"
strScreenSaverIsSecure = "1"
strScreenSaveTimeout   = "300"
strScrnSave            = "scrnsave.scr"
' ------ END CONFIGURATION ---------
const HKEY_USERS = &H80000003

set objReg=GetObject("winmgmts:\\" & strComputer & "\root\default:StdRegProv")
objReg.EnumKey HKEY_USERS, "", arrSubKeys

for each strSubkey in arrSubKeys
    WScript.Echo strSubkey
    objReg.EnumValues HKEY_USERS, strSubkey & "\Control Panel\Desktop", _
                      arrValues, arrTypes
    if IsArray(arrValues) then
        WScript.Echo "  setting screen saver values"
        objReg.SetStringValue HKEY_USERS, strSubkey & "\Control Panel\Desktop", _
                          "ScreenSaveActive", strScreenSaveActive
        objReg.SetStringValue HKEY_USERS, strSubkey & "\Control Panel\Desktop", _
                          "ScreenSaverIsSecure", strScreenSaverIsSecure
        objReg.SetStringValue HKEY_USERS, strSubkey & "\Control Panel\Desktop", _
                          "ScreenSaveTimeOut", strScreenSaveTimeOut
        objReg.SetStringValue HKEY_USERS, strSubkey & "\Control Panel\Desktop", _
                          "SCRNSAVE.EXE", strScrnSave
    else
        WScript.Echo "  NOT setting screen saver values"
    end if
    WScript.Echo
next
```

Discussion

If you want to implement a login script or batch file to enable screen saver locking for the currently logged on user of a system, you need to modify the following Registry values:

```
HKEY_CURRENT_USER\Control Panel\Desktop
"ScreenSaveActive"="1"
"ScreenSaverIsSecure"="1"
"ScreenSaveTimeOut"="900"
"SCRNSAVE.EXE"="scrnsave.scr"
```

This configures the *scrnsave.scr* screen saver to turn on after 15 minutes (900 seconds) of inactivity.

See Also

MS KB 281250, "Information About Unlocking a Workstation"

17.6   Disabling Storage of the LM Password Hash

Problem

You want to prevent the LanManager (LM) hash for new passwords from being stored in the local Security Accounts Manager (SAM). The LM hash is susceptible to brute force attacks and is primarily used for backward compatibility with Windows 95 and 98 clients.

Solution

Set `NoLMHash` the DWORD value entry under the `HKEY_LOCAL_MACHINE\SYSTEM\CurrentControlSet\Control\Lsa` to 1. You can accomplish this by modifying the Local Security Policy as described next.

Using a graphical user interface

1. Open the Local Security Policy snap-in.
2. In the left pane, expand Local Policies → Security Options.
3. In the right pane, double-click on Network security: Do not store the LAN Manager hash value on next password change.
4. Click the Enabled radio button.
5. Click OK.

Discussion

The LM hash uses an old algorithm (pre-Windows NT 4.0) and is considered to be relatively weak compared to the NT hash that is also stored. The LM hash is generated only for passwords that are shorter than 15 characters. So if you are one of the few people who have a password (or passphrase) longer than that, the LM hash is not stored for you.

See Also

MS KB 299656, "How to Prevent Windows from Storing a LAN Manager Hash of Your Password in Active Directory and Local SAM Databases"

17.7   Requiring Strong Passwords

Problem

You want to enforce the use of strong passwords for user accounts.

Solution

Using a graphical user interface

1. Open the Group Policy Object Editor and target the Default Domain Policy.
2. In the left pane, expand Computer Configuration → Windows Settings → Security Settings → Account Policies → Password Policy.
3. In the right pane, double-click Password must meet complexity requirements.
4. Make sure the box beside Define this policy setting is checked and Enabled is selected.
5. Click OK.

This setting does not have any effect on users' current passwords. Password complexity is required only after the next password change for each user. For more on how to force users to change their passwords, see Recipe 6.21 in *Active Directory Cookbook* (O'Reilly).

Discussion

Most users, if given a choice, pick really simple and easy-to-remember passwords. No matter how tight the security is on your systems, if an attacker can crack a user's password, it is all for naught. To combat this, you can enable password complexity on the Default Domain GPO to require users to choose a password that meets the following criteria:

- Not contain any part of the user's account name
- Contain at least six characters
- Contain characters from three of the following:
    Uppercase
    Lowercase
    Digits
    Special character (e.g., %(@!)

By enabling this, you can feel a little better that once users change passwords, they won't choose something trivial (although passwords such as "Mypassword!" still pass the complexity test).

See Also

MS KB 225230, "Enabling Strong Password Functionality in Windows 2000"

17.8   Getting Notified of New Security Vulnerabilities

Problem

You want to be notified when new security vulnerabilities in Microsoft products are found.

Solution

Microsoft provides a notification service that anyone can subscribe to. Simply visit *http://www.microsoft.com/technet/security/bulletin/notify.mspx*.

You'll need to provide an email address to send the notifications to. You may want to use a group mailing list so that multiple people get the notifications.

Discussion

To get a list of the latest security bulletins, visit the following page: *http://www. microsoft.com/technet/security/current.aspx*. From there you can view monthly security bulletin summaries along with on-demand webcasts that describe the technical details of bulletins.

CHAPTER 18

Performance Tuning

18.0 Introduction

How fast does your computer run?

Ask that question of most people, and you'll get a variation on this answer: not fast enough.

But you don't have to put up with a sluggish PC. There is a lot you can do to make it run faster and more efficiently—and to do it without having to install a faster processor, or buying more RAM.

In this chapter, you'll learn how to tune XP for top performance. You'll use a wide variety of tools built into XP, such as the Task Manager, the Task Scheduler, Disk Cleanup, the Disk Defragmenter, and other tools as well.

Don't expect those tools to do the job by themselves, because when it comes to tuning an operating system for a PC, you have to put a great deal of work into it as well, including some detective work.

But if you follow the recipes in this chapter, you'll be able to do the job well. You'll find out how to get more out of RAM, how to fine-tune applications and utilities, as well as XP itself, and more as well.

So try some of the recipes, and you'll find yourself with a faster PC.

18.1 Speeding Up System Performance with the Task Manager

Problem

You want a quick way to speed up system performance.

Solution

The Task Manager does more than manage tasks, show all programs and processes running on your system, and let you shut down any that they don't want to run any longer. It's also an excellent tool for tuning system performance. There are three ways to start the Task Manager:

- Press Ctrl-Alt-Delete.
- Press Ctrl-Shift-Esc.
- Right-click on the Task Bar and choose Task Manager.

When you run the Task Manager, shown in Figure 18-1, you'll see that it has five tabs. You'll use only three of them to improve system performance, the Performance, Processes, and Applications tabs. Figure 18-1 shows the Performance tab. At the bottom of each tab, you'll find a quick summary of the current state of your system, including current CPU use, the number of processes running, and how much memory is dedicated to your system.

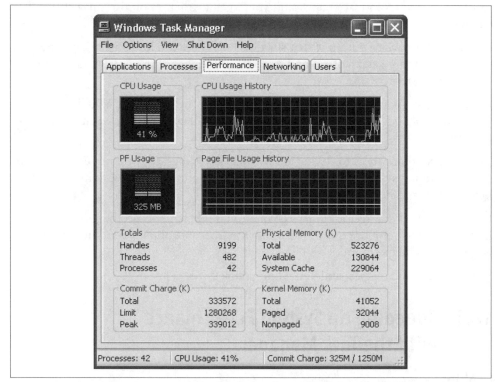

Figure 18-1. The Performance tab of the Task Manager

When you run the Task Manager, the tabs and menu bar may not be visible. To make them visible, double-click the top border of the Task Manager window.

Using the Task Manager to Monitor CPU Use

A PC running at 1 Ghz or higher can usually handle most basic tasks easily, but CPU-intensive software or tasks such as computer-aided design (CAD) programs, CD burning, and games can slow a system down significantly. The Task Manager can help by monitoring your CPU use and, based on what you find, letting you configure your system to make it run faster.

Monitor your CPU usage using the Processes and Performance tabs. You'll check total CPU load and how much of the CPU any individual process or program uses.

Finding out how much of the CPU individual programs and processes use. A common cause of PC slowdown is that one or more programs or processes take up too much of the CPU's attention. You can check the percentage of the CPU that any individual program uses. Look for those that take up too much CPU time; they're slowing down your other applications. Close down any that are CPU hogs, and your system will get a quick performance boost. If you need to run that application, close down any other applications that take up too much CPU attention.

To do it, from the Task Manager's Processes tab, double-click on the CPU heading. It will reorder the list of processes and programs in descending order, with those that use the most CPU time at the top. Note that, frequently, the top listing will be titled System Idle Process, which reports on the percentage of your CPU that is idle. Look for any programs or processes that use a considerable amount of your CPU. If you find any, close them down before starting any other CPU-intensive applications, such as CAD programs and CD-burning software.

Tracking CPU usage in real time. If your CPU regularly uses a high percentage of its capacity, you should either upgrade your CPU or run fewer programs. To find out whether it uses too much CPU capacity:

1. Run Task Manager and choose Options → Hide When Minimized from the menu. Now, whenever you minimize the Task Manager, it will sit in the Notification Area.

2. Minimize the Task Manager. It will display as a small bar graph in the Notification Area that lights up green as you use your CPU.

3. To see your current CPU usage, hold your mouse over the Task Manager icon in the Notification Area. Try running different combinations of programs and monitor your CPU use with each combination. If you find that your CPU is overburdened on a regular basis, it's time for an upgraded CPU or a new computer.

Give programs and processes more of your CPU's attention

XP gives a base priority to every program and process running on your PC; the base priority determines the relative amount of CPU power that the program or process gets, compared to other programs. Here are the priorities that XP assigns:

- Low
- BelowNormal
- Normal
- AboveNormal
- High
- Realtime

Most programs and processes are given a Normal priority. But if you have a CPU-hungry program, like a CAD or graphics program, you can give it more of your CPU's attention so that it runs more smoothly and quickly. And if there are programs or processes that normally run in the background or rarely need your CPU, you can give them less of your CPU's attention.

Use the Task Manager to change the priorities assigned to any process or program. The priorities of Low, BelowNormal, Normal, AboveNormal, and High are self-explanatory, but you might not quite understand RealTime. RealTime devotes an extremely high amount of CPU cycles to the given task—so much so that even Task Manager might not be able to interrupt any program or process assigned that priority. So, you shouldn't assign a RealTime priority to any program or task, unless it will be the sole program or task running on the PC. Of course, if it's the only program or task running, you really don't need to give it a high priority, because it already has your CPU's complete attention.

To change the priority of a running program or process from the Processes tab, right-click on the program or process whose priority you want to change, highlight Set Priority and choose the priority for the program, as shown in Figure 18-2.

Be careful when using this feature, because it can lead to system instability. If you find that it causes problems, stop using it.

 When you assign a new priority to a process or program, that new priority stays only as long as the program or process is running. Once the program or process ends and you then restart it, it defaults to the priority assigned to it by XP.

Discussion

If you want to use the Task Manager to tune system performance, you'll find it helpful to get more background about each tab. Here's what you need to know.

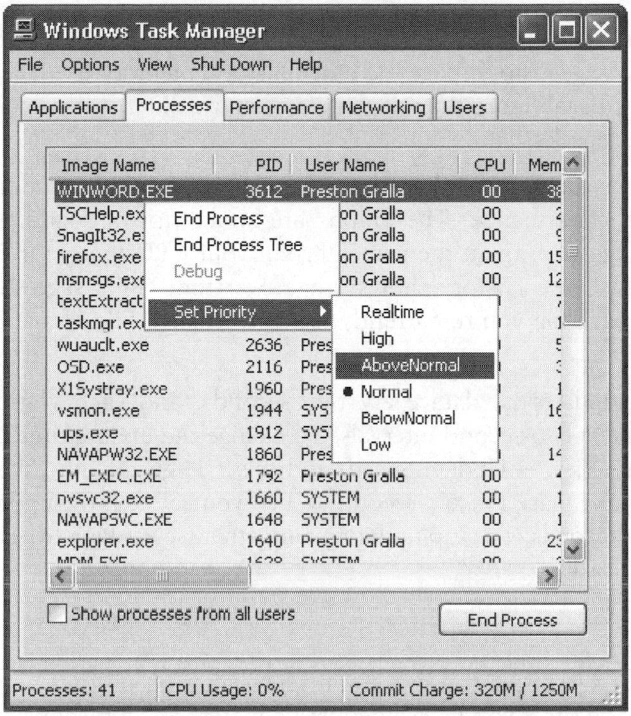

Figure 18-2. Devoting more or less CPU power to an individual program or process

Applications tab

The Applications tab displays a list of every application currently running on your PC and reports on the status of each application—mainly, whether the application is running or not responding to input.

When you right-click on any application, a menu of choices lets you manage the application in several ways: you can switch to the application, move the application to the front, minimize it, maximize it, or close it, as shown in Figure 18-2.

Processes tab

The Processes tab reports on every process running on your computer, as well as a variety of services run by the operating system. It reports on the percentage of the CPU that each process uses, as well as how much memory each process uses.

When you right-click on any process, you get a menu of choices that allow you to manage the process in a variety of ways, including closing the process and any related processes down, as shown in Figure 18-2.

Performance tab

The Performance tab shows a variety of performance measurements, including total CPU use, CPU usage history, page file usage history, memory used, and other statistics. You'll use this tab more than any other when tracking system performance and unstopping bottlenecks.

The Performance tab has tabular material and four graphs that detail your computer's current performance. The graphs are straightforward and easy to understand. CPU Usage shows you the percentage of your CPU that your PC is currently using, and CPU Usage History shows usage over time. PF Usage shows you how much of your page file you're currently using, and Page File Usage History shows usage over time.

Task Manager updates its data every two seconds, and each vertical line of the graphs represents a two-second intervals. To change the update time, from the Task Manager choose View → Update Speed, and select High or Low. When you select High, updates take place twice a second. When you select Low, updates take place once every four seconds. To stop updating altogether, select Paused. To do an immediate update, press F5.

Networking tab

The Networking tab displays a live graph representation of your network's performance. It only appears if you have a network adapter. The tab shows the quality and availability of your network connection. If you are connected to more than one network it will show you information about both.

The tab will show you network adapter name and description, as well as a wide variety of information about each connection, including your throughput measured in bytes sent and received, your overall connection speed, and other similar information.

If you're looking for an alternative to Task Manager, get Process Explorer from Sysinternals (*http://www.sysinternals.com/ntw2k/freeware/procexp.shtm*). Besides being much more robust and powerful, it is also free.

18.2 Tracking System Performance with the Performance Console

Problem

You want to track the performance of your system, so that you can see whether there are any problems or bottlenecks.

Solution

The Performance Console is an excellent way to track and graph the activities of Windows XP and its components. To use it, you first set up a log, then have the console monitor your PC, and finally examine the logs.

Setting up your logs

1. To run the Performance Console, choose Start → Run and type perfmon. The Performance Console appears as shown in Figure 18-3; you'll see the Microsoft Management Console (MMC), with the title bar Performance.

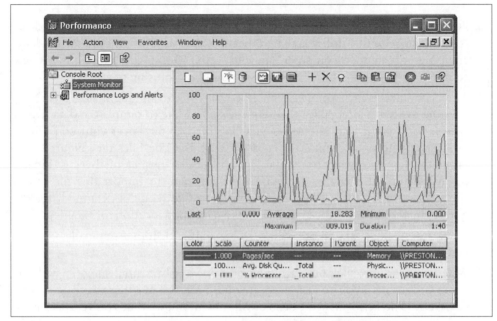

Figure 18-3. The Performance Console, tracking your system's performance

2. In the left-hand pane, click System Monitor to see a graph of your current system performance, including your processor, memory, and disk. You can use the toolbar buttons to configure the graph data and format. This graph is useful for seeing what's going on now, but useless for looking at the long-term picture.

3. To create log files of your system's performance, click Performance Logs and Alerts in the left pane of the MMC. You can create counter logs (with the values of performance indicators, measured on a regular basis), trace logs (with the values of performance indicators when something happens, like a program crash), and alerts (an action for Windows to take when a counter hits a specified value). Log files stored in text format contain one line per observation, with values separated by either commas or tabs, and are usually stored in the *C:\Perflogs* folder.

You can import these log files into a spreadsheet or database for analysis, reporting, and graphing. SQL and binary (nontext) log file formats are also available.

4. Create a counter log by right-clicking Counter Logs in the left-hand pane and choosing New Log Settings from the shortcut menu. Type in the name you want to give the log and click OK.

5. A log dialog box appears. Specify what statistics you want to log by clicking Add Counters on the General tab of the Properties sheet for the log, as shown in the nearby figure. To select a counter, first select the performance object (that is, the part of the computer system you want to monitor, such as memory or disks), from the Performance object drop-down list and then choose Counters from the list.

6. For each counter you want to track, highlight it, click Add, and then click Close. A nice feature of this utility is that you can choose whether to monitor the local computer or another computer on your LAN. Don't add more than a few counters, or your log file will grow quickly and be confusing to analyze.

7. After you choose each counter, you'll be sent back to the log dialog box. Now it's time to set the interval for the frequency you'd like to sample the data. Don't choose too frequent an interval or your log file will take over your entire hard disk (start with once a minute). To do it, click the Log Files tab (Figure 18-4). From the Log file type drop-down list, choose the format of the log (binary, comma delimited text file, and so on—if you plan to import this file into a spreadsheet or database program, choose Text File [comma-delimited] for the type). Then in the Example box, type in the name and location for your log.

8. Click the Schedule tab. Specify when the log start and stops—manually, or automatically on a schedule.

9. When you're done, click OK. If you haven't previously created a log file with the name and location you've just given it, you'll be asked whether to create it now. Click OK. The Performance Console will now monitor what you've asked it to, and write the information to a log file.

 The Performance console itself can slow down your computer considerably. Run it only when you need it, and don't set the logging interval to be too short. Set logs to stop after a day or two—otherwise, they run until your hard disk fills up.

You can also use the command-line tool logman.exe for creating and managing logs, although it offers fewer features than the Performance Console. Typing Logman create will create a new log; Logman start will begin logging; and Logman stop will stop logging.

Discussion

Recipe 18.1 showed you how to monitor your system performance with the Task Manager. So why bother to use the Performance Console?

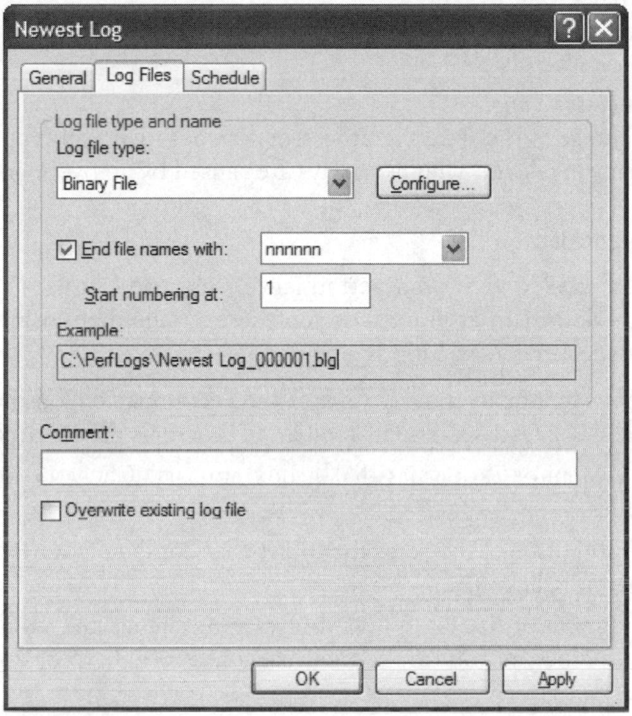

Figure 18-4. Creating a new log file

The primary difference between the two is that the Task Manager provides only a quick snapshot, while the Performance Console lets you create log files that can track performance over a longer period of time, and that you can examine. Additionally, the Performance Console lets you monitor a wider variety of metrics than does the Task Manager. And the Performance Console can set alerts as well as monitor remote systems, neither of which the Task Manager can do.

What to watch for in your logs

There are a lot of counters from which you can choose, but the following may be the most useful because they'll give you important information about system performance:

\Memory\Pages/sec
> Number of pages read from disk or written to disk when Windows runs out of memory. Swapping information to and from the disk can slow down your system a lot. Consider adding more memory if you see frequent swapping.

PhysicalDisk\Avg. Disk Queue Length
> How many read and write requests are waiting for the disk to respond. High numbers indicate that a faster disk drive would speed up performance.

PhysicalDisk\% Disk Time

What percentage of the time the disk was busy. This is another indicator of a slow or overloaded disk.

Processor\% Processor Time

What percentage of the time the processor was busy with all types of processes. This counter can tell you whether delays are caused by an overloaded CPU.

Viewing performance logs

There are several ways to view your performance logs. You can use the Performance Console itself to view them as graphs, or you can examine them using another tool, such as a spreadsheet. To view a log as a graph:

1. Click System Monitor in the left pane of the Performance Console window and click the View Log Data icon on its toolbar. (The icon is the fourth from the left.)

2. The System Monitor Properties dialog box appears. Click the Source tab and select Log files.

3. Click the Add button. Browse to the folder that contains your log, and double-click the log file. Click OK.

4. You'll see a graph of the log file. If you want to change the way the log looks, click the Properties button on the toolbar. You'll be able to customize the log's appearance.

To look at the contents of a comma-separated (*.cvs*) log file in Excel or your default spreadsheet program, double-click the filename in Windows Explorer. Excel may complain that the file is still open (since the Performance Console is still appending information to it); click Notify to see what's in the file so far. In Excel, you can analyze, graph, and print the counters.

Performance alerts

The Performance Console can alert you when there's a performance problem with your PC. To set this up, you create an alert that lets you know when a counter exceeds a specified value. For example, the Performance Console can let you know when the idle processor time drops below 10%:

1. Right-click Alerts in the left pane of the Performance Console window and choose New Alert Settings.

2. Type in the name you want to give to the alert, and click OK.

3. The Alert dialog box appears. Add one or more counters that you want to track, by clicking Add, selecting the counter for which you want to set an alert, and then clicking OK. When you've added all of the counters you want to track, click Close.

4. You'll be sent back to the Alert dialog box. On the General tab, specify the limit (upper or lower) beyond which Windows should take action.

5. Click the Action tab. Specify what Windows does when the alert occurs. You can have it add a note to an event log, run a program, send a network message, or start a new log.

6. When you're done, click OK. The alert will monitor your system and perform the action you requested when it reaches the limit you've set.

See Also

You can also use command-line tools to manage some aspects of your logs. For details, see MS KB 303133.

To learn how to log data directly into an SQL database, see MS KB 296222.

18.3 Using Memory More Efficiently

Problem

You find that your PC runs slowly because it runs up against its RAM limit, but rather than buy more RAM, you want to make the most out of the memory that you already have.

Solution

The Task Manager offers an excellent way to see how your RAM is being used. Then, based on what you uncover about RAM use, you can configure your system to make more effective use of the RAM that you have.

The Task Manager's Performance tab, shown in Figure 18-2, monitors your memory use. To get there, run the Task Manager by pressing Ctrl-Alt-Delete, then clicking the Performance tab.

The most important parts of the screen are the charts that report on Page File use and the tabular material below it that give a more detailed view of your current use of memory.

The charts relating to the Page File show current usage as well as usage over time. If Page File use is frequently high, it means that your system either isn't making the most efficient use of RAM, or you need more RAM. To make more efficient use of RAM, see the section "General Advice for Making Better Use of RAM" later in this recipe. The data below the Page File chart can be difficult to decipher. So use Table 18-1 to understand that data and, based on what you find, to make better use of RAM.

Table 18-1. *Understanding Performance tab memory reporting*

Category	Subcategory	What the data means
Totals	Handles	A handle lets a program use system resources such as Registry keys, fonts, and bitmaps. Sometimes poorly written programs don't close their handles down when the program closes, leading to memory loss. As a practical matter, you won't need to monitor this number.
	Threads	A thread is a discrete portion of a program executing a single task independently of other parts of a program. Again, as a practical matter, you won't need to monitor this number.
	Processes	This reports on the number of programs and services—processes—currently running on your system. Monitor this to see whether you have too many programs and services running on your PC. To shut down unnecessary services, see Recipe 18.8.
Commit Charge (K)	Total	The total amount of physical memory (RAM) and virtual memory (page file) currently in use, in kilobytes. The more programs, files and data you have open, the greater will be your commit charge. The greater the commit charge, the more demands put on your system. To reduce the commit charge, close programs and files, especially large files.
	Limit	Reports on the total amount of physical and virtual memory that is currently available for your PC, measured in kilobytes. To increase the limit, you can increase the page file size or add RAM to your system.
	Peak	Reports on the highest total amount of memory, measured in kilobytes, that has been in use during your current session. Check this value each session to see whether the peak value is frequently at or near the limit value. If it is, you need to increase your memory, either by adding RAM or by increasing your page file size.
Physical Memory (K)	Total	Displays the total amount of RAM in your PC, in kilobytes. This number can be confusing—to find out the amount of RAM in megabytes, divide it by 1024.
	Available	Reports on the total amount of RAM, in kilobytes, currently available. When available RAM is used up, your system begins to use its page file.
	System Cache	Reports on the total amount of RAM, in kilobytes, that is being used for the most recently accessed data and programs. Programs and data can be in the system cache even after they have been closed down; the PC looks to the system cache first when opening a program or file, since it can be opened from the cache faster than from the hard disk.
Kernel Memory (K)	Total	The total amount of memory, in kilobytes, in use by the primary components of XP—its kernel. The kernel is the core programs and files that make up the operating system.
	Paged	The total amount of memory in a page file, in kilobytes, used by the primary components of XP.
	Nonpaged	The total amount of memory of RAM, in kilobytes, used by the primary components of XP.

Here's how to use the information on the tab to make better use of RAM:

If the Total Commit Charge exceeds the Total Physical Memory, you probably need more RAM. When the Commit Charge is regularly higher than the Physical Memory available, it means that you have to regularly use a Page File, which slows your system down. Buy more RAM—it's relatively inexpensive and will boost system performance.

Before running a memory-intensive application, use the Processes Tab to identify memory-hogging applications, and close them down. The Processes tab of the Task Manager lists every process and program in use, and shows the total amount of memory each uses. Click twice on the Mem Usage heading on the tab to reorder the list of programs and processes so that those that require most memory show up at the top. Close down programs that you don't really need before running a memory-intensive application.

If the Peak Commit Charge is frequently at or near the Limit Commit Charge, you need to increase your memory. When this occurs, it means that your PC is frequently out of memory, or close to being out of memory. Either add RAM, or increase your Page File size.

General advice for making better use of RAM

The Task Manager can help you make better use of your RAM, as you've seen in the previous section of this recipe. But there is also some general advice you can follow for making better use of RAM as well.

Remove DLLs from cache memory

If you notice your system slowing down after XP has been running for some time, or if your RAM seems to be getting low, the culprit may be left behind DLLs from programs that are no longer running but that XP still keeps in memory. Sometimes XP keeps DLLs in cache memory even when the program that required them is no longer running, and this cuts down on the memory available to other applications.

You can edit the Registry to have XP automatically remove DLLs from cache memory that are no longer needed by programs:

1. Run the Registry Editor by typing Regedit

2. Go to HKEY_LOCAL_MACHINE\SOFTWARE\Microsoft\Windows\CurrentVersion\ Explorer.

3. Create a new DWORD value named AlwaysUnloadDll

4. Give it a data value of 1.

5. Exit the Registry and reboot in order for the new setting to take effect.

 This Registry setting may cause problems with some programs. Some Windows programs—especially older and 16-bit programs and Access—may issue error messages with this setting in effect. If that starts happening, delete the key or give it a value of 0 (zero).

Reduce the number of colors

Using 32-bit color takes up a great deal more memory than 16-bit color, and additionally, puts a greater strain on your processor. If you primarily use business applications such as word processors and spreadsheets, you most likely won't notice a difference between 16-bit and 32-bit color, so going with 16-bit color is a good bet. To change your color depth, right-click on the desktop, then choose Properties → Settings and in the Color Quality box, choose 16 bit.

Avoid DOS applications

DOS applications don't allow XP to manage memory properly and hold onto the memory they use; they don't allow it to be swapped out for use for other programs or processes. If you use any DOS applications, replace them with Windows versions.

Reduce the number of icons on your desktop

Every icon on your desktop uses up memory. Delete those you don't use regularly. Run the Clean Desktop wizard, which will automatically delete icons that you don't regularly use. To run it, right-click on the desktop and then choose Properties → Desktop → Customize Desktop → Clean Desktop Now. The wizard will step you through the process of deleting unused icons. If you want the wizard to run every 60 days, check Run Desktop Wizard every 60 days.

Reduce applications and services running in the background

You may have many programs and services running in the background without realizing it. Look at your Notification Area for programs running that you don't require. Shut them down, and make sure that they don't load at startup. Also, XP frequently starts services on startup that you might not need. For example, if you don't use a wireless network card, you don't need the Wireless Zero Configuration service.

To see all the services running on your PC, run the Task Manager and click the Processes tab. That shows you all the programs and services currently running on your system. To close one, highlight it and then click End Process. If you're not sure what a process is, do a Google search on the filename—you'll often out what the service is, what it does, and whether it's necessary to keep running.

Discussion

If your system doesn't have enough RAM, or uses what it has improperly, your system slows down. That's because in those circumstances, it moves data and programs to a paging file on your hard disk, and your hard disk is slower than RAM. A certain amount of this is normal, but if you use a paging file too much, or if even your paging file can't handle the memory load, you run into system slowdowns and problems.

As explained in this recipe, examining the paging file is one way to see whether you need more RAM or are making most effective use of what you have.

If after using the advice you find in this recipe, your system still runs sluggishly, and your paging file is used too much, there's only one solution to your problem: Install more RAM. RAM is relatively inexpensive, and installing extra RAM is one of the least expensive ways to give your system a performance boost.

See Also

For more information about using the Task Manager for troubleshooting, see Recipe 18.1. To turn off unnecessary services and programs that run on startup, see Recipe 18.9. And to make more effective use of a paging file (also called a swap file), see Recipe 18.5.

18.4 Balancing System Performance and Visual Effects

Problem

You want to speed up your system performance by turning off some of XP's special effects.

Solution

Using a graphical user interface

1. Right-click My Computer and choose Properties → Advanced.

2. The Advanced tab of the System Properties dialog box appears.

 For a quicker way to get to the System Properties dialog box, type sysdm.cpl at the Run box or command line and press Enter. When it opens, click the Advanced tab.

3. Under the Performance section, click Settings, then select the Visual Effects tab.

4. To turn off visual effects entirely, choose "Adjust for best performance." To use all visual effects, choose "Adjust for best appearance." To let XP determine which effects to use, select "Let Windows choose what's best for my computer." And to pick and choose individual effects yourself, choose Custom, then check the effects you want to use (and uncheck the ones you don't). You may have to experiment with different choices to see how they affect your system's performance.

5. When you've made your choice, click OK, and then OK again.

Discussion

Windows XP's visual effects—such as fading and sliding menus, background images for folders, and drop shadows for icon labels—make it a visually pleasing operating system. But all those effects can take their toll on system performance, especially if you have an older computer.

Turning off some or all of these special effects is a simple way to speed up a sluggish PC. The fewer effects you use, the faster your PC will perform. So experiment turning some on and off, for the best balance between visual effects and system performance.

See Also

For more advice on using the Performance Options dialog box to improve system performance, and for other related performance-related tips, see the CNet article "Give Windows XP a performance tune-up" at *http://cma.zdnet.com/texis/cdsamples/winxp_sample.html*.

18.5   Optimizing Page File Size

Problem

You want to optimize your page file size, because you're getting out-of-memory errors, or so that you can make the most efficient use of your RAM and speed up system performance.

Solution

Using a graphical user interface

1. Right-click My Computer, choose Properties, and click the Advanced tab.

2. The Advanced tab of the System Properties dialog box appears.

3. In the Performance section, click Settings and choose the Advanced tab.

4. In the Virtual memory section, click Change. The Virtual Memory dialog box appears, pictured in Figure 18-5. The dialog box shows you the location of your swap file, as well as the file's initial size and maximum size.

5. Click Custom, then type the initial size and the maximum size you want for your swap file and click Set.

6. You have three options for changing the size and behavior of your swap file:

   Custom size
   > This is the default setting on most XP systems. It lets you set the minimum and maximum sizes for the swap file. By default, the minimum size is 1.5 the size of your RAM, and the maximum size is twice the size of the minimum size. The minimum size XP allows is 2 MB. If youve been getting "out of memory" errors, increase the initial size by at least 25%. Set the maximum size to twice the initial size. If you have 512 MB or more of memory, and you haven't been getting "out of memory" errors, consider reducing the initial size by at least 10%. Doing this will give you more hard disk space, but in all likelihood wont adversely affect system performance. If you shrink the

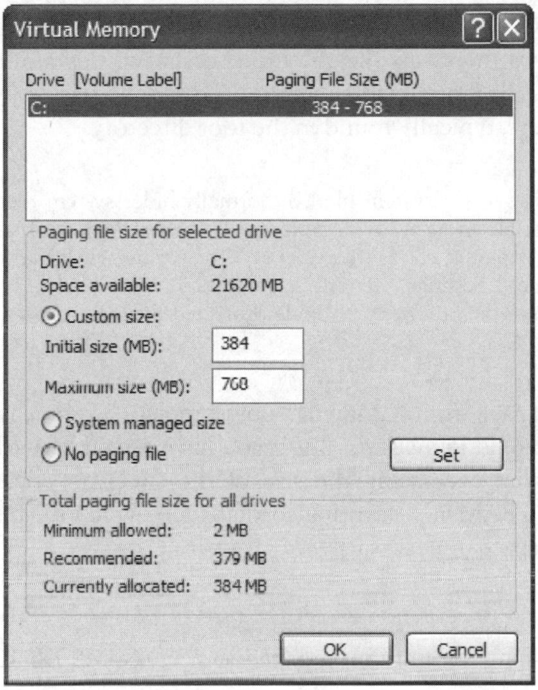

Figure 18-5. Customize the size of your swap file to get better performance

default sizes and you get an "out of memory" message at some point, increase the size of the swap file.

System managed size

When you choose this option, you'll let XP determine the minimum and maximum swap file sizes by itself, automatically.

No paging file

This option lets you run XP without a swap file. No matter how much RAM you have, it's not a good idea to choose this option. Some programs require the presence of a swap file, and Windows itself may behave erratically without a swap file.

7. Click OK, and OK on each dialog box until you've closed them all. If you've chosen to decrease the minimum size of the swap file, you probably won't have to restart for the changes to take effect. But if you've increased the minimum size, you have to restart your PC.

Discussion

The paging file, also called a swap file, is a file that XP creates to store data or program files on your hard disk when they can no longer fit into your system RAM. XP sets your initial swap file size at 1.5 times the amount of RAM on your system. So if you have 1 GB of RAM, your initial swap file size would be 1.5 GB. As you use your computer, XP allows the swap file to shrink or grow, depending on whether the operating system needs more or less memory. To see the size of your swap file, look for the file *pagefile.sys*, typically found in the root directory.

 pagefile.sys is a system file. XP normally hides system files so they're not visible in Windows Explorer. To make them visible, run Windows Explorer, choose Tools → Folder Options, click View, and in the Advanced Settings section, select "Show hidden files and folders." Uncheck the box next to "Hide protected operating system files" and click OK.

If you ever get a message from XP saying "out of memory," it means your swap file is too small, so you should increase it. But if you have a system with 512 MB of memory or more, consider decreasing the size of the swap file, because XP probably doesn't need all the RAM it's devoting to that file—which means you're giving up precious hard disk space unnecessarily.

See Also

For help in determining the minimum page file size, see MS KB 101220, "Minimum Paging File Size"

18.6   Cleaning Up Your Hard Disk

Problem

You want to clean up your hard disk by getting rid of useless and unnecessary files.

Solution

Using a graphical user interface

XP's Disk Cleanup tools provide a simple way to clean your hard disk of unnecessary files. To use it, choose Control Panel → Performance and Maintenance → "Free up space on your hard disk" and you'll see the screen shown in Figure 18-6. Check the boxes next to the files you want Disk Cleanup to delete, and click OK. If you want to view the files before deleting them, highlight the kind of files you want to view (such as Temporary Internet Files), and Windows Explorer will open to the folder containing the files. You can now view them before deciding whether you want to delete them. Once you're in the folder with Windows Explorer, you can delete files manually. That way, you can delete some, but leave others intact—after you've deleted some files, don't tell Disk Cleanup to delete the remaining files.

Using the command-line interface

Disk cleanup does a good basic job of cleaning your hard disk. But using it can be time consuming, because you have to check and uncheck so many options. Also, there may be times when you want only certain files deleted and you want to keep others. For example, your temporary Internet files speed up web browsing by keeping on hand the graphics files associated with sites you frequently or have recently visited. So there may be times when you want those files kept, but you want other files deleted.

You can solve the problem by creating separate disk-cleanup profiles. That way, whenever you want your hard disk cleaned in a certain way, you can run just that one profile. For another set of cleanup options, you can choose a different cleanup profile.

To create separate profiles, you use the command line version of the Disk Cleanup tool: `cleanmgr.exe`. To do it:

1. First, you need to create a new disk-cleanup profile. At the command line, type `cleanmgr /Saveset:n` where *n* is any number between 1 and 65535.

2. The Disk Cleanup Settings dialog will appear, as shown in Figure 18-6, allowing you to select which items you would like to be deleted using this profile.

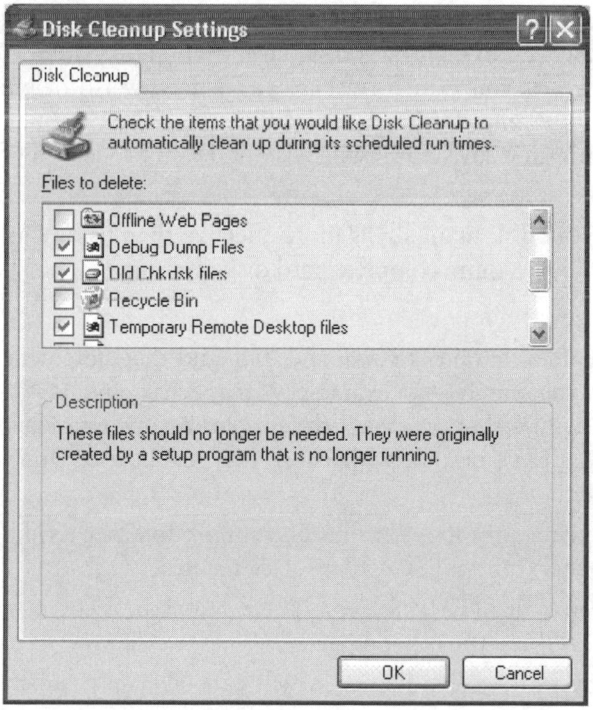

Figure 18-6. Disk Cleanup Settings screen

3. Note that this dialog box is similar but not identical to the GUI version of Disk Cleanup. You're offered several more cleanup options. Depending on what files are on your hard disk, you're able to automatically remove debug dump files, setup log files, catalog files for the Content Indexer, temporary setup files, old Chkdsk files, and various other items that the GUI version doesn't offer.

 If you're creating a profile to clean a drive other than the one that contains Windows, most of these options won't be enabled. You'll be able to automatically clean only the Recycle Bin and catalog files for the Content Indexer.

4. Make your selections and click OK to create your cleanup profile. To run this profile at any time, type `cleanmgr /Saverun:n` where *n* is the number of the profile you've just created.

 When using Disk Cleanup, from either the command line or the Windows GUI, be careful about letting it delete downloaded program files. These are often ActiveX programs and Java add-ins that are frequently useful, so delete them only if you know there are none that you use.

Manually clean your hard disk

Neither the graphical or command-line version of Disk Cleanup are necessarily the most effective way to clean your hard disk, even though they are the easiest. The tool won't find all the files you want to delete, and it might also delete files that you'd prefer to keep. For example, Disk Cleanup won't delete all the files in your *TEMP* directory, even though it says that it will. Also, it doesn't touch files that are less than one week old.

Often, cleaning your disk manually is more effective than using Disk Cleanup. Here are the steps for doing a more complete hard disk cleaning:

1. Empty the Recycle Bin.
2. Search for all files that end in *.bak* and *.tmp* and that start with ~ (use the wildcard * when you search—for example, *.tmp, *.bak, and ~*.*). Delete them all, except for any files that are dated the current or previous day. You might find that some files can't be deleted because they are in use. Don't worry about it; just leave them.
3. Delete your temporary Internet files by running Internet Explorer and choosing Tools → Internet Options → General → Delete Files.
4. Delete files in your *TEMP* folders. There might be two of these folders: one named *C:\TEMP* and the other named *C:\Windows\TEMP*.
5. Delete old System Restore Points, which can take up a substantial amount of space. You can delete all your old System Restore Points except the most current

one, but before doing this, make sure you don't need any old points. Run Disk Cleanup by clicking on "Free up space on your hard disk" from the Performance and Maintenance section of the Control Panel. Then, choose the More Options tab and click the Clean Up button.

Discussion

Hard disks are large enough so that you might think that there's no need to ever clean them. After all, with dozens or hundreds of gigabytes of free hard disk space, why bother?

But many unnecessary files can cause system problems, so cleaning them out regularly is a good idea. For example, some people have reported that when directories contain too many temporary files, their system behaves oddly—for example, causing problems with applications like Word.

See Also

There are a number of pieces of software you can download that do a better job than Disk Cleanup or manual cleanups. CleanUp! (*http://www.emesoft.se*, $18.00, trial version available) expands on XP's Disk Cleanup tool by finding and deleting shortcuts and favorites that are no longer valid, giving you a list of Registry entries that point to files no longer on your hard disk, and letting you examine and delete Internet Explorer AutoComplete entries. System Mechanic (*http:/www.iolo.com*, $59.95, trial version available) is far more than a disk-cleanup tool. In addition to normal cleanup tasks, it finds and deletes obsolete and junk files that are left behind by uninstalled programs, finds and deletes duplicate files, finds and fixes broken shortcuts, cleans out the Registry, lets you fine-tune Windows settings, has privacy protection, and more. In all, it has a suite of 15 utilities.

18.7   Converting Your Hard Disk to NTFS

Problem

You have a hard disk that uses the FAT32 file system, and you want to convert it to the more efficient and useful NT file system (NTFS).

Solution

Using the command line

To convert a volume to NTFS, you use XP's convert utility. To convert a volume to NTFS, use the following command:

```
> convert c: /fs:ntfs
```

where c: is the volume you want to convert.

You can also use a number of parameters along with the utility:

/v

This runs the utility in verbose mode, so that it provides information about the volume being converted.

/nosecurity

This sets the security privileges on the converted disk so that its files and folders can be used by anyone.

/x

Use this parameter if you're on a network and want to make sure that another user cannot disrupt the conversion process by trying to access the drive when you're converting it. The parameter dismounts the drive from the network and then converts the drive.

Discussion

NTFS is superior to FAT32 in several ways. It lets you open and save files more quickly, offers more security by letting you encrypt files, and gives you more hard disk space by letting you compress files and folders. Of course, before converting, you want to make sure that your hard disk is FAT32 and not already NTFS. To find out what file system your drive uses, right-click the drive in Windows Explorer and choose Properties → General. Look for the information next to File System; if you have an NTFS system, it will say so here.

Also, keep in mind that on drives under 1 GB, the NTFS system may be slower than a FAT32 system, so if your drive is that small, you may see a slower performance when you convert. However, on drives over 1 GB, NTFS is faster. And the NTFS file system gives you benefits other than speed, notably being able to compress and encrypt files and folders.

 If you have a multiboot system on your FAT32 drive that lets you boot into different operating systems, don't change your file system to NTFS. If you do, you won't be able to use multiboot capabilities.

Make sure the Master File Table is defragmented when you convert to NTFS

The Master File Table (MFT) is an index of all files and folders on a volume. You will be able to access files more quickly if the MFT is defragmented. XP's defragmentation utility can defragment the MFT, but only if the first fragment on the hard disk is capable of being moved. To make sure that the MFT can be defragmented when you convert to NTFS, follow these steps before converting your hard disk to NTFS:

1. Before converting to NTFS, defragment your hard disk using XP's Disk Defragmenter, as outlined in Recipe 18.8.

2. Estimate the amount of space that the MFT will require. As a general rule, the MFT uses 12.5% of a partition's space. So a 40 GB drive will require 5 GB.

3. Create a placeholder file in the root of the partition. This file should be the size of the MFT. Eventually, the placeholder file will be moved out, and the MFT will take its place. If you were going to create a placeholder file called *mftholder.txt* in a C: drive of 5 GB, you would issue the following command. Note that you can give the file you're creating any name that you want:

```
> fsutil file createnew c:\mftholder.txt 5000000000
```

4. After you've done that, convert the drive to NTFS by using the convert program with a special parameter:

```
> convert c: /fs:ntfs /cvtarea:mftholder.txt
```

5. After the volume has been created, run XP's Disk Defragmenter. The MFT will be moved to the front of the partition and defragmented. After you run the Disk Defragmenter, you can delete the placeholder file that you created.

> FAT32 drives don't have an MFT, so in this recipe, you're first defragmenting your FAT32 drive, and then creating a placeholder for the MFT for when you convert to NTFS. When you convert to NTFS, the newly created MFT will then be defragmented.

See Also

For more information about using the command line to convert a partition to NTFS, see MS KB 314097, "How to Use Convert.exe to Convert a Partition to the NTFS File System"

18.8 Disabling Startup Services and Programs

Problem

You want to disable unnecessary services and programs that automatically launch on startup, because they take up processor power and RAM, but you don't use them.

Solution

Stopping programs that run on startup

Stopping programs from running at startup is especially difficult, because there is no single place you can go to keep them all from running. Some automatically start because they're put in the Startup folder, others because of Registry settings and so on. But there are steps you can take to track them down and kill them.

Cleaning out the Startup folder. Start by cleaning out your Startup folder, which you can find in *C:\Documents and Settings\<User Name>\Start Menu\Programs\Startup*, where <User Name> is your Windows logon name. Delete the shortcuts of any programs you don't want to run on startup. As with any shortcuts, when you delete them, you're only deleting the shortcut, not the program itself. (You can also clear out the startup items by going to Start → Programs → Startup and right-clicking on items you want to remove.) Next, clean out your Scheduled Tasks folder. Go to *C:\ WINDOWS\Tasks*, and delete the shortcuts of any programs that you don't want to run automatically on a schedule.

 You can bypass all the programs in your Startup folder on an as-needed basis. To stop XP from loading any programs in the Startup folder, hold down the Shift key during bootup. No programs in the Startup folder will run, but the items will still remain there, so that they will start up as they would normally the next time you boot.

Using the System Configuration utility. Cleaning out the Startup folder will stop some programs from running, but not all of them. An even better way to disable hidden programs that run on startup is to use the System Configuration utility, shown in Figure 18-7.

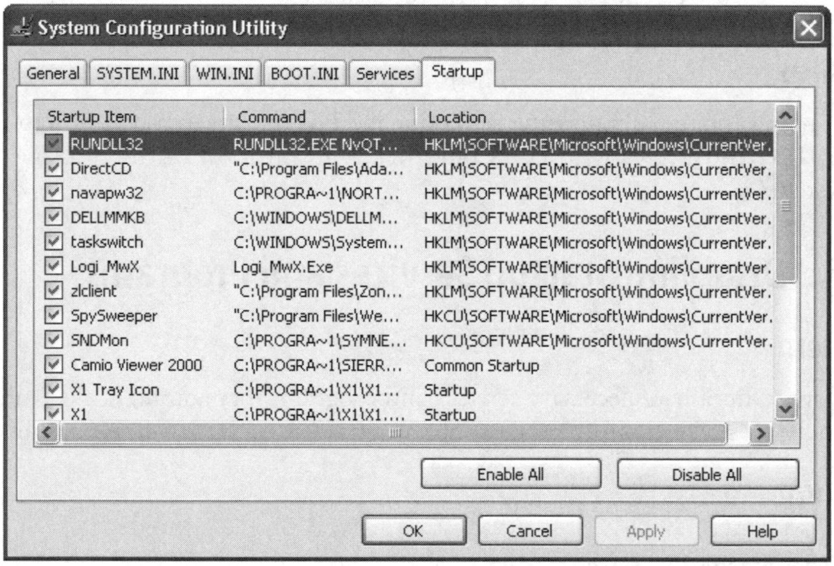

Figure 18-7. The Startup tab of the System Configuration utility is the best way to halt programs from running on startup.

To run it, type msconfig at a command prompt and press Enter. Click the Startup tab, and to stop a program from running on startup, uncheck the box next to the program. It can be difficult to understand what programs are listed on the Startup tab. Some, such as America Online, are clearly labeled. But often, you'll see a phrase or collection of letters, such as zlclient. To get more information about the listing, expand the width of the Command column near the top of the Startup tab. Expand it enough and you'll see the startup command that the program issues, including its location, such as *C:\Program Files\Zone Labs\ZoneAlarm\zclient.exe*. The directory location will be another hint to help you know the name of the program.

If that doesn't help, search for the file name on Google. Click through enough search results, and you'll find out enough information about the file to decide whether you want it to run on startup or not.

When stopping programs from running at startup, it's best to stop them one at a time rather than in groups. You want to make sure that you're not causing any system problems by stopping them. So stop one and restart your PC. If it runs fine, then stop another and restart. Continue doing this until you've cleared all the programs you don't want to run automatically.

After you've used the System Configuration utility to identify programs that run on startup, you may want to try disabling them from within the programs themselves. Run each program that starts automatically, and see if you can find a setting that allows you to stop it from running on startup.

Using the Registry

Even the System Configuration utility won't necessarily let you identify and kill all programs that run on startup. You may also need to edit the Registry to disable them. To do so, run Registry Editor and go to HKEY_CURRENT_USER\Software\Microsoft\Windows\CurrentVersion\Run. The right pane will contain a list of some of the programs that automatically run at startup. The Data field tells you the path and name of the executable so that you can determine what each program is. Right-click on any program you don't want to run, and choose Delete. That will kill any programs that run specific to your logon. To kill programs that run for every user of the system, go to HKEY_LOCAL_MACHINE\SOFTWARE\Microsoft\Windows\CurrentVersion\Run and follow the same instructions for deleting other programs you don't want to run at startup.

Disabling services that run at startup

To disable services that run at startup, see Recipe 10.18.

Table 18-2 lists some common services you might want to halt from running at startup.

Table 18-2. Services you might want to turn off at startup

Service	What it does
Portable Media Serial Number	Retrieves the serial number of a portable music player attached to your PC.
Task Scheduler	Schedules unattended tasks to be run. If you don't schedule any unattended tasks, turn it off.
Uninterruptible Power Supply	Manages an uninterruptible power supply (UPS) connected to your PC.

Table 18-2. Services you might want to turn off at startup (continued)

Service	What it does
Automatic Updates	Automatically checks for Windows updates. (You can check manually by going to *http://windowsupdate.microsoft.com*.)
Telnet (service available on XP Pro only)	Allows a remote user to log in to your computer and run programs. (This will not be found on all versions of XP Pro.)
Wireless Zero Configuration Service	Automatically configures a WiFi (802.11) network card. Disable this only if you're not using a WiFi network card.
Universal Plug and Play (UPnP)	Automatically configures devices connected to a network. It is considered a security risk.
Simple Service Discovery Protocol (SSDP)	Enables discovery of UPnP devices on your network. It is considered a security risk.

Discussion

One of the best ways to speed up your PC is to stop unnecessary programs and services from running whenever you start up. When too many programs and services run automatically every time you start up your system, startup itself takes a long time, and too many programs and services running simultaneously can bog down your CPU and hog your memory.

Some programs, such as antivirus software, should run automatically at startup and always run on your computer. But many other programs, such as instant messenger software, serve no purpose by being run at startup.

You usually see programs that run on your PC, but you rarely see services. Services are processes that help the operating system run, or that provide support to applications. Many of these services launch automatically at startup. While you need many of them, there are also many that aren't required and that can slow your system down when they run in the background. And while you need a variety of background services running on your PC in order for XP to function, there are many unnecessary services that run on startup. For example, on many systems, the Wireless Zero Configuration Service runs to automatically configure a WiFi (802.11) network card, even though no such card is present in the system.

See Also

The System Configuration utility can also be used as a troubleshooting tool. For details, see the MS KB, "How to troubleshoot by using the System Configuration utility in Windows XP"

A utility that shows you everything on your PC that starts by default is the autoruns utility (*www.sysinternals.com/ntw2k/freeware/autoruns.shtml.*)

18.9 Removing Unnecessary Items from the Notification Area

Problem

You want to stop unneeded programs from running automatically and displaying icons in the Notification Area.

Solution

Using a graphical user interface

1. Run the Registry Editor by typing Regedit at the command line or Run box.
2. Go to HKEY_CURRENT_USER\Software\Microsoft\Windows\CurrentVersion\Run and remove any listings of software that you don't want to run on startup.
3. Go to HKEY_LOCAL_MACHINE\Software\Microsoft\Windows\CurrentVersion\Run and remove any listings of software that you don't want to run on startup.
4. Close the Registry Editor.
5. Right-click the Start button and select Explore All Users.
6. Go to ...\Start Menu\Programs\Startup and delete any shortcuts to programs that you don't want to run on startup.
7. Close Windows Explorer and reboot.

Discussion

Stopping unneeded programs from running and displaying in the Notification Area can save substantial amounts of RAM. For example, MSN Messenger takes up nearly 15 MB of RAM, and other programs use a substantial amount of RAM as well. You can always run those programs when you need them; programs like MSN Messenger do not need to run all the time.

See Also

Recipe 18.9; to find out how to stop the clock and network connections icons from appearing in the Notification Area, see MS KB 310429.

18.10 Improving Startup Performance

Problem

You want your system to start up more quickly.

Solution

When you turn on your PC, press the Delete, F1, or F10 keys (it varies by computer manufacturer) to get to the BIOS screen. Then make these choice and changes to your BIOS settings. Depending on your BIOS manufacturer, they will appear on different screens.

Quick Power-On Self-Test (POST)
> When you choose this option, your system runs an abbreviated POST rather than the normal, lengthy one.

Boot Up Floppy Seek
> Disable this option. When it is enabled, your system will spend a few extra seconds looking for your floppy drive—a relatively pointless procedure, especially considering how infrequently you use your floppy drive.

Boot Delay
> Some systems let you delay booting after you turn on your PC so that your hard drive gets a chance to start spinning before bootup. Most likely, you don't need to have this boot delay, so turn it off. If you run into problems, you can always turn it back on.

Discussion

When you turn on your PC, it goes through a set of startup procedures in its BIOS before it starts XP. So, if you speed up those initial startup procedures, you'll make your system start faster.

You can speed up your startup procedures by changing the BIOS with the built-in setup utility. How you run this utility varies from PC to PC, but you typically get to it by pressing the Delete, F1, or F10 keys. You'll come to a menu with a variety of choices.

You may also want to look in the Registry key HKEY_LOCAL_MACHINE\SOFTWARE\ Microsoft\Windows\SharedDLLs for DLLs loaded at startup from software that is no longer installed on your PC.

See Also

If you stop programs and services from running on startup, XP will start more quickly. See Recipe 18.9 for details.

CHAPTER 19

Backup and Recovery

19.0   Introduction

As the saying goes, an ounce of prevention is worth a pound of cure. This statement applies perfectly to using your Windows XP computer. Unfortunately, most users ignore this golden piece of advice even though they are well aware of how important it is to put this advice into practice. Ask yourself this question: if your hard disk suddenly crashed, would you grimace in pain, knowing all of your data has been lost, or manage a smile, knowing that you'll be able to restore your important files?

In this chapter, you will learn how to back up your important files so that when—not if—disaster strikes, you will be able to recover whatever you saved on your computer. And when that disaster rears its ugly head, you will see the options open to you for recovering your system back to its pristine condition.

The recipes covered in this chapter all make use of the utilities that shipped with Windows XP and are applicable to both the Home and Professional Editions. You will see how to use the Microsoft Backup utility to back up your important files as well as Registry. You will also learn how to restore your system back if you made changes that resulted in your system becoming unstable. And if everything fails, you will see how to manually resuscitate your Windows XP installation using the Recovery Console.

19.1   Performing a Backup

Problem

You want to perform a backup of your system using the built-in application for Windows XP.

Solution

Using a graphical user interface

To back up the contents of your machine to a file or to another removable media device:

1. From the Start Menu, select All Programs (or just Programs if you're using the classic Start menu) → Accessories → System Tools → Backup. The wizard starts by default. Click the Advanced Mode link.

2. Navigate to the Backup tab, and then select New from the Job menu.

3. Click the box to the left of a file or folder to select the files and folders you want to back up.

4. In Backup destination, choose File (the default selection) if you want to back up to a file on disk. Choose another device if you want to back to a tape or something similar. You currently cannot back up to CDs.

5. In Backup media or file name, if you are backing to a file, choose a location for the backup (*.bkf*) file. Otherwise, choose the tape you want to use.

6. Make sure you've configured this backup operation the way you want by selecting Options from the Tools menu and verifying the choices there.

7. Click the Start Backup button, and then make any changes to the Backup Job Information dialog box.

8. Click Advanced to configure options like compression and verification. Then click OK.

9. Click Start Backup.

Using a command-line interface

To back up to a file or tape, use:

```
> ntbackup backup [systemstate] "@FileName.bks" /J "JobName" [/P "PoolName"]
[/G "GUIDName"] [/T "TapeName"] [/N "MediaName"] [/F "FileName"]
[/D "SetDescription"] [/DS "ServerName"] [/IS "ServerName"] [/A] [/V:yes | no]
[/R:yes | no] [/L:f | s | n] [/M "BackupType"] [/RS:yes | no] [/HC:on | off]
[/SNAP:on | off]
```

See the discussion section of this recipe for some examples of the command-line functions in use in common situations.

Discussion

NTBACKUP can perform several different types of backups:

Copy

> Copies all selected files but does not mark each file with a cleared archive attribute. Copy backups can be performed completely independently of other backup procedures without affecting their sets.

Daily

> Backs up all files modified since the previous day. With a daily backup, the archive attribute is not cleared.

Differential

> Copies new files and other files modified since the last normal or incremental backup. It does not mark files as having been backed up. To restore a complete backup, you'll need the last normal backup (covered later) in addition to the last incremental backup.

Incremental

> Backs up files created or modified since the last normal or the last incremental backup. It does mark files as having been backed up. To restore a complete backup, you'll need the last normal backup (covered next) in addition to the last incremental backup.

Normal

> A normal backup (sometimes called a full backup) copies all selected files and marks each file as backed up. You create these to start a backup scheme, and use them in conjunction with differential and/or incremental backups, depending on what you choose. Normal backups can be used independently; they don't require another accompanying set.

If you issue NTBACKUP from the command line without any parameters, Windows will launch the GUI for the Backup applet. If you specify parameters for NTBACKUP from the command line, the GUI isn't launched and the program runs entirely from the command shell.

Table 19-1 explains the variable options for the command line NTBACKUP program.

Table 19-1. NTBACKUP command-line options

Option	Explanation
@FileName.bks	Specifies the name of the backup selection file (.bks file) to be used. The @ character must precede the name of the backup selection file. The .bks file must be created using the GUI version of NTBACKUP and is essentially of summary of what a particular job is supposed to back up.
	Alternatively, you could supply the path to the drive or file to back up, for example, D:\.
/J "JobName"	Specifies the job name to be filled in the postbackup report.
/F "FileName"	If you back up to a file, this specifies the path of that file.
	You *cannot* use the /P, /G, and /T switches when using /F.
/T "TapeName"	If you back up to a tape, this specifies to tape to which to overwrite or append data.

Table 19-1. NTBACKUP command-line options (continued)

Option	Explanation
/P "PoolName"	If you back up to a tape, this specifies the media pool to use. This is usually a subpool of the media specified with the /N switch.
	You *cannot* use the /A, /G, /F, and /T switches when using /P.
/G "GUIDName"	If you back up to a tape, this specifies to tape to which to overwrite or append data.
	You *cannot* use the /P switch when using /G.
/N "MediaName"	If you back up to a tape, this specifies the new tape name.
	You *cannot* use the /A switch when using /N.
/A	If you back up to a tape, this specifies to perform an append operation.
	You *must* use either the /G or /T switch when using /A. You *cannot* the /P when using /A.
/D "SetDescription"	Specifies a label for each backup.
/V:yes | no	Specifies whether to perform a verification pass when the backup is complete.
/R:yes | no	Restricts access to the tape to members of the Administrators group only.
/L:f | s | n	Specifies the type of log file to be written. f indicates a full file, s indicates a summary, and n instructs NTBACKUP not to write any logs.
/M "BackupType"	Specifies the type of backup. Replace "*BackupType*" with one of the following: copy, daily, differential, incremental, or normal.
/RS:yes | no	Backs up the migrated data files located in Remote Storage. (This is also backed up when you select the system root folder to be included in a job.)
/HC:on | off	If available, uses hardware compression for the job.
Systemstate	Includes system state data (Registry and other critical system information) in the backup.

There are two important limitations of NTBACKUP from the command line: one, you cannot restore files from the command line, and two, you cannot back up system state data on a remote computer.

Switches /V, /R, /L, /M, /RS, and /HC default to the setting in the GUI version of the Backup applet unless you explicitly set them on the command line.

There are some considerations if you use either Removable Storage or Remote Storage. You should make a note to back up the contents of systemroot\System32\ Ntmsdata and systemroot\System32\Remotestorage on a regular basis. If not, then it's possible (although somewhat unlikely) that Removable/Remote Storage data could be lost and unrestorable.

The files that NTBACKUP creates are very large when compared to commercial products such as Veritas BackupExec. Keep that in mind when justifying the cost of sticking with the built-in product versus investing the money in a third-party backup product—how much might additional storage cost you?

Command-line examples

The first example executes a normal backup named Nightly of the *c:\mydocs* directory. This example selects media from the Tapes pool and names the tape Nightly NTBACKUP 1. The description of the backup job is "Standard evening backup." A verification pass is done, access to the tape is open to all, only a summary log will be produced, hardware compression will be used, and Remote Storage data is not backed up.

```
> ntbackup backup c:\mydocs /m normal /j "Nightly" /p "Tapes" /n "Nightly NTBACKUP 1"
/d "Standard evening backup" /v:yes /r:no /l:s /rs:no /hc:on
```

The next example starts a copy backup named Lunchtime of the E drive on the machine itself. The backed up files and folders are appended to the tape named Nightly NTBACKUP 1. Since no other switches are present, the default settings in the GUI version of Backup are used:

```
> ntbackup backup e:\ /j "Lunchtime" /a /t "Nightly NTBACKUP 1" /m copy
```

The following example performs a backup using the GUI Backup program's current setting. The program looks at the file *weekend-backup.bks*, located in the *C:\Program Files\Windows NT\ntbackup\data* directory, to select the particular data to back up. The backup job is named Weekend and it overwrites the tape named Weekend NTBACKUP 1 with the new name Weekend NTBACKUP 2. It also includes system state information:

```
> ntbackup backup systemstate "@C:\Program Files\Windows NT\ntbackup\data\weekend-
backup.bks" /j "Weekend" /t "Weekend NTBACKUP 1" /n "Weekend NTBACKUP 2"
```

The final example backs up a particular directory to a file named *backup.bkf* using the Backup program's default values for the backup type, verification setting, logging level, hardware compression, and access restrictions:

```
> ntbackup backup c:\xpckbk /j "To File on MWF" /f "E:\backup.bkf"
```

When running this command again, to simply append another backup to the existing file, simply add the /a switch, as shown. Otherwise, you will overwrite the existing file automatically:

```
> ntbackup backup c:\xpckbk /j "To File on TH" /f "E:\backup.bkf" /a
```

See Also

MS KB 283592, "No Error Message Appears to Explain Why NTBackup Does Not Start from the Command Line," MS KB 283547, "Cannot Find Windows NTBackup Folder and Catalog Files in Windows XP," and Hack #96, "Build a Better Backup Strategy," in *Windows XP Hacks* (O'Reilly)

19.2 Restoring from Backup

Problem

You want to restore files that were previously backed up with Microsoft Backup.

Solution

Files created by Microsoft Backup have the *.bkf* extension. To restore from a backup file, you can either double-click on a *.bkf* file or launch Microsoft Backup from Start → All Programs → Accessories → System Tools → Backup:

1. In the Backup or Restore wizard, select the "Restore files and settings" option and click Next.
2. Click on the Browse... button to locate the backup file to restore. Select the items to restore by checking the items in the tree. Click Next.
3. Click on the Advanced button to specify additional restore options.
4. You have three options to restore the files: to their original location; to an alternate location that you specify; or to a single location that you specify.
5. In the event that Microsoft Backup encounters existing files in the process of restoring the files, you have three options: leave them, replace them with newer files, or replace them. Click Next.
6. Finally, there are three advanced options you can choose to take advantage of: restoring the original security settings of each file and folder; restoring junction points, but not the folders and file data they reference (useful for restoring mounted drives); and preserving existing volume mount points, if you're restoring data to an entire drive or partition. Click Next.
7. Click Finish.

Discussions

Even though Microsoft Backup can back up and restore data on FAT16, FAT32, or NTFS volumes, if you have backed-up data from an NTFS volume it is recommended that you restore the data to an NTFS volume. Or else you could lose data as well as some file and folder structures.

The command-line NTBackup utility cannot restore files. You must use the GUI to restore files from a backup set.

See Also

For more information on the various advanced option for restoring your backup, refer to Windows XP Help topic "Set advanced restore options."

19.3   Using Automated System Recovery

Problem

You want to back up your Windows XP Professional system state information to a single diskette, and you want to be able to take that data and restore your system to a bootable, functional state with it.

Solution

To back up your Windows XP Professional system state data to an Automated System Recovery (ASR) disk:

1. From the Start Menu, select All Programs ⟶ Accessories ⟶ System Tools ⟶ Backup. The wizard starts by default. Click the Advanced Mode link.
2. Click the Automated System Recovery wizard button.
3. Select the destination for your backup file, and then insert a floppy disk. After the floppy is created, a full backup of your system will proceed. You'll have the opportunity to cancel that if you just want to make the ASR disk.
4. Click Finish.

To restore your system to a bootable state, use the ASR disk:

1. Boot off your Windows XP installation CD.
2. When prompted for an ASR diskette, press F2. Note that this happens right after the blue tinted screen appears, so watch carefully for it.
3. Insert your ASR diskette. Windows will copy files to your hard drive, and then prompt you to reboot.

Discussion

Using ASR is a great idea when you've simply made a configuration change that has resulted in a system that won't boot. It saves time by not requiring you to restore the entire contents of your hard disk—spreadsheets, Word documents, music, movies, and other personal items—and only focusing on system configuration data that might have become corrupted or invalid.

You can access the restore portion of ASR by pressing F2 when prompted in the text-mode portion of Windows Setup, which you can access by booting off the Windows CD. ASR will read the disk configurations from the file that it creates in step 3 of the first part of this recipe, and then restore all of the disk signatures, volumes, and partitions on at least the disks needed to boot the computer—it will try to restore all disk configurations, but might not be able to do so for a variety of reasons. ASR then installs a simple installation of Windows and automatically starts a restoration using the backup created by the ASR wizard.

If you're a fan of the GUI, in Windows XP Home Edition, you can't use Automated System Recovery (ASR), which limits your backup options. ASR can only be used in Windows XP Professional. To make matters worse, you can actually create a backup using ASR in Windows XP—but don't be fooled, because you can't actually restore that ASR backup.

See Also

Recipe 19.4 for creating an ASR disk "after the fact"

19.4   Creating an ASR Disk "After the Fact"

Problem

You need an ASR disk for a system, but that system isn't running. You do, however, have current backup media for that system generated from an ASR-based backup and would like to create an ASR disk based on that data.

Solution

To create an ASR disk from an already existing ASR-based backup media set:

1. Insert a formatted diskette into a system running Windows XP.

2. In System Tools, start the Backup program. When the Backup and Restore Wizard is displayed, click Next.

3. Click Restore Files and Settings, and then click Next.

4. In the What to Restore dialog box, select the media that contains the ASR backup. Ensure that the media is inserted, and expand the Automated System Recovery Backup Set that corresponds to the ASR floppy disk that you want to create.

5. Expand the second instance of the drive letter that contains the system files, and then expand *%systemroot%\Repair*.

6. Select *Asr.sif* and *Asrpnp.sif*, and then click Next.

7. The Completing Backup or Restore Wizard screen appears. Click the Advanced button.

8. Set Restore Files to "screen Single Folder," and then set the Folder Name dialog box to the root of your floppy drive. Click Next.

After the wizard finishes processing, the ASR floppy disk is ready for use in the event of an ASR restore operation.

The *Asr.sif* and *Asrpnp.sif* files must be on the root of the floppy to be used during an ASR restore procedure.

Discussion

When you perform an ASR backup, Windows puts the *Asr.sif* and *Asrpnp.sif* files on the backup media. In the event that you've lost the ASR disk, or that it's otherwise unavailable for the restore procedure, both the *Asr.sif* and *Asrpnp.sif* files can be extracted from the backup media and then transferred to a floppy disk to be used for an ASR operation. If you do not perform an ASR backup, these files will not exist.

See Also

MS KB 299526, "How To Re-Create a Missing Automated System Recovery Floppy Disk in Windows XP"

19.5 Using System Restore to Revive a Broken Machine

Problem

You have installed a new piece of software, and your system begins to behave erratically. Uninstalling the application did not solve the problem. You want to restore the system to its previous stable state.

Solution

Using a graphical user interface

To restore your system to a previous state:

1. Go to Start → Help and Support.
2. Under the "Pick a task" category, select Undo changes to your computer with System Restore.
3. In the System Restore window, check the "Restore my computer to an earlier time" option and click Next.
4. You will now be able to select a restore point by selecting a day in the calendar (see Figure 19-1).
5. Once a checkpoint is selected to restore, you will see a confirmation screen. Basically, you need to close your existing program and Windows XP will reboot to restore to the checkpoint selected.

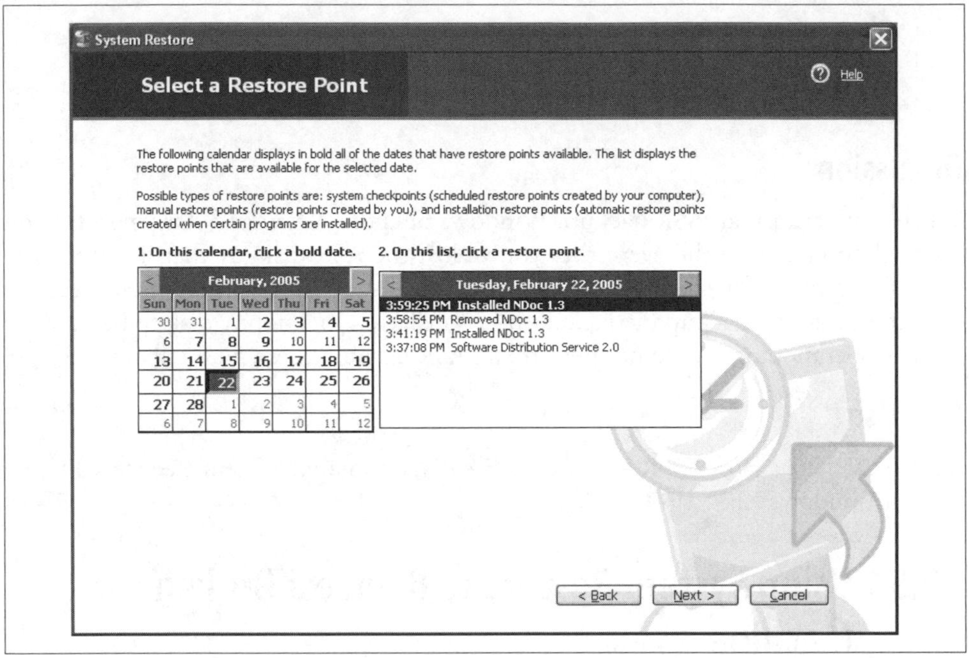

Figure 19-1. Selecting a restore point

6. After the reboot, you will see the Restoration Complete window.

7. If you did not get your desired result after the restoration, you can undo the last restoration by checking the "Undo my last restoration" option and then clicking Next.

Using a command-line interface

1. Start your computer, and press F8 during the initial boot.

2. From the boot menu, select Safe Mode with Command Prompt.

3. When the computer finishes booting, log on with an account that has administrator credentials.

4. Enter `%systemroot%\system32\restore\rstrui.exe`.

5. Select the restore point to restore your system to, and then reboot.

Discussion

Use Windows XP's built-in System Restore feature (enabled by default) to roll back your system to a state before a configuration-changing event, such as a software installation, occurs. Windows takes snapshots of your configuration, known as restore points, before installations take place, hardware is changed, drivers are installed, and other similar events. These restore points serve as markers, to which you can roll back your configuration in the event something goes wrong.

Besides the checkpoints created by System Restore, you can also create your own checkpoints. To create your own checkpoint, go to Help and Support off the Start menu, and under the "Pick a task" category, select "Undo changes to your computer with System Restore." In the System Restore window, select "Create a restore point," click Next, give a description to this restore point (something like "Restore point at 3 March 2005 3.15pm") and click Create.

While System Restore can restore your system to its previous state, do not rely totally on this technique to back up your system. As System Restore takes up a significant amount of disk storage, Windows XP will start to delete old checkpoints when the storage allocated for System Restore runs out, much like Recycle Bin items are purged when the disk allocation for it is filled. By default, System Restore uses 12% of each disk's maximum capacity. To change the amount of disk space allocated to System Restore, you can do so in the System Restore tab of the System Properties window, as shown in Figure 19-2.

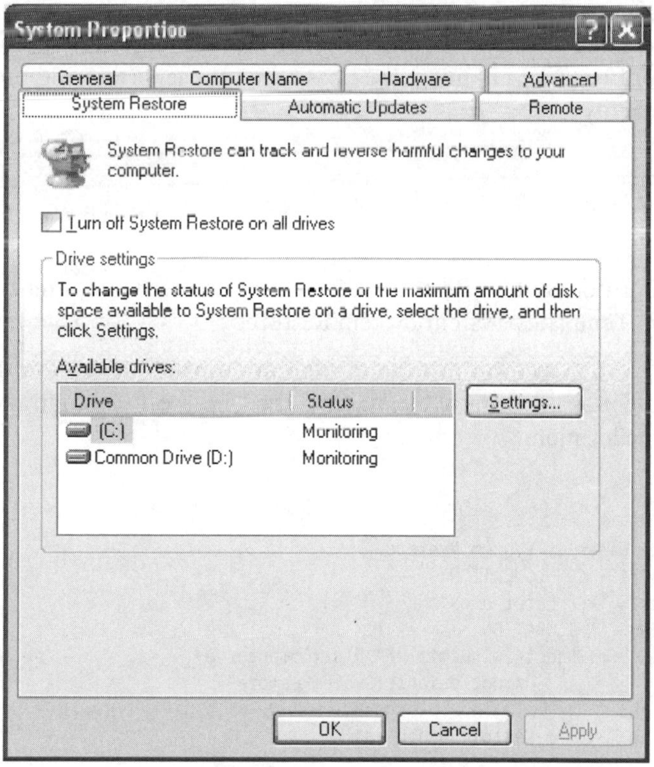

Figure 19-2. Configuring disk space for System Restore

If you have more than one drive in your computer, you will see a list of available drives that System Restore can use. To change the settings of each drive, select the drive and click Settings. You can selectively turn off System Restore for other drives by checking the Turn off System Restore on this drive option, but if you want to turn off System Restore for drive C, then you need to check the Turn off System Restore for all drives option.

One important thing to remember: System Restore does not touch data—it only handles system configuration changes. So you can't use it to get a copy of a document you have accidentally deleted.

See Also

MS KB 302796, "Troubleshooting System Restore in Windows XP," and MS KB 306084, "How to restore Windows XP to a previous state"

19.6   Disabling System Restore Remotely

Problem

You want to disable all, or portions of, System Restore remotely to save disk space, reduce user confusion, or eliminate the possibility of users restoring previous configurations mistakenly.

Solution

Using Group Policy

Enable the "Turn off System Restore" GPO setting under Computer Configuration\Administrative Templates\System\System Restore.

You can also elect to turn off just the configuration panel (and leave the actual System Restore functionality intact) by enabling the "Turn off Configuration" GPO setting in the same location.

Using VBScript

```
' This code disables System Restore.
' ------ SCRIPT CONFIGURATION ------
strComputer = "<ComputerName>"
' ------ END CONFIGURATION ---------
set objWmi = GetObject("winmgmts://" & strComputer & _
                       "/root/default:SystemRestore")
objWmi.Disable("")
WScript.Echo "System Restore disabled"
```

Discussion

If you choose to use the Group Policy and disable the "Turn off System Restore" setting, System Restore will be turned *on* for all systems to which that GPO applies, and it's enforced—meaning that users will be unable to turn it off.

See Also

Recipe 19.5 for more on using System Restore

19.7   Retrieving a Shadow Copy of a Corrupted or Deleted File

Problem

You have inadvertently deleted or modified an important file, and you want to restore a copy of it from before the mistake was made. You know your administrator has enabled shadow copies (sometimes called previous version functionality).

Solution

Using a graphical user interface

To restore a previous version of a file:

1. Open a window in Windows Explorer.
2. Navigate to the location where the damaged file resides.
3. Right-click on the file, and select Properties. (Alternatively, you can select the Previous Versions link in the left pane of the window if you have Folder Tasks enabled.)
4. Click on the Previous Versions tab, as shown in Figure 19-3.
5. Select the appropriate version of the file, called a shadow copy, from the list of previous versions on the tab and either copy the previous version to a different location using the Copy button, or restore it to its location at the time the copy of the file was made by using the Restore button.
6. Click OK. The file will be restored.

Discussion

A shadow copy is essentially a previous version of the file or folder at a specific point in time. Shadow copies are great when you accidentally delete or change a file and save over your old copy—you can simply retrieve the previous version of it and continue as you were, without the hassle of restoring from tape or involving an administrator.

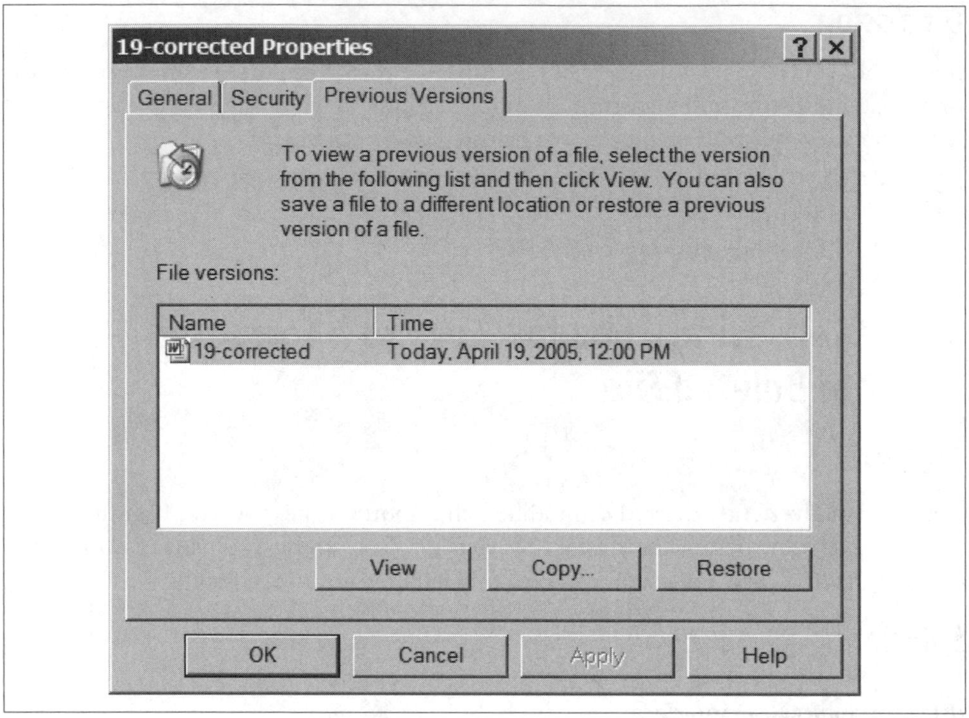

![19-corrected Properties dialog box. Tabs: General, Security, Previous Versions (selected). "To view a previous version of a file, select the version from the following list and then click View. You can also save a file to a different location or restore a previous version of a file." File versions: Name column shows "19-corrected", Time column shows "Today, April 19, 2005, 12:00 PM". Buttons: View, Copy..., Restore, OK, Cancel, Apply, Help.]

Figure 19-3. The Previous Versions tab

Windows XP is currently the only client operating system that supports shadow copies. The Windows XP clients that require the Previous Versions update can find it (on any Windows Server 2003 system) inside the *%systemroot%\system32* folder; its name is *TWCLI32.MSI*. It is installed by default on all Windows Server 2003 machines. It can also be pushed out through IntelliMirror, a part of Group Policy.

To reduce user confusion, when you access the Previous Versions link in the Explorer view of a particular share, you are only presented with a list of unique copies—that is to say, a list of versions that differ from each other, a condition that indicates the file or folder changed. In addition, shadow copies are read-only, in that you can copy, drag and drop, and perform any other function on them as usual except overwriting or deleting them.

 Viewing an executable file through the Previous Versions tab in Windows Explorer (i.e., selecting the file and clicking View) will launch the program.

The actual making of the shadow copies—a process known as taking a snapshot—is configurable only on a Windows Server 2003 machine and is not user controllable.

Some restrictions on shadow copies from an administrator standpoint are noted as follows:

- Local views of folders on a disk do not permit accessing shadow copies.
- For the Previous Versions link to appear in a folder's view, you must be accessing that folder from a network share.

See Also

Chapter 3 of *Learning Windows Server 2003* (O'Reilly), and MS KB 881789, "The Previous Versions tab for a file or for a folder in a DFS share is not displayed in Windows Server 2003 and in Windows XP"

19.8   Using XCOPY for Interim Backups

Problem

You want a simple, straightforward way to make backups of your current working data throughout the day, and you don't want to have to launch the Backup applet.

Solution

Using a command-line interface

Use xcopy from the command line to perform easy, relatively fast incremental backups. This recipe assumes that you're connected to a network with available shares to map to a drive letter or that you have multiple hard drives that are assigned different drive letters and that you (and other users on your machine) store data within your individual *My Documents* folders.

Type the following into Notepad and save as *backup.bat*:

```
@echo off
Cls
Net use k: \\machinename\backupshare
K:
xcopy c:\docume~1\*.* /s /e /a /h /c
c:
cd \docume~1\
attrib *.* -a /s
net use k: /disconnect
```

To run the file, double-click on it, open a command prompt and type its name on the command line, or set it as a scheduled task to run at a specified time during the day regularly.

Discussion

This script maps drive K to a target share on another machine, and then copies the entire contents of the *Documents and Settings* path on your local hard drive to the remote share using the xcopy command. The /s option tells xcopy to copy subdirectories of *Documents and Settings*; the /e option tells it to copy subdirectories that contain no files; the /a option tells it to copy only files that have the archive bit set on—in effect, the copy will process only those files that have been created or changed since the last backup; the /h switch copies hidden files and folders; the /c option tells xcopy to continue the operation even if it encounters an error, like a PST file being open. Without that /c option, xcopy blows up and dies on the first error it encounters.

Once the xcopy operation completes, the batch file runs the attrib command on the local *Documents and Settings* folder, which sets the archive bit off for all files (the /a switch) and processes subdirectories (the /s option). All files within that folder are marked as being backed up, so the next time the batch file is run it copies only files that have been created or changed since the last time it was run.

See Also

MS KB 128756, "Command Line Switches for the XCOPY Command," and MS KB 289493, "Switches That You Can Use with Xcopy and Xcopy32 Commands"

19.9 Using the Recovery Console During Boot Failures

Problem

Your Windows XP computer fails to boot and displays some error messages. You need a way to get it back to life.

Solution

If switching to Safe Mode does not help you solve your startup problem, the next-best solution is to use the Recovery Console. There are two ways to invoke Recovery Console: either boot up Windows XP using the installation CD and choose the option to repair a Windows XP installation, or install the Recovery Console as a boot-up option. The former approach is more common, as users generally do not prepare for disasters. For the latter approach, insert your Windows XP installation disk and issue the following command:

```
> D:\i386\winnt32.exe /cmdcons
```

where D is the CD-ROM drive letter. This will install the Recovery Console as another item in the boot-selection menu that is displayed when you boot up your computer.

Once the Recovery Console is invoked, you will see a command-line interface prompting you to select the Windows installation to repair. You would also need to supply the administrator password. Some of the most common tasks you might want to accomplish are listed in the rest of this section.

The following commands copy files from the installation CD to the root directory on the hard drive:

```
> copy d:\i386\ntldr c:\
> copy d:\i386\ntdetect.com c:\
```

The following command will write a new boot sector on your disk:

```
> fixboot c:
```

The following command will write a new master boot record on your hard disk:

```
> fixmbr
```

To get a list of services installed on your system, you can use the following command:

```
> listsvc
```

To start, for instance, the WMI service (just to use an example; you wouldn't necessarily act on this service) at boot time:

```
> enable Wmi SERVICE_BOOT_START
```

To disable that same service:

```
> disable Wmi
```

You can see a list of all available commands by typing Help at the prompt.

Discussion

The Recovery Console is a text-based operating system extension that allows you direct access to the disk on which Windows XP is installed, and similar access to key configuration files and data. It also provides a convenient way around DOS's inability to read NTFS-formatted drives, which is an issue any administrator with troubleshooting experience has come up against.

To use the Recovery Console, you must first set it up. If you are using a working system, it's prudent to go ahead and set the console up; that way, if it fails, using the console is as simple a procedure as selecting it from the startup menu at first boot. To do so, run winnt32 /cmdcons off the installation CD from within Windows. Setup will copy files and modify your boot configuration file to list the Recovery Console as a startup option.

Table 19-2 lists all available commands for the Recovery Console.

Table 19-2. Selected commands for the Recovery Console

Command name	Function
DISABLE	Prevents a service, named in the argument syntax of this command, from starting up upon a normal boot.
DISKPART	Executes a disk partitioning utility much like that used in the initial text-based phase of Setup.
ENABLE	Explicitly instructs a service named in the argument syntax of this command to start upon a normal boot.
FIXBOOT	Like the old `fdisk /mbr` command from DOS days, this will restore boot sector information and make the drive contained in the argument syntax the default drive for booting.
FIXMBR	This command is like `fixboot`, but it will only touch the master boot record of the drive; it won't alter default boot drives or create *BOOT.INI* files.
HELP	Lists all commands available in the Recovery Console.
LISTSVC	For use with the `disable` and `enable` commands, this lists all available services that can be started and stopped.
LOGON	Logs you out of an existing console and lets you select another installation on which to perform recovery functions.
SYSTEMROOT	Goes to the default Windows directory without grappling with unwieldy CD (change directory) commands.

See Also

MS KB 296251, "Recovery Console That You Create from a Sysprep Image Does Not Work," and MS KB 258585, "Recovery Console Prompts for Administrator Password Even If Administrator Account Has Been Renamed"

Also, BartPE, from *http://www.nu2.nu*, is a free tool that lets you create a GUI OS with useful system tools. The OS is Windows PE, which Microsoft uses for their installation environment. It takes a little time to set it up, but it's a lot of help when a system crashes.

19.10 Creating a Password Reset Disk

Problem

You want to create a disk that will allow you to reset your Windows XP password in the event you forget it, eliminating the need to reinstall the operating system.

Solution

You can create a Password Reset disk that contains your login credentials. In the event that you forgot your password, you can use this disk to reset your password and log in again.

To create the Password Reset disk, perform the following steps:

1. Go to Start → Control Panel → User Accounts.

2. Select your current account and on the left of the window click the "Prevent a forgotten password" link.

3. The Forgotten Password wizard will then be launched. Click Next.

4. You need to insert a formatted floppy disk into the A drive.

5. Enter your current password when prompted.

6. Your password information is then saved onto the disk. Click Finish.

To use the Password Reset disk, log in to Windows XP using an incorrect password. When an incorrect password is entered, Windows will display an error message asking if you would like to use the Password Reset disk. Insert the disk and you will be able to supply a new password (and password hint).

Discussion

As with any piece of data or software that relates to authentication in any way, exercise care in creating, storing, using, and distributing the Password Reset disk. Anyone with physical possession of the disk can successfully log in as you and reset your password.

If you have created a Password Reset disk and later change your password, you need to create the password disk again. Otherwise, the disk you created will be useless.

 If your Windows XP machine is a member of a Windows domain, you can only reset the password for a local user account on a specific machine. Domain user account passwords cannot be reset using the password reset disk.

See Also

MS KB 308273, "You Cannot Decrypt Files After You Reset Your Password with a Password-Reset Disk," and MS KB 306214, "How to create and use a password reset disk for a computer in a domain in Windows XP"

19.11 Recovering and Decrypting an Encrypted File or Folder

Problem

You need to recover and/or decrypt a file that was encrypted using Windows XP's encrypted file system (EFS) technology.

Solution

Using a graphical user interface

You must be a designated recovery agent to decrypt a file. To view the recovery agents for an object:

1. Log in as the owner of the encrypted object.
2. Right-click the object and select Properties.
3. Click the Advanced button, which opens the Advanced Attributes dialog box.
4. Click the Details button to bring up the Encryption Details box.
5. The recovery agents for the specified object are listed in the bottom box.

To decrypt a file or folder, follow these steps:

1. Right-click the file or folder to encrypt, and then select Properties.
2. Navigate to the General tab, and then click the Advanced button.
3. Uncheck the Encrypt contents to secure data checkbox, and then click OK.

Using a command-line interface

To decrypt a folder, use the following command:

```
> cipher /d <Foldername>
```

To decrypt a single file within a directory, use the following command:

```
> cipher /d /a <Filename>
```

To decrypt a single file for which you are the recovery agent, use the following command:

```
> cipher /u /a <Filename>
```

Discussion

It can be somewhat disconcerting that, in an emergency or recovery situation, encrypted files can be decrypted by someone other than the user who encrypted the file originally. This is actually a feature, and it really is quite secure. When they are created, designated user accounts, called recovery agent accounts, are issued recovery agent certificates with public keys and private keys. These are used for EFS data recovery operations. The Windows user accounts that function as recovery agent accounts can be designated by a GPO or a local security policy object (under Security Settings\Public Key Policies\Encrypting File System), depending on the machine's participation in a domain. By default, they are the highest-level administrator accounts available. Depending on the network environment of a particular machine, this is either the local administrator or the domain administrator for the first domain controller installed in the domain. The private key from the appropriate agent certificate must be located on the computer where recovery operations are to be conducted.

When a recovery agent certificate is issued, the certificate and private key are installed in the user profile for the user account that requested the certificate. An EFS file can contain more than one recovery agent account, and each EFS file can have a different private key. However, data recovery discloses only the encrypted data, not the user's private key or any other private keys for recovery. This ensures that no other private information is revealed to the recovery agent administrator unintentionally.

See Also

MS KB 255742, "Methods for Recovering Encrypted Files," and MS KB 308993, "How to Remove Encryption in Windows XP"

19.12 Backing up and Restoring Activation Data

Problem

You need to reinstall Windows and want to back up your activation data to avoid repeating the process; you then need to restore that data once your system is refreshed.

Solution

After activation, Microsoft stores associated data in the files *wpa.dbl* and *Wpa.bak* in the folder *%systemroot%\system32*. You can back up these files to a diskette or other media for storage while you're performing the reinstall.

Once your system is back up and running, you can restore the activation data by starting Windows XP in safe mode and opening a command line to the *%systemroot%\system32* folder. Then, rename the new *wpa.dbl* to *wpa.none* and *wpa.bak*, if it exists, to *wpabak.none*. Finally, copy your backed-up *wpa.dbl* and *wpb.bak* files to the *%systemroot%/system32* folder, and then reboot.

Discussion

This procedure will work only if you are reinstalling XP onto the same exact physical hardware. If you try to restore the activation data onto a system with hardware that is significantly different than the original system from which the activation data was created, the process may fail. Indeed, it may fail on systems with the exact make and model of hardware, since activation takes into account the MAC address of the machine's network card—an attribute unique to every machine.

See Also

MS KB 302740, "Running Repair on Windows XP Requires the User to Re-Activate the Product," and MS KB 305056, "Windows XP Prompts You to Re-activate After You Restore Your Computer"

19.13 Auditing Backup and Restore Actions

Problem

You want to audit who performs tasks associated with backup and restore on a Windows XP system.

Solution

Using Group Policy

Through Group Policy, you can choose to audit any action related to back up and restore. The GPO setting, for those in a domain environment, is found in Computer Configuration\Windows Settings\Security Settings\Local Policies\Security Options, and is called "Audit: Audit the use of Backup and Restore privilege." This setting is also available through Local Security Policy (you can access this through the Administrative Tools applet within Control Panel) in the Local Policies/Security Options tree.

Discussion

This GPO setting tells Windows whether to write an event in the Security event log when users exercise Backup and Restore privileges, but only when the Audit privilege use policy GPO is enabled. It also generates an audit event for every file that is backed up or restored. All audited events are caused by actions stemming from the execution of NTBACKUP—for example, creating an ASR backup will trigger a log entry, whereas doing an xcopy backup will not cause anything to be logged.

See Also

Chapter 6 on Group Policy in *Learning Windows Server 2003* (O'Reilly)

19.14 Caring for Backup Media

Problem

You want to take care of your backup media so that when you need to use it, it works properly.

Solution

The following are some guidelines to remember when using, handling, and storing the various backup media you use:

- Spot-test your files periodically and transfer the data if readability problems develop. After all, a backup is no good if it can't be restored.

- Keep your tapes boxed until you need to use them. Opening tape boxes prematurely will unnecessarily increase a new tape's exposure to dust, moisture, and sunlight, and could eventually erode a tape's quality and dependability.

- Do not attempt to load a tape into the drive if you notice dents, cracks, or moisture in the tape's cases, hinged doors, or file-protect selectors.

- Store your tapes at room temperature.

- Avoid magnetic fields. Speakers, microwave ovens, and printer heads can all produce fields that can erase part or all of your backup.

- Purchase quality disk media, be it CD-Rs, CD-RWs, or DVDs. Cheap media—not to be confused with inexpensive media—causes many longevity problems.

- Don't store CDs or DVDs in soft sleeves, or stack them without protective covering. All of these actions will cause scratches of the surface of the disk, which can result in unreadable sections.

- Limit your disks' exposure to light.

Discussion

The most reliable method of testing your existing backup media to ensure its validity is to perform a test restore of certain files at random points of the backup set. If you have a particularly critical backup, perform full test restores regularly—as often as every six months—to make sure the media isn't prematurely wearing out.

The lifetime ranges of certain media under standard storage conditions are things to consider when storing backup media. The following are good estimates of specific media lifespans:

Read-only CDs
    5 to 100 or more years depending on disk manufacturing quality

CD-R
    5 to 200 years depending on disk type and manufacturing quality

CD-RW
    5 to 100 or more years depending on manufacturing quality

DVD, DVD-R, DVD-RW
    Similar to that of a CD

Tapes
    10 to 30 years

Diskettes and hard drives
    5 to 15 years

You should also take into account the life or popularity of a specific media type's playback machine. The media may survive for 100 years, but the technology to play the media may have disappeared in that time. Replacement machines might disappear from stores before you have made the change to a new format. Remember to keep backups refreshed as technology changes.

Also consider the following: cheap mass-produced CD-R disks and similar disk media are actually worse than floppies: the quality of the media depends on the dye substrate. There are a lot of studies on this; *http://www.mam-a.com* is just one company selling archival quality CD-Rs. A lot of photographers use them for backups.

See Also

The Ontrack Data Protection Guide, at *http://www.storagesearch.com/ontartic.html*

CHAPTER 20

Crashes and Errors

20.0 Introduction

Blue screens, locked-up systems, cryptic error messages, missing operating system files, dead keyboards and mice, unresponsive devices—all in a day's work for many PC troubleshooters.

When Windows crashes, it's easy to believe that the operating system itself is to blame. Indeed, Windows probably has untold vulnerabilities that allow the core of the operating system to be blown up to the point of having to restart, but the crashes and errors are usually caused by a misbehaving application, driver, bad memory, faulty disk, or mixed-up piece of hardware.

As user-friendly as Windows XP is supposed to be, it still presents and logs many error conditions using cryptic numeric codes, or text that sometimes defies the rules of grammar, and provides no help in arriving at a solution. This chapter is full of solutions to those mysterious error codes and how to decipher the ones that are too numerous to list.

20.1 Using Safe Mode

Problem

Windows hangs, restarts by itself, or crashes with a blue screen error, or your video display is garbled and you cannot get control of the display resolution.

Solution

1. Restart your PC and press the F8 key at the end of the BIOS to access Windows' start menu.

2. Select the Safe Mode option and let Windows start up.

3. Log onto Windows if prompted.

4. Click OK or Yes to acknowledge the "running in safe mode" dialog.

5. Use Safe Mode to reset any recent configuration changes, uninstall recently installed hardware, or run System Restore to return the system to a working state.

Discussion

Safe Mode uses only basic files and drivers (mouse, except serial mice; monitor; keyboard; mass storage; base video; default minimal system services; and no network connections). In Safe Mode, your desktop display is limited to 640 × 480 resolution, allowing you to select another resolution to be used after restart—helpful if you have video driver or resolution selection problems. Many 32-bit device drivers are not loaded, limiting the number and types of programs you can use—for instance a Pinnacle PCTV tuner card cannot be used in Safe Mode. As well, entries in Windows Registry Run and Run Once keys are bypassed in Safe Mode—an essential feature for removing spyware and unwanted programs that will not go away in Normal Mode. If your computer does not start successfully using safe mode, you might need to use the Recovery Console feature to repair your system (see Recipe 20.5).

Additional Safe Mode options exist—Safe Mode with Networking and Safe Mode with Command Prompt. Safe Mode with Networking adds basic networking components to the Spartan mix of few device drivers and features so you can access LAN and web-based resources as needed. Safe Mode with Command Prompt presents the command-line interface instead of the Windows GUI, most useful if you are having trouble with and need to repair displaying Windows' graphics.

See Also

Safe Mode is one of the most limited ways to run Windows XP, but it lets you get under the skin of the OS. For a couple of non-Microsoft views of Safe Mode, visit *http://www.pcstats.com/articleview.cfm?articleID=1643* and *http://www.youthtech.com/techstuff/explore_windowsxp/xptroubleshoot.htm*.

20.2   Using Last Known Good Configuration

Problem

Windows will not boot or function properly due to recent changes in hardware or system configuration.

Solution

Using Windows startup menu

1. Restart your PC and press the F8 key at the end of the BIOS to access Windows' start menu.
2. Select the Last Known Good Configuration option and let Windows start up.
3. Log onto Windows if prompted.
4. Reset any recent configuration changes, uninstall recently installed hardware or run System Restore to return the system to a working state.

Discussion

The Last Known Good Configuration boot option uses Registry information and drivers saved at the last proper shutdown. Any system changes since the last proper shutdown are lost. Missing drivers or files necessary for operation of new devices will have to be replaced with proper versions. This is the next best thing to restoring the system to a prior system Restore Point and does not affect installed applications unless they involve device drivers.

See Also

Very little seems to be known about what precisely happens with the Last Known Good Configuration, but the simplest reference comes from Microsoft itself at *http://support.microsoft.com/default.aspx?scid=kb;en-us;307852&sd=tech*

20.3 Using Boot Log to Trace Problems

Problem

You need to determine which driver and services are starting at boot-up and may be causing Windows to malfunction due to recent changes in hardware or system configuration.

Solution

Using Windows startup menu

1. Restart your PC and press the F8 key at the end of the BIOS to access Windows' start menu.
2. Select the Enable Boot Logging option and let Windows start up.
3. Log onto Windows if prompted.

4. Open Windows Explorer, navigate to the Windows directory.

5. Locate and double-click the *NTBLOG.TXT* file to open it with Notepad or the default editor for text files. Review the log file contents to determine suspicious drivers or services that could be causing Windows to malfunction.

Discussion

The boot log function records all of the drivers and services loaded (or not) during Windows startup when you run Safe Mode, Safe Mode with Networking, and Safe Mode with Command Prompt. This wealth of information can tell you a lot about the state of drivers and bootability of your system configuration. You can also turn on the bootlog feature by checking the /BOOTLOG checkbox on the BOOT.INI tab using the MSCONFIG program.

See Also

More information about the boot log, options, and log entries can be found at MS KB 127970 and MS KB 833721.

20.4   Using VGA Mode to Solve Video Problems

Problem

You need to access Windows to correct an improper video configuration.

Solution

Using Windows startup menu

1. Restart your PC and press the F8 key at the end of the BIOS to access Windows' start menu.

2. Select the Enable VGA Mode option and let Windows start up.

3. Log onto Windows if prompted.

4. Install the proper video driver for your video adapter the restart Windows normally.

Discussion

Starting in VGA Mode is useful when Windows does not to start or display properly after you have installed a new, likely improper, driver for your video card. VGA Mode is also used when you start in Safe Mode, Safe Mode with Networking, or Safe Mode with Command Prompt.

See Also

More details about Safe Mode and recovering from startup display problems may be found at:

- *http://www.microsoft.com/resources/documentation/Windows/XP/all/reskit/en-us/ Default.asp?url=/resources/documentation/Windows/XP/all/reskit/en-us/prmb_tol_ hyec.asp*

- *http://msdn.microsoft.com/library/default.asp?url=/library/en-us/xpehelp/html/ xeconheadlessdevicevideodriverprocessing.asp*

20.5 Using Recovery Console

Problem

You are experiencing problems booting into Windows XP in either Normal or Safe Mode, or encounter missing files during startup.

Solution

1. Insert your Windows XP installation CD-ROM and boot from the CD-ROM.
2. On the Windows XP Setup menu, select R for repair.
3. Select C to use the Recovery Console as the repair option.
4. Select the Windows installation to repair (usually just 1).
5. Enter the Administrator password for this installation of Windows. At the command prompt you can type help to see the list of available commands. For help on each command, type the command followed by /?. In the recovery console you have access to the root directory of all disks, Windows system directory (and all sub-directories), as well as diskette and CD-ROM drives.
6. To recover from startup problems use either the fixmbr command to write a new Master Boot Record on the boot disk, the fixboot command to replace damaged or missing NT boot files, or both commands to ensure the system can boot up, and not have to run this process again.
7. Run the chkdsk command to check for and repair any damage to the file system.
8. Type exit to restart the system. If the Windows installation is intact, you will be able to get back into Windows. If the Windows installation is damaged, you can repair the installation or reinstall Windows.

Discussion

Repairing the bootability of a Windows system drive should be a lot easier than this, but at least the Recovery Console gives you access to some easy critical fixes to get you going again. Recovery Console may be the only way to regain the use of a Windows XP installation without having to reinstall the entire operating system. Beware that writing over the Master Boot Record will disable third-party boot manager/multiboot software that uses the MBR as a start and run point for the boot manager program, including multiboot features of Linux/Unix operating systems that offer different operating system choices to boot from.

See Also

An excellent step-by-step guide to the Recovery Console with screen shots of the process can be found at *http://www.wown.com/j_helmig/wxprcons.htm*, and a superb explanation of the options is available at *http://www.kellys-korner-xp.com/win_xp_rec.htm*.

An exceptional tool for restoring and fixing nearly all system problems is Barts PE disk. Downloads and documentation available at *http://www.nu2.nu*.

20.6 Repairing *AUTOEXEC.NT* or *CONFIG.NT* Errors

Problem

You are getting errors referring to the inability to run 16-bit programs, or an error similar to:

```
The system file is not suitable for running MS-DOS and Microsoft Windows
applications. Choose 'Close' to terminate the application.
```

Solution

1. Navigate to the *%SystemRoot%\REPAIR* folder.
2. Copy the *AUTOEXEC.NT* and *CONFIG.NT* files to the *%SystemRoot%\SYSTEM32* folder.
3. Run your application again to verify this fix works.

Discussion

Similar to the *CONFIG.SYS* and *AUTOEXEC.BAT* files for DOS and Windows 9x, *CONFIG.NT* and *AUTOEXEC.NT* establish a runtime environment to support CD-ROM drives, network redirection, sound, and mouse features for DOS and 16-bit applications running under Windows XP. For no good reason it seems one or both of these files can mysteriously disappear due to a recent software installation or disk fault. The cure is simple—if only the error message made more sense.

See Also

Scouring the Web and Microsoft's site turn up no clues as to how or why the *AUTOEXEC.NT* or *CONFIG.NT* files disappear and cause these errors, as *http://www.annoyances.org/exec/forum/win2000/1106422202* and other help forums indicate frequently.

20.7 Fixing Cryptographic Services Error

Problem

You get an error message about Cryptographic service when you try to install security updates or XP Service Pack 1.

Solution

Using a graphical user interface

1. Go to Start, select Control Panel, and then double-click Administrative Tools.
2. Double-click Services.
3. Right-click on Remote Procedure Call (RPC) and select Properties.
4. For Startup type, ensure Automatic is selected.
5. For Service status, click the Start button, wait for the service to start, and then click OK.
6. Right-click on Cryptographic Services and select Properties.
7. For Startup type, ensure Automatic is selected.
8. For Service status, click the Start button, wait for the service to start, and then click OK.
9. Close the Services window and then try your application again.

Using a command line interface

Run the following commands:

```
net stop cryptsvc
ren %systemroot%\system32\catroot2 oldcatroot2
net start cryptsvc
regsvr32 softpub.dll
regsvr32 wintrust.dll
regsvr32 initpki.dll
regsvr32 dssenh.dll
regsvr32 rsaenh.dll
regsvr32 gpkcsp.dll
regsvr32 sccbase.dll
regsvr32 slbcsp.dll
regsvr32 cryptdlg.dll
```

Then reinstall the updates or service pack.

Discussion

Microsoft's current patches and service packs carry a digital signature that authenticates them as having a valid origin from Microsoft and suitable for application to Windows. If any component of Windows' cryptographic services that validates these digital signatures is corrupt, improperly installed, or not running, you may not be able to install any updates or service packs. Resetting these services and associated files as indicated above allows Windows to properly authenticate and accept updates. Cryptographic services also depend on the Remote Procedure Call (RPC) service, which may have been disabled as a security measure. Re-enabling and starting RPC then cryptographic services should set things right.

Cryptographic services are at the very heart of Windows XP's security—almost everything you do with Windows is checked through cryptographic services, from startup to shutdown. These services provide the core for encryption, the Security Access Manager (SAM) database, authenticating users for login, file and program access, file and printer sharing, and validating security certificates for applications and patches from Microsoft and other vendors.

See Also

An excellent guide to the various ins and outs of cryptographic service errors is available at *http://www.updatexp.com/cryptographic-service.html*, and Microsoft covers this error specifically in MSKB 813442.

20.8   Fixing NTOSKRNL Errors

Problem

You receive the "NTOSKRNL Missing or Corrupt" error message at startup.

Solution

1. Insert and boot from your Windows XP CD.
2. At the first R=Repair option, press the R key.
3. Press the number that corresponds to the correct location for the installation of Windows you want to repair. Typically this will be number 1.
4. Change to the drive that has the CD-ROM and cd into the \i386 directory.
5. Type the following command into the command shell:

        expand ntkrnlmp.ex_ %SystemRoot%\System32\ntoskrnl.exe
6. Take out the CD-ROM and type exit at the command prompt, then press the Enter key to restart the PC normally.

Discussion

NTOSKRNL is the heart of the operating system, running as a privileged process with direct access to system data and hardware. With direct awareness of the system hardware, NTOSKRNL extracts information from the Registry to know which device drivers to load and in what order. A virus, boot.ini, or a file system corruption may have made the *NTOSKRNL.EXE* file unusable. NTOSKRNL gets device information to pass on to the Hardware Abstraction Layer (HAL) driver so the core operating system can function. Replacing the file is an easy sure cure.

See Also

Tips for correcting this problem and related issues are available at *http://www. computerhope.com/issues/ch000646.htm*.

20.9   Fixing a HAL Error

Problem

You receive the "HAL.DLL Missing or Corrupt" error message at startup.

Solution

1. Boot from your Windows XP CD-ROM.
2. At the first R=Repair option, press the R key.
3. Press the number that corresponds to the installation of Windows you want to repair. Typically this will be number 1.
4. When prompted, type in the administrator password.
5. Enter the following command. (If you are running *bootcfg* from CD_ROM, *d:\ path* is replaced by the actual drive letter assigned to the CD ROM drive; otherwise *bootcfg* is available directly within the Recovery Console.)

   ```
   > d:\<path>\bootcfg /rebuild
   ```
6. Remove the XP CD-ROM, type exit at the command prompt, and press the Enter key to restart the PC normally.

Discussion

This error often occurs during an installation of Windows XP, especially if you have used a boot utility or have otherwise modified the root *BOOT.INI* file, causing the NTLOADER process to lose track of where the Windows files are located. Rebuilding the boot configuration or removing modifications to the *BOOT.INI* file is a sure fix. You can modify the *BOOT.INI* file using the *bootcfg* command line program available if you run the Recovery Console after booting from a Windows XP installation CD or the command line within XP. *Bootcfg* is a rudimentary editor specific to adding, deleting, or changing entries in the *BOOT.INI* file.

See Also

MS KB 314477, "Error Message: Windows Could Not Start Because of a Computer Disk Hardware Configuration Problem"

20.10 Fixing Corrupted or Missing \WINDOWS\ SYSTEM32\CONFIG Errors

Problem

You receive an error message indicating that either *WINDOWS\SYSTEM32\CONFIG\ SYSTEM* or *WINDOWS\SYSTEM32\CONFIG\SOFTWARE* is missing or corrupt.

Solution

Using a command-line interface

1. Boot from your Windows XP CD-ROM.

2. At the first R=Repair option, press the R key.

3. Press the number that corresponds to the installation of Windows you want to repair. Typically this will be number 1.

4. When prompted, type in the administrator password.

5. At the command prompt type:

```
> cd \windows\system32\config
> ren software software.bad
> ren system system.bad
> copy \windows\repair\system
> copy \windows\repair\software
```

6. Remove the XP CD-ROM, type exit at the command prompt, and then press the Enter key to restart the PC normally.

Discussion

The system and software files are records of the initial or latest Windows install. Overclocking your system or disk corruption can cause these files to become useless. Much like using System Restore and Last Known Good Configuration, using the original copies of the *SYSTEM* and *SOFTWARE* files will take your PC back to a previous point in time, without altering the Registry, then Windows updates these files according to the current configuration.

See Also

MS KB 307545, "How to recover from a corrupted Registry that prevents Windows XP from starting"

20.11 Fixing NTLDR or NTDETECT Not Found Errors

Problem

You receive the "NTLDR is not found" or "NTDETECT is not found" error message at startup.

Solution

Using a command-line interface

1. Boot from your Windows XP CD-ROM.
2. At the first R=Repair option, press the R key.
3. Press the number that corresponds to the installation of Windows you want to repair. Typically this will be number 1.
4. When prompted type in the administrator password.
5. Enter in the following commands (d: is replaced by the actual drive letter that is assigned to the CD-ROM drive):

   ```
   > COPY d:\i386\NTLDR C:\
   ```

   or:

   ```
   > COPY d:\i386\NTDETECT.COM C:\
   ```

   Remove the XP CD-ROM, type exit at the command prompt, and then press the Enter key to restart the PC normally.

Discussion

Loss of the *NTLDR* or *NTDETECT.COM* files may be caused by a disk error, differences in disk configurations between operating system versions, or a virus. After making this repair, run CHKDSK and do a complete virus scan to ensure your hard drive is bug free. If the problem recurs, the fix may be reinstalling the operating system, reformatting the hard drive in the process to correct disk configuration problems.

See Also

MS KB 314057, "'NTLDR is missing' error message when you install or upgrade Windows XP over Windows 95, Windows 98, or Windows Millennium Edition." Many other possibilities related to system and disk corruption are documented at *http://www.computerhope.com/issues/ch000465.htm*.

20.12 Configuring Error Reporting

Problem

You want to configure Windows' error reporting to report or ignore specific error conditions.

Solution

Using a graphical user interface

1. From the Start menu, right-click My Computer, and then click Properties.
2. Click the Advanced tab.
3. Click Error Reporting, then follow the dialog to configure it.
4. By default, error reporting is enabled. To disable error reporting, click "Disable error reporting."
5. To continue to be notified when errors occur without being prompted to report the errors, click to select the "But notify me when critical errors occur" checkbox.
6. Specify whether you want to use error reporting for the Windows operating system, for programs, or for both Windows and programs.
7. To report errors only for selected programs, click Choose Programs, click All programs in this list, and then deselect the programs that you do not want to include.
8. To add a program that is not listed, click Add and type the name of the program or click Browse to find the program on your computer.
9. If many programs are listed, you may want to create an exclude list. In the Do not report errors for these programs box, click Add and type the name of each program that you want to exclude from error reporting or click Browse to find the program on your computer.

Discussion

When an error occurs, a dialog box is displayed that prompts you to report the problem to Microsoft. Windows Error Reporting (WER) is an anonymous and secure method for reporting the error condition and technical information about it to Microsoft over the Internet. Microsoft will analyze the data provided with the report to try to determine the cause of the error condition. Errors specific to non-Microsoft applications may be reported to all related program vendors for analysis and correction. Of course, not all reports get detailed scrutiny—errors with the most reports get looked at first. If a similar problem has been reported by other users and information about the problem is available, you receive a link to a web page that contains information about the problem.

See Also

Comprehensive documentation about Windows Error Reporting and its uses are covered at *http://www.windowsdevcenter.com/pub/a/windows/2004/03/16/wer.html*.

20.13 Troubleshooting Blue Screen Error Messages

Problem

You need to know the specific cause and solution for Windows' Stop or "blue screen of death" error messages.

Solution

The known causes of and typical solutions to Stop or blue-screen error messages are listed in Part VII, Appendix C of the Windows XP resource kit documentation at *http://www.microsoft.com/resources/documentation/Windows/XP/all/reskit/en-us/Default.asp*.

Table 20-1 lists general troubleshooting and repair tips for each known Stop error.

Table 20-1. Troubleshooting tips for Stop errors

Error message	Troubleshooting recommendation
Stop 0x0000000A	Replace/remove hardware, roll back, or update driver.
Stop 0x0000001E	Recently installed or defective software crashed the OS. Report the error and update or remove the software.
Stop 0x00000024	Probable disk or file system error. Run CHKDSK to determine disk problems.
Stop 0x0000002E	Defective or mismatched memory, including motherboard, Level 2 cache, or video RAM. Replace memory or system board. May also be caused by pagefile or disk error. Run CHKDSK to determine disk/file system problems.
Stop 0x0000003F	Removing or reinstalling upgraded software may solve this problem.
Stop 0x00000050	Replacing RAM memory, L2 RAM cache, video RAM, or incompatible software, including remote control and antivirus software, are possible fixes.
Stop 0x00000077	Run a virus protection scan to locate and remove any possible virus infections. Run CHKDSK or other disk-repair diagnostic or replacing the hard drive may resolve this problem.

Table 20-1. Troubleshooting tips for Stop errors (continued)

Error message	Troubleshooting recommendation
Stop 0x00000079	This error most often occurs when ACPI firmware settings are changed. For example, you might install Windows XP Professional on an x86-based computer with the firmware ACPI enable option enabled and later decide to disable it.
	This error can also result when mismatched single and multiprocessor configuration files are copied to the system.
	Re-enable ACPI or run Windows installation to repair the installation to match the present hardware configuration.
Stop 0x0000007A	Run CHKDSK or other disk-repair diagnostic or replacing the hard drive or controller may resolve this problem.
Stop 0x0000007B	Installing incorrect device drivers when installing or upgrading storage adapter hardware typically causes stop 0x7B errors. Stop 0x7B errors could also indicate possible virus infection.
	Run a virus protection scan to locate and remove any possible virus infections. Run CHKDSK or other disk-repair diagnostic or replacing the hard drive may resolve this problem.
Stop 0x0000007F	This could be caused by software problems or hardware failures. Removing and reinstalling updated drivers, software, or hardware may solve this problem.
Stop 0x0000009F	The Stop 0x9F message indicates that a driver is in an inconsistent or invalid power state. Restarting the PC may resolve this problem.
Stop 0xBE	Removing and reinstalling updated drivers may solve this problem.
Stop 0xC2	This message is typically due to a faulty driver or software. Removing and reinstalling updated drivers may solve this problem.
Stop 0x000000CE	This message indicates that a driver failed to cancel pending operations before exiting. Restarting the PC may resolve this problem.
Stop 0x000000D1	Drivers that have used improper addresses typically cause this error. Removing and reinstalling updated drivers may solve this problem.
Stop 0x000000D8	Drivers that have used improper addresses typically cause this error. Removing and reinstalling updated drivers may solve this problem.
Stop 0x000000EA	Removing and reinstalling updated drivers, software, or hardware may solve this problem.
Stop 0x000000ED	This error might also occur during an upgrade to Windows XP Professional on systems that use higher throughput ATA disks or controllers with incorrect cabling. In some cases, your system might appear to work normally after you restart. Installing an 80-wire IDE cable may solve this problem.
Stop 0x000000F2	Edge-level and level-interrupt-triggered devices are incorrectly assigned the same IRQ (for example, a serial port and a peripheral component interconnect (PCI) SCSI controller). Resetting Plug and Play/ESCD values in BIOS may solve this problem.
Stop 0xC000021A	Windows security system is unable to function. Running Windows setup to reinstall/repair may solve this problem.
Stop 0xC0000221	Indicates driver, system file, or disk corruption problems (such as a damaged paging file). Faulty memory hardware can also cause this Stop message to appear. Replacing memory or resetting the pagefile may solve this problem.

Discussion

The "blue screen of death" is the scourge of any Windows user—such errors are fatal, in that the error conditions cause Windows to completely fail without any capability of logging, traces, event log entries, or other indication resembling a direct pointer to the device or program that blew up. In most cases, the condition can be traced back to recent system changes in hardware, drivers, or software that can be undone, upgraded, removed, replaced, or diagnosed with common tools to identify disk or file system faults. If you can identify a specific BIOS version, component, device, driver, program, or operation that causes "blue screen" death, collect and report as much information as possible to the related vendor for diagnosis.

See Also

If you want to see what Windows is really thinking when errors happen, dig into Microsoft's searchable error databases at *http://www.microsoft.com/technet/support/ eventserrors.mspx* and *http://www.microsoft.com/resources/documentation/windows/ xp/all/proddocs/en-us/event_overview_01.mspx*.

20.14 Setting Up and Using Dr. Watson to Troubleshoot Errors

Problem

You want to get more detailed logs on application and driver errors to determine possible causes.

Solution

Run Dr. Watson

Go to Start, select Run, type in drwtsn32.exe, and click OK.

Enhance the debug information available to Dr. Watson

1. Open My Computer and navigate to the *%systemroot%* folder (usually *C:\ WINDOWS*) on your computer.

2. Select File, then New, and create a new folder named *Symbols*.

3. Insert your Windows XP CD-ROM.

4. Open My Computer and navigate to the *Support\Debug\i386* folder on the Windows XP CD-ROM.

5. Copy the symbols to the *Symbols* folder that you created on your computer in Step 2.

6. Right-click My Computer, and then select Properties.

7. Select the Advanced tab, and then click the Environment Variables button.

8. Click New under System variables.

9. Type _NT_SYMBOL_PATH for the Variable name, then %systemroot%\Symbol for the Variable value.

10. You can add symbols for hot fixes, patches and service packs by including additional variables—for example, the Variable value could read:

    %systemroot%\symbol;%systemroot%\hotfixes;%systemroot%\symbolsSp2

    if you've copied symbols from the different patches to these folders.

11. Click OK to close the dialogs.

Discussion

Unless you've installed another debugger application to handle programs errors and exceptions, Microsoft's Dr. Watson logs the error data for you. By default, Dr. Watson tracks only 10 instructions and 10 errors, and collects a mini-dump log file of the system state at the time of the error. The Dr. Watson dialog allows you to configure logging of more instructions and errors, a more verbose log, and log program symbol tables if they are available.

Excerpts from a *C:\Documents* and *Settings\All Users\Application Data\Microsoft\Dr Watson\drwtsn32.log* file below show you just how much information can be collected about a single error event:

```
Microsoft (R) DrWtsn32
Copyright (C) 1985-2001 Microsoft Corp. All rights reserved.

Application exception occurred:
        App: F:\Program Files\Thumbs7\Thumbs.exe (pid=1156)
        When: 6/30/2004 @ 06:09:52.593
        Exception number: c0000005 (access violation)

*----> System Information <----*
        Computer Name: SIRAH
        User Name:
        Terminal Session Id: 0
        Number of Processors: 1
        Processor Type: x86 Family 6 Model 10 Stepping 0
        Windows Version: 5.1
        Current Build: 2600
        Service Pack: 1
        Current Type: Uniprocessor Free
        Registered Organization:
        Registered Owner:
```

```
*----> Task List <----*
   0 System Process
   4 System
   ...

*----> Module List <----*
(0000000000330000 - 0000000000362000: C:\WINDOWS\System32\ODBC32.dll
(0000000000400000 - 0000000000f94000: F:\Program Files\Thumbs7\Thumbs.exe
 ...

*----> State Dump for Thread Id 0x230 <----*

eax=00000038 ebx=00000000 ecx=0012f5c4 edx=eed33d64 esi=00390608 edi=00000000
eip=7ffe0304 esp=0012f2cc ebp=0012f354 iopl=0         nv up ei pl nz na pe nc
cs=001b  ss=0023  ds=dbc8  es=1f80  fs=0038  gs=0038            efl=00000202

function: <nosymbols>
        7ffe02f2 0000              add     [eax],al
        7ffe02f4 0000              add     [eax],al
        7ffe02f6 0000              add     [eax],al

*----> Stack Back Trace <----*
*** ERROR: Symbol file could not be found.  Defaulted to export symbols for C:\
WINDOWS\System32\ntdll.dll -
WARNING: Stack unwind information not available. Following frames may be wrong.
*** ERROR: Symbol file could not be found.  Defaulted to export symbols for C:\
WINDOWS\system32\msvcrt.dll -

*----> Raw Stack Dump <----*
000000000012f2cc  34 c5 f5 77 68 9f f6 77 - 70 03 00 00 00 00 00 00
000000000012f2dc  00 00 00 00 00 00 39 00   d0 c3 39 00 00 00 00 00
```

The actual log file goes on for several hundred lines, indicating minute details for each and every running process. Dr. Watson logs are most useful to programmers who have access to symbols tables for their specific programs, and who understand the sequences of instructions that are related to the application. The log file output may make some sense to nonprogrammers by telling you which program caused an error, potentially conflicting applications, and related error codes which may help you search for solutions in a program vendor's web site or the Web in general. Occasionally an application vendor may ask you to send the log file to their technical support department for further analysis.

See Also

Microsoft documents Dr. Watson, with specific examples and explanations of the log contents, at *http://www.microsoft.com/resources/documentation/windows/xp/all/ proddocs/en-us/drwatson_overview.mspx*.

Summary of Windows XP Versions and Service Packs

1.0 Introduction

There were no parallel home and office versions of Windows 95, 98 or Me, nor of Windows 2000 Professional which was accompanied only by Server versions. Windows XP is the first Windows operating system to be available in both Home and Professional versions. This makes maintaining (patching and updating) the operating system a lot less complicated for everyone, from Microsoft to home users. To most users the differences between XP Home and Professional are almost negligible, which is good news for users because you only have to deal with one look-and-feel. To system administrators placing hundreds or thousands of Windows PCs in a network environment, or simply managing a handful of them in a small office, the difference between XP Home and Professional is like night and day—at least for networking and maintenance.

Like every Microsoft operating system before it, Windows XP has gone through myriad security, bug, and feature patches, as well as two major comprehensive service packs. Patches and service packs apply equally to home and professional versions. The variations between the operating system versions and the significant changes to them through their common service packs are summarized in this Appendix.

Differences Between Windows XP Home and Professional Editions

Microsoft chooses to label these two versions of Windows as "editions." Editions, versions—it's all marketing, which means it all comes down to features and benefits, and of course cost. The differences between XP Home and Professional may appear subtle and seemingly unnecessary to the home and small business PC user, since they can run Word, surf the Web, print documents and photos, and play music as well as their professional counterparts can. To medium and large businesses with modest to complex networks, and business-oriented services interconnecting users, customers, products, and revenue, the significance of XP Professional is mission-critical.

The top 10 differences between XP Home and XP Professional are:

Two CPUs

The kernel of the XP Professional operating system recognizes and uses up to two CPUs. XP Home users are limited to the use of one CPU no matter how many are in the box.

Remote control

XP Professional users can take control of other Windows PCs through Remote Desktop services, as well as have their PC controlled by other XP Professional users. XP Home users can get remote-control support from an XP Professional system, or third-party software to remotely control another PC, but they cannot control other PCs.

Remote software installation

A Windows system administrator can deliver and upgrade applications on XP Professional systems over a Windows-server-based network. XP Home users have to manually install applications one at a time on each PC.

Centralized control

XP Professional users can take and maintain control of Windows systems with Microsoft's server-based system management tools. XP Home systems cannot participate in Windows domains or server-based management processes.

Group control

XP Professional allows you to maintain user rights by group, so you can keep the work and resources of different departments separately and manage or entitle different working groups separately. XP Home systems do not have the benefit of distinct workgroups and Windows-server-based domain or management processes.

Roving users

Sometimes you just have to work at another PC. XP Professional and a Windows-server network allow you to move to other systems and bring your PC environment with you. XP Home users have to create their environment one PC at a time.

File encryption

XP Professional users can keep the work and resources of different users separate from one another on the same PC through local system security and file encryption features. XP Home users cannot keep files truly private from one user to another—for instance, parents (presumably having administrative rights) can access the files of children's accounts.

Restricted File Access

Not only can others' files be inaccessible, applications can be restricted on a user-by-user basis with XP Professional. Applications installed on XP Home systems are available to all users.

Offline File Access

XP Professional lets you take your laptop off the network and keep working with your net-based files by keeping local copies through the Offline Files feature in Folder Options. This feature synchronizes local and network-based files. XP Home users may not have a network, or they have to copy, copy, and copy again to keep files in synch with those on a shared or network drive.

Localized User Interface

This feature of XP Professional allows you to change display and input languages and work equally well within the same installation, and use any properly developed multilingual application in any language under any installation of XP Professional. XP Home users must pick a single language to work with and stick with it.

XP Service Pack 1

Windows XP Service Pack 1 contains more than 250 security, compatibility, and bug-fix patches to the original Windows XP Home and Professional releases. We've listed what appear to be the most significant feature, security, and bug-related issues, and the appropriate Microsoft Knowledge Base article, below. For a complete list and links to each and every item covered by the service pack, visit Microsoft's list of fixes in Windows XP Service Pack 1 and Windows XP Service Pack 1a at *http:// support.microsoft.com/default.aspx?scid=kb;en-us;324720.* For details about Windows XP Service Pack 1 and Service Pack 1a, visit *http://www.microsoft.com/ windowsxp/downloads/updates/sp1/default.mspx.*

If you are the administrator of any number of Windows 2000 or XP systems, you'll want to review this list of fixes and consider the problems you may be facing in your environment, especially centered around the many hardware-related issues. If your PC is connected to the Internet, many of these patches are a minimum requirement of preserving your PC's sanity, or you may find it easier to jump to Service Pack 2 because SP1 will be unavailable and you will have to apply SP2 to keep up. Summaries of the patches and enhancements to the various features and functions of both XP Home and Professional are:

Enhancement and fixes for the Windows environment

Program count for the Most Frequently Used Programs list; installing the Multilingual User Interface Pack from a long path; *Msconfig.exe* not responding if user does not have administrator rights; selecting a JPG image for background; data loss may after reinstalling, repairing, or upgrading; content search does not search all file types; software restriction policies not recognizing 16-bit programs.

Repairs to application-specific issues

Text overlap viewing Excel spreadsheets saved as HTML, PowerPoint turning off screen saver, Macromedia Flash 5.0 installation causing Windows Protection error, access violations with OpenGL-based programs.

Hardware-related updates
> DVD drive may not play automatically with Roxio Easy CD Creator 5.1 and Norton Anti-Virus 2002 running, resume when you press a key on a USB keyboard, Usbhub.sys driver if used as a composite driver, add Universal Serial Bus 2.0 support, Suspend mode leaves backlight on, SpeedStep process causes hang when waking up from an S4 state, USB keyboard does not work after standby or suspend, "Stop 0x0000000A" error message changing from AC power to DC power, incorrect Thrustmaster Dance pad functions, 1394 storage device not working after changing another 1394 device, system hangs using Zip drive, problems with 16-bit programs, 2.0 GHz and faster systems, inability to shut down, UPS service won't start, add support for AMD PowerNow! Technology, USB isochronous data transfers issues, Files and Settings Transfer Wizard doesn't transfer, slow hard drive performance.

Patches for Internet Explorer
> Internet Explorer not retrying bad proxy server configuration, and access violations when running ASP or VBScript programs.

Security vulnerability patches
> Unchecked buffer issues in Outlook Express, in network share provider, in Remote Access Service Phonebook, in the multiple UNC provider, in SNMP service, and in Universal Plug and Play may lead to denial of service. Attacks on Port 1720 may cause NetMeeting to fail and URL error handling vulnerability.

Repairs to networking issues
> Windows File Protection inability to restore files from a mapped network drive, Cisco VPN Client won't install, inability to print to a Windows XP print server, and multiple issues with Novell NetWare networking performance and functions.

MultiMedia issues fixed
> Problems with the InterActual DVD program, connecting two digital video cameras to two different IEEE 1394 adapters, inability to play DVDs, black video window in Movie Maker using a variable data rate digital video 1394 device, and error message when a user with limited rights tries to play a stream with Media Player.

XP Service Pack 1a

Windows XP Service Pack 1a, released February 3, 2003, differs from Service Pack 1 by the removal of the Microsoft Virtual Machine support for Java applets. Users wishing to have Java applet support should download the Java Runtime Environment from *http://www.java.com*. Refer to Microsoft's statements of transition and end-of-life statements regarding Java support at their web page, *http://www.microsoft.com/mscorp/java/*.

XP Service Pack 2

Released August 10, 2004, Windows XP Service Pack 2 (SP2) may well be what turns XP into the operating system it should have been at first release—truly more reliable, more secure, and ultimately more satisfying.

It is not necessary to apply Service Pack 1 (SP1) or 1a before applying SP2. SP2 is comprised of patches for all known security vulnerabilities up to a few weeks before its date of release, significant alterations to all aspects of networking and network applications to preclude or help mitigate many forms of attack from inside and out, new default settings in the Windows firewall to keep out more threats to the local computer, and better program execution awareness and prevention to mitigate internal threats that can affect the host computer and other computers on a network and through the Internet.

Simply stated, Service Pack 2 is a must-have for any Windows XP PC connected to other PCs or the Internet, and it will be required for ongoing update and patch support in the future. Download Windows XP Service Pack 2 directly from *http://www.microsoft.com/downloads/details.aspx?FamilyId=049C9DBE-3B8E-4F30-8245-9E368D3CDB5A&displaylang=en*. SP2 includes the following:

Rework of TCP/IP stack to restrict outgoing Raw Sockets functionality
> Increases security by preventing creation and use of nonstandard IP protocols to cause possible outbound infections or attacks upon other systems.

Improvements to Remote Procedure Call (RPC) feature
> Makes it more difficult to exploit the system.

Improved security around Distributed Common Object Model (DCOM)
> Reduces exploitability of the system.

Data execution prevention
> A protective and cooperative layer of hardware and software monitoring that prevents malicious code from running from data regions of memory, and alerts you to any attempts.

Improved firewall
> Firewall is enabled and active by default.
>
> UDP ports 137 and 138 and TCP ports 139 and 445 accept inbound connections only from the local network.
>
> When Universal Plug and Play services are enabled they will accept only inbound connections on UDP port 1900 and TCP port 2869 from the local network.
>
> The ability for a user to reset the firewall to a default configuration instead of having to undo individual changes manually.
>
> Multiple user profiles can be setup for the firewall, if the system is joined to a domain.

Security Center

Provides access to the status and control of the Windows Firewall.

Provides virus protection monitoring, which is aware of several popular virus protection programs, whether one of them is running, and the status of virus definition file updates.

Provides access to the status and control of Windows Updates.

Revisions to Outlook Express

Protects users from execution of malicious code contained in HTML-formatted email by rendering it as rich text format.

Attachment Execution Service prevents execution of code attachments in email messages.

Limits the downloading of certain HTML code that would notify a spammer that the email address receiving the message is active and potentially generating more inbound SPAM.

Improvements to Internet Explorer

Add-ons and crash prevention

Provides more visibility to more and often hidden add-ons (plug-ins) to help users determine presence of suspicious software, and allows them to be disabled.

Crash prevention monitors IE add-ons and provides the ability to disable them if they cause crashes.

Pop-up blocker for Internet Explorer

Intended to prevent unwanted pop-up messages while user is browsing.

Information bar

Notifies user of blocked pop-ups, ActiveX controls, downloads, and active content.

Group Policy Control

Allows system administrators to control IE security by user groups/privilege levels.

General security

Tighter security on IE's Local Zone to prevent ActiveX code from running without operator awareness. Intended to reduce infections from spyware, adware, and other unwanted or malicious programs.

MIME file type handling enforcement to better protect users from content or files downloaded abnormally.

Preventing code from one web site from processing cached files from another site, as a method to exploit a system from several sources.

Stronger prevention against untrusted publisher code execution.

Restrictions on the type of Windows pop-up activities allowed.

Reduction of vulnerabilities from HTML code coming through ports not normally used for HTML content.

Local Machine Lockdown can impose security restrictions on local HTML files, normally considered safe but that a hacker could exploit.

Enhancements to downloads, attachments, and authenticode features
Better indication of downloads, risks, and downloaded program source to help users determine whether a file is safe to run.

Revision of Automatic Updates feature using BITS 2 technology
BITS provides and supports the transport of updates to PCs, handles disconnection in the middle of a download, retains partial downloads, and allows picking up the download where it left off.

Windows Installer 3.0
An update to the Windows Installer service to provide more consistent and capable software installation for all vendor and Microsoft applications.

Windows Update Services
Provides better service for administrators to deploy critical and security updates to user systems, forcing some updates without user discretion. Also supports updates and patches for Microsoft applications.

Add/Remove Program List Filtering
Allows user to display (or not) Windows Updates, and provide for their removal.

Attachment Execution Service API
A protective layer that is intended to stop code embedded in email and instant messages from running. Affects and protects only Outlook, Outlook Express, and Messenger applications.

Windows Setup
New features and control over the SETUP program for operating system.

Added native support for Bluetooth devices
Allows creation of links between personal devices (PDAs, cell phones, headsets) and other computers, requiring fewer third-party drivers and applications.

Reduction in the number of vulnerable system services that start automatically
Lets the operator control the services they need/want versus leaving the system vulnerable by default. The Alerter and Messenger services are turned off/disabled.

Inclusion of new administrative tools to better manage local and remote computers
Allows remote management of other PCs. However, the TCP port 445 used to do this is blocked by the new firewall, so TCP port 445 needs to be configured in the firewall to allow this to work.

Improved security for WebDAV services
Prevents user password from being sent in the clear when connecting to remote servers for SharePoint and other applications.

Wireless Provisioning Service
> A new feature with enhancements to Windows' built-in wireless networking support. Designed to make it easier and more secure to connect to wireless hotspots, and home and corporate networks.

Windows Messenger
> Security enhancements to require a user display name and block unsafe file transfers in the Windows Firewall unless and until specifically allowed.

Media Player 9
> Media Player 9 contains security enhancements merged with more secure handling of broadcast and multicast content through changes in TCP/IP networking.

Enhancements for Tablet PC

Security Enhancements for Microsoft Data Access Components

Read-Only Control for Block Mode USB Devices
> Provides control over writing data to USB storage devices.

Security for Distributed Transaction Coordinator
> By default, network communications from this service has been disabled until changed by a system administrator.

See Also

http://www.microsoft.com/technet/prodtechnol/winxppro/maintain/sp2netwk.mspx

Index

Numbers

802.11b standards, 435, 455
802.11g devices, 455
802.11g standards, 435

A

access
    CD-ROMs, restoring, 87
    events, restricting, 519
    hotspots, 458–460
    Internet, increasing speed, 395
    physical (security), 539
    Registry, restricting, 285
    restricting, 269
    screen saver locking, 547
    shares, restricting, 269
    Telnet
        configuring, 403–405
        managing, 405
    WPA, 443
        configuring, 453
accounts
    computer
        creating, 497–498
        joining, 499–501
        renaming, 501–504
        resetting, 504
    deleting, 547
    group
        adding/deleting, 495–497
        creating, 488–490
        viewing, 491–495

passwords, requiring strong, 550
renaming, 544–546
SAM, 550
security, 539
services, configuring, 327
users
    creating, 469–471
    domains, 483–485
    enabling, 478–480
    modifying, 474–478
    passwords, 480–482
    profiles, 485
    searching last logon time, 487–488
    troubleshooting, 473
    unlocking, 471–473
actions
    auditing, 539
    events, triggering, 525–527
    services, performing upon failure, 329
activating
    TIP, 176
    Windows XP, 32
activation data, backing up, 601
Active Directory
    searching, 381–382
    shares, publishing, 271
ActiveX, configuring, 419
ad hoc networks, configuring, 456–458
adapters, installing wireless
        networking, 434–437
Ad-Aware, 417
Add Hardware Wizard, 49, 436
Add or Remove Programs dialog box, 93

We'd like to hear your suggestions for improving our indexes. Send email to *index@oreilly.com*.

adding, 47, 129
   Address Bars to Taskbars, 129
   group accounts, 495–497
   hardware, 47
   shortcuts to Taskbars, 130
Address Bar, 119
   Taskbars, adding to, 129
addresses
   IP
      configuring, 373–375
      limiting, 449
      releasing, 375–377
   MAC, filtering, 448
administrative account security, 539
administrator accounts, renaming, 544–546
Advanced Encryption System (see AES)
AES (Advanced Encryption System), 453
alarms, configuring power, 187
alerts, performance, 562
aliases, creating, 244
alternate credentials, running tasks
      with, 304–306
Alternative User Input Text Input Processor
      (TIP), activating, 176
America Online icons, deleting, 122
analog video cameras/videotape, capturing
      video, 356
analyzing security
   configurations, 540–541
   MBSA, 540
anonymously surfing the web, 431–432
antecedent services, viewing, 330–333
antennas, 446
antispyware definitions, updating, 539
applets (Control Panel)
   hiding, 139
   recategorizing, 141
   viewing, 137
Application Compatibility Toolkit, 102
Application Compatibility Wizard, 100
applications
   Ad-Aware, 417
   aliases, creating, 244
   Backup, 581–585
      applying ASR, 587
      creating ASR, 588
      restoring files, 586
   base priority, assigning, 556
   compatibility, troubleshooting, 105
   customizing, 97–99
   default locations, modifying, 94
   deleting, 88–91

disabling, 547
DOS, running, 106
Dr. Watson, troubleshooting events, 536
EMS Free Surfer mk II, 411
EventCombMT utility, 335
Excel, starting, 98
firewalls, bypassing, 422–425
GhostSurf, 431
ImageConverter .EXE, 364
IrfanView, 363
keyboard shortcuts, 95, 109–110
Microsoft Windows AntiSpyware, 418
Most Frequently Used Programs List,
      customizing, 133–136
moving, 111–113
MusicMatch Jukebox, 349
NTBACKUP, 582
older versions
   formatting styles, 107
   running, 100
PerfectDisk, 212
Pinned Programs List, customizing, 136
Pop-Up No-No!, 411
PowerDesk Pro, 247
PowerPoint, 98
QFixApp, 103
RegSpy, 92
remote installation, 113–115
remote redeployment, 115
remote uninstallation, 116
services, running as, 322
Spybot Search & Destroy, 417
startup, shutting down unnecessary
      at, 175–180
SymmTime, 164
System Restore
   applying, 589–591
   disabling, 592
uninstalling, 91
   deleting from Add or Remove
      Programs dialog box, 93
WAVClean, 348
WaveCorrector, 348
Webroot Spy Sweeper, 418
WinZip, 253
ZoneAlarm, 429
ZoneAlarm firewalls, 428
Applications tab, 557
applying
   ASR, 587
   Dr. Watson, 619–621
   EFS, 599

Last Known Good Configuration, 606
Recovery Console, 596–598, 609
System Restore, 589–591
system standby, 187
TweakUI, 153
VGA Mode, 608
XCOPY, 595
archiving events, 523
ASR (Automated System Recovery)
applying, 587
creating, 588
assigning
base priority, 556
packages, 114
attacks, taking action against, 540
audio (see sounds)
auditing
actions, 539
backups, 602
enabling, 542–544
policies, configuring, 543
restoring, 602
Auditing Entry dialog box, 260
auditpol command, 260
authentication, networks, 452
Autoexec.bat files, 106
AUTOEXEC.NT errors, 610
Automated System Recovery (see ASR)
Automatic Updates, configuring, 40–42
automatically synchronizing time, 161
automating Windows XP deployment, 18
auto-restart, Automatic Updates
installations, 41
autorun, troubleshooting CDs, 83
AUTORUN.INF files, 79–81

B

backgrounds, modifying Internet
Explorer, 408
backing up
activation data, 601
auditing, 602
maintaining, 540, 602
Registry, 287
systems, 581–585
applying ASR, 587
creating ASR, 588
restoring files, 586
XCOPY, applying, 595
BackupEventLog method, 524
balloon tips, turning off, 127
bandwidth, USB, 58

base priority, assigning to
applications/processes, 556
basic disks, converting to dynamic disks, 204
batch conversions, images, 363
batteries, extending life of, 187
BIOS
devices, resolving conflicts, 57
editing, 198
firmware, updating, 60
hardware, 47
parameters, troubleshooting, 81
bit rates for music files, 342
blocking pop-ups, 409–412
blue screen error messages, 617–619
boosters, installing, 446
Boot Delay, 580
Boot Up Floppy Seek, 580
booting
clean boots, 174
defragmenting, 198
Last Known Good Configuration, 52, 606
logging, enabling, 528, 607
multiboot menus, creating, 167–171
screens, modifying, 182
System Restore, 54
troubleshooting, 25
applying Recovery Console, 596–598
boot.ini file, 167
switches, 170
BootXP, 182
browsers
Firefox, 412
IE, 414
Internet Explorer, 415
Navigator and Mozilla, deleting
cookies, 415
(see also interfaces)
burning
CDs, 344–346
troubleshooting, 346–349
DVDs, 360
bypassing firewalls, 422–425

C

cables, changing, 60
caches
DNS, flushing, 380
troubleshooting, 398
capturing video, 356–360
CD-ROMs
access, restoring, 87
troubleshooting, 84

CDs
   autorun software installation, 83
   installing from, 11–14
   music
      burning, 344–346
      ripping, 339–342
      troubleshooting burning, 346–349
chkdsk utility, 215
Choose Programs dialog box, 191
class ID (CLSID), 121
clean boots, 174
clean installations, 10, 11–14
cleaning
   desktop icons, 128
   Disk Cleanup tool, 210
   hard disks, 570–573
   Registry, 198
   Scheduled task folders, 176
   Startup folders, 176, 575
   volumes, 209
clearing
   events, 518
   paging files, 181
ClearType, optimizing resolution, 149
Client Installation Wizard, 23
clients, Dhcp, 381
clocks, configuring, 160–164
cloning installations, 20
CLSID (class ID), 121
columns, Windows Firewall logs, 427
commands
   aliases, 244
   auditpol, 260
   dir, 237
   diruse, 307
   DISABLE, 27
   DISKPART, 27
   dsadd, 489
   dsmove.exe, 545
   ENABLE, 27
   FIXBOOT, 27
   FIXMBR, 27
   HELP, 27
   inuse, 257
   linkd.exe, 242
   LISTSVC, 27
   LOGON, 27
   netdom, 166, 501
   netsh, 371
   netstat, 386

   netstatp.exe, 300
   prompts, opening, 145
   psexec, 237
   pslist, 300
   Recovery Console, 27, 598
   runas, 237
   runas.exe, 304
   sidtoname, 546
   subst, 220
   SYSTEMROOT, 27
   tIntadmn, 406
compact privacy statements, 414
comparing
   files, 248
   Registry, 284
compatibility
   Application Compatibility Toolkit, 102
   applications, troubleshooting, 105
   older versions of applications, 100
   tests, 29
Compatibility dialog box, 100
components
   IIS, 400
   unremovable, uninstalling, 88–91
compress.exe utility, 253
compressing
   files, 252
   volumes, 213–215
computer accounts
   creating, 497–498
   joining, 499–501
   renaming, 501–504
   resetting, 504
Computer Name Changes dialog box, 165
computers, renaming, 165–167
CONFIG.NT errors, troubleshooting, 610
Config.sys file, 106
configuring, 325
   ActiveX, 419
   audit policies, 543
   Automatic Updates, 40–42
   computer accounts, 497–498
      joining, 499–501
   desktop, saving, 156
   Dr. Watson, 619–621
   environment variables, 193
   error reporting, 616
   events, retention policies, 516
   group accounts, 488–490
      adding/deleting, 495–497

viewing, 491–495
labels of volumes, 208
Last Known Good Configuration, 52
networks
    ad hoc, 456–458
    disabling connections, 371–372
    DNS, 377–379
    filtering TCP/IP, 388–391
    installing IPv6 stacks, 392
    IP addresses, 373–375
    managing routes, 383–384
    measuring latency/link speed, 391
    registering DNS, 380
    releasing IP addresses, 375–377
    searching Active Directory, 381 382
    troubleshooting, 387
    viewing, 368–370
    viewing ports, 385–387
power
    alarms, 187
    schemes, 185
privacy, 412–416
Registry
    Group Policy, 280
    values, 277–280
security
    analyzing, 540 541
    services, 327
Setup Manager, 16
startup services, 325
System Configuration Utility
    clean boots, 174
    cleaning applications and services at
        startup, 576
    shutting down unnecessary
        applications at startup, 176
Telnet, 403–405
time, 160–164
transferring files, 111
user accounts, 469–471
    domains, 483–485
    passwords, 480–482
    profiles, 485
    troubleshooting, 473
    unlocking, 471–473
WEP, 450
Windows Movie Maker profiles, 359
Wireless Zero Configuration service, 442
worms/viruses during installations, 44
WPA, 453
conflicts, resolving, 56–58

connections
    devices, resolving conflicts, 56–58
    DNS, troubleshooting, 396–399
    Ethernet cables, 438
    Internet Connection Sharing,
        troubleshooting printing, 69
    modems, troubleshooting, 50
    networks
        configuring IP addresses, 373–375
        disabling, 371–372
        filtering TCP/IP, 388–391
        installing IPv6 stacks, 392
        measuring latency/link speed, 391
        releasing IP addresses, 375–377
        troubleshooting, 387
        viewing ports, 385–387
    USB
        bandwidth errors, 58
        hung devices, 59–61
        troubleshooting, 61
    wireless networking, 440
        configuring ad hoc, 456–458
        encrypting, 450–455
        hotspots, 458–460
        mixing 802.11b/802.11g devices, 455
        security, 447–450, 464
        sending email from hotspots, 460–462
        speeding up, 445–447
        stuttering (hotspots), 463
        troubleshooting, 442 445
ContextMenu Plus, 147
Control Panel applets
    hiding, 139
    recategorizing, 141
    viewing, 137
controls
    ActiveX, configuring, 420
    older programs, forcing to use, 107
conventions, UNC, 114
converting
    basic disks to dynamic disks, 204
    to classic Windows interfaces, 150
    hard disks to NTFS, 573–575
    ImageConverter .EXE, 364
    images, 362–363
Cookie Pal utility, 394, 413
cookies, 414
    configuring, 412–416
    examining and deleting manually, 415
    exporting, importing or backing up, 415
    IE cookie handling, customizing, 413

cookies (*continued*)
    IE privacy settings, effects of, 412
    related terminology, understanding, 414
    supercookies (Windows Media
        Player), 353
    third-party cookie managers, 413
    (see also privacy)
Copy To Folder option, 145
copying files, 246
CPU usage, tracking, 555
crashes
    Last Known Good Configuration,
        applying, 606
    Safe Mode, starting in, 605
    (see also troubleshooting)
critical patches, installing, 539
Cryptographic service errors,
        troubleshooting, 611
current installations
    creating multiboot installations, 29
    troubleshooting multiboot
        installations, 31
Customer Experience Improvement
        Program, 353
Customize Notifications dialog box, 131
Customize Start Menu dialog box, 133
customizing
    applications, 97–99
    events, logging, 512
    Internet Explorer, 406–408
        security, 419–422
    Most Frequently Used
        Programs, 133–136
    Pinned Programs, 136
    power alarms, 187
    sounds, 183
    video recording, 358

D

datatypes, Registry, 279
DDK (Driver Development Kit), 371
decompressing files, 253
defragmenting
    boot files, 198
    volumes, 211
delaying booting, 580
deleting, 495–497
    accounts, 547
    America Online icons, 122
    applications, 88–91
    desktop icons, 120–123, 124–126

    files, 232
        security, 235
        undeleting, 235
    folders, 233
    items from Notification Area, 579
    Registry, 277–280
        keys, 275–277
    services, 547
    shares, 266
    tasks, scheduling, 318
dependent services, viewing, 330–333
deployment
    applications, remote redeployment, 115
    automating, 18
desktop
    icons
        cleaning, 128
        deleting, 120–123, 124–126
    settings, saving, 156
    versions, viewing, 126
Desktop Items dialog box, 124
DEVCON, 48
devcon.exe tool, 371
Device Manager, 48
    error codes, 70
    USB devices as unknown, 62
devices
    802.11b/802.11g, mixing, 455
    adding, 47
    conflicts, resolving, 56–58
    drivers, troubleshooting updates, 51
    hidden, searching, 64
    hung USB, 59–61
    unknown
        resolving, 49
        USB, 62
    USB, troubleshooting, 61
DHCP Client (Dhcp), 381
dialog boxes
    Add or Remove Programs, 93
    Auditing Entry, 260
    Choose Programs, 191
    Compatibility, 100
    Computer Name Changes, 165
    Customize Notifications, 131
    Customize Start Menu, 133
    Desktop Items, 124
    Disk Cleanup Settings, 571
    Environment Variables, 194
    Open, 114
    Performance Options, 568
    Pop-up Blocker Settings, 410

Power Options Properties, 185
Shortcut Properties, 96
Sounds and Audio Devices
　　　Properties, 184
Start Menu Properties, 131
Windows Firewall, 422
digital media
　　images
　　　converting, 362–363
　　　sizing, 364–365
　　Internet radio stations, playing, 350
　　music
　　　burning CDs, 344–346
　　　ripping, 339–342
　　　troubleshooting burning
　　　　CDs, 346–349
　　privacy, protecting, 351–353
　　searching, 354–356
　　video
　　　burning DVDs, 360
　　　capturing, 356–360
digital video cameras, capturing video, 357
dir command, 237
diruse command, 307
DISABLE command, 27
disabling, 42
　　applications, 547
　　applications at startup, 575–578
　　error reporting, 190
　　firewalls, 42
　　LM password hash, 550
　　network connections, 371–372
　　services at startup, 178, 575–578
　　System Restore, 592
　　user accounts, 478–480
Disk Cleanup Settings dialog box, 571
Disk Cleanup tool, 210
DISKPART command, 27
diskpart utility, 202
DiskPie Pro utility, 222
disks
　　ASR
　　　applying, 587
　　　creating, 588
　　basic to dynamic, converting, 204
　　I/O errors, 25
　　monitoring, 205
　　quotas
　　　enabling, 224
　　　limiting, 226
　　　viewing, 228

read-only, 216
shortcuts, adding, 130
space
　　requirements for installations, 13
　　troubleshooting, 24
viewing, 202
(see also hard disks)
distribution points, creating, 113
DLLs (dynamic-link libraries), 25
DNS Cache (DnsCache), 381
DNS (Domain Name System)
　　configuring, 377–379
　　registering, 380
　　troubleshooting, 396–399
Domain Name System (see DNS)
domains
　　clocks, configuring, 160–164
　　computer accounts, joining, 499–501
　　systems, renaming, 165–167
　　user accounts, configuring, 483–485
DOS
　　applications, running, 106
　　USB printers, printing from, 68
Dr. Watson
　　configuring, 619–621
　　events, troubleshooting, 536
dragging music, 343
Driver Development Kit (DDK), 371
Driver Verifier tool, 65
drivers
　　devices, troubleshooting updates, 51
　　rollback, 52
drives
　　letters, setting, 207
　　networks, mapping, 218
　　viewing, 202
　　virtual, creating, 220
dsadd command, 489
dsmove.exe command, 545
DVD-ROMs, troubleshooting, 84
DVDs
　　installing from, 11–14
　　movies, troubleshooting, 86
　　music, burning, 360
dynamic disks, converting from basic
　　　disks, 204
dynamic-link libraries (see DLLs)

E

ECP (Enhanced Capability Port), 67
Edelman, Ben, 419

editing
    BIOS, 198
    video, capturing, 356–360
efficiency, increasing memory, 563–567
EFS (encrypted file system), applying, 599
email
    hotspots, sending from, 460–462
    images, sizing, 364–365
EMS Free Surfer mk II, 411
ENABLE command, 27
enabling
    auditing, 542–544
    boot logging, 528, 607
    disk quotas, 224
    NetLogon logging, 530
    Outlook logging, 535
    screen saver locking, 547
    user accounts, 478–480
    user environment logging, 529
    web sharing, 270
    Windows Installer logging, 531
    Windows Time service logging, 534
encrypted file system (see EFS)
encryption
    AES, 453
    files, 255
    WEP/WPA, 443
    wireless networks, 450–455
End-User License Agreement, accepting, 16
Enhanced Capability Port (see ECP)
Enhanced Parallel Port (see EPP)
environment variables, creating, 193
Environment Variables dialog box, 194
EPP (Enhanced Parallel Port), 67
errors
    codes (Device Manager), 70
    disk space, 24
    reporting
        configuring, 616
        disabling, 190
    USB bandwidth, 58
    volumes, checking for, 215
    WER, 193
    (see also troubleshooting)
Ethernet cables, connecting, 438
Event Comb utility, 507, 523
Event Viewer, 507
EventCombMT utility, 335
events
    actions, triggering, 525–527
    creating, 509, 512
    logging

archiving, 523
    clearing, 518
    configuring retention policies, 516
    Dr. Watson, 536
    enabling boot, 528
    enabling NetLogon, 530
    enabling Outlook, 535
    enabling user environment, 529
    enabling Windows Installer, 531
    enabling Windows Time service, 534
    monitoring, 540
    restricting access, 519
    searching, 520–523
    sizing, 515
    troubleshooting, 525, 527
    viewing, 510–512
        sizing, 514
Excel, starting, 98
exceptions, adding to firewalls, 422–425
explicit consent vs. implicit consent (for use
        of personal information), 414
exporting Registry files, 281
extender antennas, installing, 446
extending life of batteries, 187

F
fields, event log messages, 512
files
    Autoexec.bat, 106
    backing up, 582
    boot, defragmenting, 198
    boot.ini, 167
        switches, 170
    comparing, 248
    compressing, 252
    Config.sys, 106
    copying, 246
        troubleshooting, 25
    creating, 232
    decompressing, 253
    deleting, 232, 235
        undeleting, 235
    hard disks, cleaning, 570–573
    hiding, 249
    HOSTS
        increasing Internet access speed, 395
        troubleshooting, 397
    ImageConverter .EXE, 364
    INF, 76–78
        AUTORUN.INF, 79–81
    MFT, 574

modifying
 performing actions on multiple, 264
 searching last one opened, 259
moving, 246
music
 dragging, 343
 sizing, 342
naming, 246
opening, searching, 261–263
ownership of, 258
paging, clearing, 181
properties, viewing, 237–239
read-only, 251
recovering, applying EFS, 599
Registry
 exporting, 281
 importing, 282
renaming, 246
replacing, 256
restoring, 586
 retrieving shadow copies, 593–595
searching, 245
security
 deleting, 235
 encrypting, 255
shortcuts, creating, 239–242
transferring, 111
viewing, 263
volumes, searching, 221–223
Files and Settings Transfer Wizard, 111
filtering
 MAC addresses, 448
 pop-ups, 410
 TCP/IP, 388–391
Firefox, blocking pop-ups, 412
firewalls
 bypassing, 422–425
 configuring to block Trojans, 430
 disabling, 42
 ICF, 429
 spyware, 417
 tracking intrusion attempts, 426–428
 versions of, 430
 ZoneAlarm, 428–430
firmware (BIOS), updating, 60
first-party cookies, customizing IE handling
  of, 413
FIXBOOT command, 27
FIXMBR command, 27
flushing DNS caches, 380

folders
 cleaning, 176
 creating, 233
 deleting, 233
 linking, 242
 My Music, 344
 Network Connections, 443
 options, 145
 ownership of, 258
 properties, viewing, 237–239
 read-only, 251
 searching, 245
 shortcuts
  adding, 130
  creating, 239–242
 startup
  cleaning, 575
  moving, 189
 virtual drives, creating, 220
 volumes, searching, 221–223
 (see also files)
formatting
 aliases, 244
 ASR, 588
 computer accounts, 497–498
  joining, 499–501
 drives, virtual, 220
 environment variables, 193
 events, 509
  logging, 512
  viewing size of, 514
 files, 232
  shortcuts, 239–242
 folders, 233
  shortcuts, 239–242
 group accounts, 488–490
  adding/deleting, 495–497
  viewing, 491–495
 images
  converting, 362–363
  sizing, 364–365
 MMC, 4
 passwords, 599
  requiring strong, 550
 power schemes, 185
 Registry
  keys, 275–277
  values, 277–280
 shares, 266

formatting (continued)
    user accounts, 469–471
        domains, 483–485
        passwords, 480–482
        profiles, 485
        troubleshooting, 473
        unlocking, 471–473
    volumes, 206
        setting drive letters, 207
Found New Hardware Wizard, 63
Frequently Used Programs List, 120

G

GDI (Graphics Device Interface), 67
GhostSurf, 431
Globally Unique Identifier (GUID), Windows
        Media Player, 353
GPO (Group Policy Object), 114
granting permissions to manage services, 336
Graphics Device Interface (GDI), 67
group accounts, 495–497
    adding/deleting, 495–497
    creating, 488–490
    viewing, 491–495
Group Policy
    Internet Explorer, configuring
        security, 421
    Registry values, 280
    remote applications
        installation, 113–115
        redeployment, 115
        uninstallation, 116
    System Restore, disabling, 592
    tasks, running via, 312
Group Policy Editor, modifying
        interfaces, 153–156
Group Policy Object (GPO), 114
guest accounts, renaming, 544–546
GUI mode, troubleshooting setup, 25
GUID (Globally Unique Identifier), Windows
        Media Player, 353

H

HAL (Hardware Abstraction Layer), 64
HAL.DLL Missing or Corrupt error
        message, 613
hard disks
    cleaning, 570–573
    NTFS, converting to, 573–575
    (see also disks)

hardware
    Add Hardware Wizard, 436
    Add New Hardware wizard, 49
    adding, 47
    Found New Hardware Wizard, 63
    Last Known Good Configuration, 52
    removing, 57
    resetting, 60
    System Restore, 54
    teaming, 372
    wireless (see wireless networking)
Hardware Abstraction Layer (see HAL)
Help and Support Center, 5
HELP command, 27
hidden devices, searching, 64
hiding
    Control Panel applets, 139
    files, 249
    icons, 122
        Notification Area, 130–133
HOSTS files
    access, increasing speed, 395
    troubleshooting, 397
hotfixes
    installing, 36
    slipstreaming, 38
    viewing, 34
hotspots
    connecting to, 458–460
    security, 464
    sending email from, 460–462
    stuttering, 463
hung USB devices, 59–61

I

ICF (Internet Connection Firewall), 429
icons
    cleaning, 128
    deleting, 120–123, 124–126
    hiding in Notification Areas, 130–133
IE (see Internet Explorer)
IIS (Internet Information Services)
    installing, 399–401
    managing, 401–403
ImageConverter .EXE, 364
images
    converting, 362–363
    sizing, 364–365
imaging (RIS), 23
implicit consent vs. explicit consent (for use
        of personal information), 414

importing
    cookies from Internet Explorer, 415
    Registry files, 282
increasing
    Internet access speed, 395
    memory efficiency, 563–567
indexes, MFT, 574
INF files, 76–78
    AUTORUN.INF, 79–81
installation
    activating Windows XP, 32
    applications, modifying default
        locations, 94
    boosters, 446
    from CDs or DVDs, 11–14
    Client Installation Wizard, 23
    cloning, 20
    critical patches, 539
    extender antennas, 446
    firewalls, disabling, 42
    hotfixes, 36
    IIS, 399–401
    IPv6 stacks, 392
    multiboot, 29
        troubleshooting, 31
    from network shares, 14
    partitioning, 13
    preparing, 8–11
    remote applications, 113–115
    RIS, 15, 21–24
    scheduling, 41
    service packs, 37
    troubleshooting, 24–28
    from unattended installations, 15–20
    upgrading, 28
    viruses/worms, 44
    wireless networks
        adapters, 434–437
        routers, 438–440
    workgroups, 14
    (see also uninstalling)
installed service packs, viewing, 34
interfaces
    Address Bars, adding Taskbars, 129
    balloon tips, turning off, 127
    Control Panel
        hiding applets, 139
        recategorizing applets, 141
        viewing applets, 137
    GDI, 67
    Group Policy Editor, modifying
        with, 153–156

icons
    cleaning, 128
    deleting, 120–123, 124–126
Internet Explorer
    customizing, 406–408
    privacy, 413
    security, 419–422
    spyware, 417
MBSA, 540
Most Frequently Used Programs List,
    customizing, 133–136
Mozilla, 412
My Recent Documents,
    troubleshooting, 158
Netscape Navigators, 415
Notification Area, hiding icons, 130–133
Opera, 412
Pinned Programs List, customizing, 136
resolution, optimizing, 149
scripting, 4
settings, saving, 156
Start menu, troubleshooting, 157
taskbars, adding shortcuts, 130
thumbnails, modifying, 147–149
TweakUI, applying, 153
versions, viewing, 126
Windows classic, converting, 150
interim backups, applying XCOPY, 595
Internet
    DNS, troubleshooting, 396–399
    firewalls
        bypassing, 422–425
        tracking intrusion attempts, 426–428
        ZoneAlarm, 428–430
    HOSTS files, increasing access speed, 395
    IIS
        installing, 399–401
        managing, 401–403
    pop-ups, blocking, 409–412
    privacy, configuring, 412–416
    radio stations, playing, 350
    RSS feeds, 432
    security, firewalls, 417
    spyware, 416–419
    surfing the web anonymously, 431–432
    Telnet
        configuring, 403–405
        managing, 405
    WISPs, 460
Internet Connection Firewall (ICF), 429
Internet Connection Sharing, troubleshooting
    printing, 69

Internet Explorer, 414
  cookie settings, customizing, 414
  customizing, 406–408, 413
  exporting or backing up cookies, 415
  privacy, 413
  privacy settings, effects of, 412
  security, customizing, 419–422
  spyware, 417
Internet Information Services (see IIS)
Internet Protocol (see IP)
Internet service provider (see ISP)
intrusion attempts, tracking, 426–428
inuse command, 257
IP (Internet Protocol)
  addresses
    configuring, 373–375
    limiting, 449
    releasing, 375–377
  IPv6, installing stacks, 392
IrfanView, 363
ISP (Internet service provider)
  troubleshooting, 398
  WISPs, 460

J

joining computer accounts, 499–501
junction points, linking, 242

K

keyboard shortcuts
  applications, 109–110
  starting, 95
keys, creating/deleting, 275–277
killing
  pop-ups, 417
  processes, 303

L

labels, configuring volumes, 208
LanManager (LM) hash, disabling, 550
laptops
  batteries, extending life of, 187
  resolution, optimizing, 149
Last Known Good Configuration, 52
  applying, 606
last logon time (user accounts),
    searching, 487–488
latency, measuring, 391
LCD monitor resolution
  messages, 75
  optimizing, 149

legacy applications, troubleshooting
    compatibility, 105
lg tool, 489
limiting
  disk quotas, 226
  IP addresses, 449
linkd.exe command, 242
linking
  folders, 242
  Registry, 289
  speed, measuring, 391
Linksys routers, 438
LISTSVC command, 27
LM (LanManager) hash, disabling, 550
load orders, viewing, 333
local printers, troubleshooting, 66
Local Service account, 328
Local System account, 328
locations, moving startup folders, 189
locking, enabling screen saver, 547
LockoutStatus tool, 473
logging
  booting, enabling, 607
  events, 509
    archiving, 523
    clearing, 518
    configuring retention policies, 516
    customizing, 512
    Dr. Watson, 536
    enabling boot, 528
    enabling NetLogon, 530
    enabling Outlook, 535
    enabling user environment, 529
    enabling Windows Installer, 531
    enabling Windows Time service, 534
    monitoring, 540
    restricting access, 519
    searching, 520–523
    sizing, 515
    troubleshooting, 525, 527
    viewing, 510–512
    viewing size of, 514
  firewalls, tracking intrusion
      attempts, 426–428
  multiboot menus, 167–171
  Performance Console, 559
  performance, viewing, 562
login scripts, running tasks via, 310–312
LOGON command, 27
logos, Internet Explorer, 406–408

M

magazines, 7
maintenance
    backups, 540, 602
    (see also troubleshooting)
management
    Device Manager error codes, 70
    IIS, 401–403
    routes, 383–384
    SAM, 550
    services, 336
    Services Computer Management
        Console, 178
    Setup Manager, 16
    systems, renaming, 165–167
    Telnet, 405
mapping network drives, 218
Master File Table (see MFT)
MBSA (Microsoft Baseline Security
        Analyzer), 540
measuring latency/link speed, 391
members
    adding/deleting, 495–497
    viewing, 491–495
memory
    efficiency, increasing, 563–567
    multiple operating systems, running, 173
    page file size, optimizing, 568
menus, creating multiboot, 167–171
messages
    event logs, 512
    LCD monitor resolution, 75
    STOP, 25
metadata, searching digital media, 354–356
methods, BackupEventLog, 524
MFT (Master File Table), 574
microphones, 184
    (see also sounds)
Microsoft Baseline Security Analyzer (see
        MBSA)
Microsoft Developers Network (MSDN), 5
Microsoft Knowledge Base (MS KB), 5
Microsoft Management Console (see MMC)
Microsoft Software Installer (MSI)
        packages, 113
Microsoft Windows AntiSpyware, 418
missing modems, repairing, 50
mixing 802.11b/802.11g devices, 455
MMC (Microsoft Management Console)
    creating, 4
    IIS, managing servers, 401–403

modems, troubleshooting, 50
modifying
    application default locations, 94
    BIOS, 198
    boot screens, 182
    files
        preforming actions on multiple, 264
        searching last one opened, 259
    interfaces, Group Policy Editor, 153–156
    Registry values, 277–280
    text, Internet Explorer, 408
    thumbnails, 147–149
    user accounts, 474–478
monitoring
    CPU usage, 555
    disks, 205
    event logs, 540
    Registry, 290
monitors
    LCD resolution messages, 75
    video, troubleshooting, 74
Most Frequently Used Programs list,
        customizing, 133–136
Most Valuable Professionals (MVPs), 6
Move To Folder option, 145
movies
    DVDs, troubleshooting, 86
    (see also video)
moving
    applications, 111–113
    files, 246
        music, 343
    folders, startup, 189
Mozilla, blocking pop-ups, 412
MP3 players
    ripping, 339 342
MS KB (Microsoft Knowledge Base), 5
MSDN (Microsoft Developers Network), 5
MSI (Microsoft Software Installer), 113
multiboot installations
    creating, 29
    troubleshooting, 31
multiboot menus, creating, 167–171
multiple computers
    cloning, 20
    unattended installations, 15–20
multiple operating systems,
        running, 172–173
multiple systems, searching event logs
        on, 522

music
    CDs
        burning, 344–346
        troubleshooting burning, 346–349
    dragging, 343
    My Music folders, 344
    ripping, 339–342
    (see also sounds)
MusicMatch Jukebox, 349
MVPs (Most Valuable Professionals), 6
My Music folder, 344
My Recent Documents, troubleshooting, 158

N

naming
    computer accounts, 501–504
    computers, 17
    files, 246
    networks (SSID), 439
    systems, 165–167
    UNC, 114
navigating
    Internet Explorer
        customizing, 406–408
        privacy, 413
        security, 419–422
        spyware, 417
    pop-ups, blocking, 409–412
    surfing the web anonymously, 431–432
netdom command, 166, 501
NetLogon, enabling, 530
Netscape Navigator, handling cookies, 415
netsh command, 371
netstat command, 386
netstatp.exe command, 300
Network Service account, 328
Networking tab, 558
networks
    Active Directory, searching, 381–382
    authentication, 452
    configuration, viewing, 368–370
    connections
        configuring IP addresses, 373–375
        disabling, 371–372
        filtering TCP/IP, 388–391
        installing IPv6 stacks, 392
        measuring latency/link speed, 391
        releasing IP addresses, 375–377
        troubleshooting, 387
        viewing ports, 385–387

DNS
    configuring, 377–379
    registering, 380
    drives, mapping, 218
    naming (SSID), 439
    RIS, 23
    routes, managing, 383–384
    shares, installing from, 14
    wireless (see wireless networking)
    ZoneAlarm, 429
New Virtual Machine Wizard, 172
newsgroups, 6
nlparse.exe utility, 508
Notification Area, 120
    icons, hiding, 130–133
    items, deleting from, 579
notification of security vulnerabilities, 552
NT Backup utility, 287
NT file system (see NTFS)
NTBACKUP, 582
NTDETECT is not found error message, 615
NTFS (NT file system), converting hard
        disks, 573–575
NTLDR is not found error message, 615
NTOSKRNL Missing or Corrupt error
        message, 612

O

object linking and embedding (see OLE)
objects
    desktop, CLSIDs, 121
    GPO, 114
OCM (Optional Component Manager), 25
older version applications
    running, 100
    styles, formatting, 107
OLE (object linking and embedding), 25
Open Command Window Here
        PowerToy, 146
Open dialog box, 114
opening
    command prompts, 145
    files, searching, 261–263
Opera, blocking pop-ups, 412
operating system (see OS)
optimizing
    disks, monitoring, 205
    Internet, increasing speed, 395
    laptop/LCD resolution, 149
    page file size, 568

performance
    memory, 563–567
    Task Manager, 553–558
    tracking, 558–563
    startup, 579
    video recording, 358
    wireless network connections, 445–447
Optional Component Manager (OCM), 25
options
    folders, 145
    power, 185
    (see also customizing)
OS (operating system), 1
    multiboot installations, 29
    multiple, running, 172 173
outbound traffic from your PC,
        monitoring/blocking with
        ZoneAlarm, 429
Outlook
    logging, enabling, 535
    starting, 98
ownership of files and folders, 258

P

packages
    assigning, 114
    MSI, 113
page file size, optimizing, 568
page-oriented printers, 67
paging files, clearing, 181
parameters
    applications, customizing, 97–99
    BIOS, troubleshooting, 81
partitioning installations, 13
passwords
    creating, 599
    formatting, requiring strong, 550
    LM hash, disabling, 550
    services, configuring, 327
    user accounts
        configuring, 480–482
        modifying, 474–478
patches
    critical, installing, 539
    security, 417
Per Site Privacy Actions dialog box, 413
PerfectDisk, 212
performance
    alerts, 562
    disks, monitoring, 205

hard disks
    cleaning, 570–573
    converting to NTFS, 573–575
    logging, viewing, 562
    memory, optimizing, 563–567
    Notification Area, deleting items
        from, 579
    page file size, optimizing, 568
    special effects, turning off, 567
    speeding up systems, 553–558
    startup, 575–578, 579
    tracking, 558–563
Performance Console, 559
Performance Options dialog box, 568
Performance tab, 558
    reporting, 564
permissions, granting, 336
personalizing sounds, 183
physical access (security), 539
Pinned Programs List, 120, 136
playing Internet radio stations, 350
Plug and Play
    conflicts, 57
    hardware, adding, 47
policies
    Account Lockout Policy, 476
    audit, configuring, 543
    retention, configuring events, 516
Pop-up Blocker Settings dialog box, 410
Pop Up No No!, 411
pop-ups
    blocking, 409–412
    killing, 417
portqry.exe, 300
ports
    printers, troubleshooting, 67
    viewing, 385–387
    (see also connections)
POST (Power-On Self-Test), 198, 580
PostScript printers, 67
power
    alarms, configuring, 187
    connections, USB devices, 59
    schemes, creating, 185
Power Options Properties dialog box, 185
PowerDesk Pro, 247
Power-On Self-Test (see POST)
PowerPoint, starting, 98
pre-installation worm infestations,
        avoiding, 44
preparing to install, 8–11

Previous Versions tab, 594
printing
    Internet Connection Sharing,
        troubleshooting, 69
    local printers, 66
    printer time-outs, 66
    to USB printers, 68
privacy
    customizing IE cookie handling, 413
    IE privacy settings, 414
    implicit vs. explicit consent for use of
        personal information, 414
    Internet, configuring, 412–416
    Windows Media Player, 351–353
processes
    base priority, assigning, 556
    killing, 303
    properties, viewing, 297
    Registry, viewing, 292
    resources, viewing, 298–301
    running, viewing, 295–297
    suspending, 302
Processes tab, 557
profiles
    user accounts, configuring, 485
    Windows Movie Maker, configuring, 359
programs (see applications)
prompts, opening command prompts, 145
properties
    files, viewing, 237–239
    folders, viewing, 237–239
    power, 185
    processes, viewing, 297
protecting
    privacy, Internet, 412–416
    against spyware, 416–419
psexec command, 237
pslist command, 300
psloglist.exe, 508, 510
public hotspots, connecting to, 458–460
publishing shares, 271

Q

QFixApp program, 103
Qualsys Browser Checkup, 422
Quick Launch, 119
Quick Power-On Self-Test (POST), 580
quotas
    enabling, 224
    limiting, 226
    viewing, 228

R

radio stations (Internet), playing, 350
RAM (random access memory), increasing
        efficiency, 565
random access memory (see RAM)
reading
    DVDs, troubleshooting, 86
    RSS feeds, 432
read-only disks and volumes, 216
read-only files/folders, 251
Really Simple Syndication (RSS) feeds, 432
rebooting
    scheduling, 197
    shortcuts, 196
    (see also booting)
recategorizing Control Panel applets, 141
recording
    sounds, 184
    video, 358
recovery
    ASR
        applying, 587
        creating, 588
    files, applying EFS, 599
Recovery Console, 26
    applying, 596–598, 609
    commands, 27
Recycle Bin, 121
    (see also deleting)
redeployment of remote applications, 115
registering DNS records, 380
Registry, 273
    access, restricting, 285
    applications, killing at startup, 577
    applications, uninstalling, 92
    Automatic Updates, 41
    cleaning, 198
    comparing, 284
    datatypes, 279
    desktop icons, deleting, 122
    files
        exporting, 281
        importing, 282
    icons, modifying, 125
    keys, creating/deleting, 275–277
    linking, 289
    monitoring, 290
    Pinned Programs List, 137
    restoring, 287
    searching, 283
    services, killing at startup, 577

Start menu, customizing, 134
startup, 178
tasks, running via, 308–310
time, synchronizing, 162
values
    configuring, 277–280
    Group Policy, 280
viewing, 292
RegSpy, 92
remote applications
    redeployment, 115
    uninstallation, 116
remote computers, mapping drives, 218
remote installation, 113–115
Remote Installation Services (RIS), 15, 21–24
    imaging, 23
remote systems, running tasks with, 306
removing
    hardware, 57
    unremovable components, 88–91
    (see also deleting)
renaming
    accounts, 544–546
    computer accounts, 501–504
    files, 246
    systems, 165–167
renewing IP addresses, 375–377
replacing files, 256
reporting
    errors
        configuring, 616
        disabling, 190
    Performance tab, 564
    WER, 193
requiring string passwords, 550
resetting
    computer accounts, 504
    hardware, 60
resolution
    laptop/LCD, optimizing, 149
    LCD monitor messages, 75
    thumbnails, modifying, 147–149
resolving
    device conflicts, 56–58
    unknown devices, 49
resources
    magazines, 7
    newsgroups, 6
    processes, viewing, 298–301
    web sites, 6
restarting in Safe Mode, 605

restoring
    activation data, 601
    auditing, 602
    CD-ROM access, 87
    files, 586
        retrieving shadow copies, 593–595
    icons, 122
    Registry, 287
    System Restore, 54
        applying, 589–591
        disabling, 592
restricting access
    events, 519
    Registry, 285
    shares, 269
retention policies, configuring events, 516
retrieving shadow copies of files, 593–595
revealing hidden devices, 64
Richards, Joe, 472
ripping music, 339–342
RIS (Remote Installation Services), 15, 21–24
    imaging, 23
Rockwell/Conextant modem chips, support
        for, 51
rollback (drivers), 52
root hubs (direct USB ports), 60
root keys of the Registry, 277
routers, installing, 438–440
routes, managing, 383–384
RSS (Really Simple Syndication) feeds, 432
Run Desktop Cleanup Wizard, 128
runas command, 237
runas.exe command, 304
running
    DOS applications, 106
    multiple operating systems, 172–173
    processes, viewing, 295–297
    in Safe Mode, 53
    scripts as services, 322
    tasks
        with alternate credentials, 304–306
        via Group Policy, 312
        via login scripts, 310–312
        via Registry, 308–310
        on remote systems, 306
    tools with alternate credentials, 3

S
Safe Mode
    restarting in, 605
    running in, 53
    System Restore, 54

SAM (Security Accounts Manager), 550
saving
    desktop settings, 156
    Registry, 287
    (see also backing up)
sc.exe utility, 162
scheduling, 41
    rebooting, 197
    Task Scheduler, 316
    tasks, 314–317
        deleting, 318
        troubleshooting, 320
        viewing, 317
schemes (power), creating, 185
schtasks.exe utility, 316
screen saver locking, enabling, 547
screens, modifying boot, 182
scripting, 4
    login, running tasks automatically
        via, 310–312
    services, running as, 322
    unattended installations, 15–20
Search Companion, 356
searching
    Active Directory, 381–382
    digital media, 354–356
    events, 520–523
    files, 245
        last one opened, 259
        open, 261–263
    folders, 245
    hidden devices, 64
    Registry, 283
    RSS feeds, 432
    user accounts (last login time), 487–488
    volumes, 221–223
security, 235
    10 Immutable Laws of, 538
    accounts, renaming, 544–546
    administrative acocunts, 539
    AES, 453
    auditing, enabling, 542–544
    configuration, analyzing, 540–541
    EFS, applying, 599
    files, encrypting, 255
    firewalls
        bypassing, 422–425
        disabling, 42
        spyware, 417
        tracking intrusion attempts, 426–428
        ZoneAlarm, 428–430
    hotspots, 464

Internet, configuring privacy, 412–416
Internet Explorer, customizing, 419–422
LM password hash, disabling, 550
MBSA, 540
passwords
    creating, 599
    requiring strong, 550
patches, 417
physical access, 539
screen saver locking, 547
services, configuring, 327
spyware, 416–419
vulnerabilities, notification of, 552
Windows Media Player, protecting
        privacy, 351–353
wireless network connections, 447–450
    encrypting, 450–455
Security Accounts Manager (see SAM)
selecting restore points, 590
sending email from hotspots, 460–462
servers
    IIS, managing with, 401–403
    Telnet
        configuring, 403–405
        managing, 405
Service Creation Wizard, 323
service packs
    installing, 37
    slipstreaming, 38
Service Set Identifier (see SSID)
services
    actions, performing upon failure, 329
    deleting, 547
    IIS
        installing, 399–401
        managing, 401–403
    load orders, viewing, 333
    managing, 336
    scripts, running as, 322
    security, configuring, 327
    shutting down, 179
    starting/stopping, 321
    startup, 325
        disabling, 178
        viewing history, 335
    Task Scheduler, 316
    unnecessary, stopping at startup, 199
    viewing, 330–333
    Wireless Zero Configuration, 442
Services Computer Management
        Console, 178
session cookies, accepting in IE, 413

setup
    troubleshooting, 25
    (see also configuring)
Setup Manager, configuring, 16
shadow copies of files, retrieving, 593–595
shares, 269
    creating, 266
    deleting, 266
    networks, installing from, 14
    publishing, 271
    viewing, 267
sharing
    Internet Connection Sharing, 69
    web, enabling, 270
Shortcut Properties dialog box, 96
shortcuts
    files, creating, 239–242
    rebooting, 196
    shutting down, 196
    Start menu, troubleshooting, 157
    Taskbars, adding, 130
    tool, 240
    (see also keyboard shortcuts)
shutting down
    services, 179
    shortcuts, 196
    special effects, 567
    speeding up, 181
    unnecessary applications at, 175–180
sidtoname command, 516
sizing
    events, viewing, 514
    images, 364–365
    music files, 342
    vents, 515
slipstreaming hotfixes/service packs, 38
Smith, Richard, 353
Sound Recorder, 183
sounds
    personalizing, 183
    troubleshooting, 71
Sounds and Audio Devices Properties dialog
        box, 184
special effects, turning off, 567
speeding up
    performance, turning off special
            effects, 567
    shutdown time, 181
    startup, 197
    systems, Task Manager, 553–558
    wireless network connections, 445–447
Spybot Search & Destroy, 417

spyware, 416–419
    definitions, updating, 539
SSID (Service Set Identifier), 443
stacks, installing IPv6, 392
standards, wireless networking, 435
standby, 187
Start menu, 120
    troubleshooting, 157
Start Menu Properties dialog box, 131
starting
    applications, keyboard shortcuts, 95
    Excel, 98
    Outlook, 98
    PowerPoint, 98
    in Safe Mode, 605
    services, 321
    Word, 98
    (see also startup)
startup
    applications
        disabling, 575–578
        shutting down unnecessary, 175–180
    folders, moving, 189
    HAL.DLL Missing or Corrupt error
            message, 613
    NTDETECT is not found error
            message, 615
    NTLDR is not found error message, 615
    NTOSKRNL Missing or Corrupt error
            message, 612
    optimizing, 579
    Registry, 178
        running tasks automatically, 309
    services
        configuring, 325
        disabling, 575–578
        viewing history, 335
        viewing load orders, 333
    speeding up, 197
Startup folder, cleaning, 575
statistics, enabling disk performance, 205
STOP messages, 25
stopping
    applications from running at startup, 575
    services, 321
stuttering (hotspots), 463
styles, formatting, 107
subst command, 220
suffixes, configuring DNS, 378
supercookies (Windows Media Player), 353
surfing the web anonymously, 431–432
suspending processes, 302

switches
    applications, customizing, 97–99
    boot.ini files, 170
    shutdown, 196
Symantec Ghost, 21
SymmTime, 164
synchronizing time, 161
Sysinternals Autoruns, 314
Sysinternals File Monitor, 263
Sysinternals Fundelete tool, 235
Sysinternals LoadOrd, 333
Sysinternals Process Explorer, 262, 296
Sysinternals Registry Monitor, 290, 292
Sysinternals TCPView, 299, 385
SYSPREP, 21
System Configuration Utility
    applications, shutting down unnecessary
        at startup, 176
    clean boots, 174
    startup, cleaning applications and services
        at, 576
System Restore, 54
    applying, 589–591
    disabling, 592
system standby, 187
System Tray, hiding icons, 130–133
SYSTEMROOT command, 27
systems
    backing up, 581–585
        applying ASR, 587
        creating ASR, 588
        restoring files, 586
    renaming, 165–167
    updating, 417

T

tables, MFT, 574
tapes, backing up, 582
Task Manager, speeding up
    performance, 553–558
Task Scheduler service, 316
Taskbars, 119
    Address Bar, adding to, 129
    shortcuts, adding, 130
tasklist.exe t, 296
tasks
    alternate credentials, running
        with, 304–306
    Group Policy, running via, 312
    login scripts, running via, 310–312
    Registry, running via, 308–310
    remote systems, running on, 306

scheduling, 314–317
    deleting, 318
    troubleshooting, 320
    viewing, 317
    viewing, 314
TCP/IP (Transmission Control
        Protocol/Internet Protocol),
        filtering, 388–391
teaming, 372
Telnet
    configuring, 403–405
    managing, 405
testing
    compatibility, 29
    POST, 198, 580
text
    Internet Explorer, modifying, 408
    mode, troubleshooting setup, 25
third-party cookies, 414
    customizing IE handling of, 413
thumbnails, modifying, 147–149
time, configuring, 160–164
time-outs, printers, 66
TIP (Alternative User Input Text Input
        Processor), 176
Titlebar (Internet Explorer), 406–408
tlntadmn commands, 406
T-Mobile, 460
    (see also hotspots)
tools
    Application Compatibility Toolkit, 102
    BootXP, 182
    chkdsk, 215
    compress.exe utility, 253
    devcon.exe, 371
    Disk Cleanup, 210
    diskpart, 202
    DiskPie Pro utility, 222
    Driver Verifier, 65
    Event Comb, 507, 523
    Event Viewer, 507
    lg, 489
    LockoutStatus, 473
    netdom command line, 166
    nlparse.exe, 508
    NT Backup utility, 287
    psloglist.exe, 508, 510
    RegSpy, 92
    running with alternate credentials, 3
    sc.exe, 162
    schtasks.exe utility, 316

Services Computer Management
    Console, 178
Setup Manager, 16
shortcut, 240
sidtoname command, 546
Sysinternals Fundelete, 235
System Configuration Utility
    clean boots, 174
    cleaning applications and services at
        startup, 576
    shutting down unnecessary
        applications at startup, 176
System Restore
    applying, 589–591
    disabling, 592
unlock, 472
wmic, 524
(see also applications)
(see also Sysinternals)
tracking
    CPU usage, 555
    intrusion attempts, 426–428
    performance, 558–563
    (see also auditing)
transferring files and settings, 111
Transmission Control Protocol/Internet
        Protocol (see TCP/IP)
triggering actions, 525–527
Trojan horses, 425
    blocking with ZoneAlarm firewall, 430
troubleshooting, 31, 341
    Application Compatibility Toolkit, 104
    AUTOEXEC.NT errors, 610
    BIOS parameters, 81
    blue screen error messages, 617–619
    booting
        applying Recovery Console, 596–598
        enabling logging, 607
    caches, 398
    CD-ROMs, 84
    CDs
        autorun problems, 83
        burning, 346–349
    clean boots, 174
    compatibility, 105
    CONFIG.NT errors, 610
    Cryptographic service errors, 611
    devices
        resolving conflicts, 56–58
        updating drivers, 51
    disk I/O errors, 25
    disk space, 24

DNS, 396–399
Dr. Watson, 619–621
DVD movies, 86
DVD-ROMs, 84
events, 525, 527, 536
files, defragmenting, 198
HAL.DLL Missing or Corrupt error
        message, 613
HOSTS files, 397
hotspots, 463
installation, 24–28
Last Known Good Configuration, 52
    applying, 606
modems, 50
My Recent Documents, 158
network connectivity, 387
NTDETECT is not found error
        message, 615
NTLDR is not found error message, 615
NTOSKRNL Missing or Corrupt error
        message, 612
POST, 580
printing
    internet Connection Sharing, 69
    localprinters, 66
    printer time-outs, 66
Recovery Console, 26
    applying, 609
Safe Mode, restarting in, 605
services, performing actions upon
        failure, 329
sounds, 71
spyware, 416–419
Start menu, 157
System Restore, 54
    applying, 589–591
    disabling, 592
tasks, scheduling, 320
USB devices, 61
user accounts, 473
video, 73, 608
    monitors, 74
viruses, 44
WER, 193
WINDOWSSYSTEM32CONFIG
        errors, 614
wireless network connections, 442–445
    speeding up, 445–447
worms, 44
turning off balloon tips, 127
TweakUI, 122
    applying, 153

U

unattended installations, 15–20
UNC (Universal Naming Convention), 114
undeleting files, 235
uninstalling
  applications, 91
    deleting from Add or Remove
      Programs dialog box, 93
    remote applications, 116
    unremovable components, 88–91
Univeral Serial Bus (see USB)
Universal Naming Convention (see UNC)
unknown devices
  resolving, 49
  USB, 62
unlock tool, 472
unlocking user accounts, 471–473
unremovable components,
          uninstalling, 88–91
updating
  antispyware/virus definitions, 539
  Automatic Updates, configuring, 40–42
  BIOS firmware, 60
  devices, troubleshooting drivers, 51
  hotfixes, 36
  security, searching
          vulnerabilities, 540–541
  systems, 417
upgrading
  installations, 10, 28
  Windows XP Upgrade Advisor, 9
USB (Universal Serial Bus)
  bandwidth errors, 58
  hung devices, 59–61
  printers, printing from DOS, 68
  troubleshooting, 61
  unknown device messages, 62
user accounts
  creating, 469–471
  domains, configuring, 483–485
  enabling, 478–480
  last logon time, searching, 487–488
  modifying, 474–478
  passwords
    configuring, 480–482
    requiring strong, 550
  profiles, configuring, 485
  troubleshooting, 473
  unlocking, 471–473
user objects, viewing groups, 493
userAccountControl, configuring, 484

V

values, 277–280
  configuring, 277–280
  Group Policy, 280
variables, environments, 193
verification, Driver Verifier tool, 65
versions, 29
  older applications, formatting styles, 107
  older versions of applications, 100
  viewing, 126
VGA Mode, applying, 608
video
  capturing, 356–360
  DVDs, burning, 360
  troubleshooting, 73, 608
    monitors, 74
viewing
  Control Panel applets, 137
  disk quotas, 228
  disks, 202
  drives, 202
  events, 510–512
    size of, 514
  files, 263
  group accounts, 491–495
  hotfixes, 34
  installed service packs, 34
  network configuration, 368–370
  performance logging, 562
  ports, 385–387
  processes
    properties, 297
    resources, 298–301
    running, 295–297
  properties, files/folders, 237–239
  Registry, 292
  services, 330–333
    load orders, 333
    startup history, 335
  shares, 267
  tasks, 314
    scheduling, 317
  user accounts, 474–478
  versions, 126
  video, capturing, 356–360
  volumes, 202
  (see also Event Viewer)
virtual drives, creating, 220
Virtual PC, 172–173
viruses, 44
viruses, updating definitions, 539

volumes, 206
    cleaning, 209
    compressing, 213–215
    defragmenting, 211
    errors, checking for, 215
    formatting, setting drive letters, 207
    labels, configuring, 208
    read-only, 216
    searching, 221–223
    viewing, 202
vulnerabilities, notification of, 552

W

WAVClean, 348
WaveCorrector, 348
web pages, sizing images, 364–365
web sharing, enabling, 270
web sites
    IIS, 400
    resources, 6
    (see also Internet)
Webroot Spy Sweeper, 418
WEP (Wireless Equivalent Protocol), 443
    configuring, 450
WER (Windows Error Reporting), 193
Wi-Fi Protected Access (see WPA)
Windows classic interfaces, converting
    to, 150
Windows Component Wizard, 89
Windows Error Reporting (WER), 193
Windows Explorer
    cookies, listing of, 415
    thumbnail, modifying, 147–149
Windows Firewall, 42
Windows Firewall dialog box, 422
Windows Installer, enabling logging, 531
Windows Media Player
    privacy, protecting, 351–353
    troubleshooting, 341
    (see also digital media)
Windows Movie Maker, 357
    (see also video)
Windows Server 2000/Windows 2003
    Resource Kit tools, 3
Windows Support Tools, 3
Windows Time service, 161
    enabling logging, 534
Windows XP Upgrade Advisor, 9
WINDOWSSYSTEM32CONFIG errors, 614

WinZip, 253
Wireless Equivalent Protocol (see WEP)
wireless Internet Service Providers (see
    WISPs)
wireless networking
    ad hoc, configuring, 456–458
    adapters, installing, 434–437
    connecting, 440
        mixing 802.11b/802.11g devices, 455
        speeding up, 445–447
        troubleshooting, 442–445
    encrypting, 450–455
    hotspots
        connecting, 458–460
        security, 464
        sending email, 460–462
        stuttering, 463
    routers, installing, 438–440
    security, 447–450
Wireless Zero Configuration service, 442
WISPs (wireless Internet service
    providers), 460
wizards
    Add Hardware Wizard, 436
    Add New Hardware, 49
    Application Compatibility Wizard, 100
    Client Installation Wizard, 23
    Files and Settings Transfer Wizard, 111
    Found New Hardware Wizard, 63
    New Virtual Machine Wizard, 172
    Run Desktop Cleanup Wizard, 128
    Service Creation Wizard, 323
    Windows Component Wizard, 89
wmic utility, 524
Word, starting, 98
workgroups, installing, 14
worms, 44
WPA (Wi-Fi Protected Access), 443
    configuring, 453

X

XCOPY, applying, 595

Z

ZoneAlarm firewall, 428–430
    configuring to block Trojans, 430
    versions, 430

About the Authors

Robbie Allen is a technical leader and solutions architect at Cisco Systems, where he has been involved in the deployment of Active Directory, DNS, DHCP, and several network management solutions. Robbie was named a Windows Server MVP in 2004 and 2005 for his contributions to the Windows community and the publication of several popular O'Reilly books. Robbie is currently studying at MIT in the system design and management program. For more information, see Robbie's web site at *http://www.rallenhome.com*.

Preston Gralla is the author of more than 30 books, including *Internet Annoyances*, *PC Pest Control*, *Windows XP Power Hound*, and *Windows XP Hacks*, all from O'Reilly. He is also a freelance journalist and columnist and has written about technology for many major national newspapers and magazines, including *PC Magazine*, *Computerworld*, the *Los Angeles Times*, the *Dallas Morning News* (where he was the technology columnist), *USA Today*, and several others. A well-known technology expert, Preston has also appeared on many TV and radio programs and networks, including CNN, MSNBC, and NPR. In addition, he has won a number of awards for his writing, including "Best Feature in a Computer Magazine" from the Computer Press Association. He lives in Cambridge, Massachusetts.

Colophon

Our look is the result of reader comments, our own experimentation, and feedback from distribution channels. Distinctive covers complement our distinctive approach to technical topics, breathing personality and life into potentially dry subjects.

The animal on the cover of *Windows XP Cookbook* is a common garter snake (*Thamnophis sirtalis*). The garter snake is the most wide-ranging and adaptable species of reptile in North America. It can be found just about everywhere in the U.S., except for parts of the Southwest, and is the only species of snake found in Alaska, making it one the nothernmost species of snakes in the world. With an unparticular diet consisting of a variety of small creatures—insects, slugs, worms, mice, lizards, fish, eggs, snails, and frogs—garter snakes are able to adapt to both wet and dry regions.

Garter snakes are harmless to humans and will always attempt to avoid them. If handled by a human, a garter snake may or may not attack, but its bite will have little or no effect on most people. The snake's other defense is a foul-smelling fluid that it secretes from its rear glands.

Adam Witwer was the production editor for *Windows XP Cookbook*. Argosy Publishing provided production services. Sanders Kleinfeld and Claire Cloutier provided quality control.

Ellie Volckhausen designed the cover of this book, based on a series design by Edie Freedman. The cover image is from the Dover Pictorial Archive. Karen Montgomery produced the cover layout with Adobe InDesign CS using Adobe's ITC Garamond font.

David Futato designed the interior layout. This book was converted by Keith Fahlgren to FrameMaker 5.5.6 with a format conversion tool created by Erik Ray, Jason McIntosh, Neil Walls, and Mike Sierra that uses Perl and XML technologies. The text font is Linotype Birka; the heading font is Adobe Myriad Condensed; and the code font is LucasFont's TheSans Mono Condensed. The illustrations that appear in the book were produced by Robert Romano, Jessamyn Read, and Lesley Borash using Macromedia FreeHand MX and Adobe Photoshop CS. The tip and warning icons were drawn by Christopher Bing. This colophon was written by Adam Witwer.

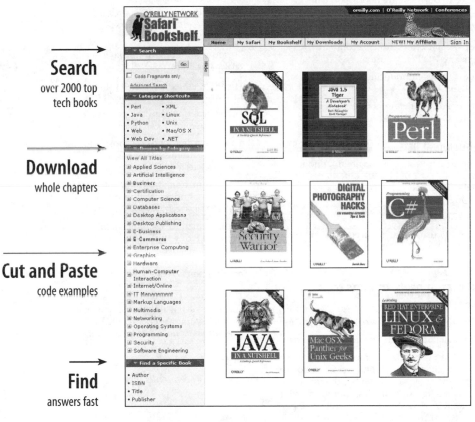

Keep in touch with O'Reilly

Download examples from our books

To find example files from a book, go to: *www.oreilly.com/catalog* select the book, and follow the "Examples" link.

Register your O'Reilly books

Register your book at *register.oreilly.com* Why register your books? Once you've registered your O'Reilly books you can:

- Win O'Reilly books, T-shirts or discount coupons in our monthly drawing.
- Get special offers available only to registered O'Reilly customers.
- Get catalogs announcing new books (US and UK only).
- Get email notification of new editions of the O'Reilly books you own.

Join our email lists

Sign up to get topic-specific email announcements of new books and conferences, special offers, and O'Reilly Network technology newsletters at:

elists.oreilly.com

It's easy to customize your free elists subscription so you'll get exactly the O'Reilly news you want.

Get the latest news, tips, and tools

www.oreilly.com

- "Top 100 Sites on the Web"—PC Magazine
- CIO Magazine's Web Business 50 Awards

Our web site contains a library of comprehensive product information (including book excerpts and tables of contents), downloadable software, background articles, interviews with technology leaders, links to relevant sites, book cover art, and more.

Work for O'Reilly

Check out our web site for current employment opportunities:

jobs.oreilly.com

Contact us

O'Reilly Media, Inc.
1005 Gravenstein Hwy North
Sebastopol, CA 95472 USA
Tel: 707-827-7000 or 800-998-9938
    (6am to 5pm PST)
Fax: 707-829-0104

Contact us by email

For answers to problems regarding your order or our products: **order@oreilly.com**

To request a copy of our latest catalog: **catalog@oreilly.com**

For book content technical questions or corrections: **booktech@oreilly.com**

For educational, library, government, and corporate sales: **corporate@oreilly.com**

To submit new book proposals to our editors and product managers: **proposals@oreilly.com**

For information about our international distributors or translation queries: **international@oreilly.com**

For information about academic use of O'Reilly books: **adoption@oreilly.com** or visit: *academic.oreilly.com*

For a list of our distributors outside of North America check out: *international.oreilly.com/distributors.html*

Order a book online

www.oreilly.com/order_new